# Suffolk County Wills

# Suffolk County Wills

Abstracts of the Earliest Wills Upon
Record in the County of Suffolk, Massachusetts

*From The New England Historical and Genealogical Register*

With an Index by Judith McGhan

CLEARFIELD

Reprinted for
Clearfield Company, Inc. by
Genealogical Publishing Co., Inc.
Baltimore, Maryland
2005


Excerpted and reprinted from *The New England
Historical and Genealogical Register,*
with added Publisher's Note and Index, by
Genealogical Publishing Co., Inc. Baltimore, 1984.
Added matter © 1984 by Genealogical Publishing Co., Inc.
Baltimore, Maryland. All Rights Reserved.
Library of Congress Catalogue Card Number 83-82826
International Standard Book Number 0-8063-1069-3
*Made in the United States of America*

# *Note*

The work primarily of William B. Trask, this long series of will abstracts appeared at intervals over a period of forty-five years in *The New England Historical and Genealogical Register.* Initiated by Samuel G. Drake in January 1848, the series was entrusted three years later to Mr. Trask, who continued it without interruption until 1866, then set it aside for ten years, returning to it in 1876 and carrying it forward for another two years. Sixteen years later, in 1894, Walter K. Watkins added the final installments.

The series embodies abstracts of the earliest wills and inventories of Suffolk County, Massachusetts, representing, in substance, the first thirty years or so of the county's estate records. When originally published, the series appeared under the title "Abstracts of the Earliest Wills upon Record in the County of Suffolk, Mass.," with later alterations in the wording to indicate that a certain portion of the abstracts derived from *unrecorded* estate papers. Although scattered throughout more than sixty issues of the *Register*, the series manifested a unity of purpose and a remarkable consistency in editorial standards. Owing to its protracted publication, however, it has remained obscure and out of reach. To make it accessible, therefore, and to bring it before a deserving audience, we have gathered up the various installments and reprinted them in this volume, to which we have added an essential index of names.

*Genealogical Publishing Company*

## ABSTRACTS OF THE EARLIEST WILLS UPON RECORD IN THE COUNTY OF SUFFOLK, MS.

[We would note that it has been our endeavour to give these Abstracts exactly as they stand recorded, and as far as practicable to preserve the orthography, capitals, &c. And, that we intend in future numbers of our work to devote some space to Wills and other documents of the 'olden time,' and hope our friends will send us copies or originals of any thing they may have of this nature. *Originals are always to be preferred.*]

A Coppye of the last will and Testament of *Richard Eles*, deceased the 29 (8$^{mo}$) 1639.

If the lord take me out of this life my will and desire is, that those things that I have should be thus disposed of as followeth:

first I desire y$^t$ fortye five shillings should be sent to owld England for *Jo: Keene* and my brother *John*, that is 35 to the one & ten to the other.

I desire y$^t$ those things that I have should be sowld, both beddinge & cloathes & tooles, except my Coverlett, and that I desire to give to my aunt for hir paines and hir love; further, I give to my Cosin *Tho. Harris* 20s. — To *William Harris* 20s. — To *Anthony Harris* 20s. — To *Jo Harris* 20s. — To my Cosin *Anne Maverick* 20s. — To my Cosin *Daniell Harris* 20s.

ffurther I give to my two little Cosins, *John & Abigale Maverick*, five shillings p peice.

ffurther I give Goodwife *Greenland* five shillings, & for the rest that

1

remaineth, I desire it shall be divided into fowre eaquall pts. for my three brothers and my sister.

———

The last will & Testament of *Edward Skiner*, now departed, while he was in perfect memory. [25: 10: 1641 in margin.]
*Imprimus.* That the lands and howse that he now possesses in Cambridge, in New England, the one half should be disposed of vnto one Mr. *Robert Ibbit* of Cambridge in Owld England, the other half vnto the Church of Cambridge in New England. Also it is his will that *Marie Hanner*, now servant vnto *Thomas Parrish*, should have 3lb; moreover his Cloake Saw & betle Hoopes, and wedges vnto Good. *Marchant;* vnto goodman *Crackbone* his best sute of Cloathes; vnto *Philemon Dixison* his stufe sute, & white russet Bootes; vnto *John Sawin* a bedd on[e] paire of sheets, a peice of Stuffe, his best hat & postnett & a handsaw; vnto *John Boutle* a iackett, a paire of fustian stivers, and a payre of leather stivers; vnto Goodwife *Marchant* all his sheetes, & 5lb stir, that the owld man knew not of; vnto the wife of *Thomas Parrish* one peice of hempinge cloath; vnto *Jeremy Barber* one p of shoes; vnto his owne man a paire of owld briches, irckin, wastcote, hatt & Capp; & for his time, he is to serve one yeare with elder *ffrost*, & on[e] other yeare [with] Good *Stoune;* vnto *Thomas Parrish* 6lb for debts and other reckoninge, & all his iron ware & tools as his voluntary gift.

Witnesses. *Jo: Sawin,*                         The ‡ marck
      *Marie Marchant.*                  of EDWARD SKINER.

Moreover I given vnto *John Sawinge*, 9 payre of Shoes, & five p. of Bootes; & vnto Goodman *Coolidge* a debt, the wᶜʰ he owyht him in his booke, about 3lb; one peice of leather, and a spade vnto *Thomas Lowe.*
*Curia dicit.*

Things to stand as they are in England.

———

The last will and Testament of *William Waltham* of Weymouth, (now deceased) while he was of perfect memory. [30: 10: 1641 in margin.]
I bequeath my sowle to god yt gave it, & my body to the Earth, vntill the resurrection.

For the better settling of my small meanes, wᶜʰ the lord hath given me, have made this my last will & testament, Intreating my loving ffather to be my Executor, wᵗʰ full power to sell all my halfe pte of the mill in Weymouth, wᵗʰ yᵉ ffiftye acres of land, vnto my parte of land belonging vnto it, the halfe of the howse, & the portinance ptaininge. And what it shall yeeld, beinge sowld, to pay the sayd monye in six monthes ffollowinge, vnto my brother *Thomas Waltham* the one halfe, and to my brother *Henery Waltham* the other halfe; but if my ffather thinke not best to sell it, then to remaine vnto them ioyntly, & to there Eares.

Also I give power vnto my sayde Attorney to sell five steeres & two Heiffers, & the mony to pay vnto my sister *Anne Waltham*, & my sister *Phillyne Waltham*, in a yeare after the sale thereof, or at the day of their marriage, Joyntly betwixt them, or to keepe them for theire better Benifitt, wᶜʰ I leave to the discretion of my ffather, to keep them to theire vse, or sell all as aforesayde.

In witness hereof have hereunto sett my hand & seale, the third of November, Anno 1640.

Witnesses                              WILLIAM WALTHAM.
  *James Laddyn*
  *Will: Jefferay.*

2

The last will & Testement of *Barnabe Lambson* (deceased) when he was of pfect memory.
ffor the dispossinge of my Children to 5 pticalor men, every one.
My daughter *Mary* to my brother *Sparahak.*
To my brother *Isaack* my daughter *Sarah.*
My soñe *Barnabey* to my brother *Parish.*
My daughter *Mary* to my brother *Stone.*
My Sonne *Joseph* to my brother *Bridge.*
Now for the some of my estate I would have it delivered unto these 5 mens hands for the bringing up of my children, & I would have it equally divided amongst them.  [Amount not mentioned.]
Witnesse
*Edward Hall*
*Joseph Isack.*

———

22 day 11th, called December, Anno Domini 1640.
The last Will & Testament w^ch I *George Alcock* of Roxbury in N: E: doe make, havinge yet my perfect vnderstandinge and memory according to the measure thereof.
Debts to be paid both in owld England & in new
My debt of 40£. to my Sonne John, w^ch I have of his in my hands. — Wife to have £100. to be paid her in whatsoever she shall chuse. — Brother *Thomas Alcocke* of Dedham all that he oweth me, & my Heifer w^ch is w^th Calfe, wh came of the great Cowe, if my goodes will howld out, else he shall have only hir Calfe, & I give his 2 Children each of them 2^lb. — To our brother *Edward Porter*, 20 bushles of Indian Corne, & to our brother *Chandler*, the monye he oweth me. — To *Elizabeth Blandfeild* 2^l; she shall [be] put forth where she may be well educated. — To my servant *Joseph Wise*, my young heifer, & the rest of his time, from after mid-somer next. — To my servant, *John Plimton*, his time from after midsomer, for 5^l — My youngest sone shall have the silver bowles, & my wife the silver spoons. — My house and lands to be improved for the best, for the eaducation of my children, and the halfe of y^e revenue of the farme shall be to eaducate my sone *John* in learninge, together w^th the wisest improvement of his 40^l — The other half to educate sone *Samuell*, for 7 yeares, begining from y^e 1st daye of y^e 11 month, called January, about w^ch time expired, my sone *John* will be 21 yeares of age. — Part of the debts to my brother *Carwithy* be layde out on the 2 Cowes I had of Mr. *Perkins.* — My lovinge brethren, *Phillip Eliot*, & *William Park* be my executors.  My brother Mr. *Hooker*, Mr. *Welde*, Mr. *Eliote*, *Isacke Heath* to overseers.
Witnesses                                          George Alcocke.
*Tho Welde*
*Thom Alcocke*
(28) 11: 1640.

———

The last Will & Testament of John Tey, deceased, while he was of pfet minde and memorye.
That 2^l be given to Mr. *Raynsford*, — 2^l to Mr. *Offley*, — To Goodwife *Wormwoode*, 1^l, besides satisfaction for her paynes, & 10^s to Goodwife *Search*, besides satisfaction for what she hath done for him; & 10^s to *John*, Mr. *Rainsford's* man; 2^l to his cosin *Jackson* of Watterton; & to *John Whight*, & to John *Wylie* such of his goods as are remayninge

3

to be devided betweene them both; & for his books to be comitted to Mr. *Eliote*, Teacher of Roxburye to be kept till his sonne *Allin* comes of age, & if he cometh over hither to be given to him safe, only one thats left w$^{th}$ *Jacob Eliote*, for his Trees, 10 to Mr. *Eliote* Teacher of Roxburye, & 10 [to] *Jacob Eliote*, & 3 to *Phillip*, & 3 to Elder *Heath*, & 3 to *ffrances Eliote* & the rest to be devided to his kinsmen; to Goodman *Dawson* 10$^s$: besides satisfaction for his labor, & 2$^l$ to the poore of boston:
Witness,
*Jacob Eliote*
in co$^{rt}$ 7$^{th}$: 10: 1641.

4

# ABSTRACTS OF THE EARLIEST WILLS UPON RECORD IN THE COUNTY OF SUFFOLK, MS.

## ABRAHAM SHAWE.

The last will & Testament of Abraham Shawe deceased.

Memorandum that if it please Almyghtye God to take me to his mercye by death. That it is my minde & will that my estate shal be disposed of as followeth (that is to say) I bequeathe to my sonne John, & Martha Shawe, beinge infants ten pownds betweene them, also betweene the aforesd Martha & Marye I leave as much quicke goods as shal be bal- * ance to eight pownds, also to Joseph in some goods twelve pownds as may be thought fitt: furder, that Joseph & John shall have my lott att Dedham equally to be devided between them. Also that all the rest of my estate whatsoever be devided, proportionate, betwene all my childron.*

Witnesses

Nicolas Biram †

Joseph Shawe.

These psons were ordered to make an Inventorye of the estate by the helpe & advice of Mr. Edward Allen.

---

## JOHN MASTERS.

19: 10^mo. 1639.

This is the minde & will of me John Masters. ‡

*Item* I give to my wife all my estate for the terme of her life & after hir decease I will & bequeathe vnto my Daughter Sarah Dobyson ten pownds.

*Item* to my daughter Lidya Tabor ten pownds,

*Item* to my Grand child John Lockwood ten pownds,

---

* There is no date at all about this will as it stands on the book. It follows next in order to that we have given date, p. 105. The inventory of his estate is recorded in book II., and dated 1638, as returned by "Edward Allen, Jo: Kingsberye, Jo: Howard and some others."

† BYRAM in Farmer's Register, where we find "NICHOLAS, Waymouth, 1638, removed to Bridgewater; d. 1687, leaving one son, NICHOLAS. Rev. ELIAB, H. C. 1740, probably a descendant, was minister of Hopewell, N. J." There is a representative, probably of this family, in Lowell at this time. Judge Mitchell has near three closely printed pages of families of the name in his History of Bridgewater, and the SHAWS as much more.

‡ MASTERS, JOHN, Watertown, freeman 1631, a proprietor of and perhaps resident at Cambridge. He died 21 Dec., 1639, and his wife died five days after him. *Farmer.* — In June, 1631, the court ordered that "Mr. John Maisters having undertaken to make a *Passage* from *Charles River* to the *new Town*, 12 feet broad, and 7 deep, the court promises him Satisfaction." *Prince*, ii. 30. There was a *Nathaniel*, Beverly, 1659, according to Farmer, but whether the one named in the will is not known. Several persons of the name of Masters have graduated at the different colleges in New England and New York.

*For balance *read* valued.

5

*It* to Nathaniell Masters ten pownds to Abraham Masters ten shillings, Also my minde & will is that the ten pownds I give to John Lockwood, & the ten pownds I give to Nathaniell Masters shal be layde out vpon somethinge that may turne to the encrease of theire portions ffurthermore my will is that these leagacyes shal be well & truly discharged wthin six monthes after my wives decease, these & all other my debt beinge discharged I give all the remainder of my estate vnto my daughter Elizabeth Latham.

------

June 26: 1638.

### JOSEPH HARVIE.

Memorandum that Joseph Harvie husbandman of Gamscolne* in Essex deceased bequeathed all such goods & chattles w^ch were then his should be sold to best improvement, & the proceed to be dd: to Joseph Isaack of Cambridge in New England It was Newtowne & to Will Beellaze a passinger in the sayde shipp wherin he dyed soe the sayd monye is to be improved or lent as they shall in Judgment see fitt for the benifitt of some pore Christians in these plantations, & the capitall stocke to be returned at 2 years end & payde to his brother John Harvie of Wetherfield in owld England or to his lawfull Attorney only five pownds w^ch he bequeaths that his sayde brother John Harvie Shall pay vnto his sister one Goodw Burke y^t lives in owld England, & that these were his expressions for the bequeathinge of his estate is witnessed by these names here vnderwritten, whom he called to be as witnesses of the same. †

Will Bullard deposed y^t
this was y^e true will of
Joseph Harvie : & his desire
was y^t should take the whole
business upon him.

------

### ROGER HARLACKENDEN.

[p. 13.] In the name of God Amen I Roger Harlackenden‡ late of Erlescolne§ in the Countye of Essex in the Realme of England gent

* The several villages, says Dugdale, distinguished by the name of *Colne*, in the Hundred of Lexden, evidently derive their appellative from the river Colne. But the student may search in vain in the topographical dictionaries to find the locality of that in the text. It is our opinion that Engaine Colne is meant; if so, it is now written Colne Engaine and sometimes called Little-Colne.

† " The inventory of the goods and chattles of Joseph Harvye w^ch were prised by John Bridge of Cambridge and John Permitor then of Watertown."

‡ In the will of Sir John Fogge, Knt., of Ashettisford, dated 4 Nov., 1533, he appoints " *Thomas Harlakynden*," one of his executors, and " Edward Lee, archbishop of York," overseer. The ancient Asshetsford (now Ashford in Kent) took its name from the family of De Asshetsford or Ashettisford. It is about 54 miles from London. The family of Fogge settled there in the time of Henry IV., though it came into Kent in the reign of Henry I., from Lancashire. Sir Francis Fogge, Knt., acquired the manor of Repton, by his marriage with a co-heiress of the Valoigns. Sir John Fogge founded a college at Ashford, and died in 1490. This was the father of Sir John, first named. This family was of high standing and much consequence for many ages, but it is entirely extinct at Ashford, and perhaps in the county. It may be a branch of this family that now flourishes in New England. There was a *Ralph Fogg* at Salem in 1634, who, Mr. Felt tells us, returned to England.

§ Noted as the birthplace of Thomas Lord Audley, chancellor of England in the reign of Henry VIII., (1488.) In the church here are carved the arms of John De Vere, the sixteenth earl. — *Dugdale.*

now of Newtowne in the Mattachusetts Bay in America doe make & or-
deyne this my last will & Testament in maner & forme folowinge. I
give & bequeath all that my lands & tenements w^th the appurtenances
commonly called Colne Parke or the little lodge now in the tenure of
March Thomas Hales and the widdowe Waford together w^th one
pcell of meadowe called Hunwickes medowe lyinge in Erlescolne or
elsewhere in the Countye of Essex into the hands of Godfrey Bosveile
Richard Harlakenden Henerye Darbey Nathaniell Bacon Esqes to such
uses as are hereafter limited & expressed, My Will & meaninge is that
m ysayd ffeoffees aforenamed shall have full power & Awthoritye to
make sale of my aforesaid lands if they shall thinke fitt for the better
performance of this my will I give & bequeath all that my land w^th the
appurtenances abovesaid to my eldest sonne & his heires for ever if I
shall have such issue by Elizabeth my now wife lawfully begotten of my
bodye comminge (in case my lands beforesaid be not sowld) Provided
all wayes that my sayd sonne pay yearlye at Michaeltide and our Ladye
dayes, or one fortnight after to Elizabeth my wife fortye pownds p anum
duringe the time of hir naturall life at twentye pownds the halfe yeare,
to begyn at the first of the sayd dayes w^ch shall happen next after my
decease, & for to continue duringe the terme, And if it shall happen that
the said rent in part or in whole, shal be behind & unpayd, at the dayes
mencoñed then it shal be lawfull for my wife to distreine or to enter
vpon the land while such moneys be payed, ffurther my mind & will is
that my sayd sonne shall pay to my daughter, Elizabeth (if she be then
living) the some of three hundred pownds of lawfull mony to be payd
w^thin six monthes after my decease, for the performance, thereof I bind
my said lands &c. nevertheless in case my land be sowld, then my will
is that the monye w^ch shal be received for the same, shal be destributed
according to the uses formerly expressed Morovver my will is if I have
noe issue male lawfully begotten then I give to my Daughter Elizabeth
all that my land abouesaid performinge the conditions before mencoñed.
ffurthermore, if I shall have another daughter then I give to the said
daughter five hundred pownds of lawfull moneye of England, to be payde
by my daughter Elizabeth unto hir one yeare after my decease for the
true performance thereof I bind my sayd lands, but in case she should
dye before the monye is due, then my daughter Elizabeth shall not be
bound to pay the same. I give to Elizabeth my wife all that my howse
& lands latlye purchased of Thomas Dudlye Esq^r in Newtowne in the
Massachusetts Baye in America or elsewhere w^th my farme to hir & hir
heires forever. And also I give my saide wife fortye pownds per Ann to
be payd as aforesaide out of my lands. In like manner I give to my
wife the one halfe of all my goods and chattles & all my lands about the
Towne w^th the interest in all the commons. Also I give to my naturall
sisters now livinge to the children of my Sister Nevile each of my sisters
livinge five pownds and five pownds to my sister Neviles children I give
to Mr. Shephard our Pastor fortye pownds and to our Elders that w^ch is
in theire hands, and to the pore brethren of o^r Congregation twentye
pownds to be ordred by M^r Shephard, to the librarye ten pownds & all
my books w^ch are not usefull for my wife. Also I give to my Cosin Sarah five pownds to be payd w^thin one yeare after my decease. Also I
give to John Bridge 5: 10 to Anna my mayde servant fortye shillings to
Mary my mayd thirtye shillings, to Gowldinge & Thomas Prentise thirtye shillings each of them. All other my lands & goods unbequeathed I

give to my Executors towards the payment of my debts & legacyes & if it shall not be sufficient to pay my sayd debts then I binde my said land in Essex for the true performance thereof & I doe constitute, & ordeine my brother Richard Harlakenden Esq^r & my brother John Haynes Executors of this my last will & Testament. And I doe further constitute my welbeloved wife & John Bridge to be Executors of this my last will & 'Testament equally to be joyned w^th them.

Witnesse  
    John Haynes  
    Thomas Shepheard  
    John Moore

ROGER HARLAKENDEN  
A Seale

---

### PETER BRANCH.

The last will & Testament of Peter Branch late of Holden in Kent in owld England Carpenter, beinge sicke in bodye but of good & perfect sence & memorye comitt vnto Thomas Wiburne, late of Tenterden in Kent my Sonne John Branch to provide for and oversee him for eleven yeares from henceforth dated the 16th daye of June, 1638 — and my whole estate to be kept by s^d Thomas Wiborne who shall pay all my debts out of s^d estate. If my s^d sonne dye before y^e end of s^d time then the saide Wiborne shall give to Widowe Igleden the late wife of Stephen Igleden or to his children or to her children she had by him five pownds. *Item.* I give to Thomas Wiborne for the keepinge of my son eight pownds. If my sonne John dye before eleven yeares what remayne in y^e hands of said Wiborne to go to the pore of those three congregations, of Concord, of Sittuate, & to that congregation wich a company that goes in the Shipp called the Castle, if there be a company of them, if not then to be devided [among] the aforesd two congregations. My son John Sole Executor & Thomas Wiborne my feafeere to whom I comit the over sight of my will.*

---

### WILLIAM BALLARD.

Nicholas Browne & Gerarard Spencer sworne affirmeth that being w^th Mr. Willm Ballard of Linn a day or two before his death, & perswadinge him to make his will [*defaced*] S^d Mr. Ballard towld him he intended to do it the next day but [*gone*] dyed before he could put it in wrightinge, he would have his [*wife Sarah?*] half his estate, and the other half to be devided amongst his children, the said William Ballard beinge then of pfect minde.

taken upon oath 1: of the 1 month  
164[1?]

Simon Broadstret  
Increace Nowell.

---

### ANNE VTTINGE.

Anne Vttinge of Dedham singlewoman did give & bequeathe hir goods in maner & forme as followeth viz : [*no date.*]

---

* In the inventory of his effects it is stated that this testator died on board the ship Castle. The above is an abridgment, but in all our abstracts or abridgments no *name, date,* or *facts* will be omitted, and when an abridgment is made it will be noted.

8

1. To George Berbor* of Dedham singleman one feather bed one feather boulster one p of sheets one blankett one Coverlett.

2. To Anna Phillips the wife of Henerye Phillips of Dedham one Bible one table cloath two table napkins one p of sheets one pillowe one Cushen.

3. To John Brocke singleman one p sheets one handchircheife.

4. To Elizabeth Brock singlewoman one stuffe Coate.

5. To Elizabeth Brock the wife of Henrey Brock one twentye shillings wch she is to receive of Joseph Clerck of Dedham.

6. Such things as were owinge from divers psons she forgave them.

7. The rest of hir goods not disposed of she gave them to Elizabeth Brock the wife of Henery Brock of Dedham.

Witnesses in Cort
    Anne Phillips to the whole will in all the pticulars.
    John Brocke to all except the 2 : 3 : & 4th.

---

## JOSEPH MIRIAM.

The 29th the 10th month in the yeare of oʳ Lord 1640.

The last will & Testament of Joseph miriam of Concord.

I Joseph Miriam† of Concord being weake in bodie, but blessed be God of good memory and sense inwardly do comit my soule to God in Jesus Christ & my body to the earth from whence it came.

Item. To wife Sarah all my whole estate towards & for the bring vp of al my children. Power to her to sell my house I now live in, it beinge larger and bigger than she shall stand in need of. The overplus of providing a lesse house shal be disposed in some way for the good and benefit of my wife & children. Wife to bring up all the children till they are one & twenty the sonnes: & the daughters either at that time or at the day of marriage. When my oldest child shall be one & twenty, the estate to be prised & wife Sarah to have one third. If she marries to have one third.

Wife whole executor & wth her my welbeloved brethren Mr. Thomas fflint Simon Willard Robert Miriam put in trust.

Testified vpon oath to be the last will of Joseph Miriam 26: 8. 1642, by George ffowle.‡

                Capt cop nobis
                die et anno superadicto
                Rich: Bellingham
                Increase Nowell

* Farmer's article (in his Gen. Reg.) on *Barber* is as follows:
"EDWARD, Dorchester, d. 9 June, 1677, a. 80. GEORGE, Dedham, 1643, memb. Art. Co., 1646; rep. 1668, 1669, and 1682, of Medfield, in which place he was principal military officer. JOHN, Salem, 1637, church memb. 3 Apl., 1646, styled carpenter. JOHN, Medfield, rep. 1677. RICHARD, Dedham, freeman, 1640, d. 18 June, 1644. This name is written *Barbore*. William, Marblehead, 1648."
*Zechariah Barber* of Medfield was probably a son of *John* of that place. On the records of that town, "1684 Zac. Barber was hired to beat the drum on sabbath days for half the year." This beating drums on a Sunday is explained in the present volume, p. 69.
† In the History of Concord by Lemuel Shattuck, Esq., will be found an account of the family of Meriam, also in Farmer's Register. Descendants are scattered over many towns. See Ward's Shrewsbury and Barry's Framingham.
‡ Date of Inventory 18 Jan., 1640. Apprizers, Thomas Flint, Lyman Willard, Robert Miriam, Tho. Brooke.

That this will of Joseph Miriams is his owne will & freely consented
to he being reasonable apprehensive of the same we whose names are underwritten do testifie this

SIMON WILLARD
GEORGE FFOWLE

This note was taken vppon oath the 26 of the 7th month 1642.

THOMAS FFLINT.

This was deposed by Lieftenant Willard 29: 7: 1642 before me.

INCREASE NOWELL.

---

## THOMAS BAGNLY.

Testimonies given concerning y⁰ will of Tho: Bagnly late of Concord deceased.* [13(3) 1643 in margin.]
John Smedly of the same husbandman swore that the sᵈ Thos: said
about 3 or 4 days before his death that he meant to leave all he had to
ffrancis Barker his partner.
James Taylor of the same, carpenter swore that about 3 weekes after
michlemas last he heard the sᵈ Bagnly say the same.
Taken vppon oath 28 (2) 1643.

Before JOHN WINTHROP Governor
Thomas fflint

---

## JOHN BRADLEY.

The last [will] & Testament of John Bradley of Salem deceased the 4 mo.
1642 as he related to vs witnesses was of pft memory.
Vrsly Greenoway deposed saith that John Bradley of Salem deceased,
being asked in the time of his sickness what was his will, & persuaded to
make a will, did ask why he should mak his will, he had no body to give
his estate but his wife, only some of his clothes & tooles he gave to his
brother in lawe William Allen.
    29 (5) 1642
        Testified before the Governor & court
        INCREASE NOWELL Secretary.

---

## THOMAS BLOGGET.

### Cambridge in America.

[24 (5) 1643 in Margin.]

I Thomas Blogget† being at this time in my right mind, give to wife Susan my whole estate after my decease, as well within doors as without.

---

* Thomas Bagnley died 18 March, 1643. — Shattuck's *Concord.*
† DANIEL, Chelmsford, 1654, freeman 1652. This name was anciently written *Bloghead,* [see I. Mather's *Ind. Wars*] and was so pronounced within 30 years. THOMAS,
Cambridge, freeman 1636. Five of the name have graduated at Dart., Mid. and Vt. Colleges. — Farmer's *Genealogical Register.*
  The individual referred to by Mather, *Brief Hist.,* 35, is *Ruth Bloghead,* who was a witness in a case, not meet now to be mentioned, with many others of Woburn. It may be
proper to state, however, that it had nothing to do with the Indians.
  We do not recollect to have seen the name in English authors, but those bearing it are
somewhat numerous in New England. There were none in the early directories of New

She to bring vp my children in such learning & other things as is meete for them, & pay oldest son Daniel £15 when one & twenty or in one month after her decease.  To my 2ᵈ son Samuel £15, as above.  To daughter Susanna £15.  Should they have a father-in-law who does not treat them well my will is that the Deacons & our brother ffessington & our brother Edward Winchship, they or either of them should have power to see unto it & reforme it by one meanes or other.  Written this 10th day of the 6th month 1641.*

In presence of us           Hereunto I set my hand
Tho: Harris                 THOMAS BLOGGET
John Mena†
Deposed by Tho: Harris & John Mena the 8 (5) 1642 before
                          INCREASE NOWELL Sec.

CORRECTION. — On a recurrence to the original, we are satisfied that *Richard Eles*, on p. 102, *ante*, should be Richard *Iles*. (See p. 1).

---

* Inventory dated 28 (10) [25 (5) 1643 in margin] apprised by Gregory Stone, Nathaniel Sparhawk, Edward Winship and John ffessington.  [Same since Fessenden, no doubt.]
† Perhaps since *Meane* or *Means*.  Farmer has "JOHN MEANE, Cambridge, buried 19 March, 1646.  Wife *Ann*, and several children.  JOHN, his son, d. Oct. 1646." The name of Means occurs in our first volume, p. 330, but that family was a recent emigration. The name MEIN is also of recent importation.  See Thomas' *Hist. Printing.*

## ABSTRACTS OF THE EARLIEST WILLS UPON RECORD IN THE COUNTY OF SUFFOLK, MS.

[Continued from p. 186, of this volume.]

### JOHN PERRY.

This 4° of June 1642.  24 (5) 1643 [in margin.]

I John Perry of Roxbury, being weake in body.  My wife shall have all my house, & land & goods, wᵗʰin doores & wᵗʰout, & to bring up my children vntil my eldest son is of the age of 21 yeares, then halfe my house & land or the benefit thereof to be equally divided vnto my three children, the other halfe vnto my wife during her naturall life, then the whole to remaine vnto my children, that is to say, a double portion vnto my oldest son, & the other theird equal portions.  Therefore furder my desire & request is vnto my beloved brethren, William Hetth & Phillip Eliot be pleased to oversee & councell my wife & children for their best comfort as they are able.                 JOHN PERRY.

Isaack Heath
Witnessed by Phillip Eliot to be the will
of John Perry, before the Court of Boston, the 7°
of the 1°. 1642 or 1643.           Increase Nowell Sec:

York, but in the *first* Boston directory, (1789,) there were " *Blodget & Gilman*, store-keepers, No. 53 State street."  They are believed to be numerous in Rhode Island.  Major William Blodget of the Revolutionary army, married Anne Phillis, daughter of Capt. John Chase of Newport.  Maj. Blodget was the father of Col. Wm. Blodget of Rhode Island, now living.  See Updike's *Narraganset Church,* 109.
* Inventory dated 28 (10) [25 (5) 1643 in margin] apprised by Gregory Stone, Nathaniel Sparhawk, Edward Winship and John ffessington.  •[Same since Fessenden, no doubt.]
† Perhaps since *Meane* or *Means*.  Farmer has "JOHN MEANE, Cambridge, buried 19 March, 1646.  Wife *Ann*, and several children.  JOHN, his son, d. Oct. 1646." The name of Means occurs in our first volume, p. 330, but that family was a recent emigration. The name MEIN is also of recent importation.  See Thomas' *Hist. Printing.*

JONATHAN WAYMOUTH.

24° (5°) 1643, [in margin.]

I Jonathan Waymouth, seaman, bound for the west Indies, giue my goods to John Sweete, shipwright of Boston, for his use till I returne. First, he is to receive from goodman ffracter of Dorchester two Ewe Goats & 21ˢ for me, from David Anderson at Long Island, 31ˢ from goodman Merry, £5. after Gd. Merry hath receiued it of John Saunder, fisherman, liueing at Pascataway, & also he is to receiue from Richard wright of Boston, £10. 5ˢ after he has receiued it of Edward Heathe, 7ˡᵇ 5ˢ, & 3£ more from Arthur Browne. Of James Davies 18ˢ. one suite of apparell & cloake wᶜʰ he is to sell for me, & as I think worth 50ˢ, as also one silver spoone of 5ˢ prise: one chest of 7ˢ worth, & bookes & other smale things in the chest, wᶜʰ the aforesaid John Sweete is to sell & improve till I, Jonathan Waymouth, do come againe.

this 19ᵗʰ day november: 1639          A hand & Seale.
Witness, John Mansfield,
deposed that this is a true Copie of
the will before the Court, 26 (11°) 1642.

Increase Nowell Sec:

---

SAMUEL HAGBORNE.*

24° (5°) 1643, [in margin.]

The nineteenth of January, 1642. I Samuel Hagborne of Roxbury, haueing my understanding & memory, do make & ordaine this my last will & Testament. *Imprimus*, wife sole executrix. I intreate the Reverend & beloved Elders & deacons of our church of Roxbury to be ouerseers, & I giue them power to order all my estate, & guide my wife in all her wayes. *Item.* My debts in England shall be paid out of my stock or lands. *Item.* Oldest daughter, Elizabeth, shall haue the greate pot & 3 silver spoones which her Grandfather gave her, — each of my daughters shall haue a bed, blanket, Rugg, boalster & a pair of sheets, only my wife shall take her choice of the best first. Out of my greate desire to promote learning for Gods honoʳ & the good of his church, my will is that when Roxbury shall set up a free school in the towne, there shall be 10ˢ p annu out of the neck of land, & 10ˢ p annu out of the house & house lot vnto it for ever. *Item.* I giue vnto my brother, Abraham Hagborne, the heifer wᶜʰ I bought of Daniel Brewer, & my suite of apparell. *Item.* I giue vnto my brother Lugg four bushels of Indian corne and my suite of apparell. *Item.* I give betwixt my dau. Elizᵗʰ, my maide Alice, & my man Nathaniel, the heifer wᶜʰ I bought of Mr. Gore, whereof one quarter being Alices already, I giue her another quarter, so that it is half hers & the other half equally between Elizᵗʰ & Nathanˡ. aforesᵈ., if he serve his time out faithfully to my wife. To my Eldest son Samuel half my house & lands called the neck, when he is one & twenty. Wife to haue the hay of 10 Acres of saltmarsh on the furder side, as long as she liueth.

---

* This name is spelt many ways. Farmer has "HACKBURNE, ABRAHAM, freem. 1645, had sons, ISAAC, b. 1642; JOSEPH, b. 1652. *Samuel*, Ms, freem. 1638," which is all he has given us. Mr. Ellis (*Hist. Roxbury*, 120,) has no *Abraham*, but gives us the children of Samuel, as follows: Elizabeth, b. 24 April, 1635; Samuel, b. 1637; John, b. 1640; Hannah, b. 5 January, 1642. Samuel, our testator, died 24: 11: 1642.

*Item.* To son Samuel my house, house lott & swamp at his mothers decease. If he die under age, my sonne John shall have half his lands, & the other half to be equally divided between my two daughters. If both my sons die, my daughters to be joint heirs. To Son John the other half of my land called the Neck at one & twenty. To oldest daughter my peece of land called the Calues pasture, when she is one & 20. To my younger daughter, my woodlot & my part of the 4000 Acres w$^{ch}$ is about 100 & four score Acres, more or lesse, when she is eighteen. If she die under age her sister shall be her heir. *Item.* I give my last Division of Land in Roxbury to my two daughters after my wifes disease. My greate desire is that one sonne be brought up to learning, if my estate will afforde it.                                         p me SAM HAGBURNE.

Witnesses
William Perkins
Joseph weld
Joshua Hewes
John Johnson
        Deposed the 8$^{th}$ day of the first M$^o$: $^{1642}_{1643}$
before the Court, witnes,                    Increase Nowel Secretary.

- - - - - - -

## RICHARD CARVER.

### 30° (8°) 1643, [in margin.]

In the name of God Amen. the eighteenth day of December, in the yeare of o$^r$ Lord God, 1638. I Richard Carver of watertowne, in New England, yeoman, being sick, but of perfect memory. *Item.* To Elizabeth Carver, my daughter, £30. in money or goods. *Item.* To Susanna Carver, my daughter, the value of £30 money or goods, all the residue of all my goods & houseing, w$^{th}$ my lott lands, chattles, Cattell, money & debts whatsoeuer, vnto Grace, my wellbeloued wife, she to pay the legacies & to keep my daughter Susanna vntil she be disposed of.

witnesses         Nicholas Guye*                A hand & Seale
        Joseph Tainter†
    Testified before the Governo$^r$, John Winthrop,
the 9° of 7°, 1641.

- - - - - - -

## HENRY RUSSELL.

### 30° (8) 1643, [in margin.]

The last will of Henry Russell of Weymouth, the 28° of the 11° Month, 1639. I giue my wife half my land & half my house, my land being eight acres or there abouts, during her widowhood. My daughter Elizabeth full & sole heire, executor & administrator of all my house, lands goods cattle, money now in possession, or otherwise in grant vndisposed of — y$^t$ y$^t$ £30. be not paid to goodman stowe his vse in England, w$^{ch}$ I took vp of him here in Cattle & goods, then shall my wife & daughter equally make satisfaction. Overseers of this my will, & also of this my child, namely Zaccheus Goold, will$^m$ Cowdery, Edward Batts,‡ Henry

---

* GUY, NICHOLAS, Watertown, a deacon, was admitted freeman, 1639. — *Farmer.*
† The same, probably, who came to New England in 1638, in the ship *Confidence* of London, from Southampton, at the age of 25 years. See p. 108 of this volume.
‡ Not clear in the record, but I doubt not it should be Batte.

Russell. Witnesses, John Vppam Edward Batte, Jeremy Gould. Further I giue & assign vnto Jane my wife, the remainder of time to be served by my seruant John Comstock.

HENRY RUSSELL X his mark.

Witnessed by [as above.]

This is a true copy of the original will proved before the Governo<sup>r</sup> by the oath of Edward Batte, one of the witnesses. 9 (8) 1640, to be entered by the Recorder.

Testor Tho : Lechford.

---

## THOMAS BITTLESTONE.*
### 30 (8) 1643, [in margin.]

He deceased the 3° of Nouember 1640. *Imp.* To my daughter, Elizabeth Bittlestone, for her childs portion, £150. To Mr. Thomas Shepherd the pastor of Cambridge £5. To Mr. ffoordam† who came over in the ship w<sup>th</sup> me, for a token, 20<sup>s</sup>. To my wife, Elisabeth Bittlestone, the rest of mine estate. I leaue to my wife my boy, John Swan, to serue her sixe years, she then to giue him £5. If my daughter dye before she come to perfect age, then her estate to return to my wife. Should they both dye, then one 3<sup>d</sup> of my estate to be giuen to my Naturall kindred in Ould England, one 3<sup>d</sup> to this church of Cambridge, the other 3<sup>d</sup> to my two friends, Thomas Cheesholand, & W<sup>m</sup>. Cutter, both of Cambridge. Tho : Cheesholand & W<sup>m</sup> Cutter shall haue the oversight of my daughters estate.

| Witnesses Richard Cutter | Deposed the 7° of the 7° month 1643 |
| Katherine Haddon | by these three before me |
| Barbara Cutter | Samuel Symons & |
| | Increase Nowell. |

---

## MOSES PAINE.‡
### 30<sup>th</sup> (8) 1643, [in margin.]

I moses Paine of Braintree in New England gent. Son moses Executor. To Steven Paine my second sonne one quarter of my goods & lands in Braintree, Cambridge, Concord & Pascataway in New England, also a quarter of my goods or debts in Ould England if they may be recovered.

---

* The inventory of his estate amounted to £271 : 2s.: 2d., £175 of which was in money. It bears date of record 30 (8) 1643, and is signed by *Thomas Cheesholme, John Sill,* and *William Cutter.* The name of BITTLESTONE is not found in Farmer's *Register.* He lived in Cambridge. We know none of the name at this time.

† Perhaps Robert, a minister, who went to South Hampton, L. I. There are many of the name on the easterly part of the island at this day. The Rev. *Robert Fordham,* probably accompanied Rev. Mr. Denton to Hempstead in 1644, as he is the first person named in Keift's patent to that town. His wife's name was *Elizabeth.* His children were, Hannah, who married Samuel Clark, another dau., who m. Lieut. Edward Howell, both of Hempstead; John, who d. 1683; Jonah, a minister, who preached a time at Hempstead, after Mr. Denton left, in 1662; Robert and Joseph. Mr. Fordham died in September, 1674. His son Jonah, above named, had a son Josiah, also a clergyman, who preached a while at Setauket, after the death of Mr. Brewster. Said Josiah Fordham was the great-grandfather of B. F. THOMPSON, ESQ, the historian of Long Island, our chief authority for this note.

‡ Inventory on record, amounting to £671 : 03s., debts to be paid out £73–5s.–5d. Date of entry 30 (8) 1643. Signed by *Robert Kitchell, William Chittenden, Benjamin Albe,* and *John Reade.*

14

To Elizabeth Paine my daughter one quarter of my goods in the fore-named places, & in Ould England if they be recovered. Out of the former houshold stuffe, that one chest of fine Linnen be giuen to her, excepting two paire of fine & stronge sheetes, to be giuen to son Moses, & two paire to son Steven, Strong & good. Sonne Steven to be vnder sonne Moses' tuition till at the age of 20 & 3 yeeres. To sonne Steuen twenty pounds sterling. To be brought vp at schoale for three months, & 6 months for the bettering of his reading & writing, to be paid for by son Moses. lastly the moity & one halfe of my estate, goods, house, lands, cattle, debts, moveables, Chatteles be giuen to my oldest sonne, Moses Payne,* & he to be sole executor. Further, to the said Moses I giue half my debts in Ould England, if they may be recouered. Daughter Elizabeth to be paid her portion wi<sup>thin</sup> three months after my decease.

17th of the 4th mo., commonly called June, 1643.

A Hand.

Witnesses John Mills,
     Daniel Weld.

As an addition to this my last will, I Moses Paine bequeath unto my wife, Judith Paine, twenty shillings, to be paid her wth<sup>n</sup> the space of ten yeares after my decease.

20th 4th m°., 1643.

     Richard Brackett,
     Henry Adams,
     John Mills.

* "Moses Pajne, Ensigne to the foote compā in Braintry being remooved from thence, the magist doe Appoint Sergt. Robert Swelus (?) to be Ensigne to y<sup>t</sup> Comp<sup>y</sup> in his stead." — *General Court Files.*

## ABSTRACTS OF THE EARLIEST WILLS UPON RECORD IN THE COUNTY OF SUFFOLK, MS.

### [George] Barrell.*

### 31. (8) 1643, [in margin.]

In feare & reuerence of the greate & dreadfull name of the Almighty Creator of heauen & earth, & only wise orderer of all things therein at his good will & pleasure, vnto whom I desire to resigne my selfe & all that I haue vnto his greate praise & glory. And according to his good hand vppon mee by w<sup>ch</sup> I am more especially required; I do now by these presents set mine house in order in manner & forme following. My house and lands in Boston I giue to wife Anne during her life, then to sons

* BARRELL, GEORGE, Boston, freem. 1643, d. 11 Sept., 1643, JOHN, Boston, mem. art. co. 1643, ensign of it 1656, d. 29 Aug., 1658. He had sons, JOHN, b. 1645; JOHN 2d, b. 1652; WILLIAM, b. 1654; JOHN 3d, b. 1656. *Thomas*, Ms., freem. 1645. *William*, Boston, d. 20 Aug., 1639. — *Farmer's Register.*

John & James. To sonne John Barrell, two thirds of primises; the other third part vnto younger son James Barrell; John to pay twenty shillings to Anne Gawod, & the like sume to Hannah Semon, my two grand-children, when they shall be 21 yeares old. To sonne John my new bed & bolster w<sup>th</sup> my new rugg; & vnto James the bed & bolster w<sup>ch</sup> I now lye vppon, & my greene rugge. To dau. Anne my other bed w<sup>th</sup> the greene couerlett, after the decease of my said wife. To John & James all my working tooles, belonging to my trade.* All the rest of my goods debts & moveables whatsoeuer to wife Anne, whom I constitute sole executrix. This 28° day of the 3° month, 1642.

Witnesses    James Everill                     A hand & Seale.
               Edward Alleyne

Testifyed by James Everill before me
                      Increase Nowell the 30<sup>th</sup> of the 8° 1643.

---

## THOMAS WILSON.

### 31 (8) 1643, [in margin.]

In the name of God Amen    I Thomas Wilson of Exeter being very sick, yet in my right witts. My loving wife & deare children I commend vnto the grace of God & to the oversight & watchfull eye of my christian brethren of the church of Roxbury, Hampton & Exeter, or where it shall please God to call them. To wife my dwelling house & new frame w<sup>th</sup> the mill, & all lands & moveables thereunto belonging, during her widowhood: & the vse of all my cattle & moovable goods for the bringing vp of my children. If she marry again, then to haue her thirds, & to leaue them to my son Humfrey. To son Samuel & son Joshua, to my daughter Deborah & my dau. Liddey, either of them ten pounds at the age of 21, or day of marriage, out of the mill goods. To son Humphrey my right & interest in house & land w<sup>h</sup>. I bought of Mr. Needam. And if wife die before my four younger children come to age, or any of them, then son Humphrey to provide for their nurture & bringing vp out of his owne dowry. To sons Samuel & Joshua, 4000 pipe staues, to buy either of them a bullock.

                                      A hand.

This 9° day of the 11° mo 1642.
Witnesses,

| | |
|---|---|
| Edward Hilton, | deposed in court the 20<sup>th</sup> |
| John Smart, | of the 7°, 1643. |
| John Legat,† | Increase Nowell. |
| John Richardson. | |

---

* He appears to have been a mason.

† He was admitted an inhabitant of Hampton, N. H., 30: 8: 1640, but was of Exeter in 1646, and in Hampton again in 1649. At this last date he agrees "to teach & instruct all the children of or belonging to our towne, both male & female, (which are capiable of learning,) to write & read & cast accounts, (if it be desired,)—this yeare insuinge, as the weather shall be fitting for the youth to come together to one place; & also to teach & instruct them once in a week or more in some orthodox Chatechise provided for them by their parents or masters." — Toppan's *Hampton Genealogies*, MS. His wife's name was Ann, but whether he left any children is not known at present.

## WILLIAM FRY.*
### 4. (10) 1643, [in margin.]

This may be to witnes & giue testimony, vnder the hands of those whom haue herevnto subscribed their names that W^m ffry of Waymouth who dyed the 26° of october, 1642, being sicke & weake in body.   To his wife after his decease his house & foure acres of land being his home lot, & after her decease to his two daughters, Elizabeth & Mary.   To his two daus. 2 acres of mead &,sixe acres of land lying by the mill, also to each of them a Goate.   To *Thomas Harris, Thomas Rawlens* & *John Meggs* his three sisters youngest children, each of them a kid.   The rest of estate to wife

Thomas Baily<br>John Burge

deposed by the above named before the court
the 9° of the 9° mo. 1643.

---

## SAMUEL HOLLY.†
### 5 (10) 43, [in margin.]

Because it is appointed for all men once to dye, & the dayes of men in this world are but like a shadowe y^t soone departeth, Therefore, I Samuell Holly doe make this my last will.   Effects to my loving wife, except Tenn acres of land to my soone according to a former writing, and the remaining part of the inclosed lott to goe to my soone & his heirs; to goe after y^e decease of my wife, but she to haue y^e vse & possession thereof, during her life.   To my soone one blue stuffe Sutte of apparall, one hatt one pr of shoos; all other my lands & goods I giue to my wife, whom I doe make my sole Execut^r.   This 22^th of October, 1643.
Witnesses     John Jackson
Edward Jackson

---

## WILLIAM BOWSTRED.‡
### 8 (1°) 1643, [in margin.]

The last will & Testament of W^m Bowstred, the 23 of Octob. in y^e yeare of o^r Lord 1642.   To the children of my sister Elizabeth Newman all my estate; my sister to haue it till the children are 21.   I put into the hand of Joseph wheeler whom I make overseer of my will, all my goods, to sell to put into cattle, & send them to my sister aforesaid.   To Richard Beten one ould grey suite of cloths, one coat, 2 shifts, 2 paire of ould hose, one paire of bootes, one bible, one paire of stockings, one old hatt, in consideration of his paines & charges that he hath beene at.

William Bowstred

W^m Hunt,
Tho: Bagnley.
Sworne before the Court 8 (1) 1643

Stephen Winthrop, Recorder

---

* He died at Weymouth, 26 October, 1642, according to *Farmer*, which is all we know of him.   The inventory of his estate, as recorded, is £36 – 2s – 11d.   Appraisers, *Edward Batts, Walter Harris*, and *Thomas Bayly*.   Dated [*defaced*] (10) 1643.
  † From the inventory of his effects we learn that he died " in y^e bounds of Cambridge." Amount, £15 – 13s – 2d.
  ‡ Mr. Shattuck notices " William Bowstree d. Nov. 31, 1642."   *Hist. Concord*, 264. The inventory of his estate is recorded, but there are no names of appraisers to it.   Amount, £20 – 16s – 4d.

March 12th 1642.   Whereas I Vennis Clearke of Dertford in the county
of Kent, husbandman, haueing formerly heard of the death of Anna my
wife, did therevppon betake my self to the companie of Olave Peddington
of Dertford aforesaid, & by her had two children in the absence of the
abovenamed Anna.   And now finding the abouesaid Anna yet to be liueing, & notwithstanding my affections not inclining towards her, but rather
towards the foresaid Olave w<sup>th</sup> whom I haue last acompanied, I do therefore by these presents testify, that I do wholely refuse to liue any longer
w<sup>th</sup> the foresaid Anna in a conjugall Society; & further, I do by these
presents freely acquitt & discharge, (as farre as in mee lyeth,) the said
Anna of all duty & conjugall bands, & leaue her at liberty to be marryed to any other man, & doe freely giue vnto her all such goods as already shee hath, either in her owne or her mothers possession.

In witness whereof I haue           The mark of Penuis Clark
hereunto set my hand &                    & his Seale.
seale in the presence of vs
John Winthrop
Richard Babington
Emman : Donning
Nehemiah Bourne

CORRECTION. — The date of the approval of the last will on p. 186 should be 8 (1)
1642, instead of 8 (5) 1642. (See p. 11).

# ABSTRACTS OF THE EARLIEST WILLS UPON RECORD IN THE COUNTY OF SUFFOLK, MS.

## EDWARD HOW.

*1644, June 3. I doe make this my last will I do thus dispose of my estate. First I giue to *Nathaniell Treadaway*† about three acres of Upland lying behinde his dwelling howse & one acre vnbroken before yᵉ said howse with nine acres purchased lately of *John Vahan* further I giue to my wife, *Nathaniel Treadaway*, & *Anne Stonne* yᵉ wife of *John Stonne* of Sudbury yᵉ wares wᵗʰ all yʳ previldges therto belonginge & all yᵗ is due to me from *Mr. Thom: Mayhew*: to either of them one third part. I give to *Mary Knowlse* & *Elisabeth Knowlse* each of them one sheep: And all yᵉ rest of my estate, howsinge Lands Chattles & Moveable goods & Debts I give to my wife. If she shall not make vse of or dispose of my estate during her life what she Leave *Anne Stonne* shall haue one third part of all yᵉ Cattle: & all yᵉ rest of yᵉ Cattle howsinge Lands Debts & movables I giue to *Nathaniell Treadaway*: my wife *Nathaniell Tread·way* & *John Stonne* Execcutors of this my last will: & I doe Appoint *John Sherman* Suprovisour of this my last will. & I giue vnto him fiftye shillings to be paid by my wife in half a year after my Decease.

By me EDWARD HOW.

witnes   *John Sherman* who
was sworne yᵉ: 25 of yᵉ 5ᵗʰ 44
in Court

*Steph. Winthrop* Recorʳ.

---

## ELISABETH HOBERT.‡

Boston in New England the 29° of the 10ᵗʰ month 1643. [In margin] 4°. (7°)1644. [Date of proof.]
The said *Elisabeth Hobert* being not well & yet being in perfect sence & vnderstanding do make this as my last will & testament, that my daughter *Hannah Hobert* & my sonne *Benjamin Hobert*, I do make them my whole executors joyntly together of all those goods wᶜʰ are mine, with this provisor, my exectitors to pay three score & ten pounds & ten shillings to *Hannah Carrington* as soone as the goods can be sould. Also to pay to the said *Stoctdell Carrington* foure pounds & some odde money: also to my sonne *Richard Hobert* twelve pence. Also to dau. *Hanner Hobert* & to sonne *Benjamin Hobert*, & to dau. *Sarah Hobert*, & to dau. *Rachhell Hobert* equall portions of what is left when all cost & chardges is paid. Youngest dau. *Rachell* to haue three pounds more than the rest of my three children, that is to say Hannah, & Benjamin & Sarah. The executors to haue a tender care of their youngest sister *Rachel*.

---

* This as well as the following wills in this article is slightly abridged; but the phraseology is always preserved.
† Spelt *Treadway* in FARMER. In the REV. MR. BARRY's *Hist. of Framingham*, are many facts concerning descendants of the name.
‡ She died 6 Jan., 1643–4, at Boston. — *Shurtleff*.

19

*Robert Hull* & *Thomas Clarke* desired to be overseers of will, to see it fulfilled as neere as they can.  ELISABETH HOBBERT.
Witnes Robert Hull
Thomas Clarke.                                      proved 4°. 7°. m°. 1644.
                                                    before me Samuell
                                                    Symonds & me
                                                    Increase Nowell.

---

### GEORG PHILLIPPS.
### D. I. (M. 5)* 1644.

Wee do hereby testify this to be the last will of *Georg Phillipps* Pastor of Watertowne. [Date of proof pr. margin] 6° (7°) 1644.
1. I giue to my wife the Thirds of all mine estate.
2. The remainder to be divided amongst my Children. *Samuel* the Eldest to haue a double portion, & the rest to haue equally alike.
    Witnes *Symon Eire*
           *Apphia ffreeman*
    The mark of *Elisabeth Child*
Presently after his wife putting him in mind of the bond in *Elder Howes* hand, he called *Samuel* to him and tould him he had given him a double portion, and bade him let the bond alone & give it in to yo^r mother when yow come to age, but if yow take that yow shall haue no more.
                                                    Witness *Symon Eyre*
This was taken vppon                                *Apphia ffreeman..*
the oathe of the said
*Symon Eyre* & *Apphya*
*ffreeman* before m^r. *John*
*Winthrop* D Gov^r. & Mr.
*William Hibbins.*

---

### THOMAS PIG.
### 14° (7°) 1644 [in margin.]

Be it knowne to all men that this is the will of *Thomas Pig*,† that he doth give to his sonne *Thomas* the house w^th the home lott, 2 acres of fresh marsh, also my lott by the dead swamp, & all the land in the neck both upland & Marsh, & the 5 acres at the great lots end.  He to pay his brother *John* ten pounds, 5 at 21 years of age, & and the other 5 a year after.  To sonne *Thomas Pig* also the land in the Calues Pasture, paying his sister *Hany*‡ *Pigg* 5 pounds, 3 pounds a yeare after his mothers death and the other three pound the year after that, and for defect not paying this six pounds at these tymes appointed, the land to returne to her.  To dau. *Saray*, dau. *Mathew* my Eight Acre Lott lyeing vppon *Pigs hill*, & I give To them also my last Division of ground.  To dau.

---

* 1° of the 5th month (i. e, 5 July, 1644.) is probably the date intended.
† The name of *Thomas Pigge* is found in our list of Roxbury people printed in Vol. II. p. 53.  It undoubtedly represents the same person.  Pigs hill, mentioned in this will, we are told is still known by that name; but that no person of the name of *Pigge* has resided there for a long time.
‡ Mr. Ellis, in his *Hist. of Roxbury*, enumerates a *Henry* among the children of Thomas Pigge, but *this* name we are inclined to think stands for *Hannah;* yet when we come to a "daughter Mathew," we confess we are somewhat puzzled.  The reader may be sure, *we have not mistaken the manuscript.*

*Mary* my allotment in the thousand Acres lyeing at Dedham. Wife to haue all I haue so long as she liues to bring vp my children. After her death my children to have their portions as aforesaid.

> *Giles Payson    Robert Williams*
> Testifyed before m^r *Winthrop* Dep: Gov: & *Mr. Nowell* the (7°) 12–1644.

---

## JOHN LOVRAN.

A true Copie of the testimony of *Elisabeth Child, Elisabeth Pierce & Margaret Howe* examined vppon oath before vs, *Richard Browne & W^m. Jennings* appointed 9° (9°)

*Elizabeth Child* being w^th *John Lovran\** of watertowne some three dayes before he dyed, did move him to make his will, to w^h he answered, That he had but little, & that his wife was sickley, & so he would leave that he had to her.

*Elisabeth* Pierce at the same tyme being present, heard him speake to this purpose, Alas, that I have is but little, & that he had a sickly wife, & what he had was little inough for her.

*Margaret How* in the presence of her Husband *Mr. How* & of the wife of *John Lovran* deceased, not long before the death of the said *John.*

Only a trifle or twoe; He would give his brother that had children one hundred pounds, & twenty pounds vnto the Church after her life.

> *Richard Browne*
> *William Jennison.*†

---

## THOMAS FINSON.
## 23. (2) 1645.

Whereas *Thomas ffinson* mariner late of Dartmouth Dyed abord the Shipp Gilbert in September last, *Oades*‡ *Bayle* being present, the said *Thomas ffinson* by word of mouth declared this to be his last will & testament. To son *Samuel* fyve pounds of English money; to his child that his wife went withall fifty shillings; to wife one Hogshead of Tobacco; to his father in lawe *Andrew Harwood* all his wages. The fifty shillings for the Child & the Tobacco to be delivered to *Andrew Harwood* for the vse aforesaid.

> Deposed the
> first of the (9°) month
> 1644 by *Oads Bayle*
> before the Court.

---

## GABRIELL WHEATLEY.
## 27 (8) 1645.

*Thomas Rogers* of Watertowne sworne before *John Winthrop* Governor 13 (5) 1637, saith that *Gabriell Wheatley* being of pfect vnderstanding

---

\* Probably since *Lovering.* On this name FARMER has but a line and one third in his *Register,* which is this: "JOHN, freeman 1636, might be the same who lived at Dover in 1665."

The "freeman" of 1636 of Farmer was probably our *John Lovran*; but that he was the same at Dover in 1665, is improbable. There are many of the name in New Hampshire at this day, and elsewhere in New England.

† Seems at first to have been written *Jennings,* like that at the commencement of the document, but subsequently altered to *Jennison.*

‡ Possibly *Oates* is meant, and perhaps *Otis Bayley.*

even to the time of his death, said in the presence of *Bryan Pendleton* and this deponent that he would haue the said *Bryan* to take charge of his estate & out of it to pay himselfe what was due to him; the rest to go to his daughter — to be gathered vp & reserued by the said *Bryan*. Vppon this the said *Bryan* was granted to administer, & to be accountable when required. The summe that was due to her amounted to £16 16s.

Witnes { *Richard Browne*
       { *Edward Howe.*

---

### THOMAS KNOCKER.*

An Inventory of the Goods of *Tho: Knocker* prised of *Will Stitson Will Brackenburye Augustion Walker* & *Jo: Allen* y⁰ 19 Nov. 1641.

[His whole effects amounted to some £30. The following names we find among the list of his debtors & creditors:]

Persons owing: *Rich^d. Graues* of Salem, 6s. *John Penticost*, 6^d. *Tho: Poyston†* of Watertown, 12s. *Nic Jewett*, 12^s. Mr. *Robert Woarye*, 4s. 6^d. *Jo Burridge*, £1. 3s. *Gd* [goodman] *Paddock*, 3 pecks of Corne. *Edward Fuller*, 4s. 6^d.

*Thomas Knocker* was debtor to *James Browne*, £1. 9s. *Austin Walker*, 5s. *Abram Palmer*, 4s. His bro: *Geog Knocker*, 4s. *Wid° Wilkinson*, *Jo Lawrence*, £3. 2s. *Ryse Cole*, 9^d. *Robt. Heath*, 1 bu. Corne. *Tho Moulton*, 14s. *Edwd. Convers*, 6s. *Jer Swayne*, 2s. *Gd Hawkins*, £8. 12s. 6^d. *Good Brackenburye,‡*     *Gon Drinker*, 3s. 1d. *Will Smith*, 6^d.

---

### ABIGAIL SUM̄ER.§

31 (8) 1643.

The goods of Abigail the late wife of Tho: Sum̄er deceased praised by the psons subscribed.

| | Amount £7. 9s. 8^d. |
| witnes | Oweth 1. 18. 0. |
| Joseph Jewet | |
| William Boynton. | |

---

* The will of this individual does not appear to have been recorded. The abstract of the inventory which we here give is taken from the 2d volume of our Registry, entitled "Inventories," and is called No. 2. FARMER seems not to have met with the name of *Knocker*, at least not in this form. It is possible that it may have been curtailed into that of *Nock*.

† I can make nothing else of this name, and it is a perfect stranger in my catalogue of New England names. Probably *Boylston.*

‡ The family of *Brackenbury* was anciently of much note in England. As late as the 32d of ELIZABETH, "*Richard Brakinbury* was an old courtier." In 1575, in a visitation, he is mentioned as Gentleman Usher to Queen Elizabeth, and was the fifth son of *Anthony Brakenbury* of Denton, by Agnes, dau. of Ralph Wycliffe of Wycliffe in Yorkshire.— *Lodge's Illustrations*, ii. 421. *Dale's Hist. Harwich*, 177.

§ Perhaps *Sumner*. We do not find either *Summer* or *Sumner* at Watertown in 1636, though we infer that this person died resident there. There is no will on record. FARMER found a *Thomas Summer* at Rowley, 1643. In the index of our volume of Inventories (a modern work,) we find "Abigail Sumner," which is probably right.

22

## EDWARD WOOD.

Inventory of goods and money belonging to Edward Wood of Charlestown, deceased being valued by Robert Long, William Brackenbury and Richard Russell the 4th day of the 18 Month 1642, in New England.

---

## EDWARD SKINNER.*
## 13 (  ) 1643.

The Inventory of *Edward Skinners* of late prised by *Gregory Stone* & *Gilbert Crackborne* November, 1639.

|                                                   | £ | s. | d. |
|---------------------------------------------------|----|----|----|
| Paid out of this estate to *W<sup>m</sup>. Merchant* for debt | 6 | 0 | 0 |
| To *Thomas Warrish* [Warwick ?]                   | 4 | 19 | 6 |
| To *Goodman Rise*                                 | 4 | 0 | 0 |
| To *Goodwife Merchant* of his gift                | 4 | 4 | 0 |
| To *Mary Slanney*                                 | 2 | 7 | 0 |
| lost in the sale of the goods & debts             | 0 | 6 | 0 |

£21 – 16 – 6

Deposed the 8 of y<sup>e</sup> first month 1642
by *Gregory Stone* & *Gilbert Crackborne*
before the Court                    *Increase Nowell* Secr.

---

## ATHAGERED KNIGHT.

An Inventory of *Athagered Knights* goods departed & prysed by Lieftenant *Mason* & Goodman *Cooledge*.

[Amount of effects,] £7. 14s. 8d.

Hugh Mason
John Coolidge.

---

## THOMAS AXTELL.
## 6 (3) 1646.

The Inventory of the goods of *Thomas Axtell* of Sudbury late deceased. Imprimus his land & house £8. 10. Cattle £8. 10. Wearing apparell & bedding w<sup>th</sup> his Armes £10. for Brasse & pewter £5. prised by *Edmund Rise, Philemon Whale, Edward Rice*. He expressed that *Mary* his wife should haue all his estate for to bring vp his children. Testifyed by Edmund Rice vppon oath the 6 (3) 1646 before the Governor, Dep. Gov<sup>r</sup>. & *Increase Nowell* Secr.

---

## ALEXANDER BRADFORD.
## 12. (4) 1646.

The last will of *Alexander Bradford* being made this xvii<sup>th</sup> day of the vi month 1644 witnesseth. I the said *Alexander Bradford* of Dorchester

---

* In extracting the will of *Edward Skinner* (Vol. II. p. 103) the inventory of his estate [1] was inadvertently omitted. The follqwing is all Mr. FARMER has in his *Genealogical Register* upon this name:
"SKINNER, THOMAS, Malden, 1653—a name common in New England, and which has furnished 14 graduates at the different colleges."

[1] See p. 2.

23

apprehending myself much weakned & naturall life impayred through Sickness & dissease. vnto *Sarah* my now wife all my Masion house & other buildings with the houshold stuffe as it now stands in Dorchester Wife sole executrix. I intreate my brother *Walter Merry* of Boston to be my Supvisor to help my wife in managing her affaires, & for three pounds w$^{th}$ my brother *John Bradford* did owe mee I release him of that, it to be equally divided among his children.

ALEXANDER BRADFORD.

Signed in y$^e$ presence of
*Philemon Pormort*\*
*Walter Merry.*

Testifyed vppon oath *Walter Merry* 2 (8) 1645 before *John Winthrop* Dep. Gov & *Herbert Pelham.*

Moreover After the death of my wife I giue unto the children of my brother *John* all my housen & lands, the said *Alexander Bradford* haue giuen to *Robert Stowton* his Moose Suite & a musket & Sworde & bandilieres & vest. *Alexander Bradford.*

William Ireland also
testified this addition to be
made by the said Alexander
Bradford being of disposing memory.

Sworne before *John Winthrop* Dep. Gov. &
*Herbert Pelham.*

---

\* Perhaps afterwards written *Pimer.* There was a *Matthew Pimer* at Dorchester, who died before 1639. See *Blake's Annals,* 58.

# ABSTRACTS OF THE EARLIEST WILLS UPON RECORD IN THE COUNTY OF SUFFOLK, MS.

## JOHN BENJAMIN.
### 12 (4) 1646.

I *John Benjamin* being in pfect memory, as touching my outward estate — do bequeath to sonne *John* a double portion, beloved wife two Cowes, fourty bushels of Corne out of all my lands, to be allowed her towards the bringing vp of my smale Children yearly such as growes vppon the ground, one part of fower of all my hous hold stuffe, all the rest of my lands goods & chattels shal be equally divided betwen seven other of my children. Provided that out of all my former estate my wife during her life shall enjoy the dwelling house I live in, & three Acres of the broken vp ground next the house, & two Acres of the Meddowe neere hand belonging to the house. That this will be truly pformed I do appoint my brother *John Eddie* of Watertowne & *Thomas Marrit* of Cambridge that they doe theire best Indevo<sup>r</sup> to see this pformed.*

JOHN BENJAMIN.

Witnes *Georg Muniage* [Muning]
    the 15 (4) 45.

This was proved to be the last will & testament of *John Benjamin*, & that he did further declare (as an addition to this his will) that his wife should have liberty to take wood for her vse vppon any of his Lands dureing her life, vppon the Oath of          Before
    *John Eddye*                         *Thomas Dudley* Gov<sup>r</sup>.
    (5) 3. 1645                          *Jo: Winthrop* Dep. Gov.

---

## WILLIAM HALSTED.
### 13 (4) 1646.

Whereas I *William Halsted* do find by dayly experience my body to decay. *Imp.* vnto the poore of the towne fyve pound to be laid out in a Cow w<sup>ch</sup> I would haue so ordered by the Deacons & my executors that may be a continual help to such as are in need, God giueing a blessing therevnto. The remander of my estate, vnto brother *Henry*, & to my sister *Edna* her child or children — to brother *Henry*, at the end of two years, except he dispose of himselfe in marriage, or haue a lawfull calling to England by his friends there, to the satisfaction of my executors, & in case he should goe to England of his owne accord, then not to have it till they heare certainly of his welbeing there. And in case he should dye before this time be accomplished, then my sister *Edna* her child or children shall haue it. And I make *william Wood* & *George Heyward* executors.                              WILLIAM HALSTED.
    witnes
    *Rob<sup>t</sup> Miriam.*
    *Luke Potter.*

---

\* The inventory of the estate of *John Benjamin* may be seen in Vol. II. on p. 25 (Suffolk Wills.) No footing appears to the various items, but we make the amount of the whole, £297. 3s. 2d.
" This was deliuered as a true Inuentory of the estate of *Benjamin* deceased vppon the Oath of *Symon Stowe John Eddye* & *Thomas Marret*, to the best of theire knowledge. Taken before *Thomas Dudley*, Gover: & *John Winthrop*, Dep. Gover. 3 (5) 1645.

The testimony of *Luke Potter* to this will was taken vppon oath the 13 (8) 1645 before *Thomas fflint.*

*Rob* Miriam* sworne 15 (8) 45 before *Joh: Winthrop* dep Govr. & *Tho fflint.*

Inventory is dated 10th 8th 1645. Robt. Miriam & Georg Heward [Heyward] apprisers. Amount, £97, 10s, 7d.

---

## SAMUEL CROWES.
### 3 (4) 1646.

I do appoint *Samuel Bitfield* to take my goods & pay my debts & take the remainder to himselfe.

This was approved to be a lawfull will by the Court & Jury in tryall of an action betweene *Thomas Skidmore* & *Samuel Bitfield* at a Court held at Boston 2 (4) 1646.

---

## MARY BENJAMIN.
### 13 (4) 1646.

I *mary Benjamin* of Watertowne do give to *Pastor Knolls* fyve Acres of Marsh at the Rocky Meddow in Watertowne bounds. I giue to my *Aunt Wines* one Cowe, I giue to my sister *Abigail Stubbs* two Cowes my best clothes w$^{th}$ my best searg Peticoate. I giue to my brothers in generall one Cows worth. To my Cosin *Anne Wyes* my best wastcoate. May 16 1646.                                    MARY BENJAMIN her owne
                                                        act & deede.

Witnes to this will
    *Jane Mahew*
    *Elizabeth Child*
both sworne in Court 4 (4) 46.

                                                        *Increase Nowell* Sec$^r$.

---

## RICHARD BARBER.
### 13 (4) 46.

I *Richard Barber* of Dedham. I haue receiued a Cow of M$^r$ *Prichard* of Roxbury as the gift of one M$^r$. *Anderson* of London. I will & bequeath the said Cow to remaine to the vse & benefit of the poore in Dedham. My house & lands in Dedham, & goods & chattles vnto my Executors. My beloved friends & brethren in Christ *Henry Brock* & his sonne *John Brock* my executors.

                                    The mark of *Richard Barber.*
    Testified in Court the 21 (3) 1646.

                                                        *Increase Nowell* Sec$^r$.

---

## LAWRENCE BUCKMASTER.
### 4 (5) 1646.

Seene that I am now bound for the sea, & soe for England, them smale things that I haue heare leve & thos desposed of if *Capt. Smith* doe not recover my wages againe, then thus I have ordered it if God take me away. That the piece of land I bought of *Thomas Spaul* I giue it to my sister *Elisabeth Buckmaster* & some smale things in my chest, as a

26

great Coate to *Thomas Spaule*, & the sixe shillings due to me from *Thomas wellens* w^th it. My black hatt to *Abigail Sherman*, the suite of apparell to my brother *Zachary Buckmaster*, & a shirt and band or two for my ffather, there wil be left a paire of Stockings; the best to *Matthew Coy*, the worster paire or two paire, & the Chest vnto the said *Thomas Spaule*, & a smale caske of Mackrells that *Thomas* is to send to Sea for me for to let them go to sea for his daught^r *Mary* till they come to some thing or nothing.

LAWRENCE BUCKMASTER in
the presence of *Thomas Spaule*.

But the land she is not to make it away nor part frō, but she is not to haue it, nor haue nothing to doe w^th it till the yeare of O^r Lord 1649, & that, Mayday. If I dye at Sea, then to demand vppon inquiry, you may true wages for the time, & to giue my ffather it.

*Robert Portous* the 27^th (9) 1645.

Deposed the 2 (5) 1646, by *Thomas Spaule* & *Robert Portous* vnter *M^r Nowells* hand.

---

### THOMAS MUSSELL.

This twenty seventh of July 1640. [4 (5) 1646 in margin.]

I *Thomas Mussell* seaman, doe giue full power to *John Sweete*, Carpenter of Boston to receiue or take up for my vse: the 4^th part of the pinnace called the Mary, & the profits of it: the said my share or part: till such time as he the said *John Sweete* by power & vertue of this my will doe sell the same: or if one *Phillip White*, my partner in the said vessell, do sell her, he is to giue *John Sweete* before named, the money or goods, what shee is sould for. To said *John Sweete* twenty three shillings due me from *William Quick*. A hand & Seale

*Nicholas Lopdell.*
*John Mansfield.*

The said *John Mansfield* did testifie this vppon oath, 26 (1) 1646, before *John Winthrop*, Dep. Gov^r., & *Increase Nowell*.

---

### WILLIAM WEALE.

15 (12) 1646.

William Weale made a Nuncoupative will the 5th (8) 1646 as was testifyed by Goodwife *Milom* & *John Harwood*. See Affidavits,* p. 42.

---

### NICHOLAS STOWER.

The last will of *Nicholas Stower* of Charlestown. 16 (3) 1646.

To beloved wife *Amy Stower* my dwelling house w^th y^e barn & all other houseing, w^th the two Acres of ground by it, & all the ground in the necke of Charlestowne. Also a hay lot on Mistick syde near the North spring next o^r sister *Rands*, also half of the hay of the other hay lots on Mistick syde. Likewise 4 Cowe Com̄ons on the stinted Com̄on w^thout the necke. Also 3 of the Acres of planting ground on Misticke syde that is broken vp, & it is now sowen w^th english corne & planted w^th Indian Corne: she

* We are informed by the very obliging and intelligent gentlemen in our Registry Office, that they know of no such book.

to haue the vse of all the aforenamed—She to haue vse of the cart & plow & its furniture: she to haue my two best working oxen—all the English Corne & Indian corne on the ground on mistick syde—except that w<sup>ch</sup> my Son *Richard* is to haue of the same crop.

When wife is deceased my sonne *Joseph Stower* to haue the house, barne & other housing w<sup>th</sup> the 2 Acres of ground, to abide with his mother to do her service while she liues, or till he be twenty & one yeare old. Hee to pay his sister *Abigail* 2 Cowes, & one to his sister *Jone* at y<sup>e</sup> decease of my wife.

To daughter *ffar* a great bible, & the great brasse pan after my wifes decease, all the rest to be my wiues for euer.

To son *Richard* my two oxen next to the best, land on mistick syde, only his mother to haue the vse of 3 Acres,—To dau. *Jone Stower* one Cowe presently, & one out of *Josephs* portion.

To dau. *Abigail Stower*, after my wives decease, two good Cowes out of *Joseph's* portion.

To dau. *ffarre* a great Bible. Wife sole executrix—loued brethren *Thomas Lyne* & *Robert Hale* to be overseers of this my last will.

Witnesses
 *Increase Nowell*
 *John Greene*
 *Thomas Lyne*
 *Robert Hale.*

---

### Thomas Williams.
#### 25 (2) 1646.

I *Thomas Williams* doe make this my will. To *John Spoore* of Boston my part in the bote, & one pound seven shillings that *John Norman* of Jeffrey Creecke haue, & is in my master *Holgraues* hand, due to mee, & that w<sup>ch</sup> he tooke order to leaue at M<sup>r</sup>. *Stodders* for me, & what els I haue, & my master *John Spoore* to pay M<sup>r</sup> *Oliver* for letting me blood & to pay M<sup>r</sup> *Ayers* & M<sup>r</sup> *Cordll* of Salem one shilling & eight pence, that w<sup>ch</sup> I did owe M<sup>r</sup> *Holgraue* haue or ingaged himselfe to satisfy *John Norman* w<sup>ch</sup> was for dyet & lines & other things axes, one at *Jeremy* the *Smith*, & another at Mr. *Holgraue*. I owed a shilling at the ferry at Salem, & *Henry Swan* I apponted to pay it. Dated, 25 (2) 1646.

Witnesses, *Bartholomew Chever* & *Edward Cowell* testifyed 5 (9) 1646. by *Bartholomew Chever* & *Edward Cowell* before the Magistrates. *Increase Nowell* Sec<sup>r</sup>.

Date of Inventory, 1 (3) 1646.

2 weekes wases due by M<sup>r</sup> *Holgraue* of Salem 8s. M<sup>r</sup> *Holgraue* debtor for a bullocke £6. Due by *Thomas Williams* to *John Norman* of Marblehead, £4.—to *John Spoore* £4. paid for him by *John Spoore* to M<sup>r</sup> *Correll* of Salem, 1s. 8d.—p<sup>d</sup>. to M<sup>r</sup> *Aires* by *John Spoore* 17s. *John Spoore* count for tendance in *Tho Williams* Sicknes, for makeing graue, coffin, & all charges, £1. 10s.

Amt of Inventory £15 10s 6<sup>d</sup>: debts £10 9s. 8d.

# ABSTRACTS OF THE EARLIEST WILLS UPON RECORD IN THE COUNTY OF SUFFOLK, MS.

### THOMAS RUGGLES.
#### The 9 (9) 1644.

I *Thomas Ruggles* of Roxbury. To Sonne *Iohn* my lott w^ch lyeth behind the great pound contains my sixteene Acres more or lesse. To sonne *Samuell* my lott butting vppon the left of *Philip Eliot* on the east, & one *A^rthur Ga^ris* north — 7 A^res more or lesse. Also my land at Dedham, containing 12 Acres more or lesse. To dau. *Sarah* three pound in such pay as my wife can best spare, to be paid her at the age of one & twenty yeere. At decease of wife effects to be divided betweene my 3 children.

Witnesses                THOMAS RUGGLES.
*Phill: Eliot*
*John Ruggles*
    Testyfied before
    the Court
      *Increase Nowell.*

---

### IOHN GRAVE.
#### November (1) 1644.

John *Grave* late of Roxbury. Vnto sonne *John* the ten Acre lott containing six Acres more or lesse. Also my two Oxen & the vse of halfe the barne during the time of his mothers life & then the barne to be divided as his mothers land is, one halfe vnto him. Also my best suite & the bed that he lyeth vppon. *John* shall pay vnto dau. *Mary* six pounds at the age of twenty-one years — but in case she dye before, *John* to pay his brother *Samuell* & *Jonathan* fourty shillings apiece.

Also vnto sonne *Samuell* my lot called the four acre lott, the lott of goodman *Lewis* between the land of *Robert Seaver* & the land of goodman *Lewis*, vnto him, &c.

vnto *Jonathan* my son that lott lying on the great hill of 5 Acres — if my two frends, *Phillip Eliot* & *Will^m Heath* exchange it for land more convenient & vsefull for my son, I give them full power so to doe.

Also my lot of Co͞mon w^ch was last divided vnto me by the towne, I give to my foresaid three sonns equally to be divided — wife to haue free liberty to fetch fyre wood.

To dau. *Mary* the bed & all that belongeth thereto w^ch her grandmother now lyeth vppon.

If wife liue fyve years after the death of my mother, then she shall pay vnto my daughter *Hanna* six pound — if she dye before, then *Iohn* & *Samuell* & *Jonathan* to pay vnto her fyve pound.

                           *Phillip Eliot.*
    Testifyed before the Court     *William Heath.*
       *Increase Nowell* sec^r.

---

### IOHN GRAVE.
#### 26 (9) 1645.

John *Grave* late of Roxbury. My land to be sould. — Vnto my brother *Samuell* Six pound, to brother *Jonathan* four pounds. — to sister *Sarah*

29

three pound — to my sister *Hanna* three pound — to sister *Marah* sixe pound w^ch I was to giue vnto her by my ffathers will — to be paid her at the age of one & twenty — vnto *Georg Brand* what he doth owe vnto mee — vnto my Mother all my wearing apparell — vnto *Phillip Eliot* what he doth owe mee, whom I doe make mine Executor. What is left to be divided between my Executor & my mother. What I was to haue by my ffathers will, after the death of my mother my two brethren, *Samuell & Jonathan* shall enjoy it equally. They to pay sister *Sarah* five pound, & to sister *Marah* three pound, & to sister *Hanna* three pound. The testimonies of *Robert Pepper, Widdowe Grave & John Hansett.* See in the book of affidavits,* fol. 43.

### Iohn Oliver.
### 25 (6) 1641.

This is my last will except any befoure beareing date after it concerning the disposall of estate w^ch the Lord hath carved out vnto mee in this world, those many ingagements that lye vppon mee being by the good hand of God discharged, w^ch may be done ptly by those ingagements whereby others stand indebted vnto mee, as also by the sale of my house at Boston & of my bookes & geometricall instruments, the remaining pt being divided into three equall parts at the discretion of my deere & reverend ffathers M^r *Tho: Oliver* M^r *Iohn Newgate*, one third vnto my deare & faithful yoake fellowe, the other two thirds vnto my deare children at theire (viz^t my ffat:) discretion, and whereas my ffather M^r *Thomas Oliver* hath according to his faithfull care, & prudence promised mee that if I should dye before him, I should have power by my will to dispose of such part of his estate, as should have fallen vnto me if I had survived, my will is that it be in like manner divided & disposed of as my owne estate. If my deare brother *James Oliver* surviue me I desire him to discharge my many ingagements w^th that part of my estate foremencioned for that end. all w^ch promises I doe in hast confirme by my own hand

Deposed by *James Johnson*
& *James Oliver* the 11 (7) 1647 before
the court by me
   *Increase Nowell*, Sec.

witncs my hand
JOHN OLIVER.

### William Brinsmeade.
### 10 (10) 1647.

This testifyeth that I *W^nj Brinsmead* being in health (this 10^th of the 10^th month 1647) do make & ordaine that my estate be divided into fyve equal parts — two of these fyve I giue vnto *W^nj* my sonne, the other three parts I giue to my three children *Alexander Ebbet & Mary*, to each one part, ffurther if sonne *w^nj* Dye before he come to the age of one & twenty, *Alexander* shall haue a double part, but if either of the other die before they come of age, then it is equally to be divided to the rest. Sonne *W^nj* to be kept to schoole; also if my other sonne be capable & willing he haue so much bestowed as may fitt him to write well & cast accounts, fit for a Navigator. My daughter to be so imployed as that there may be so much saved for theire future portions as may conveniently bee

* See note, page 179, ante. (See p. 27).

30

ffor the good incouragement that I haue of my sonne $w^{rj}$ concerning his learning. I therefore giue to him all my bookes, only a Bible w$^{ch}$ I had of my ffather, that I giue to *Alexander*. I giue to $W^{rj}$ my *Negro Symon*. to my daughters I giue my wives cloathes. I appoint M$^r$ *Nathaniell Patten* of Dorchester to be my childrens guardians. I assigne him to receiue what is due to mee for the vse of my children.

W$^{NJ}$ BRINSMEADE

This will was p$^r$sented to the Court 15 (3) 1648. by *Nathaniell Patten* & *David Sellocke* written in a booke of M$^r$ *Brinsmeads* & subscribed w$^{th}$ his hand as to the Court it did appeare, who ordered M$^r$ *Patten* to bring in an Inuentory of M$^r$ *Brinsmeads* estate.

---

AGNES BENT.

7 (9) 1648.

*Thomas Blancher* testifieth that *Agnes Bent* made her will & gaue her estate to *Richard Barnes* & *Elisabeth Plimton*, & to pay fyve pound to *Elisabeth Plimton* & twenty pounds to *Richard Barnes*, & gaue ten pounds to *John Bent* & fyve pound to *Thomas Plimton*, the rest to be divided betweene *Richard Barnes* & *Elisabeth Plimton*. Deposed the first of the 9$^{th}$ month 1648. before me *Increase Nowell.*
*Peter Noyce* testifyeth the same, all but the two debts, the same day before me *Increase Nowell.*

---

THOMAS NELSON.

I *Thomas Nelson* of Rowley in the County of Essex (in N. England) being called now to make a voyadge into Ould England, giue to beloved wife *Joan*, my Mill & Millshouse in Rowley, & all the ground neere vnto the said mill, w$^{ch}$ was lately in the occupation of *Joseph Wormahill*, all my land betwene Rowley oxe pasture & the Com͞on & the mill River. Two acres in the Pond field next M$^r$ *Rogers* leaving out the Pound to build her a house on. The remainder or reversion I giue to my children, as well that child w$^{ch}$ my wife is w$^{th}$all as the rest. To oldest son *Phillip* a double portion, to son *Thomas* & to daughter *Mercy*, & the child or children shee is w$^{th}$all theire equall parts: If any of them dye before they come to the age of twenty & one yeares, then their part to be equally divided among the other children.

My will is that *Ri: Bellingham*, Esq., & my honoured vncle *Richard Dumer*, gent. shall haue the education of my son *Phillip Nelson* & *Thomas Nelson*. Wife & vncle *Richard Dumer* shall have the education of my dau. *Mercy* & the other child my wife is w$^{th}$all. To wife (*Joane*) foure choice Cowes, one choise mare & ten pounds to build her a house. To son *Phillip* ten pound w$^{ch}$ was giuen him by my Aunt *Katherine Witham*, & his plate marked with his own name P. N: & to my second son *Thomas*, a wine bowle & one spoone. M$^r$ *Richard Billingham* & my vncle *Richard Dumer* my executors. M$^r$ *Ezechiell Rogers* of Rowley & M$^r$ *John Norton* of Ipwich to bee mine overseers. To wife all her apparell, her chest boxe & bed & furniture & a silver beaker

THOMAS NELSON.

December 24. 1645.            & a seale
sealed signed & deliuered
in the presence of *Jeremie Houtchin*
               *Ezechiel Northend.*

A schedule to be annexed to the Will of *T. Nelson.* These are to certifie all whom it any waies may concerne, that I *Thomas Nelson*, about to returne to Rowlowe in New England, being at present sick, confirm my last will made in New England w^ch my wiues vncle M^r *Richard Dumer*, only w^th the addition of these provisions that my youngest child *Samuel Nelson*, being borne since that will was made, if my wife be now w^th child, & shall bring forth a child, that *Samuel*, & this may enjoy each a childs portion proportionable to the rest of my children. I earnestly desire of our Reverend Pastor & Elder M^r *Rogers*, & of that whole Church at Rowley that they may not mistake themsels concerning the eleven pounds & seventeene pounds w^ch I payd to goodman Seatchwell for his fferme, & I did not giue these in w^th other moneyes that I laid out for the plantation least this being a wrong to mee, bee to theire griefe at the day of Jesus Christ: as also fifteene pounds payd to Mr. *Carltons* hundred pound w^ch I ought not to pay. This I intreat them seriously to lay to hart, & righting mee in all these particulars. Witness my hand the sixt day of Sextiles here called August, 1648. THO: NELSON.
Testifyed as his Act & deed, &
subscribed by him in the p^rsence of vs witnesses
   *Henry Jacie* alias *Jesse*
   *Daniel Elly* his marke
   *Sarah Appleyard* her marke

---

### NICHOLAS TAILOR.
### 19 (11) 48.

I *Nicholas Tailor* of the p^rcincts of st Katherins neere vnto the tower London, mariner, bound to sea to New castle in the good shipp called the pilgrime of London. — To the poore of the parish twelve pence, loueing wife *Elisabeth* all my lands house or houses, being in Kingshire in the County of Norfolk or any other Country. Wife sole executrix. This 26^th day of July, Anno Dni 1637. Anno Regni Regis Caroli Anglie xiii°.

p me signum dicti
Sealed & D D in                          *Nichol^s* + *Tailor* & a seal
the pñce of vs.
& on the back side.
Sealed & D D published & really declared in the presence of vs
   *Richard ffairefield.*

---

### THOMAS CROMWELL.
### 3 (9) 1649.

I *Thomas Cromwell* of Boston doe by these p^rsents make my last will & Testament. Deere wife *Anne* sole executrix. To dau. *Elisabeth Cromwell* fyue pounds sterling at marriage, or at one & twenty. To wife all the remainder of my estate, excepting the ship Anne — to pay to goodwife *Sherman* ten pounds sterling, & to goodwife *Spaule* fyve pound sterl. I giue my six bells being in the Custody of *Henry Walton* vnto the towne of Boston, This 29^th of August, 1649.

THOMAS CROMWELL & a seale
Sealed signed & D D in pñce of
   *John Clark*
   *Henry Walton*              Deposed that this was the will 26 (8) 1649
                                            *Increase Nowel, Sec:*

# ABSTRACTS OF THE EARLIEST WILLS UPON RECORD IN THE COUNTY OF SUFFOLK, MS..

## ISRAEL STOUGHTON.
### 17th of July, 1644. [London.]

Being now likely to run some pt. of the hazard of warre. For my outward estate — those [affairs] in ould England as they stood the day of the date of these pntes, and for those in New England, they are manifest by what I left there at last ptng. Debts in England & what goods also I shall leave here vndisposed of. As for those in New England, they are by bookes left there, best discovered, & both are rtly discovered by my Alphabeticall booke here in England, though I dcubt in some points, imperfectly, through hast.

To Deere & worthily honored wife the entire pfitt of all my land vppon Dorchester neck (being about 50 acres all in tilth) during life ; & furthermore a third of the clear pfitts raised or raisable of all my other lands or mills, w$^{th}$ the buildings & p$^r$snt stock — during life & single estate ; also one third of all my moovable goods ; free habitation & vse (w$^{th}$ the children) of house in Dorchester towne, w$^{th}$ the garden, orchard & yard roome, being about two acres of land. Lastly, my wearing ring, all my plate, best downe bed, & her tapestry, coverlett, with all the best furniture thereto belonging ; stooles, chaires, curteines, cupboards, Andyrons, &c.. And one ffetherbed more.....& only begg of her not to weep for mee, as one of those w$^{th}$out hope. If I now dye, what love shee owed vnto mee, that it may be bestowed (after mee) vppon o$^r$ poore deare children for my sake.

For my children, I will them to the government & ordering power of my s$^d$ Deere wife, during their minority. Eldest sonne Israel a double portion, unlesse he prove himselfe unworthily ; in such case, his double portion to goe to *William ;* if *William* prove himself unworthily, then the same to be given to the next sonne, *John.* Or if yet there be another, him to be judged of as aboue ; provided if the difference in matter of grace and vertue appeare not very euident, or the eldest his vice not very euident, then let the double portion remaine his absolute due.

And for the way of accounting the Double portion, I will it thus. In case my number be seven (as I hope) *Israel* is to have two pts of the seaven ; then the remaining five pts to be cast againe into seaven pts, if I had seven children all, or six parts if six all, or fiue pts if fiue all, and one pt of the s$^d$ seven, six or fiue to be equally distributed amongst my other sonns. Remainder of estate to be equally divided by even portions to the sonnes & Daughters alike. [Provisions of contingencies and consequent subdivisions omitted.]

Moreover to sonne *Israel* one fourth part of [my] smale Library, & vnto *John* another fourth pt, & vnto *W$^m$* the other halfe, for his incouragm$^t$ to apply himself to studies, especially to the holy Scriptures ; vnto w$^{ch}$ they are mostly helpful ; if either of these dye before age, & if now unknowne I haue another sonne, if one that had a fourth pt dye, let the fourth sonne take his pte ; or if no fourth sonne, let the student take the dead sonnes pte. Provided also, concerning the Bookes, that my wife retaine to her vse during life what she pleaseth, & that my daughters chose each of them one for theire owne, that all may haue something they may call theire ffathers.

Vnto Harvard College, two hundred Acres of land, out of my purchased

33

lands on the northeast side of Naponsett, about Mother Brooke,* that is on the vtmost bounds of my ffarme next to Dorchester towne. To some meadow & some vpland about mother Brooks may in time be something worth towards the advance of learning : & one hundred acres more, I giue to the same vse out of my dues on the blew hills side, provided the towne will allow it to be laid in due opposition to those former two hundred, that the riuer only may part them ; to remain to the College vse forever.

Wife & sonne *Israel* joint Executo<sup>rs</sup>, *John Winthrop* Sen<sup>r</sup>, Mr. *Thomas Dudley*, Sen<sup>r</sup>, Mr. *Richard Bellingham*, Mr. *Richard Saltonstall* & Mr. *Increase Nowell*, & also my deere brother Mr. *W<sup>m</sup> Knight*, Mr. *Thomas Stoughton*, Mr. *Thomas Clarke*, Mr. *David Yale* overseers this seventeenth of July, 1644, in London.

ISRAEL STOUGHTON.

Concerning my deere mother — not to be abridged of her twenty pounds pr ann during her life, in regard of the cattle I had of hers, though they proved of little worth to me. Also, to dwell in the house with my wife, during her pleasure, and any other comfortable accommodation my estate may reach vnto. If God take my wife before mee, or before this will be settled, or the estate of things altered by my wife, then I in her steed doe ordaine my deere brother Mr. *Tho: Clarke*, & my loveing frends Mr. *Thomas Jones* of Dorchester, & Mr. *Edward Johnson* of Roxbury as overseers in speciall — & to haue twenty pounds each, & my brother *Clarke* to have over & aboue that, as much as his services meritt, being judged of by the gentlemen before mentioned. The same day and time aforenamed.

ISRAEL STOUGHTON.†

---

CHRISTOPHER STANLEY.

19 (12) 1649.

I CHRISTOPHER STANLEY of Boston being now sick.— Vnto *Richard Benit* three Acres of land adjoyning my orchard, w<sup>th</sup> half a house neere *John Gallop's* point. The other half to *George Benet*. To *Sarah Cotton*, dau. of Mr. *John Cotton* fyve pounds. To *Mary Wilson*, the dau. of Mr. *John Wilson* fyve pounds. To the Church of Christ here at Boston foure pounds. For the maintenance of the free schoole at Boston, a pcell of land lying neere to the water side, & fovre rodds in length backward. To each of o<sup>r</sup> teaching & ruling Elders of Boston, & to their wives a paire of gloves of fyve shillings ⌐rice. All the rest of my estate, viz<sup>t</sup>. my now dwelling

---

* "*Motherbrook* is a stream flowing spontaneously from Charles River in Dedham, though its channel has been enlarged by cutting. It crosses the S. W. corner of the town, and falls into Neponset."—*Harris' Hist. Dorchester.*

† He settled in Dorchester, freeman, 1633, representative from 1634 to 1636, mem. ar. co. 1637, its captain 1642, assistant 1637 to 1644. Returning to England, was a Lieut. Col. under Rainsborough, and died, in the time of the civil wars, at Lincoln, Eng.

*Farmer.*

He seems to have been actively employed while in New England. In the Pequot War he was a Captain, and there are extant letters which he wrote while upon that service. Vide *Book of the Indians*, Book II. 107, and *Winthrop's Journal*, Savage's Edition.

Gov. WILLIAM STOUGHTON was son of the testator, H. C. 1650. He went to England and had a fellowship at New College, Oxford, was a preacher in Sussex, ejected after the restoration, returned to N. England, became an assistant in the government of Ms. 1671, in which he was continued till 1686; agent for the Colony in Eng., 1677, one of Sir E. Andros' Council 1687, counsellor under the new Charter, 1692, Chief Justice, Lieut. Gov nine years, 1692 to 1701, Commander in Chief 1694 to 1699. Died unmarried, at Dorchester, 7 July, 1701, æ. 70.—*Ibid.*

house out houses & garden, my house & and land lying towards Charls-towne, land about twelve acres, w^th all the rest of my estate vnto my wife *Susan*, sole executrix. 27th day of the 1^st month, 1646.

In presence of
*Tho: Savage*   Deposed by *Th. Savage* & *Tho. Marshall*,
*Thomas Marshall*.   the 19 (11) 1649, before the Court in ppet-
uam rei memoriam, & to be recorded.
*Iner. Newell* Sec:

The Inventory of the estate of *Christopher Stanley* amounted to £349. 16s. He deceased about the 27^th 1^st mo. 1646.

---

## JACOB ELLIOTT.

### 28 2 m°. 1651.

The last will of JACOB ELLIOTT this 28 of the 2 m°: 1651. To sonne *Jacob Elliot* the howse & backside adjoyning to *Edward Rainsford* w^th the vse of half the barne with all the land at Muddy Riuer, except the tenn acres purchased of *Jonathan Negoos*, & this to haue at his day of marriage, & during the time of his single estate to liue with his mother. To daughter *Hanna Eliot* the howse that was *John Cranwetts* with all the back-side beloing to it, if she shall marry before her mother's death — all the rest of my estate to wife during life or widowhood — then to go to my children — to son *Jacob* a double portion — daughters to receive their portions at the day of marriage or at eighteen. *W^m. Colbron* & *James Penn* overseers.                                        JACOB ELEOTT.

20: 9: 1651. Mr. *W.^m Colbron* & Mr. *James Penn* deposed before the County Court, that this was the last will & testament of JACOB ELIOTT deceased, which the Court approved of. *Edward Rawson* Recorder. Recorded this 21 : 9 : 1651. p *Edward Rawson*, Recorder.*

Inuentory £579. 2s. 8d. *Margery Elleott* wife to *Jacob Elleott* dec^d, deposed, 29 : 11 m°: 51, that this was & is a treue Inuentory of her late husband.

---

## RALPH HUDSON.

### 24th 7th mo. 1638.

To the treasury of the Church of Boston, forty pounds — to *John Hudson*, my brother, forty pounds at the age of 24 years,— to my man *Benjamin Thwing*, tenn pounds at the end of his time,— to my majde *Judith Keieke*† five pounds — to dau. *Hannah Hudson*, one hundred pounds at the age of 21 yeeres,— to wife *Mary* my new builded howse in Boston, with the yard lying vnder it, also my new taken in garden and my great lott of 46 acres at Pullen Point. wife sole executrix.

witnesses                                        P mee RALPH HUDSON.
*Thomas Oliver*
*Thomas Leverett*
*James Penne*

Proved, 20 : 9 : 1659 by the testimony of Mr. *James Penne* & Mr. *Thomas Oliuer*.

*Edward Rawson*.

---

* This is the first will recorded by the new "Recorder," it being in his regular well known (to the searchers of our records) hand. It commences on the 58th page of the first volume of that old venerable book of wills of the Suffolk registry. There are in the volume 542 pages, foolscap, and we hope to be enabled to continue our labors through it.

† The MSS. is hardly to be made anything else of than the reading we give it, and yet, we are led to think it should be "*Kerbe.*"

## MARY HUDSON.
### 26 : 7 : 1651.

of Boston, widdow being very sicke, make my last will and testament To *Hudson Leverett*, my grandchild, my howse & land adjoyning to it, which Mr. *Edward Ting* dwells in, & which joynes to Mr. *Richard Parker*, as also my land at Pullen Pointe, with a garden in possession of *Robert Walker*, — to *Hannah Leuerett*, my grandchild, my two howses now in the occupation of *Nathaniell Duncan* & Mr. *John Tincker* bounded by Mr. *webb* on the east & Capt. *Robert Keajnes* on the west,— to my sonne Capt. *John Leueret*, forty pounds, & to his wife forty pounds, & to his dau. *Elizabeth*, forty pounds,— to Reverend friend & teacher, Mr. *John Cotton*, tenn pounds — to my Honoured ffreind & pastor, Mr. *John Wilson*, eight pounds,— to Mr. *Thomas Olliuer*, six pounds,— to my sister, Mrs. *Ann Leuerctt*, sixe pounds,— to Mr. *Isacke Addington*, sixe pounds,— to *Benjamin Thwing*, sixe pounds,— to the vse of the school in Boston, tenn pounds,— my meaning is that the six score pounds I haue given to my sonne *Leuerett*, his wife & daughter, Shall be out of that sixteene pounds I lent him at his first trading, when he married my daughter,— the rest of my estate, in plate howsehold goods, &c. not herein mentioned, to my grandchildren, *Hudson & Hannah Leuerett*, equally, whom I make executors. If both grandchildren dye, their portions to goe to my brother *Peacock*s two sonnes *Thomas & William*, which he had by my sister,— to Mr. *Richard Bellingham*, the some of sixe pounds.

Witnesses
  *William Colbron,*
  *James Penne.*

Proved 20 : 9 : 1651, by the same witnesses. The Court approved it excepting a howse & land giuen herein contrary to hir husbands will, prooved the same time as this was: *Edward Rawson*, Rec. And being the children of *Capt. John Leuerett* are vnder age, and not yet capable of choosing their oune Guardian, nor to be executors, the Court appoints Capt. *John Leuerett* their father their Guardian, & impoures him to Act in right of his two Children. 3 December, 1651. *Edward Rawson*, Recorder.

The Inuentory of the estate of *Mary Hudson* wyddow was taken by *W^m Colbron, James Penn, Antho: Stoddard, Capt. John Leuerett. Edward Rawson*, Rec. Boston, 20 : 1 mo. 1651.

---

### ROBERT WING.
### 21 : 9 : 1651.

*Thomas Walker* of Boston, & *Elizabeth Baker* wife to *Alexander Baker* of Boston, Depose that ROBERT WING late of Boston, being on his death bed, sent for them, & said, in their presence, he would leave all he had into his wives hands praying her to be good to his children : this being three dajes before he djed, & that was his last will & testament.

*Edward Rawson*, Recorder.

Itt is ordered that *Johanna Wing*, wife to *Robert Wing*, deceased, shall be Responsable to the fower children she had by him. 3 : 10 : 1651.

E. R. Rec.

Inuentory of his estate £124. 7*s*. 6*d*.

# ABSTRACTS OF THE EARLIEST WILLS UPON RECORD IN THE COUNTY OF SUFFOLK, MS.

## JOHN MILLS.

### (22<sup>th</sup> October 1651.)

I JOHN MILLES of Boston, being sicke, Doe nominate my loving freinds *Samuell Mauerick, Rob<sup>t</sup> Knight & Paul*: *White* my executors — To *Lyddja Tounesend*, servant to Mr. *Rucke* in pte Requitall of paines taken about me, fforty shillings,— to *John Peirse* his fower children, to each twenty shillings,—to Mr. *Cotton* forty shillings,— to Mr. *Wilson* forty shillings,— remander to my loving freinds, Mr. *fferdjnyndo Bodry* & Mr. *David Stephens*, marchants in the Canarjes,—witness my hand & Seale, this 22<sup>th</sup> day of October, 1651.

*Thomas Rucke*  
*Richard Wajte*

JO MILL & a Seale

*Richard Wajte* deposed, 3: 10: 1651, to the above. Recorded the same day. *Edward Rawson*, Rec<sup>r</sup>

Inventory, £815. 12: 9½, in which demands are enumerated against Mr. Vallentine Hill, Mr. John Manning, Mr. Thomas Lejgh in Virginea, Mr. John Treworgie, Mr. Nicholas Treworgie, Major Generall Gibbons, Mr. Dauid Yale & Mr. Daves, Nehemiah Boarne, Samuell Mauericke, Mr. John Turner, Perregrine whitt, Henry Sherman, Robert Nauney, John Jarves, Thomas Mayhew, Mr. Phillip Lewes, Mr. Thomas Lake, Mr. George Newman, dead, Mr. Richard Towgood, dead, Mr. Rob<sup>t</sup>. Saltonstall, dead, Mr. John Codington, Mr. Simon Kempthorne, Thomas Pacey, Mr. Jon<sup>a</sup> Steevens, John Dunbarr, Major Rob<sup>t</sup>. Sejuke [Sedgwick], Joseph Armitage, Darby Feild, Antipas Mauericke, Hugh Gunnison, Capt. Frauncis Champroune, as p accon in y<sup>e</sup> court of Douer — Deposed in court by Mr. Rob<sup>t</sup>. Knight, 3: 10: 1651. *Edw<sup>d</sup> Rawson*, Rec<sup>r</sup>

---

## ROBERT TURNER.

### (14<sup>th</sup> August 1651.)

The last will &c of Robert Turner Shoomaker of Boston is as ffolloweth: ffirst halfe of my estate personal and real to wife *Elizabeth Turner*, and the other halfe of my estate the one halfe of it to sonne *John Turner*, and the other halfe undevided to *Habacuk Turner* and *Elizabeth Turner*. Provision is made in case of another child being born, that it shall have a portion out of the whole equal with the two younger children. In case of decease of wife and children, then one halfe of estate is to be given to *Abigail Death* the daughter of my brother *Peeter Turner*, and the other halfe to *Hanna Hill* daughter of *Frances Hill* my wifes sister. Five pounds to *Abigail Death*, five pounds to *Hanna Hill*, and forty shillings unto *John Spurrs* wife. Wife *Elizabeth Turner* to be sole Executrix, and ffriends *Vallentyne Hille, Richard Treusdale Joshua Scotto* and *Hezekiah Usher* to be overseers. Provision is made for other overseers in case his legatees remove to Old England. ROBE<sup>T</sup> TURNER.

witnessed by us  
Richard fairebanck.  
Joseph Pendelton.

Joseph Pendleton deposed before the County Court 3ᵈ Dec. 1651 to the above. Recorded on the same day by Edward Rawson, Recorder.

26 (7). 51. Inventory of moveables and goods belonging to Mʳ Robert Turnor shoomaker lately deceased taken by Robrt Scott, Rich Cooke & Benjamine Negus. £384: 04: 11.

Elizabeth Turner deposed before the county Court 3. 10. mo 1651 that this was a full and true Inventory of the goods and estate of Robt Turner hir late husband to her best knowledge, and p'mised on oath that if afterward ought else shall appeare shee will bring it into the Courte.

Edward Rawson, Recorder.

---

THOMAS SATELL. (Nuncupative)

[14 (5) 1651]

To his brother Richard Sattell he giveth his bedding, iron pot, skillett, beetle and ring, eathen things, chest and lines, and what of his in the keexing [keeching] and under the trust of brother and sister Kenricke at Muddy River. Unto Mr Cotton teacher of Boston church twenty shillings in signe and token of his love and thankfulnes and likewise vnto me twenty shillings vppon the like respect. Item vnto my daughter Mary Wilson he giveth twenty shillings if what he leaveth in my house or land will reach so far. Item he giveth his muskett, his sword and his bandeleeres to his sajd brother's eldest sonne, and whatsoeuer else he hath or is dew vnto him for three quarters wages the premises discharged he doth give vnto his sajd brother Richard for the good of him and his family and children. This he did with his owne mouth declare vnto me this 14ᵗʰ day of the fifth month 1651.

witnes John Wilson.

This was deposed by the sajd John Wilson to be the last will and testament of Thomas Satell 18. 9mo 1651. before the Court. The Court approoved of this will and did graunt administration thereof to Richard Satell brother to the sajd Thomas Satell deceased, who is to see the sajd will performed. 18. 9mo 1651,        Edward Rawson Recorder.

An Inventory of the goods of the deceased Tho; Sautell Octobʳ 11ᵗʰ: 1651.

This Inventory was brought into the Court after yᵉ will was prooved 18: 9mo: 51 & administration was graunted by yᵉ Courte to Richard Sautell who is to see the will ꝑformed.

Recorded ꝑ Edward Rawson Recorder<br>20. 9mo. 51.

---

WILLIAM HEATH.

(May 28, 1652.)

"The last Will & Testamᵗ of Willm Heath of Roxbury in manner and forme following.

Item I give vnto my loving wifc during her natural life ye newe end of my house that I nowe dwell in both aboue & below and half the great barne and half the barne yard togeither wᵗʰ all my Arable land and meadowe that I am nowe possessed of Togeither wᵗʰall my Cattell & moveable goods vpon this Condition following ffirst that shee shall pay all my debts, secondly that shee shall pay my daughter Mary Spere Tenne pounds wᵗʰin one yeare after my death. Thirdly that shee shall pay my daughter Hanna

38

Tenne pounds w^{th}in two yeres after my death And when shee hath paid all my debts & legacies the remainder of the benefitt I giue wholley vnto my wife as better expressed during her naturall life and I doe make her my whole executrix.

Item 2ly. I giue vnto my sonne Isaac p^rsently to possesse the old end of my dwelling house" &c. After death of wife "my two soones shall haue all my howse and lands in Roxbury" "sonne Isaac my eld_st sonne a double po^rcon and my son Pelig a single porcon."

"Item 3ly I giue vnto my daughter Mary that I had by my ffirst wife fforty shillings a yere out of all my lands to be paid by both my sonns that is to say my sonne Isacke to pay twenty shillings a yere & my sonne Pelig twenty shillings a yere during the whole tyme of her natural life and they to begin at the tyme of their mother's death and they enter on the land and I doe intreate my wife in the meane season to haue a motherly care ouer hir and see y^t shee want nothing that is convenient for hir.

And I doe intreate my three friends that is to say my deare brother elder Heath John Rugles & Phillip Elliott to see this my will ꝑformed & my lands equally deuided according to y^e true intent of this my last will.

Witnes *Isaac Heath Phillip Elliott*
    *John Rugles*

The X m^rk of<br>
WILLM HEATH.

21 day 8mo 1652 taken vpon Oath by *Phillip Elliott John Rugles* to be the will of *Willm Heath* as above before me *John Glover.*

The Magistrates approue of this will so as they bringe in the Inventory by the next Court. 17 Nov 1652      *Edward Rawson* Recorder.

---

JOHN HOLLAND.

[16. (10.) 1651.]

In the name of God amen I *John Holland* of Dorchester in Newe England being by the ꝑmission of the Lord bound for Virginia and knoweing my life to be mortalle & at the disposeing hand of the Lord, ffor the ffurther setling of my estate after this life if the Lord Jesus shall call me to himself before my returne from this ꝑnt Vioage I do herefore bequeath my estate in manner following ffirst I giue to my wife all ye one half of my estate a moveable or vnmovable my Iland of Munings Moore excepted which I giue to my eldest sonne John Holland ouer & aboue a double portion w^ch ye rest of his brethren & sisters the rest of ye moytie of my whole estate to be deuided amongst my Children onely I giue to Mr Mather as a Remembring of my Loue to him fforty shillings to be bestowed in a siluer Cupp all this to be ꝑformed when my debts are honestly paid that shall appeare to be dew And for executo^r I leaue my wife & my sonne *John Holland* to see this my will ꝑformed I intrust *Elder Minott Elder Withington & John Smith* and *Willm Robbinson* and that this is my last will and testam^t I haue sett my hand this 16^th 10^th 1651

JOHN HOLLAND.

Witnes *Mathew Ball*

Mathewe Ball deposed before ye Magistrates vlt Septemb^r 1652 that he sawe *John Holland* signe this as his last will & testam^t and that he was of a disposeing minde when he made & signed it to best vnderstanding w^ch they approue of      *Edward Rawson* Record^r

An Inventorie of the estate of M^r John Holland nowe Deceased dat the

39

tenth of the 7<sup>th</sup> m° 1651. Amount consisting of land at Dorchester and
Boston and other property and dues £3325. 17s 00d
In debts by computation 1000. 00 00
Mo<sup>r</sup> an Ileland comonly called Manings Moore 28 00 00
Wee priseres of the said goods doe here subscribe our names
*George Mynot, Henry Withington*
The wife of *John Holland* this 16th Septemb<sup>r</sup> 1652 deposed before M<sup>r</sup>
*Bellingham* & M<sup>r</sup> *Nowell* that this is a true Inventorie of her husband
*John Hollands* estate to the best of her knowledge and that if more comes
to her knowledge shee will certifie the Recorder thereof w<sup>ch</sup> the Magistrates
approued of and ordered the acceptance of the said Inventorie to be kept
on file *Edward Rawson* Record<sup>r</sup>

---

### HENRY BROCKE.

"I *Henry Brocke* of Dedham in Newe England being sicke in body but
p'fect in minde doe make & ordaine this my last will and Testam<sup>t</sup> as
followeth:—"
"I giue & bequeath vnto Elizabeth my beloued wife my house & lands
in Dedham dureing her naturall life and after her decease I giue my said
house and lands in Dedham to my sonne John Brocke & to his heirs for
euer. Item I giue vnto Elizabeth my said wife the vse of all my moveables household & Cattell during her naturall life to maintaine herself and
educate my daughter Anne and what shall remaine of it after her decease
my will it should be equally diuided betweené my two daughters Elizabeth
& Anne or to their heires. And being I haue all readie giuen vnto my
daughter Elizabeth part of her portion my will is that what she hath had
all readie shall bee vallued by my executo<sup>rs</sup> and at the decease of my wife
shee shall have so much lesse that my daughters portions might be equall.
And I doe ordaine Elizabeth my beloved wife and my sonne *John Brocke*
to be executo<sup>rs</sup> of this my last will. In witnes whereof y<sup>t</sup> this is my will
I haue sett to my hand this 22<sup>th</sup> of ye 2<sup>d</sup> m° 1646.
HENRY BROCKE.

In the vnse of vs
*Henry Phillips Michaell Powell*
*Henry Phillips* deposed saith that this is the last will and Testam<sup>t</sup> of
Henry Brock late of Dedham and that hee sawe him subscribe the same
and that he was of a disposing minde when hee subscribed it 19<sup>th</sup> October
1652 w<sup>ch</sup> will the Magistrates approue of
*Edward Rawson* Record.
"A true Inventorie of the goods Chattell & other moveables being the
estate of Henry Brocke late of Dedham deceased whereof he died seized
made & taken the 3<sup>d</sup> of the 8 m° 1652 by the men whose names are
underwritten."
Among the items mentioned is the "wairing wollen apparell of Eliz:
his wife nowe deceased."

Signed by Henry Chickering Nathaniell Aldis
Anthony ffisher Henry Phillips
Eleazer Lusher John I Dwight
his mark

M<sup>r</sup> *John Brocke* deposed saith that to his best knowledge this is a true Inventorie of the estate of *Henry Brocke* his father, and when any more
comes to his knowledge he will bring it in to the Recorder 19<sup>th</sup> Octob<sup>r</sup>
1652 *Edward Rawson* Record<sup>r</sup>

# ABSTRACTS OF THE EARLIEST WILLS UPON RECORD
## IN THE COUNTY OF SUFFOLK, MASS.

### HENRY PLIMPTON.

Mr. *Hibbins*, Mr. *Glouer & Recorder*, did graunt power to Administracon to ye estate of *Henry Plimpton* of Boston to *Richard Waight* on ye behalf of ye creditors and friends of ye deceased ptie [party] and order that he bring in an Inuentory of ye estate to ye next County Court.

### DOROTHIE KING,

Wife of *John King* of Waymouth, seaman, will made ye 14th day, 4 mo., 1652. — To dau. *Sarah Hunt*, all my wooden moveables, w$^{ch}$ were mine before I married with my now husband, *John King*, as also one bed with ye furniture, also one piece of stuffe for a suite p$^r$ped [prepared] by her owne father for her, w$^{th}$ my haire couler water chamlett gowne. The charge and care of the oversight of her I comitt to Mr. *Thomas Thatcher*, Mr. *Richard Collicott* and *John Kinsley* of Dorchester, to dispose of her and her estate for her best advantage.

To dau. *Ruth Barker* the rest of my wearing cloathes, w$^{th}$ y$^e$ greater half of my larger linen, ye lesser half being reserved for my dau. Sarah ; also to dau. *Ruth* one bed w$^{th}$ ye furniture ; to dau. *Susanna Heath* one little flockebed.

My husband *John King* to be saued harmless from all his debte and disburstments laid out of any other way. it being answered out of my pticular estate ; — That my sonne *Joseph Barker* be my executor, wholly and solely, to whom I give the rest of my estate w$^{th}$ any right in *Thomas Perriman* my seruant. In case *Ephraim Hunt* shall sue my sonne *Joseph* as executor, and recover any thing of him for disbursements to myselfe, that then it shall arise equally upon y$^e$ whole estate, as well legacies as else.

I entreat Mr. *Thomas Thatcher*, Mr. *Rich'd Collicott* and my husband to be overseers.

| | | | her | |
| --- | --- | --- | --- | --- |
| Witnes to this will | *Wllm Tompson* | DOROTHY | X | KINGE |
| | *Jone Smyth* | | mark | |

Taken upon oath 21st day 8 mo. 1652 by *Wllm Tompson*. Proved 17th November, 1652, at a Countie court before me *John Glouer*.

At a Counte courte, 21st of y$^e$ 7$^{th}$ 8 month, 1652.

*Edwd Rawson, Recorder.*

At a Countie Court held at Boston, 18 : 9 : 1652, power of administracon to the estate of *Enoch Hunt*, late of Waymouth deceased not yet administred, is granted to *Ephrim Hunt* his sonne.

*Edw'd Rawson* Recorder.

### WILLIAM BLANCHARD.

The 27th of y$^e$ 7 mo. 1652. *William Blanchard* of Boston, taylor being sicke : — To *Hannah* my wife the third pt of my estate, debts being paid, also all my household goods, paying vnto *John* my sonne XX *ls* out of it when he shall accomplishe the age of 20 years, and tenne pounds to my dau. *Hanna* when 18. *John* to have a double portion, and dau. *Hannah* half so much of ye rest of my estate ; and if either dye before accomplishing their ages aboue said, the survivor shall have half of its porcon, and wife y$^e$ other half. Brother *John* my best Cloake ; sister *Garlicks* children shall haue 40 *s* a peece.  My deare and loving mother, *Anne Blanchard* to haue the Heyfore that is in the hands of *Richard Barnes*; and if an adventure made by Capt. Henfield come well from Engl, that she to have a suit of the best cloth of y'.  To my father-in-law, *Everrills* three children, 20 s. apeice; and loving wife *Hannah* the benefit of my servants towards the bring vpp of my children.  Wife *Hannah* my sole executrix.  I do intreate Mr. *James Penne*, Mr. *Edward Tinge*, and my loving father-in-law, *Iames Everill* to be ouerseers.  And haue published this my last will in y⁰ prence of y⁰ said *Iames Everill, Iohn Barrell* and *Nathaniell Sowther*, the day and yere aboue said.  It was farther added that his said ouerseers should haue 5 *s.* apeice for their paines.

In presence vs                            WILLM BLANCHARD.
*James Everrell*
*John Barrell*
*Natha: Sowther*

Proved by the deposition of *Sowther & Everill* before ye County Court 18 Novr. 1652.                    *Edwd. Rawson*, Record.

---

### BARNARD CAPEN.

Octo. 9th 1638.  Sonne *John* five acres of land out of my great lott, next adioyning to his lott y⁰ which he is to possess immediately after my decease. w^ch is to fulfill a promise made at his marriage.  To wife all such lands and goods as I now possess during her life.  And when it shall appear her dayes drawe to an end, that she w^th ye rest of my friends whom I put in trust, to divide theis lands and goods to my children equally.  If she change her name by marriage with another man, then she shall, w^th y⁰ aduise of those my friends give porcons equally to my children.

Now theis my friends w^h I put in trust, to see theis things done according to my will are Mr. *Minit* the elder, my brother *Dyer* & *Willm Sumner*, & *George Dyer* & *Will Sumner* deposed before County Court, 19th November, 1652, that this was the last will of *Bernard Capen*.

                                        *Edwd Rawson*, Record.

*John Capen* deposed before y⁰ County Court, 19th November, 1652, that the tyme when his ffather made the will was in y⁰ yere 1638.

                                   Per *Edwd Rawson*, Recd.

---

### JOHN COTTON.

I *John Cotton* of Boston in New England, do make and declare this my last will and Testament.  First, my soule w^ch God hath chosen and redeemed, my body to be committed to the earth till y⁰ day of resurrection of y⁰ just.  The outward estate which God hath giuen me, as it is y⁰ will of God, so my will is.  Out of it my debts be first paid, then my wife and children should liue of y⁰ rest.  And because y' small part of my house, w^ch S^r *Henry Vane* built, whilst he sojourned with me, he by a deed gave it (at his departure) to my sonne *Seaborne*, I doe y'fore leave it unto him as his by right, and together y^rwith liberty of comonage with his mother in y' south garden, w^ch lyeth vnder it; he carrying himself, (as I hope he will) respectively and obediently to his mother.  My books I estimate to y⁰ value of 150*l*. (though they cost me much more) and because they are of vse only to my two sonnes, *Seaborne* & *John*, therefore I giue them unto them both, to be devided by equal portions; and what is wanting in their worth of 200*l*. to be supplyed to y^m out of my other goods.  The like portion of an 100*l*. apiece I give to my two daughters, *Elizabeth* &

*Mary*, to be paid unto y^m by their mother, at 21 yrs. of age, or at day of marriage. And because God hath called me to expend y^e moneyes I have received, so y^t I leave my wife little or noe ready money at all, y^rfore for y^e discharge of my debts, legacies and portions, I give vnto her, my well-beloued wife, first all rents of hir house & garden in y^e market place of Boston, in Lincolnshire, w^ch are myne by right of ·marriage with her during my life. — I giue unto hir what moneyes were left in my brother *Coneyes* hand, and are now in y^e vse of my sister *Mary Coney* his wife, or my cosigne *John Coney* their sonne, so far as any psell y^rof remayneth in their hand. — I giue vnto her ye dwelling house wherein I now live, with all the plate, goods, and furniture, in every roome in y^e house, together with all y^e barnes, edifices, gardens, backsides and fences w^ch lye about y^e same, y^t is, y^e goods plate and furniture, for her owne prper vse, during her naturall life, also my farme at Muddy River, with y^e building thereon, and y^e stocke, for y^e better education of my children, as by name my sonne *John* at Cambridge, and for her owne maintenance. Should my wife dye before my children, my estate to be divided amg my child^n. my eldest sonne *Seaborne* to have a double portion, and my yonger child^n. equall single pertions. But if it shall please y^e Lord to take my wife & children by death, without heires descending fro me, or if they shall transplant y^mselves from hence into Old England, then my will is (& I trust acceptable to y^e will of God) and I do hereby bequeath and devise my ffarme and grounds at Muddy River, by two equall moityes, the one moitye to Harvard Colledge at Cambridge for y^e vse of y^e Colledge foreuer, & y^e other moity to ye^e Deacons of y^e church at Boston, towards y^e maintenance of y^e free schoole in Boston foreuer. I give to my cosigne *Henry Smith*, whilst he liveth with my wife, (for an acknowledgement of his former seruice & an encouragement to be farther helpful and seruiceable to her) his dyet and lodgeing with such apparell of myne as my wife shall see meete ; also 20*l* worth, in cattle or goods, to be kept for him at the farme. To my cosigne *John Angier*, with his wife and child (who now live in my house) y^e sume of 10*l*, over and above what moneyes I have laid out for him formerly. To my kinswoman *Martha Mellowes*, fiue marks. To *Elizabeth Clarke* my maide XX *s.* The rest of my goods and chattells to my deare wife *Sara Cotton*, whom I make sole exutrix.

This 30th of 9 : 1652          By me JOHN COTTON.

     Witnes *James Pen.*

For a shdule I give to the church of Boston a silver tunn to be vsed amongst the other comvnion plate. To my grand child *Betty Day*, my seconde silver wine boule.

This 12 : 10 mo. 1652          By me JOHN COTTON.

     In witness *James Penn.*

         Jno. Leverett.          Proved by the oaths of Mr *James*
         Wm. Davis.            *Penn* & Mr. *William Davis*, be-
         Nathaniel Williams.     fore the County Court, this 27
                                January, 1652 [1653]

[In the Will of *Daniel Maud* of Dover, N. H., dated 17th 11mo. 1654, and proved 26 June, 1655, are some interesting facts connected with the present subject — "my body to be layd in the place of ordinary buriall near to my last wife" — "what few books I have I leave [to my successor] for the use and benefit of such a one as may be fit to have improvement, especially of those in the Hebrew tongue ; but in case such a one be not had, to let them go to som of the next congregation as York or Hampton ; except one boke titled " Dei [*illegible*] w^ch I woul have left

for Cambridge library, and my little Hebrew bible for Mr. *Brock*" —
" And of my wifes 4 children, seeing I received some of her debts since
my marriage, of about 11 *l*, to have, (if my estate will reach) to the value
of 20 ackers" — " my best outward receiving coate to Mr. *Pembleton*, &
14 *s*. to Mr. *Cutts*; 10*s* [due] to *George Walton* w^h *Tho: Beard* is to
pay; 4*s* to goodwife *Tucke* of Hampton [*Joanna* wife of *Robert Tucke*,
who d. 4 Feb. 1673] & 20*s* to one *George Feild* [who was] dwelling in
Boston, but was removed as was sayd, to Sudbury, w^h I owed him for som
conveighance of som comoditos hither fro Boston. Something I am indebted Mr. Newgate — bout 7*s* to Mr. [illegible] for som bokes — I desire
Mr. *Brock*, *William Pomfret* and *John Hall* to undertake [illegible.]
One thing there is of som greater importance, w^h is a little [*manuscript?*]
wrayped up in my deske w^h I would have comitted to Mr. *Brock* to put
into the hands of Mr. *Dauenport*, who as I heard, is intended go for England, that he would pruse, and for putting it forth I would leave it to his
wise and godly ordering of, — w^h I think there is a trust of God in, and
som benefit to redound to som by. There is a booke of Mr. Nortons
which is entitled Orthodox Evangelist, w^h I would have my sister *Cotton*
to have, and another booke I borrowed of my brother *Cotton*, is to come
to his son *Seaborn*. [*much illegible*] *Susan Halsted* — *his* bro. and sister
& sister-in-law who have no need of supplyes for me, I desire to be heartily remembered to those, they are ch — in years. In presence of *William
Wantworth, Job Clements*.
Approved in Court, Jun 26th 1655. *Renald Fernald.*" — *Copied from
the original at Exeter, N. H., by Mr. A. H. Quint.*]

## Iohn Holman.

Whereas Almighty God having laid upon me a great affliction I think it
my duty to dispose of y^e small estate God haue giuen mee to p^rvent trouble
for tyme to come. And whereas the honorable Court haue established a
lawee the eldest sonne shall haue a double porcon, my earnest desire is,
& to my griefe I speake it, my sonne being groune to some yeres proueth
disobedient & stubborn against mee my desire is he may be depriued of
that benefit w^ch others may justly enjoy, & I giue onto him my sonne *John
Holman* 50*l*. at 20 yrs of age. To *Mary Holman* 50*l*. at 18 yrs of age, or
at day of marriage. To my foure yongest child^n 50*l*. each at y^e age of 20
yrs. To my two sonnes *Thomas & Samuel Holman*, & to daus. *Abigal &
Hannah Holman* 50*l*. each, at day of marriage or at 18 yrs. of age. My
housing & land at Dorchester to my wife during her life; & after her
death, halfe to sonne *Thomas & Samuel Holman*, the other half wife to dispose of as she see fitt. Rest of estate to wife, her I make executrix. In
case any child die before their porcon be due, then to bee att my wifes dis-
pocing. My four yongest child^n to remain w^th their mother till they come
to age menconed. I appoint my beloved brethren *Richard Collocott &
William Robeson* to be overseers unto my wife & children. This 10 day
4 month 1652.
*Rich: Collicott & Willm Robinson* both of Dorchester deposed before
the Majistrates, that on their pfect knowledge this was y^e las will of *John
Holman*, owned by him bfere his death.

*Edward Rawson*, Recorder.

## ABSTRACTS OF THE EARLIEST WILLS UPON RECORD IN THE COUNTY OF SUFFOLK, MASS.

### THOMAS RUCKE, JUNIOR,*

Of Boston in New England. To *John Rucke* of Salem in New England, all my wearing apparrell & lynnen & my sea instruments & books. To *Samuel Rucke* of Salem 10*l.* of lawful money of England. To *Joane Kalsoe*, my sister, 10*l.* Goods unbequathed to Mr. *Thomas Rucke* my father, whome I make my sole executor.      THOMAS RUCKE.
    In presence of *William Crofts,*
                *Zachary Cullen.*

This being belieued to be yᵉ act and deede of *Tho : Rucke*, Junoʳ, though the witnesses that should prove it are in England, & so not cappable of giueing their testimony, at the request of Mr. *Tho : Rucke*, Senʳ, the magistrates doe graunt administracon to the estate of *Tho : Rucke*, Junʳ, to *Tho : Rucke*, Senʳ, he acting with the estate as neare as may bee to the will. 26 June,† 1653.      *Edward Rawson*, Recordʳ.

---

### THOMAS DUDLEY,

Of Roxbury in New England, made in perfect health, the 26th of Aprill, 1652; for my sole I coňend it unto the hande of my God in whome I haue beleued, whome I haue loued, which hee hath promised to receiue in Iesus Christ my redeemer & sauiour, with whome I desire euer to bee, leaueing this testimony behinde mee for the Vse & example of my ppsteritie, & any other vpon whome it may worke, that I haue hated & doe hate euery falce way in religion. not onely the old Idolitry & superstition of Popery which is wearing away, but much more (as being much worse) the more herisies blasphamies & error of late sprunge vpp in our natiue country of England & secretly receieied & fostered.—My body I desire to bee buried neare my first wife, if my present wife be liuing at my death. My temporall estate I intend to despose of it as iustly and equally as I can contriue it, betweene the posteritie of my childn by my first wife, and my children by my last wife, accounting *Thomas Dudley* & *John Dudley* my grand children (whome I haue brought upp) in some sort as my immediate children. First what I couenanted at my marriage with my pʳsent wife, to giue to her, & such childⁿᵉ as I should haue by her, bee made good vnto them, with this condition & explanacon; that all my lands in Roxbury, being duely vallued by my executor, wᵗʰ all my goods, debts, plate, household stuffe & bookes.—My sonne *Joseph Dudley* to haue a double portion, & *Paule Dudley*, & *Deborah Dudley*, each a single porcon;—land to goe to *Joseph* according to my foremenconed couenant, & yᵉ Goods & debts to *Paule* & *Deborah*. If the land amount to more then a double porcon, then to take ovt of yᵉ same from *Joseph*, and giue it to *Paule* & *Deborah*. My present wife & my three children to haue all my lands, goods & debts,

---

* This will is twice recorded in the original volume. The second time, what follows was added : " The originall will by order of yᵉ majests, Depᵗy Gounʳs, *Mr. Nowell*, & Mr. *Hibbins*, was deliuered to Mr. *Thomas Rucke, Senʳ*, yᵗ so he might prooue it in England.      *Edwᵈ Rawson*, Recʳ·

† This date is given by the Recorder, when he recorded it the second time, " 16 June."

45

(except what I giue to others) I giue to the children of my sonne *Samuell Dudley*, the 6th part of my mill at Watertowne, & of the house & ffteene acres of land in Watertown, together w$^{th}$ a 6th part of y$^e$ debt w$^{ch}$ *Thos: Mayhew* his heires doe owe me for not performing their bargaine w$^{th}$ me, for w$^{ch}$ the said myll was pte of my assurance—to be equally divided among them.—To the childn of my dau. *Bradstreete*, another 6th. To the childrn of my dau. *Denison*, another 6th.—To the children of my dau. *Woodbridge* another 6th. Also vnto the aforesaid *Thomas Dudley*, another 6th; & to the aforesaid *John Dudley* the other 6th. If my sonne *Samull Dudley*, or any of my three daughters, *Bradstrecte, Denison*, or *Woodbridge*, have any more children, they shall haue equal shares with the rest. To enter upon said mill & lands the 20th day of October next, after my death & not before. They to pay my dau. *Sarah Pacy*, half yearly, 20 *s.* apiece yearly. To the deacons of the church of Roxbury, 5 markes, by them to be distributed to the poor of said towne. Worthy & beloued friends, *John Elliott*, teacher of the church at Roxbury, *Samull Danforth*, pastor of the said church, *John Johnson*, Surveyor Generall of the Armes, & *Willim Parkes* of the said church, giueing to each of them, if they shall liue, 2 years after my death, 5 *l.* apiece—that they will doe for mee & mine as I would haue done for them & theirs in the like case. In my former will I have named my sons executors, but better considering of their remote dwelling, &c., I have chosen my aforesaid friends to be executors. THO: DUDLEY.

To grand-childe *Thomas Dudley*, 10 *l* a yeare, for 2 yrs after my death, besides what I shall owe the colledge for him at my death. To grandchilde, *John Dudley*, 15 *l.* a yeare, for 3 yeares after my death. To wife I give the tyme & interest I haue in *John Ranken*, also all my rent & profitts of my mill at Watertowne, from the day of my death till the 20th of October, then next following, on condition that she giue to my dau.—*Sarah Pacy*, her diett, &c., or after the rate of 6 *l.* by the yeare, till she is to receive what I haue giuen her out of my will—I meane her first payment thereof. Whereas my sonne, *Samuell Dudley*, hath beene importunate with me to mayntaine his sonne, *Thomas*, at y$^e$ colledge at Cambridge, untill the month of August, 1654, when he is to take his 2d. degree, I haue consented thereto, but soe that the case of the Educacon of my younger children doth compell me to retreate and revoake from my said sonne, *Samuell*, and his other children & their heeres, the 6th part of my mill & lands at Watertowne, and do revoake & call back also 20 *l.* I gaue to the said *Thomas Dudley* his soone, & 45*l.* I gaue to *John Dudley*, another of the sonnes of my said sonne *Samuell Dudley*, w$^{ch}$ I hereby doe, yett because it is not equall that *John Dudley* aforesaid (who hath been seruisable to mee) should losse any thing by my benefycence to his brother, I do hereby giue vnto him, the said *John Dudley*, all the said 6th part of my myll & land at Watertowne, w$^{ch}$ I had formerly giuen to his father, or his yonger brothers & sisters, so that I haue settled a 3d part of the said mill vpon him the said *John Dudley*, & a 6th part vpon the said *Thomas Dudley*. Witness my hand, this 13th day of Aprill, 1653. THOMAS DUDLEY.

My will is that this schedule be annexed to my will, & be as authenticall as the same, and my meaning is, that this 6th part of the mill at Watertowne be charged w$^{th}$ 40*s.* a yeare, to be paid to my dau. *Sarah Pacy*, as before this schedule was made. My dau. *Pacy* to haue guen her a feather bed & boulster, w$^{ch}$ shee had when she liued last at Boston, one yellowe Rugg & 2 blanketts of the worser sort, 2 paire of little sheetes, & a chest.
May 28th, 1653. THO: DUDLEY.

The charge of my long sicknesse, I thereby being disenabled to make bargaines as I was wont for the vpholding of my estate, I finde my estate thereby, and by other meanes soe weakned, that the due care of my thre youngest children's education compelleth mee to reuoake & detract a 6th part of what I had giuen to mine other children & grand child$^n$ out of my will, & settle it vpon my three younger child$^n$, I do therefore recall from my other child$^n$ a 6th part out of euery share w$^{ch}$ by my will I had formerly giuen them. And I giue the said 6th parts to my said three youngest children. Witness my hand to this Schedule also. Witness, *Samuel Danforth*, who wrot this, as *Mr. Dudley* dictated to me by his direction, this 8th day of July, 1653. THO: DUDLEY.

My three youngest child$^n$ shalbe rateably charged for what is here giuen them to my daughter *Sarah Pacy*, as the others are.

*Jno: Dudley* *

Mr. *John Johnson*, on the 15th of August, 1653, appeered before the Magistrates, & did on his oath present this as the last will of *Tho: Dudley*, late of Roxbury, Esqr. w$^h$ was found in the chest of the said THOMAS DUDLEY, psently after his decease, vnder locke & key.

Edw$^d$. Rawson, Recorder.

The magistrates did allow & approue of this will with the schedules annexed. Present, *Richard Bellingham*, Esq. *Mr. Nowell*, & *Mr. Hibbins*.

Edw$^d$. Rawson, Recorder.

---

### JAMES BATE,

Elder, of Dorchester in New England, 22$^d$ day of the ninth month called November, 1655, giue vnto my Sonne M$^r$ *Richard Bate* of Lid Towne in Kent in Old England, all my Lands, moveable goods & debts y$^t$ I now haue or hereafter may haue in Old or New England, to be disposed of by him, according to his discretion; yet desireous y$^t$ he would attend vnto such directions thereabout, as I shall send in writing, vnless I shall See ground & reason afterwards to alter the said directions in any of the pticulars thereof. Said Sonne whome I haue all wayes found faithfull, my sole Executor.

Subscribed as well as he in y$^e$ want of his bodily sight could write in ye p$^r$sence of *Gabrell Mead* & m$^r$ *Rob$^t$ Howard*, Not$^y$ pub$^{cus}$

JAMES BATE.

Codicil——Sonne *James Bate* shalbe joyned Executo$^r$ with Sonne *Richard*, only for this purpose, that, sonne *James* may receiue such debts as are owing vnto me in N. England, also to Sell such Lands & goods as I have, excepting what is mentioned in my directions, to be giuen vnto my Grand child *James ffoster*, provided he doth make a true Inventory y$^r$of, and convey y$^e$ said Estate vnto my said Sonne *Richard*.

26$^{th}$ Nov. 1655     JAMES BATE the Elder,

*Rob$^t$ Howard* deposed to the above, 14 Jan 1655.     his 1 U$^5$ mrke.

*Roger Clap*, aged forty six yeares or thereabouts, saith—he being w$^{th}$ m$^r$ *James Bate* to visete him in his sicknes,—he intreated him to take

---

* This fac simile has been loaned for our use by Mr. Capen, author of the State Record.

some wittnes with himselfe, that it was his will his daughter *Gibson* haue tenn pounds for hir owne vse & at hir disposing, & not to her husbands; the said *Roger* said to m^r *Bate*, if you haue any written will, it must be added thereto, he replyed with earnestness y^t he would haue done.

*Edw^t Roger* & *Nicho Clapp*—haue all three taken theire Oathes to the truth of the Testimony—written 17: 11^th mo. before me, 22 Jan. 1655.

*Jo: Endecott*, Gov^r

I *Jas Bate* testify,—I heard my father *Bate* say the Sabbath day before he dyed, y^t he would giue vnto his dau. *Margret Gibson* tenn pounds—at her disposing, & not at her husbands, which he said he would add vnto his written will. *James Bate* came before me, 19: 11^mo. caled Jan^y 1655, and took oath to the truth of the p^rmises.                 *Jo Endecott*, Gov^r

Know That whereas I *James Bate* the Elder haue made a will,—22^d 9^mo 1655, wherein I make son *Rich^d* Sole Execut^r expreseing in Said will further direction, in writing to be given vnto him—as followeth, vdizt.— he to giue vnto sonne *James* three children *Sam^l Allice* & *Mary*, £100 a piece, when one & twenty yeares of age; son *James* to have the profit of sd portions, vntill then for & towards their bringing vp; in case he doth goe with his family to Liue in Eng. Allso sonne *James* putt in good security to pay said £300.   my house, Orchard & three Acres of planting Land adjoyning with the meadow, also adjoyning, on y^e back of said dwellinghouse, in Dorchester, New England, I giue vnto *James ffoster*, his Grandchild provided y^t dear wife *Allice Bate* haue her maintenance out of said house &c.   Also I will m^r *Mather* Teacher of the church of Dorchester haue £20 and y^e now wife of *Gabriell Mead* £20.   These directions bearing date with said will.         JAMES BATE y^e Elder

*Rob^t Howard* No^ty pub.                                                 ♦ a marke

14 Jan 1655 deposed by *Robt Howard*.

---

## W^M DAVIS.

*W^m Davis*, seaman—giue *Isaac Colemore* of Boston all to me belonging—only to *Henery Tite* my pistoll, what debts I doe owe be pajd out of my Estate.—14 Sep. 1655.                         WILLIAM DAVIS.
Witness *Nath^l Williams*
Marke of I ♭ *John Sanders*.

10. 9 : 1655 *Nath^l Williams* & *Jno Sanders* deposed before Court, that this schedule was the true mind of *W^m Davis*.

10: 9: 55.   Power of Administration graunted to *Isaac Cullemore*.

---

## TIMOTHY JONES.

11: 10^mo 1655—*Timothy Jones* of Dorchester—appoint *John Kingsley* of Dorchester & *W^m Robinson* of same towne executors; they shall dispose of what is mjne for the best good of my wife & child ;—vnto wife third p^t of all I haue here or in England, my son to have the rest.—Executors sell Land to the paying wife her Legacy & the keeping of my child.   If father *Kingsley* desire to buy any of my Land *W^m Robinson* shall choose two men to judge the value of it—he paying for it as much as another would doe.                                  TIMOTHY JONES (his marke)

3 Jan 1655 *Rob^t Spurr* & *Thos Pearse*
deposed that this was the Last will
of TIMOTHY JONES.

Witness   his marke R
*Rob^t Spurr*
*Thomas Pearse*

## JOHN CLEMENS.

*John Clemens* seaman—giue *Isaac Cullemore* that I have due vnto me
in the Adam & Eue; foure pounds vnto my sister liueing in wakerin
within Sixe miles of Lee named *Mary Clemens* to pay what I owe in the
shipp.—I owe *Nicholas Pris* one shilling,—*Rich⁴ Cletherly* one shilling
& sixe pence;—the rest giue vnto *Isaac Cullemore.*

The marke of  *John* i h *Sanders.*    The marke of *John* w *Clemens.*
 *Benj Thwing*
 *Wᵐ Steuenson*

more—one pound ten shillings to be allowed vnto my wages for short
allowance
 County Court 10. 9: 1655
*Jno Sanders* & *Wᵐ Steuenson* deposed—Administration granted to
*Isack Cullemore.*

---

## SAMUELL MORSE.

2: 10: 1654. SAMUELL MORSE, Estate whether movables or jmmova-
bles, as house, Lands, Chattle, house houlde stuffe, bequeath all vnto *Elizabeth Morse* my wife;—after her decease to be devided amongst my children, *John Morse, Daniell, Mary Bullin,* & *Ann Morse,* the wife of my *son
Joseph* deceased, who with my sajd children shall haue an equall portion—
for the childrens sake of my said beloued *Joseph*—the above named *Ann*
shall make an equall distribution when they & euery one of them shall
grow vp to the age of one & twenty  wife *Elizabeth* executrix.

           SAMᴸ MORSE 2 his marke.

*Henry* H *Smith*     *Ralph* 0 *Wheelock*
 marke
    *Samuell* ſ *Bullin.*
     marke

---

## BEZOUNE ALLEN

Of Boston; beloued wife Third part of Estate Reall & psonall, besides
my best bed bedstedd, Curtaines, vallaints & furniture in yᵉ Chamber wᶜʰ
I now lye in, with all my plate, not doubting hir motherly Care and Loue
to bring vp my Children in yᵉ feare of god,—being allowed necessary
Charge for diet & Clothes. Overseers, Mr *Edward Rawson,* & mr *Jeremiah Houchin.* Eldest sonne a duble portion; all yᵉ rest of my children,
as well yᵗ wᶜʰ shee goeth withall, haue equall porcons paid them at yᵉ age
of one & twenty yeares or day of marriage, wᶜʰ shall first happen. In
case any of My Children die the portions to be equally devided amongst
yᵉ rest; if all should die before they attaine yᵉ age or tyme aforesaid, then,
wife haue one halfe, yᵉ other halfe to be deuided between sister *Eliz: burcham,* & sister *Joanna Pecks,* thejre Children; to Mʳ *Hubbard* my friend
& pastoʳ Ten pounds, ffiue pounds whereof I formerly promised him
towards his house—to *Mathewe Hawkes* fiue pounds; my eldest Son my
Ring; & yᵗ he haue my mares as pᵗ of his double porcon at aprizmᵗ now,
and to Runne till he be of Age; my man fiue pounds at yᵉ end of his time,
if he proue faithfull to his mrs: 20ᵗ to my maid.   BEZOUN ALLEN.
 9ᵗʰ Sep. 1652.
*Jeremiah Beales,*
*Josiah Hubberd.* memorandum, yᵗ yᵉ seale of this will was accedentally
torn off by yᵉ deputyes before mʳ *Hills* brought it vp to yᵉ magistrates:
wᶜʰ is to stand as firme as if it were sealed as it was: 28 oct. 1652. yᵉ

magistrates consid$^r$ this act to be necessary. *Jo: Endecott,* Gov$^r$. w$^{ch}$ was ordered by y$^e$ vote of y$^e$ whole Court to be as Athenticke w$^t$hout y$^e$ seale as with it, & as it was before. *Edw$^d$ Rawson,* Secret" Recorded 10 July, 1653.                                                 *Edw$^d$ Rawson,* Sec$^y$.

### RACHELL BIGG

(17. Nov$^r$. 1646) of dorchester, widdow, hauing soulde my house and land wherein now I dwell vnto Nephew *Hopestill ffoster* for one hundred & twenty pounds, to be payed w$^{th}$in halfe one yeare after my decease, he shall paie vnto *thankfull Stowe* Threescore pounds within halfe a yeare next after my decease, & I giue more vnto *thankfull Stow,* Twenty pounds, which is due from said *Hopestill* to be paid her w$^{th}$in three months after my decease; if the said *Hopestill* do not pay the three-score pounds so giuen, then I giue the house & land vnto her; he performing y$^e$ payments. I giue him three score pounds the remainder of the said ƒome of one hundred & Twenty pounds, & the Rent of the said house & Lands so it amountes not to aboue Eight pounds, out of w$^{ch}$ he shall giue three pounds vnto his dau. *Thankfull,* to bee layed out vpon a siluer Pott for her, marke w$^{th}$ R. B. and twenty shillings to his sonne *Hopestill* to buy for him three siluer spoones,—also fforty shillings to his dau. *Patience,* to be lay$^e$d out vpon sixe siluer spoones for her; all the spoones to be marked w$^{th}$ R. B.—also I giue vnto him the said *Hopestill* a ffeather Bed & boulster. My sonn in Law *John Stow* oweth me one hundred and fforty pounds, which he promiseth to pay out of his house and lands in Roxbury, out of w$^{ch}$ I giue vnto his Eldest sonn *Thomas Stowe* Thirty pounds, he paying out of it fforty shillings to be layed out vpon sixe siluer spoones to be marked w$^{th}$ R. B. of w$^{ch}$ I giue three of them to his dau. *Marie,* the other three to his son *Sam$^l$.* Vnto his Eldest sonn *John,* a siluer cup, w$^{ch}$ I bought of his father;—vnto *Elizabeth Stow,* wife of *henery Archer,* Thirty pounds, ffiue pounds out of it in fifteene spoones marked R. B. sixe to her dau. *Rachell,* three to *John,* three to *Isaac,* three to *Theophilos,* ther three sonnes;—vnto *Elizabeth Stow* my siluer Pott, and my Booke of dockter Preston to be deliuered by executors. Vnto *Nath$^l$ Stow,* Twenty pounds, hauing giuen him formerly a small Tenement & land; vnto *Sam$^l$ Stow* Thirty pounds, to be paid vnto them by their ffather w$^{th}$in one year after my decease;—vnto *Peter Masters,* my sonn in law, now liuing in England, Twenty shillings;—to his dau. *Elizabeth* Tenn shillings; to his wife, *Katherin,* my fille kirtle;—vnto m$^r$ *Richard Mather,* fforty shillings.;—to the poor in Dorchester, Twenty shillings, to be distributed to them by the deacons where they see most need;—vnto m$^r$ *Newman* & m$^r$ *John Miller* tenn shillings apeece;—vnto *James Batte* senio$^r$, ffiue shillings, to his sonne *James,* ffiue shillings; the now wife of *Thos. Lyme* ffiue shillings;— *Clement Batte* Twenty shillings;—his dau. *Rachell* ten shillings;—to the residue of his Children, ffiue shillings apeece;— *Thos Beatts,* Twenty shillings; *Thos Beall, John Compton,* Goodwife *Turner,* wife of *Rich$^d$ Brittaine,* Goodman *Meade,* Old *margery,* & Goodwife *Place,* to euery of them ffiue shillings;—poore Goodwife *Hill,* & goodwife *Patching,* tenn shillings apeece;—some considerations moueing I further giue *Thankfull Stow* all my household stuffe & plate.—All the residue of my goods &c to louing sonne in law *John Stowe,*—my executor.—Dated the day & yeare aboue written,                                    The marke of  R. B.  RACHELL

1646. In p$^r$sence of                                                         BIGG & seale
    *Rich$^d$ Peacocke,*
    *Gabrell Meede.*

*Rich<sup>d</sup> Peacocke* Testified that this was the last will of *Rachell Bigg*
    Taken vppon oath &c        30 (4) 1647        *W<sup>m</sup> Aspinuall*
                                                      Record<sup>r</sup>
Entr<sup>d</sup> & Record<sup>d</sup> 20 Feb. 1653 at Request of Ensigne *Hopstill foster*
                                            *Edw<sup>d</sup> Rawson* Recor<sup>d</sup>

---

## WILLIAM POTTER

(14 Jan. 1653)—of Roxbery, being sicke. Vnto m<sup>r</sup> *Tompson,* Pasto<sup>r</sup> of y<sup>e</sup> church of Brantrey, Tenn Pounds, to be pay<sup>d</sup> within one yeare after my death ; m<sup>r</sup> *fflint,* Teacher of y<sup>e</sup> church of Brantrey, tenn pounds, to be payd within one yeare as before ; vnto brother *John Potters* wife, in England, her foure Children w<sup>ch</sup> she had by my brother, sixe pounds, thirteene shillings foure pence;——vnto Brother *Geo. Potter,* if he be liuing, [the same] if he be dead to be equally deuided betweene all his children then liuing ;—to sister *Jane* three pounds sixe shillings, eight pence, if Liuing, if dead to her children, if she hath none, then itts go to brother *Jn<sup>o</sup> Potter's* children ;—sister *Annes* dau. wife of *John Coking,* three pounds, sixe shill<sup>s</sup> eight pence, if liuing, if not, to her children, if none, to bro. *Geo. Potters* children.—my wifes dau. *Hannah Graue,* Twenty pounds, to be payd her at y<sup>e</sup> day of her marriage ; also Twenty pounds more to be payd her at my wifes death. Vnto y<sup>e</sup> Schoole in Roxbery, Twenty shillings : to y<sup>e</sup> Colledge at Cambridge, Twenty shillings; all y<sup>e</sup> rest of estate Lands & debts with the debt y<sup>t</sup> mr. *W<sup>m</sup> Brenton* of Boston doth owe me, three score & tenn pounds or thereabouts, vnto loueing wife, Executor, she & her heires foreuer. My desyer is my wife wil be carefull to send to my friends in England, & if they desyer to haue this twenty pound sent them, y<sup>t</sup> she will be carefull to advice w<sup>th</sup> M<sup>r</sup> *flint,* y<sup>t</sup> it may be conveyed to y<sup>m</sup> as safely as it may be, but my wife not to stand to any hazard of y<sup>e</sup> goeing of it The marke    of
                                                    W<sup>M</sup> X POTTER

Witnes—*Phillip Elliot*
        *Rob<sup>t</sup> Pepper*
        *Phillip Curtis*
p<sup>r</sup>sent m<sup>r</sup> *Nowell*
       *m<sup>r</sup> Hibbins*
       *Cap<sup>t</sup> Gookin*
       & Recorder

*Phillip Elliot* & *Rob<sup>t</sup> Pepper* deposed before y<sup>e</sup> Court y<sup>e</sup> Last day of Jan<sup>y</sup> 1653, y<sup>t</sup> they saw *W<sup>m</sup> Potter* signe this as his Last will, & y<sup>t</sup> he was of a Sound mynd, &c. The Court approved thereof.

---

## JOHN GLOVER

Of Boston.—I haue by deede giuen to sonne *Thos.* all my Lands in England, w<sup>th</sup> pmise they shalbe freed of my wiues dowre & promised to him four hundred pounds ;—to sonne *Nath.* so much in good payment, as would make Lands, the which I deliuered him, worth foure hundred pound; haue also giuen sonne *Habakucke,* one halfe of the new house in Boston nearest m<sup>r</sup> *Webbs* house with halfe of all the other housing, halfe of y<sup>e</sup> yeard, & pitts in it, & other accomodations for tanning, & promised to make it vp foure hundred pounds, these with all other my debts to be duely payd out of goods, debts due me, profitts of Lands in Dorchester & Boston, saueing wiues dowre. my two sonnes, *John* & *Pelatiah,* either of them, one hundred pound payd them out of my goods.—y<sup>e</sup> profitts of my two farmes on the further side of the River in Dorchester & out of the one halfe of my house, yeard, other housing & tan pitts not herein exprest, to be giuen my sonne *Habacucke,* as soone as my wiues necessary maintenance out of the aforesaid estate will p mitt ; my beloued wife relinquish-

51

ing right of dowre in England shall haue all the rest of my goods, profitts of two farmes in Dorchester aforesaid, half house, yeard, housing and tann-pitts in Boston vndisposed of. sonn *Habacucke* halfe of my house in Boston next goodman *Hudsons,* w^th half of yeard &c [he] paying in one year to sonne *Thos Glover* ten pounds; son *Nath^l* forty pounds, & to Harvard Colledge at Cambridge, towards y^e maintenance of a fellow there, fiue pounds a yeare foreuer, if my beloved wife can spare to giue the said fiue pound a year in her life time, I doubt not she will giue it; wife Executor. m^r *Rich^d Mather* & m^r *Henery Withington* overseers.

If sonnes *John* & *Pelatiah* haue occasion to sell m^r *Newberys* farme, it be sould to sonne *Nath^l* if he desyer to buy it—11 Aprill, 1655.

JOHN GLOVER

Vpon further Consideration of what Sonnes *John* & *Pelatiah* haue already receiued in their education, y^t after the decease of my wife, they receiue out of my farmes in Dorchester either of them y^e sume of two hundred pounds, w^ch sume of four hundred pounds being first payd them, I giue the Reversion & Inheritance of the said farmes to *Habacuke, John, Nath^l* & *Pelatiah,* & their heires foreuer, to be equally devided. 26: 11: 1653.

JOHN GLOUER.

*W^m Hibbins.*

9^th ffeb: 1653 m^r *Habacucke Glouer* appeared before y^e Magistrates & presented y^e aboue to be y^e Last will & Testam^t of his father m^r *John Glouer* deceased m^r *W^m Hibbins* being wittnes. Approved,

m^r *Hibbins* Record^r

---

W^M DENNING.

Being now sick; Louing friends & Brethren *Edw^d ffletcher* & *John Hull* of Boston, overseers. To wife *Ann Dening* y^e vse of all my estate shall not haue power to alienate any part;—after her decease, if son *Obediah* come over into N. E. then one half of estate to be his, in case he doth not come p sonally into y^e Country, then I giue vnto said sonne twenty shillings, and no more; y^e Remainder shal be giuen, together with y^e other halfe, after the decease of my wife, vnto my kinswoman *Mary Powell,* Provided y^e said *Mary* continue with my wife dutifull dureing her life, if not, vpon just complaint made to *Edw^d ffletcher* & *Jno Hull,* I giue full power to disinheritt her;—also giue them power to sell one piece of ground of about half an Acre lyeing below my garden, bounded with the highway one side, & ground of *Maudil English* on the west, & *Dea Marshall* & Cap^t *Rob^t Keayne* on y^e North, only reseruing one Roud broad at y^e end next my garden from the high way, for a passage into my other ground; also any other part of estate to pay any just debt withall; if my wife stand in necessity for further maintenance she shall haue liberty to sell such things as may best be sould for necessary support, provided it be with y^e consent of overseers. 18^th 11^mo 1653. WILLIAM DENNING.

Attestants, *Gamalell Waite.*
*Benj Negus.*

*Gamaliell Waite* & *Benj^n Negus* deposed before the Magistrates that they saw *W^m Denning* signe this will; he was of a disposing mind to the best of their knowledge this 31 Jan^y. 1653.

---

JN^O ROBINSON

2d day of June, 1653.—Due to me from My maister, *W^m Phillips,* for wages, Eight pounds seauen shillings, also seauen pounds ten shillings

from m⟨r⟩ *Richard Lord* & m⟨r⟩ *Goodier* of Newhauen, for wages vpon a
Barbadoes Voyage, my request is y⟨t⟩ the docter be satisfyed, & what I
owe to my Landlord, *Rob⟨t⟩ ffeild*, for dyett, Lodging, & Attendance ; what
I owe my maister, & what may be over & aboue I leaue to [him] & *Rob⟨t⟩
ffeild*, [but] in case y⟨t⟩ ṁy mother or sister may be aliue and demand it,
then they to haue it, if not aliue, then to keepe it   P⟨me⟩ *Comfort Starr.*
                                                              *Elias Hosking.*
  m⟨r⟩ *Comfort Starr* deposed before Magistrates, 9 June, 1653,—was present ẃhen *Jn⟨o⟩ Robison* declared this to be his will—Administration granted
to *Rob⟨t⟩ ffeild.*

-----

JOHN COOPER.

  Now resident in Weymouth being sicke, doe make this my will ; y⟨t⟩ y⟨e⟩
wife of m⟨r⟩ *Henery Waltham*, in whose house I now sojourne, may be fully ˙
satisfyed for charges in Phisicke, Attendance or otherwise w⟨ch⟩ being done,
if any thing remaine, y⟨t⟩ *Hazillpenah Willockes*, dwelling now with m⟨r⟩
*Waltham*, haue tenn shillings—all the rest of my goods & cloathes vnto
Louing friend *Thos Dyer* of Weymouth, executor.   JOHN COOPER.
  witnesse  *W⟨m⟩ Torry,*
          *Jonatham Waltham.*   Deposed by *W⟨m⟩ Torry*, Oct 21. 1653.

-----

JOSEPH SHAW.

  12. Dec⟨r⟩ 1653,) of Weymouth ; to *Mary* my Louing wife, one halfe, of
all my Estate & Lands, the other halfe to be devided amongst my Children, with respect of a double portion to *Joseph*, my Eldest Sonne ; wife
& my Brother *Nicholas Browne*\* Executors ;—*Ephraim Hunt* & *Joseph
Bicknall*, both of Weymouth [overseers]        JOSEPH SHAW.
  Witnesses  *John Clarke*
            *W⟨m⟩ Cotton*
            *Nath⟨t⟩ Souther*, Not. pub.
  m⟨r⟩ *John Clarke* & *W⟨m⟩ Cotton* deposed before the Magistrates y⟨t⟩ they
saw *John Shaw* signe this as his Last will, &c.  3 ffeb. 1653.

-----

REBECCA WEBB

  Grandchild *Rebecca Armitage*, sole execuțrix ; to pay all my debts, possesse all my goods, debts & estate.   Loveing friends *Thomas Butolph*
Senio⟨r⟩ & *Peter Olliver* administrators.   Committ vnto y⟨m⟩ the care of said
grandchild & my said goods debts or Estate to improoue to the best be-
hoofe of said grandchild, also to dispose of her in marriage (if she liue till
she be capable thereof, or at sixteene yeares of age, then she hath liberty
to dispose of hir estate hir selfe, in case God take hir away by death
before marriage, at twenty yeares of Age she hath power over hir
estate, but not of hir pson in marriage without Consent of hir father *Godfrey Armitage, Thomas Butolph* & *Peter Olliver.*   If God take away
said *Rebecca* by death before the age of sixteen yeares, then Administrators & sonne *Armitage* have all my estate to be equally devided betweene y⟨m⟩, they paying such Legacys as followeth, (vizt) to *Seaborne Cotton* & *John Cotton* forty shillings a piece, to m⟨r⟩ *John Wilson*, Junior, forty
shillings, to his sister *dauenport* forty shillings ; m⟨rs⟩ *dauenport* forty shillings, for her loue & care of said grandchild ; & sixe pound a yeare with

-----

  \* The name Byram written with a pencil in the margin and a line drawn under
Brown.

53

hir for two yeares. Aboue named Administrator⁸ & said sonne in Law twenty shillings a piece : wittnes my hand the 10ᵗʰ Decʳ 1654.

in pʳsence of           REBECCA WEBB   W   her marke
*James Johnson.*
*Jonath Negus.*

Leift *James Johnson* & *Jonathan Negus* sworne before yᵉ Magistrates 23 feb. 54, saith they saw *Rebecca Webb* signe this as hir Last will, &c.

---

### WILLIAM LANE of Dorchester.

Vnto *Thomas Rider* my Sonne in Law, & dau. *Elizabeth* his wife, my new dwelling house in Dorchester with all the outhousing, garden, &c. only to & for the vse of my dau. & ħir children : ffor euer : except my great Lott within the great Lotts of Dorchester within Pale & without, Estimated 24 Acres more or lesse, wch I giue vnto dau *Mary Long;* also such psonall Estate as I dye possesed of shall by my Executors be thus distributed ; vnto sonne Thomas *Linckhorne* of Hingham, £8. in silver ; vnto Sonne *George Lane* of Hingham, £8.; sonne *Nath Baker* of H. £8.; sonne *Andrew Lane* of H. £8. the discharge of these Legacyes in Siluer aforesaid £60. due vnto me vpon Bill frō mʳ *John Glover,* the Remainder of the Bill after £32. in Legacyes (being Twenty Eight) I giue vnto *Mary Long,* my dau. together with all my psonall estate, except one standing bedsteed in the Parlor, also one table & one chest in the house, & also two fatts in the Leantoo to wett Barly in, wᶜʰ I giue vnto my sonne *Rider,* & his wife to Remaine at the house, vnto *Mary Long* all my Cattle, haye, Corne, mault, swine, Pewter, brase, beding, & all my Estate ; funnerall charges & Legacyes being discharged ; vnto *ffredome Kingley,* who hath beene my faithfvll Servant. 20⁹ *Mary Long* to haue liberty in my dwelling house after my decease for the Removall of hirselfe & goods frō thence, such time as my executors thinke convenient, not exceeding sixe moneths after the day of my Buriall, also such liberty in the Barne & vpon the Land Concerning hir haye, Corne & Cattle, wᶜʰ is thus to be vnderstood, that it shall not at all pʳjudice or hinder *Tho Rider* from the vse of the Land at all ; in case I dye in such Season as the Land is to be planted or Sowne, he haue liberty so to doe, & she haue liberty to Reape & take what was by me planted or Sowne. Louing Brother *Joseph ffarnworth* & *John Wiswall* executors. 28. 12mo 1650.

Signed in pʳsence of          the marke of H WILLIAM LANE
*Thomas Wiswall*
*ffreedome Kingsley*
pʳsent yᵉ *Gover*ʳ        *Thomas Wiswall* deposed before yᵉ magist
mʳ *Nowell*           this 6ᵗʰ of July 1654 yᵗ this was yᵉ Last
mʳ *Hibbins*          will of *Wᵐ Lane.*
Capt *Gookin* & *Record*ʳ

---

### THOMAS JEWELL of Brantrey.

All yᵉ estate to my wife to be hers as long as she is a widdow, if she mary then to deuide it into three parts, two parts among my children the third to be hirs. *William Needom* & *Tho: ffoster* to take the care & over sight of Estate for my wife & Children.    THOMAS JEWELL † his marke

10. 2 mo 1654          That this is the true will of *Tho: Jewell*
in the pʳsence of        testifyed by *Wᵐ Scant* & *Hannah*
*William Scant*        *Harbor* before me *Samᵗ Basse* Comis-
*Hannah* H *Harbor* witnesses     issionʳ

Administration granted to *Grisell Jewell* his Late wife who is to see the will pformed & giue security that the children shall haue their parts out of it; this 21 July, 1654.

Att a meeting of the Magists & recorder the 5ᵗʰ October 1655.

*Humphry Griggs* of Brantrey who with Gods leaue is Suddenly to *mary* the,Relict of *Tho: Jewell*, Appeared before the magists & acknowledged yᵗ it was agreed betweene him, *Tho: ffoster*, & *Wᵐ Needom*, yᵗ the said *Griggs* haue sole benefitt of the Estate of *Tho: Jewell*, & at his owne charge bring vp all the children of said *Jewell* till they were fitt to be putt Apprentice, causing them to Read, & the said *Griggs* did binde himselfe & estate, vizt. yᵉ house & Land of said *Jewells* besides his owne, to pay to each of the said children the sume of seauen pounds & ten shillings when they come to the age of twenty one yeares yᵉ sonnes; at day of marriage or eighteen yeares yᵉ daughters, & to yᵉ Eldest sonne fiueteene pounds at his age of twenty one ycares; in witnes said *Humphry Griggs* subscribed his name before yᵉ magistrate & Recorder, yᵉ day aboue mentioned, wᶜʰ Agreement was approved of & vpon the former, *Humphry Griggs* bond of *Wᵐ Needom* & *Tho: ffoster* is to be giuen vp

witnes *Wᵐ Needom, Tho: ffoster*

---

### Thomas Wheeler of Boston.

Wife *Rebecca* Sole-executrix; to said wife all my Estate dureing Life, if she continue a widdow; if she mary then vnto sonne *Joseph Wheeler* my house and Land, reserving vnto my wife her thirds, vnto my dau *Rebbecca* out of my moveables £20. at hir marriage or at yᵉ age of nineteene yeares *Richᵈ Trusdall Nathˡ Williams* & *Edwᵈ ffletcher* [overseers]

6: 3mo 1654                                             Tho: Wheeler

witnes  *Wᵐ Colbron,*        Proved by *Nathˡ Williams*, 25 July 1654
  *Nathaniell Williams.*

---

### Richard Wilson of Boston.

Being very sick, bequeath all my Estate vnto *Sarah* my wife, debts being payd, said estate kept & improued for yᵉ vse of said wife.  *Wᵐ Kilcop* & *Richard Knight* overseers, forty shillings a peece as a token of my Loue        19 Aug. 1654.                         Richard Wilson

*Wᵐ Holloway,*
*Thomas Harwood.*

---

23 Dec. 1654.   Barnabas ffawer of Boston.

Debts being payd, vnto *Grace ffawer* my wife & *Eliazer* my Sonne the Remainder of my Estate, wife sole Executrix. I will yᵗ sonne *Eliasar* shalbe kept at Schoole with mʳ *Chevers* at Ipswitch for one yeare to be brought vp at Learning.  mʳ *James Penn*, mʳ *Wᵐ Paddy*, mʳ *Tho: Lake*, & *Tho Marshall* all of Boston, overseers, to see my will truely p formed, Viz! that when my sonne shall come to the age of twenty & one yeares, the estate to be equally devided betwixt them.

Witnes *Thos Marshall*        Will proved 2 feb. 1654 by Elder *James*
    *James Penn*           *Penn* mʳ *Wᵐ Paddy* & mʳ *Thos Lake.*
    *Wᵐ Paddy*

---

12: 2ᵐᵒ 1654    Jefery Turner of Dorchester,

Husbandmān, being Sicke knowing it to be yᵉ minde & will of God yᵗ a man should Sett his house in order before he depart this life, all my

outward estate house Lands & other goods to be employed for y^e maintenance of my wife *Isabell*, & two sonnes *Praiseeuer* & *Increase*, & for the
increasing of a stocke, if God shall please to blesse the same vntill the time
y^t my sonne *Praiseeuer* shall haue accomplished the age of one & twenty
yeares, then one halfe of all vnto my wife dureing life, & y^e other halfe
to my two sonnes after wifes decease ; a double portion to sonne *Praise
ever*, saveing the sume of twelfe pounds to be abated in regard of a trade
w^ch I haue putt him out to Learne, haue bestowed y^t cost vpon him in
regard of his apparell, & haue wanted that helpefullnesse from him in
pointe of his Labour, w^ch otherwise he might haue afforded if he had liued
with me as y^e younger sonne hath done, his porcon (except here excepted)
to be double to sonne *Increase*, & deliuered to him in house & Lands, if
what I leaue in y^t kind extend so furr ; sonn *Increase* to haue his in household stuffe or other goods, if my goods extend to such a value ; if either
my sonnes dye before *Praiseeuer* haue attayned the age of 21 yeares,
then y^e portion shalbe to my other sonne surviving ; if my wife depart
this life before sonnes receiue their portions the outward estate shalbe used
for the benefitt of both by my overseers, & by the Survivo^r of them, to
witt, *Lieft Roger Clap*, & Ensigne *Hopestill ffoster ;* wife *Isabell* executor.
witnesses *Richard Baker*        JEFFERY TURNER
 *Richard Leedes* (—p his marke Will Proved 25. 3^mo 1654 before me
 *John Gornell*        *Humphrey Atherton.*
    *m^r Nowell*
    *Cap^t Atherton*   Will allowed 25 Mch, 1655.
    & *Recorder*

---

 23 Sep. 1654   GEORGE DAVIS.

 Wife *Barbara* & *Dan^l Turell* Executors ; whole Estate to wife she allowing thirty pounds to Eldest sonne *Samuell* when he is in age, & twenty
to sonne *John* when he is in age, provided this estate by a crosed hand of
p vidence be not wasted ; if wife mary another husband, then Executor^s
shall pay to *Sam^l* one hundred pounds when he is in age, & to *John* sixty,
if God so despose of *Barbara* my wife, y^t she change not her condicon
into a state of marriage, then I bequeath all to hir disposing she allowing
the forenamed portions to my sonnes.   GEORGE DAVIS.
In the p^rsent of *Nath^l Greenwood*,
   *John Brimblecome.*  Proved by them 25 Aprill, 1655.
         p^sent y^e *Governo^r.*
          *m^r Nowell.*
          *Cap^t Atherton.*
          *Edwd^d Rawson* Record^r

### JAMES JORDAN, OF DEDHAM.

**APRIL 24, 1655.**

vnto *Thomas Jordan* my Sonne & to his heyres for euer that my feather bed bolster & pillow wherein I vsually Lodge together with all y° bedding whatsoeuer therevnto belonging as well woollen as Linnen, & also my other Linnen, only Reserving & excepting such as shall be necessarily vsed about y° decent buryal of my body, & further I giue to my Said Sonne *Thomas*, all my wearing Apparell whatsoeuer & all my working tools. Vnto *Mary* my eldest daughter whom y° Lord hath visited w^th blindnes y° Some of thirty pounds to her and her heirs for euer w^ch thirty pounds is in y° hand of *Tho: Jordan* my Sonne pvided y' if it shall please y° lord y' I shall yet liue & be necessarily occasioned to expent any pte y^r of then my daughter shall haue y° remainder, otherwise she shall haue the whole to be payd to hir or hir heyres or assigns, as by bill from *Thomas* my Sonne it ought to be payd to me. Vnto y° fiue children of my daughter *Anne* the wife of *Abraham Jaquith*, Late of Charles Towne the Sume of fiue pounds; y' is to say, to each of y^m twenty shillings, to be payd to the said *Abraham* their father to their vse in Currant Countrey paym^t & at prize then Currant deliuered with in one whole yeare after my decease, in Dedham. *Eleazer Lusher* of Dedham sole Executor, vnto whom I bequeath whatsoeuer of my Estate is hitherto vndisposed of towards charges aforesaid.

In the psence of vs
  *Henery Chickering*
     his

JAMES ⚔ JORDAN

his
  *Edward* I-I ¹¹¹ *Hawes*
    marke

              Testifyed vpon Oath by the ptyes aboue named
                   Before me *Eliazer Lusher.*

p'sent y° Governo'
  dep' Gov^r
  m' *Nowell*
  major *Willard*
  & major *Atherton*

Proved at Boston 1 Aug 1655.
   by *Henery Chickering* & *Edward Hawes*
Will Produced by Cap' *Eliazer Lusher.*

Inventory taken by *Henery Chickering* *John Lason* I his marke.
4. 3. 55 deposed by them 1 Aug 55 £53. 07. 02.

----

### JAMES SNOOKE OF WEYMOUTH.

being Sicke in body but in good Memory I giue to my Sister *Gouer Tice* of Chester in old England in Dorcet shyre, & her foure children twenty shillings to Each of them; to my sister *Joane Snooke* of ffiffed Magdelene in old England in Dorset shyre, twenty shillings: to my Sister in Law *Elizabeth Snooke*, & hir three children foure pounds, & to each of them alike to *John Rogers* of weymouth in New England Linnen weaver, fiue pound: But it is not my will y' these legacyes should be payd tell after the decease of my wife whom I make my Sole Executrix.

      In the p'sence of vs. 22 June, 1655.
witnes, *Thomas Dyer*              JAMES SNOOK.
  *Stephen ffrench* proved 19.5.55 by *Thos: Dyer & Stephen ffrench.*
*Margaret Snook* widow of James of Weymouth will made 9.2.60.

Inventory of the Estate of *James Snook* of Weymouth taken 14.5.55. by *John Rogers* & *Tho Dyar*, £88. 07. 08d.

___

## JOHN SPYERS.

Being very sicke. Well beloued friend, *Euan Thomas*, Vintner of Boston, Executor, to receiue all my goods in *ffoster* his celler, that is to say, two double Anckers & one Single Ancker of Strong watters, with one Barr⁰ᶠ of Cannary Wine. The foresaid *Evan Thomas* Executoʳ for the recovering of Seaven pounds of sterling money of *William Brenton*, m'chant in Boston, as a debt due to me from the said *Brenton* for Tobaccoes sould by me vnto *Edward Tapley.*

I doe Ordaine the aforesaid *Evan Thomas* [?] *Blith* of Boston Marriner Amounting to the Sume of two pounds ten shillings sterling money.

for yᵉ recovering of *Ralph Earle* of Road Island one Mare Colt which I bought of the said *Ralph Earle* of the age of fifteen moneths old.

For the recovering A shallop of *Henery Perin* of Road Island, wᵗʰ I bought of the said *Perin* with Rigging according. These words being deliuered by the aforesaid *John Spyers.*

25. July 1655.

wittneses *Joseph Read*

*W Hamilton Francis Newbery* they deposed before Court 6ᵗʰ Aug. 55. p'sent yᵉ *Evan Thomas* acknowledged before the Court that it was Governor *John Spyers* Request, after debts & expences payd, the rest of depᵗ Govʳ his Estate should be Sent to his wife & Child, wᶜʰ he pmised mʳ *Nowell* should be done.

Maj *Atherton* Inventory taken by *Wm. Tilly* & *John Sunderland* 3:6ᵒ.55, *John Spiers* £35. 09. 06.

deposed by *Evan Thomas*, 6 Aug. 55.

___

## ROBERT KNIGHT.

Wife *Anna Knight* Executrix; Leaving my Sonne *Edward Knight*, & my dau. *Martha Knight*, the two children which God hath beene pleased to giue vs, soly to hir custody, desyering hir to bring them vp in the feare of God & to such Learning as they shal be capable of, not doubting with all, but that in convenient time she will alott & giue vnto them such a pporcōn of yᵉ Estate as shal be fitting for their future comfortable Liueing.

Have set my hand & seale this 8ᵗʰ of May, 1655.

Witness                                           ROBᵀ KNIGHT.

*Samuell Maverick*
*Joseph Bastar*            Aug 1 55        Samˡ *Mauericke* &
*Amos Richison*                             *Amos Richison* deposed.

___

## GEORGE DELL OF BOSTON.

Marriner being by yᵉ p'vidence of God bound on a Voyage to Sea frō England to Ireland & frō Ireland to Virginia & frō Virginia to New England do hereby bequeath mine Estate to my wife Dureing hir life one halfe of my Estate Moueables & vnmovables a fourth part of my sᵈ Estate two my two youngest Sonnes to be devided equally betwixt them for overseers, Capᵗ *Thomas Clarke* of boston in New England m'chant & mʳ *Henry Webb* of the towne & Countrey aforesaid what Estate I haue in England I leaue it to be overseene by my brother, mʳ *Richard Barachew* Liueing at Hackney neare London, & my brother *Ralph Dell*, they to be accomptable to mʳ *Thomas Clarke* & mʳ *Henry Webb*, of New England. 3 of 9ᵇᵉʳ 1658.                                                P mr GEORGE DELL.

26 Aug. 1655. Power of Administracon graunted to *Abigall* his Late wife. An Inventory of the Estate of Cap *George Dell* apprised by *James Euerell* & *John Anderson*, 6 Sep. 1655. £1506. 14. 07½.

### 11. 5. 1655.    JOHN CLAP OF DORCHESTER.

To my wife, my 'new dwelling house with all my lands both in y° necke & in the woods w⁺ to me doth appertayne, dureing hir naturall life, & after my wife's decease I giue my said house & land to the maintenance of the ministry, & a Schoole in Dorchester foreuer; to Brother *Ambros Clap* what is due me still from brother *Richard Clap* in England, wᶜʰ is three pound or there about; to brother-in-Law, *Edward Clap*, three pounds of y° wᶜʰ is in his owne hands; vnto Cousins *Richard* & *Elizabeth*, Children of my brother *Richard Clap*, one platter which I haue at my brother *Richards* aforesaid; to Cousene *deborah Clap*, daughter of y° brother aforesaide, one Siluer Spoone w⁺ Spoone is in his fathers hand; to Couseins *Nathaniell, Ebenezer, Sarah & Hannah Clap*, brother *Nicholis* Children, tenn shillings a piece; to Couseins *Elizabeth Prudence* & *Samuell Clap*, Children of my brother *Thomas Clap*, eight shillings a piece; y° rest of his children each of them fiue shillings; to Couseins *Prudence, Ezra, Nehemiah & Susannah Clap*, each of them eight shillings a piece; all y° rest of my goods; my funerall discharged, & just debts being payd, I giue to my deare wife whome I make my sole Executrix.

postcript

Allso I giue to my Couseine *John Capen*, 2s 6d, to Couseine *Roger Clap's* children, one shilling a piece; I desyer my brother *Nicholas*, Brother *Edward*, & my Couseine *Roger Clap*, to be my overseers for the pformance of this my will.                                                JOHN CLAP.

witnesses

*Edward. Clap*            At a meeting of the Govᵉ Mʳ *Nowell* & Recordʳ
*Sarah Clap*                          30 Aug 1655.
*Jone Clap*                  *Roger Clap* deposed.

An Inventory of the goods Chattells of *John Clapp* of Dorchester, deceased, 24ᵗʰ July, 1655. Taken by *Edward Clapp, Nicholas Clapp, Roger Clapp*, £140.04.10. 30 Aug. 55. *Jone Clapp* widow of the deceased deposed.

### ZACHEUS BOSWORTH.

23ᵈ 5. 1655. beloued wife *Ann Bosworth*, sole Executrix of all my house & lands with my Cattle & household stuffe. It is my will y' my sonne *Samuell* shall at y° age of twenty years haue the best paire of working oxen with all their furniture, & fiue acres of land y' lyes in Center field, & he shall haue one part of the house w⁺ I now dwell in; I giue to my daughter *Elizabeth Bosworth*, two acres of land with a mare, or else y° barne with a piece of ground to it to be layd out by y° overseers of this my will; my wife I doe giue unto hir hands all y' I haue vntill my sonne come to y° yeares of twenty, & then y' shall haue one pte of y° house while she liues, & after hir death my sonne *Samuell* shall haue y° whole house & ground, & for the rest of y° household stuffe, I doe leaue it to my wife for hir to dispose of & vse it dureing hir life, & as she shall haue opportunity to giue of it to yᵐ when she shall dye. Elder *Penn* Deacon *Johnson* Deacon *Trusdall* & *Leift Cooke* overseers.     the marke of
                                                                A C *Zacheus Bosworth.*

*Wittnes Harwood Elisha Cooke.*

p'sent y°                              Will Proved by *Elisha Cooke*, Oct. 5. 1655.
dep' Governo'      Inventory of Estate made 15. 6. 55. by *Nathan¹ Williams*
Moʲor *Altherton*    *Thomas Bumsteed*, £142. 07. 10. *Ann Bosworth widow*
& Recorder.            of *Zacheus* deposed, Oct. 5. 55.

CHRISTOVELL GALLOP.

24ª of yᵉ 5 mo. 1655. I doe give vnto my Sonne *John Gallop* halfe my
money wᶜʰ is about £15 & doe giue him yᵉ bed I lye on with one boulster,
one coverlid & blanckett, alsoe one of yᵉ best brasee Kettles a sea Chest, a
great bible one pewter platter one paire of sheets one pillowber fiue napkins, one holland board cloth & halfe my waring clothes, I doe giue
*Hannah* my sonne, *John Gallop's* wife; I giue to my daughter *Joane Joye*,
halfe my money with on great brasee pott, with on of yᵉ best brasee
Kettles, also a great white chest one bedsteed one flocke bed two blancketts
also one paire of my best sheetes one beareing sheete one odd sheete one
pewter candlestick one porringer, one pewter platter, & fiue napkins,
with halfe my wearing clothes all these I doe giue to my daughter *Joane
Joy* yᵉ rest of my goods I doe giue to be deuided betweene my sonne *Samⁿ
Gallop* & my sonne *Nathaniell Gallop*, each of them equally. *James Penn*
& *Edward Rainsford* to be yᵉ overseers of this my will.

wittnes            CHRISTOVELL GALLOP
*John Search*                  and a marke
*Dorothy Vpshall*        Power of Administration granted to
                    Elder *James Penn* & *Edwᵈ. Rainsford.*
*Christobell Gallop* Inventory £36.14. 31 Oct. 1655.

———

I. JOSHUA FFOOTE Cittizen & Iremonger of London, being by Gods
pvidence now resident in pvidence in New England, being sick, doe make
this my Last Will. I comitt my whole estate vnto Lifteᵃ *Joshua Hewes*
& *Henry ffowler* for to take care of that it may be preserued for my wife
& children, & such as I am Indebted vnto; also to reckon & gett in my
debts, & to sell of houses goods lands & to satisfye such debts I am ingaged
with as much speed as may be, so farre as it will goe to my wife & children. 2. 8. 1655.

Witnes *William Blaxton*            JOSHUA FFOTE
      The marke of [] *Richard waterman* ⎫     and a marke
prᵉsent           *Thomas Harris* ⎬ deputies
dep Govᵗ         31 October 1655 ⎭
major *Atherton* Power of Administration granted to Leift *Joshua Hewes.*
& Recorder.

———

THOMAS DUDLEY.

hauing a Long tyme through the patience & goodnes of God Layen
vnder his afflicting hand, doe make this my will.

To mʳ & mrs *Norton* three pounds a piece, as a smale remembrance for
theire exceeding Large Love & kindnes they haue showne vnto me wᶜʰ I
jntreate them to accept of, with my Hebrew Lexicon yᵗ *Paynin* made, wᶜʰ I
giue further to mʳ *Norton* over & besides my djet & other many charges
that they haue beene at with me Since my coming vnder theire Roofe,
wᶜʰ I desire my executors hereafter mentioned to satisfy to the full; Vnto
my Loueing friends mⁿ *Greene* & goodwife *Langhorne*, both of Cambridge,
forty shillings a piece; Vnto my Aunt *Pacy* my best cloake, wastcoate,
& forty shillings; Vnto the two majde servants of mⁿ *Norton* a piece of
kersy of three y'ds, & all my poore Linnen to be devided as mⁿ *Norton*
shall Judge fittest; to my two sisters by my mother, *Margaret* & *Ann*, tenn
pounds a piece, wᶜʰ I desire my Execuoʳ mʳ *Thomas Danforth* to take into
his custody & to improoue it to their best advantage in some way of encrease in sheepe or otherwise, as he shall see meete; they to haue the
principall & increase at the day of theire marriages, or with in tenn dayes
after my fathᵉ's decease; Vnto mʳ *Thomas Danforth* & mʳ *Samⁿ Danforth*

of Cambridge & Roxbury, my Loueing friends, the some of forty shillings a piece, & I make y^m my Sole Executers.

I giue vnto my only deare brother *John Dudley* the rest of my estate, be it tenn pounds more or lesse, executor' to dispose of & improve it as before, till he comes to liue of & by himselfe, after he hath attained the age of twenty one yeares, & my mjnd is y^t if either of my sisters or broth^r should dye before their appointed time to receiue w^t I giue [then the sum to be divided betwixt the survivors] my mjnde is y^t out of my brother *John's* legacy, my father most Honnored & deare, might haue twenty shillings pajd him p^rsently to buy him a ring, as a smale token of y^t duty I owe to him & I further giue my brother *John* my new suite, y^t is now a making, my mjnd is y^t my bookes debts & pte of the mill my grandfathér *Dudley* gaue me, be all sold & improoved by Executors.

In p^rsene of vs          THO DUDLEY.
*Peter Olliuer*
*Eleazer Mather*       Will proved 7. 9. 1655.
An Inventory of the Estate taken of m^r    by m^r *Edward Rawson*
*Thomas Dudley* Jun^r lately deceased at    & *Peter Olliver.*
Boston. £65. 15. 02.     21 June, 1664.

---

GEORGE STEVENS.

I doe bequeath all that I haue vnto my Landlords, *Isaack Collemore*, in whose house I sojourne, that if I dye & it please God to take me, I shall as I haue said to bequeath all y^t I haue to him, but if the Lord doe restore me to my health to enjoy it my selfe, & this is the true jntent of my mjnd at p^rsent; this is my true meaning what is aboue written.

By me *James Lambert* ⅃ marke      GEORE STEVENS
the last of the Eight moneth, 1655.     & a marke.
Wittnes *Edward Smith*       *James Lambert* & *Edward Smith*
*Henry messinger*        deposed before Court 10 Nov 1655
*James Bushell*

Inventory of the goods of *George Stevens*, Cooper prized by *Bartholmew Barlow*, & *James Merrit*. £7. 6. 6.    deposed by *Isacke Cullemore.*

---

INCREASE MATHER.

I INCREASE MATHER of Boston in New England being not only sensible y^t I am (as all men are) a poor mortal but having moreover in respect of some bodily Infirmities especially that Ephialtes w^ch I have been often afflicted with reason to think y^t my breath will suddenly be stopped so that it is possible and probable, y^t when dying I shall not have Liberty to express my mind.

And considering y^t God (of his abundant mercy) has given me to accomplish those things which w^n sick near unto death, many years ago I desired life & health y^t I might finish them, I wold be in a readiness y^t when Christ shall call for me I may have nothing else to do, but to dye & go to him. And that remembering, that it is according to the will of God that a man before his death set his house in order, I do make & appoint this to be my last will & testament in maner following.

Concerning my soul, I have long since (even from my youth for more than threescore years ago) given it to God in Jesus Christ trusting y^t he who has y^e Keys of hell and death, will comand his holy Angels to conduct me into his blessed presence when once death has separated between my mortal body & my imortal spirit I am the chief of sinners & have nothing in y⁰ world to depend upon but only the Righteousness of Jesus Christ (and the remembrance of that Righteousness does make me to triumph not only over death & devils but over all my sins When my soul is out of my body, let my dear Lord Jesus Christ do what he will with it for into his hands I do comĩt my spirit. If he will send that soul which he has redeemed with his own blood, and wᶜʰ he has made above all things desirous to glorify his Name, if he will send yᵗ soul down into eternal darkness I am yⁿ content to perish, but that can never be

Concerning my body I comĩt it to y⁰ earth, there to sleep in hope until y⁰ Resurrection of y⁰ just

As to y⁰ outward estate wᶜʰ y⁰ Lord of his goodness has bestowed on me, It is my mind & will (& I trust y⁰ will of God also) yᵗ it be disposed of as followeth I would in y⁰ first place give order for ye payment of any debts if I had any, but I bless y⁰ Lord yᵗ I owe no man any thing but Love I give five pounds to y⁰ poor in yᵗ church to which I am related

Concerning my wife yᵗ now is, there was an agreement before marriage, & writings signed accordingly, yᵗ I should not be concerned wᵗʰ any part of her estate nor she wᵗʰ mine If she shall (as hitherto she has not) bring anything to me I wold have it returned to her again or double y⁰ value.

Concerning my son *Cotton Mather* he has been a great comfort to me from his childhood having bin a very dutiful son & a singular blessing both to his Fathers Family & flock. If I had any considerable estate I ought to bequeath the greatest part of it to him. It has bin thought yᵗ I have bags by me wᶜʰ is a great mistake. I have not twenty pounds in silver, or in Bills. But wᵗever I have (be it more or less) whether in Silver or Bills I give it to him my eldest son. Item, I give to him my pendulum watch. Item my pendulum clock, Item my silver tankard: And I bequeath to him all my manuscripts, & y⁰ one halfe of my Library, desireing yᵗ my Books & manuscripts may not be sold, nor embezeled.

Concerning my son *Samuel Mather*, I have expended more in his education, yⁿ on any one of my children. I gave him a considerable number of Books at his going for England And a considerable part of his uncle *Nathaniel's* Library has fallen to his share He liveth where he may furnish himself wᵗʰ variety of Books & is blest wᵗʰ an estate able to do it. Never y⁰ les Considering yᵗ he has bin a dutifull son an honor to his Fathers name I bequeath to him a fourth part of my Library, in testimony of my Paternal affection. The remaining fourth part thereof I bequeath to my Fatherless grandson, *Mather Byles*, in case he shall be educated for & employed in y⁰ work of y⁰ ministry (wᶜʰ I much desire & pray for) leaving wᵗʰ my executor to order & determine what particular Books shall be his, only I give him (in case aforesaid) particularly [poti synopsis criticorum?] in five volumes in folio, & his english Annotations wᵗʰ y⁰ continuation in two folios.

I give to my grandson *Samuel Mather* [thesauris Cöentari or piscacoris comentarium] in Biblon in three folios

I give to my grandson *Thomas Walter* the English Annotation in two folios, Also y⁰ dutch [Anentodiah?] in two folios

The remainder of my estate in houses or moveables I give to be equally divided among my beloved daughters *mariah, elizabeth, Sarɪh & Abigail* what I give to my daughter *elizabeth* I desire may (if his mother can) be improved towards y⁰ education of her only son (my grandson *Mather Byles*) in Learning, because he is a child whom God has blessed with a strong memory & ready capacity & aptness to learn I leave it as my dying Request to his uncle my son *Cotton Mather*, to take care of y^e education of y^t child as of his owne. If he shall obtain subscriptions for his education for y^e ministry (as he knows I have done for more fatherless children y^n one) I am persuaded y^t his owne children will not fare y^e worse for his being a Father to a fatherless child. To prevent his being chargable as much as I can I give him my wearing apparel excepting my chamber cloak w^ch I give to my executor.

If y^e Lord shall take away *Mather Byles* by death before he is of full age (or if he shall not be employed in y^e work of y^e ministry,) it is my mind & will, y^t then y^e Books bequeathed to him, shall be given to such other of my grand children as shall be preachers of y^e Gospel of Christ according as my executors shall dispose.

I dy believing y^t God will bless my children after I am taken from them And my persuasion is grounded on these as well as other Scriptures, Gen. 25. 11 & 48. 21, psal 37. 25. prov. 20. 7 unto God in Jesus Christ I Comit my selfe and all mine forever.

Finally I constitute & appoint my beloved son *Cotton Mather* To be y^e sole executor of this my will entreating my worthy friends m^r *Thomas Hutchinson* m^r *Adam winthrop*, m^r *Edward Hutchinson* m^r *John Ruck* & m^r *John Frissel* to be assistants or overseers praying y^m y^t for my sake, but especially for y^e sake of y^e glory w^ch I ·hope may come to God y^rby they will be kind to my Fatherless grandson *Mather Byles*.

This I declare to be my last will & Testament. And I have accordingly written this with my own hand & hereunto affixed my seale the seventh day of y^e fourth month called June in y^e year of o^r Lord one thousand seven hundred & eighteen.

witnesses y^t I declare this to be my will

    *Jonas Clarke*                                INCREASE MATHER
    *Edward Wilder*
    *Joseph Woodwell*

    I do hereby signify to my executor that it is my mind & will y^t my Negro servant called [*Speedgood?*] shall not be sold after my decease, but I do y^n give him his liberty let him y^n be esteemed a Free Negro
June 4 1719

Suffolk sc.

    By the *Hon^ble Samuel Sewall Esq*
              Judge of Probate &c

The within written Will being presented for probate by y^e Executor therein named *Jonas Clarke & Edward Wilder* two of the Witnesses to the s^d Will personally appearing made oath that they Saw the Rev^d *Doctor Increase Mather*, deceased, the subscriber thereto, sign & seal & heard him Publish & Declare the same as his Last Will & Testament, and that when he So did he was of Sound disposing mind and memory according to these Deponents best discerning, unto which they (with *Joseph Woodwell* lately also deceased) Set to their hands as Witnesses thereof in the said Testators presence.            Jurat Cor.

Boston September 23^d 1723             SAMUEL SEWALL.

    [Endorsed in *Dr. Increase Mather's* handwriting,
        "Last Testament June 7. 1718"]

---

### SUSANNA PHILLIPS.

Whereas my beloved husband *William Phillips* hath by his Last will bearing date with these p^rsents confirmed vnto me y^e house w^ch was my husband *Stanleyes*, together with the great pasture close & y^t w^ch was bought of

63

*Christo: Lawson*, together with plate & household goods, & further hath giuen me power to dispose of all or any part y^r of whilst yet he is liuing, This writing doth declare that I *Susanna Phillips* doe dispose as followeth   To dau-in Law, *Mary field* fiue pounds ; dau. *Martha Thurston* fiue pounds ; dau. *Rebecca Lord,* fiue pounds ; Sonne *Wm Phillips* twenty pounds ; Sonne *Nathl Phillips* twenty pounds ; *Elizabeth Phillips* my dau. fiue pounds ; dau. *Phebe Phillips* twenty pounds ; dau. *Sarah* twenty pounds ; to *Elizabeth Aspinwall* fiue pounds ; vpon *Wm Aspinwell,* if any of my brother or sisters children come over to liue within two yeares after my decease, six pounds a piece, to the value of Eighteene pounds, the first three that come to demand it ; to *Richard Bennitt* & *George Bennitt,* w^ch were my Servants, fiue shillings a piece ; all the residue both y^e house w^ch was my husband Stanleyes, & y^e great close in the mill field, & the field w^ch was *Christo: Lawsons,* withe plate & househould goods vnto my husband, *Wm Phillips,* as his own proper inheritance, & doe make him sole executo^r.
10 (7) 1650                                   Susanna Phillips.
                                                       & two seales
my true meaning is not necessarily to reserue any title to his heire (further then he shall see cause) I freely giue him whatsouer right my husband *Stanley* or I had vnto any other house or Land not here mentioned.
   10 :7: 1650   with this addition in p^rsence       Susanna Phillips.
        of *Wm Aspinwall* Notarius publ.
            p^sent y^e *Governer*                      Approued Aug. 2. 1655.
               *dept Gov* m^r *Nowell*
               *major Atherton.*

# ABSTRACTS OF THE EARLIEST WILLS UPON RECORD
## IN THE COUNTY OF SUFFOLK, MS.

Last will and Testament of Mr Robert Keayne, all of it written with my owne hands & began by me Mo : 6 : 1 : 1653 comanly called August. [This will extends from page 116 to 274 — 158 pages, in the original volume.]

I Robert Keayne, Citizen and M$^r$chant Taylor of London by freedome, now dwelling at Boston, declare this to be my Last Will and Testament. —[Having spoken of his Faith &c he continues] Haveing beene trayned vp in Millitary Discipline from my young$^r$ yeares, & haveing endeavoured to promote it the best I could Since God hath brought me into this Country, & seeing he hath beene pleased to vse me as a poore Instrument to Lay the foundation of that Noble Society of the Artillery Company in this place that hath so far prospered by the blessing of God, as to helpe many with good experience in the vse of theire Armes, &c. a Nursery to raise vp many able and well experienced Souldiers therefore to declare my affections to that exercise & to the society of Souldiers I shall desire to be buryed as a Souldier in a Military way.

Debts to be paid which at this tyme doth amount to about One hundred and fivety pounds, besides what I owe vnto the poore boxe ; The particula$^r$s of w$^{ch}$ my executo$^r$s may find in a Long paper booke in my closet at Boston with a white Parchment cover, intitelled my Inventory booke, which debts of myne if God be pleased to spare me health while next spring I hope I shall pay the most of them myselfe except that only which I owe to the poore Boxe being about Eighty pounds——My will is after my Death a true Inventory betaken of all my Lands, Houses, Cattle, Bookes, Household Stuffe, Marchandize, Jewells &c of all the Corne I have at home or at my farme with all things there

The thirds of all my Lands & Housing both at Boston & at my ffarme at Rumne Marsh or any where else that I shall be possessed of at the tyme of my Death I bequeath vnto my wife m$^{rs}$ Anne Keayne during her Naturall life, a greate if not the greatest part of my Estate Lying in my Housing & Lands.

The rest of my whole Estate both personnall & Reall I deuide into two parts, the one part I give vnto my wel beloved & only Son Benjamine Keayne, the other part I reserue as my owne right to dispose of as I please which is as herein shall after be expressed.

And because I am not Ignorant that formerly there hath beene many claymors & evill reports raised vp against me here & else where, as if I had gott my Estate by vnjust dealing and wronging of others, That all might take nottice, that I durst not allow myselfe in any such knowne wickednes, I did in some of my former Wills and also in my Last before this of Anno 1649 (which I still keepe by me though cancelled & made Null by this, and will be needful to be preserued—to be read over by my executors—severall things mentioned therein, which I leaue out in this & may be of some help to them) Set apart Two hundred pounds, that if any man or woman in old England or New, could justly make it appear that I had in any thing vnjustly wronged them, that they might have had full satisfaction allowed them, though I know of no such thing that can justly be layd to my charge—having lived in New England 17 or 18 yeares, and none such haueing appeared I thinke it needles to continue any Longer what I formerly Sequestered for such ends.

65

Haueing thought of the want of some necessary things for the Towne of Boston, as a Market place & Cundit, the one a good helpe in danger of fyre, the want of which we haue found by Sad experience &c. the other vsefull for the Country people, that come with theire provisions for the supply of the Town, that they may have a place to sitt dry in and warme both in Cold, Raine & durty weather, a place to leave theire Corne or any other things safe, that they cannot sell, till they come againe, to haue some Convenient Roome or two for the Courts to meete in both in Winter & sumer & so for the Townes men & Comissiors, in the same building or the like a Convenient Roome for a Library, & a gallery or some other handsome Roome for the Elders to meet in, also a Roome for an Armory—If it should not be thought convenient that all these be vnder one Roofe or in one place, if advice were taken with some Skillfull workmen & others that haue good heads in Contriving of Buildings, Such as mr Broughton, mr Clarke the Chirirgion &c there might such a Model be drawne vp that one building may be contrived that would accomodate all these vses, without extraordinary Cost & yet be a great Ornament to the Towne as well as profitable other wayes, but if the Cheife of the Towne be of another minde I should propose That the Cundit & Markett House be sett in the Market place Some where betweene mr Cogins House & mine, or any where in that great streete betweene mr Parkers House & mr Brentons or rather mr Webbs if it should be judged there to be more convenient, He also proposes a Roome for the devines & Schollors, [another,] for Merchants mr of Shipps and Strangrs as well as the Towne—if it be thought not convenient to have it in front of the meeting House, it may accomplish the same ends if placed on that Side of the meeting House from Seargeant Williams shop to Deacon Trusdalls House [if it be thought proper to have a Cunditt elsewhere] it may be sett vp alone, about the place where the Pillary stands—I give Three Hundreth pounds in good Merchantable pay, one third part when the frame is brought to the place & raysed &c, the seconde part when the Chimneyes are built, the House covered and floores Layd, the last part when it is quite finished provided it be gone about and finished within two or three yeares after my decease—when finished [that the Buildings prove not] as Shaddowes & stand as Emptie Roomes without Substance I shall be willing to cast in my Mite, & bring my Lime & hare possibly God may Stirr vp the hearts of others to bring in their Badger Skines & Silke & others more Costly things that the worke may goe on.

To the Granere I giue one Hundred pounds to be payd in Corne, and that to be improved for a publicke Stocke.

The Library & Gallere for devines being finished, I giue to the beginning of that my 3 great writing bookes wch are intended as an Exposition or Interpretation of the whole Bible, as also a 4th great writing booke in which is an Exposition on the Prophecy of Daniel, of the Revelations & the Prophecy of Hosea not Long Since began, all which Bookes are written with my owne hand So farr as they be writt, & could desier that some able Schollar or two that is active and diligent & addicted to reading and writing were ordered to Carry on the same worke by degrees as they have Leasure and opportunitie, & in the same Methode and way as I have begun (if a better be not advised to) it shal be esteemed for the profitt of it to young Students (though not So to more able and learned devines in these knaving times) worth the Labor as I haue & doe finde it to my selfe worth all the paines & Labour I haue bestowed vpon them, so that if I had 100lb Layd me downe for

66

them, to depriue me of them, till my sight or life be taken from me, I should not part from them.

Further my will is that my Son Benjamine Keayne my Executor haueing first made choyce out of my study of Such Bookes as he shall desier for his owne vse and reading (not to sell) whether Diuinitie, Hystory, or Milletary, or any of my written Sermon bookes excepting those fower before giuen to the Library : & my wife also some few for her vse, if she shall desier any other than those she hath already, the p'mised my will is that my Brother Wilson & m' Norton with my Executor & Overseers view ouer the rest of my Bookes, and to choose from them Such as they shall thinke profitable for such a Library, they being all English none Lattine or Greeke the rest which remaines may be Sould for there due worth both the written and printed ones : And though my bookes be not many, nor very fitt for Such a worke, being English & smale bookes, yet after the beginning the Lord may stirr vp Some others that will add more to them, & helpe to carry the worke on by bookes of more valew, Antiquity vse and esteeme, & that an Inventory may be taken & kept of those bookes they Set apart for the Library. I doe will fower pounds a yeare be payd out of some of my shops in Boston by quarterly payments to provide some refreshing for [the Elders] when they meete, or now and then dinn'rs as farr as it will goe, this fower pounds pr Anno I give for the space of ten yeares, if that meeting continue. If a Convenient fayre Roome in one of the buildings be Set a part for an Armory & the meeting of the Artillery I give five pounds for the incouragem' of that Company to be Layd out in Pikes & Bandal'rs for the vse of such Souldiers of that Company that Liue in other Townes, so farr as it cannot be convenient for them to bring there Armes with them &c.

I giuie further to this Artillery Company fiue pounds more, towards the Erecting of a platforme for two mounted peeces of Ordinance to stand vpon, a greater & a smaller, with a Shead of boards raysed over it, to keepe them dry, in the most convenient pt in the Trayning place in Boston against some Hill or riseing ground that may receive the Shott of these peeces, & may be free from endangering any that vnexpectedly passe by that the Company may Learne how to Traverse, Lade, Mount Levell & fyre at a mark wch is as needfull a Skill for a Souldier as the Exercise of theire ordinary Armes. I suppose the Countrey will willingly Send the Company two such peeces for so good a vse & a Barrell of powder or two.

The bullets wil be most of them found & saued againe if the Hill or Butt against wch they Shoote be not so Low & narrow that they over mount & shoote aside at Randome—as many of the Company, or others, wch desire to Learne that Art of gunnere may enter there names to be Schollers of the great Artillery & giue so much for Entry and so much a yeare afterwards, &c. I give Two Heifers, or Cowes, to the Capt & Officers of the Company to be kept as a stocke Constantly, the increase or profitt of these Cowes yearely to be layd out in powder, Bulletts, &c. If the Company neglect to accomplish, this before expressed above two yeares after my decease these three Legacyes both the fiue pounds & the two Cowes to be voyd & to be the vse of my Executor, If the things be accomplished [he desires Security for the Cows] that the Stock be preserued, if the Company breake off the Cows to be returned.

[One half of the former grant of 100 lbs] with the increase thereof I giue to the vse of the free Sehoole at Boston, to helpe on the Trayning vp of Some poore mens Children of Boston (that are most towardly &

hopefull) in the knowledge of God & of Learning, not only in the Latine Tongue but also to Write & Cypher, as farr as the profitt of it will reach, as the Townesmen or ffeofees of the free Schoole from time to time shall Judge best takeing advice of my Executo^r.

The other fivety pounds with the profitt of it, I give for the vse & Releife of the poore members of our owne Church or to any other good vse that shal be accounted as necessary or more necessary then this.

Now if that Scoole should be sufficiently provided for before I dye, then I would propound it to be kept as a Magazine of store from yeare to yeare & as a stocke for the Towne, if either a famine or warre should happen amongst vs, which may tend much for the p^rseruation of the Towne especially the poorer sort 400 bushells of Indian may be bought for 50 lb & 250 bushells of Rye if not 300 for 50 lb & 80 pease, & how easy a thing would it be for the Towns to make it vp a 1000 bushells or more by euery family putting in but a pecke of Corne or such a matter but once in a yeare.

[He adds 20 lb to the former stock for the poor making in all 120 lbs this stock was gained] by taking one penny out of euery shilling which I have gotter by my Trade &.  So that when I gayned much in a weeke there hath beene the more layd aside for any good vse, & when Trayding hath beene dead & the gaines Lese, there hath beene the lesse layd a Syde for this stocke & vse, which course I haue constantly kept above this 40 yeare, which I now mention not in any way of boasting, but y^t all that know it may take nottice of the blessing of God vpon such a voluntary course, w^ch some others it may be wil be willing to Imitate by w^ch means I have had comonly Lyeing by me 50 lb 60 lb or 80 lb ready money, especially in old England, & some pretty quantity here, till now Lately Since money hath beene so Scarce amongst vs, whereby I haue beene fayne to borrow out of that stocke my selfe, for my owne necessary vse when I have wanted money of my owne, & a good comfortable helpe it hath beene to me that way in many pinches, but doe still keepe a carefull account what at any time I take out & pay it in againe as money comes to hand, out of w^ch Stocke vsually lying by me I haue had opportunitie to Lend to any poore godly Christian or Minister in neede (besides what I giue away).  Vnto w^ch Stocke I am indebted One Hundred pounds sterling or 101 lbs as nere as I can gesse, besides all the money that is now in Cash in 2 private boxes within my Cabinet in my Closet at Boston there being as I remember ten pounds in New England money with some old England Silver, & some what more then Tenn pounds in the other secret box in which is two ten shillings pieces of Barbere gold & 258 Single two pences pence & halfe pence, w^ch boxes are to be vn locked or opened with any Ordinary pinne or needle thrust into a Small pin hole, that is there against a piece of Steele, which easily will giue backe. [Good security is to be given for the 120 lbs otherwise it is to go] to Harvard Collidge they takeing care to secure the Stocke.

[In relation to the 300 lb. given to the Towne for the purpose of a Condit Market House, &c.] if the Towne of Boston slight or vndervalue this gift & neglect to finish these buildings in manner & time before mentioned these gifts with relation to these buildings, as my Bookes to the library, &c. shal be & remaine to the sole vse of the Collidge at Cambridge.

68

# ABSTRACT OF THE EARLIEST WILLS UPON RECORD IN THE COUNTY OF SUFFOLK.

### Will of Robert Keayne

If the Towne of Boston shall sett vpon one or two of these workes & neglect to Carry on the rest as if they should build only the Condit & Market House & not a Townes house or Library & Gallere, or a Grannere & not a Condit, &c. then my will is, [that they have only a proportional part] compared with the value of the other buildings left vndone, [The residue,] for the vse of the Collidge.

Now if any part thereof fall to the Collidge, my desire is, that should be improved, [not about the buildings or repaires,] but for the helpe of Such poore & hopefull Scholl^rs whose Parents are not comfortably able to maintaine them there for theire dyett & Learning, or for some addition yearely to the poorer sort of fellowes or Tutors whose Parents are not able nor themselves haue not abillitie nor supplies otherwise, to defray there charge, and make there studyes Comfortable &c. [To be referred to the President, Overseers, &c. of the Collidge.] Concerning my bookes giuen to begin the Library with, all in Boston, if the Towne should not within five years after my decease build a handsome roome for a Library, &c. that then they may be delivered to the Collidge.

I had in some of my form^r wills set a part some Legacies for the Trayning vp of some of the Indians, as also of theire Children to be taught to write & read, & to Learne the English Tongue & had thought vpon and proposed some wayes how to get of theire Children and youth that they might be so taught, as also that some of our young students might be incouraged to Study the Indian Tongue & instruct the Indians, & to Preach or Prophecy to them in theire own Language, as they should haue been directed by y^e Magistrates or Eld^rs. I had also left some pledge of my Loue to m^r *Elliot* & some others that haue taken paines to instruct y^e Indians, but the truth is, that vnkinde Carriage of m^r *Elliott* (that I may putt noe worse Tittle vpon it) in Seeking to interrupt, yea to take away, not only from my selfe, but from some others also, Certain ffarmes not giuen to vs by the Genn^rall Court, but my owne bought with my money, of the wor^pp my Brother *Dudly* & some others, but after it was graunted by the Court to be in that place, & I had been at the charge to Survey & Lay it out & after it was againe ratifyed to me by the genn^rall Court—There was Land enough granted to them by the Court with out the bounds of any of our ffarms; the action it selfe being very vnsavory not only to our selues but to many oth^rs, Therefore I would make it my request to the Reverent Eld^rs of this Country not to be too Stiffe & resolute in accomplishing theire owne wills & wayes, but to harken to the advice & counsell of there Brethren, & to be as easily p swaded, to yeeld in civill & earthly respects & things as they expect to p^rvayle with any of vs, when they haue a request to make for one thing or another, Least by too much Stiffness, they hinder many good workes that may be p fitable to themselues and to the whole Country. But God hath beene pleased to provide Such a Comfortable Supply, from Larger & fuller purses, to carry on this great & good worke amongst the Indians, that they shall not neede the helpe of p tiall p sons to make any addition that way.

I giue one hundreth pound of that which I had formerly set a part, for the Indians, to the vse of the Collidge, [on condition that the people of

Boston accept his former offer, " or any thing vnder the one halfe of the whole sume which is Two hundred & Ten pounds fall to the Collidge "] w^ch 100lb will purchase Twenty Cowes & these Cowes will Let for Twenty pounds a yeare, which Twenty pounds p Anno I desire may be disposed of to the best good of the Schollrs. If the whole 420 or one halfe of it Come to the Collidge, then this Legacy of one Hundred pound shall become voyd.

I giue to my Loveing Son Majo^r *Benjamine Keayne*, over and above the third part of my Cleane Estate as before mentioned, the great Gold Emerod Ring that was my wives fathers & now in my wiues keeping, which I desire that he may keepe by him, & neither sell nor giue away as long as he Liues, Except Some great necessitie should force him therevnto.

Item, I giue to him further, as my Speciall gift to him, my little written booke in my Closet upon i Cor: ii: 27: 28: w^ch is a Treatise on the Sacram^t of the Lords Supper p m^r Briarly a little thin pocket book, bound in Leather, all written with my owne hand, which I esteeme more pretious then gold, & w^ch I haue read over I thinke a 100 & a 100 times & hope he will read it over no Lesse, but make it his Constant Companion, & that it may be as pretious to him, as euer it was to me ; to let any one that desires haue a Coppie of it.

In some of my former wills I did bequeath to him likewise my 3 great written bookes vpon the Exposition of the Bible & request that he would carry on the same worke, which will be a worke of his whole life ; but considering Since that he will be hardly able, nor it may be willing to take so much paynes, & considering also that such a worke should be appropriated to one man only, may be beneficiall to a Society of men, I have Since thought it would be more vsefull to giue them to some publicke library, as now I haue done.

There wilbe found may bookes both printed & written that haue diverse Leaues turned down thicke in them, they are only such choyce places w^ch I intended to transcribe into these 4 great paper bookes.

I giue to my Loueing wife m^rs *Ann Keayne*, over & above her third part of my Lands &c. one ffeather Bedd & Beddsteede, with a ffeather Bowlster & one pillow, two white blanketts, one Rugg, two paire of sheets two pillowbers, with a paire of Curtaines, & valence Suitable to her owne Vse ; not the best of all that I haue in my house, but the bedd with the furniture before mentioned, to be Second, or next to the best of all, if there should be any matteriall difference betweene them.

I give to hir, that great Silver beare bowle that was giuen to vs both br m^r Prescot, at the time of his deathe ; I meane he gaue vs 3lb to buy a piece of plate, with which & some additions of my owne money putt to it, I bought this Cupp, which ingraven vpon the boule thereof to be the gift of m^r Prescott to vs.

I have allready giuen to my Son *Benjamine Keayne* a Comfortable portion at his marriage w^ch is all that he can challenge by agreement betweene my Brother Dudley, myselfe & Son, at the Consumation of that vnhappy match betweene them ; therefor I hope my Son will not thinke much of what I doe here giue away by legacyes out of my owne estate but will be studious to p forme them according to my true intent. My motion about my Sonnes keeping his Lands &c. rather then goods, is because my desire is that he would resolve to Liue in this Country so Long as he can enjoye his peace, & keep a good conscience, which I thinke he may doe as well, if not better, then in any other part of the world.

I giue to *Hannah Keayne*, mv Son *Benjamins* Daughter, Three hundred pound for a Legacy, to be payd to hir on the day of hir Marriage, or at the Age of Twenty yeares which of them shall first happen. So hir Marriage be not before the Eighteenth yeare of hir age; the Ordering of which 300 lb. I leaue to the care of my Executor, hir father, with Aduice of hir Grandmother, not only how the Stocke may best be ordered, but, how she may best be Educated; the profitt of which money yearely may be for hir dyet, clothes, & learning, (a part of which my desire is, may be to teach her to write well & to cipher in a reasonable Manner, & if I thought she would not addict hir selfe to it, or that hir father or Grandmother should neglect to haue hir Taught therein, I would take away a good part of this Legacy giuen to hir) till she come to receiue it hir selfe. More I would haue giuen to hir, but that I know hir father will haue a good Estate & haueing yet no other Child but She, wilbe able to giue her more then she will deserue, besides what the affection of hir Grandmother will Lead hir too; This of itself wilbe a comfortable portion for hir maintenance, So She be not Cast away in hir Match, if God be pleased to bring hir to that Estate, My desire to hir father, Grandmother & my Overseers, [is] that all care be taken for hir Marriage, that she miscarry not that way, but be bestowed of Some man, truely fearing God. And my Speciall Charge to hir is, that she would not dare to set her affections vpon any in that kind, without there advice & helpe in such a choyce.

[If *Hannah* dye, before the time specified, & *Benjamine* haue any other Child or Children of his own,] if he haue but one, then I giue Two Hundred of that 300lb. to that one; if two, then they to haue the 300lb. between them; if three, then they to haue One Hundred pound a peece to be payed to them; when either of them shalbe marryed, &c. If my son haue but one child, then the odd Hundred pound I giue to himselfe & the other 200lb. to his child as before. [If Hannah dye] before she comes to enjoye her portion & my Son haue noe other Child, I giue *Hannah* liberty to dispose of 10 or Twenty pounds in Legacyes to her friends; if she die but a yeare before [she] receiued it Then I giue one Hundred pounds thereof to my wife, if living; the other Two Hundreth vnto my Son *Benjamine;* if he surviue her, And if my wife should be dead, before the Grand Child comes to Age, that Hundredth pounds that I giue to her, I giue to the Collidge at Cambridge, If my Son [die] before his daughter, & Leaue no issue, & *Hannah* die before she receive her portion, Then I giue that Two hundredth pound likewise vnto Harvard College.

And because my Son, Major *Benjamine Keayne*, is now in Old England, & may dye before me; in such a case, my will is, [that his whole property accrue to his other children, if he have any,] but in fayle thereof, I dispose of it in manner following — His Debts to be payed — My Legacyes made good out of it — 400lb. of it to daughter *Hannah*, [In case of her death, to go to one of Benjamins childien,] or, if he have more than one, to have it equally devided amongst them.

If my Son leaue a Son, or more, behind him, his Eldest Son to haue one halfe of the remaineing part of his fathers portion & the rest to be equally devided amongst his other children; *Hannah* also haueing a proportionable part in this also. If he haue not aboue two Children more Lieuing, then, besides herselfe, though it be by another wife then her mother; if he should haue but one Son & noe other daughters but *Hannah*, then that Son to haue one halfe of his fathers portion. If he haue one or more daughters besides *Hannah*, then one halfe I haue giuen to my Son to be devided between them, & to be Sequestered vpon good Securitie, that they may Enjoye it when they come to Age, the profitt to be imployed for their foode & Rayment & carefull Education. If my Son haue no other Child but her & he dye before he knows what I haue giuen him, Then my will is, that *Hannah* haue Two Hundred poundes more out of her fathers part, that is, sixe hundred pound in all, besides the Three hundreth pound that I haue giuen to her of my owne; & to my wife One hundred poundes if then aliue. To my Overseers 10lb. a piece, Also, out of my Sons part in the cases before mentioned, vnto my Sister *Grace Jupe*, her three children, of whome I haue yet the care of, viz.ᵗ *Anthony Jupe*, my Couzine, *Mary Jupe*, mrs *Mary Mosse*, & *Benjamine Jupe*, that now liues in my house, one hundreth pound to be equally devided between them. If either dye before they Come to Enjoy it, then the other two to haue fifty pounds a peece; if but one remaine, that one to haue the whole hundreth pounds—also in such case, to my Brother & Sister *Wilson* with their two Children in this country; my Cousine, m^r *John Willson*, Preacher at Medfaild, & my Cousin, m^rs *Mary Davenport* at Roxbury, One hundred & twenty pounds; to each forty pounds a piece. In case either my Couzine *John*, or my Couzine *Davenport* dye before they come to Enjoye it, these parts to be giuen to there Children.

The rest of my Sons & childrens portion, in such case, I leaue to my Overseers, with the consent of my wife, while she remains aliue, to dispose of to any Publicke or charitable vse; to the Towne of Boston, Collidge of Cambridge, or else where that they in theire wisdome & consciences shall judge to be most vsefull.

And my desire is to my Overseers, in case my Son dye before *Hannah* be of age, that they be assistant to my wife in their best Counsell & advice, to dispose of her for her future education, vpon some Such wise & Godly m^rs or family, where she may haue her carnall disposition most of all subdued, & reformed, by strict discipline; & also that they would show like care & assistance in Seasonable time, to provide Some fitt & godly match, proportionable to her Estate & Condition, that she may liue comfortably, & be fitt to doe good in her place, & not to suffer her to be circumvented, or to Cast away her selfe vpon some Swagering gentleman, or others, that will Looke more after the enjoying what she hath, then lieuing in the feare of God & true Loue to her.

Item. I giue to the three children of my owne Sister mrs *Grace Jupe*, now deceased, namely, *Mary Jupe*, now *Mary Mosse*, wife to *John Mosse* of Boston, Thirtie pound; vnto Couzine *Benjamine Jupe*, (because he is Lame and dime Sighted & not like to doe much, if any thing at all, towards his own maintenance,)I giue fortie pounds, if he be liueing, two years after my death. [These 100lb. to be given, in addition, to the same sum before mentioned. He hath] fower pounds a yeare left him by his mother, in a house at London; also by some Tenements in London left him by his vncle m^r *Nicholas Jupe*, which will produce 8 or ten pounds P Anno to him for 18 or 20 years, besides what I haue left him in this will.

I giue to my Loueing brother, m^r *John Willson*, our Pasto^r at Boston, Ten pounds.

Vnto my Loueing Sister, his wife, my wiues owne Sister, Ten pounds.

To my Couzine, m^r *John Willson* my Broth^rs Son, now Preacher at Medfield, Thirty pounds.

Twenty pounds to Couzine *Mary Willson*, his sister, now m^rs *Davenport*, at Roxbury.

Vnto m^rs *Cotton*, wife of our Reverend Teacher, m^r *John Cotton*, deceased, Three pounds.

Vnto o^r Elder *Olliver*, if he be aliue one year after my decease, forty shillings. In case he be dead, I bequeath said legacy to his Grand child, son of m^r *John Olliver*, deceased.

To our Elder *Colborne*, and o^r Elder *Pen*, Thirty shillings a peece.

Vnto Major Gen^rall *Gibbons*, Three pounds, to buy him a Ring, or a peece of Plate.

Vnto my ancient friend, Reverend m^r *Norton*, Three pounds, in case his aboad be with vs here in Boston, two yeares after my decease.

Vnto our Brother *Renolds*, Shoomaker, Senio^r, Twenty Shillings; not forgetting a word he spake, publiquely & seasonably, in the time of my distresse, & other mens vehement opposition against me.

Vnto *Sarah Baker*, daughter of *John Baker*, that was sometime my Bayle, & the Child borne in my House, forty shillings, in a Heifer Calfe worth so much, two yeares after my decease, if the child be then liueing.

To *Edward Hall*, of Lyn, Carpenter, as an acknowledgm^t of his Loueing seruice to me, (though of Later yeares he hath Carryed it lesse deseruing, & fuller of more Just provocation,) Three pounds.

To *William ffeavo^r*, Sometime my Servant, forty shillings. To *Alice*, his wife, who was also my Servant, Twenty shillings. If they owe me any thing, then deduct it, as I doe to *Edward Hall*.

To *Robert Rand*, of Lyn, Sometime my Servant, forty shillings.

Vnto *James Pemerton*, & his wife, sometimes my Servant, now partner with me at my ffarme, forty shillings.

To my Three Negars, namely *Angola Negar*, & *Richard* my Negar, fforty shillings, [apiece.] To his wife, *Grace*, Twenty shillings, to be paid to them in some young Heifers, to rayse a stocke for them.

I giue *Richard Negars* Legacy, to his daughter *Zipora*, if she be aliue at my death.

To m<sup>r</sup> *Whiting*, one of the Teaching Eld<sup>rs</sup> at Lyne, fforty shillings.

To m<sup>r</sup> *Cobit*, the other Teaching Elder at Lyn, forty shillings.

To the two Children of my wiues Brother, m<sup>r</sup> *John Mansfeild*, * Ten pounds, to be equally devided between them ; to be payd in two Cowes, to be kept for [their] vse. If any be inquisitiue, why I doe no more for him or his, being a Brother, My Answer is, I haue done very much for him, in England, in releasing him out of Prisons, furnishing him with a Stocke to set vp his Trade &c. when he had spent all his owne in takeing vp many quarrellsome businesses, which he in his distempered fitts had plunged himselfe into ; yet I compounded them, sent him over into New England, when his life was in some Hazard, paid his passage & some of his debts for him in Eng. & lent him money to furnish himselfe with Clothes & other necessaryes for his voyage, till for his distempered Carriages, I was fayne to putt him out of my house. He was never quiet from disturbing my whole family, pursueing me with complaints to our Eld<sup>rs</sup>, that he would haue cutt my throate with his false accusations, if it had lyen in his power. All my kindnes hath been putt into a broken bag ; an vnthankfull p son, y<sup>t</sup> hath euer rewarded my good w<sup>th</sup> euil, though I desire to forgive him. Some may thinke these things had beene better buryed, yet seeing God hath not helped him to acknowledge his Sine, nor truely to repent of it, I thinke it is of vse. They that doe expect Loue from their friends, had not need abuse them, but rather show Love & respect to them I haue the rather made mention of these things, to vindicate myself from the censures of others, who Else might haue thought the hardlier of me for seeming to neglect him.

---

* *John Mansfield*, of Charlestown, *Anne*, wife of Capt. *Robert Keayne* and *Elizabeth*, wife of Rev *John Wilson*, of Boston, appear to have been the children of Sir *John Mansfield*, Master of the Minories, and Queen's Surveyor. See Mather's Magnalia, Bk. 3, p. 42, in connection with the following.

A petition of *John Mansfield*, on the Middlesex Court Files, dated 25 June 1661, states, that his mother died some 27 years previous, in London, at the house of her daughter, then (1661) *Mansfield's* sister *Cole*. His father was a rich man, a Justice of the Peace, and a Knight. His " cossen " *Mansfield Hassell* received estate in England for him. £2000 was due for a Parsonage that his mother had. She had it for 3 lives ; her own, that of his sister *Wilson*, now dead, and that of his sister *Keane*, now married to Mr. *Cole*. He also mentions his " cossen *Hannah Lane* " and " cossen *Royson's* (*Rawson's*) daughter.—[*Wyman's Middlesex Abstracts* i. 129.

Boston, this    day of ffebruary 1674.

Whereas, y<sup>e</sup> Generall Court of this Mattachusets Colony gaue unto y<sup>e</sup> late m<sup>rs</sup> *Anne Cole*, y<sup>e</sup> Relict & Executrix of y<sup>e</sup> late Cap<sup>t</sup> *Robert Keayne*, fiue hundred acres of land, as they did also fiue hundred acres † to m<sup>rs</sup> *Anna lane*, y<sup>e</sup> Grand child of y<sup>e</sup> sd late *Robert & Anne Keayne*, as in consideration in y<sup>er</sup> Records is exprest, *John Wilson*, Pastor of y<sup>e</sup> church of Medfeld, Nephew to y<sup>e</sup> s<sup>d</sup> *Anna Cole*, formerly *Keayne*, doth depose & say y<sup>t</sup> in a short time after y<sup>e</sup> s<sup>d</sup> fiue hundred acres was layed out unto his aboue mentioned *Annt*, & confirmed to hir by the s<sup>d</sup> Court, as in their records may appeare, his s<sup>d</sup> Annt m<sup>rs</sup> *Anne Cole*, formerly *Keayne*, not once only but seuerall times, Spake to him, & desired him to take notice, & remember y<sup>t</sup> she had giuen & did giue her aboue mentioned farme to her Nephew, *John Mansfeild*, y<sup>e</sup> son of y<sup>e</sup> late m<sup>r</sup> *John Mansfeild*, her onely Brother y<sup>t</sup> dyed lately at charlstone, & y<sup>t</sup> he should haue at his owne dispose for euer, & y<sup>t</sup> he perceiued his s<sup>d</sup> Annt's mind, [on] such was intent & solicitous about it, & further saith not.—M<sup>r</sup> *John Wilson*, & *Edward Weeden* made oath to the testimony aboue written ffeb. 11, 1674-5. Before us,     *Edward Tyng*,
*Suffolk Deeds.*]     *William Stoughton.*

† Granted, 1659-60, in consequence of *his* [*Keaynes*] liberal donations to the country."

73

[He then Speaks of his own "haynous offences," for which the Court fined him 80 lb.] For selling a good bridle for 2ˢ, now worse are sold without offence for 3ˢ & 6ᵈ; nayles for 7ᵈ & 8ᵈ; nayles for 10ᵈ p lb. frequently for a great deal more, & so in other things; selling gold buttons for two shillings nine pence a dozen, that cost aboue 2ˢ in London, & yet neuer payd for by them that complayned. These were the great matters in wᶜʰ I had offended.* [In another connection he says] If the Lyon will say the Lamb is a foxe it must be so; the Lamb must be content to bear it. [About 30 pages is here taken up in his own vindication.]

One halfe of wines thirds after her death, to Son *Benjamin*. One of the other two parts, to his Daughter Hannah. [The residue] to Harvard Collidge. If *Benjamin* dyⁿ before his mother, then his Children to have it, [if he have other beside *Hannah*, otherwise,] to be for the benefitt of the library. [If that fail,] to go to Harvard Collidge.

It is my will, that mʳˢ *Sarah Dudly*, now *Sarah Pacye*, may haue no part of my property, that I have bestowed upon her daughter. In such a case *Hannahs* legacy to cease, & go to the Collidge. [All forgotten kindred, who lay claims within 2 years,] to have ten Shillings apeece. All the overplus, to son *Benjamin*, my Executor. [He then leaves directions as to his Accompt books. In these, particular mention is made of his Cattle, &c. what are lost by the wolues; how many remain; ages, value; p ticulars of the ffarm, value, &c.

At my ffarme, also, many printed bookes, both great and smalle, Devinitie, Hystory, Millitary bookes, &c. and Some written Sermon bookes, both in Closet & Chamber; also some Plate, as a Silver Porringer, a Sacke Bowle, Siluer hot water cup, &c. bedding, Linnen, household Stuffe, dary vessells, Carts &c. At Boston, my Receipt Book, Pocket Booke of dayly Expences, as what is payd to Bakʳˢ, Butchers shops, Carting of wood, Rates & divers such charges; for I am as carefull to charge my selfe with what I owe, as what is oweing to me. There is, [are] 2 other bookes, bound up in vellum, wᶜʰ I call Number bookes, of vse, when I kept Shop in London, & here, but not now; also a paper booke, quarto, sent me from London, by my Son, mʳ *Gray*, and my brother *Jupe*, who was Sub executor to my Sisters will, in my Steed; which bookes containes only the accoᵗˢ belonging to the 3 children, *Anthony, Mary, & Benjamine Jupe*.

It may possibly fall out, that my Son, who is my Executor, may be out of this country, (as now he is,) at the time of my death. If it should so proue, my desire is, that my Laueing Brother, mʳ *John Wilson*, Pastor, of Boston, would be pleased to stand in my Sons roome, or, to desire my Cozine, mʳ *Edward Rawson*, Secretary, or leiuet *Johnson*, our Deacon, or some other, to be Assistant to my wife, till my Son come to take charge of it; wᶜʰ seruice I did willingly p form for my Brother *Willson*, When his Brother, Doctor Willson, dyed; himselfe being in this country.———If my Son dyⁿ, before he comes, then my wife to be Executrix, during the time of her widdowhood, & no Longer, with the assistance of Brother *Willson*.

If my Estate Suffer many fold Losses, then my will is, that all my Legacyes bear a proportionable share, or, by omitting wholly of gifts to publique uses, wᶜʰ shall be judged of Least concernment, & best spared. My Son, to haue his first choyce—wife next provided for—*Hannah Keayne* next—*Mary Mosse*, Anthony, & *Benjamin Jupe* next—then, Brother *Willson* & wife—next, or indeed next after *Hannah Keayne*, Overseers to be taken care of.          I value my Estate at 4000lb. or thereabouts. [If any in Authority seeke to raise vp to trouble diuers public gifts, such gifts to become voyd.] Then out of those gifts 100lb. to my wife,— 100lb. to *Anthony* and *Benjamine Jupe*, & *Mary Mosse*, 100lb to *Hannah Keayne* —100lb to wife of Brother *John Keayne*, who did liue in Chesson, not far from London. To his children, & my poore Kindred; & 100 lb. to my Overseers. Remainder to Son *Benjamine*—2lb. to mʳ *Bellingham*—3lb. to mʳ *Edward Winslow*, in England—Legacyes giuen to *Benjamine Jupe*, & *Mary Mosse*, for some just

---

* He was "cleared," as he says, in one instance, from the charge of extortion, relative to the price of "nayles," "by good Testimony from an honest man in his own Towne, Goodman *Medcalfe*." Possibly *Michael Metcalfe* Senʳ of Dedham.

74

occasions of offence giuen to me, to become voyed—Overseers of this my will, m^r *Symon Bradstreet*, Major *Denison*, his brother, m^r *William Hibbins*; also m^r *Edward Winslow*, of Plymouth, if he returne to abide in N. England; also, Brother *John Wilson*, m^r *Norton*, Minister, Cozen *Edward Rawson*, & Leiut *Johnson*.

And my desire is, that my Overseers have three or fower Coppies of this my will, writt out at my Chaige, or, of the most matteriall parts of it. (If they thinke the whole too Long, or needles,) to keepe alwayes by them to view, when they meet together about it. If a few could be printed at no great charge, I would think that the better way; & then eu^ry one concerned, may haue a Coppie of the whole by him.

To Ouerseers, fiue pounds a peece, to buy eu^ry one of them a piece of Plate.

I haue set my name to euery page, in these nine sheets, So in the last page of the Last Sheet, haue putt to my hand & Seale, the fourteenth day of November, 1653, when I finished. Sealed, declared, &c. it be my Last will & Testam^t, in the presence of vs, who Testifye, that this will, containes Nine Sheets of paper, written full on all Sides.

*John Willson, Rich^d Parker, Edw. Tinge.*

*Robert Keayne*, & a seale.

[CODICIL.] I giue to *James Bitts*, the Scotch man, if he be in my Seruice when I dye, Twenty Shillings.

To *Nan Ostler*, my maide Seruant, Twenty Shillings, if in my Seruice when I dye.

It is very likely, those w^ch Come to heare, or reade over this my Will, may meete with Some Tawtollegies, w^ch they may thinke to be vaine repetitions; & some censure it to be of an vnsettled minde, as if I was not Compus Mentis; I would pray them not so to thinke, but impute it to the weaknes of my memory, not being made at one time, being begun Mo 6 : 1 : 1653, finished Nov^r 15, & this addition, Dec^r 15. 1653.

I giue to m^r *Buckley*, Senio^r, Minister of Concord, Three pounds; & to m^r *Tomson*, Minister of Brantrey, forty shillings.

I haue forgott one Loueing Couple more, that came not to my minde till I was now Shutting vp, that is, Cap^t *Bridges* & wife, to whom I giue forty shillings.

Written this Dec^r 28. 1653.

*Robert Keayne* & a seale.

*John Wilson, Edw : Ting, Richard Parker,*
*Rob^t Hull, Edw. ffletcher.*

Will Proved, May 2, 1656. Deposed, m^r *John Willson* senr., m^r *Richard Parker* & m^r *Edward Tyng* as Attests.

*Edward Rawson*, Recorder.

P^rsent, y^e Gov^rnr, dep^t Goun^r, major *Atherton*.

Inventory of Cap^t *Robert Keayne's* Estate, taken April 23, 1656 £2427. 12. 01 —Debts oweing to the deceased £416. 07. 02. Debts due from Estate £274.

*Wm Colbron*.
*Anthony Stoddard*.

*Anna Keayne* deposed 19. 9. 1657

Present y^e Gov^r ,Dep^t Gov^r, Major *Atherton*.

*Edward Rawson*, Recorder.

County Court for Suffolk held at Boston, 29th Jan 1683.

The Executo^rs of the will of Capt *Robert Keayne*, being both dead, Power of Adm^con granted unto m^r *Nicholas Paige*, and *Anna*, his wife, Grand daught^r of *Robert Keayne*. They to give bond, one thousand pounds.

Attest Js^a *Addington*, Clerk.

# ABSTRACTS OF THE EARLIEST WILLS ON RECORD IN THE COUNTY OF SUFFOLK.

## ANN HIBBINS, OF BOSTON.

I, Ann Hibbins, widdow,* being in health of Body and in pfect memory for causes me hereunto moveing, doe make this my Last will.

I giue vnto my three sonnes as followeth : vnto my Eldest sonne, Jno Moore, A double portion of my whole Estate, in pt, two Chests and one deske, with all the things therein Contained, as they now are. Vnto my other two sonnes, Joseph and Jonathan, Each of them an equall portion. Now, because none of all my three sonnes, aforesaid, are here to take the Administratio of ye p^rmises, I haue made Choyce of Capt. Thomas Clarke, Leivt. Edward Hutchinson, Livt. William Hudson, Ensigne Joshua Scottowe and Cornet Peeter Olliver to be overseers and Admrs of this my Last will, giving them full power to make sale of Land or houses, for the best advantage of my Sonnes aforesaid or otherwise to see y^m improved for their profitt vntill such time as my Eldest Sonne shall come over, whom, when he shall come, I make whole Executo^r to my will.

In Case my Sonne John Come over but be dead, his portion to be to his heires, and my youngest Sonne Jonathan to be sole Executor, in wittnes whereof I y^e said Anne Hibbins, haue here vnto sett my hand and seale, dated in Boston, in the yeare of our lord One thousand sixe hundred fifty-sixe, vppon y^e twenty-Seventh day of May, in the p^rnts of vs.                                                    *Ann Hibbins*, & a seale.

*William Salter, James Johnson.*
[Codicil.]

I doe earnestly desire my Loueing freinds, Capt. Johnson & m^r Edward Rawson to be added to y^e rest of y^e Gentle^n mentioned as overseers of my will, to whom I comitt viz^t to Cap^t Johnson, Care & trust my two Chests & deske with all things y^r in, to be kept Intirely whole & in kind, till my said Sonne Jn° or his order Athenticated by a Publicke Notary shall come, & demand y^e same, & to the said m^r Rawson I haue deliu^red the keyes of the said Chests & deske with all my pap^rs that

---

*She was the widow of William Hibbins, a merchant of Boston. He was made freeman in 1640; representative, 1640, 1641; elected assistant 1643 to 1654; was an agent for the colony in England; d. July 23, 1654.—*See Farmer.*

Mrs. Hibbins, in the year 1655, was tried and condemned for the supposed crime of *witchcraft*, and in June, 1656, was executed. "This was the second instance upon record," says Hutchinson, "of any person's being executed for witchcraft in New England." (*Hutch.* i. 174.) Margaret or Alice Jones, executed June 15, 1648, was the first. (*Reg.* i. 73.)

Mr. Beach, a minister in Jamaica, in a letter to Dr. Increase Mather in the year 1684, says, "You may remember what I have sometimes told you your famous Mr. Norton once said at his own table, before Mr. Wilson, the pastor, elder Penn and myself and wife, &c. who had the honor to be his guests : That one of your magistrates wives, as I remember, was hanged for a witch only for having more wit than her neighbours. It was his very expression; she having, as he explained it, unhappily guessed that two of her persecutors whom she saw talking in the street, were talking of her, which proving true, cost her her life, notwithstanding all he could do to the contrary, as he himself told us."—*Hutchinson*, i. 178.

J. B. Moore in his "Lives of the Governors of Plymouth and Massachusetts Bay," p. 344. states, that this same Mrs. Hibbins was a sister of Governor Richard Bellingham.

concerne me, whom I haue desired not only to keep y^m but send such copies of them, to my Sonne as he shall see meete, & y^t he will giue my Sonne or Sonnes his best Councill & advice in improoving what I haue left y^m. My desire is y^t all my overseers would be pleased to shew so much respect vnto my dead Corps, as to cause it to be decently Interd, & if it may be, nere my Late husband; & y^t if my sone Jno shall neither come himselfe fully impowered with Authority to receive what in this my will is bequeathed to him and his brothers yet if any other of my Sonnes shall come with sufficient Authority from their broth^rs, my will is my estate left shall be deliu^red to such Sonne or Sonnes, or to any other Impowred by them. If any part of my Estate left in y^r hands, [the overseers] by fyre or other Causalties not foreseene should Suffer losse, my children should beare it. After one yeare, in case my sonnes come not, then any three of my overseers are hereby Impowred with m^r Rawsons consent to sell my ffarmes at Muddy River, &c. & Improue y^e same for the best advantage of my Children in y^e countrey. I giue to my Couseine, Cap^t marke Cooe, y^e sume of forty shillings as a Legacy to be payd him out of what is due to me from m^r Tilly in London, whose care I earnestly desire to procure y^e whole debt for y^e good of my Sonnes, & y^t he will further y^m with his best councill to procure them y^e benefitt of y^e houses & Lands I bought of his brother. I giue to Georg Dod y^e tenn pounds he owes me. In testimony to which, I haue subscribed my name this 16th day of June, 1656.

I giue my Sonne Jonathan twenty pounds over & above what I haue allready given him towards his paines & Charge in coming to see me, w^ch shalbe first payd out of my Estate.          *Ann Hibbins.*

Signed               my further mind & will is out of my sence of
*James Johnson,*      y^e more y^n ordjnary affection & pajnes of my
*William Salter.*     sonne Jonathan, in y^e times of my distresse, I
                     giue him as a further legacy tenn pounds.
                     Subscribed 19th June, 1656.

p^rsent dep^t Gov^r                              *Ann Hibbins.*
Major Atherton    Will Proved 2 July, 1656.   Capt. James Johnson
& Recorder.       & W^m Salter deposed. *Edward Rawson*, Record^r.
        At a County Court held at Boston, 30th July, 1656.
It is ordered y^t y^e Overseers of this will, at Request of Jonathan Moore, one of y^e sonnes of mrs Hibbins lately deceased in y^e absence of y^e Eldest sonne are jmpowred to act as y^e said Jno Moore might doe, & pay vnto y^e sd Jonathan his portion.
Entred & Recorded 20th August, 1656.   *Edw Rawson*, Record^r.
Inventory of the Estate of Mrs. Ann Hibbins, taken 30 Aprill, 1657, by Amos Richeson, John Lake.   Amt. £344 14.   Capt. James Johnson deposed.
                         _____

### CAPT JAMES TOUNG.

I giue vnto my welbeloved wife Elizabeth Toung, all my personall Estate, all bills, bonds, legacies, Cloathes & what else I haue in any place or places whatsoeuer.   This being done in my full memory.
I desire my loving friend James Lasells to deliuer this my last will vnto my Loving wife Elizabeth Toung, & such goods & Cloathes as is now in y^e said James Lassells vessell now riding at Jamica.
                                                *James Toung.*
    testis   *Thomas Brunel, William Hippen, Jno. Langham, Jno. Mudd,*
1655.     17 July, 1656.   Power of Administration granted to Elizabeth Toung.
*Jno. Langham* deposed.

## SARAH COTTON.

Whereas the Reverend m<sup>r</sup> John Cotton, deceased, did by his last will,* bearing date 30<sup>th</sup> 9 mo. 1652, leaue vnto his wife m<sup>rs</sup> Sarah Cotton, his whole Estate, for such ends & purposes, as in y<sup>e</sup> said will is at large expressed.  The Providence of God Calling the said m<sup>rs</sup> Sarah Cotton to change her condition [by] Intermarriage w<sup>th</sup> the Reverend m<sup>r</sup> Richard Mather of Dorchester for divers good Reasons her therevnto mooving, she hath resigned into the hands of her trusty & wellbeloved friends Elder William Colbron & Elder James Penn dureing y<sup>e</sup> noneage of her Children, John & Marja, all her power of y<sup>t</sup> Estate Left vnto her, by her Late husband to mannage & Improve y<sup>e</sup> same for the benefitt of her selfe & y<sup>e</sup> said m<sup>r</sup> Richard Mather, for y<sup>e</sup> Education of her fore-mentioned Children, with y<sup>e</sup> paym<sup>t</sup> of such debts & legacjes as were made, or giuen by y<sup>e</sup> late m<sup>r</sup> Cotton, excepting only fifty pounds worth of such of the goods, pte of y<sup>e</sup> said m<sup>r</sup> Jn° Cotton's Estate, w<sup>ch</sup> she shall choose & carry with her to the said m<sup>r</sup> Rich<sup>d</sup> Mather.

In Consideration whereof y<sup>e</sup> aboue mentioned Elder W<sup>m</sup> Colbron & Eld<sup>r</sup> James Penn doth hereby engage according to theire best abillityes to p forme & shall eu<sup>r</sup>y year, during the life of y<sup>e</sup> said m<sup>rs</sup> Sarah Cotton, pay vnto m<sup>r</sup> Rich<sup>d</sup> Mather, y<sup>e</sup> Sume of twenty pounds out of y<sup>e</sup> yearely Rents of y<sup>e</sup> houses, farmes & lands of m<sup>r</sup> Jn° Cotton deceased, over & aboue what is her owne estate in England, & after y<sup>t</sup> John & Marjah shall attain to full Age & theire portions payd them, they shall deliver up the Estate jnto the hands of m<sup>rs</sup> Sarah Cotton, to Remaine at her owne dispose.  In case m<sup>r</sup> Richard Mather depart this life before m<sup>rs</sup> Sarah Cotton, then Mr Mather shall leaue vnto her, out of her owne Estate, at least one hundred pounds : i. e. fifty pounds in speciall good pay over & aboue y<sup>e</sup> value of y<sup>t</sup> fifty pounds w<sup>ch</sup> he rec<sup>d</sup> at his Marriage with y<sup>e</sup> sajd m<sup>rs</sup> Sarah Cotton.  In wittnes whereof y<sup>e</sup> partyes in this writing have sett to their hands & seales this twenty-eight of July, 1656.

In presence of vs

*John Wilson*, senio<sup>r</sup>
*Edward Rawson.*

*Sarah Cotton* & a seale.
*Wm. Colbron* & a seale.
*James Penn* & a seale.
*Richard Mather* & a seale.

Approved 31 July, 1656.

*Edw. Rawson*, Record<sup>r</sup>.

## THOMAS WEYBORNE, of Boston.

I, Thom Wyborne,† vpon my Bed of weaknes, though through favo<sup>r</sup> enioying my witt, senses, & memory, doe apoynt my two Eldest sons, viz. Thomas & James Weyborne to bee my executo<sup>rs</sup>; then, I doe will y<sup>t</sup> all my debts shall be iustly paid.  I doe freely giue vnto my Wife Elizabeth Weyborne, the one halfe of y<sup>e</sup> Windmill in Boston, as also y<sup>t</sup> my sd executors shall pay vnto my said wife forty Shillings by y<sup>e</sup> yeare vntill Shee marry.  I giue vnto sun Jno Weyborne, forty Pounds, to bee paid at y<sup>e</sup> age of twenty and one years; vnto my daughter Elizabeth Merrit, Twenty pound; vnto my daughters Child Deborah Merrit, fiue pound; vnt my daughter mary Weyborne, twenty pounds to bee paid at y<sup>e</sup> age of sixteene yeares, & also y<sup>t</sup> Shee liue not at y<sup>e</sup> finding of my executors, then I giue her fourty Shilings a yeare vntill y<sup>e</sup> Age of six-teene ; to my wife Elizabeth y<sup>e</sup> vse of one fether bed & furniture for it, & all other Household necesarys while Shee remaines A Widdow. Louing ffreinds m<sup>r</sup> Edward Ting & Jno Hull of Boston, to bee y<sup>e</sup> ouer seers of this, my will; that this is my testament I heer acknowledge

---

* See abstract of the Will, in Vol. V. of this work, p. 240. 241. (See pp. 42, 43).

† Thomas Wyborne, Boston, 1653, d. 2 Oct. 1656; Farmer says, he had a son Na-thaniel, b. in 1654.  Was he not the son of Thomas, Jun<sup>r</sup>?

by subscribing my hand this Twelveth of Septb^r, 1656—(moreouer, I will that my best fether bed and great Bible Shall peculierly bee for my eldest son.                                    *Thomas Weyborne.*
attestants, *Edmond Eddenden, Jno. Marion, John Hull.*
Will Proved, 28 Oct^r, 1656.    *John Hull* and *Edmond Eddenden* deposed.
Inventory taken by *Edmond Eddenden, Nathaniell Bishope,* 14, 8, 1656. Amt. £386. 1*s.* "desperate debts" included.   *Thomas Wieborne* and *James Wieborne* deposed, 28 Oct., 1656.

### SAMUEL WILLBORE.

30th April, 1666.   I, Samuell Willbore of tanton, in plimouth patten, doe make this my last will.* Vnto my Louing wife Elizabeth, all y^e moueable goods y^t is or shalbee in my house in Boston, where at p esent I doe inhabit at y^e time of my decease, and allso my sheep and Lambs at dorchest^r there kept to halues, Also A Mare & Coult At Jno. Moores of Brantry—vnto Samuell Wilbore, my eldest Sonne, all my Lands at Road Island, and all my debts dew to mee theire, first from Richard Smith y^e eld^r & also A debt from Henry Bull, w^ch is foure pounds, and an ewe of 2 yeares owld, also one Cow in y^e hands of James Badcock, also one Cow y^t is at Bridg Water, togeth^r w^th y^e rent for y^e sd Cattell, according to agreement; also Six hundr^d of Iron leying at Tanton in my dweling house their.   I giue vnto sonne Joseph Wilbore, my house and Land where hee, my sd Sonne, doth inhabit, also twelue Acres of ground graunted by y^e towne of tanton, being by y^e Iron Mills, also my share in y^e sd Iron workes.   Vnto my yongest Sonne, Shedrick Wilbore, my house and Lands there vnto belonging at Tanton, wherein I dwell with all y^e moueable goods w^thin and w^thout dores, and Cattell, excepting halfe y^e orchyard and halfe y^e sd dweling house & two of y^e best Cowes & hay to bee taken of y^e meadow ground convenient for y^e wintering w^ch I giue vnto my Wife, prouided shee Continew theire, but In Case my wife shuld marry Another man & inhabit else where, y^t my said Sonne shall haue y^e Sd [land,] alowing my wife or her Assignes, y^e summ of Ten pounds, to bee pd in such goods As y^e Cuntry doth aford.
I giue vnto Sonne Shedrick y^e dbt of James Lenard, Ralph Russell, & Henry Newland.   Wife Elizabeth and Sonne Shidrak, executors.
I giue my white Horse vnto Shedrick, & what other Cattell or goods I haue not disposed of, I will y^t my executors haue, beetwixt them equally to be divided.   I giue vnto Robert Blot, of boston, twenty shillings.   I giue vnto goodman fflack, twenty Shills—vnto my sonn Shedrick, the time of service of my man Jno. Mockcliet, A Scotchman. I giue Joseph A peece of blue trucking Cloth of 8 or 10 yds, w^ch sd Cloth is included amongst y^e goods in y^e house at Boston Where at p sent I doe inhabitt.   I will y^t my executors pay my sonn Joseph within two yeares aft^r my desease, ye somme of tenn pounds in Iron, viz : one fiue pounds at Six moneths end, and y^e other fiue pounds at ye two years end.   I haue herevnto sett my hand seale y^e day and yeare aboue-said.                                    *Samuell Wilbore*, Seale.
Attests p *Robert Howard*, Notorius Publis.
p^rsent Govrn^r, dept Gov^r & Record^r.
Proved, 6^th of Nov. 1656, on deposition of M^r *Willm Colbron, and* M^r *Robr^t. Howard.*

---

* A brief abstract of this Will was given in the Reg. Vol. V. p. 385, copied from the Probate Office, Plymouth.
Mr. W. was made freeman, March 4, 1638-4, died 29 Sept. 1656.

# ABSTRACTS OF THE EARLIEST WILLS ON RECORD IN THE COUNTY OF SUFFOLK.

## THOMAS BUCKMASTER.

2 of ye 7th mo. 1656. I, Thomas Buckmaster * of Muddy Riuer, being now sick & in my owne apprhension neare ye day of my death, yet being in my pfect sences doe make this my last will.

I giue to my Son Zackery, fourty shillings, to my daughter Elizabeth spowell, daughter Mary Stevens, daughter dorkas Corben, fourty shillings [each]. To my Son Thomas, Son Joseph, Son Jabesh, fourty shillings [each to be paid when severally " one & Twenty yeares of Age."] To my daughter spowells two Children, twenty shillings, to be put into ye deacons hands to be improued for ye Childrens learning. Vnto my daughter Stephens two Children 20s, daughter Corbens Children ten shillings, to my Son Zackrys Child ten Shillings—wife Joanna, Executrix, giueing vnto her all my land and goods. It is my will that my two youngest Sons, Joseph and Jabesh, dwell with my wife and faithfully serve her till they be one and twenty yeares of Age, but if my wife shall marry before they Come to yt Age they shall be free.

I giue to my daughter Sarah fourty shillings, to be paid at hir day of mariage or at ye Age of one and twenty years—this was forgott to be sett in place wth ye rest; this is my will. wittn Jno winchester.

present                                    ye mark of X Jnᵒ Lawrence.
    dept Go ;        Jnᵒ winchester deposed before
    mʳ Atherton     ye magistrates 23 Nov. 56 ; Saith
    & Recordʳ.      yt he writ this paper wch he also Read
                  To Thomas Buckmaster, who declared it
                  to be his Last will.     Edw. Rawson, Recordʳ.

Inventory of Estate taken 2, 9, 1656, by Peter Oliuer, John winchester. Amt. £112. 16s. 06d.

---

## JOHN BURRELL.

August 3, 1654. I *John Burrell* of Roxbury, shoomaker, being at this time afflicted by the hand of God wth sicknes doe make this my last will. Vnto wife *Sarah & Sarah* my daughter, my house wherein I now dwell, the barne & outhouses, my home lott and the orchard and all things belonging therevnto, also fiue acres of land more or lesse, lying neere the Great pond, leading from the High way wch Goes to Jnᵒ *Weld's* farme, toward the Great Pond, wth a Cart way two Rod wide, lying betweene *Christopher Peake* and *Robert Pepper*. Also another parcell of land lying from the head of said land vnto the Pond, being foweʳ Rodd wide & thirty Rod in length, more or lesse, having two marked trees at each Corner next the Pond also : seven acres of wood lott, more or lesse, lying in two Severall places, as by the Towne booke it may Appeare, Also twenty acres & a halfe of wood lott, being part of the midle devission, lying betweene *John weld* and *Thomas Pigg*. Also tenn Acres of Land

---

\* Progenitor of the late Joseph Stevens Buckminister of Boston. Barry, in his history of Framingham says, " the name of Buckminster first appears in a deed to Joseph, son of Thomas, dated July 23, 1660, (Suff. Deeds,) and that "Buckmaster is the name given upon the Records to all of the first and second generations." Thomas was made freeman 1646, d. at Muddy River, (now Brookline,) Sep. 20, (Bos. Rec. say 28,) 1656. His wid. m. Edward Garfield of Watertown, Sep. 1, 1661. Barry's Framingham, p. 199–203. See abstract of the will of Lawrence Buckmaster, son of Thomas, in Gen. & Hist. Reg. Vol. III. p. 178, 179. (See pp. 26, 27).

in the great lott, lying betweene *John Stebbin & Thomas waterman* on the one side, and daniell Brewer on the other side, one acre of land in the vpper Calves pasture. Also nine acres of Salt marsh, and a high way leading through m^r Dudley' necke ; all the aforesayd lands &c., debts being paid, shall be equally devided betweene *Sarah Burrell* my wife, and *Sarah* my daughter. *John Boules & Thomas weld* overseers.

*John Burrell.*

Subscribed & deliuered being his owne wille & *Sarah* his daughter Interljnd.

*Daniel Weld, Isacke Morrell.*

19 feb. 1656. Power of Administration Graunted to *Sarah Burrell*, y^e late wife of the sajd *John & Richard Davis* in behalfe of his wife late dau. to y^e sajd *John*, they bringing in an Inventory of y^t Estate & p forming this Imperfect will as neere as may be.

*Edward Rawson*, Record^r.

Inventory taken, 23. 12. 1656, by *John Johnson, William Parke, Isaack Morrell*. Amt. £188. 17. 08.

30 July 1657. *Sarah Burrell & Richard Davis* deposed.

---

WILLIAM REPLYE, of Hingham.

I *William* being sick and weake, doe make this my Last will. Vnto my eldest sonne, *Jn° Replye*, the dwelling howse he now dwells in, with all y^e barnes &c, but my Sonn *Abraham* shall haue Liberty to Vse y^e new barne for his Corne & other occasions : & y^e new leaneto for his Cattle for y^e terme of fower yeares, w^thout molestation. Vnto my sonn *John*, all y^e Land w^thin that feeld, namely y^e lott y^e towne gaue mee, lying for fower Acres, and y^e lott w^ch I bought of *Jno. ffoulsham*, lying for fower Acres, and y^e lott w^ch I bought of *Thomas Thackster* lying for fiue Acres, and y^e lott w^ch I bought of *Stephen Payne*, lying for fower Acres, with all prividlidges belonging to these lotts. Vnto my Sor. *Jn°* my planting lott w^ch I bought of *Jn° Prince*, lyeing for three Acre. vpon y^e world's end, next vnto *Jn° Tucker* north : next vnto *Jeremy Beales* Eastward : butting Vpon y^e sea West & south. Vnto my Sonn *Jn°* fouer Acres of salt meadow, w^ch I bought of *Jonas Austen*, lyeing at Lyford's Likeing, next vnto *Thomas Lincorne* west : next vnto *Nathaniel Beales* east, butting vpon y^e old planter's hill north, and vpon y^e neck South. I giue vnto my Sonn *Jn°* of fresh meadow, w^ch I bought of *Thomas Vnderwood*, lyeing in Crooked meadow, With a little peece of meadow belonging to y^e same, Lyeing next vnto *Samuell Ward*, Eastward, and y^e Riuer Southward. Vnto my sonn *Jn°* A peece of Salt meadow lying at Conyehassett : for three Acres more or lesse ; it is in y^e third deuision. Vnto sonn *Jn°* my horse, y^e horse Colt y^t Came of my mare : two Oxen, Collier & Buck, fouer Cowes, three sheepe Ewes, with 3 lambs : eight goates : halfe y^e dry goates and halfe y^e kids. Vnto sonn *Abraham*, y^e home lott, which I bought of *Thomas Vnderwood*, together with the orchyard and fencing and other appurtenances thereto belonging ; w^ch lott lyeth for fiue Acres, next Vnto *Jn° Lasell* east : next to *Jn° Otis* west ; also vnto Sonn *Abraham* : all y^e fresh meadow y^t lyeth at y^e end of y^e said home lott ; all y^e salt meadow w^ch I bought of *Thomas vnderwood*, lyeing at y^e wear : next *ffrancis James* southward, and *Robert Joanes* north : y^e great lott w^ch I bought of *Thomas vnderwood*, lying for fifteene Acres, next vnto *Jn° Lasell* South East, & next vnto *Cornelius Cantleburry* north west, butting on y^e riuer ; y^e planting lott, which I bought of *Thomas vnderwood*, lyeing in the neck for thre Acres : next vnto *Mathew Cushen* north, and *Jn° Beales* South : butting

vpon the sea westward, and *Michaell Pearse* eastward. Vnto Sonn *Abraham*, two old oxen, Called Broad and Browne, two stears of fiue yeares old, one young steere 2 yeares old, three young Cowes, and eight milch Goates, halfe yᵉ drie Goates & halfe yᵉ kids, two Ewe sheepe two lambs, fiue wether Sheepe and two Rams, my Mare of 3 yeares old, my ffether bed and greene Rug, one blankett and one broad brasse kettle, one Iron Pott and A Chest yᵗ yᵉ Cover is Loose ; A little Cofer and three empty Barrell : The Cart and Wheeles, plowes and plow Irons, with all yᵉ Chaynes, shall be equally devided betwene my Sonn *Jnᵒ & Abraham*. Vnto Sonn *Abraham* one Swine of A yeare old and yᵉ vantage. Vnto Sonn *Jnᵒ* my best Cloake and 2 peeces of Cloath of yᵉ sáme, So much as will make a sute of apparrell, one paier of Shooes, A payer of stockins, my best hat, And my great bible. Vnto Sonn *Abraham*, my book of Masters, and all my other apparell ; debts due vnto mee from severall psonˢ, as they doe receive any, they shal be equally devided betwene yᵉ said *Jnᵒ & Abraham*; debts due for me to pay, *John & Abraham* Shall pay it equally together. John and Abraham Executors.
30 June 1656.                                              *Wm. Ripley* & a seale.
Wittnes *Mathew Cushin*
            *John Thaxter*

24 Jan. 1656, *Mathew Cushin* and *Jnᵒ Thaxter* deposed.
Inventory taken, July 20, 1656, by *Joshua Hubbard, Mathew Hawke.*
Amᵗ £332. *Jnᵒ Ripleye* deposed before yᵉ Court, 29ᵗʰ Jan. 1656.

---

### EDWARD BULLOCK.

The twentie fifth day of the fifth Moneth in yᵉ year of oʳ Lord God One thousand Six hundred and fortie Nine, I *Edward Bullock* of Dorchester, having by the Providence of God a Calling and determinacion to goe for England, with all Expedicon, and not knowing how the Lord of Heaven and Earth may dispose of me, doe for the better settling of my Estate and goods & Cattles here in N. England, & for my wife's more Comfortable maintenance while shee liues, & for the more carefull Ordering & disposing of the same in such mannʳ as may Conduce for a Sufficient Competencie for my wiues maintenance as before, and dischargeing of such debts as are Specifyed in a writing annexed heere vnto ; and to this Ende I haue jntended my speciall good friends & neighboʳs heereafter mentioned, to looke vnto, & to haue a respect vnto my wife, yᵗ she may haue a Competent Maintenance out of yᵉ p fetts & yearely incomes of my Estate, pvided, they also haue respect vnto yᵉ discharging of my debts, also, out of ye p fitts of my goods, videlicet, of my corne, now vpon the ground. And also vnto my friends heereafter named, I doe giue vnto them, & yᵉ Major part of them, full power to sell, lett, Manage & dispose of my house, Lands and gardens, so as may be for yᵉ best p fitt and benefitt, that they conceive, may be made of the Same, & also to order yᵉ Cattle & goods heere left, by selling or exchanging but not diminishing of yᵉ same, so as in theire best discretions may be the likelyest way of p fitt & encrease to & for yᵉ ends aforesaid, dureing my wife's life. And after my Said wife's death, my will is that my daughter in Law, *Hannah Johnson*, shall haue all my goods, Lands and Estate, that then shal be Remaining, to be delivered heere at tjme of her marriage, or of Lawfull age. And for yᵉ ordering of my said Estate, I doe intend my friends Capt. *Humphery Atherton, Augustine Clemens, & George Weeks* to be my overseers & rulers, and to order the things abovesaid, Provided that if Providence so fall out yᵗ I doe returne againe, yᵗ then this Will and minde of myne to be voyd and of noe Effect & y^e p mises to haue again as form^rly. In witnes whereof, I y^e said Edward Bullocke, have herevnto set my hand and seale ; dated y^e day & yeare first above written.

*Edward Bullocke* & a seale.

Signed, sealed & delivered in the p^rnts of
    *Edward Clap*
    *Roger Clap.*                     29th January 1656.

Memento, y^e waxe of        It is ordered y^t y^e Estate mentioned in
y^e seale, when brought,    y^e paper should remaine in y^e hands of
was as now it is,          Major *Atherton*, m^r *Patten* and *Austine*
rubbed of.                 *Clemens*, to Improve according to y^e
                          Purport thereof, till further order Come
                          from him, or they heare from him, or
                          take further order.

    The debts w^thin specifyed are as followeth :

To *John Holland*, two pounds, one halfe in wheate and halfe in peas ; to *Barnabas ffawer*, two pounds, all in peas ; to *Richard Baker* fifteene shillings Sixe pence, some wheat, some peas.

To *Jane Pope* vidzt 20 shills 15 in Rye & 5 peckes of peas.

*Edwd. Clapp*, 8 shill.    *Wlli Weekes* a bush. of Indian.

Deacon *Wiswall*, a bush of wheate.

To *Jn° Gill*, about 2 shill^s for 7 lb ¾ of beefe at 3^d per lb.

To *Jn° Burchill*, 5 peckes of Rye.

To *Sampson Mason*, for my wiues shoes.

To *George Badcocke*, for cheese, three shillings Sixe pence.

To *Nich° Woode* for cheese, one shill. seaven pence.

To m^r *Patine* for a pecke of wheat.

To *Jn° Wheple*, five shill^s for stockings & a Cocke.

To *Walter Harris*, a pecke of Rye, for tryming for a hatt 7^d or 8^t

To *Augustine Clemens*, £6 w^ch he is to be answered in a steere, w^ch if he Comes not so much to he is to [be] satisfyed out of the corne, and if he yeeld more, it is to be good to Edw^d Bullocke, or his vse, for two q^rts of Sacke, for his vse, in y^e shipp to bro: Clemens.

To Brother *Wales*, for weaving, 0 : 2^s : 7^d

To *Abraham How*, for weaving, 0 : 6 : 3.

To Mr. *Perpointe* of Roxbery, 4 peckes of wheat, 3 peckes of Rye, 2 peckes of Indjan.

To m^r *Perpoint*, for a Howe, 0 : 18 : 02

To *Thomas Burch*, for *Sam^ll Vulet* 0 : 06 : 08

*Edward Bullock.*

    The five shillings Widdow *Pope* was to receiue of the sume aboue said, she doth owe *Hannah Johnson*, 5^s she sayes it shall pay hir more, she sayes y^t I, *George Weekes*, shall haue 2^s 6^d in Corne Rye, of what is due to hir above said 9 shill : 8^d.

# ABSTRACTS OF WILLS OF THE EARLY SETTLERS OF NEW ENGLAND.

Note.—The Abstracts which follow, are from the *originals* on file, and are not among those recorded, unless the contrary is mentioned.        W. B. T.

The Last Will and testament of M\_r\_ Thomas Newberry of the Church of Christ at dorchester, who beeinge in pffect memory the 12th of the 10th month Anno Domm: 1635 is as followeth;

Imprimis. I give vnto my wife *Jane Newberry*, twoo hundred poundes, w\_th\_ all the house hould stuffe w\_ch\_ shee brought w\_th\_ her at her mariage.

Itt. I give all the rest of my goods vnto my Children, to bee equally devided betwixt them, vnlesse 3 of my younger daughters, it is my will y\_t\_ these three shall have 50s. a peece lesse than the rest.

Itt. it is my will, if any of my Children dye before they bee of the age of one & twenty, y\_t\_ then his or theyre portion thus deceased, shall be equally devided amongst the rest of my Children y\_t\_ are alive.

Itt. it is my farther will, if there doth fall out any controversy betweene my Children, that then these my overseers shall end it or any such s\_d\_ controversyes & they are to take advise by them.

Itt. I doe ffurther make my wife my whole executrix.

Lastly, I doe make m\_r\_ *John Warham & William Gaylord* my overseers of this my s\_d\_ will.\*

---

### ANTHONY COOP.  (Hingham.)

Inventory taken Feb. 26, 1635.  Amt. £580. 5s. 10d.  Prized by *Richard Betscomb & Nicho Baker.*  Witnesses, *Peter Hubbert, Tho. Lorain, John Stronge.*

---

### BENJAMIN COOPER.  (Salem.)

Inventory taken 27. 7. 1637.  Am't £1014. 16s. 6d.  Mention is made of *Ester Cooper. Laurence Cooper,* son to *Benj.* had sister *Rebeka.* Signed, *Townsend Byshopp, John Woodbery, Robt. Moulton.*

---

### EDWARD BLACKLEY.  (Rocksbury.)

Inventory 25. 10. 1637.  Am't £130. 17s. 2d.  Signed, *John Stow, Isack heath, Joseph Weld, John Johnsone, Thomas sems, William Parker, samm well basse.*

---

\* The above is a full Copy of the Will of Mr. Newberry, as found on Suffolk Files, without Seal or Signature.

Sep\_t\_ 1, 1634. It is ordered that m\_r\_ *Newberry* shall have 30 acres for his accomodation in the Plantation.

It is ordered that m\_r\_ *Newbery* is to have for his purchase that he bought of m\_r\_ *Pincheon,* the house m\_r\_ *Pincheon* built, 40 acres of upland ground to the house, 40 of Marsh 20 acres in Quanty necke.

Nov. 2. 1635. An hundred acres of meddow vnto m\_r\_ *Thomas Newberry* as that was likewise graunted him by order of Court togeather with an hundred acres of Vpland ground.

And likewise it is ordered and agreed upon whereas M\_r\_ *Newbery* hath relinquished a former graunt from the Plantation of 40 acres of Marish and 20 acres of Vpland in squantum Necke he is now to take all the ground from his house to m\_r\_ *Willsons* farme, in consideration thereof.—*Dorchester Town Records,* Book I, p. 11, 17.

Inventory of the goodes of M\_r\_ Thomas Nuberie, made the 28\_th\_ of Jan An\_o\_ 1636, Amt. 1520.04.07. including " Land in England, 300l." Signed. *Israel Stoughton.*

ROBERT POND. (Dorchester.)
Inventory 27. 10. 1637, by *Capt Atherton, Leiftenant Clappe & George weekes.* £165. 5*s. Roger Clap, Geo. Weekes.*

---

THOMAS BEECHER. (Charlestowne.)
Inventory 29. 5. 1637. £485. 16*s. Ralph Sprage, Abr. Palmer, Thomas Ewer.*

---

SAMUELL HAULE. (Charlestowne.)
Inventory taken the m. 16. 1637. Am^t £444. 13. *Raphe Sprage, Raphe Mousell.*

---

JOHN GREENE.
Inventory of *John Greene* lately dwelling with danill brver of roxbery 14 feb. 1638. Am't £5. 11*s.* 03*d. Edward Porter, S^nmm well basse.*

---

THOMAS FFAYERWEATHER.
Inventory taken 8. 11. 1638. Am't £111. 18*s.* 8*d.* By m^r *william Colborne, John Edlin.*

---

Will of EDWARD WILSON.
Vnto my brother, *Thomas Wilson* all my household stufe, halfe that mony w^ch is in the bills to my brother *Will Wilson;* halfe the corn w^ch I haue, the other half of the sayd mony & corne to my brother *thomas willson,* but if my brother *Will wilson* do not come ouer to new england then my brother *thomas* is to haue all the sayd money & corne.
witness *Robert hawkins.* 1638, the 19 of aprill.

---

M^R WOLCOTT.
Inventory taken 17. 5. 1638. By *Georg Philips, Richard Browne, Abra: browne,* the m^rke + of *Symon Stone.*

---

REBECCA BACON.
Inventory taken 1. 8. 1638, by *John Russell, Edward Collins.* Am't £19. 07*s.* 4*d.*

---

RICHARD ILES.
Inventory taken 29 Nov. 1639, by *Ralph Moushole, Robert Hall.* Am't £22. 14*s.* 02*d.*

---

Will of GEORGE HOLMES. (Rocksbury.)
My loving wife sole executresse. I giue vnto her my whole estate, to be improved for the education of my children, but none of my lands to be sould vnlesse in case of necessity & by the advice of my overseers. After my wives decease, my houses & lands shall be equally divided amongst all my children; yet if it shall please the Lord to convert my sonne *Joseph* in the meane time, so as y^t he is in charity accepted among the saints, my will is y^t he shall haue two parts, & the rest but each of them one. And my request is to my Dearly beloved brethren Elder *Heath,* broth^r *Eliot* & broth^r *Parks* our Deakens & my broth^r *Ruggles* & broth^r *Riggs* to be my overseers to counsell & guide my wife in all her affaires. I giue full power to them to make the fore named division of my lands in the most equal & peaceable mañer they can, & if any of my children will not rest in what they doe, my will is y^t child shall lose

his part, & it shall be given to such as my overseers see most fitt, & I intreate my deare wife to doe nothing of moment w<sup>th</sup>out the advise of these my overseers.—Also my will is y<sup>t</sup> there shall not be strip & wast made of timber & fire wood from my ground, only so much as may be for the necessary vse of my family.

witnesse     John Eliot,           mark of *George* + *Holmes.*
John Scarebrow.

Mr *John Eliot* deposed before Court, 30. 11. 1651 that *George Holmes* was of a disposing mind the yeare 1646 or thereabouts.

Edw Rawson Recorder.

NOTE. The above Will is in the hand writing of the Apostle *Eliot*.

## Will of GEORGE HUNNE.

3.<sup>mo</sup>. 25. day. 1640

I *George Hun* weake in body, but of right vnderstanding doe heare by my last will giue the 3 ackers of planted ground at long Iland to *An* my wife and my sonns laboure till the crop of corne this yeare be gotten Home. I allsoe giue my stock of Coates that now are together with m<sup>r</sup> *Colbornes* to hir when they are deuided, onely one of them I giue to my sonn *nathanell*, the Second Coate in worth, which either he ore his freind shall make choise of. I allso giue to my wife my present dwelling House and beding and pewter and Houshold stuf there in, except a box of linnins that my Son hath the key of, and one great trunck, all my weareing aparell, as all soe a wooll bed, a bolster and tow pillows, a couerled and a blancket, the which I giue to my sonn *nathanell*, together with one little trunck, as allsoe 5 or 6 Acres of land at mount Wolleston which is in Use by *steuen kinsley*, and the rent of it to be receiued by *James Johnson* and He to improve it for my son *nathanell* till His time of seruis be expired ; as allsoe I giue to my wife of the 31 acors at menactecote riuer : 21 : and the other 10 acors to my sonn *nathanell*, equally to be deuided, that both may haue the benefites of the riuer ; and I give the 3 : Swine to my wife. I desire that my wife should pay my debts and receiue what is oweing to me.

by me *George Hunne.*

in witnes heare of we
haue set to our hands
*Robert Hull*
*James Johnson*

It is all agreed that my sonn *nathanell* shall be seruant to *James Johnson* and his wife for fiue years, his seruis begining in the 9 month, and for his waiges to be apointed yearely by the decons and Bro : *Hull*, and he to find himselfe aparell there out.

so dysposed by me, *George Hunn.*
soe acxsepted of by me, *James Johnson.*
soe agreed vnto by me, *nathaniell Hun.*

## GEORGE ALCOCK.

Inventory of the Estate of George Alcock, late of Rocksbury, deceased, taken by us the thirtyeth day of december, 1640.

Will<sup>m</sup> *Denyson*          *Will Parrks.*
[torn off]    *Welde.*           *Philip Eliote.*
                           *Steph : Winthrop*, record<sup>r</sup>.

SIMON RAYES of Brantry.

ffeb this 20<sup>th</sup> 1641.

Inventory of the goods of *Simon Rayes* praised by *Martin Sanders* and *Richard Brackett* of the same toune ; Am<sup>t</sup> 122-14-4.

---

JOHN BRADLEY.

Inventory of the Estate of *John Bradly*, deceased, taken 21. 4. 1642. By *William Hathorne, Thomas Putman*, including "A ten acre lot on Cape An side" and " 25 Acres at Jaffrys Creeke." A part of this inventory is gone.

---

THOMAS COYTMOR.

I *Thomas Coytmor** beeing in health of body beeing bound forth to Sea. And for as much as in thes vncertaine times its very difficult if not impossible to set a due valuatio vppon temporal estates, therefore I conceive it most Convenient to Consider my estate in Sixteene partes, Either to remaine in an anuity & Soe to bee pportionably distributed yeerly. Vnto my wife Six pts of the sixteene—son *Thomas* six sixteenth pts. As times are very hazzardous in Europe Therfore in case things should soe passe in England that my deere mother *Katherin Coytmer* bee deprived of her estate, then for her support I bequeath vnto her ffoure sixteenths of my estate to have as an annuity dureing her life, after which it shall returne to my child or children equally.—If my wife haue another child by me, then, wife haue but five pts, & son *Thomas* ffive, mother three, & youngest childe three. If the latter child die in nonage, then my will is to stand as before—if son *Thomas* dye in nonage, then if a second or latter bee liveing hee or shee to enjoy the same, &c. Bro *Increase Nowell* & m<sup>r</sup> *ffrancis willoughby* overseers ; vnto each ffourty shillings ; wife sole executrix : witnes my hand & seale this 25<sup>th</sup> 6<sup>mo</sup> 1642. *Thomas Coytmorr.*

Witness *John Perce.*

On the back of the document is the following :

Wheras *Joseph Hills* of Charles Towne bought of *Thomas Squire* five acres of Land.

This was testified upon oath by *John Peirce*
before the Cort, *Increase Nowell*, sec.

---

SUSAN HUNT.

An inventorie of the goods and lands of m<sup>rs</sup> *Susan Hunt* of Soodberie, Amt 48. 11. 2, taken by *Peter Noyes, Walter Hayns*, who deposed the 24<sup>th</sup> of the 9<sup>th</sup> mo 1642, before the gov<sup>r</sup>nor & my selfe, *Incr: Nowell* secret.

---

DANIELL SHEOPARDSON. (Charlestown.)

Blacksmith. I comit my body to the ground to be buried in the usuall buring place.—estate to my wife as long as she liveth ; after my wifes dedecease, my house w<sup>th</sup> garden, three acres of ground in the neck, with my armes & tooles to my sonne daniell, whom I would have brought up in the trade of a smyth—the rest of my estate after my wifes decease to be divided betweene my two daughters *Lidia* & *Johanna*,—wife sole

---

\* Mr. C. was of Charlestown. The inventory of his estate was there taken, 21 : 5 : 1645.

87

executrix—m<sup>r</sup> *Nowell*, bro. *Heborne* & bro. *Cutler* my overseers. 16. 5. 1644.

in p<sup>r</sup>sence of<br>
*Increase Nowell*<br>
*Thomas Carter*<br>
*Rice Coles*

the marke of<br>
*Daniell Sheopardson.*

If his wife & 3 children dyed hee gave mee, Incr : Nowell his house, house plot, at the same time before the same witnesses.

---

WILLIAM HALSTED.* (Concord.)
Inventory taken 10th day of th X month 1645. Amt 97. 10. 6
*Robert Merriam*
*Geo Howard* apprisers.

---

Will of JOSEPH WELD of Roxbury.

Ipswich 2. 4 moth 1646.

To the Colidg In Cambridg Tenn pounds to be payd In fiue yeeres, viz 40ᵉ p Annum, to the helpe & fertherance of such In larning as are not able to subsist of themselves, & herein I referr my Say to m<sup>r</sup> *Dunster* & m<sup>r</sup> *Eliot*, to be disposed as they Judg meet, only by this I recall the 20ᵉ a yeare back againe, w<sup>ch</sup> I put to my hand to giue to Dr *Ames* sonn ; yet If those fournamed Judg it fitt to give him the 40ᵉ p annum I leave it to ther wisdoms.—To my sonn *John* who is now my eldest sonn, sonn *Thomas*, sonn *Edmond* & my Daughter *mary* my howse called the farme, with barne, & all the erable land, midow pasture ground contayning 80 acres & vpwards, with all the howsold stuff I haue ther, oxen & cowes, with cart, plows, yoks, Chaines & all the furniture : also my last devission of land being the 22 or 23 lott, being about 130 akers more or less ; also, 3 akers of land somtimes *John graues*, lying next to the grounds of *Josuah Hewes ;* allso, six akers of salt marsh, more or less, that was bought of the Hairs of *Samuell shoreman*, lying next the marsh of *John watson ;* all these howses & moveables, cattell & p<sup>r</sup>cells of land named I giue to these 4 of my children named, viz, sonn *John* a dubble ption, the other three an equall ption.—If god take any of them away by death vnder the age of 21 yeares, the survivors of these 4 shall Injoy his or there ptions. I giue to *hanna*, my youngest dau. by my first wife, my ground comonly cald the leauen akers, lying next mudy riuer, also 20<sup>lbs</sup> to be payd out of my goods by my wife *barbara*, at the age of 21 or day of marriage—If god take her away before her ption be devided among the children I had by my former wife, my will is, lf I dy before that time be expired, that I am engaged to m<sup>r</sup> *Hoocker* to find her clothes out of her portion—Children by my former wife all of them a payer of sheets & all the beding, except that I shall hereafter name—[To the children severally] the rent due from *William dauis*. That my overseers doe see p<sup>r</sup>formed out of the corne w<sup>ch</sup> william davis is to pay that my Brother *edward* porter ? have Ten bushells of rie, allso bro. *mayes*, bro. *Jones*, bro. *lewis*, bro. *peake*, bro. *gamlin*, [each] 5 bushells.—Because my house in the towne have little wood belong to it my wife and children that are to inioy that shall have liberty to take soe much In the Sothermost grounds as will serue for ther vse for fiering, puided [they] cutt it out & make no stroy ; this to Inioy for the space of Ten years after my decease.—Those chil-

---

* An abstract of the *Will* of *William Halsted* may be seen in *Reg.* Vol. III. p. 177. (See p. 25).

88

dren named shall haue each of them a boock, & ther be 3 of doct *prestons*, one of Dr *Sibb*, m$^r$ *rogers* 7 treatises ; the eldest to take his choyse first. Sonn *John* my best stuff suit, son *Thomas* my frise suit & *Edmond* a ption as may be equall.—To sonn *John* my cloth cloke, to sonn *daniell* a suitable ption of my apparrell, equally parted among all my sons except my black tawny cloke to m$^r$ *John Eliot* o$^r$ Teacher, my best sword to sonn *Jonn* & my other sword and black belt to son *Thomas:* The share I haue fr the Iron works the yearly pfit may be disposed to bring vp my son *Thomas* at Cambridg till he com to be m$^r$ of Art, and if my son daniell be capiable of larning, my desire is, that he allso after my son *Thomas* haue the like benefit, till he com to be m$^r$ of art ; after that the whole to be equally devided among all my children. Wife *barbara* (my executrix,) together with my son *daniell*, dau. *Sara*, dau. *mara*, my howse, the 15 akers in the neck, also that cow I bought at watertown, for the other is my son *Johns*, together with too young steeres that are som-ering at *John woods* at sudbury. Those excepted, I giue all my other cattle at home to my wife & her children ; the downe bead, bolster &c on the best chamber ; one fether bedd & the beadsted on the hall cham-ber ; with the yellow rugg, largest green rugg, 4 pillows, 2 payer of blankets, allso on flock bead &c. My dau. denison affirmes the down beads, my wiues mother gaue to her, after my decease, I know no such thing ; yet, being soe confidently affirmed by her, my will is, after the decease of my wife, [they] shall be my dau. denisons.—Debts to be paid, also m$^r$ *cuddingtons* anewity of 20$^{lb}$ a year, till 7 yeares be expired ;— 40$^{lbs}$ a year for 5 years to the Colidg. Mr *John Eliot*, Elder *heath*, *Ed-ward Clapp* of dorchester, & *William parks*, [overseers,] 10$^{lb}$ to be payd them.

p m$^r$ *Joseph weld*. 22. 5. 1646. My desire is, that Leuetenant *Hewes* & bro. *bell*, allso, bro. *John Johnson* may be added to the overseers, [they to have power to make the portions of the children equal.]

p me Joseph Weld

Witness p vs,
*Joshua Hewes*
*John Johnson*
Proved 10$^{th}$ (8) 1646. Lieftenant *Hues* & *John Johnson* deposed.

W$^m$ Aspinwall Recd$^r$.

NOTE.—This will is in the form of a letter, with the superscription—"To the Rev-erende his Esteemed In the lord m$^r$ John Eliot giue this not to be opened till after death."

Inventory* of *Joseph Weld*, late of Rocksbury, by *Barbara*† his wid. 4 (12) 1646. Am$^t$ 2023. 14. 9. Apprizers, *Isack heath*, Will$^m$ Deny-son, *John Johnson*, *William Parke*. The name of W$^m$ *Pirkines* is men-tioned. Proved 4 (12) 1646.

---

THOMAS COOKE, (Watertown.)
Inventory taken by *Nath$^l$ Bowman* and *Thomas Hastings*. Mentions Mr. *Mayhu* and goodman *Childs*. Amt. £5. 03. 00.

---

* This Inventory is also *recorded* in the first book of Inventories, in the Suffolk Probate office, page 29.

† Her maiden name was Clap. For farther information relative to *Joseph Weld*, see *Ellis' Hist. Roxbury*, p. 134.

JOHN OLIVER.

Inventory taken 23. 2. 1646, by *James Penn* and *Nathaniell Williams*. Amt. £205. 6. 4. [See *Abstract of the Will of John Oliver*, Reg. Vol. III. p. 266.]

---

Will of HENRY ADAMS, of Braintree. 1646.

First, my will is, that my sonne *Peter* and *John*, and my dau. *Vrsula*, shall have the ground in the Neck, both vpland and meddow, during the terme I was to enjoy it, vntill it returne into the townes hands againe from whom I had it. Also the Aker in the Mill feilds. My will is, that my bookes shall be devided amongst all my Children; that my wife shall have and Enjoy all my other Goods so Longe as shee liveth vnmarried. And if she marry, then my will is y^t *Josephe*, *Edward*, and my dau. *Vrsula*, should enjoy all my ground in the feild that lyeth in the way to Waymouth ferry, and my house Lott, with all the houses and fruit trees, and all my moveables, at the death or marriage of my wife; Provided, they and their mother shall pay to my sonne *Samuel* that w^ch is due to him for the ground I bought of him, to be payd in Convenient tyme. But in case God should soe deal w^th my wife that shee be constrayned to make vse of something by way of Sale shee may.

finally, for moveables, my will is, that my sonne *Peter* and *John* shall have an equall share with my sonne *Joseph* and *Edward*, and my dau. *Vrsula*.

Beniamin All be

8. 4. 1647.

Richard Brackett.

Increase Nowell sec.

The Inventory of Henry Adams of Brantry is recorded in Suffolk Probate Records, Vol. 2, p. 32. Amt. £75. 13. Deposed in Court 8 (4) 47.

Increase Nowell sec.

---

ROBERT MILLER, (Concord.)

Inventory made the 26: 12: 1646. Amt. £10. 6s. 2d. By *John Smedly*, Timothy miller (?)

THOMAS GRIGES.

Inventory 25. 3. 1646. Taken by Phillip Eliot & John Ruggles. 1. 5. 1647. Wm. Aspinwall Recorder.

---

JOHN HILL, (Boston.)

Blacksmith. Deceased the 21 July, 1646. Inventory taken by *Thomas Marshall*, *Thomas Clarke*, Tho: Dennæ or Vennar (?) *Isaac Waker*. Amt. £255. 03s. 08d. Mentions goodman *Godfrey* of duxberry, his pt of *George Adames*, m^r *Treworthy*, Mr *Lux*.

---

WILLIAM BRANDON, (Weymouth.)

Inventory taken by Edward Bate, John Frissyll (?) Nicholas Λ Phillips 23: 9: 1646.

his
marke

---

Will of JOHN LOWLE Late of Newberry.

9. 4. 1647. I give vnto my Wife *Elizabeth Lowle* one halfe of my Estate also Twenty pounds out of the residewe of the Estate w^ch came by her mother. The rest of my Estate to be devided Equally betweene Sonu *John, Mary Lowle, Peter, James, Joseph, Beniamine & Elizabeth Lowle*—my bro. *William Gerrish, Richard Lowle, John Sanders, Richard Knight, & Nicholas Noice* to be my Executors. If any of my first Wifes

90

Children dye before they have their portion, that it be equally devided amongst the rest that are Living; the same Concerning my second Wifes Children, *Beniamine* & *Elizabeth*, these portions to be paid them 'when the Court Judge them wise and able to manage an Estate, as theie shall receive information from Sixe of the Wise, Godly men of the Towne, with the Elders. Alsoe, that dau. *Elizabeth*, shall take tenn pounds worth of their own Mothers Clothes; dau. *Mary*, [likewise.] If my Wife Marry, my dau. Mary shall Live with my sister *Johan Gerrish*, if my Sister please, if dau. *Mary* Chuse to Live with my sister before my Wife.

Witnes                                       p me *Jnᵒ Lowle.*

*Edmond Grenleife*    Proved 27. 8. 1647.   *Edm. Greenleife & Willi:*
*Willⁱ Gerrish*            Gerrish.

*Robert Long*                               Increase Nowell sec.

Inventory of the Estate of *John Lowle* taken by *Edward Rawson, & Abraham Tappan*, the last of June 1647.   Amt. £245.

---

## Will of GEORGE MARSH of Hingham

2 July, 1647.   Vnto wife *Elizabeth*, fower pound tenn shillings a yeare; on fether bed, on payer of sheets &c. after hir desese to returne to my sonne *Thomas Marsh*.   To sonne *Oneseferes*, one yerling stere, an one to yerling hefer, one hefer Calfe, one Ewe, &c.   Dau. *Elisebeth Turner*, one yerling hefer.   Dau. *Mary padge*, to Ewe gotes, &c.   Sonne *Thomas Marsh*, my house and all my land in Hingham.

Witnes    Ralfe Woodard
          William Hersee.

---

## Will of JOHN PRATT, of Dorchester.

3. 1. 1646.   Wife sole executrix.   When my debts are discharged she shall haue yᵉ Rest, soe to improoue to bringe vp the Children, and when as the Come to age and able to manage it, to giue to ech one a portion alike.   Mine Eldest sone to haue a double portion, prouided that hee soe distributeth as her selfe may haue a Competency, if shee liue a widdow; if she mary againe, shee shall haue a third part to inioy during her life, and after to returne to the Children, euery one alike; and I desire our deacon *wiswall* and Brother *hopestill foster* to take the pains as to my ouerseers, to Counsell and guid my wife in all her afairs.        John pratt.

Witness    *Thomas Dickerman.*

*Thomas Dickerman* deposed 27 (11) 1647.

Inventory of *John pratt* of Dorchester.   Taken 11: 3: 1647.   By *Tho: Dickerman, Will Clarke, Hopestill ffoster*.   Amt. £81.

# ABSTRACTS FROM THE EARLIEST WILLS ON FILE IN THE COUNTY OF SUFFOLK, MASS.

### PHILLIP DRINKER.

*Phillip Drinker,** late of Charlestowne, who deceased 23 : 4 : 1647. Being sick—doe make this my will 21 : 4 : 1647. Vnto wife *Elizabeth,* the Howse my son *Edward* lives in, w$^{th}$ the garden, &c. one Aker of Arable land y$^t$ is broken vp, w$^{th}$ 2 Cowe Comons and 2 Hay lotts ; after her deseace, to bee my son *Johns ;* Vnto wife, twoo Cowes, one yeareling, the best Bed, twoo par of sheets, &c. ; also 4 pounds in mony, w$^{ch}$ is in the Howse, to bee hers for ever. The residew of the monies in house, with the debts due, &c. to bee equally parted between my wife an son *Edward.*

Vnto son *Edward* the Howse I now live in, w$^{th}$ the Kilne and garden, w$^{th}$ the peece of marsh meddow adioyning. Alsoe the boat I bought of *Elias Maverick,* he being payd ; To son *Edward,* one Aker of Arrable land broken vp, the lower Aker, one Cow Comon, one hay lott on *willsons* syde, w$^{th}$ A 10 Aker lott on mistic syde, w$^{th}$ all the lead, wood and fagotts I had of bro. *James,* w$^{th}$ all the tooles belonging to my trade ; Vnto my two sons *Edward* and *John,* the other half of my household stufe and bedding, to bee equally divided between them. Vnto son *John,* my great lott at woeburn ; alsoe twoo Oxen, my best dublet, w$^{th}$ a peece of cloath to make him a payre of breeches, w$^{th}$ my best hatt, to bee his for ever. Vnto son *Edward,* my next best suight, & my best great coate. My will is that *John Gouldsmith* serve the rest of his tyme w$^{th}$ my son *Edward,* he to fulfill the Indenture ; only instead of the 12$^s$ there mentioned, my son *Edward* shall give him 5$^s$, when his tyme is expired. Alsoe, that my wife and son *Edward* haue 40$^s$, w$^{ch}$ comes from the hire of the Oxen this yeare.—son. *Edward,* Executor.

*Increas Nowell,* overseer. 21. 4. 1647.
witnesses, *Ralph Mowsall, Thomas wilder.*
> *Tho*$^s$ *Wilder* deposed. 3 (5) 1647.
> > *W$^m$ Aspinwall* Record$^r$

Inventory† of the Estate of *Phillip Drinker,* of Charlestowne, 1647. Taken by *Thomas Wylder,* the marke of *John Roper.* witnes *John Greene.*
*Edward drinker* & *Thomas wylder* deposed. 3 (5) 1647.
> > Recorded 15 (5) 47 by *William Aspinwall*
> > > V. Recorder.

---

* Died in Philadelphia, 17 Nov., 1782, *Edward Drinker,* æ. 102 years, having been born the 24th of Dec., 1680, in a cabin near the corner of Second and Walnut streets, where the triangular block now stands. When Dr. *Franklin* was questioned in England to what age we lived in this country, he wittily said he could not tell until *Drinker* should die and settle it. " The parents of *Edward*," says *Watson,* " came from Beverly, and settled on the site of Philadelphia before *Penn* came, which was in 1682. *Edward* had all his 18 children by his first wife, having had four wives in all. He was never sick—always cheerful."—Watson's *Historic Tales of Olden Time,* 72, 246. See *Hist. Gen. Reg.,* Vol. IV, p. 373.—[See also Watson's *Annals of Philadelphia,* where there is a long and interesting biography of Edward Drinker.—EDITOR.]

† This Inventory is also *Recorded.* See Probate Records, Vol. II, p. 31.

Will of JOHN GOVE of Charlestowne.

I do give & bequeath, w^th my wifes full consent, my dau. *Mary Gove* to *Ralph Mousall* & his wife, as their own child, forever. Unto *Ralph Mousall*, a silver porringer & five pound out of the house I bought of goodm *Larkin* in Charlestown, to bring up y^e child. To my two sonnes *John* & *Edward*, fifty shillings a piece, to be paid out of the brasse that is in the house, or out of the brasse that is to come out of England, by m^r *John Allen*, to be delivered into the hand of the said *Ralph Mousall*. The rest of my goods & the other halfe of my house, to my wife, she paying what I owe to others—wife executrix. 22 : 11 : 1647.

John Gove.

Inventory 25 : 11 : 1647. £9. 12. 6.

Mentions maior *Sedgwick*, *Jonathan Brust^r*, goodm *Hall* of duxbry, goodm *Park^r* of Dedhā; 3¼ bls pease at sec : *Greens*, goodm *Jackson*, Eld^r *Champny*, goodm *Stimes* son, goodm *Shrimton*, m^r *Alford*.

---

### FFRANCES BLOFFE (Cambridge.)

Widow. Inventory, prised by *John Bridge* & *Roger Bancroft*. Amt 14. 10. 8.  7 : 10 : 1647.

---

### ABRASA HAWKINS.

Inventory taken 28 : 7 : 1647 by *William Stitson, Randoll Nickolls.* Amt lb 44. 1. 8. *Elizabeth Hawkins* deposed, 18 (1) 1647 or 1648 before *Increase Nowell.*

Know all to whom this may conserne, That this o^r brother, who is deceased, did in his sicknes tho of perfect vnderstanding and memory, say vntoo mee that all that hee had hee freely gave it vnto his wife *Elizabeth Hawkins*, which I testify.

31 : 11 : 1647.  John Greene.

Proved 18 : 1 : 1647 or 1648, before me, Increase Nowell.

---

### JOHN RIGBEY,* [Dorchester.]

Inventory taken by Capt *Humfrey Atherton, William Robinson*, & *Geo. Weekes.*  16 : 2 : 1647.  Proved 9 : 10 : 1647.

---

### ELIZABETH GOODALLE,

Of Newberry, late of Yarmouth. Inventory taken 27 March, 1647, by *Edward Rawson, Henry Shorte, Richard Knight.*

---

### DANIEL BREWER of Roxbury,

12 : 11 : 1645. Husbandman. Vnto wife, *Joanna*, my dwelling howse with the buildings, reserving one chamber, & halfe the barne, and halfe the other outhouses, w^ch I giue vnto my sonne Daniell, soe longe as he shall remaine vnmaried. Vnto wife my home lott, fiue acres more or lesse ; also, sufficient Tymber for repations of the buildings & ffences, for her to sell & fetch off from my sonn *Daniell's* lands, hereafter giuen to him, and sufficient ffier wood. Vnto my sonn *Daniell* two Oxen, one

---

* See *Register*, Vol. V, p. 465.

Steere Calfe, w<sup>th</sup> one Carte & Plowe, w<sup>th</sup> the furniture therevnto belonging, and Sixe accres of Land lying neere the greate Lotts, And Sixe accres of swampe ground, w<sup>th</sup> the wood therevpon, lying neere vnto the howse of *Edward Bridge*, and fforty accres, more or lesse, lying in two p cells, sixteene accres thereof lying neere my meadow at Stony riuer, the other pte beiond Rocky swampe, neare the greate Meade ; all my mowing ground, ffresh & Salt, conteining ffower accres & a halfe, lying in two p cells ; also my best Bed & bedstedd, furnished, and my Iron pott, after his mothers decease, he paying these legacies hereafter mentioned ; to sonn *Nathaniel*, Tenn poundes ; to my dau. *Ann*, tenn poundes ; dau. *Joanna*, ffiue ; dau. *Sarah* ffiue ; to be paid in Cattell or Corne ; one third pte of each within one yeare after the death of their mother ; one third pte the yeare next enesueing ; the last third pte the next year after that. If any of my dau<sup>s</sup> dy before the dayes of payment, the surviving dau<sup>s</sup> to enioy their pte. Vnto wife sufficient hey, ffresh & salt, for the keeping of three Cowes, and the plowing & soweing of the said home lott, she finding seed & halfe the dunge, & the bringing in of herr corne into the barne ; also sufficient Wood for fiering. Legacies to be paid by sonn *Daniell*. Also ffower poundes & Tenn shillings to *John Watson*, when it is due, it being for his two oxen before mentioned. Vnto sonn *Daniell*, my howse with all the buildings and the home lott, with a Table & a Cupboard, after my wifes decease. To my daus. at day of marriage or after my Wiues decease, these legacies ; to dau *Ann*, a fflock bed furnished, & my biggest Chest, one little Iron pott, & one pewter dish ; To dau. *Joanna*, my great kettle, & my next great chest, one fflock bed furnished, & a pewter dish ; To dau. *Sarah*, a fflock bed furnished, my new kettle, & a pewter dish ; Vnto wife, my three Cowes, and my Redd Steere, and all my Swine. The residue of my goodes to my wife, whom I make my executrix. I heartily intreate my loving brethren in Christ, *Isaac Morrell* and *Edward Bridg*, to be Ouerseers of this my last will. It is my will that my sonn *Daniell*, shall not onely plowe his mother's ground sufficiently & well for her seed, but shall also Cutt downe & bring in her corne, & her fier wood to her howse, & lay out the dung all of it if he keep his owne Cattell else where.

Witnesse heerevnto  
*Willm Denyson.*  
the marke ——) of Edward Bridg.

the marke **D B** of  
*Daniel*   *Brewer*

Proved by *W<sup>m</sup> Denison* & *Edward Bridge* 20 (3) 1647.  
*William Aspinwall* V. Record<sup>r</sup>.

12 : 3 : 1647. Inventory of the goods of *Dannill Brver*, of roxbery, late deseased, prised by vs whose names are vnder wrightten. *Edward Porter*. Amt. £166. 4. 0.

———

26 : 3 : 1647. at a generall Corte. Upon p<sup>r</sup>sentment of the will &, inventory of *Daniell Shepardson*, It is ordered, that the land should go according to the fathers will to the sonne, or recompense according to the value of 21. 10<sup>s</sup> & because the moth<sup>r</sup> hath bene at great charge in educating the sonne three yeares, & is still to be, shee should be alowed the tooles & bellows & armes for that, & that the daughter shall have of what their fath<sup>r</sup> hath given them onely to the value of nyne pounds each of them for their pt.

by the gen<sup>r</sup>all Co<sup>r</sup>te *Incr: Nowell* sect.

JOHN GEORGE of Watertown.
Inventory 12 (4) 1647, by Left. *Mason, John Coolage, John Shearman.*
Debts dew from *John Raulinge* in ould England ; from m$^r$ *Dunster, John Springe, James Cuttler ;* Dew to *Willyam Knoxe,* Junior, is the titel of land purchased of him, be made good to the heire *£3. Anne George,* wife of *John George,* late deceased, proves the Inventory, 29 (4) 1647.
*William Aspinwall.* V. Record$^r$.
12 Jan. 1647. The Inuentory of *John George,* is debtor to his Sonne *Robert,* and his dau. *Susan £50.* 12$^s$. mother in lawe, *Anne George,* Guardian, before *John Winthrop,* Gov$^r$, *Tho Dudley* dep$^t$. Gov$^r$, *Increase Nowell* sec. & *W$^m$ Hibbins.* 7 : 1 : 1647.
*William Aspinwall.* V. Record$^r$.

———

WILLIAM BRANDON.
Last day 6 month, 1646. To Wif, *Mary Brandon,* my dwelling hous, & out houses, & 3 acers of land joyning, be it more or less ; To sonn *Thomas,* the 8 acers by the mill path, my gret pot, & my two guns, musket & fowling pece ; To dau. *Sarah,* on Cow, when she Come to 13 years of age : To dau. *Mary,* on Cow when she Com to 13 years of age ; 'To dau. *Hanah,* on Cow when she Comes to 13 years of ag ; To Sonn *Thomas,* all my houses, & lands, only entering vppon on half of it at 21 years of age ; the other half to wif. she to save out of it to my thre daus. 15 lb when they Com to sixteen yeares of ag ; £5 each daus. *Sarah, Mary, Hanah ;* Sonne *Thomas* pay to 3 daus. 15 lb within 3 yeares after he enters vppon the on half of the Lands. If wif dy befor legases be due, then, sonne *Thomas* pay the other 15 lb allso. If sonne *Thomas* dy before he Com of age, I giv to Brother *William,* his eldest Sonn, the worth of 10 lb of the howses & lands. The Rest of thes howses & lands to the Rest of my Children surviving, equally. My will is, if any Child. dy, 30 lb be paid to other Child or Children Surviving.
*Edward Bates* testifyeth vppon oath that *William Brandon* was of a disposeing mind when this will was written, only he is doubtfull concerning the last clause about his brothers sonne, whether he was then of sound memory. Swore before the Court 28 (8) 1647.
*Increase Nowell* sec.

———

EZEKIEL RICHARDSON of Woburn.
20 : 5 : 1647. I, *Ezekiell Richardson,* of Woebourne, being in perffect memorie. Wife *Susanna,* and Eldest Son, *Theophilus,* Executors. To son *Josias,* thirtie pounds, to be paide in mony, Cattell or corne, when 21. Vnto son *James,* £30 ; Vnto dau. *Phebe,* £30. I discharge whatsoever demands haue bin between my brother, *Samuel Richardson,* and my selfe. Vnto brother, *Thomas Richardson,* his Son *Thomas,* 10$^s$. Overseers, *Edward Converse* and *John Mousall* of Woebourne. In case either die before the accomplishment of this my will, the surviuer, with the consent of *Thomas Carter,* pastor of the church in Woebourne, shall haue power to chuse an other overseer in his place. Vnto the Overseers 30$^s$ a peece. Debts discharged, all the rest to Executors, provided wife may peacablie injoy her habitation in the house.

*Thomas Carter,* scribe          *Ezekiel richardson.*
*Edward Convars*          Proved by *Edward Convers* & *John*
*John Mowsall*          *Mowsall.* 1 (4) 1648, before the Gov$^r$ & my selfe.
         *Increase Nowell,* sec.

Inventory taken 9: 18: 1647, by *Edward Convars, John Mowsall, Thomas richarson.* The debts of our sister *Susanna Richarson,* 6–10– 0. Her legasie, 93–10–0. The remainder to the Executors, £90–6s.–6.

## Will of JOHN MERRICKE, of Hingham.

24 June, 1647. Vnto my seu.ᵗ [servant] *John Scathe,* Sonne of *Elisebeth Hilleard,* all my housing an home lot, an my twelfe Acker lot vppone the greate playne mall. I giue him too Ackers of fresh medo that lyeth too the East of *Thomas Joslenes* medo. Allso one Cow lot of sallt Marsh, at Waimoth riuer, next *John Winchesteres* medo; Capt. *Ward,* an he the sayd *John Scathe,* to haue them after the desese of my wife, Elisebeth, but shee to hould them [for life]   to sister *Hiller* 20,' wich is in her husbands hand; to *Anne Scathe,* dau. of *Elisebeth Hiller,* £5 too yere After my desease; vnto *William Heley,* that deat that is in his hand that is dew to me; to Mʳ *Hubbart,* 10ˢ; to wife *Elizabeth* all the rest of my lands, goods, &c., making hir Execter; she shall giue vnto the aboue named *John Scathe,* an *Anne Scathe,* £5, each; but If my nesse, *Elizebeth Merricke,* an *John Fisher,* an *Anne Fisher,* shall hapen to Com suer before the desese of my wife *Elisebeth,* that £10, shee should pay to *John* an *Anne Scathe,* shee shall pay it to *Elisebeth Merrick,* an *Anne Fisher* by Equall shares; and tho aboue named *John Scathe,* shall pay to *John Fisher,* fiue pound, out of the land, after my wiues desese. I do leue *William Hersee, John Winchester, Thomas Samson,* fefers in trust, to se the will performed, an to see that my wife be not ronged.

*John Merrick.*

Tis my will that *John Scathe* shall stay with my wife tell A month after milliestid, 1647;* that *William Hersee,* an *John Winchester* haue the disposing of my neuey [nephew] *John Scathe,* to bind him to a trad, what trad he shall most desier Excepting any trad that belongeth to the seeay [sea].

In presence of
*William Hersee*
*John Winchester*

*John Merrick.*
deposed 9 : 7 : 1647
*Increase Nowell.*

## MARGARET GRIMSTONE.

Inventory, by *Thomas Clarke & Edmond Eddenden,* 7 (12) 1649. Amt 27ᵗʰ. 13.

## THOMAS COLLIER.

I *Tho: Colear,* of Hingehame, this sexᵗ of April 1647, being sicke, Vnto sonne, *Moses Colear,* house and houseinge, wᵗʰ home lott and plantinge lott, & great lott and meadowes, with all other my lands and Commons in the towne of hingehame; wife to haue the vse of the afoore named houses; to sonne, *Moses,* my two Cowes, twoe steeres, fife gootes & one Calfe; wife, *Susan,* have the vse & profit of thease Cattell deueringe heere life. To dau. *Susan,* one Cowe, my feather bead & thinges belonginge to it, wᵗʰ one pewter platter, one holland sheet, & one pilow

---

* That is, 30 March, 1647, as I suppose; for, among the Saint's Days in the Roman Calandar, that of *St. Mille* is 30 March, hence Mille's-tide is probably meant.

EDITOR.

96

beere, after my wiues deses. To sonne, *Moses*, rest of househould stufe, after my wiues deses. To *Susan* my wife, & *Moses* my sonne, my two hogges betweene them. To sonne *Tho Colear*, one goate.

witnesse.                                    *Tho Coliar*
> *Nico Baker*                        his ⋈ marke
> *John Otties*

Testified on Oath of *John Otis* to be the Last Will of *Thomas Collier* and that he was of sane memory. 29. 8. 1647. *Jo Winthrop:* Gouer.

9 M^rch 1659. *Nicholas Baker* deposed. Power of Administration granted to *Susannah Collier* & *Moses Collier* to pforme this Imperfect will. *Edward Rawson* Record^r

Booke No : 5 : p 142.

Entered & recorded* word for word & compared therew^th 15^th of x^br 1671.                              *P^rffree Grace Bendall Cler.*

Inventory of the Estate, Recorded in Book 3. p. 198. Suffolk Records. *Moses Colier* deposed, 27 April 1660. *Edward Rawson*, Record^r.

---

### HENRY KEMBALL OF WATERTOWNE.

Inventory 22 (5) 1648. by *Henrie Bright, Nich: Bairstow, John Sherman.*

A note of what goods & debts m^rs *Sarah Barnes* acco^d of to be hers at y^e marriage of *Jn° Tinker.* Amt 13.ᵉ10. beside wereing Apell, both linen & wollen ; prised by 2 men & 2 women. Amt 08. 10. 06. Whole Amt, of goods & debts £45. 16s. Debts due by m^r *Jarvis, Wm. Berry,* m^rs *Stee. Winthropp,* goodm *Perry,* m^r *Addis, Jn° Gallop,* goodm *Windows,* goodm *forde, Jn° Seers,* goodm *Norton.* In Charles Towne, Boston &c. m^r *Dunster, Amose Richeson,* m^r *Deane Winthrop,* m^r *Addam,* m^r *Adkinson,* m^r *Rainsford,* goodm *ffeild,* g: *Arnell,* g: *Weight,* g: *Moone,* g: *Williams,* m^r *Saltestone, Stro: ffurnell,* m^r *Russell,* g: *Hagborne,* m^rs *Walton,* m^rs *Scarlet, Jn° Dones, Juner,* at Castle, m^r *Mansfeild,* g: *Streete,* m^r *Gunnison,* g: *Cutler, George Vahan,* m^r *Cowdell,* g : *Blanch,* m^r *Hill,* g: *Cutter.* There is 8^lb : 10ˢ pd vnto *Richard Cooke,* in Lew of bringing vpp y^e eldest of the 2 Children, which he doeth accept of with one halfe of y^e debt of m^r *Addis :* w^ch is doubtfull. all the rest of the estate, both good and doubtfull, to remaine to *Jn° Tinker,* for y^e bringing vpp of the yonger Child : & is according to the last will of the wife of *Jn° Tinker,* deceased.

13 (10) 1648. The Court doth allow of this returne so that the two children haue 6^lb. 13ˢ. 4^d. a piece : the Eldest by *Richard Cooke,* that brings her vp, and the other, by m^r *Tinker* that brings her vp.

                                  *William Aspinwall,* Record^r.

---

### NICHOLAS BROWNE.

Inventory 10^th May, 1648. The marke of *frances* F M *Mathues.* Signed also by *Nic: Shapleigh, William Serrnay, Humfry Lux, John Rayes.* Amt 223.^lb 01. 06. One third pt appertaines Vnto m^r *John Seelly.* The property of *Nicholas Browne* consists, in part, of one house, 6¼ Acres of Land settuated on the South side of y^e riuer of pescattaque vallued at £ 6. Two houses & 8 acres of land on same river—£12. An apprentice boye, for his tyme, Eight years, vallued at £30.

---

* No such record has been found in the proper office. The book referred to is probably lost.

97

Proved by *John Seely*, 6 (4) 1648. *Increase Nowell*, secret.

An Account of *John Seely*, tendered into Court of the payments he hath made for m$^r$ *Nicholas Browne*, deceased, to the full discharge of the Inventory. Paid m$^r$ *W*$^m$ *Hinckson*, Major *Sedgwick*, m$^r$ *ffoster*, m$^r$ *Knight*, vppon *Richard Walderns* Acct, *Henry Sherborne*, *Chr: Lawson*, in all £310. 13. Deposed 28 : 5 : 1648. *Increase Nowell*, sec.

---

### JOHN LEVINS of Rocksbury.

Inventory taken 30 : 6 : 1648. By *John Stow, William Park.*

---

### THOMAS FRATCHFORD.

Inventory taken 3 : 3 : 1648, by *Robert Hull* & *James Johnson* according to their best Judgment & Conscience.

---

### WILLIAM JOICE.

Inventory 25 : 8 : 48, by *Thomas Savage, Anthony Stoddard*, Amt. 19. 10. Itt is further desired by the said *William Joice*, that *William Hudson* should call m$^r$ *Aspenholl* to Acco : and receaue w$^t$ soeuer is of his in his hands, and vpon payment of all chardges what soeuer is left, to send it vnto his wife, in Rattlife in London.

Wittnesses  *Henr Walton*

 *Bartholmew Barloe*

26 (8) 48. Administration granted vnto *W*$^m$ *Hudson* of the estate of the said *Joice*, to be accountable to his wife, or to the Court, when he shall be there vnto called.

*William Aspinwall*, Record$^r$.

---

### GEORGE LUDKIN.

Inventory of *George Ludkin*, Late of Brantree, deseased, Valued 18 : 2 : 1648. Taken by *Daniel Weld*. The marke ⌐ of *Thomas Mekins, William Allis, Aaron Ludkin* delivered in this Inventory before the Gov$^r$, m$^r$ *Dudley* dept Gov$^r$ & m$^r$ *Hibbins*. 31 (6) 1648.

---

### JOHN WINTHROP.

Inventory of the goods & Chattles of *John Winthrop*, Esq : late Governo$^r$ of the Massachusetts, deceased, taken by *James Johnson*, & *William Aspinwall*, the 17$^{th}$ of the 2$^d$ mo. 1649.

---

### NATHANIEL SPARROWHAWK.

Inventory of the Estate of m$^r$ *Nathaniell Sparowhauke*, of Cambridge, who departed this life, June 27$^{th}$, 1647. Apprized by m$^r$ *Henry Dunster; Edward Goffe ; Tho: Chesholme* & pt. by *Gregory Stone.*

M$^r$ *Sparowhauks* Estate, By Debts oweing to it in Rowly from *W*$^m$ *Addams, Isacke Cousens, Nath. Stow, Obediath Holmes*. *W*$^m$ *Sparowhauks* Estate, Debtor, To *Nath ffrench, Robert Daniel*, Goode *Betts, W*$^m$ *Mannig* Senior, *Robt fface, Edw: Goffe*, m$^r$ *Edw: Jacson, Rich: Champnies*, Widdow *Lumpkin, W*$^m$ *Mans* wife, *Edw Okes, Rich: Oldam*, m$^m$ *Tompson, Abra Waluer*, m$^r$ *Cooke* of Charlstown, *Edmund Angier, Tho Beale*, m$^r$ *John Bukly, Rich Lord, W*$^m$ *Manning*, Jr. m$^r$ *Button*, m$^r$ *Alford, Edw. Brasier*, m$^r$ *Aires, George Haddings* p tion, *W*$^m$ *ffrench*,

*Easter Sparowhauke*, to yᵉ (2) Virginia boyes, 10.ˢ *Chandler* of Boston, *Tho: Chesholme, Goode Bucke, Theoder Adkins, Rich: Cutter, Wᵐ Cutter, ffrances Smith,* Sister *Holban, Mary Lemon,* mʳ *Henry Dunster, Joseph Magit,* mʳ *Wᵐ Ames, John ffesington, Robt Homes,*Goodm *Witherell, Abra Errington,* Goodm *Knights, Tho Longhorne, George Doubty,* Goodm *Brookes* at Concord, mʳ *Dauis petecharie* at Boston, mʳ *Belcher* at Boston, old Goode *Prentice, John Taylor, Percefell Greene, John Russell,* mʳ *Russell* at England, *Mary Peirce, ffrances Moore,* senior. To *Barnebe Lampsons* Children, Sister *Meene, Daniel Stone,* mʳ *Tho Shepard,* pastor, mʳ *Tho Lake, John Rogers* & Goodm *Stilson,* mʳ *Bennit* of Virgenia, *John Trumble,* mʳ *Caltor* of Rowly, Goodm *Rainer, Tho: Hall, John ffuller, Wᵐ Pattens* wife, Goodm *Eaton,* Goodman *Penticost,* ffranck*len* of Boston, *Jonathan Padlefoote,* mʳ *Star, Edw: Shepard,* mʳ *Dumer,* mʳ *Wᵐ Payne,* mʳ *Robt Payne,* mʳ *Apleton,* Goode *Smith* at Watertowne, old mʳˢ *Browne,* mʳ *Russell* of Charlestowne, mʳ *Palsgraue,* mʳ *Norton, Tho. Oaks,* Goodm *Grimes* in England, *Besaliel Angier* in England, *John Sparauhauke* at Copell in England, mʳ *Tanner* at Copell in Eng. *Edw. Micherson, Jonathan Michell, George Hutchine, John Parish, Gilbert Crackbone, John Sill, Goulden Moore, Tho Swetman, Robert Parker, Sam. Green, Robt Stedman, Joseph Cooke, Daniel Kempsters, Tho Danforth, Matt. Hancocke, Steeuen Day, Richard Jacson* for *Chare Griffin, Joseph Miller, Sam. Hides. Wᵐ Bull, Richard Hildreth, Jnº Cooper, Isacke Amsden,* Sister *Willows, Tho: Sawjer, Philip Cooke, John Stedman, Richard Robbins, Wᵐ Towne, Wᵐ Hamlet, Rich: Parke, Capt Coogine,* [*Gookin,*] *Euens* at Virginia, *Tho: Marrett, John ffounel, Cristo: Cane, Mary Isacke, Jonathan Danforth, John Boutaile, James Luxford* in *Tho: Brighams* acct.

Watertowne Debts—Good: *Philbricke,* Good: *Leapet, Henry Kemball,* old *Mihel Basto, Robt Jupe, Christo: Grant, Isacke Mixture,* old *Warren,* old *Hamund, John Benjamin,* old *Taylor, Natt: Treadaway, John Shearman,* old *Wincol, John Wakefield.* In Yarmouth, *Roger East, Swift, Jordan, Dogget, Robinson* of Duxbery, *Randol,* mʳ *Come, Richards, Zachery field,* at Conectecut, *Dauid Carpenter,*—New Hauen, *Mary Adkins, Benjamin Wilmut, Joseph Midlebrooke*—England, *Robt Meadford, ffaithfull Chapman.* In Holland, *Sam: Angire.*

Sudbury Debts, *Rich. Newton, Wᵐ Browne.* Charlestowne Debts. *Wᵐ Buckman, Gool, Johnson, Lepingwell.* In Hingom, *Thomas Nicoles,* Goodm. *Stet* at Nantascut. *Nath: Baker.* Goodm *Lausun.* In Hampton, *James Dauis.* In Rowly, Widdow *Huginsworth.*

---

### JOLLIF RUDICK.

Inventory 12 : 8 : 1649. By *Henry Webb,* & Henry Sandys. Amt. 299ˡᵇ: 6ˢ. 2ᵈ. Administration granted 21 : 10 : 1649 to *John Ruddock, Increase Nowell,* sec.

---

### THOMAS SANDBROOKE.

Inventory Prised by *John Lake* & *Richard Chrichley,* 14. 5. 1649. Amt. £123. 18. 10. Debts due from mʳ *Shrimpton,* Goodm *Jewet* of Rowley, Goodm *Halstone,* taylor, *Leonard Haryman,* of Rowley, Goodm *Bumsteed, James Wood,* of Longe Island, mʳ *Kinge,* of Linn.

## ABSTRACTS FROM THE EARLIEST WILLS ON FILE IN THE COUNTY OF SUFFOLK, MASS.

[Prepared by Mr. Wm. B. Trask of Dorchester.]

Thomas Sanbrock of Boston.

Loving friend *Henery Shrimpton* of Boston, Executor. For the Estate, the best of it I Leave in the hand of my Executor to satisfie my debts. [The residue to be divided into three parts,] to parts to Wife *Elinor Sanbrock*, the other part 20s. to bro. *William Sanbrock*, to sister *Alce Sanbrocke*, 40s.; to Cosen *Samvell Sanbrock*, 20s. and 40s. to the pore members of the Church of Boston; my fowling pec to my Executor, & my halfe picke to *Jonathan Shrimpton*. The Residew of the third part, to Loving Cosen, Mᵣ *William Pynson*, and in Case he shall be ded to be distributed Equally amongst his Children. In Case Aney goods, bils or Leters shall be sent from England, or aney other parts, Executor to Receve them, and to despos of them, for the best Advantag, and to make Returns to thos that hands them. [Dated] 16 (3) 1649.

Wittnes, *Edward ffletcher*      *Thomas Sanbrooke*
       *Samuell Shattock*      *Edw. ffletcher & Samuell Shattock*
                           deposed. 6 : 12 : 1649.
Inventory printed p. 176.            *Increase Nowell.*

---

John Gallop,* of Boston.

Wife executrix. To Sonne, *John Gallop*, my new shallop, after my death. To my dau *Joane*, my heaffer, my two youngest Sonns, shall Imploy my barcke, the first year after my decease, wholly for theire mother, and after one yeare to haue two thirds for themselves and one third for theire mother, and to repajer and majntejne the bark themselves, looking for no helpe from theire mother, only shee shall haue the third of profitt; also my wife shall haue the vse of howses, lands and goods for hir Comfortable majntenance So long as shee shall live; after hir decease, it shall wholy Remayne & equally devided to my two youngest Sonns, *Samuell Gallop & Nathaniell Gallop*, If they carry themselves as obedient children to theire mother, but if they be rebelljous, than shee shall haue liberty to dispose of all as shee shall thinke Good ; & if one Sonne dye before theire mother, then all to remajne to the other ; if both dye before theire mother, then my wife shall dispose of all as shee shall thinke Good. 1 doe Giue to *John Joy*, my daughters sonne, £5, to be Pajd to him at 21 yeares of Age, & if he dye before, It shall remajne to his brother *Joseph*. I doe Giue forty shillings to the building of the new meeting howse. Dated the 20th of the 10 mo 1649.

Witness heerevnto,           the marke   I   of
*Nich Vpsall*     *John Search*        John    ✝   *Gallop.†*
*John Sweete.*

---

* This abstract was made from the Will as recorded. It is *not on file*.

† The editor of *Winthrop's Journal*, i. 97, misjudges the chirographical attainments, at least, of this veteran and substantial old early settler of Boston, by unreflectingly pronouncing him as possessed of " less education than most of our early inhabitants," because he made a mark for his name when he executed his will. Now that editor did not require to be told that such execution of a will is no proof *at all* of a man's inability to write his name. I shall show elsewhere that *no* man of that time wrote his name handsomer than John Gallop, if he were a fisherman ; he was a merchant likewise.—Editor.

9. 12. 1649.  *John  Search  &  John  Sweete* deposed before the Court, *Increase Nowell* Sec.   Recorded at Request of *Samuell Gallops* Sonne to yᵉ Sajd *John Gallop*, deceased, this 3d of October 1657.

Edwᵈ *Rawson* Recorder & Secrety.

---

JOHN GALLOP.

Inventory, 26ᵗʰ of yᵉ Last Monthe, 1649.   Owne house and ground Lyinge in Boston, being bounded vpon yᵉ weste with yᵉ Land of *Matthew Chafine, John Sweet* Vpon yᵉ Easter sid ; that is to say, yᵉ Howse and Garden, together withe yᵉ towne shoare vpon yᵉ flattes, for Liberty of Wharfengeʳ granted by yᵉ towne.   The Island, Called by yᵉ name of Gallupe's Island, Containeinge about 16 Acres. £12.—foure Acres Lyinge at Long Island, of Meddo ground—£6; owne Vessell or Pinnis, called by yᵉ name of yᵉ Buck—£100.   Whole Amt of Inventory £311. 10s. 8. Wittnesed by *Nich Upsall*

Ed. *Raynsford*          Given in to the County Coᵗ 12ᵐᵒ 1649.
Willi *Beamsley*                         Incr *Nowell* sc.

---

OSOMANT BRAY of Weymouth.

Estate prized by *Robert Tucker*. 23 of the last mo. 48.   Testifyed before mʳ *Bellingham* 24 (8) 1650.   *William Aspinwall*, Recordʳ.

---

ISACK GROSSE of Boston, brewer.

29 : 3 : (49)   Being sicke.   To wife, the house I nowe liue in, wᵗʰ the onset, and one hundred pounds starlinge, £12 in money, the other in goods : Vnto *Edmund Grosse*, £200.   Vnto *Clement Grosse*, £100 ; Vnto *Matthew Grosse*, £100 ; Vnto Mʳ *John Cotten*, teacher of the Church off Boston, £10 ; To *Philemon Pormort*, off Wells, £10 ; To *Willm Wardayle*, off Wells £5 ; To *George Baytes*, off Boston, £5 ; To my Grand Child, *Isack Grosse*, £20 ; To my Grand Children, *Hanna* and *Susanna Grosse*, each £5 ; To my Grand Child, *Tho Grosse*, £10 ; To the Child wᶜʰ my sonn *Clements* Wiffe goeth wᵗhall, iff borne aliue, £5 ; To my Wiffe, besides the above mentyoned, my ser[uant] the Indyan, named *Lewes*.   My sonn *Edmund*, executor.          The testator *I. Grosse*. Witnesses hereto

*Tho Marshall*
*Isaack Waker.*

This is my further Will, iff my estate shall not extend to make good the bequests aboue sayd, that they be abated according to their several pportions, saue only Mʳ *Cotten* and Mʳ *Pormort*—and my executor shall haue six monthes to pay the one halfe, and six monthes the other halfe. Wittnesses to this last clause                         *I Grosse.*

*Tho Marshall*
*Isaack Waker.*

Debts owing to the testator.—By *Thomas Philps*, off Damaralls Cove, By *ffrancis Knight* of Pimaquid, ffor halfe a tun off strong beare.  3. 10s. By the Towne off Wells, ffo mʳ *Pormorts* Passage £5.   By *Willm Wardayle, Willm Wentworth*, and *Willm Cole*, wᶜʰ they owe me ffor wheat.   By Widdowe *Puddington*, of Aggamenticus, for moneys owinge by her husband, beffore his deceas, 22*lb.*   By *Willm Hilton*, of Pascataqua, by wine and beare 26*lb.*   By *Thomas Willms*, of Puscataqua, by wine and beare 33*lb.*   By Mʳ *Lane*, of Strawbury banke, ffor the hire of a barke 46*lb.* 06.   More by Mʳ Lane, ffor the hire of a barke and ffor

101

damage ffor want off the barke, as also ffor the barke it selfe w<sup>ch</sup> he sold w<sup>t</sup>hout order, and ffor damage othe<sup>r</sup>, 128*lb*.13*s*.   By *Tho Waye*, off Isle off Sholes.   By *Tho Yeo*, off Boston.   By *Rice Codogen* off **Aggmentycus** in the p<sup>r</sup>vince off Mane ;  By *Samson Anger*, off do.   *Oliue Ellen*, off the same<sup>*</sup>, to wine ;  *John Ball*, off the Isle of Sholes.   *Rice Jones*, of Boston ; M<sup>r</sup> *John Truworthy* ;  *Blasden* off Salsbury ;  *Samuell Winsley* ;  *Sherwood*, off Pentucitt, M<sup>r</sup> *Coppen*, off the new towne at Newbury ;  *Willm Welster*, the Brewer, off Strawbury Banke ;  *James Oliuer*, 42 Bush ½ Malt ;  M<sup>r</sup> *Perry*, off Newhaven ;  *Sentyon*, the Baker, off Wethersfeild ;  *Tho Sadler*, off Wethersfeld ;  *Tho' Stanton* ;  Capt. *Clarke*, off Road Island ;  Mr. *Throgmorton*, *Henry Bull*, off Road Island, 10 bushells of Barly, to be payd in ffatt Weathers ;  *John Stow ;*  M<sup>r</sup> *Holland*, of Dorchester ;  *Roger Amadowne*, of Waymoth ;  M<sup>r</sup> *Stowman* and *Callycott ;*  *Heugh Clarke*, off Watertowne ;  *John Loe*, off Boston ;  *Robt Nashe*, a butt off Muddary sack 12*lb ;*  *Willm Payne*, off Ipswich.

Inventory 5 : 4mo : 49, by *Tho Marshall, Isaack Waker*, Amt. 783*lb*. 16. 09.

------

JOHN STONNARD, of Rocksbury.

Inventory 20 Aug. 1649, by Isack Heath, John Johnson, William Parke. Amt. 135*lb*. 00. 6.

------

JOHN POPE, of Dorchester,

Who dessesed the 12 of the Second month, 1646.   Vnto wif, all my Land, and my howse in the great Lots ;  35 Ackers in the great Lots, 2 Ackers of Meadow in the Calves pastur, 9 Ackers by the mill, 9 Ackers by the 20 Acker Lots, my 20 Acker Lote, also 12 Ackers of Land 1 bought of M<sup>r</sup> *Borne ;*  my Right in all the Common of the Meadow, also own Acker at M<sup>r</sup> *Stowtones* great Lots, end of Meadow ;  Vnto my daughter my dwelling house, and ground belonging to it, provided she be willing that hir Mother should abide in It, As Long as her mother doth se Cause. If she be not Willing, hir mother shall have the disposing of it as she do se Cause, and all my goods I give vnto my sarvant mayd, *Ane Wellmoton*, [?] 15*s.;* vnto my sarvant, *Hannah Janson*, 5*s*. at the end of hir time ;  Vnto *William Smead*, my Littell boy, my Lomes, and such Taklinge as do be- long vnto them, which is to the vallew of 3*lb*, provided he be willing to dwell with my Wife after his time is out, also provided he be willing to Learn my Trad, and that their be A comfortable Agrement mad betwene the[m] Afterward.   I do Consider *Stephen Hoppen*, in Regard of his meannes [poverty,] and also in Regard of his Willingnes to the Trade, to set him in a way of work, I give him A lome I have half mad, likewise a Reed I have, which I do vallew in 5*s.;*  To my bro. *Thomas*, my new stufe sut of Azell <sup>*</sup> ;  To my bro. *Joshua*, my sisters husband, I give tow vper Coats, and som other Azell.

Witnes, *Henry Kibby*

    *John Peirce.*   Proved 5 (4) 49, by *Henry Kibby* & *John Pierce.*

                                     *William Aspinwall*, Record<sup>r</sup>.

*Henry Keeby* & *John Pierce* further witnes, the testator did declare to them, it was his will  his wife should have the goods & dispose of the same, whether his dau. be willing her mother abide in the house or no. Testifyed vppon their former oathes, in presence of *Increase Nowell*, sec :

------

* Hazel, (a light brown color) is no doubt meant.—EDITOR.

Inventory of the goods of *John Pope*, sen$^r$ of Dorchester. Taken 1 June, 1649, by *Humprey Atharton, Walter Harris, Hopestill ffoster*. Am$^t$. 184*lb*. 12. 06. Debts due £66 10. 06. Witnessed by *Geo Weekes* & *Richard Baker*.

---

## Will of WILLIAM HOMES.

12 Nov, 1649. I, Maior *William Homes*, being sick, Vnto loving kinswomen, *Margarett Homes* & *Mary Homes*, now residing at the Island of Antego, and dau$^s$ of my deceased bro. *Thomas Homes*, all my Plantation, w$^{th}$ the appurtenances vpon the said Island; all my estate, goods, &c that belong and shall be due vnto me from Captayne *Joseph Lee*, or any other person vpon said Island, to be equally devided betweene them; To said kinswomen, all the lands, goods, &c. I haue in New England, except what I shall otherwise dispose of, to be equally devided betweene them. Vnto my sister in Law, *Margarett Webb*, alias *Homes*, the late wife of my bro. *Thomas Homes*, and to *Rachell Homes* and *Bathsheba Homes*, two other dau$^s$. of my said bro., all now living in London, if they hereafter come over into New England, all my farme, w$^{th}$ the appurtenances, lying in Scituate, in N. E., now or late in the possession of *William Brooke;* one halfe said farme to *Margarett Webb*, als *Homes*, during her life, after her decease to *Rachell* & *Bathsheba*. The other half, to said *Margarett* towards bringing vp said *Rachell* & *Bathsheba* till they attayne the age of 16, or be married, each of them at said age or marriage to take possession of one quarter part of the said farme. If neither my sister *Margarett, Rachel*, or *Bathsheba* come over into N. E. then my will is, that the farme, &c. remaine to *Margarett* & *Mary Homes*, equally to be devided betweene them. Whereas there are certaine arreres due vnto me for being a souldier & Comander in the army & seruice of the King & Parliament, my desire to my sister in Law, *Margarett*, also to my executors, [is] that they take care for obtayning said arreres, w$^{ch}$ being effected, I give the same vnto my aforesaid kinswomen, *Margarett, Mary, Rachell* & *Bathsheba*, at 16 years of age, or marriage. [In case of the decease of either to be equally divided among the survivors.] Vnto my kinsman, *Job Hawkins*, of Boston £20. w$^{th}$in 2 months after my decease. *James Penn*, & *Robert Scott*, Executors, [each] £5. *William Homes*.
Witnesses.—*John Dane.*

    *John Bosworth*      *John Richbell* deposed 30 (9) 1649.
    *Nicholas Simknes* [?]
    *John Richbell*         *William Aspinwall*, Record$^r$

---

## MICHALL BACON, of Dedham.

14 : 2 : 1648. Vnto *Michall Bacon*, my Eldest sonne, one tipped pott, [torn off] siluer spoones, after my decease, [and] my stuff coate and my stockings. Vnto *Daniell Bacon*, my second sonne, the best kowe & the best steere that shall be mine at the time of my decease, pvided, said kowe or steere be let out vpon hyer at [torn off] of my decease. At the end of the tearme of hyer they shall be deliuered vnto said *Daniell*. In case of losse of said cattell, my executor shall make it good. Vnto sonne *Daniell*, my best Iron kettle, and three pewter dishes, of middle sort in value; my own best [torn off] Coate, & my wiues best Gowne. Vnto *John Bacon*, my third sonne, my pcell of vpland, Comonly called the twelve Acre Lott, with all buildings, &c thervpon; also that pcell of Meadow adioyning, allso, four Acres of Meadow Lying in ffowle Meadow,

in Dorchester; all woodlands & swamps granted me by the Town of Dedham, excepting that Swampe that Lye one the North [of] Charles Riuer. To sonn *John*, my best ffeather bedd, except one, [torn] twoo pillowes & pillow bieres, one blancket, best couerlet except one, one payer of [torn] fine ope seamed sheetes, my bigg [torn] pott, & one trammell. Vnto *Sarah Bacon*, my dau. my Tenement, wherin I now dwell, with all the houses, lands, &c. ther vnto belonging, also seauen acres of meadow in Broade Meadowe, & twoo Acres of my pcell of six acres in ffoule meadow, to be differently deuided from the other four Acres formerly in this my will giuen to my sonn *John*; also, four Acres of Land vpon the great playne, lately purchased of *Richard Ellice*; allso, that pcell of wood land I formerly purchased of *Edward Culluer*. If *Sarah* decease, without leaueing issue, all Lands giuen her shall at the end of one year after her decease returne to my twoo sonnes, *Daniell & John*, to be equally devided betwixt them. If *Sarah* leaue issue that shall not liue to the age of 18 yeares, it shall returne as before said, to my two sonnes. If her issue liue to the age of 18, then my gift shall be of full force to them & their heires. To *Sarah*, all my cattell not formerly disposed of; all my swine liuing or dead, my household stuffe not here in bequeathed, w^th all instruments of husbandry, my Cart wheeles with what doe belong to them, reserueing the Corne & debts due me, to the use of my executor; To *Sarah*, my [orchard?] being on the Iland playne; Vnto *Thomas Bancroft*, my Sonne in Law, 20s, to be payd within one yeare after my decease. *John Bacon*, my sonne, Executor, vnto whom I giue all my goods not disposed of.

sign

Michaell (O Bacon.

In p^rsence of
John (K Kingsberry,        *Daniell ffisher* deposed 26 (2) 1649.
Eleazer Lusher,                *Increase Nowell*, sec^y
Daniell ffisher.

Memorandum. *Anthony Hubbert* is to paye to for that bullock he bought, the same price he agreed for vpon purchase he is to paye the executor; as for that bullock of 3 yeare old, Anthony Hubbert receaued vpon condicion to bring vp another steere to the same age, he is discharged of that engagement, if the Testator recouer not. *Anthony Hubbert* is to pay for the testator 10s. to *Mr. Allen*, pastor, & 7s. 6d. to *John Morse*. Inventory of *Michaell Bacon*, of Dedham, taken by *Eleazer Lusher, John Eaton, Daniell Fisher*, 20. 2. 1649. Amt 54*lb*. 15. 04. *John Bacon* deposed 26 (2) 1649.

---

12 : 12 : 1649. Mr. *Comfort Starr*, sen^r testfyeth, That M^r *W^m Hanberry* of Boston, merchant, about four or fiue dayes before his death, very affectionately vttered these words in my heareinge, vnto his wyfe saying, that shee had beene a good wyf vnto him, and that yf he had a thousand tymes so much more than he had (or a thousand worlds) he would that shee should have it all, at w^ch tyme hee was sound in memory to this dep^ns judgment and vnderstanding.      *Comfort Starr.*

Deposed 13 : 12 : 1649.    *Isaac Waker & Mary Souther* testified and deposed to the same.      *Increase Nowell*, sec^r

---

Inventory of M^r *W^m Hanbury*, late of Boston, merch^t, deceased. 21. 12. 1649 by m^r *John Clark*, Chirurgeon, m^r *Jn° Hughson*, merch^t, & *Nathaniel Sowther*. Amt. £1453. 01. 08.

There is a farme at Joanes Riuer in question betwixt him & his brother

*John* of £100, and also £100 w<sup>ch</sup> wil be, at old m<sup>rs</sup> *Hanburies* decease, in England, w<sup>ch</sup> I tooke not at for p<sup>r</sup>sent. out of w<sup>ch</sup> estate I intend to giue two thirds (debts being payd) to my foure children, of what will be gott in w<sup>th</sup> respect to the Eldest, according to his byrthright, and to the rest as I shall think good, and the remaynder I reserue to myself.
[Signed as above.] 12<sup>mo</sup> 1649. Increase Nowell sec.

---

### THOMAS RICHARDS of Weymouth.

17. 10. 1650. At present in the towne of Hull, in the house of *Tho. Loring*, beinge sicke. When my sonne *John* Come home my whole estat shall be Cast vp, what it Comes too, and Sonnes *John, James, Samuell, Josephe*, and *Beniamine* shall have all of them alike : dubble portions to my daus. Sonne *John*, haue beene at greater Charge w<sup>th</sup> him then with aney of the other Daus *Mary, An, Alce* and *Hannah* shall haue halfe so much as my sonnes ; all alike, only dau. *Mary* shall haue teene pound moore then aney of the other. My wife shall haue suffitient maintaine-ance allowed heere out of my estat, that is to say, thirty five pound a yeere, deurringe life, the manner of it at discretion of [overseers.] To bro *Tho Loringe*, £5 for the troubell they have beene at with me. To *Thomas Prosser* 20s. Sonne *John* shall have sonns *Josephes* and *Ben-iamines* portions in his hand Vntill they be twenty and one yeares of age ; in the meane time *John* shall alow them for the vse of it what shall be thought fet by the overseers, sonne *John, Thomas Loringe* and *Nicolas Baker*, Both of Hull ; what Charge they be at the shall be satisfied out of my estat.

Witnesse                                My hand    *Thomas Richards.*
*Thomas Loringe*
*Nico Baker*                        Proved by them in Court 28 (11) 1650.

The same day the above named Heirs *James, Joseph, Benjamin* & *Hannah* petition Court that their Mother M<sup>rs</sup> *Welthian Richards* have power to improve the Estate vntill our brother *John Richards* shall returne, he being now in England, or, in case of his not returninge, vntill the Court thinke good to dispose otherwise, and that our Mother may returne an Inuentory of the Estate." Signed also by *Ephraim Hunt, Thomas Loringe, Nico Baker*. M<sup>r</sup> *Thomas Hinckley*, & M<sup>r</sup> *Willm Bradford* by letter desire the same.

Inventory of Estate taken by *Michael Powell, Thomas Loringe, Thomas Dyer*, 25 (11) 1650. Amt. £1300. 17. 11. Mentions *John Parris* in Barbadoes, *John Richards* at Kinebek. Goods sent over by M<sup>r</sup> *Richards* to sell for *Henry Powell, John Hatch, William Hatley*. Mrs *Richards* testifyed. 28 (11) 1650.                *William Aspinwall.* Record<sup>r</sup>.
Another Inventory taken 3 : 10 : 1651.

---

### ELIZABETH MORICKE.

Widdow of *Jno Morricke* deseased ; at Hingham But now Dwellinge in Roxbery, Not deprived of my witt & sences. *Robert Hull* of Boston & *Leonard ffellowes* of Great Bowden in old England. Executors. Vnto *William ffellowes* of Ipswidge, £10. *Richard fellowes* of Conecticot, £10. *Samuell ffellowes* of Salisbury, £10 ; *William Healy*, of Roxbery, £8 ; M<sup>r</sup> *Eliut*, of Roxbery, 20s. ; M<sup>r</sup> *Danforth*, of Roxbery 10s ; M<sup>r</sup> *Hubbert*, the minister of Hingham, 10s. *Ann Hillard*, of Hingham, *John Scath* & *Ann Scath* 1s [each,] *Jeames Johnson* & *Jno Hull* of Boston, Overseers. To each 5s. 14 March 1649. That £8 expressed in the 9<sup>th</sup> line is £4

to himselfe & the other £4 betweene the two eldest children of the s^d *William Healy.* I giue to my sister *Grace Allam* In Linckconeshire £5.
Witness                                        The marke ⌒⌐ of
RW    *Robt Waker*                              *Elizabeth Moricke.*
*John Hull.*    Deposed 5 : 7 : 1650.    *Encr : Nowell*
Estate of *Elizabeth Moricke,* prized. 5 : 7 : 1650, by *James Everill,*
*James Johnson.*

---

## ELIZABETH PURTON of Boston.

Widdow.    Vnto *Robert Blott,* of Boston, the full worth of 40s., to be
paied him suddeinely, after my Departure by Death, in such things of
mine as now he hath in his possession. Vnto my sonn, *John Purton,*
whatsoeuer shall Bee Left Remaining of mine ; whether in the Custody
of *Joseua Scottow,* or in Possession of *Robert Blott* or of any other.    [If
*John* die] my feather bed shall be giuen vnto M^r *John Cotton,* teacher of
Boston church ; 40s. vnto *John Mellowes,* of Boston.    In Case the Adventure Comitted vnto sonn *John* by s^d *Mellowes* be not Returned vnto s^d
*John Mellowes* or vnto any for him.    My Bible vnto *Robert Blott.*    What
shall be Left, Legasies taken out, shall be Comitted vnto the Deacons of
the church of Boston for s^d churches vse.    18 : 12 : 1650.
Witnessed by Vs                                The mark          of
  *John Hull*                                  *Elizabeth* Ⴀ *Purton.*
The mark R of            Testefyed in Court 29 (2) 1650 by *John Hull*
*Ralph*       *Greene.*                        *William Aspinwall* Record^r

---

## DAVID PHIPPENY.

Vnto wife *Sarah,* the house I dwell in, & my shopp with the shore, also
what tooles are mine, there being an hundred foote taken out for to
three houses vppon from the hygher end of it, I meane westward, what
shal be remainge shall belong to the house giuen to my wife.    The three
hous lotts is appointed, one for *Benjamin,* another for *Gamaliel* & the
other to my sonne *George,* & another house, being in the streete leading
out to Roxbury, vppon the left hand, in the outside of goodman *Woodward.*
Also, vnto *Thomas Yeo* my sonne in lawe, that plott of ground betweene
good man *Batts* ⌒⌐ & my selfe, from the streete backward, fourty foote.
Also to my sonne *Georg Vickars.* a Cowe, to be made good by my wife
to them.    Sonne *Joseph Phippenie,* joint Executor, w^th my wife, pertaineing all my land in Hingham.                    *David Phippeny.*
This will was accepted & approved at the Court at Boston, 31 (8) 1650.
                                        *William Aspinwall,* Record
Inventory accepted same day.    Prised by *James Everill.*    Am^t £220.
19. 09.—" a dwelling house wherein *George Deere* liues £22 ; " " a pcell
of land giuen vnto his son in lawe *Thomas Yew,* lyeing betweene his
dwelling house & *Bartholmew Barlow* £8."

---

## CLEMENT BRIGE of Waymouth.

1648.    To son *Thomas,* my home Lott at Plemouth, 20 acres, and my
Bigest Iron Pott.    To Son *Jonathan,* 3 acers of Land Joining *John Rees*
Lands, That is not Brak vp, and to Enter to it when hee is of the aige of
18 ; When 21 to haue 4^th pt of all my land in Waymouth ; after the
decese of my Wiff one 4^th more.    If Shee die Before *Jonathan* Be 21,
then it be for the Bringing vp of my Children.    To Son *Clement,* my
housing & the other halfe of my Land in Waymouth.    To Sons *Thom,*

106

*Dauid, John & Remond* my other Land at Plemouth Equally amongst them.  After *Clement* do Enter to the fors^d. Land hee shall giue his Brother *Remond*, 20s., *John* 10s.; *Jonathan* shall giue 10s. to his bro. *Dauid &* to his bro *Thom.* 10s. in one yeare after hee do Enter to half my land.  Wife Executrix ; degon *Rogers* and *Robert Tucker* ouerseers. Wittnes

| | The mark | ᗑ of |
|---|---|---|
| John Rogers | Clem^t | ᗒ Brige |
| Robert Tucker | Testifyed 24 (8) 1650, before M^r *Bellingham* vppon Oath. | William Aspinwall. |

---

JEREMIAH MORE.

Inventory taken 13 (11) 1650   by *Henry* H Evans,  his DS mark
*Richard Walker*, Amt. £87. 17.
                                        his                Samuell
                                        mark               Dauis,

---

PHILIP LONG of Boston.

Being bound to Seass.  Wife *Ann*, Executrix. 27 Oct. 1658.
*Thomas Squire*                         *Philip Long.*
*Walter Salter*          *Zackery Phillips & Benjamin Brisco*
*Zackery Phillips*       deposed. 13 Nov 1659.
*Beniamin Briscoe*                   *Edw. Rawson*, Secrety.

---

JOHN WOODDY of Roxbury.

Inventory taken  4 : 4 : 1650 by *John Cogan, William Park, Mary Woody* testified to the truth of this Inventory of her husband's Estate, 15 (6) 1650. *Increase Nowell.*

---

JOSEPH PELL of Boston.

Butcher.  Inventory taken by *Tho. Marshall, James Johnson.*  23 : 2 : 1650.  Amt £25. 02. 05.  Debts owing £13. 15. 02.  Mentions Bro. *Robte Scott*, M^r *Stodder*, bro. *Bumstead*, bro. *Willm Hudson*, bro. *Grubb*, *Robte Waterman, Richard Havens, Theodo^r Atkinson, Robte Wallker, Willm Hely* of Roxbury, *Amos Richardson, Francis Dowse, Francis Ingollds* of Lin, M^r *Whyting* of Lin, *Henny Bridgham*, of Boston, M^r *Henry Webb* of Boston, goodm : *Jones* of Charlestowne, *Edw. Kowdale, Willm Blanton, Joseph Jewett* of Rowley, *Robte Turner* of Boston.  Agreement of *Elizabeth Pell* and the Children of her deceased Husband.  The estate amounting to £21. 7, 3. the Children to have £13. 5. 8. the widdow the remaynder, accepted by the Court 25 (2) 1650. *William Aspinwall*, Record.

---

NICOLAS WILLIS.

Inventory taken 20 . 4, 1650, by *William Colbron, Jacob Eliot.*  Amt. £681. 02. 01.

---

M^r THOMAS LEVERETT of Boston.

Nvncupative Will. 1 : 2 : 1650.  Debts of Estate being paid by *Ann Leverett*, wife of Thomas, vnto said *Ann* all the rest of the estate. Wittnes, *William Hibbins, Will Colbron, Jacob Eliot.*
Inventory of Estate, taken by *Will Colbron, Jacob Eliot.*  £Amt 328. 17.  " House & ground at Muddy Riuer, cont. 175 Acres more or less £100 ; 3 Acres on Centry Hill £30 ; old houses & lands lyeing neare the old meeting house in Boston, £50.

# ABSTRACTS FROM THE EARLIEST WILLS ON FILE IN THE COUNTY OF SUFFOLK, MASS.

[Prepared by Mr. Wm. B. Trask, of Dorchester.]

Note.—In the July No. of the Reg. p. 227, it is stated that the Will of John Gallop is not on file. This is a mistake. It has since been found.                    W. B. T.

Leiftenant collonel Israell Stoughton.
Inventorie of his lands, goods &c. Taken by *John Johnson, William Parke*, 2 : 2 : 1650. [Land] by *Thom. Birches ;* Neck of Land y^t was *Mr Bournes ;* 100 Acres y^e Indians have, they to have 40, y^e other 60 Mr *Stoughton*, when he calls for it ; 3 Acres in 2^d Division of y^e Cow walke y^t was *Whites.* The Mill,* £50. 966 Acres Commons, 200 given to Harvard College ; 100 acres [more] to the College ; 100 Acres bought of M^r *Newberry ;* halfe the Tide Mills at Boston ; 9 Acres, at Boston, next Mr. *Newgates ;* 26 S. of y^e Ship America, M^r *Haddock*, Master ; 10 Acres, sold to Goodman *Robinson*, the Orchard, &c. &c †
Debts due in New England from *Micheson Marshall*, Good *Fairbanks*, *Geo. Holsey.* Mr. *Hopkins.* G. *Cheesbrooke.* M^r. *Hil.* G. *Prate, Jo. Blake, Nich. Clap, James Cudworth, Rob Paine,* M^r *Wil Knight,* M^r *Indecotte, Thom Boyes,* Good. *Grinnoway, G. Munnings. Thom. Tilestone, G Wrighte, George Proctor, John Scudder,* of Bastable, Mr. *Corwine.* Signed by Geo. *Weekes, George Minott, Thomas Jones.* Mrs. *Stoughton*, deposed 9. 6. 1650.
Mr *Fran Willougby* testifyed before the Court at Boston that m^r *Hickok* s^d there was a box delivered to him by m^r *Israel Stoughton* sealed vp to be kept & not opened vntill he came againe or dyed. And when M^r *Stoughton* was dead, M^r *Willoughby* was called to see the opening of the box in w^ch was this writing or Will ‡ of the s^d M^r *Stoughton.* rec'd by Court.
Test

*Humphrey Atharton*
*John Johnson.*        Court graunted that m^r *Rawson* should deliver
                        the originall Will vnto M^rs *Stoughton* the Exec-
                        utrix. **30 : 5 : 1652.**        *Increase Nowell.*

---

* " This Year [1633] y^e Plantation Granted Mr Israel Stoughton liberty to build a Mill upon Neponsit River, which I suppose was y^e first Mill built in this Colony, and y^e s^d River has been famous for Mills ever since." [Blake's *Annals of Dorchester,* p. 12.
This may have been the first *water* mill, in *Massachusetts* Colony ; there was a *wind* mill, however, in Boston, for grinding corn, as early as 1632. See Drake's Hist. of Boston, p. 144. See also Reg. Vol. V. p. 378, for a notice of Stephen Deane's " water worke to beate Corne," in Plymouth Colony, in 1632. Hayward, in his lately published U. S. Gazetteer, erroneously states, that the first water-mill in America was erected in Dorchester. Probably the first water mill for *grinding* was built by Stoughton, in that town. We know of none earlier.

† The total amount of Land specified, as belonging to said Estate, in Dorchester, is *five thousand six hundred and thirty-five Acres.*

‡ See abstract of the Will, in N. E. Hist. Gen. Reg. Vol. IV. p. 51. (See p. 33).

GEORGE WEEKES of Dorchester,
Who departed this life 28 Dec. 1650.  Sum Total of Inventory £254.
04. 07.  Taken 22 : 11 : 1650 by *Edward Clap. Roger Clap, Hopestill
Foster.*  Debts due, additional, £10.

---

ROBERT BUTTON of Boston.
One half of my estate to wife *Abigall;* half of [remainder] to son
*Samuell;* the [rest] to be divided equally betwixt my three daus. *Abigall,
Hannah & Sarah Button.*  Estate to be impoued by wif. for the education
of them, vntill the age of twentie yeares of age or marriage.  In Case my
wif mary before my Children liue to the ag afores^d, estate to be disposed
of as my overseers shall Judg most convenient.  [In case of the death of
any of the children, before the time mentioned,] the survivors to share
equally.  Wife Executrix.  *Thomas Savage & Hezekiah Vsher,* overseers. 9. 11. 1650.
In psence of
*James Penn*   Testifyed in Court 28 (11) 1650 by M^r *Penn* & M^r *Oliver.*
*James Olliver*   p me   *Robert Button.*

---

STEPHEN SERGENT.
Inventory of Estate, taken 29. 9. 1649, by *John Monk, Antipas Mavericke,* the Sine of R C.  *Richard Cuminges, John Thompson* testifyed
27. 2. 1650.  p^d *Hercules Hunckin,* £4.

---

ROBERT SALTONSTALL.
Vnto bro. *Samuell Saltonstall,* £20 starling.  To each of my [Execu-
tors ?] £10 starlinge, also [    ] Pounds starlinge, towards releaseinge Aunt
*Clarkes* Sonne from Capt. *Midlton,* in the Barbadoes.  To *Henry Walton,*
£10 starlinge.  Estate in England, after debts are satisfyed vnto my ffather
*Richard Saltonstall* and my bro. *Richard.*  Out of it to be paid to Sister
*Roseamond,* £20 ; to bro. *Henry,* £20 ; to Sister *Grace,* £10, Vnckle *John
Clarke* and *George Munninges,* Executors.  To Vnckle *Clarke,* my best
blacke suite & plush Cassock.  Vnto *George Munninge,* my gray Cloake.
My Sadd Coulered Cloath suit & Cloake, vnto *Henry Walton,* Vnto M^r
*Adam Winthrop,* the black beauo^r hatt I am to receaue from Captaine
*Keine.*  The rest of my bootes, shooes, stockins & Lynnen to *George
Munninge.* 13 June 1650.  Postcript.  I giue M^r *Thomas Lake,* £5 out
of that estate due mee, either from M^r^s *Whiteinge* or *Capt. Wiggons.*
In p^rence of                                    *Robert Saltonstall.*
*John Sanford*
*Will Norcutt*     Testefyed on Oathes of *Henry Walton* & *John
Henr Walton*          Sanford,* 15 (6) 1650.
I *John Clerke* renounce the Executorship of this will of my Cosen, *R.
Saltonstall,* & desire the Court to enter it vppon Record.
                15. 6. 1650.                  *John Clark.*

---

EDWARD MELLOWES of Charlestowne.
Who deceased 5. 3^mo 1650   Amt £82.19.

---

THOMAS ACRES.
11.11.50.  Estate prized by *Richard Russell, Thomas Savage, Richard
Sprague.*  Amt £118.07.

## ROBERT SHUTE.

Vnto mr *John Cotton,* Teacher of ye church of Boston 50s. Vnto mr *Jnº Wilson,* pastor 50s. To *Richard Russell,* £10. Vnto *Sara Phippeny,* £4. Vnto mr *Zakeria Sims,* Pastor of Charlstown, 40s. Vnto mr. *Thomas Allen,* Teacher of the same church, 40s. Vnto my Loving Bro. *Richard Shute,* liveing neer Pemmaquid, all my depts dew to mee from the Indians about those parts, and acquitt him from all depts Dew from him vnto mee. Remainder of Estate to my bro. *Thomas Shute,* my Sister *Marie,* and my Sister *Sara Hollyes* children, to each, one third pt. Alowing out of the whole vnto bro. *Thomas* whatt hee may Expend In receauinge the same. Out of the three last Legacyes the expenses requisite to a decent buriall of mee be deducted. In Case bro. *Thomas,* Sister *Marie,* & children of sister *Sara,* [die, legacies] to bee devided betwixt survivors children. *Richard Russell,* Executor. 24 : 1 : 1651.

My bro. *Thomas Shute* [added as joint Executor.]  *Robert Shute.*

Allowed & accepted 29 : 2 : 1651, wth the Inventory wch amounted to £84.15s.11d.  *Increase Nowell.*

---

## JAMES BROWNE of Boston.

9 : 3 : 1651. It is my will that my wife *Grace Browne* have my house & land during her life, & all my goods & moveables dureing her widdowhood, or till my sonne *James* come to the age of 21. In case my wife marry, sonne *James* shall have one half of my goods.—I comend the care of his education vnto my wife, & request her to be tenderly carefull of placeing my sonne to some such trade as he shall be most capable of. In case God take away my sonne ere he come to 21 yeares of age, then the children of *Thomas Stocker* of Rumney Marsh shall haue £10 out of my sonnes halfe of the goods, & the rest of the goods, also the house & land to service of Christ in this Church of Boston whereof I am a member, after the decease of my wife to be disposed of by the hands of the deacons. Wife executrix. In case of her death I comitt the care of my sonnes education vnto Elder *James Pen* & deacon *Ri : Truesdale.*

*James Penn*                                            *James Browne*
*William Aspinwall*      Testifyed in Court 7 (6) 1651 by *James Penn*
                                                      *Wm Aspinwall.*

---

## HENRY SANDYES.

Inventory taken by *Will Tynge & Thomas Clarke.* Estate Dr among others to *Samuell Skarlet; Nathaniel Hanford; Jnº Heard; Isaack Grosse;* mr *Jnº Turner; Joseph Jewet;* mr *Hill* yt liues wth mr *Wory;* mr *Samll Winslowe; Henr Phillips,* of Dedham; *Samll Carwithen* of Salem; *Edw Gillmon;* mr *Robert Pitts;* mr *Tho Cossen; James Henewood; George Gillum; Henr Chaplin;* mr *Marce Toker; Samuell Mayew; Tristrom Hull; Joseph Perry* of Seaquonck; *Jnº Yates* of Duxbery; mr *Huse,* Roxber; *Richard Benet,* of Virginia; *Richd Hougge; Tho Clarke,* smith; *Jnº Nash,* shoomaker; Nurce *meddowes; George Kendrick;* Goodm *Severn,* of Salsbery; *Tho Burges; Martin Stebbins; Euan Thomas; William Lane;* mr *Iverts,* of Linn; *Angell Hollet; Bartholl Barlowe; Tho Lunn;* Goodm *Craft;* Capt *Bridges; David Nicholls; Jnº Sunderland; Aurther Kane; Richard Andres,* for sheepe; *Jnº Myllum; Daniell Kinge; Jacob Greene,* of Charlestown; *Edw Preston;* mr *Ares; Jnº Tinker; Ben Gillum;* Goodwife *Buckmaster; Francis Smith;* mr *Oliuer,* in *Jnº Spurs* house; *Math. Ganet;* mr *Wm Phillips; Tho*

*Gardner,* of Roxbery ; *Hugh Drewry ; Robert Sharpe; Rich Harden,* of Brantre ; mʳ *Geo Parthurst ; Jno Harte ; Jnᵒ Browne,* of Providence ; *Jnᵒ Bradly ; Joseph Wormhull ; Mariam Wormhull ;* Goodm *Johnson* glover ; Goodm *Jackson,* of Sittuat ; *Elnathan Dunckly ; Math. Bright ; Jnᵒ Collens ; Tho Roberts ; Richʳᵈ Withington ;* Goodm *Wix* [Weeks ?] ; *Jno Balden ;* mʳ *Smith,* of Warwick ; mʳ *Makepeas ;* mʳ *Phillpot ; Mary Harris ; Nicho Hodsden ;* mʳ *Smith,* of Seconque ; *George Brume ; Nicho Vpshall ;* Goodm *Tyler,* of Linn ; *Phillepp Wharton ; George Benet ;* Goodm *Brackelbery ; Jobe Haukins ;* Goodm *Batemans* sister ; *Mary Duke ; Nathl Ganet ; Jnᵒ Gennings ;* Goodm *Southick ; Maxamill Jewet ; Jnᵒ Lake ; Will Basset ; Richʳᵈ Waiere ; Robʳᵗ Brick ; Edw Page ; Roger Clapp ; Moses Kaine ; James Wiseman ;* Goodm *Hall,* of Linn ; mʳ *Jnᵒ Vassell ; William Winborn ;* Goodm *Barnes,* Miller ; *Robert Darvell ; Richʳᵈ Norton ; Jnᵒ Crandell ; Nicho Clapp ; Wm Blancher ; John New-marsʰ ;* mʳ *Roger Williams,* of pvidence ; mʳ *John Hill ; G French,* Bran-tree ; Leift *Waker,* Winesimet ; *Robert Huly,* of Duxbercreeke ; mʳs *Mro-ly,* Brantre ; *Tho Holbrook,* Waymouth ; Goodm *Cooke,* oʳ Neighbor ; *Hen Chamberlin ; Hen Leonard,* of Linn ; *Tho Chamberlin,* Woeborn ; *Math Boyce,* Rowly ; Goodm *Lamb,* Roxbery ; *Daniell Baker,* for scotch cloth ; *Robert Nash,* on *Jer Goold's* accᵗ ; mʳ *Christo. Clarke's* wife ; *Jno Bond,* Nubery ; Good *Rugles,* Dorchester ; *Will Pond ; Edw Gills,* Salem ; *Samᵘ Jackson ; Wm Marchant,* Watertowne ; *Nicholas Norton,* Waymouth rest ; *Tho Pratt,* Doctoʳˢ wife, of Roxbery, widdo ; *Andrew Bellcher,* Cam-bridge ; *Hen Moslyes* wife ; Good *Borrell,* Noxbery ; Good *West,* Tanner ; mʳ *Pendleton,* Watertowne ; *Jnᵒ Wipple ;* Good *Eliot,* Brantree ; *Casarma-kine* Indian ; *Matt Bridges ; G Porter,* Roxbery ; Goodm *Pope,* Dorches-ter ; *Jno Yates,* Duxbery ; Good *Speere,* Brantre ; *Jno Keysly,* Barnstable ; *Jnᵒ Tinkers* other wifes sister ; *Nathᵘ Adams* wife, of Lin ; Goodm *Bow-man,* Watertown ; yᵉ Coop. by Goodm *Thomases ; Wᵐ Griggs,* at mʳ *New-gats* farme ; *Wm Poole,* at mʳ *Endicots ; Lidia Gulifore,* Dorchester ; *Mathew Knight,* Carpenter ; *Jnᵒ Watkins,* of Cambridg ; mʳ *Simkins,* Tay-loʳ ; *Math Dove ; Jno Harris,* Rowly ; *Wm Ludington,* Charlestow ; *G Waite,* Taylor ; *G. Killcupp ; Steephen Hoppkins,* Dorchʳ ; *G. Davis,* Carpenter ; *Nicho White ; Edw Hall,* Duxbery ; Goodm *Griffin,* of Ips-wich ; *Jno Morse ; Tho Andrews,* Dorchʳ ; *Robt Noyce,* Sudbery ; *Peeter Lials* wife, Roxbery ; *Nicho Allen,* Dorchʳ ; 7 : 11 : 1651.
  30 : 11 : 1651. *Jeremiah Howchin,* Admʳ.

---

### JOHN MILLS of Boston.

  Being sicke. *Samuell Mavericke, Robᵗ Knight, & Paull White,* Exec-utors. To *Liddia Townsend,* servant to Mʳ *Bucke,* in the requitall of paines taken about me, 40ˢ. To *John Peirse,* his foweɩ children, each, 20ˢ. To Mʳ *Cotton,* 40ˢ, Mʳ *Wilson,* 40ˢ. Debts & legacies pᵈ [remain-der] to be remitted to my friends, Mʳ *Ferdinando Bodey* and Mʳ *David Stephens,* marchants in the Canaries. 22 Oct 1651.
  *Thomas Parke*                               *John Mills.*
  *Richard Waite.*
  *Richard Waite* deposed 3 Dec. 1651. Mʳ *Sam : Mauericke* & mʳ *Rob-ert Knight* being willing only to accept of the executorship to yᵉ will, wᶜʰ the Court approved of. *Edw Rawson,* Recordʳ.

---

### SUSAN HAUGHS.
  Inventory 29 : 3 : 1651. £68. 12. 3. By *Thomas Savage* & *Edward Hutchinson.*

111

NATHANIELL BYOM.

Inventory. 7 May 1651. By *George Dell* m<sup>r</sup> of the Shipp. Witnesseth *Marcke Handes, Samuell Shattock. John Vassall* of sittuate, Administrator. 26 Oct. 1652.

JAMES ASTWOOD, of Boston.

Estate bee deuided into seven partes; to my wife *Sara* two partes of the seuen; sonn *James* two partes; sonn *John* on part, sonn *Joseph* on part; dau *Sara Astwood* on part. Portions to be paid my sonnes at the age of 21, to my daus at the age of 16. If any of the children die, legacies to be divided equally among the survivors. Wife to enjoy children's portions till theire several ages aforesayd. What estate I haue in our native Country in England whether in house or lands my executrix hath power to sell; debts discharged the remainder to be devided between my wife and sonn *James.* Wife Executrix. To bro. *John Astwood* £5. To Capt. *Thomas Clarke,* m<sup>r</sup> *Jaacob Sheath,* of Boston, and M<sup>r</sup> *William Parkes,* of Roxbury, my overseers, each £5. 17 Sept. 1653. Farther, my will is, to giue M<sup>rs</sup> *Jane Maverick,* 20s. *Dorothy Andrewes,* 20s. and my mayd servant *Sara Jackson,* 10s. I desire that I may haue my body buried at the feet of M<sup>r</sup> *Cotton,* as neere to him as I may, though not to hinder my betteres.

*John Astwood*                                         *James Astwood.*
*John Wilson*
*Thomas Rucke*

13 Oct 1653. mrs *Sarah Astwood,* late wife to M<sup>r</sup> *James Astwood* Appeared before the magists and did Renounce hir executrix ship bec. of hir going to England. *Edward Rawson,* Record<sup>r</sup> m<sup>r</sup> *Turner,* m<sup>r</sup> Deputy, m<sup>r</sup> *Nowell,* m<sup>r</sup> *Hibbins,* m<sup>r</sup> *Glouer.*

---

JOHN ROBERTS.

Deceased in the house of goodman *Stebbins,* 1652. Goods apprised by *William Reade, Godfree Armettage.*

*James Johnson & Robert Hull* having by the appointment of the Court administered on Estate desire that what remaineth may be given to the bro. of s<sup>d</sup> *John Roberts,* who liveth with Goodman *Buswell,* of Sallsbury; his Name is *Samuell Roberts.* There was as wee vnderstand A token of 20s. Comitted to the trust of this *Jn°* *Roberts,* by one in England, to be delivered to one *Jn° Fish,* that Liveth in the Jurisdiction of Conecticutt. Inventory, proved in Court, by *Capt. Johnson & Robt Hull,* 2 Feb. 1653, present m<sup>r</sup> *Nowell,* m<sup>r</sup> *Hibbins* & Recorder.

---

JAMES SMITH.

Lately died at Seacuncke. Power of Administration granted to *Amos Richardson,* of Boston. 7 Sept 1653.

---

RICHARD WALTER of Marden, Co. Kent. Eng.

Marriner, appoint Major *Symon Willard,* of Concord, & *Jacob Sheafe* of Boston, New England, Mchants, my lawfull Atturneys. 26 Aug. 1653.

*Thomas Savage*                                         *Richard Walter.*
*Edward Hutchinson,* sen Esq.

On representation of Cap<sup>t</sup> *Thomas Savage, Edward Hutchinson,* senio<sup>r</sup> & *Nathaniell Sowther,* the Court grant Power of Administration on Estate of s<sup>d</sup> *Walter* to *Symon Willard & Jacob Sheafe,* 7. Sep 1653. in behalfe of the wife of s<sup>d</sup> *Walter* or his neerest kindred. *Edwd Rawson* Record<sup>r</sup>

### ABRAHAM PALMER.

Marchant, late Inhabitant of Charltowne, who lately deceased at Barbados. Taken in Charltowne, New England; 29: 6: 1653. £165. 03. By *John Green, Robert Lyale, Thomas Lynde.* Proved 23: 7: 1653. Powor of Administration granted *Grace Palmer* on the Estate of her husband.

---

### EZRA CAVE.

Inventory of Estate prised 9. 7. 1653 by *Ricd Wayte, Robert Rayner* Amt *£25, 11. 02.* mentions *Martin Stebins, John Tilly;* A lad *Tho. Brumble.*

---

### ELIZABETH HOWING.

Estate prised 6 : 8 : 53. by *Rich : Truesdall.* Amt. *£83. 01. 03.* Paid Goodman *All cocke* for the Cow keepeing, 3s. 2 : 11 (53)

---

### DAVID SELLICK

Inventory taken 6 : 10 : 1654 by *Edward Hutchinson, Willm Paddy.* *Thomas Clark.* £478 ; one horse prised by *Christopher Gibson.* *Thomas Clark.* Thomas Clarke & deacon Wiswall deposed 4 Feb. 1657.

---

### JOHN SWEETE of Boston.

Bond 16 Jan 1654. for Administration on Estate of *Arthur Gill*, in behalfe of children of sᵈ *Arthur.*

$$\text{Jno} + \text{Sweete} \quad \text{marke}$$

Teste *John Gill*
    *William Awbrey*    Bond cancelled by order of Court
                           28 March 1656.        E. R., R.

---

### Bond of WM. FOLLETT of Oyster Riuer.

To the amount of £20. starlinge to *Edward Rawson.* dated 19 Sept. 1654. in behalfe of Laur. [rest of the name gone] Signed by *William Follett.* Witnessed by *Rachel Awbrey, Margaret Rawson.* [On the back] —" Folletts bond abt Amorys Estate."

---

### JONATHAN POND

*Steven Meares,* aged about 18 yeares testifieth and saith, That Liveing in Goodman *Sheppards* house, in Cambridg, a little before *Jonathan Pond* went last to sea, who lived in the same house when he was not at sea, the said deponent being in the Chamber wᵗʰ the said *Jonathan,* & seing him put his Clothes into a Chest, as[ked] him if he would carry them to sea, the said *Jonathan* answered no, I will leaue these with my mother, that if I com not agayne, shee may dispose of them, & so of all that I haue, onely that she out of thence first pay my debts, and I haue writt my mother a note to that purpose, & shew it vnto me, & I red it ouʳ, and I the deponent affirme that this hereto annexed is the very same note. Sworne In Court 19. 9ᵐᵒ· 1657.        Edw Rawson Recordʳ.

*Sara Pond,* neere 17 yeares of age, testifieth and saith, that she did see *Jonathan Pond* her brother, wright the said note & deliu'ed it to her mother, & thus said vnto his mother, I desire you to dispose of my estate if I com not agayne, & her[e] is a note to that purpose. Sworne In Court 19 : 9ᵐᵒ· 1657.        Edw Rawson, Recorder.

---

### JOHN WOODY, of Roxbury.

Debts due his Estate, &c. *Rich : Woodde, Isaac Woodde & Edmond Sheffield,* husband of the late *Mary Wooddy,* petition General Court,

" Whereas it hath pleased God by death to rmove *John Wooddy*, oᵣ kinse-man, the sonne of *John Wooddy*, late of Roxbury, oᵣ brother, being next heires unto said John," &c. do therefore desire power of Administration upon the estate 15. 8. 1657. Mr Coggan petitions in their behalf. The Estate consisted of a house, pᵗ of a mill, the rest in goods & Cattle, he haueing a wife & Child. The Court accept of mᵣ Coggans securitie for 70*lb.* as the Childs pᵗ in that estate, and 7 p añn. vntill the Childe com to the age of 21 yeares;—the house & pte of mille being before sold by the overseers—alowed so to do by order of Court—the Child dyes in its minoritie. Quest. who in right ought to enjoye the estate of this childe, deceaseing in its minoritie? The deputyes Voted, the Child or Children of the Woodyes, wᵗʰ reference to oᵣ honʳᵈ magistrates.

Signed, *Samuel Symonds, Eleazer Lusher, Roger Clap.* William Tor-rey, Clerk. The magistrates Consent heereto. Edw. Rawson, Secty.

-----

## THOMAS ROWELL.

Inventory. The marke of *John ʃ Farnum*, the elder, the marke of *Gorge Orriss.* Witness, *Walter Salter.*

*Richard Bradley* deposed 16. 9. 58.          Edw. Rawson, Recordʳ.

Mentions *Tho : Chamberlin*, off Chensford.

-----

## WILLIAM PADDY.

Inventory, taken 18 Sepᵗ. 1658. by *Josh. Scottow, Thomas Savage.* £537. 12. 00. Debts due the estate £2221. 6. 1½. Deposed p. Wᵐ Davis, 14 May 1663.

-----

## THOMAS ROWELL.

I *Thomas Rowell*, now resident in Boston, Wosted-comer, being sick—debts vnto the householder where I ly sicke be paid, and my Phisicke paid for, and funerall expences; what shal be Left ouerplus, (all my cloathes and what soeuᵣ else appertaineth vnto me from any pson) I giue vnto *Richard Bradly*, of Boston, shoemaker, whom I make my sole executor. 10 Sepᵗ. 1658.

Witnessed by *Philip Longe*                The marke  of

*David Ludecus Edling.*                          R

                                                          Thomas Rowell.

15 Oct. 1658. *Philip Long* deposed. pʳsent Depᵗ Govʳ, majʳ Atherton & Recordʳ.                                   Edw. Rawson.

I *David Ludecus Edling* doe declare by these presents that I Would Willingly haue tacken my Oath, iff Capt. *Josua Hobbertt* hath had the power Concerning this Will and Testament off *Thomas Rowell*, but that some Certaine occasions about sick poeple doeth hinder mee that I cannott come att present to Boston, butt if occasion requireth When 1 Come to Boston, shall bee ready as aforesayd, etc.

Witnes : *Joshua Hubberd.*                     *David Ludecus Edling.*

-----

## RICHARD WOODY of Roxbury.

Being sick.—Vnto Eldest sonn *Richard*, his Heyers the Howse, yard, barne, orchard, home lott & wood lott, Prouided that *Richard* lett my wife haue his owne howse in Roxbury & the Chambers ouer it for her Comfortable dwelling duringe life, and soe much of the yard as belonge to it, and the stable & his parte of the orchard vnto the Crosse fence that part the orchard and the Land, this in Consederation of her thirds of my land : to my wife all my Corne in my howse, all my Hay and my Horse,

114

vnto her and her too Children, the wood in the yard, my butter, Cheese, frute and hoggs; also I giue her halfe of the linnen I haue purchased since I married her, and halfe that w^ch she made her selfe, also all the Cotton [      ] woole, that is in the howse, and flax, the twoo wheeles, the bedstead in the little Chamber, a Chayer.    Vnto son *Isaack*, all the moueables in the Hall Chamber, the beds and its furniture, Table, forme, Chayer and Chest.    My will is that my Exector pay my sonn *Isack* £15. within one yeare after my departure.    To my dau. *Mary Sheffield*, the bed whereon I lye in the kitchin, w^th all the furniture belongeinge thervnto, and my Byble, also £10.    My mynde is, that all thinges my wife brought w^th her when we married & since may be returned vnto her back againe. The rest of myne estate, sonn *Richard* myne Exector to diuide between my thre Children.    The other halfe of the Linnen, to be to the proper vse of my sonn *Richard* ; also the warminge pann & a kettle, I giue my wife duringe her life. 24 Sept. 1658.                              Richard Woody. Witnesse *Daniel Weld, Thomas Weld.*

    *Thomas Weld* deposed 16 Dec^r 1658.    Edw. Rawson, Record^r.

# ABSTRACTS FROM THE EARLIEST WILLS ON FILE IN THE COUNTY OF SUFFOLK, MASS.

[Prepared by Mr. Wm. B. Trask, of Dorchester.]

[The following Abstracts are of Inventories from the second volume of the Probate Records, which volume consists entirely of Inventories. The first volume is of wills.—W. B. T.]

Peter Fitchew.—Boston 3 : of yᵉ 18. 1639. Before *Jo: Winthrop* Esq. Governoʳ. upon vieue of the dead bodye of *Petter Fitchew* found drowned in the salt-water neere the house of Mr. *Rainsford.*

Jury. Tho: Grubb, Rich: Gridley, Tho: Wheeler, Rich Cooke, William Penye, Jo: Sparowe, Tho: Savage, Willᵐ Netheland, Rich Truesdale, Alexander Beck, Jo Webbe, Nathanell Woodward.

Sworne and Charged to enquire how the sᵈ *Petter Fitchew* came to his death.—Did find that he had wilfull drowned himselfe and so was felo de se, & guilty of his owne death. The reason of there verdict was—:

1. That it was not neere any path—2: it was in the day time ; he had layed by his hatt & Coat & 30*s* in money : it was not his depth in Watter ; he came passinger in the Champion & did Atempt to distroy himselfe in the Ship.

Inventory of his Goods preised by *Jo: Long, Edward Converse* and *Richard Brackett.* £4: 18: 10. Charges to *Rich. Brackett*—to those that buried him, 5*s* ; to Goodᵐ *Winge* foʳ Atendance, 6*s* ; to him that found him, 2*s* ; to the Records, 2*s* ; to *Richard Trigge* for his payns wᵗʰ him in the ship, 10*s.*

---

Tho. Blainfeeld.—Inventory. [no date.]  Amt £50.

---

Alice Jones, of Dorchester.  Inventory of her goods signifyed wᵗʰ her hands the 2ᵈ day of 12ᵐᵒ. 1642. £52. 6. 8.—to her son *Timothie,* £4 : 4*s : 8d.* [She was widow of Richard Jones of Dorchester. See *Hist. Dorchester*, p. 61.]

---

Thomas Bagnley.—Inventory. 28: 8: 1643.  £22: 08: 9.  [See vol. ii. (1848) p. 185.] | (See p. 10)

---

George Barrell of Boston.  Inventory. 31: 8: 1643.  " 2 Acres of land at Spectacle Island 2*lb*" &c. &c.  Amt £133. 6ᵈ.  Testifyed by *James Everill* before Mʳ *Nowell* the 30ᵗʰ of the 8ᵐᵒ. 1643. [See Will of Geo. Barrell, vol. ii. p. 383.] (See p. 15).

---

Elisabeth Hubbard.—Inventory of Elisabeth Hubbard, widdowe of Boston, who deceased the 6: 11ᵐᵒ. 1643. By Robert Hull & Thomas Clarke, given in the 4 (7) 1644 before mʳ Increase Nowell. £239. 18. Mention is made of Mr. & Mrs. Corington.

---

George Phillips.—July 22. 1644. [Margin, 6 (7) 44.]  Inventory

116

taken by Ephraim Child, Thomas Hastings, Nicholas Guye, Symon Stone. Amt. £553. 02. 09. " It<sup>m</sup> the study of bookes, £71. 09. 09."

NATHAN HALSTED.—Inventory of the goods of *Nathan Halsted*, late of Concord, deceased, taken the 5: 12: 1643. Amt. £213. 13s. 02d.

EDWARD PARILL of Watertown. Inventory. 24 June, 1644. Mentions *John Winter*, marsh by *Eph Child* in Cambridge bounds, *Thomas Mayhew, Samuell Shepherd, Isack Stearnes, Rob<sup>t</sup>. Lockwood*, also M<sup>r</sup>. *Treyrice* of Charltow.

JOHN GOSSE of Watertowne. Inventory, taken 14: 3: 1644, [margin, 12: 9:] by *Rich. Beeres, Thomas Hastings*. Amt. £85. 05. Testifyed by *Robt. Nicholls* before *John Winthrop*, dept. *Increase Nowell*, secret.

THOMAS KING of Watertowne. 24: 10: 1644, [margin, 23 (2) 1645.] Debts at Sudbury, Pastor *Browne*, £1 ; *John Rutter*, £2 ; *B. Smith*, £2. 3s ; Mr. *Will<sup>m</sup> Pellam*, 14s ; Debts at Cambridge ; *John Jackson*, 11s ; m<sup>r</sup> *Way* 19s ; Debts at Boston ; m<sup>r</sup> *Coggan*, £6. 10s ; *George Oris*, 6s ; *Anthony Beares*, £1. Debts at Watertowne ; *Thom. Winkle*, £4 5s ; *John Stowers*, 4s ; *John Sternes*, £1. 10s ; *John Kemball*, 5s ; *John Merchant*, 5s ; *John Prescote*, 12s ; *Joseph Bearesto*, £2 ; M<sup>r</sup> *Kiers*, 9s ; *James Cuttler*, 10s ; of the Indyans, £18 ; of *James Luxford* by a verdict of Court, £32, &c. &c. Taken by *Joh: Sherman, John Coolidge, Hugh Mason*.

MR. JOHN SIMSON of Watertown. Dyed intestate. Amt. of inventory, £74. 05. 04. Taken by *Richard Browne, Mallachie Browning, Nicholas Guye, George Parkhurst, Susanna Parkhurst*. Sworne by *Geo. & Susanna Parkehurst* before the Court, 24 (2) 1645. p. Mr. *Nowell*. Mentions homested of 12 Acres ; 6 Acres of land neere vnto the meeting howse sould vnto *W<sup>m</sup> Page* for £9 ; sould to *Symon Heyers* 4 Acres on the plain, of plow land, for £1. 12s ; 2 Acres of Meddowe in piggs gusset, sould to *Boyden*, £6.

JOHN GRAVE the yonger, late of Roxbury. Inventory taken 13 (4) 1646. Testifyed by *Philip Eliot*. Mentions *James Morgin*, Mr *Prichard, Griffin Craft* ; 17 bushels of wheate measured by *John Stonehard* vnto me at 4s p bushel ; 8 bushells of Indian and Rye vnto his mother ; 5s received of *Thomas Reeves*. *William Aspinwall*, v Record<sup>r</sup>.

AMY STOWER.—Inventory of *Amy Stower* wid of *Nicholas Stower* late deceased. Taken 1 (5) 1646. Amt £165. 04: 06. [See Will of Nicholas Stower, vol. iii. (1849) p. 179.] (See p. 27).

JOHN SCARBARROW, of Roxbury. Inventory, 17: 12: 1646. Land bought of *Isaac Heath*, £50. &c. Total £91: 06: 04.

THOMAS LAMB, of Roxbury. Inventory, taken this last of the first mo. 1646, prised by *W<sup>m</sup> Denison, Joshua Hues, W<sup>v</sup> Parke*, Amt. £112: 08: 08.

*Thomas Atkinson*, of Concord.—Inventory 16 (9) 1646. *Simon Willard, Tho. Brookes, Georg Wheeler*, prizers. Indebted, £9. 10s. The sum w^ch debts pay, £59. 05s. : 1d. He had £80 in England to rec. & some little he hath rec. but it is not knowne what, vntill intelligence comes the next yeare. Administration granted to *Susan*, his wife, 25 (9) 1646.

THOMAS COYTMORE, of Charlestowne.—Inventory taken 21 (5) 1645. Amt. £1255. 04. 06. " Part in the new mill, £124. 6s. 6d." [See Will, vol. vii. (1853) p. 32. (See p. 87).

ROBERT STARKE—28 : 8: 1846. Amt £10. 08. 04. Debts due from estate £13. 13s 8d. Capt. *Willard, Joseph Wheeler, Richard Lettin* (?) allowed Administration. 31. (8) 1646.

WILLIAM GOODRICH, of Watertowne.—Inventory taken by *Samuel Thatcher* & *Thomas Hastings*, Apr. 3, 1647. Due from *Henry Ambrose*, of Hampton, £1. 12s. *Margaret*, wife of s^d *William*, testifyed, 15 (2) 1647, before *John Winthrop*, Gov^r.

ROBERT EDWARDS, of Concord.—Inventory 18 (10) 1646. Amt. £56. 14. 03. Witness, *Symon Willard, Joseph Wheeler, Geo. Heiward*.

WIDDOW ANN GOULDSTONE.—An Inventory of all such goods as were widdow *Gold stones*, & in her possession before she entred into a Married estate.
*Anne Geor[ge]* late wife of *Henry Gouldston* testifies that is a true Inventory of his estate. Before Court 29 (4) 1647.

HERMON ATWOOD.—Inventory prised 13 : 8 : 1651, by *James Johnson, Nathañiel Willjams*. £34. 03s. Proved 19. 9. 1651. Power of Administration granted to *Ann Atwood*, wife of the deceased, in behalfe of hir selfe & two children. Edward Rawson, Record^r.

RICHARD JARRETT.—Valluation of his goods taken by *John Bayly* & *John Peach* the 4. 8. 1651. £13. 01. 02. A true Inventory, deposed by *John. Sunderland*, excepting two Se^rvants, wch are £8 a peece. 20. 9. 1651. Edward Rawson, Record^r.

PEETER THORNTON.—Att a County Court held at Boston. 9 Feb. 1651. Inventory aprized by *John Sunderland* & *William Ludkin*, 22 : 11, 1651. £45. 17. Debts he owed £5. *Mary Thornton* deposed 9^th Feb., that this was a true Inventory of hir husbands estate. *John Sunderland* & *William Ludkin* deposed, that being with *Peeter Thornton*, as he lay on his death bed, they heard sajd *Thornton* say, that the little goods & estate he had he left to his wife to bring vp his children. The Court Graunted Administration on y^e Estate, to *Mary* his widdow. Edward Rawson, Recorder.

MARY SEARES.—Administration on Estate granted to *John Sunderland*, on behalfe of *Daniell Seares*, hir husband, now at sea, 9 Feb. 1651. Inventory signed, *John* I^mark *Sunderlands*, *John* ⋈^mark *Cuenfeild*.

118

HENRY SANDIS,—Inventory of Estate Apprised p *Richard Parker*, *Edward Ting, Thomas Makepeace, Bozoone Allin*, 17. 10. 1651. *Jeremiah Hauchin*, Adm^r.

---

GRACE BROWNE, Wid. of James Browne.—Inventory of estate prized by *James Johnson, Nathaniell Williams*, 10 : 9 : 1651. £246. 17. 09. Elder *James Penne* deposed, 28 : 11 : 1651. [See Will, vol. vii. p. 335.] *

JOHN SHEPPARD of Braintry.—Intestate. Inventory taken by *Beniamin Albie, Henry Adams*, 22 : 7 : 1650. £78. 06. 01. *Margaret*, wid. to *John Shepperd*, deposed, 27 April 1652. Same day, Administration granted her, provided, if shee marry againe before her marriage, s^d estate shall subiect to the distribution of the Court respecting her children. *Edward Rawson*, Record.

---

WILLIAM LUDKIN, who deceased the 27. 1^mo. 1652.—Inventory taken by *Tho. Mason, John Odlin*. Amt. 158. 16. Administration granted to *Elizabeth* wid. of *William Ludkin* for herself & two children. Wid. to have the vse of the whole estate, till the Children come to age, or shee change hir condicon, in w^ch case she to haue one third pt, the sonne two parts of what remaynes, the rest to the daughter. *Elizabeth Ludkin*, deposed, 29 April, 1652.

---

GEORGE BENNETT of Boston.—Inventory £90. 03. 08. 6 Aug. 1652, *Adey*, wid. of *George Bennett* deposed. Administration granted to s^d *Andrey* 29 Aprill 1652, in behalf of herself & child now liueing, & that shee goeth withall, & the Court orders that she haue a third pt of the estate, eldest child a duble porcon, the rest to yt shee goeth w^th all. In case that child dies or that it comes not to life, then the widdow to have half of y^e whole estate. Debts due from *John Lowe, Nath^l Hunne, Rob^t Woodward*. Estate indebted to Mr. *Michalson*, the marshall ; Mr *Thomas Lake*, Mr *Rob^t Lord*, *Joseph Bastor, John Wilkey*, Mr *Shrimpton*, goodwife *Prior, Zacharie Phillips*, goodman *Vpshall*, goodwife *Burton, Edward Yeomans, Thomas Swetman*, of Cambridge ; *John Beedeman*. Whole estate, debts discharged £87. 14. 7½.

---

ELIZABETH FISHER of Dedham, Who died intested, 21 : 11^mo. 1651 ; praised by *Henry Chickrin, Anthony Fisher, John* 11 the mark of *Luson*, 10. 12. 1651. Amt. 54. 09. 08*d*. Debts due from her to others, £4. 9*s* 3*d*.

---

BAZELIELL PAYTON, Mariner.—Inventory taken by *Barnabas Fare, Thomas Lake* 21 (9) 51. Amt. £265, 19. 08. " To goodman *Foster* in England, £3. 10." Balance of estate, debts deducted, £186. 03. 06.

---

WILLIAM BUTLER.—Inventory brought in by Mr. *Nowell* who was the Administrator. [No date.]

---

ABRAHAM MELLOWES.—Inventory prized by *Tho : Marshall, James Everill*. [No date.]

*See p. 110.

119

Mr. Guy.—Wee vnder written, being desired to apprize a p'cell of Goods for *Mr. Guy* estimate as followeth, &c.   Amt. £62. 11.  p. me *Richard Russell, John Allen.*

---

Capt. Howsen—County Court, Boston, 13. 10. 1652.  Mr *Sam¹ Maverick*, Mr *Robert Knight*, Mr *Benj. Gillam* & *Joshua Scottow*, as agent for Major *Edward Gibbons* ; & Capt. *Tho. Clarke*, agent for Mr *Dauid Yale*, who was admitted to Joyne wᵗʰ the other three as Administratoʳ to the estate of Capt *Howsen*, depose, estate ought to have (p. Shipp Brocke sold at £380. old iron sold by *Benj Gillam*.  Bills of *Thomas Chambers*, *Thomas Pacy, John Turner*,) £425. 15       *Edward Rawson*, Record.

---

Mr. Adam Winthrop.—Inventory taken by *Edward Rawson, Thomas Lake*, 4 Sept 1652.  Mrs *Elizabeth*, wid. of *Adam Winthrop* deposed, 27 Jan. 1652.  Due the estate by bill of sale of a pte of ship Expectation & Cargo ; more from Mʳ. *Turner*, from Mr *Jno Treworgy*, £25, and from Mʳ *Jno Paris*, a negro, wᶜʰ I Attest.  *Edw Rawson*, Recorder.

Robert Button.—Inventory taken 21. 11. 1650.  Amt £66. 17. 07. Signed by Capt Bozoone Allen, Edward Tinge 10 (1) 1652.  Debts recᵈ from Mʳ Tho. Venner, Tho. Ford, Mʳ Browneing, Robt Moone, John Stowe, Mr Sands, Peter Pitford, Tho Yeew, Joseph Phippeney, John Langdon, John Lake, Henry Warwicke, Marke Hams, Docter Steuens, Robert Collins, Sampson Shoare, George Mullings, Math. Abdie, Good Carley, Geo. Dod, Joseph Hardin, Edward Hasty, Emanuell Clarke, Edward Jackson, Job Judkin, Tho. Swetman, Joseph Moore, Robert Gray, Capt. Shaplej, Rich Waite, Willm Kirbey Jun, Peter Paine, Tho. Scottowe, John Culliner, Isac Tasker, Math Coe, Ralph Parker, Nicholas Laurence, Mr Willᵐ Paine, Christopher Gibson, Franc Littlefield, John Lewis, John Wilkey, Humphrey Milam, Edward Sturges, Edward Arnald, Ed. Cowell, James Dennis, Wiliᵐ Philpott, James Hawkins, John Hardin, Dauid Tichborne, Angell Holland, Willm Briggs, good. Collins, Math Hawke, John Prince, Joshua Stubbs, Peter Truesdell.  The above debts presented to the Court 10. 1ᵐᵒ. 4̷9̷ by vs, Tho. Sauage, Hezekiah Vsher.

Debts oweing to Rich Lippencut, Capt All, Sam. Oliver, Antho : Newland, Robt Wright, Brother Sauage, Henry Messinger, Tho : Jenner, &c. £441. 09. 09.

Doubtfull debts, &c —Mʳ Francis Johnson, Mʳ Willᵐ Alford, Roger Hanniwell, Mʳ Isac Walker, Ambrose Berry, Edward Wells, Mr Holgraue, Mʳ Hohnan, John Trumball, John Crabtree, Tho : Bowen, John Keagle, Peter Dier, Rich : Coman, Goody Wormod, John Ball, Tho Tilleston, Willᵐ Evans for Tho. Finder, Peter Pitford, Macklin Hucstable, Erasamus James, Siluester Stovard, Math Gillit, Thos Turpin, John Harker, Mr Ed. Mittison, John Marable, Mʳ Spencer for Henry Warvicke, Mr Bud, Tho : Warner, Willm Gibons, Sam : Jewell, Rowland Yonge, Robt Barrett, Mr. Hust, John Milam, Lauce Baker, John Bushe, John Lorans, John Bushenell, Mannell Clarke, Edward Coleman, John Comer, Good Healy, John Swasey, Strong Furnill, Nath : Beales, John Marchant, Willm Beamesley, Peter Paine, Phill : Gurwell, Rich : Hutton, Goodman Farrey, Hugh Gullison.

Pettie Debts —Tho Gaige, Nicho : White, John Taboies, Mrs Goose, Adam Westgait, John Beckett, Phillip Swadden, Robt Field, Humphrey Horne, Robt Edmunds. John Loker, Math : Mayhew, Isac Woody, Edw :

Gilman, John Stone, Rich Harine, Willm Bassitt, John Hardin, Caleb Corwithie, Robt Henfield, Franc Smith, Nath: Greene, Sam: Lincolne, Henry Tailer, Jo: Andras, Nich: Whitmarshe, John Tode, Good Codman, Tho: Welsh, Arthur Clarke, good Pitts, Laurence Walter, Henry True, Jo: Dawes, Franc Perrie, Tho: Gardner, Philemon Dickeson, Philip Longe, Benj: Boseworth & Ralph Smith, John Nuemarke, Mʳ Francis Knight, John Wilkie, Ben Waire, Edward Clarke, Jo: Bennett, Henry Singleman, John Bodman, Tho: Mercer, John Demericke, Jonathan Webb. Taken out of the bookes of Mʳ Robᵗ Button by vs this 10: 1ᵐ⁰ $\frac{42}{53}$ Tho: Savage, Hezekiah Vsher. Mrs Abigell Hutchinson formerly Wife to Mʳ Robert Button, deposed. *Edward Rawson*, Recod. [Will, vol. vii. p. 334. (See p. 109).

---

EDWARD HOWE.—Edward Howe who deceased at Watertowne 24: 4. 1644. Inventory taken by *John Knowles, Wᵐ Jenison, John Sherman*. Mentions land by *John Winters*, vpland by *Gregory Taylors*, marsh by *Ephraim Child*, in Cambridge bounds. Debts owing him a bond vppon *Thomas Mahew*, £400; due from *Samuell Shepheard*, £15; from *Isaac Sterne* & *Robert Lockwood*, £21; from Mr. *Trereise*, of Charlestowne Village: £8.

---

JOHN BENJAMIN of Watertown.—Inventory taken by *Symon Stowe*, [*Stone ?*] *John Eddye, Thomas Marret*, before Thomas Dudley Gover. & John Winthrop dep. Gover 3. (5) 1645. Mentions the lot bought of *John Bernard*, land of Capt *Sedg[wick]* &c. &c.

HENRY PLIMPTON,—Inventory—Taken by *Rich: Waite*. Proved 3 Feb. 1652, before Mr Bellingham, Mr Nowell, Mr Hibbins & Mr Glouer. Amt. £34: 03: 03. [Will, Vol. V. (1851) p. 239. (See p. 41)

DOROTHIE KING, Deceased wife of *John King*, of Waymouth, Seaman—Inventory taken by *Nicholas Phillips*, 18. 8. 1652. The Magistrates approue of his Inventory so as the husband acknowledgeth yᵉ goodes by his Consent to be so disposed of on oath of the Executor. Edwᵈ Rawson, Recordeʳ.

---

JOHN HOLMAN.—Inventory taken 18: 1ᵐ⁰: 52 or 53. Some totall £739. 16. This Inventory Accepted prouided yᵉ executrix Appeare before the next County Court giue in securitie for the Childrens porcons. Edward Rawson Recordʳ. Praysers of the goods, Rich: Collicott, Willᵐ Robenson of Dorchester. [Will, Vol. V. p. 242.] (See p. 44).

CAPT. BOZONE ALLEN.—Inventory taken by Mr Edward Hutchinson & Mr Joseph Rocke, 22 Sept 1652. Mentions land in England purchased of Mr Josiah Stanborough.
Debts due the estate from individuals belonging to the following towns: *Boston*—Mr Parker, Franc Robinson, Mr Cooke, Willm Cotton, Mr Walker, Mr Webb, John Heard, Capt Thomas Clarke, Mr Gibson, Isaack Woody, Thomas Grub, John Shawe, good Fawer, Mr Batt, good Armitage, Henry Blacke, Mr Sowther, Rich Woodowes, goodⁿ Eddington, good Lewis, Hugh Drury, Capt Tinge, John Harrison. Mr Harwood, John Sunderland, John Baker, smyth; Mr Auberry, goodman Lowe, John Lang-

ley, John Hart, Euan Thomas, Henry Rust, Math Williams, Tho : Wilshire, Mr Martin, Mr Bushnell, Thomas Joy, Will^m Lane, Mr Knight.

*Hingham*—Thomas Johnson, John Fearing, Mr Woodward, Stephen Gates, Edward Pitts, Will^m Hearsey, Marke Hams, Thomas Mashe, Daniell Lyncolne, Tho : Lincolne, John Oates, John Sutton, Nicho : Jacob, Franc James, James Whitten, Nath : Beales, John Lasell, Will^m Ripley, John Smyth, Will^m Backland, Sam : Parker, John Foulsome, John Louit, Edmund Hubbard, Mathew Cushion Jun^r, Mathew Cushion sen, Mathew Hawke, Daniell Cushion, John Lobdon, John Balls Jun^r, Thomas Thaxter, Nathaniell Baker, Mr Hubbard, Henry Wade, Tho : Lewit, Isaack Wright, Robert Jones, Ralph Smyth, Moyses Colyer, Michaell Perce, Joseph Jones.

*Weymouth*—Left Torrey, Mr Kinge, Ensigne Whitman, Nicho : Norton, James Nashe, Goody Bridges, George Fray, Good Kingman sen^r, James Prest, Edward Pode.

*Hull.*—John Prince, Nicholas Baker, Tho : Jones, Tho : Loreing, Ralph Greene, Nathaniell Boseworth, Richard Stubbs, Mr Ward, goodma Bonson, [       ] Stevens.

*Rehoboth.*—Thomas Cooper, Stephen Paine, Mr Pecke, Daniell Smyth, Judeth Smyth.

*Charlestown.*—Capt Allen, Mr Garrett, Mr Russell, Aaron Ludkin.

*Dorchester.*—Mr Collecot, Mr Leads, good : Way, [John?] Grinaway, Mr Foster. *Cambridge*—Mr Swetman, Mr Michelson. *Roxbury.*—Mr Gore, Mr Alcock, goodma Chenney, Sera^t Craft, Will^m Healey. *Rowley*—Mr Joseph Jewett, Mr Rogers. *Salem*—Samuell Archer. *Misticke*—Rich : Dexter. *Lynn*—Jos : Jenkes, Capt Bridges. *Nashaway*—John Prescott. *Taunton*—Tho : Lyncolne, Jonas Awstin. *Yarmouth*—Mr Hedge. *Providence*—Mr John Sailes. *Reading*—Sam Walker. *Sudbury*—Peter Bent. *Nodles Island*—Mr Mauericke, John Gore. *Ipswich*—Edward Gilman. *Scituate*—John Palmer, Geo. Russell, *Malden*—Tho : Hett. *Weniey Symett*—Leift Walker. *Plymouth*—Mr Paddy, Mr Groomes. *Braintree*—Henry Adams. *Exeter*—Edward Gilman. *Accomenticus*—goodm Knight. *Newhaven*—Mr Pecke. *Pascataq^a*—Mr Gunnison. *Longe Island*—Mr Joseph Yonge. *London*—Mr Caleb Foote. *Virginia*—Michaell Williams.

Other names, places not mentioned :—Edw Arnall, butcher, Tho : Boyden, carter, John Collins, shoemaker, George Allen, bricklayer, Bartho : Barlowe, cooper, good Rawlins, brickmaker, Goodma Euins, shoemaker, John Johnson, saylemaker, Christopher Perkins, porter, Mr Baughtons, brewer, Geo : Halsall, the smyth, Robt : Nashe, butcher, Edward Jackson, shoemaker, Mr Clarke, shipma^r, Thomas Baker, the smythe, Nathaniell Williams, glouer, goodman Ward, shipwright, Widd Grosse, John Bersto, at Mr Hibbinses farme, Mr Atkinson, Lieut Joshua Hubbard, Mr John Hill, Mathias Briges, Mr Thomas Hawkner, Anthony Hams, Robt Bradford, Mr James Oliuer, Mr Samuell Oliuer, Mr Peacock, Angell Hallett, Thomas Noble, Mr Henbury, Franc Dowse, Capt Dauenport, Mr Will^m Phillips, Capt Simpkins, Mr Richard Woody, Mr Alford, Tho : Shawe, Hugh Durdell, Daniell Church, Jeremiah Burrowes, John Porter, Josiah Keayne, John Stoddard, Widd Hourle, Goodman Gridley, Mr Edward Tinge, Will^m Norman & ptners, Mr Philip Sweden, Mr Burt, Mr Dauison, Mr Cole Jun^r, Mr Cutting, Mr Hopkins, Mr. Lampere, Thomas Phillips, Mr John Ainger, Stronge Furnell, Ralph Hill, Left Will^m Hudson, John Garnett, Mr Astwood, Thomas Gill, John Goure, Thomas Harmon, Mr Halgraue, Zachery Phillips, Capt Daniell Hough, Geo : Vicory, Mr Blackleach, Mr Fishe, Benj Phippen, Elder Elliots, sonne, Mr Leader, Job Hawkins, Mr Venner, Mr Samson, Samuell Norden, Mr Coles daughter, Sampson Shoare, Tho : Thorowgood, Edward Gold, Edward Kingman, Jun<sup>r</sup>, Cornelius Cantlebury, Will<sup>m</sup> Woodcocke, Mr Silliocke, Roger Amydowne.

Debts to be p<sup>d</sup> out of the estate, to Mr Brettle ; John Chickley, John Beales, of Hingham ; Rob<sup>t</sup> Turner at the Ancor ; Mr Makepeace ; Mr Powell ; Stephen Lyncolne ; Mr Chickering of Dedham ; Mr John Woodmansey ; Mr Tinker, Mr Rucke ; Will<sup>m</sup> White ; Capt Breedon ; Mr Glouer, of Dorchester ; Mr Bradstreete ; Nicholas Phillips ; Mr John Vassell ; Mr Maddocks ; Tho : Roberts the hatter ; John Bacers, of Plymouth ; Mr Busby ; Mr Wood ; Mr Ruggles ; Mr Wilson ; Mr Denison ; Tho : Duer ; Mr Dauenport ; Mr Johnson ; Mr Starr ; Will<sup>m</sup> Penne ; goodwife Bennett ; Richard Trewsdell ; James Richards ; M<sup>rs</sup> Perrey ; Zachey Boseworth ; Mr Samuell Hutchinson ; M<sup>r</sup> Houchin ; Goodman Messenger ; John Lake ; Goodman Stibbins ; Will<sup>m</sup> Kilcup ; Mr Powell ; Mr Marshall ; Mr Hubbard w<sup>th</sup> what was giuen by Will, £10 ; Debts in England to Leift Coll Cushion & others.  Boston Vlt, Aprilis 1653. *Mrs Anne Allen* deposed.  *Edw<sup>d</sup> Rawson*, Record<sup>r</sup>. [Will, Vol. V. p. 299.] *

---

Capt William Tinge, of Boston.—Inventory made 25 : 3 : 1653 by *Natha : Duncan, Antho : Stoddard, Willm Dauis.*  Amt £2774. 14. 04. Mentions *Geo: Spencer's* farme. Also the names of about seventy vols ot Books in folio, quarto, &c.  Mr *Edward Tinge* bro of Capt *William Tinge*, deposed, before *Mr Nowell, Mr Hibbins. Mr Glouer* & y<sup>e</sup> Record. er.  *Edward Rawson*, Recor<sup>d</sup>.

---

John Cooper.—Inventory.  [No date.]  *Thomas Dier* deposed, 9 June, 53.

---

James Astod, of Boston.—Inventory taken. 6 : 8. 1653. Signed *James Euerill.*  The Sum £85: 10 : 20 : 1653, *John Johnson, Phillip Eliot, William Potter.*

---

Samuell Bass, the younger, of Brantrey. Yeoman, deceased.—Inventory made by Capt *Humphrey Atherton*, Deac. *Parkes, Richard Bracket, Francis Elliot, Edmund Sheffield* y<sup>e</sup> 15. 3<sup>m</sup>. 1653. Sum totall, £201. 18. 05.  *Mary Bass,* widdow, deposed, 22 Dec. 53.

The Magistrats, on y<sup>e</sup> widdowes Relinquishing her Right in y<sup>e</sup> Thirds, did Judge it meete that y<sup>e</sup> whole Estate be equally deuided betweene the Mother and the Child ; that M<sup>r</sup> *Howard* in behalfe of his daughter, giue securitje to deliuer s<sup>d</sup> Child of *Sam<sup>l</sup> Basse* one halfe of s<sup>d</sup> Estate at y<sup>e</sup> Age of 14 yeres.  *Edward Rawson*, Record<sup>r</sup>.

---

William Blanchard, of Boston.  Taylor.—Inventorie of his goods taken 20 Oct. 1652, by *Edmund Jackson, James Everell, Nath<sup>ll</sup> Sowther.* Sum total £236. 03. 02. Debts oweing by him £88. 14. *Hannah Everill* deposed 18 Nov 1652 that this is a true Inventory of the estate of *Will<sup>m</sup> Blanchard*, her late husband, so far as she knowes.  [Will, Vol. V, p. 239.] (See p. 41).

*See p. 49.

## ABSTRACTS FROM THE EARLIEST WILLS ON FILE IN THE COUNTY OF SUFFOLK, MASS.

[Prepared by Mr. WM. B. TRASK, of Dorchester.

MR. JOHN COTTON.—Deceased 23d Dec. 1652. Inventory of the estate taken 17 Jan. 1652, by *Jo. Leveret, Willm. Colburn, Ja: Penn.* Amt £1038.04. Proved 27 Jan. 1652, by *Mrs. Sarah Cotton.* Mentions, the dwelling house at Boston, yᵉ ground before & backside & other side of yᵉ hill, besides yᵉ fourth pt built by Sʳ *Henry Vaine.* The farme at Muddy River, 260 acres. [Will, vol. v. p. 240.] (See p. 42).

JOHN LOW, of Boston.—Inventory, 28 (11) 1653. Amt. £500: 11ˢ. Taken by *Josh: Scottew, Jnᵒ Barrell.* Estate indebted to goodman *Cuke,* Mʳ *Padishall,* Mʳ *Scotaway,* Mʳ *Workeʳ,* Goodman *Packer,* Goodman *Tomas,* good wife *Benitt, Richard Benit,* Mʳ *Stoder,* goodman *Holsey,* good wife *Vane,* goodman *Gridley,* and others. Amt. £214. 01. Power

of Administration granted to *Anthony Lowe,* his sone, so as he duely prouides for his Mother Comfortable Maintaineance dureing her life. *Anthony Lowe* deposed.

---

SAMUELL OLIUER.—Inventory taken 5 (11) 1653, by *James Johnson,
Jn° Floyd, Thomas Clarke.* Amt. £450. Accepted 12 (11) 1653.

---

ROBT WOODWARD.—Inventory taken, 3 March, 1653. Amt £119.09.06.
Deceased oweth to *Thomas Sauage,* £7. 5ˢ. 7ᵈ. 7 March, 1653. Power
of Administration granted *Rachell Woodward,* his wife, in behalfe of her
selfe & Children. *Rachell Woodward* deposed.

---

THOMAS THAXTER, of Hingham.—Inventory taken 20 Feb 1653, by
*Joshua Hubbard, Matt. Hawke.* Amt. £213. 18ˢ. 04. *Elizabeth Thaxter,*
his wid. deposed March 9, 1653–4. Signed, by *Joseph Hubbard, Matt.
Hawke, Jn° Leavitt.* Recorded yᵉ 7ᵗʰ of May, 1654.
In Book 2. Suffolk Records, p. 15, is a petition to the Court, for a
Division of the Estate of *Tho: Thaxter* of Hingham, who died intestate,
leaving an Estate to the value of about £230. Wid. to have a 3ᵈ pte.—
eldest son a double porcon, the other 3 children equall shares, *Elizabeth,
Sarah, Samuell;* eldest Sonne out of his share to pay his bro. *Samˡˡ* £14;
his sister *Sarah,* £2; and his wid. to have 40ˢ by yeare payd to hir during
the time of hir widdowhood. Hingham 20 Aprill 1654.

| John Thaxter,<br>Abraham Harden | Guardians to<br>Samˡˡ & Sarah<br>Thaxter. | Elizabeth ✕ Thaxter<br>hir marke<br>Mathew Hauke<br>Wy Pitts |

*Capt Joshua Hubbard* deposed.
Since the giueing in of the Inventory there is found a debt of £2. 17ˢ.
Approved by the Court, who desire that *John Thaxter,* yᵉ sonne out of his
porcon pay the last sume of 40s. mentioned as a debt the estate oweth.

---

ELIAS MAINEYERD, of Sidmoth, County of Deuon in England.—Debts
dew him from Mʳ *Tho. Brawton* for his wages, *Raphe Mason,* Mr. *Robt
Scotte, Wˡˡ Foy, Robt Walker,* Mʳ *James Oliuer, Henery Lamper.* Debts
owing by him to Ric. *Norton,* yᵉ Coop; *William Tolbut,* Mr *Hogsfleshe.*
Mentions *Jn° Shawe,* Fisherman; & *Gamaliell Waight.* Due by bound
from *Elias Parkemane* to be paid in England, £30. Last year pd £18;
due for ought I know, £12. *Edward Rainsford* deposed, 16 March, 53.

---

JAMES IVEY, of Brantrey.—*Thomas Thaxter, Gregory Belcher, Edmond
Quencser* depose that *James Ivey,* late of Brantrey, who deceased theire
the 3ᵈ of March last, did declare his last will and testament to this purpose. He gaue to the Elders of Brayntree, namely, Mʳ. *Thompson &
Mr Flynt,* £5 to be divided equally; debts being pd, rest of his estate to
*Jn° Ivey,* his brothers sonne. *Tho. Thaxter & Gregory Belcher* to be his
overseers. *Thomas Thaxter* deposed 26 Aprill, 1654. In the Inventory
is mentioned *Jno Mills* of Brantry, *Samˡ Dearing, Tho. Thaxter,* junʳ,
*Samˡ Stables.*

---

MICHAELL METCALFE, of Dedham.—Inventory taken 31, 1 : 1654, by
*Eleazer Lusher, Francis Chickering, Jno ✕ Dwight, Petter ✕ Woodward.*
his marke. his marke.
Amt. £164. 09. 10. Power of Administration granted 26 April 1654 to

125

*Mary Metcalfe*, widow, in behalfe of her selfe & 5 children. The Court Judge it meete y^t the widdow haue £50 out of the estate; y^e 4 youngest children £20 apeece. The debts discharged, the Eldest to haue the Rest of y^e Estate w^ch the Court Conceiues but just bec y^e Eldest after y^e grandfathers Metcalfe decease is to have another portion by virtue of both Grandfathers agreem^t. *Mary Metcalfe* deposed. Edward Rawson, Record^r. [See Metcalf Genealogy, vol. vi. (1852) p. 171, &c.]

---

ISACKE ADINGTON.—Inventory prised 10. 10. 1652, by *John Clarke, Anthony Stoddard, Rob^t Scott.* Amt £998. 09. 01. Ann, wid. of Isaac Addington deposed 22 Dec· 1653. The magistrates agreed that the wid. relinquishing her interest in the thirds of the land should have a third pt. of the estate, the rest to be divided between y^e children; the eldest to have a duble portion. Agreed to by *Ann Addington*, 29 Dec. 1653. Witness, *Edward Rawson, Anthony Stoddard.*

---

THOMAS DUDLEY, Esquire.—Inventory, taken 8. 6. 1653, by *Isaac Heath, Wm. Denison, Daniel Weld.* Amt. £1560. 10. 01. Mr. *Jn^o Johnson* deposed 27 Aprill 1654. Mentions a servant, of Mr Dudley, *John Rankins*; about 40 volumes of books, severall pamphlets, & new books.

---

WIDDOW GROSSE.—Inventory, taken 29. 10^mo. 1653, by *Richard Parker, Edward Hutchinson, Jeremy Houchin.* Amt. £360. 13. 02. Mr *Edward Ting* & Deac. *Tho^s Marshall* affirmed that this was a true Inventory of the Estate, w^ch was accepted, 6 Jan 1653.

---

WILLIAM HUMPHERYES.—Inventory taken by *John Clarke* & *Comfort Starr.* Amt. £45. 5. 8. Due vnto *Jeremy Houchin* p money delive^red him when he went vnto England, £9. 10.; vnto *Henery Shrimpton*, for fraight & passage for himselfe and goods &c; vnto M^r *Dickery Carwithe.* Mr. *Jeremiah Houchin* deposed, 3 Feb. 53.

---

SIMON EIRE, JR.—Inventory of *Simon Eire*, Jun^r & *Lydia* his wife deceased 10. 6. 1653. Taken by *Bartholmew Cheever, Wm. Wenborne,* 19. 6. 1653. Amt. £120. 08. Power of Administration granted to Mr *Comfort Starre* in behalfe of his grandchild, *Simon Eire*, till it come to the age of 14 years. Mr. *Starre* to give security that the principall be ready for the Child, being 12 Jan. 1653. Mr. Comfort Starre deposed y^t this was a true Inventory of y^e Estate of his dau. *Lydia Eire*, to y^e best of his knowledge.

---

EZRA KANE.—Inventory, taken by *Richard Wayte*, Robert *Raynold.* Amt. £25. 17. 02. Layd out in debts payd by *Rob^t Hull* & *James Johnson*, to *Martine Stebbins, John Tilly* & *Tho. Trumbull*, a lad, £9. 19. 06. Rests in our hands, £15. 17. 08. Accepted by the Magist^r 12 Jan. 1653.

---

WILLIAM DENNING, of Boston.—Inventory apprised by *Richard Gridley* & *Gamaliell Wayte*, of Boston, 18. 11^mo. 1653. *Edward Fletcher* & *John Hull* deposed, 31 Jan. 1653. [Will, vol. v. p. 302.] (See p. 52).

ABSTRACTS FROM THE EARLIEST WILLS ON RECORD*
IN THE COUNTY OF SUFFOLK, MASS.

[Prepared by Mr. WM. B. TRASK, of Dorchester ]

JAMES ASTWOOD.—Inventory giuen in to the Court 25 Oct. 1653. Estate indebted to Maister Drudgham, John Moss of Dedham, Edward Brudall, Richard Bolden of Milford, Joseph Godfrey of Newhauen, dead ; Mr John Mills, he is dead ; Mr John Gove ; William Peacocke ; George Brand ; Tho Clarke of Boston ; James Burges ; Richard Cutter ; George Griffin, Boston ; Edw Estwicke, Richard Bennett of Boston ; John Shaw, Boston ; John Browne ; John Hart, Boston ; John Maynard, Boston ; Richard Thurston ; John Watson ; John Dane ; Mr John Alcocke ; Ephraim Child ; Paul Allestree ; Nath: Vty ; Mr Edwd Collins ; Griffine Craft ; John Budman ; Mr Richd Leader ; Mr William Alford ; William Gurly, Boston ; Mr Dauid Sellicke ; John Griffin ; Thomas Hawkins ; Robert Feild ; Good· Baker, Smith ; Tho. Joy ; Good Row ; Saml Winslow ; Wm Phillips Junr ; Marke Hans ; Henry Lamprey. Creditors—Robert Seuer, of Roxbery ; John Swet ; Benj Gillam ; Willm Blanton ; Leift Richard Cook ; Hugh Stone ; James Matux ; John Farnum ; Mr Joshua Foot ; Tho Thurry ; George Munnings ; Ed Pason ; Phillip Torry ; Stephen Paine ; Mr John Glover ; Danl Kempthorne of Cambridge for keeping his sonns ; Tho. Roberts ; Peter Tracy ; Mr Belcheere ; John Weselld ; Mr Jacob Sheafe ; Mr Powell ; Joseph Wise ; William Helly ; Isaack Johnson ; John Bouls ; Tho Caruer ; Robert Shefeld ; Capt Danford ; Tho Kemball ; Leift William Phillips ; Mr William Peake of London ; William Whitweld ; William Vocy ; John Woodmancy ; Mr John Dudley ; Mr Davison ; Mr Abraham Palmer ; Mr John Newell ; Mrs. Dell ; Goodman Chapman ; Abraham Browne ; Mrs. Hanbury ; goodman Wullocks ; Capt Asten Walker ; James Graues ; Tho Phillips ; Mr Avery ; Mathew Paine ; Mr Francis Willoughby ; Mrs Nash ; Mr John Fredericke as Leift John Hewes affirmes ; Goodman Goodwin for two lighter load of stones ; Mr Tho Broughton ; Richard Gardner ; Adam Wight ; Mr John Maverick ; Mrs Elizabeth Foot ; Francis Hudson ; William Arnald ; Mr Booth ; Arthur Clarke ; Mr Same Cole ; Mr Norton the Cooper ; Randall Nichols ; Good Jacksons daughter his servant by pmise vpn his death bed ; Mr Butcher ; John Viall ; Isaack Heath ; Ed Mattux ; goodman Nash of Weymouth.

Taken by Tho. Clarke, Jacob Sheafe, William Parke. 31 : 11 : 1653. Amt of Debts due, £928. 18. 03.

1 Feb 1653. By order of Court all persons clayming ought from sd estate are to appeare before Mr Anthony Stoddard & Mr Edward Ting at ye Anchor Tauerne, ye 10th Feb. & make due proof of their debts. In ye mean time Deacon William Parks is appointed to Sett ye house to Sale, & ye debts by him to be gathered in. [Will. vol. vii. p. 337.] **

SAMUELL GOODYEARE.—Inventory prised 9 : 7 : 1653, by *William*

---

* The abstracts of inventories given in the present volume. pages 55 and 128v. are from the Records, and not from the *Files* as there indicated (See pp. 116, 124).
**See p. 112.

*Read, Ri Wayte.* Power of Administration granted to Marshall *Richard Wayte.* Pay *Martin Stebbins £7.* Signed *Ri: Bellingham.*

THOMAS EDINSELL.—Inventory taken by *Nath Sowther, Joseph Armitage, George Halsall.* Mr *Bucke* deposed, 3 Feb 1653. £11. 16s. 07d. The advance 4ᵈ. p shilling comes to £3. 10. 10.

JOHN WIGHT, of Medfield.—Inventory taken, 3: 8: 1653, by *Ralph Wheelocke, Tho: Grubb, Rob Hensdell* Amt. £171. 02. 09. Power of Administration granted to *Ann* late wife of *John Wight* in behalfe of herselfe & yᵉ child she goes withall. *Ann Wight* deposed, Oct. 53.

ROBERT SCOTT, of Boston. Inventory. 21. 12. 1653, prised by *Jacob Sheafe, Henery Shrimpton, William Francklin.* Amt. £439. 17. 05½. Estate indebted £298. 12. 09. Power of Administration granted to *Elizabeth Scott,* his widow, who deposed 24 March, 1653.

MAJOR GENERALL EDWARD GIBBONS.—Inventory prised 15: 10: 1654, by *Thomas Clark, Edward Hutchinson,* Amt. £535. 06. 07½. Deposed by Mʳ *Thomas Lake,* & Ensigne *Joshua Scottow,* 4 Jan. 1654. Maj *Gibbons* had property at Pullen Point, at *James Bills* house, at *John Brownes,* 4 acres of Land at Hog Island. &c.

ROBERT SHARP.—Inventory taken 19: 11: 1654, by *Peter Olliver, Edward Clap,* Amt. £172. 07. 06. Estate indebted to Elder *Colbrvn;* debt yᵗ was due frō Mʳ *Pilbeame* of Rehoboth; payd to *Peter Aspinuall* for so much of yᵗ he lent yᵉ said *Sharp;* to *Robert Hake, Abraham Hoe, William Fugrame,* for Labour; Mr *Gore,* for goods; to *Mary Read* for seruice; to goodman *Dunckin;* goodman *Voysy;* Capt *Johnson* of Rox: for a horse Coller; *Edward Devotion, Tho. Clarke, Peter Olliver.* Whole Estate, £172. 7. 6. Debts, £83. 06. 08. The house & land, prized at £110, at the request of the widdow & her friends set apart for the childrens portions, so farr as it goes, the rest the widdow is to make good. Said land & house is bound over to the Court for sᵈ childrens portions, the Sonne paying his sisters theire portions; the house & land sᵈ *Robert Sharpe* his father desyred is to be wholy his. 26 Jan 1654.

DAVID MATTOX, of Roxbury.—Inventory taken by *Isaac Heath, John Johnson, Robert Williams.* 18 May 1654. Sum total £55. 3. 04. *Sarah Mattox* wid. of *David,* deposed. The Magist. 25 May 1654 determined the widdow should haue one third pt of the estate, & the other two parts, they will order a direction to afterwards.

8. June 1654. the Magist. mett againe and on Sight of yᵉ maide yᵗ was decrepit, they ordered yᵉ estate to be thus devided, £10. to the maid; £8 to yᵉ sonne & and yᵉ mother to haue the rest.

Present yᵉ Govʳ, Mr Nowell & Recorder.

WILLIAM LANE, of Dorchester.—Inventory, prized by *John Wiswall, Wᵐ Clarke,* 5 July 1654. Amt. 82. 10. 08½. *Joseph Farnsworth* deposed. [Will, vol. V. p. 364.] (See p. 54).

THOMAS WHEELER, of Boston, Deceased about the 18ᵗʰ May 1654. Estate prized by *Nathⁱⁱ Williams, Edward Fletcher,* Amt. £100. 18s. *Rebeccah Wheeler* wid. of *Thomas,* deposed, 25 July, 1654. [Will, vol. V. p. 305.] (See p. 55).

RICHARD WILSON, of Boston.—Inventory of Estate prized by *William Holloway*, *Thomas Harwood*. Sum total. £104. 07. [no date.] This Inventory was accepted w^thout Oath because all the Estate was giuen to the widdow. Mentions goodman *Sawer*, *John Biglaw*, goodman *Jones*, doodman *Oakes ;* Mr *Broughton*, goodman *Chevers*, goodm. *Wenborne*, Mr *Cooke*, goodman *Carter*, goodman *Knight*, goodman *Grose*, Mr *Snellin*, goodman *Hagburnes* daughter, her mother & sister *Elizabeth ;* M^r *Barnard*, goodman *Burton*, goody *Whetwell*, goodman *Gridley*, goodman *Bosworth*, goodwife *Cowell*. *John Benham* [      ] haueing marryed *Sarah* y^e [wife of ?] *W^m Killcup*.
*Sarah Benham* appeared & made y^e same acknowledg^mt. [Will, vol. V. p. 305.] (See p. 55).

———

THOMAS ROBERTS, of Boston.—Inventory of *Thomas Roberts* taken on the testimony of *Joshua Scottow* & accepted ᵒᶜ by y^e Gov^r, Mr *Nowell* &c. without oath. Signed, *Tho: Buttolphe*, ᐯ᠁ .*Villioms*, *Joshua Scottow*. 25 July, 1654. On the margin *Theodore* ᐧtkinson, *Joshua Scottow*.

———

JOSEPH MORSE, of Dorchester.—Inventory of y^t pte of the Estate w^ch he had at Meadfield, taken 20 : 4 : 1654 by *Thomas* T *Wight*, *Robert Hensdall*, *George Barbar*. Sum. £183.
[End of Vol. I. Suffolk Inventories, being Vol. 2d Probate Records.]

———

[The Abstracts that follow are from the first volume of Suffolk Wills, in continuation from Vol. VI. p. 356, of this work.]
ALICE FERMACE.—I, Alice Fermace of Boston, Widdow, doe ordaine this my Last will. I giue unto my sister Joan Towne my old Cloth gowne ; daughter Ester Estick my best stuffe gowne ; vnto my Grand Child, Susan Goose, my box & my muffe ; vnto my daughter Sary Langdon, my red Petticoate ; all my wearing linnen vnto my daughter Sarah Langdon and my daughter Ester Estic & Pilgrim Edee & Elizabeth y^e Negro : servants vnto my Son m^r Edward hutchinson, to be equally divided by my daughter Susan goose & my daughter Abigall Hutchinson ; all the rest of my Estate I giue unto all my Childred to be equally disposed of among them—my Son, m^r Edward Hutchinson to be Executor. I haue hereunto set my hands the eight day of february, in the yeare of our Lord one thousand Six hundred and fiuety & Sixe.
Witness                    The marke of ⌣⌣⌣⌣⌣ Alice Fermase.
Jonathan Negus : Elkenah Cooke.
Jonathan Negus & Elkenah Cooke deposed 24 Aprill, 1656.
                                        E ᆜward Rawson, Record^r.
Inventory of y^e goods of Alice Fermase, widdow, Late of Salem, deceased, aprized the 20th day of the 12 moneth, 1655, by Jefferey Massey, Henry Skerry Sen^r. £18. 03. Inventory of goods at Boston 11 March, 1656, taken by Richard Cooke, Ben : Gillam, £11. 10.
                              Edward Hutchinson deposed.

———

GEORGE BURDEN.—I make my loving wife *Anne Burden*, my Executrix. I giue y^t Estate, goods & Chattells whether in England, or heere in New England, to be in y^e hands of my wife vntill my two children Come to y^e Age of Eighteene yeares or marriage, w^ch comes first, & then they, my two Children are to haue two parts of that Estate y^t God hath betrusted me with all, & to my wife yᵉ third part, & if my wife shall mary, then I will yᵗ my Children shalbe at yᵉ oversight and disposall of my father *Soulsby*, if it please God he surviue me, with my owne Brothʳ *Timothy*, & if my wife & children Stay in England, but if wee Returne to New England, then I make my Atturneys yᵉ overseers of my will, & yᵗ this is my Last will, if none appeare to beare date After this.

I witnes by my hand and seale, this 15th day of yᵉ eight moneth, 1652. the pʳents of vs 　　　　　　　　　 *George Burden* & a seele.

James Johnson
Thomas Downes 　　　　 30 April 1657. Capᵗ *James Johnson* & *Richᵈ*
Joseph Webb 　　　　　　 *Webb* deposed.
Edmund Jacklin

———

JOHN MORSE, of Boston.—Now undertakeing a voyage for England, being not without much hazzard, & although I doe Carry a Considerable part of my Estate to venture at sea, with my selfe, yet I thinke it my dutie to take care of my wife & Children. Therefore now, this Eighteenth day of december, Anno: 1655, I, the said *Jnᵒ Morse*, doe declare this my minde and will, vnto my beloved wife, *Annas*, forty pounds ; the rest of my Estate, I Comitt into the hands of my Executoʳs, to be equally devided to my Children ; yᵗ is to say, to my daughter *Ruth*, my Sonne *John, Joseph, Ezrah, Abigall, Ephraim, Bathia* and *Nathaniell*, each of them to haue a like proportion & not one to haue more then another, because the Elder of them are brought vp, & yᵉ younger of them are yet to bring vp ; if my executors see Cause, they shall pay my daughter *Ruth* her proportion, within one yeare after my decease ; yᵉ rest of my Childrens portions as aforesaid, at theire severall ages of one & twentie yeares ; my Estate to remaine in yᵉ hands of my wife vntill my Children come of age ; in Case my Estate I carry with me be pʳserved, then my wife shall haue yᵉ vse of that ; as of yᵉ rest of yᵉ Estate, the said forty pounds to my wife, I giue twentie pounds thereof to her, the other 20ˡᵇ to my Children, after her decease, to be equally devided. And in case any dye before they come to the age of one & twenty yeares, their pportion be devided amongst yᵉ rest surviving, alwayes pvided my debts be satisfyed ; my beloved brother & friend *Francis Chickrin*, with my wife *Annas*, Executoʳs.

Temperance Smith 　　　　　　　　　 *Jnᵒ Morse* & a seale.
　　his C marke & of
one *Robert Howard* Notᵗ Pubᶜᵘˢ.

18ᵗʰ June 1657. Mʳ *Robert Howard* deposed ; at yᵉ same time *Francis Chickerin* publiquely refused to pforme yᵉ officer of an executor to this will, & desired his Renunciation might be entered & Recorded as was graunted.

June 9ᵗʰ 1657. Inventory of the Estate of *John Morse*, Taylor, of Boston, Late deceased. Prized by *Francis Chickerin*, Pet: H *Woodward*,
　　　　　　　　　　　　　　　　　　　　　　　　　　　　　　　　　　　　 his marke
*Daniell fisher.* Amt. 385ˡᵇ 09. 05ᵈ. *Annas Morse* deposed.

———

NICHOLAS BUSBY.—Being sicke, doe make this my Last Testament. I doe appointe my three sonns that are here in New England, that is to say, my Sonne *Abraham Busby*, my Sonne *William Nickerson* & my Sonne *John Grout* to gather vp all my debts mentioned in my debt bookes, to make them of a true accoᵗ, & to deliuer it as they shall receiue it vnto my Executrix. I doe make my Loving wife whole Executrix of my Estate, & to possess this my dwelling house wherein I liue, dureing her life, and all my household Stuffe plate & money ; & for my farme if she will consent thereto, that it be sold & she to receiue the price thereof, to add to it my stocke & discharge the seu*r*all Legacies ; the Remainder to be for her maintenance dureing her life. Vnto *John Busby,* my Eldest Sonne, seaventy pounds more then that I sent him the Last yeare, w*ch* was thirtie pounds, & this Seaventy pounds to be payd in such goods as are gathered in by the Brethren, within Seaven monthes after my decease. Vnto *Abraham Busby,* my Sonne, sixtie pounds. And after his Mothers decease, this my new dwelling house, with the garden & fruit trees, being in Boston. Vnto *Anne Nickerson,* my Eldest daughter, fiftie pounds ; vnto my daughter, *Katherine Savory,* fortie pounds, (more then that I sent her the Last yeare.) Vnto *Sarah Grout,* my youngest daughter, Sixtie & five pounds ; vnto my grand Child, *Joseph Busby,* Sonne of my Sonne *Nicholas,* deceased, Twenty pounds ; vnto *Sarah Grout,* my grand child, tenn pounds ; vnto my two Sonns *John Busby* & *Abraham,* my printed bookes, in manner following ; to *John,* all my Phisicke bookes, as *Glendall* practice, *Barrowes* method, Dutch Phisicke & garden of health, M*r* *Coggans* treatis, and the Dialogue of Phisicke Surgery, with *Plinnys* Naturall Hystory. Vnto *Abraham,* my bookes of Divinitie, vizt. M*r* *Perkins,* M*r* *Willet* sinops and Comentary on the Romans, & M*r* *Hieroms* two bookes ; as for the rest of my bookes of divinitie, or Hystory, my desire is, they may Loveingly & Brotherly devide them betweene except the three Bibles ; first, the thicke Bible, I giue vnto *Anne Nickerson.* The Best Bible, to *Sarah Grout,* and the bible in my Hamper, to *Katherin Savory.* As for my Apparell, I giue vnto *John,* my Sonne, my blacke Stuffe Cloake, & the remainder of my apparell to my wife to dispose of. As for my weaving tooles, as the two Loomes, the one, I giue to *John Busby* in case he come over to New England, or else to *William Nickerson* the same. And the other Loome & warpins, bobings, wheeles, shettells & other Implem*ts* thereto belonging, vnto Sonne *Abraham;* as for my household stuffe, plate & money, I leaue vnto my deare wife. I haue heereunto set my hand & seale, this five and Twentieth day of July, One thousand Sixe hundred fifty and Seauen.

In p*r*sence of vs.          By me *Nicholas Busby* & a seale.
     *Nathaniell Woodward, W*ᵐ *Pearse.*
10 Sep 1657.   *Nathaniel Woodward* and *W*ᵐ *Pearse* deposed.
Will Recorded, 14ᵗʰ Oct. 1657. Inventory of the Estate taken 1ˢᵗ Sept*r* 1657, by *Nathaniel Woodward* and *Robert Saunders.*
Amt. 973. 11. 08¼.   10 Sep 1657.   *Abraham Busby* deposed.

JOHN OTTIS, of Weymouth.—Will made 30 : 3 : 1657. To my dau. *Margaret Burton* & her three children 20ˢ amongst them, and a smale brasse pott and a Canvass sheete. To my dau. *Hannah Gile* two feather boulsters, one Rugg and Cotton blankett, my biggest brasse kettle. To *Mary Gile,* one Cowe and one pillowber. To *Thomas Gile* junio*r*, one Muskett. To my dau. *Anne* and my dau. *Allice* 5s apiece. To my wife 40s. My son *John Ottis* executor.            *John* χ *Ottis.**
     Witness *John Rogers*
         *Thomas Dyer*

---

* Debility, no doubt, obliged the Testator to sign his will by a márk ; he wrote a handsome Autograph in early life. See vol. ii. of the *Register,* p. 283.

*John Rogers* deposed, 28 July 1657. Recorded 14 Oct. 1657. Inventory taken 16: 4: 1657. *Jn° Ottise* deposed before Court 28 July to this Inventory of the Estate of his late father. Edw Rawson Record<sup>r</sup>.

---

NICHOLAS JACOB, of Hingham.—Will made 18 May 1657. Being sicke. My wife *Mary* executor; vnto [her] the bed and bedding she vsually lyeth vpon, with all the furniture there vnto belonging, to dispose of it vnto whom she please, [also] £30 out of the estate in what she sees meete, to be for her propper vse, dureing life & after her decease, to be divided amongst all my children in proporcon as the rest of the Estate is divided. Vnto *Joseph, Hannah* and *Deborah Jacob* £10. apiese, to be payd out of the estate before it be devided, in Lue of what my other childred have had before; the rest of the estate to be devided as followeth: vnto my Eldest sonne *John*, a double portion, vnto the rest of my Children, namely, *Joseph Jacob, Mary Ottis, Elizabeth Thackster, Sarah Cushen Hannah Jacob* and *Deborah Jacob*, Equall shares, and euery one of them shall pay vnto theire mother, *Mary Jacob*, 18d. p. pound yearely for so much Estate as shall be putt into there hands; to be payd in Corne or Cattle, at the Current prize, euery halfe yeare dureing her widdowhoode; and in case she shalbe maryed vnto another man, then they shall pay but the one halfe of the Revenue, that is to say, but 9d. p. pound yearely.

    *Edm: Pitts*                     *Nicholas Jacob.*
    *Thomas Marsh*
    *Mathew Hawke*       *Thomas Marsh* and *Mathew Hawks*
               deposed 28 July 1647. Recorded 14<sup>th</sup> Oct.
                       p Edward Rawson Record<sup>r</sup>

Inventory of estate taken 12 June 1657 by *Mathew Hawks, Thomas Marsh.*
Amt. £393. 08. 06. *Mary Jacob* deposed. 28 July 1657.

---

SAMUELL JUDSON, of Dedham.—Will made 7 June 1657. Vnto *Mary*, my wife, the third pt of all my houses and Lands for her maintenance. After my decease all my estate being equally and indifferently aprized, the moueables or the value of them being devided in fower equall parts, one fourth part I giue vnto my wife & her heires, the other three pts to my 3 dau<sup>s</sup>, *Mary, Sarah* and *Esther*, to each an equall third pt. to be payd them at my now dwelling house in Dedham, at the time they shall generally attaine the age of 18 yeares, and at the same to receiue theire respectiue pt in my house and Lands, the third pt being reserued for the vse of my wife. After her decease my said dau<sup>s</sup>. shall possesse the whole of my houses and lands, each an equall pt. Said wife shall possess my whole estate vntill my dau<sup>s</sup> attain the age aforesaid; the vse whereof I allow vnto her towards the education and bringing vp of my said three dau<sup>s</sup>. to the age aforesaid, as also for her owne vse otherwise, or for the benefitt of her two Sonnes, which were hers before she was my wife being the Sonnes of *Henery Aldridge*, deceased; to which her two sonnes I leaue that Land that was sometimes theire fathers to Inheritt according to Law. My wife *Mary*, sole executrix. If any of my dau<sup>s</sup> depart this life before they attaine the age of 18 yeares their portion to be equally divided vnto them that shall be then surviuing.     *Samuel* X *Judson.*

In the p<sup>r</sup>snts of vs
    *Thomas Fuller*
30 July 1657. Cap<sup>t</sup> *Eliazer Lusher* deposed.

4 Aug 1657 *Thomas Fuller* deposed before *Eliazer Lusher*, Commis-sion<sup>r</sup>. Edw Rawson Recorder.
Inventory of the Estate, taken 24 July, 1657, by *Eleazer Lusher Nath: Aldis, John Cawards, Tho Fuller. Mary Judson* deposed 30 July, 1657.

---

PHILLIP ELLIOT, of Roxbury.—Will made 21 : 8 : 1657. All my debts to be in the first place payd. To testify my love to Christ I giue vnto the Treasury of the Church of Roxbery where I haue in my poore measure found Christ, 5£. to be payd within two yeares after my decease. Whereas my sonne *Aldis* oweth me £5. vpon a Late bargaine, my will is, y<sup>t</sup> his dau. *Sarah Aldis* haue that as a Legacy from me. I giue to my Grand Child, *Henry Withington*, £5. towards the bringing him vp in Learneing. I giue £5 to *John Perry* when his time is out, pvded he liueth with, and is seruiceable to my wife, but if my wife putt him away, my will is that he be not put to any against his will, and to whomesoeuer he be put I giue him £5. out of the value of his time, being indifferently prized. My will is that £60 be payd my dau. *Lydia,* for her portion equall with her other sisters, this is to be payd in any thing saueing in moveables, as may fall to be theire share at last ; for my will is that all my 3 dau<sup>r</sup> have equall shares therein, as also in all the rest of my Estate after my wiues decease. I make my wife sole executrix, to whome I Comit the Residue of my Estate dureing her life. If my wife change her estate she shall haue her thirds of my Estate, and the rest devided to my Children. My will is that my wife doe nothing of moment without the ap-probation of my Brother John Elliott our Teacher, Elder Heath, Deacon Parks, John Rugles, senior, whome I make my overseers. If any differ-ence arise among my Children & executrix about any devision of my Es-tate, my will is that they shall not goe to Law, but be determined by three of my next of kindred then surviueing ; & if any should be troublesome (which God forbid) my will is y<sup>t</sup> such shall loose theire part of my Estate about w<sup>ch</sup> they so striue. I desire my Brother Deacon *Parks*, with the Elders, to pfect & finish such of my Church accompts as are not yet pfected.

      wittnesse *Griffine Craft*              *Phillip Elliott.*
            *John Rugles*
11 Feb. 1657. Sworne by the witnesses to be the Last will of Phillip Elliott
                    before me. Jo: Endecott Gov<sup>r</sup>.
[Inventory recorded, without date, vol 3. fol. 121. It was probably taken in 1658.] *Elizabeth Elliot*, his widow, deposed.
    Amt. £554. 01. 10.                   Edw Rawson Record<sup>r</sup>

---

THOMAS BIRCH, of Dorchester.—Will made 4 June 1654. I appointe M<sup>r</sup> *Nathaniell Patten, John Pearse* senio<sup>r</sup> and *John Minott* to take care of my Children and estate ; for my Land I would haue none of it to be sold. I giue all my estate to my Children only ; for my man *Richard,* I would haue him to serue out his time, and then that his Indenture should be pformed, & besides I giue him 40s. I giue to my dau. *Mary,* £8. more than her pporcon towards the bringing her vp, and to my sonne *Jer-emiah,* 40s. for his bringing vp, more than his proporcon. I would haue my estate divided into seven parts, and then *Joseph* to haue two pts, the other fiue pts to the other fiue children, after the former Legacies are Satisfyed.  I would haue my Sonne *Joseph* to be of my owne Trade.

Boston 22 May 1657.  At a meeting of yᵉ magistrates & Recordʳ, Power of Administration to the estate of Thomas Burch, of Dorchester, deceased, is graunted to *John Gurnel* & *John Minot* in behalfe of the Children of the said Burch, they bringing in an Inventory of that Estate to the next County Court.  Present yᵉ Governoʳ, Depᵗ Govʳ, Major Atharton & Recordʳ.

Inventory taken, 27 Oct. 1657, by *William Blake*, and *Richard Davis.* Sume totall £170. 11. 11.  *John Minott* & *Jnᵒ Gurnell* deposed, 5 Nov 1657.

It is also Ordered that the said *Jnᵒ Minot* & *Jnᵒ Gurnell* shall & is hereby Impowered to dispose of the children of the said *Burch*, in binding them forth Apprentices, with Consent of the Court, as they shall see cause.

E. R., R.

---

JOHN GORE, of Roxbury.—Being sicke.  Debts to be paid in old England and New ; for the discharge thereof, all my debts that are oweing me should be speedily gathered vp to pay as farre as they will goe, & the rest to be made vp out of my stocke and Sale of Land by my executors, that the remainder of my Estate should be improved together, untill my sonne *Samuel* be of the age of 23 yeares, except my sonne should, before this age, change his estate or my wife hers, wᶜʰ of this time comes first that then the remainder of my Estate be equally prized, and my sonne *Samuel* to Receive one fourth pt of my whole estate then remaineing, and my two dau'. *Abigall* and *Hannah*, to receiue equally one fourth pt more at the age of 21 yeares, or the day of marriage, wᶜʰ shall be first.  The other halfe of my Estate vnto my wife dureing life, whom I make my sole Executrix.  After the death of my wife all that estate she did enjoy shall be equally devided betweene my 5 children, *John Gore, Mary Mylame, Samuel, Abigail* and *Hannah Gore.* The Reason why I did not giue my Eldest Sonne, *John Gore* and my dau. *Mary* no more, is because they have received there full proporcon before and my will is that if any of my 3 younger Children dye before Marriage that those three should be one anothers heires.  If my wife should Liue a widow Long and by Reason of any hand of God as sicknes or the like should be in any want, I giue her full power, with the Consent of my overseers to sell some Land and spend the same for her Comfort.  I desire my beloued Brethren *Phillip Elliot, John Pierpoint, Amos Richeson*, to be overseers of this my last will, and doe Intreate them to be helpfull vnto my wife and Children, and doe desire my wife that she would doe no matters of moment without their advice and Consent, according to the true intent & meaning heereof.

p me *John Gore*

22 : 3 : 1657   In the pʳents of vs

*Phillip Elliott*          Proved by *Phillip Elliot*
*John Ruggles*         *John Ruggles, Robert Pierpoint*
*Robert Pierpoint*      30 July 1657

Jo Endecott Govʳ.

Inventory of Estate taken 22 : 4 : 1657 by *Isaack Heath, Isaack Morrell.*  Amt. £.812 : 07 : 6   *Rosa Gore*, his widow, deposed.

# ABSTRACTS FROM THE EARLIEST WILLS ON RECORD IN THE COUNTY OF SUFFOLK, MASS.

[Prepared by Mr. Wm. B. Trask, of Dorchester ]

Thomas Olliver, of Boston.—Will made 13 March 1652. Executors of this my will, my sonne *Peeter* and *James Olliver*, with my sonne in Law *James Johnson*. I giue to my wife all that her Land and goods was sold for, the value of 60£, w^ch is in her Childrens hands, for her vse, to be payd to her when she shall require it; and further now I doe giue her £10 dureing her life in such Comodities as is Convenient; and I doe giue in household stuffe those things for her vse, foreuer, mentioned in a Shedull hereto Annexed. My will is, to pay this, my farme & state shal be Either to be Let or sould, as my said executors or any two of them shall agree, and all my Land and goods and house being sould to be devided in fiue Equall pts. My will is, that my sonne *John*, his wife and Children, shall haue two pts as being my Eldest; that the Children of my sonne *John* & *Peeter* & dau *Abigail* shall haue 20ˢ euery one of them, and my executors to haue the rest, provided that all that w^ch I haue deliuered to any of them before, shall come into that equall devision Amongst them. I also giue to *Hannah Tarne*, £5, to be payd at the age of 21, or at the day of marriage; to all my grand Children, 10ˢ apiece, both in old England and heere in New England. My sonne *John* Receiued of me £74 in goods and money; my sonne *Peeter*, £40; my sonne *James*, £40; & my sonne *Samuell* a portion, and to my dau. the wife of *James Johnson* he Receiued £20. I giue to my sonne *Peeter*, a Siluer boule, and to my sonne *James Olliver*, my watch; and to my dau. *Abigail Johnson*, my siluer salt. My will is, to giue to my wife these things, vnder written, the feather-bedd in ye Parlour, with the greene Rugg, and the 3 Blanketts & 3 Pillowes, with the boulster and Matterise & Curtaines with the dornix over it, and bedsteed, the Round Table, 4 Joyne stooles, 2 Low stooles, 4 Pillow bers, 4 paire of shetts, 12 napkins, 3 broad Cloathes one of them the shortest of the lest, one paire of Cobirons, with the spitt and dripping pan, 4 platters, 2 Candlestickes, one brasse and one pewter, the siluer wine Cup & 4 Siluer spoones, with one dornix Carpitt, with a third of the brasse. 15: 1: 1652.

I giue to my dau. *Woollfall* and my dau Havens [?] £40 to be equally devided betweene them; to *Richard Woollfall*, at Muddy River, 40ˢ. provided my Estate hold out, if not, then to abate with an equall proporcon, and this I witnes to as my act. 2: 3: 56.  *Thomas Olliver.*

Power of Administration graunted vnto Leiut *Peter Olliver*, Capt *James Olliver* & Capt *James Johnson* to p'forme this Imperfect will, & bring in an Inventory of the Estate. 27 Jan. 1657.

Inventory of Estate of Elder *Thomas Olliver*, taken 15: 11: 1657, by *Edward Porter, Robert Turner.* 30 Jan. 1657. Capt *James Olliver* & Capt *James Johnson*, deposed.*

---

John Glover, of Boston.—Inventory of his goods and chattells at his Farme, in Dorchester, beyond Naponset, now in the occupation of *John*

* See Drake's *Hist. and Antiq. of Boston*, p. 293, for a pedigree of the family of Thomas Oliver.

135

*Gill* & *Roger Billings*, prized 6: 2: 1653. Amongst the items are "one Cannon" and "one Indian plow." Whole amount at sd farme, £1151 17.

6: 12: 1653. Inventory of his estate at his Farme in Dorchester, behind Neponset, now in the occupation of *Nicholas Wood*. Amt. £505. 11. 04.

Goods and chattells at his house in Boston: 7: 12: 53. Amt. £1688. 18. 11. "fiue servants at 8£ p' servant."

Signed by *Humphrey Atharton, John Wiswall, John Smith*. Mrs *Anne Glouer*, widow of John, deposed 4 Jan. 1654.

Debts oweing the estate by *Wᵐ Phillips* at yᵉ ship Taverne in Boston; goodman *Coleman*, of Boston, shoemaker; *Wᵐ Robinson*; Mr *Thomas Lake*, of Boston for principle forbearance & not paying in old England; Mr *James Astwood*; Mr. *Valentine Hill* principle & for not paying in old England; Capt *John Leuerit*; *Wᵐ Shattocke*; *Joseph Jewett*, of Rowley; *Sampson Mason*, of Dorchester; Capt *Gookins* to pay in England; Mrs *Holeman*, of Dorchester; Mr *Thomas Broughton*, of Boston; *John Gornell*; Mr. *Rawson*. [Will. Vol. V, p. 301.] (See p. 51).

---

JOHN STOCKBRIDGE, of Boston.—Will dated, 4: 7: 1657. I giue to my Eldest sonne *Charles*, my Water mill at Sityate, 6 acres of meadow, & the house, ground & orchard belonging to it; and the said *Charles* is to pay out of this mill and ground to his sister *Elizabeth*, £10, at her day of marriage or at the age of 21. To my wife *Mary*, my house and ground at Boston and all things belonging to it, & my house at Sityate yᵗ *Gilbert Brocks* doth Liue in, & ground, orchard & meadow that doth belong to it. If my youngest son doth liue, he is to enjoye it after his mothers death, paying £10 to his sister, *Mary Stockbridge*; if said *John* doth not liue, then it is to be devided equally betweene all my children. To my dau. *Ester Stockbridge*, my house at Sityate, that *William Ticknor* doth liue in, with orchard, ground & meadow, the land at Brush hill, & Land at yᵉ fower Clift, after her death to be devided equally between all my children. To my dau. *Hannah Ticknor*, 40ˢ out of that wᶜʰ her husband hath in his hands. To my dau. *Sarah*, £10, to be payd her at marriage or when 21 yeares old & to be payd out of yᵗ wᶜʰ I haue giuen my wife. I giue all my working toules to my Eldest sonne; to my wife, all my household goods. My wife & Eldest sonne, Executor.

John Stockbridge.*

Witnesse *Henry Allin, Mathew* ⋈ *Eirounes*.

8 April 1658. *Hen Allin* deposed.

Inventory of the Estate of *John Stockbridge*, wheelewright, taken by *Richard Gridley*, & *Henry Allin*, 3: 2: 1658. *Charles Stockbridge* deposed, 8 April, 1658.

---

RICHARD HARDIER, of Brantrey.—Will made 18: 10: 1657. To my wife *Elizabeth* all my Estate during her life & then to be disposed of as she shall thinke good. Vnto *Jnᵒ Hardier* or his dau. *Mary* £30, to be payd them within 2 yeares after yᵉ decease of my wife. My wife sole executrix.

*Richard Hardier*.

Inventory taken 25: 11: 1657, by *Richard Brackett, William Allis*.

In the pʳnts of vs, *Margery Flint, Liddia Scottoo*.

*Margery Flint* and *Elizabeth Hardier* deposed 8 July 1658.

---

* See Deane's *Scituate*, p. 342, for an account of John Stockbridge.

WILLIAM WEARE, of Boston, shoomaker.—Will, 26 March 1656.
Vnto my dau. *Sarah Weare* after her mothers death, my house in Boston,
with all y$^t$ doth appertaine vnto it ; my house, Barne, Orchard & Garden
in Dorchester, and all my goods, only her mother to haue all for her vse
as Long as she doth Liue. If my dau. *Sarah* dye vnmarryed, or if marryed & haue no Children, then my dwelling-house in Boston I giue vnto
my Grand Child *Obediah Gill*, & vnto my Grandchild *Elizabeth Gill* my
house and Barne and Orchard and Garden & all that doth belong vnto it :
But if any of these shall wrong her, either y$^e$ Parents or the Children,
then I giue her full power to dispose of it as shee seeth good. 26 March
1656. *William Weare.*
Only if I dye in debt my debts to be payd of my land.
Power of Administration granted to *Elizabeth Weare* his late wife to
p'forme this imperfect will. 1 Apl. 1658.
There is on File an Administration Bond in the sum of £300, given by
Elizabeth Ware to Ew$^d$ Rawson, 14 Apl. 1658, witnessed by *George
Shove, Margarett Rawson.*
Inventory of Estate taken 24: 1: 1647-8,* by *Richard Webb* & *Rich-
ard Collicott. Elizabeth Weare* deposed. 1 April 1658.
On the same Document, on file, is written—" Power of Administration
to y$^e$ Estate of Rice Davies deceased, is Graunted to Evan Thomas & Mr
Tilley they bringing in a true Inventory of the Estate. 15 Aprill 1658.
p. Edw. Rawson, Recorder."
A Bond for settling said Estate, given by *Evan Thomas*, W$^m$ *Tilly*, 13
April 1658 ; signed also by *Benj. Brisco, Elkanah Cooke.*

---

COTTON FLACKE, of Boston.—Will dated 2: 9: 1654. Wife *Jane* executrix ; she [to] haue my house and Garden Lott in Boston, with all my
goods and moveables. I giue my sonne *Samuell Flacke* out of it 40$^s$ to
be payd within one yeare after my decease ; and the reason I give him
no more is, I gaue him my Land at Mudy Riuer containing 20 Acres In
my life time. My Loving Brethren *John Lake* and Bro. *Petter Oleiver*
overseers. *Cotton* ⋈ *Flacke.*
*Will. Colbron, Henry Alline.*
*Henry Allin* deposed, 5 Aug. 1658.
Inventory made 31: 5: 1658 by *Peeter Olliver, Henry Allin.* Amt.
£42. 15. This Inventory was taken in 5: 6 mo: 58 by Henry Alline,
without Oath, the whole estate except 40$^s$ being by will given to *Jane*,
his late wife.

---

JOSEPH SHAW, of Weymouth.—Inventory of estate taken 2 Feb. 1653,
& apprised by *Nathaniell Sowther, Nicho. Byrome,* & Mr *Isaack Walker.*
Debts owing by *James Smith* ; *Henery Crabb* ; goodman *Emons* ; *Mordicha Graner* ; *George Davis*, the smith ; Elder *Bates* ; Mrs. *Richards* ;
goodman *Parker*, for Rent ; *John Bicknall* ; *Henery Lamprey* ; *John
Turner*, of Weymouth. Debts oweing by the Testator. To Mrs *Ruth
Stanley*, at Barbadoes ; M$^r$ *Cullet* ; *John Porter* ; Mrs *Hanberry* ; Widdow *Roberts* ; *William Bellantine* ; Mrs. *Preistley*, in England.
1 Feb. 1654. *Mary Blake,* late wife to Joseph Shawe, deposed.
[Will, Vol. V, p. 303.] (See p. 53).

---

* So reads the Record, but it should be, evidently, 1657-8.

JOHN AVERY.—Goods prized by *John Sunderland* and *Godfrey Armitage*. Administration to the Estate granted to *William Follett*, of Oyster River in Pascattoway, in behalfe of his brother *Laurence Avery*, 19 Sept. 1654.

---

GOODMAN HURST.—Inventory of Goods Apprized by goodman *Fletcher*, Goodman *Kilcop* & goodman *Lake*, 23 Dec. 1653. Amt. £46: 19: 11 M<sup>r</sup> W<sup>m</sup> Brenton deposèd, 25 Aprill, 1654.

---

JEFFERY TURNER, of Dorchester.—Inventory of Goods prized 22: 2: 1654, by *John Wiswall*, *John Smith*. Amt. £164. 04. 09. *Isabell Turner*, his widow, deposed, 25 May 1654. [Will, Vol: V, p. 305.] *

---

GEORGE MUNNINGS.—Will. Being very sicke. To my wife *Johannah*, £100, and such things as she brought with her. A note of the p'ticul<sup>rs</sup> is in Mr *Isaac Wakers* hands, and to this I have subscribed my hand, this 23 of Aug. 1658. *George Munnings.*
*Isaack Waker Will Hudson*
16 Sept 1658. Leift. W<sup>m</sup> Hudson & Isaack Waker deposed. Power of Administration granted to *Johannah Munnings*, his widow.
21: 7: 1658. Goods prised that were *Symon Boyers*, now the goods of *Joanna Munnings*, w<sup>ch</sup> she had before her marriage with said *Munnings*, amounting to £25. Inventory of the Estate of *George Munnings*, taken 17: 7: 1658, by *James Euerill*, John ✕ Button, *Francis Douse*. Mentions *Thomas Hawkins* ; *Randall Nichols* ; *Thomas Myrricke*, of Springfield ; *John Chayneies* and *Jn° Emeryes*, of Newbery ; *Theophylus Munnings* ; *Francis Buers* ; *John Jarvis* ; *Henry Way*, of Dorchester ; *Thomas Jones* ; Capt *Robert Harding* ; *Phillip Long* ; *John Shaw* ; *John Smith*, of Redding ; *Hugh Gunnison* ; *Edward Colcord* ; *Edward Kibby* and *George Way* ; *Job Lane* ; *Abraham Shurt* ; *John Giffard* ; *John Hawthorne* ; *Henry Lamprey* ; Sarg<sup>t</sup> *Cotton* ; *John Hammon*, of Wa:ertowne. The Inventory of debts was taken by *Richard Cooke* and *Richard Collicott*, 8 Jan. 1658.
Inventory of Estate of George Munnings, on file, taken 21: 7: 1658, by James Euerill, John ✕ Butten, Francis Douse. 28 Jan. 1658. Amt. £16. 19. Johanna Munnings wid. of George deposed.

---

JOHN BARRELL.—Will. 27: 6: 58. I giue all my proper Estate that is my owne to my wife to bring vp the Children, and to maintaine my mother. Mr *Gibbs* I desier may have his goods returned to him so farr as they will goe, at the same prise they came at. The old house and ground is my mothers dureinge her life. I desire my debts may be payd as farr as my Estate will reach. I make my wife sole executrix.
*James Olliver Will. Hudson* *John Barrell*
16 Sept 1658. Capt *James Olliver* and Leift. *Hudson* deposed.
Inventory of the Estate taken by *Josh: Scottow*, *Thomas Dewer*, John ✕ Andrewes £434. 13. 05. *Mary Barrell*, widow of John, deposed 18 Nov. 1658.

---

WILLIAM HERSIE, senior, of Hingham.—Will. 9 March 1657. Being now sicke. I giue to my sonne *William* y<sup>e</sup> house and home Lott that he
*See p. 55.

138

now Liues in and yᵉ penn plott before his gate, and yᵉ Lott I bought of *Mathew Chafey* at yᵉ Capᵗ Tent, with one great Lott at Nuttey hill, yᵗ Lyes outmost to yᵉ South East, to him and his heyres for euer.   To my sonne *John*, one Lott at Nuttey hill, yᵗ lyes Northward of *Moses Colliers*. To my sonne *James* the Lott yᵗ Lyes next yᵉ aforesaid Lott giuen his Brother *John*, Lyeing to yᵉ Northward of the Lott of *George Lane*.  To my dau. *Francis** £5 sterling; dau. *Elizabeth* £5 sterling; dau. *Judith*, £5 sterling; [each of these at yᵉ decease of their mother, or yᵉ day of their mothers marriage.]   I giue my Grand Child, *John Croade*, after my decease, when Liueing to 4 yeares of age, 40ˢ.; my grand child, *William Hersie*, 40ˢ in like manner.   All yᵉ rest of my Land, housing goods &c. to my wife *Elizabeth*, during her life, or liues in a Widdowes Estate; but if she marryes, then to distribute it amongst my Children as she may see good, allwayes p'vided not to Lay any restraint vpon her for matter of time in disposall of what she may see meete to any of my Children; making her my only executrix.   Overseers, Cousine *John Farrington*, Thom-
as *Marsh* & my sonne in Law *Richard Croade*.

   Witness
     *Thomas Marsh*         *Thomas Marsh* deposed, 29 April 1658.
     *Richard Croade.*     *Ri: Croade* deposed, 12: 2: 58.
   Inventory of the Estate of *William Hearsie*, senior, of Hingham, deceased the 24ᵗʰ day of March ⁵⁷⁄₅₈, apprized at Hingham the 28ᵗʰ of April 1658, by *Moses Collier* and *Tho. Marsh*.   Amt. £419. 13. 06.   "Land wᶜʰ was *John Princes* and *Stephen Gates*; a piece of ground at the rotten tree; land at Hockley; at Conahasset; at ware neck," &c., &c.   *Elizabeth Hersie* deposed, 28 April 1659.

---

   WILLIAM PADDY, of Boston, merchant.—Will.   Being at present vnder Gods visiting hands of sicknes, I giue to my wife, *Mary Paddy*, one third of my Estate.   In case she liue a Widdow, and dye in an Estate of widdowhood, that then at her death she shall haue libertie to dispose of yᵉ one halfe pt of yᵉ Estate she shall dye possessed of, to whom she pleases, the other halfe shall be equally deuided among mine and my wiues 11 children, or to as many of them as shall be aliue at her death.   In case yᵉ Lord dispose of my deare wife againe in marriage, my will is yᵗ she shall before her marriage giue to euery one of my Eleven Children 10 or 15£, or to as many as shall be then aliue, vnlesse yᵉ p'vidence of God take away this Estate giuen to my wife before yᵗ time, wᶜʰ I leaue to my Executors to judge of.   To my wife over and above her third part, a new Siluer Cawdle Cup and porringer, as a token of my endeared Love.   The other two thirds of my Estate vnto my 9 children, *Elizabeth, John, Samuell, Mercy, Thomas, William, Nathaniell, Hannah, & Benjamine Paddy*, to be equally deuided among them; portions to my sonnes at yᵉ age of 21 yeares and dauˢ at the day of theire Marriage, or at the age of 19 yeares. In case my deare wife should prooue to be with Child and it Liue, it shall come in for an equall share with my other Children.   [In case of death, provision made for the survivors, and for the education of the chiidren.]

---

   * *Frances* m. *Richard Croade* of Hingham, and afterwards of Salem.   Her sister *Elizabeth* m. *Moses Gilman*, and her sister *Judith* m. *Humphrey Wilson*, both of Exeter, N. H.

She shall have libertie to keepe as many of them with her as she pleases. And whereas there are 11 of myne and my wiues Children, formerly said to be named, it is to be vnderstood of my nine Children already named, and *Sarah* and *Mary Payton*. I giue to my dau' *Elizabeth* and *Mercy* £50, more or lesse, w^ch is a debt in y^e hands of Mr *Val. Hill*, as shall appeare by my bookes, w^ch fiftie is over and above theire forementioned portions, to be equally devided betweene them, w^ch is in Consideracon of a debt I owe them, for my former wife and theire deare mother. To my sonne, *John Paddy*, 6 Siluer spoones as a debt I owe him. For y^e disposall of y^e rest of my children y^t my wife shall not keepe, and leaue y^m to y^e care of my Executors and overseers. I giue 40' for a Ring to Mrs. *Mary Willet*, y^e wife of Capt *Tho: Willet*, of Plymouth; to Mr *John Endicott*, senior, and Mr. *John Wilson* senior and Mr. *John Norton*, of Boston, each £5. 1 giue £10 to be disposed of by y^e select men of y^e towne of Boston, for y^e poore; to my sister, *Margarett Baxter*, 50'; to *Thomas Coachman, Francis Golder*, and Goody *Pratt*, all of Plymouth, each, £4. Debts being payd, residue of my Estate to be disposed of as before mentioned. *Thomas Willet*, of Plymouth and Mr. *W^m Davis*, of Boston, Apothecary, sole Executors. Overseers, Mr *Henry Shrimpton*, Mr. *Jacob Sheafe*, Mr *Thomas Lake*, Mr. *John Hull*, 20 Aug^t 1658.

In presence of vs    *Peter Olliver,    Samuell Prince.*

*Codicil.*—I further giue, to *Elizabeth Tilson*, 20'' and to *Hannah Churchill*, 10'' and to *Mary Andrewes*, 10''.

Acknowledged by y^e Testator before sealing, in presence of *Peeter Olliver.    Samuell Prince.*

*Peeter Olliver* deposed, 9 Sept 1658.

Inventory taken Sept. 1658, by Josh. Scottow, Thomas Savage. [See Reg. Vol. VII, p. 339.] (See p. 114).

---

RICHARD WALTERS, Mariner.—Inventory taken 30 Aug 1653. Major *Symon Willard* and Mr. *Jacob Sheafe* deposed 22 June 1654. [Seè Vol. VII, (1853) p. 337.] (See p. 112).

---

JNO. SAMSON, late of Marblehead.—Inventory taken 28: 7 mo: 1654, by *Francis Johnson, John Smith*. Amt. £32. 14'. *W^m Sampson* deposed.

---

ARTHUR GILL.—An Invoyce of such goods and debts as were left in the hands of *John Sweete* by *Arthur Gill* at his goeing for England. One bill of *W^m Garscay*, one of *Alexander Adams*; due from *Andrew Ayger, John Gill, W^m White, Thomas Chadwell, Francis Hutson*, &c. &c. Amt. £106. 04''· 09^d·  Rec^d from *W^m Elliway* of Cape Anne, 20s. *John Sweete* deposed 10: 11: 1654.

---

REBECCAH WEBB, Widdow. Late of Boston, deceased.—Inventory taken 22 Dec. 1654, by *W^m Davis, Robert Sumner, Tho: Clarke*, Leift *Peeter Olliver, Thomas Buttolph, Godfrey Armitage*, overseers of the Last Will of Rebeccah Webb, deposed 16 March 1654. [See Will, Vol. V, (1851) p. 303.] (See p. 53).

# ABSTRACTS FROM THE EARLIEST WILLS ON RECORD IN THE COUNTY OF SUFFOLK, MASS.

[Prepared by Mr. Wm. B. Trask, of Dorchester ]

Abraham Harding.—Inventory of his Estate taken by *Thomas Weight*, *Robert Hensdell, Ralph Wheelocke*, 6 : 2 : 1655. Am$^t$ £322. 09s. *Elizabeth Harding.* [Entered on the *margin* of the book, the following Will :—] I *Abraham Harding* hath appointed vpon my Last will y$^t$ my whole Estate shall remaine in my wiues hands 10 yeares except shee see other cause & and then my wife to haue y$^e$ third part & then y$^e$ rest shall be devided to my Children with y$^e$ Child y$^t$ is to be borne, but John my sonne shall haue a double porcon. Witnesses *Peter Adams, Prudence Frary, Hannah Alby*, w$^{th}$ others. At a County Court held at Boston 24$^{th}$ Aprill 1655, Power of Administration granted to *Elizabeth Harding* his late wife, to see this imperfect will p'formed as neere as may be.

Edward Rawson, Record$^r$.

---

George Davis —His Estate prized by *Daniell Turell & Barbary Davis*, 20 Aprill 1655. Am$^t$. £569. 09s. 06d. Mentions ¼ & 1/16 part of *Benj$^n$. Munjoys* ship called the Delight, also ¼ part of *George Munjoys* ship called y$^e$ Swan. *Barbary Davis* widow of *George*, deposed, 24 Aprill 1655. [See Will, Vol. V, (1851) p. 306.] (See p. 56).

---

John Coggan, of Boston.—Will dated 16 Dec$^r$ 1657. Vnto my Loving wife *Martha Coggan* during her life, ⅓ p$^t$ of my Estate ; after her decease, to be vnto my son *Caleb.* Also to my sonne *Caleb* I give my now mansion house and the house adjoyning thereto, wherein Goodman *Bomstead* doth Liue, and my two shopps* Adjoyning to my dwelilng house & my house wherein Mr *Sheafe* doth now dwell & my garden plott by Eld$^r$ *Penns* house, and all my farmes & Land at Rumney Marsh & my Corne Mill at Maulden, & ¼ p$^t$ of the Corne mill at Charles Towne, with all my Lands at Maulden, & 500 accers at Woburne. If *Caleb* dye before the age of 21 yeares, the legacy to be divided ; Unto my dau. *Robinson*, one third p$^t$ during her life ; after her decease to be Equally devided amongst her Children. To my dau. *Rocke* ⅓ p$^t$ during life, y$^e$ remainder to be equally devided amongst y$^e$ children of my dau. *Robinson*, to be improoued in some stocke vntill they Come of age. Vnto my dau. *Robinson*, £10. p ann. during life to be payd to her out of the farme at Rumney Marsh. To my dau. y$^e$ wife of *Joseph Rocke* I give £10. To my 3 grand children of my dau. *Robinson*, £10. apiece. To my sonne *Caleb* £10. My will is that the said £40 be putt into y$^e$ Custodie of my sonne in Law *Robinson* & by him improued in a joynt stocke as sheep, horsc, &c. at his discreccon for y$^e$ benefitt of y$^e$ aforesaid Legatees vntill they Come at age. In case any dye, before they arrive to age, the survivors shall haue y$^e$ porcon of y$^e$ deceased equally devided among them. I giue vnto y$^e$ Church at Winsor £20 to be Layd out in Lands or otherwise at their discretion and the same to be improved for the benefitt of a schoole

---

* John Coggan opened the first shop in Boston, for merchandise, in 1634. It was located on the Northeast corner of what is now Washington and State streets. See Drake's *Hist. of Boston,* p. 166.

master for teaching Children to write and read, provided securitie be giuen to my Executors that said stocke shall frō time to time be made good & not diminished.  I give vnto my sonne *Caleb* all the remaining part of my Estate not diposed of.  None of the aboue named Legacies to be payd until the end of two yeares.  The one third pᵗ given my wife shall be delivered into her hands without requiring any securitie more than her owne, during her Widdowhoode, but in case she mary againe My will is that her husband give securitie vnto my executors.  In case my sonne *Caleb* dye before he arive vnto 21 yeares of age, my will is that my wife shall injoy the sᵈ third pᵗ of my estate.  In case my sonne *Robinson* or dau. *Robinson* or any theire heyres or assignes shall not fully acquiesce in this my Last will, but shall make any further Claime or demand to any pᵗ of my Estate, whether in refference unto the estate of my sonne in Law *Woody* deceased or any ingagemᵗ by me made to my sonne *Woody*, or to his wife my dau. *Robinson* or to any other freinds or other relaccon, or by vertue of any order of the Generall Court or upon any other account what soeuer make any further claim to any pᵗ of my Estate then as is before named, then all those gifts shall be vtterly voyd.  None of my houses or lands to be sould, or leased for any Longer terme then 7 yeares.  My wiues thirds of the Lands shall be annually payd her out of yᵉ rents arising from the same; my Executors shall let out the whole together & Assigne her one third pᵗ of the rents thereof, to be payd by the tennants that occupy the same, Provided alwayes for just Cause & religious Ends so judged & determined by the Eldʳˢ of that Church in Boston for the time being, whereof Revᵈ Mr *Wilson* is now Pastoʳ, being giuen undʳ theire hands in Writing to be theire advice & Counsell, it shall be lawfull for any my heires to make sale of said Houses & Lands, otherwise all such sales, mortgages &c. to be Voyd.  I nominate my wife *Martha*, my sonne in Law *Joseph Rocke* and my Loving friend Mr *Joshua Scottow*, Executors.  I also desire the Revᵈ Mr *Norton* Teacher of the Church of Christ at Boston, my Loving friend *Thomas Danforth* & my sonne in Law *Robinson* to be overseers of this my Will.  I giue vnto my sonne *Rocke* and to Mr *Scottow* 5£. apiece, and vnto my overseers 40s. apiece, intreating them to accept of it as a remembrance of my Loue vnto them.  My booke of Martires I giue vnto my sonne *Caleb*, my dau. *Robinson* & my dau. *Rocke*, the Longest Liuer of them, to enjoy the same wholly, & in the meane time to enjoy the benefitt thereof equally as they shall judge most equall yᵐselues.  Vnto *John Coggan* sonne of my brother *Humphery Coggan* I giue my gould Ring.  3 August 1658.

*Natha: Duncan. Thomas Bumsteed.*      John Cogan.
*Henry Powning. Ignatius Hill*      *Joseph Rocke* did not accept of the
*Samuel Robinson.*      executors place.  Mr *Nathaᵉ Duncan*
      & *Thomas Bumsteed* deposed.

Inventory of Estate taken 3 Augᵗ 1658, by *Richard Parker*, *Jacob Sheafe, Thomas Bumsteed.*      Amᵗ. £1339. 01. 01.  Debts due from yᵉ Estate—£454. 17. 03.  Mrs. Martha Coggan deposed.

[There is on file a declaration of the Overseers respecting this Will, two of the Executors nominated having disclaimed the proving thereof, so that it rested wholly upon Mrs. Coggan, the widow, " to undertake a business of so troublesome a nature, or otherwise the will of the deceased must be wholly frustrated."  The Overseers taking the matter into consideration, endeavor to resolve some of the queries proposed by Mrs. Coggan.  In answer to one of these, touching the education of her son Caleb,

" The overseers do Judge meet to declare that £20 p' Ann. dureing the time the s⁴ Caleb shalbe brought vp at English or Gramʳ schooles, & £30 p' Ann dureing the time he shalbe at the Colledge, shalbe accounted a meet recompence to the executrix, with allowance for wᵗ she shall lay out for his bookes & Extraordinary Expenses for phisicke, &c."
John Norton, Thomas Danforth.
Thomas Danforth deposed 3 Aug 1658.]

WILLIAM BEAMSLEY.—Will. Being sicke, make my wife executrix & Administratrix of all my houses, Lands Orchards, goods, &c. as Long as she shall Liue, Provided she Let *Mercy* haue that Chamber wherein she now lyes for her owne, and there shall be with all Conveniency made therein a Chimney, and she to enjoy it dureing her Widdowhoode. And I desire that my wife may take yᵉ Care of her, and see that she wants neither meat, drink nor Cloathing during the time of her Widdowhoode. My Will is that after my wifes decease my whole Estate shall be prized and sett to sale   The whole Estate that is then left to be equally distrib-uted amongsᵗ all my Children, Namely, *Anne Woodward, Grace Graues, Mercy Wilborne, Hannah Beamsley, Edward Bushnell, Elizabeth Page, Mary Robison;* and in case any of those dye vnpossessed, it shall returne to the next heyre. My desire is, that *Thomas Clarke, Richard Gridley, Alexander Adams,* see this my will fullfilled. 14 Septᵗ 1658
In the pʳnts of vs                                   William Beamsley.
*Thomas Clarke*                      *Thomas Clarke, Alexander Adams,*
*Alex: Adames sn*                   *Richard Gridley* deposed, 28 : 8 : 1658.
*Richard ⋈ Gridley*
*John Ferniside*
Inventory of yᵉ Estate of yᵉ Late Ensigne *Wᵐ Beamsly* (who departed this life the 29ᵗʰ Septᵗ last,) taken this 15 Oct 1658. Apprized p. *Tho: Clark, Allex Adames, Jnᵒ Richards.* Amᵗ. £251. 14. 01. " House & Land at Boston £140. Land at Muddy River £4 " " Due Mr *Wᵐ Payne,* £4." *Martha Beamsly,* widow of *William,* deposed, 28 : 8 : 1658.

JOHN DANE.—[On file in his own handwriting.] Vpon the sevth day of the seventh month in 1658.—To son John Dane, ten pounds out of my now dwelling house, which will appear ln deed, dated 2d. feberi in fift one [1651.]—To son Francis my wood lot, about two & twentie ackers, mor or les, as it doth appeer in Town-book.—To dafter Elizabeth How, a black cow now att Andiver in the hand of Georg Abet [Abbot] to be deliuered to her after my deseas emediatly.—To Son John Dane, on feather bede & on feather boster & two fether pillows & a yellow rugg, & also a pewter platter.—To son Francis, on great ketle, also on flaxen sheet & a saser.—To dafter Elizabeth How, a litl kittle, & on pewter candlestick.—To Son Frances, my old black cow, now at Roxburie, & my bible.—To louing wiff Anic, whom I mak sooll exseekitrix all my movable goods that is not expresed.
In witnes heer vnto I hav set my hand this seueth day of the seveth month 58   By me
Isaac Heath,
John Johnson, Isack Morrell.
At a county court held at Boston 16 Oct. 1658, Mr John Johnson de-posed that he saw Jnᵒ Dane sign & publish it as his last will, &c.
                                        Edward Rawson Recordʳ.

143

STEPHEN LINCOLN senior, of Hingham.—Being very sicke. It is my will that *Joane Lincolne* widdow, my mother, shall haue for her habitation during her life the new End of my house that is to say, the Parlor, the Low roome only, and that she shall haue the vse of what houshold things are necessary for her occasions. My will is also that my said mother shall haue one Cowe, with two Goates, kept winter and sumer at the Charge of my sonne *Steuen Lincolne.* I giue also unto *Thomas Sayer* one blacke Ewe : and the Lambe of that Ewe I giue unto *Susanna Lincolne,* Daughter to my brother, *Thomas Lincolne.* I giue also my Cloake vnto my brother *Thomas Lincolne.* It is my will also that *Steuen Lincoln,* my sonne shall haue all the rest of my estate, houses, Lands, Chattells whatsoeur, whome I make executor to this my Last will.

Steuen his Lincolne marke

Witnesses, *Peter Hubberd*, Signum **O** *Johannis Lowe.*

Mr *Peter Hubbard* and *John Lowe* deposed, 18: 9: 58. Inventory of Estate made 18: 8: 1658, by *Joshua Hubbard, Mathew Hawke.* Amt. £179. 10s. "A pcell of meadow in broad Cove meadow, £20 ;" "A great Bible, 10s." &c. *Stephen Lincoln* deposed this to be a true Inventory of his late father, 18: 9: 58.

---

JOHN EATON of Dedham, though sicke, yet sound in memory, doe make this my Last Will.—I giue vnto *Abigall* my wife, the free vse of my Parlor in my now dwelling house, & the Leantoe thereunto adjoyning, and all the household stuffe at present in them, to her vse all the tearme she shall remaine a Widdow ; & sufficient firewood for her vse, to be provided and Layd in the yard at her assignmt. I giue my wife, the annuitie of 6 pounds p ann. to be payd at the End of each halfe yeare after my decease, in such things as she needeth out of my estate hereafter to be disposed of, during her life ; or the third pt of my Lands during the same tearme ; her selfe to choose which of these two she best liketh. I giue unto my wife so much of my other household stuffe as come to the value of 5 pounds, such as her selfe shall make Choyse of, and also one Cowe her selfe to choose. I giue to *John Dammant,* of Reading, £5 ; to *John Plimpton,* of Meadfeild £5 ; vnto *Edward Hodsman,* my kinsman, 40s. The remainder of my Estate shall be devided into two equall pts. and that pt of her portion which my dau. *Mary* haue receiued to be accounted therevnto ; the one halfe whereof I giue to *John Eaton,* my sonne, and his heyres foreuer, and the other halfe to *Mary* and *Abigall,* my two daughters and theire heires ; my sonne and my two daughters to pay to my wife, their mother, that £6 p ann as aboue written. I nominate *Abigall,* my wife, to be my executrix. 2: 9: 1658. *John ⋈ Eaton.*

*John Allin Eleazer Lusher. John Allin* and *Eleazer Lusher* deposed. Inventory of the Estate taken 30: 9: 1658 by *Eliazer Lusher, Henry Chickering, Jnᵒ Harvard.* Amt £392. 10s. "Land in the Island playne £28 ;" two pcels in the great plaine £19 ; by South Plaine, at foule Meadow ; Right in an Island in the swampe, &c. &c. *Abigall* relict of *Jnᵒ Eaton* deposed, 16: 10: 58.

---

JOHN BEALES.—Being by a pvidence of God to goe to old England doe make this my Last will. Vnto my Cousen *Mary Whiton,* the wife of *James Whiton,* 30s ; vnto *Elizabeth Lasell,* wife of *John Lasell,* 30s. The rest of my Estate shall be disposed of as followeth : one halfe of it to yᵉ use of my father *Edmond Beales* or his heyers or assigns ; the other

halfe, one third part of it to my Cosen *Jeremiah Beales*, one third to my Cosen *Sarah Marsh*, the wife of *Thomas Marsh*, one third part to my Cosen *Rebecca Beales*, dau. of *John Beales* senio<sup>r</sup>. There is due vnto me from *Josiah Hubbard*, the sonne of Mr. *Peter Hubbard*, 44s. w<sup>ch</sup> some if *Josiah* pay it I giue it unto Mr *Peter Hubbard*. I appoint my Cosen *Thomas Marsh* sole executor. 26 Oct<sup>r</sup> 1657.              *John Beales.*
Witness *Mathew Hawke John Fering.*
*Mathew Hawkes* and *John Fering* deposed 28 July 1658.
Inventory taken by *Mathew Hawke, John Ferring, Nathanyell Beales.* Am<sup>t</sup>. £37. 03s.

---

THOMAS MARSH, of Hingham, being sicke, doe make this my Last Will.—I giue all my Estate, Land & Cattle whatsoeuer vnto *Sarah Marsh*, my wife & vnto my 4 Children, *Thomas, Sarah, Ephraim & Mary.* My intent is that my wife whome I ordaine executrix of this my Last Will shall carefully educate & bring vp my Children w<sup>th</sup> what Estate I Leave her. And my will is, that when my youngest Daughter *Mary* shall attaine the age of 14 ycares, or my sonne Thomas vnto 21, then what remaines of this Estate shall thus be devided amongs<sup>t</sup> them, the one halfe of that Estate that is left to *Sarah* my wife, & y<sup>e</sup> other halfe to my 4 Children, as followeth: my Eldest sonne *Thomas*, two shares; my other three Children, single shares. I appointe as overseers to this Will, my friends *Mathew Hawke, John Fering & Nath<sup>ll</sup> Beale*, with *Sarah* m<sup>v</sup> wife. 31 Aug. 1658.                                        *Tho : Marsh.*
Witnesses *Peter Hubberd Tho : Hubberd.*
Mr *Peter Hubbard* deposed, 18: 9: 58.
Inventory of the Estate of *Thomas Marsh* taken by *John Fearing, Mathew Hawke, Nath<sup>ll</sup> Beales.* Sum £320. 06. Debts due from him £12. " Part of a home Lott bought of *John Lobdin*, 5 Acres of planting Land vpon Bakers hill, 5 Acres vpon Weriall hill, 2 smale Lotts vpon Squirrell hill," &c. &c. *Sarah Marsh*, widow of Thomas, deposed 26 Aprill 1659.

---

SIMON EIRE, of Boston. 5 July 1658.—I giue vnto *Martha*, my wife, the thirds of my dwelling house at Boston, with y<sup>e</sup> Garden & appūr<sup>ces</sup> belonging to it, & also the thirds of my Farme at Watertowne with the houses, Barne, Orchard &c. belonging to it, now in y<sup>e</sup> occupacon of *Joseph Tainter* during her life, & the other two thirds towards the bringing vp of my two youngest children, *Maria & John*; & after my wifes death y<sup>e</sup> said *Maria & John* to haue my said house at Boston & Farme at Watertowne w<sup>th</sup> y<sup>e</sup> houses, &c. belonging to them, to be equally devided betweene them, & if y<sup>t</sup> either the said *Maria* or *John* shall dye, before they marry or come to y<sup>e</sup> age of 20 yeares, y<sup>e</sup> survivor to enjoy it, but if both dye before they mary or come to y<sup>e</sup> age of 20 yeares, then y<sup>e</sup> said house at Boston and farme at Watertowne, with all y<sup>e</sup> appūr<sup>ces</sup> belonging to them, I will y<sup>t</sup> they be equally devided amongst my Children, both sonnes & daughters, & if any of them be dead, theire Children Living to Enjoy theire part.
Also to *Martha*, my wife, towards y<sup>e</sup> bringing vp of *Mary & John*, my two youngest children, & for y<sup>e</sup> paym<sup>t</sup> of my debts, y<sup>e</sup> £115 due me, as appeare by y<sup>e</sup> executor account in Dec<sup>r</sup> 6<sup>th</sup> 1657. I giue to *Martha*, my wife, the woolen & Linnen Cloth in y<sup>e</sup> presse, with my apparrell Phisicke & Debts due to me, with all y<sup>e</sup> Mares & Colts at Ipswich & Watertowne, to make good y<sup>e</sup> Cattle & moveables I had out of y<sup>e</sup> stocke Left

for her vse. I giue to *Maria*, my youngest daughter, all my household stuffe, Bedding, brasse, iron, Pewter plates. I giue to *John*, my youngest sonne, all my booke manuscripts, mortars, scales & weights, stills, potts & Glasses. I giue to *Thomas*, my Eldest sonne, the 200 Acres I am to haue Layd out at Watertowne for a farme, with y^e 17 accres of remote meadow & y^e 16 accres Called *Seelyes* Lott, Lying in Watertowne, to make vp his double portion. I giue to *Dorothy*, my Daughter, forty pounds of English goods, being Linnen & woollen cloth, to be payd at Boston within one yeare after my death at m^rchants price out of the £115 due to me. Also to *Dorothy*, one halfe headed bedstead with y^e Curtaines & valance of Dornix, one feather bed, one boulster, on pillow, one greene rugg & two blanketts in y^e Hall chamber. The rest of my children hauing had their portions.                    *Simon Eire.*
Witnes, *Richard Parker, Theodore Atkinson.*
   I make Mr *W^m Hubbard* Jun^r, of Ipswich, & Mr *James Penn*, of Boston, my Executors, & doe give to each of y^m £5, & doe also make *Martha*, my wife, executrix.
   Mr *Richard Parker*, & *Theodore Atkinson* deposed, 4 March 1658.
   Inventory of the Estate of *Simon Eire*, deceased this last Dec^r 1658 ; taken by *John Clarke, Richard Parker, Theodore Atkinson.*  Sum Totall, £577. 05s.  Mrs *Martha Eires*, widow of *Simon*, deposed, 11 Aug^t 1659.

---

   JAMES ASTWOOD.—The Estate y^t *W^m Parkes*, y^e Administrator, Receiued,* was, by Inventory in the Court, besydes the houses and Lands, £74. 2s. 8d.  The house & Land at Roxbery w^ch is in the said Inventory £85. sould to *Joseph Wise*, one of the Creditor^s for £60: 08s. and his owne debt payd. The house & Land at Boston, sould by Mr *Michaell Powell*, Mr *Thomas Kimball* & *Edward Burt*, being three of the Creditors, sould for £65. & their debts payd.  So y^t all the Estate y^t came into the hands of the said Administrato^r is, £199. 10s. 8d. w^ch is payd out as followeth, to W^m Sweet, Mr Booth, W^m Vesey, W^m Whetwell, Robert Turner, Mr Davison, John Dudley, Mr John Newell, Edward Goodwin, W^m Phillips, Sampson Shore, George Boner, Cap^t Sperlin, George Munnings, Richard Cooke, Richard Norton, John Hull, W^m Hudson, Edward Maduck, Tho. Roberts, John Viell, Zachary Phillips, Joshua Foote, James Madocke, John Lewis, Benj^a Gillum, Heugh Stone, Thomas Thorowgood, Edward Pason, Randall Nichols, John Shaw, Phillip Tory, Peter Tracy, Caleb Foot, John Bowles, Robert Shefieles, John Woodmancey, George Dell, Goodman Chapman, Abram Browne, Thomas Phillips, Cap^t Rich^d Walker, Matt Payne, W^m Hawley, John Farnam, Mr W^m Peake, Robert Seuer, Abram Palmer, Richard Garner, Adam Wright, &c. &c.  *Anthony Stoddard* & *Edward Ting* were ordered, by the Court, to take proofe of the Debts owing by Mr James Astwood & make devision of his Estate among his Creditors ; who " find it to reach in paym^t as nere as we could compute it, to 6s. a pound." Deacon *W^m Parkes* deposed 2 Feb. 1654.

---

   THOMAS BELL.—Inventory of Estate proved 4 July 1655 by *Ann Bell*, widdow of *Thomas*.  Mentions, " 4½ acres of Land at Long Island of planting ground & meadow, £10 ; 21 Acres of Land at Brantree, £3 ; from *John Hurd*, £2." &c. &c.

---

* See p. 275, Vol. VIII.  (See p. 127).

## ABSTRACTS FROM THE EARLIEST WILLS ON RECORD IN THE COUNTY OF SUFFOLK, MASS.

[Prepared by Mr. WM. B. TRASK, of Dorchester.]

EDMUND GROSSE.—Inventory of his Goods prized by *John Butter*, *James Euerill*, 5: 3: 1655. Amt. £149. 14s. Power of Administration granted to Mr. *Jer: Houchin* and Leif. *James Johnson*, in behalfe of yᵉ widdow and children. Mentions "50 Acres of Land Lying at Muddy Riuer, £7. 10s." The Estate is in Debt to Mathew Grosse, Mr. Cole, goodman Weeden, Clement Grosse, Mr. Starr senʳ, Mr. Starr junʳ, Mathew Barnes, Brother Burton, Goody Carter, Sister Davis, Mrs. Bowyer; to Mr. Garrets father in England for lyquors; to Barnard Squire, &c., &c. *Jeremy Houchin* deposed, 4ᵗʰ July, 1655.

NATH SOWTHER.—The goods of Mʳ *Souther*, Lately deceased, Aprized by *Samuell Betfield, Thomas Bumsteed, Godfrey Armitage.* 17 July, 1655. Amt. £150. 16. 6. Goods of Mʳˢ *Souther*, wᶜʰ she brought to Mʳ. *Sowther.* Amt. £83. Power of Administration granted to *Sarah Souther*, his widdow, who deposed, 31 July 1655.

BARNABAS FAWER.—Inventory of the Estate that was belonging to *Barnabas Fawer* deceased the 19ᵗʰ of the 10ᵗʰ moᵗʰ 1654, apprized by *Jacob Sheafe, James Eurill, Richard Cooke.* Amt. £596. 17. 06. "Due from *Wᵐ Hudson*, £30; in beefe and flower from *Wᵐ East*, of Milford, £117. 11. 06; Mr. *Wᵐ Phillips.* £12; in Mr. *Wᵐ Paddyes* hands, Received in debts from Connecticott and sundry places, in flower, wheat, Rye, and Porke, £60; from *Richard Fellowes*, of Connecticott, £3. 10s.," &c., &c. Values "2 mares runn away in the woods and 1 horse runn away suposed to be at Dedham, £30." The Estate in Debt to good *Oliver*, the Taylor; goodman *Henfield*, of Millford; Mr. *Pell*, of Fairefeild; Mr. *John Webb*, &c. *Grace Fawer*, widow of *Barnabas*, deposed, 9 August 1655. [Will, Reg. (1851) Vol. V. p. 305.] (See p. 55).

ELIZABETH PITTS.—Inventory of the goods of Mrs. *Elizabeth Pitts* deceased at Waymouth, prised by *John Whitmarsh, Thomas Bayly, Samuell Packer, James Nash.* Amt. £16. 06. 06. "My Mother Mrs. *Pitts* oweth to me and to other in her sicknes and health as followeth, 6 Weekes attendance in her sicknes, at 6s. 8d. per weeke, £2; 20 weekes attendance in her sicknes, at 8s. per weeke, £8; Mr. *Allcocke*, for Phisicke and Cordialls, 7s; Mr. *Allcockes* Journeyes hither, 7s; for things fetched at *Thomas Dyars*, 12s. 02d; debt to *John Phillips*, of Boston, 3s. 6d., &c. Whole amount £13. 16s. 8d. Administration to the Estate of Mrs. *Elizabeth Pitts* granted to *Wᵐ Holbrooke & Elizabeth*, his wife, 1 Aug. 1655.

HENERY GLOVER.—Inventory of the goods of *Henery Glouer*, of Medfield, deceased the 21ˢᵗ of the 5ᵗʰ moᵗʰ 1655, taken by *Thomas Wight, Robert Hensdell, Ralph Wheelocke.* Sume totall, £88. 05. Administration granted, 13 Sept. 1655, to *Abigail Glouer*, his late wife, who deposed, 29 Novʳ 1655.

147

JOHN CODDINGTON.—Inventory of the goods of *John Coddington*, deceased 27ᵗʰ Augᵗ 1655 prized by *Richard Peacocke, Edmund Jacklin.* Power of Administration granted to his Estate by *Emm,* his late wife, who deposed same day.

---

SAMUELL NAULTON.—Inventory of his goods. " Due to him in wages for 9 moᵗʰ, at 35s. per moᵗʰ, £15. 19s.," &c. Owing *Lorance English* 7s., &c., &c. *Jnᵒ Naulton* deposed, 22 Sepʳ 1655, yᵗ this is a true Inventory of his brother, *Samᵘ Naulton* estate, to the best of his knowledge.

---

THOMAS DUDLEY, junior.—Inventory. " Parte of Water Towne Mill estimated at £40." &c., &c., £63. 15. 02. Mr. *Thomas Danforth* and Mr. *Samᵘ Danforth* deposed, 6: 9: 55.* Mr. *Sam: Danforth,* Informed of a Bed, bedding, Corne &c prised at 40s. wᶜʰ I here set down. 21 June 1664. *Edw: Rawson,* Recordʳ.

---

GREGORY BAXSTAR, of Brantree.—Being sicke—doe make my last will —wife and sonne *John* executors. I giue to my sonne *Dearing* my little piece of salt meadow adjoyning his own house, being in quantitie about an acre of ground ; to his dau. *Bethia,* £10, to be payd her when she is 16 yeares of age, also on blake Calfe of a year old, and one black young Ewe sheepe, to be delivered to her father, to be improved by him for her vse, as he shall see meete, till she is 16 yeares of age. Vnto my sonne *Joseph Adam* and my dau. his wife, 6 acres of Land lying in the great feild, being all the Land lying vpon the right side of the Cart way to the ferry, be it more or lesse ; also my lettle Island of Salt Marsh, wᶜʰ lyeth at the head of the Salt Creeke, that Cōmeth up towards the Towne land, lying neare to the ende of *Peter Georges* lott, and also halfe my Lands at the Captaines plaine. I giue to his sonne *Joseph,* the Child of my Daughter, and if he dye without any heyre, then it shall goe to my Daughtʳˢ next eldest sonne, or dau. if she haue no sonne. Also, I giue to my sonne, *Joseph Adams,* my old Mare. All yᵉ rest of my Estate I giue to my wife and my sonne *John,* my wife to haue all yᵉ vse of it while she Liueth ; after her decease my sonne *John* to haue it all, only my wife shall haue two Cowes to dispose of as she pleaseth at her death ; only I giue my horse, two oxen, one Cowe, and one Steare, to my sonne *John.* Also, I giue to my wife those two Cowes she hath power to dispose of at her death, to be for her owne vse while she liueth. 2ᵈ day of the 4ᵗʰ moneth, cōmanly called June, 1659.

his<br>GREGORY ⋈ BAXSTAR.<br>marke

his<br>
In the pʳnts of *John* ⋈ *Gurney, Moses Payne, Richard Brackett.*<br>
marke

Whereas in this my last will I haue giuen to my sonne *Deareing* A little piece of Salt Marsh, I now make voyd that act, and giue that piece of Marsh to my wife and sonne John, for them to vse together, while she liueth, and after her death to be wholy my sonne *Johns* as yᵉ rest of my Estate is ; and I giue to my sonne *Dearing,* in the room of that, two weather sheepe. 19: 4ᵗʰ: 1659.

his<br>GREGORY ⋈ BAXSTER.<br>marke

Witnès, *Moses Paine, Richard Brackett.*
14 June 1659. Capᵗ *Richard Brackett* and Ensigne *Moses Paine,* deposed.

---

* There is an omission of this date in the Abstract given, Reg. Vol. V. 1851, p. 445. (See p. 61).

An Inventory of the Goods of *Gregory Baxtor* deceased, Brantrey 7: 5ᵗʰ. 1659. Taken by *Jnᵒ Gurney, Moses Paine, Edmund Quinsey.* Amt. £417. 19s. *Margaret Baxter,* relict of *Gregory Baxter &* *John,* theire sonne, deposed, 14 July 1659. Present yᵉ Governoʳ, Depᵗ Governoʳ, Major Atharton & Recordʳ.

---

Mʀ. Joshua Foote.—Inventory of his goods in and about Boston. Amt. £13. 5d. " 96 acres Land at Brantrey not prized." " Wee did not medle with the Land, as wittnes our hands this 30ᵗʰ of the 8ᵗʰ moᵗʰ
the marke of
1655. *Richard Woodde, Jeremy* ⋈ *Morell.* One Warehouse in Boston, and house and land at Roxbury, morgaged and forfeited for his debts. Lieut. *Joshua Hewes* deposed, 15 Nov. 1655. The following persons, among others, are mentioned in the inventory of debts :—George Hallsall, Benjamine Negus, William Helds, Tho Rider, Jnᵒ Bowlles, Tho Kemball, Jnᵒ Lambett, Wᵐ Dawes, Tho Whitmore, Samuell Bennett, John Diven, Richard Bennett, Robert Burmop, Mr Ware, Shipwright ; John Hathorne, Mr John Cutts, Joseph Jencks senioʳ, Mʳ Edward Hutchison, Mathias Briges, Mr Samuell Mauricke, Mr Tho Broughton, Benjamine Child, Jnᵒ Phillips, Thomas Rallings, Joseph Jenkes Junioʳ, Charles Presus, Richard Sute, Henry Kimball, Joseph Bastarr, Thomas Williams, Isaack Nash, Samuell Hart, Roger Tiler, Jasper Rawlings, Richard Knowles, Amos Richison, Richard Chard, William Pittman, Mʳ Valentine Hill, Jnᵒ Sunderling, Fardinando Tare, Tho Tare, Sidracke Tare, Ralph Mason, Mr William Paine, Robert Burden, Jnᵒ Welke, Jnᵒ Barnes, Richard Clarke, Jnᵒ Hanmore, Strong Furnall, Mr Tho Mayhew, Samˡˡ Jackson, Jnᵒ Millam, Jnᵒ Rogers, Edwᵈ Weden, Quinton Pray, Nicholas Pinnion, Tho Paine, Hen Greene, Joseph Saundʳs, Joseph Armitage, Richᵈ Post, Jnᵒ Bee, Phillip Leonard, Edward Gardner, Francis Perry. [Will, Reg. (1851) Vol. V. p. 444.] (See p. 60).

---

Roberт Reynolds.—Will. Now liueing in Boston. I giue to my wife, my house with all that appertaine vnto it, with my Marsh ground at Muddy River, with one lott of Ground at Long Island, so long as she liveth, with all my house stuffe in my house, and what money there is left. After her decease I haue given my house and orchard to my sonne *Nathaniell* and to his heyres foreuer, and if he should dye without Children, or any one Child lawfully begotten of his owne body, then his wife to enjoy the said house and Orchard so long as she liueth, and after her decease, to Returne to my fowre daughters Children, that is to say, my dau. *Ruth Whitney* and to her Eldest sonne ; to my dau. *Tabitha Abdy* and her sonne *Mathew Abdy,* and if he should dye, to her two dauᵗ. either of them alike ; to my dau. *Sarah Mason* and her sonne *Robert Mason,* and if he dye, to her dau. *Sarah ;* to my dau. *Mary Sanger* and her sonne *Nathaniell* and if he dye to her next child, either sonne or daughter. [Also, to his four dauˢ. £20 each.] For the paymᵗ of these legacies I haue eight acres of Marsh land, which if my sonne *Nathaniell* will pay £20 in good pay towards this fower score pound, then he to haue my Marsh land and his heyres foreuer ; but if he refuse to pay the twentie pound, then to be devided equally to my fower dauˢ. and to theire Children, or else that it may be sold for as much as it will yeeld, and devided among them equally. The other threescore pound to be raysed out of my owne estate ; what is over and aboue, my will is, my wife shall haue, and I do make her my executrix; also, I joyne my sonne *Nathaniell* with her, to be as helpefull to my wife, his mother, as possibly he can. These legacies to be payed within one yeare and a day. If it should please God that I doe liue so long as any of my Estate should be spent, as it is likely it may, I & my wife being stricken in age & are almost past our Labour, then, for euery one of them to abate proportionably alike. 20 : 2 : 1658.                                                              Robert Reynolds.

27 July 1659.  *Thomas Grubb & Nathaniell Bishop* deposed, that being a visiting of *Robert Reynolds*, a little before his death, the said *Reynolds*, in their p<sup>r</sup>nce, declared this paper to be his last Will.  Inventory of the Estate prized by *Nathaniell Bishop, Richard Woody.  Mary Reynolds*, widow of *Robert*, deposed 27 July 1659.  House & Land in Boston, valued at £110.

----

JOHN RUGGLES.—Inventory of *John Ruggles* [senior] late of Boston, deceased, taken by *James Johnson*, Deac. *Richard Trusdell* & *Robert Walker*, 21 Jan. 1656.  Am<sup>t</sup>. £147.02.08.  Estate indebted to Richard Parker, W<sup>m</sup> Browne. W<sup>m</sup> Brenton. Bonniface Burton, Margery Lever, Joseph Mosse, &c.  22 Jan. 1656.  *Georg Ruggles* & *James Wiseman* deposed.

----

RICHARD HAWES.—Power of Administration to y<sup>e</sup> Estate of *Richard Hawes* late of Dorchester, granted to Majo<sup>r</sup> *Humphrey Atherton* and Leiftenant *Roger Clap*, they bringing an Inventory of y<sup>e</sup> estate into y<sup>e</sup> Court. Edward Rawson.

----

PHILLIP ALLEY.—Inventory of his Estate prized by *Richard Gridley, Gamaliell Waite, Hope Allen*, 11 Dec. 1655.  Amt. £77. 11s. 06d.  Power of Administracon graunted to *Susanna*, wife of s<sup>d</sup> Alley, 13 Dec. 1655.

----

RICHARD WEBB.—In sicknesse, doe make this my last Will.  I giue to my Eldest sonne *Joseph* that part of my now dwelling house in Boston w<sup>ch</sup> is next to M<sup>r</sup> *Glover*, & the roomes over it, with halfe both sell<sup>r</sup>s, & halfe the yard behind it.  I giue to *Nehemiah*, my youngest sonne, the other part of my house, with the other halfe of the Cellars, and y<sup>e</sup> one halfe of the yard, one feather bed with its furniture, the two middle brasse potts, fiue siluer spoones, sixe pewter platters of them that be at my dau. *Pearces*, one plate and lesser Kettle, one of the best Quishons, one Muskett sword & bandel<sup>r</sup>s, one old great Bible, & M<sup>r</sup> Elton his works, one of M<sup>r</sup> Boultons works, one of M<sup>r</sup> Whentleys, one smale bible, one paire of sheets, one paire of pillowkers, one silver wine taster.  I giue to *Ester Pearce*, my dau. in law, £5. p Annū. to be payd yearely by my two sonnes, or whosoeuer shall enjoye my now dwelling house in Boston, vizt. each part of the house, yearely, to pay £2. 10s. which paym<sup>t</sup> is to beginne when the house is finished & made tenantable, & to Continue during the life of the said *Ester*, If the house continue so Long in being.  I giue to *Moses & Ester* my said dau. in lawes two children, to each, 20s.  I giue the rest of my goods & Estate, after my Just debts be payd &c. & my now dwelling house finished, vnto my sonne *Joseph Webb*, whom I make Executo<sup>r</sup>.  Also I appointe Deacon *Vpham*, of Mauldin, Deacon *Clap*, of Dorchester, & Leif<sup>t</sup> *Roger Clap*, of Dorchester, to be my overseers, In-

treating them to assist & Counsell my Children for theire best good.  1st
of July 1659.                                          Richard Webb.
In the prncē of *Roger Clap*,
*Joan Clapp, Nathaniell Bishop.*
21 July 1659.  Present Goverʳ, Depᵗ Govʳ & Recordʳ. Leifᵗ. *Clap* &
*Nath: Bishop*, deposed.  *Joseph Webb* declared that he chose his vncle
*Vpham*, leiuᵗ *Clap* & Deacon *Clap*, to be his guardian.

---

Mr. James Bate, of Dorchester.—Inventory of Estate taken 8 : 11mo :
1655. by *Joseph Farnworth, Henery Cauliffe, Richard Withington.*
Amᵗ. £413. 9d.   14 Jan. 1655. *James Bate* sworne saith this is a true
Inventory of his late father *James Bate* Estate.  [Will, Reg. (1815) Vol.
V. p. 297.] (See p. 47).

---

John Ruggles, sonne of *Thomas Ruggles*, being weake, I thinke good
to settle things to Leaue peace behind me.  My house & lands with yᵉ
rest of my Estate, the debts being discharged, I giue vnto my wife &
children; yᵉ whole Estate to remaine in my wifes hands so long as the
Children Continue with her, & the Children at yᵉ age of 21 yeares to
possesse yᵉ one halfe, and my wife yᵉ other halfe, for her life time, &
after her decease to be yᵉ Childrens ; the halfe of yᵉ Estate wᶜʰ I giue·
my Children to possesse at yᵉ age of 21 yeares my sonne *John* to haue
yᵉ one halfe of it, & my sonne *Thomas*, & my sonne *Samuell*, yᵉ other
halfe, equally betwixt them ; the other halfe, wᶜʰ I giue to my wife her
life time, after her decease, to be devided to my children , yᵗ is to say, to
my sonne *John*, the one halfe, & my sonne *Thomas* & my sonne *Samuell*
the other halfe : also, this power I giue to my overseers, yᵗ in case my
wife Mary againe, if then my overseers doe not like yᵉ vsage of my
Children, then I giue my overseers power to take away my Children, &
to take yᵉ halfe of my Estate wᶜʰ I leaue in yᵉ hands of my wife, & dispose of it as they thinke best, for yᵉ good of my children, & she to haue
her halfe Remaining vnto her as aforesaid.  My overseers are my Vncle
*Ruggles*, my father *Craft*, & my Brothér *Samuel Ruggles*.  What Lands
I haue sold & haue not giuen an assurance my overseers shall haue power
to giue an assurance, as likewise what Lands I haue bought & haue not
receiued assurance, my overseers shall haue power to receiue for my wife
and children quiet possession.  I Leaue my wife & my father *Craft* to be
mine Executors, with power to sell any Cattle, or Cart, or any other thing
yᵗ may be necessarily spared for the paymᵗ of my debts, and likewise
his house & Orchard vpon the hill neare yᵉ meeting house ; the overseers
to giue full assurance.  9th 7 ber 1658.            John Ruggles.
Witnes, *Robert Pepper, Peleg Heàth*, who deposed 15 Oct. 1658.
Inventory of the Estate of Seargᵗ *John Ruggles*, deceased, prized the
20 Sept 1658, by *Thomas Weld* & *Peleg Heath.* Amᵗ. £185. 11. *Abigail
Ruggles* & Leiuᵗ *Griffine Craft* deposed 15 Oct. 1658.  The Estate indebted to widdow Ardell, for bricks ; to father Hull ; to Goodman Roote,
for Rent ; Tobias Davis, for Smiths worke ; Thomas Weld ; Mrs Sands,
for spice, Goodman Bloors, for Sugar ; William Peacocke, for swine ; to
yᵉ Glazier Bushnell, for glasse ; Henry Farnham, for joynery worke ;
Shuball Seaver ; John Johnson, deceased ; Phillip Wharton ; Tho. Haly ;
Joseph Wise, for mault & meate ; Brother Porter, for Candle ; John
Mather ; John Stebbin, for bran ; Isaac Morrill ; Goody Roote, for Ap-
ples ; Robert Prentise, for worke ; Richard Woodde, for sacke & beere ;

Joseph Griggs, for goods; Hugh Clarke, &c. &c. Debts oweing to y^e Estate by John Crafts, Samuel Finch, Edward Morris, Sam^u Ruggles, Leiut Rimington, James Trissell, & John Bridge.

The Accompt of Cred^r & Deb^r Relating to John Ruggles Junio^r Estate, Late of Roxbury, proved, & allowed by the Court 26 Aprill 1660. Edw: Rawson Record^r.

---

JOHN WILLIAMS.—Power of Administration to y^e Estate of *John Williams* is graunted to Robert *Williams*, his father, 15 Oct. 1658.

Inventory of s^d John Williams, who deceased the 6^th of Oct. 1658, taken by *Thomas Madson & Daniell Turell.* Amt. £55.10.03. " His tooles with the Anvill, Iron, steele, Coles, locks & Rubstones, £24.08.09." *Robert Williams*, deposed 2^d Dec. 1658.

---

WILLIAM POTTER, of Roxbury.—Inventory taken 23 Jan. 1653, by *Phillep Elliott, Isack Johnson, Robert Seaver, Robert Pepper.* [Will, Reg. (1851) Vol V. p. 301.] (See p. 51).

---

JOSEPH FARNWORTH, of Dorchester.—2 Jan. 1659. Being of reasonable health & memory, doe by this my last will dispose of my Estate as followeth :—vnto *Mary*, my wife, £37, in money or other moveable Estate at money price; also £13. 6s. 8d. more out of my moveable goods as they shalbe indifferently prized. I giue vnto my wife *Mary*, the same of fowrescore pounds for portions for her two Children w^ch she had by her other husband, namely, *Joseph Long & Thomas Long*; to dispose of the same to them, w^ch & as she shall see meete, whether alike proportion to both, or to one & y^e other lesse, Considering theire dutie & behavio^r towards her as theire mother. I giue to my dau. *Elizabeth*, wife of *John Manfeild*, £18. 5s. w^ch maks vp y^t w^ch she haue allready received y^e sume of £40 ; to my dau. *Ester*, £36 ; to my dau. *Mary* y^e wife of *Abraham Ripley* £24. 11s. w^ch makes vp what she haue allready receiued y^e sume £40 ; vnto my grand child *Joseph Peck*, y^e sonne of *Simon Peck* (who marryed with *Hannah*, my Daughter, now deceased) £5, to be payd vnto him by my Executrix when he shall accomplish y^e age of 21 yeares, or day of marriage, w^ch shall first happen. In case said *Joseph* dept. this life before he accomplish said age, or disposeth himselfe in marriage, then my will is that said Executrix dispose thereof to *Samuell*, my sonne. I giue unto my dau. *Rebecca*, £40. For my Eldest sonne *Joseph*, although he haue already had from me a Considerable Estate, more then a double portion, yet I giue vnto him for a Remembrance, 20s. to be payd him when Lawfully demanded. Legacies to my 4 dau^s. [to] be paid within one yeare after my decease. In case my moveable Estate will not pay said Legacies, Then my will is, y^t my Executrix sell any p^t of my Lands to satisfye said Legacies. All y^e rest of mine Estate in Land & goods I giue vnto my sonne *Samuel* when he shall accomplish 21 yeares or day of marriage, vntill which time my wife shall possesse y^e same for his Education, giueing accompt to him when he comes of age, or within three monthes after his marriage. In case my wife continue in y^e Estate of Widdowhood as left of me, then my will is, y^t she possesse halfe of all my said houses & lands with my sonne *Samuell* during her life. In case she mary, then my will is, y^t after such time, as my said sonne shall accomplish his age of 21 yeares or marriage, That he then shall possesse all my said houses & lands. [If the son die before

either of the times mentioned, the halfe of s⁴ property is to go to his
mother; the other half " to be equally devided betweene all yᵉ rest of
my Children & her Children " now, & then, aliue in New-England.]
Mary, my wife, executrix, my friends *John Minot* & *William Pond*, both
of Dorchester, overseers                                    Joseph Farnworth.
   In the pʳnce of *Richard Withington,*
*Joseph Weekes, Enoch Wiswall.*
   1 Feb. 1659. *Richard Withington* & *Joseph Weekes,* deposed.  Inventory of the Estate of Joseph Farnworth, taken yᵉ 20th: 11mo. 1659,
by *Hopestill Foster, Lawrence Smith, Richard Withington.* Amᵗ. £206.
18.02. Lands yet not prised.  House, Orchard, Lands &c. about 2¼
acres; about 23 acres in the necke of Land, so called; in the Calue pasture, salt marsh, 4 acres; in yᵉ feild Called yᵉ great Lott, 12 acres within yᵉ fence & 12 acres without yᵉ fence; in the Cow walke 5 acres, &c.
*Mary Farnworth* deposed, 1 Feb. 1659.  *Rebecca Farnworth* came into
Court & Chose Wᵐ *Pond* to be her Guardian.

---

   WILLIAM DAVIS.—Inventory, taken by *William Salter, Robert* ⋈ *Meare,
John Hudson.* 10 : 9 : 1655. *Isaack Cullemore* deposed. [Will, Reg.
(1851) Vol. V. p. 298.] (See p. 48).

---

   JOHN CLEMONS.—A Note of what *John Clemens* Clothes came vnto
with a Chest. Amᵗ. 12s. prized by *William Salter* & *Robert Meare.*
10 : 9mo : 55. *Isack Collymore* deposed. [Will, Reg. (1851) Vol. V.
p. 299.] (See p. 49).

---

   SAMUELL MORSE.—Inventory of *Samuell Morse* of Medfield, taken
10 : 5 : 1654, by *Tho Wight, Georg Barber, Ralph Wheelocke.* Sum
totall, £124. 07s. *Elizabeth,* wife of *Samuell Morse,* deceased, deposed.
Taken vpon oath the 27 : 11 : 1654 by me, *Tho: Grubb,* one of the
Comission⁻ʳs for the towne of Medfield.  Att a County Court held at
Boston 30. Jan. 1654 this Inventory was accepted by yᵉ Court, on the
Oath here incerted. [Will, Reg. (1851) Vol V. p. 299.] (See p. 49).

---

   MATHEW KENNIDGE.—Inventory taken 22: 10 : 1654, by *Jonn Phillips, Daniell Turell* & *Edward Woods,* of a pcell of goods of *Mathew
Kennidge* lately deceased in Boston.  By the desire of *Nathaniell Gallop,*
who deposed, 4 Jan. 1654.

---

   DAVID SELLECKE.—Power of Administracoñ to the Estate of Mʳ *Da-
vid Sellecke,* graunted to Mʳ Wᵐ *Brenton,* Capᵗ *Tho Clarke* & Deacon John
Wisewall. [See Reg. for Jan. p. 58.]  Accompt of what wee finde due
from the estate of Mr. David Sellick, deceased, 18th : 12th : 1655.
   [Signed by] *Anthony Stoddard, Edw: Ting.*
   To Mr Henry Shrimpton, Anthony Stoddard, Tho. Scottow, Mr Webb,
for Mr Abraham Browne; Mr Webb, for Mr Nicholas Opie; Mr Tho
Lake, Mr. William Paddy, Edward Johnson, Jonas Fairbanks,* Mr Thos.
Marsh, Mr Edward Ladd, Mr Richard Hutchinson, Phillip Long, Stephen
Buttler, Mr Thomas Broughton, Capᵗ Thomas Savage, Tho Roberts, Mr
Robᵗ Pateshall, Tho: Boyden, John Webb, Mr William Paine, Tho:
Walker, Augustine Clement, &c. Amᵗ £560.08.

---

* See Reg. (1852) Vol. VI. p. 30.

THOMAS BUTLAND.—Inventory of the Estate, made by his father, *William Butland*, Administrator—" for wages due in yᵉ hands of Capᵗ Clarke £4. 3s." *William Butland* deposed, 6 Nov. 1655.

Wᵐ AMES.—Inventory of the goods of *William Ames* deceased. £45. 11s. Taken by *William Allis, William Needome, John Deffet*. Power of Administration, graunted vnto *Hannah Ames*, widow of William, for her selfe and Children, 6ᵗʰ Mᵗch 1654. She deposed the same day.

JOHN ROBERTS.—Inventory of yᵉ Estate. Debtor to *Evan Thomas & Mathew Coy*. Creditor for 2 monethes seruice on yᵉ shipp good Fellow £5. 10s. Capᵗ *Tho Clarke* deposed 7 : 9 : 1655.

FRANCIS BENNET.—Inventory, 4 Dec. 1655. Prized by *John Lewis* and *Ralph Sames*, of Boston, yᵉ 15th : `11mo : 1655. Amᵗ £49.08. Debts due to Sᾳmpson Shoare, Mathew Barnet; Good Walker, brick maker; Good Clarke, Ironmonger; Thomas Nocke, Edward Couzens, John George, &c. Power of Administration graunted to *Alice* late wife of sᵈ Bennett in behalfe of her selfe & Children. 7 Feb. 1655.—deposed the same day.

THOMAS TRESCOTT.—Inventory of goods prized by *John Farnum* & *Ralph Sames*, 20 : 3 : 1654. Amᵗ £17.03.1. 20 Mᵗch 1655. *Wᵐ Trescott* deposed this to be a true Inventory of his late brother.

SAMUELL KOKER.—Inventory of goods pʳsented by *Daniell Turell*, Constabel, to be prized, wᶜʰ were the goods of *Samˡˡ Koker*, drowned ; prized this 15ᵗʰ of the 2ᵈ moᵗʰ 1656. by *Thomas Savage, Joseph Rocke*. Amᵗ. £25. 17. 01½. More of the goods of sᵈ Koker, prized by *Phillip Wharton, John Peas*. One third pᵗ of a barke & furniture appertaing, with a smale boat.
*Michaell Martine* & *John Brookeing* deposed, 18 Aprill 1656. Power of Administration granted them, 17 : 2 : 1656. on behalfe of *Elizabeth Kaker* yᵉ said *Kakers* mother & *Ormanell Kaker* & *Elizabeth*, his sisters, of Holberton, in Devonshire, nigh Plymouth ; they putting in sufficient Caution, to the Recorder, within two dayes, that they will Administer according to Law.

JOHN HOLMAN.—*Jnᵒ Holman* came before the Magistr, & with their allowance chose *Robert Badcocke* to be his guardian. 17 Aprill 1656. [See Will of John Holman, the father, Reg. (1851) Vol V. p. 242.] *

ANNE LOOMAN.— *Thomas White*, aged about 60 yeares & *John Thompson* aged about 40 yeares, saith, they were with Mrˢ *Anne Looman* of Weymouth, about six weekes since, & yᵉ same day that she dyed, & she was in perfect memorie; she made her will, and made *Hannah Jackson*, her grandchild, her Executrix, & gaue 2s. to *John Monticue*, her grand child, yᵗ dwells at the East ward ; & Left all yᵉ rest of her Estate to *Hannah Jackson*, & appointed us two to be overseers. 21 : 8 : 1659.
*Thomas White* & *John Thompson*,     Thomas White.
                marke
deposed 20ᵗʰ October, 1659.       John L Tomson.
Inventory taken 24 Sept. 1659, by *Thomas White* & *John Rogers*. *Hannah Jackson* deposed, 20 Oct. 1659.
*See p. 44.

# ABSTRACTS FROM THE EARLIEST WILLS ON RECORD IN THE COUNTY OF SUFFOLK, MASS.

[Prepared by Mr. WM. B. TRASK, of Dorchester.]

COMFORT STARR.—22 Aprill 1659. Will. My body to be burryed within yᵉ vsuall place of buriall in Boston, so neere my late wife as may be possible with conveniency. I giue vnto *Samuell Starre*, my large book of Martyrs, with yᵉ frame belonging therevnto; vnto Euery one of my Grand Children, 12d apiece, in English money; vnto yᵉ fiue dauᵗ. of my dau. *Maynard* (deceased) £10. apiece, to be payd to either of them, as they come to yᵉ age of 16 yeare; vnto my sonne *Thomas Starre*, (deceased) his children, £10 apiece, to be payd vnto each as they either of them come vnto 18 yeares of age; vnto my sonne *Thomas*, his fower youngest, one Mare to be disposed & equally devided at yᵉ discretion of my Supervisors; if they thinke meete, yᵉ Mare to be sold, then, my will is, either of them Children should have one quarter pt of what said Mare is sold for; vnto my grand Child, *Symon Eire*, £6. p. Annu to be payd him yearely, vntill he come vnto yᵉ age of 18 yeares; it being so giuen by me vnto him for yᵉ Advancemeⁿᵗ, helpe & furthering him in Learneing. For yᵉ assurance of yᵉ due paymᵗ of yᵉ said £6. yearely, I Engage my now dwelling house, That he, or his Guardian, or those who have yᵉ oversight of him, shall and may lawfully enter into yᵉ said house, and distreine for euery defect so much as shall satisfy yᵉ said sume yᵗ is not payd, & yᵉ charge or charges yᵗ ariseth by reason of such distresse for yᵉ non paymᵗ of yᵉ said £6. yearely, yᵉ overplus to be returned. My minde & will is, That if yᵉ said *Symon Eire* desist goeing forward in Learneing, yᵗ is yᵗ he doe not goe vnto some Gramar Schoole & to some Academia, or to be with some godly Minister whereby he may be instructed in yᵉ Toungs, Arts & Sciences, then ye said Annuall paymᵗ of yᵉ said £6. shall cease. My minde is, yᵗ yᵉ said *Symon Eire* should enjoy his house & land yʳ vnto belonging wᶜʰ apptaineth vnto him, of right, by inheritance, And also, yᵗ my Executoʳ shall pay vnto him yᵗ wᶜʰ I am Engaged vnto him by yᵉ Honoʳed Court, yᵗ is, about £60, wᶜʰ is as much as I haue receiued of his, by my Administring of his moveable goods after yᵉ death of his pʳents. My sonne *John* I giue to be my Executoʳ. The rest of my Estate in New England I giue to my sonne *John Starr*, and vnto my dau. *Elizabeth Ferniside*, equally to be devide betweene them; then, yᵗ my sonne *John* shall devide his share into three pts; one third of it shalbe given vnto his Children, vnto Euery one a equall share, [The portion of Elizabeth to be divided in the same manner.] If my dau. *Hannah Starr* come into New England, my mind is, yᵗ [she] shall haue my siluer guilt double salt Celler. I giue vnto my dau. *Hannah Starr*, all my debts due vnto me in old England. I giue vnto said *Hannah*, £50 sterling to be payd vnto her, out of yᵉ Rent, as it ariseth of my house & land, wᶜʰ I haue in Eshitisford, in Kent, in old England. I giue vnto my sonne, *Comfort Starr*, my before mentioned house & land in Eshitisford, pvided my said dau. *Hannah* be payd yᵉ aforesaid £50; And also provided, yᵗ my sonne *Comfort* Cause to be payd at Boston, for yᵉ vse of my Grand Children, for my Executoʳ, to distribute to Euery one of my Grand-Children in good Kersy & Peniston & Cotton to yᵉ worth of 40s. a peece, to be payd within 4 yeares after my decease. Vnto my dau.

155

*Elizabeth*, all my Right of y^t Land wherevpon her now dwelling house is built, & also y^e Land adjoyneing, from y^e high way before theire house, downe backward, vnto y^e mill pond. I appointe my beloved Broth^rs in Law, Mr *John Morley & Faithfull Rouse* my Supervisors, vnto either of w^ch I will, 20s. a peece. I giue vnto my dau-in-law y^e late wife of my sonne *Thomas Starr*, one siluer bossed wine Cupp. It is my minde (in regard of y^e scarcitie of money in this Countrey) y^t my Executo^r shall pay my Legacies, if hê Can Conveniently, with shop pay, but if he Cannot so suite or fitt them, then he shall pay them in such Comodities as this Countrey brings forth, except such legacies y^t is Expressed to be payd in money or siluer.                                        COMFORT STARR.
in y^e p^rnce of *Christopher Gibson.*
*John Collins, Rich^d Taylor, William Read.*
2 Feb. 1659, *Rich^d Taylor, & W^m Read* deposed.
Inventory of the Goods & Chattells of Mr Comfort Starr Deceased 2d Jan. 1659, prized by *John Chickering, Edward Burt,* 3 Feb 1659, when *John Starr* deposed. Sume totall, £613. 02. More apprized 8: 1: 59-60. £32. 14. 11.
Debts due the deceased from John Carrey, Faithfull Rouse, Sam^u Bryant, James Vahan, Johannah Mills, W^m Wenborne, Alexander Waits, James Luxford, John Borne, Georg Clarke, John Rogers, Joseph Ramsden, John Howard, Francis Weston, Hen Sampson, William Spowell, Rebecca Taylor, John Harding, Edward Hall, Phillip de La Noe, Margaret Vassall, Job Hawkins, Bourne, of Muddy River; Edmund Weston, Jonathan Brewster, junio^r; Joseph Gallop, Evan Thomas, Pate Feild, Joseph Pryor, Edward Page, Joseph Harding, Thomas Wheeler, George Wheeler, Symon Tuttell, Mr John Cutts, Boson Russell, Will Edmonds, Mathew Grosse, Jno Holloway, Arthur Keayne, Mr ·Westmerland, John Hanmore, Good. Wheat, Good. Wooley, Tho Walker, John Matson, Doman Mathewes, Good. Felt, Tho. Call, Mr George Broome, Anthony Dodson, Georg Turner, Tho Fox, Will Hartwell, George Howard, John Hill, Zachary Phillips, Humphrey Turner, John Tuckerman, Daniell Aleborne, Cornelius Wright, George Dobson, David Faulkner, Good. Pecke, Mr Auldine, senior; Good. Baker, W^m Dickerman, Sam^u Norden, Vrsilla Batten, W^m Read, Mr Euerill, for John Fris; W^m Clarke, Joseph Bettle, John Coles, of Lovells Island; Edw Bruffe, Charitie an old maide; John Aymes, &c.

---

JOHN JOHNSON, of Roxbury. Will. 30: 7^th. (59.) My dwelling house & Certaine lands I haue already giuen to my beloved wife, dureing her life, according to a deed extant, wherein also I haue given her £60. for her household furniture, w^ch house & Lands, after my wifes decease, I giue vnto my fiue Children, to be Equally devided, my Eldest sonne hauing a double portion, according to y^e word of God. Vnto my two Grand Children, who haue liued with me, *Elizabeth Johnson & Mehetable Johnson,* each of them £5. to be payd within one yeare after my decease. I haue given to my sonnes, *Isaac Jonnson, & Robert Pepper* a p^rcell of lands of 55 acres in y^e third devision of y^e towne, w^ch I heartily Confirme. All y^e rest of my Lands, debts, &c. I giue to my fiue Children to be equally devided; my Eldest sonne haueing a double portion. I make my sonne *Isaac Johnson & Robert Pepper,* my Executors. 1 request Elder *Heath &. Deacon Parke,* to be overseers, and in token of my Loue I giue them each 40s. If my Children disagree in any thing, I order them

to choose one man more to these my overseers & stand to theire determination. JOHN ⋈ JOHNSON.

Witnes, *John Elliot, John Alcocke,*
*Edward Denison.* The last two deposed.

15 Oct. 1659. Inventory of Estate taken by Capt *Isaac Johnson &*
*Robert Pepper,* who deposed, 15 Oct. 1659.

---

ROBERT BRADISH.—Will. My wife executrix. To my wife, *Vastie*
*Bradish,* my whole Estate, both in Boston & in Cambridge, or else where,
so long as she liueth ; to be at her disposing, both house & lands & what
is in them, or vpon them. After her decease, I giue to my sonne, *James*
*Bradish,* 20s. To my sonne, *John Bradish,* £40. & a bedsteed, & all yᵉ
bedding yᵗ doth belong therevnto. I giue my sonne in Law, *Ezekiell*
*Morrell,* £10. & a bedsteed therevnto belonging; yᵗ wᶜʰ he hath now in
possession. To my sonne *Joseph,* a flocke bed, & a trundel .bed. To
my dau. *Mary Gibbs,* a flocke bed. After my Goods are prized & Legacies payd, yᵉ Remainder shall be equally devided amongst fower of my
children, *James, Joseph, Mary & Hannah.* If any of these be deceased,
then theire pᵗ. to goe to theire children. If *John Bradish* dye, without
heyres, his £40. to be equally devided between these fowre of my Children last mentioned ; & yᵉ bed to *Ezekiell Morrell.* If *Ezekiell Morrell*
dye, without heyres, then his £10. & yᵉ bed, to be equally devided between these fowre Children, or theire Children, if theire Parents is dead.
My Loveing Brother, *Isaac Morrell,* to be my overseer, if he be aliue at
yᵗ time. 12 : 3mo : 1657. Robert Bradish.
in yᵉ pʳnce of *John Wiswall, Isaac Morrell,* who deposed 29 Oct 1659.

Inventory of yᵉ Goods & Chattells of Robert Bradish of Boston, deceased, taken by *John Wiswall & Thomas Butolph* 28 : 7 : 1659. Amᵗ
£207. 02. 02. *Vashty Bradish,* Relict of *Robert,* deposed 29 Oct.
1659.

---

PHILLIP LONG, of Boston, being bound to sea, doe make this my last
will. Wife *Anne Long,* my Executrix of all my worldly goods, moveable & immoveable.

27 Oct 1658 Phillip Long.

Test : *Thomas Squire, Walter Salter.*
*Zachary Phillips, Benjamine Brisco.* Phillips & Brisco deposed.

Inventory taken 3 : 9 : 1659, by *James Euerill, Will English, Will*
*Nickerson.* Mentions, Thomas Browne, Hen Lamprey, George Broome,
Roger Seaward, Edwd Page, Benjamine Brisco, &c. 13 Nov 1659.
*Anne Long* deposed this ⁺o be a true Inventory of her late husbands,
*Phillip Longs,* Estate.

---

JARVIS GOULD.—Inventory of the goods of *Jarvis Gould,* deceased,
of Boston, shoomaker, 4ᵗʰ July 1656. Amᵗ. £66. 08. 07. *Jnᵒ Parke,*
*Alexander Adams, Henry Bridgam & Edward Goodwin,* deposed, 8
July, 56.

---

THOMAS FAULKNER.—Inventory of the Estate of the late *Thomas*
*Fawkner,* of Boston, taken 22 : 5mo : 1656, by *Richard Russell, Robt*
*Pateshall, Josh Scottow, Tho: Lake.* Amᵗ. £153. 09. *James Hawkins,*
*& David Fawkner,* deposed, 29 July 56.

THOMAS RAWLINS.—Will. Being very weake. All my worldly goods y⁣ᵗ I haue here resident at Boston, that is to say, my house and Land, I bequeath vnto my wife *Sarah*, & vnto my sonne, *Thomas Rawlins*. My wife [to] enjoy it for her life time, with all yᵉ moveable goods therevnto belonging, & yᵗ my sonne *Thomas* shall not sell nor any way hinder my wife of yᵉ enjoymᵗ of any of my goods belonging vnto my house, yᵗ is to say, all mannʳ of houshold stuffe & bedding & other household necessaries, & yᵗ my wife shall not hinder my sonne *Thomas* of his right of yᵉ enjoymenᵗ of a habitation ın yᵉ house, & yᵉ vse of such necessaries as he stands in need of, as is to say, yᵉ vse of my tooles, bedding for his supply, &c. And it is my desire yᵗ my wife & my sonne *Thomas* Liue together peaceably, as formerly they haue done. My house & Land lyeing at Scituate, Called by yᵉ name of Rawlins Farme, I giue vnto my sonne, *Nathaniell Rawlins*, being in quantitie about 40 acres of vpland, & 10 acres of marsh, belonging vnto yᵉ foresaid house & Farme. Yᵉ 20 accres of Land yᵗ lyes by yᵉ end of *William Parkers*, I leaue vnto yᵉ disposeing of my sonne *Thomas*; as for yᵉ Lott yᵗ lyes by goodman *Boords*, I giue vnto my sonne *Thomas*, being about fowre score accres of vpland & six of Marsh, more or lesse, provided yᵗ he let my sonn *Nathaniell* haue two accres of Marsh for a supply of fodder for his Cattle next vnto Goodman *Boords*. 12ᵗʰ March 1660.

witness herevnto *John Lovewell*          *Thomas Rawlins.*

And for yᵉ better execution hereof, I appoint my wife, & my sonne *Thomas*, executors.

Attest, *John Hall.*

And further, I giue vnto my sonne *Nathaniel* one of yᵉ two Cowes yᵗ he hath now of mine in his keeping, provided he raise a Calfe for my wife.

4 Aprill 1660. *John Louewell* deposed. Edw: Rawson Recordr.

Also, *Thomas Rawlins*, yᵉ sonne, declared yᵗ knowing his father to haue left his mother in Law, *Sarah*, too little, he was free and willing & did giue her £10. more then his father gaue her.

Inventory made 23 March 1660, by *Thomas Buttolph* & *Richard Woodde.*

---

PHILLIP LOCKE.—Inventory of his Estate rendered by *Hugh Williams*, Administrator, who deposed, 31 July, 1656. Amt £16.09. Mentions Mr *Robert Long*, senior, of Charlestowne; Mr *Booth*; *Tho. Hawkins*; *Mrs. Ann Knight.*

---

THOMAS PADDENS.—Inventory taken by *John Barrell*, and *Thomas Dewer*. Amᵗ. £5.11.09. Wᵐ *English* deposed, 1ˢᵗ August 1656.

---

JAMES KEMON.—Inventory of his goods taken yᵉ 18ᵗʰ of yᵉ 8 moneth 1656. *Willm Blake, Thomas Iwitt, Mr Clarke*, deposed 30 Octobʳ 1656.

---

NICHOLAS SIMKINS.—Inventory of his goods and Chattells taken by *Thomas Savage, Joshua Scotto*, 30 : 8 : 1656. Amᵗ. £72.00.06. Power of administration graunted to *Ishabell*, his Late Wife, in behalfe of hir selfe & Children. Deposition made by her, the same day.

---

SAMUEL SHERMAN, late of Boston, deceased. Inventory, taken 2 : 1 :

1644. *William Colbron*, *Mr Hills*, & *Jacob Eliott*, deposed 28 July 1652. *Richard Parker* received for yᵉ vse of yᵉ stocke yᵗ remained, £33.10. The magistrates received this Inventory wᵗʰ yᵉ bill of Charge Annexed and Conceive that the 50 odd pounds remaindʳ being due to yᵉ Children be secured. The petition of *Mary Eliott* may be graunted to hir. Edward Rawson Recordʳ.

Disbursements out of the Estate to Thomas Bayly, of Hingham; Thomas Painter, of Boston; Richard Blake, of Dorchester; Mr. John Oliver, of Boston; Thomas Marshall, of Boston; Jnᵒ Locke, of Boston, for Samuell Sharman; Jacob Sheafe, of Boston; Martha Sharman; Mary Sharman, &c., &c. [The $50 above mentioned, to be paid the children.] £20, to yᵉ Eldest, & £10 a peece for the other 3, & one of yᵉ said 3 being dead, *Phillip*, his portion shalbe equally deuided amongst yᵉ survivers, which order shall be Recorded.

Edward Rawson Recordʳ.

---

RICHARD SHEARMAN.—Being weake, doe make my last Will. I giue vnto my two dauˢ. *Ann Shearman* & *Prissilla Garett*, wife of *Martine Garet*, to each, £10; to my dau. *Martha Browne*, £10; to my dau. *Abigail Damine*, £10; all which Legacies I appointe to be payd out of my Estate that shall remaine after the decease of my wife *Elizabeth*, within sixe monethes after her decease, by my overseers. Provided my wife shall see Cause with yᵉ advise of my overseers to sell yᵉ dwelling house & yᵉ ground adjoyning to it during hir life time, then said Legacies shall be payd within six moneths after such sale; the two tenn pounds to my two dauˢ. in England into yᵉ hands of my Cousine, Mr [Edmund ?] Anger, of Cambridge, to be sent vnto my said two daus. if then liueing, or else to yᵉ Child or Children of them. If either die without issue before yᵉ time mentioned, then yᵉ survivor, or hir children, to receive it. If both die, leaving no issue, yᵉ £40 [to] be disposed of to my two dauˢ. *Martha* & *Abigaile*, or to their Children, at yᵉ discretion of my Overseers. I giue vnto *Mary* & *Elizabeth Spawle*, my Grand Children, to each of them, £5, vpon yᵉ same terms as yᵉ legacies of my dauˢ. aboue specifyed, to be payd by my wife or her successors. In Consideration of wᶜʰ I discharge my wife from yᵉ paymᵗ of £15, mentioned in a deed of sale, whereby I haue made over my orchard to my wife, the said deed bearing date the 25ᵗʰ Aug. 1658, & I doe Confirme said deed of sale to my wife, wᶜʰ deed was made to *Mr. John Joyliffe* on hir behalfe, who is hereby discharged. I appointe my wife, sole Executrix of this my Last Will. I also appointe my friends and Kinsmen, Mr. *Edmund Anger* and *John Lovermore*, of Watertown, Overseers. 7 April 1660.

signed & deliuered by *Richard*      *Richard Shearman.*
*Sherman*, with yᵉ clause on yᵉ
margent, being in these words,

leaueing all yᵉ rest of my estate vnto my said wife & Executrix. Witness, *William Bartholmew, John Joyliffe.*

31 July 1660, *William Bartholmew*, deposed.

Inventory of Estate taken 26ᵗʰ June 1660, by *William Colbron, William Bartholmew.* Amᵗ. £105.10.06. *Elizabeth Shearman* deposed, 31 July 1660.

---

SAMUEL JOHNSON.—Inventory of *Samuell Johnsons* goods deceased the 23 of the 11 mo. 1656. Taken by *Benjamin Ward, Edw. Raynsford.* Amt. £56.00.5. *Mary Johnson*, wid. of *Samuel*, deposed.

ARTHUR GILL.—*John Sweete*, Adm͞r–tor to yᵉ Estate of *Arthur Gill*, renders his account. 19 March 1656, which the Court allows. Mentions " *John*, yᵉ Eldest sonne "; " his sonne *Tho.* dyett for above a yeare, for his passage to England ; " &c. " his dau. *Frances Gill*, Edwᵈ Goodwine, Richᵈ Sanford, Peeter Hill, George Davis, Allexander Adams, Jnᵒ Sunderland, Wᵐ White, Andrew Anger, goodman Elliway, Tho. Chadwell, Wᵐ Gorgray, Mr Coker," &c.

---

SAMUEL BASSE, JUNIOR.—*Jeremiah Houchin* and *Peeter Brackett* having examined the Estate of *Samuell Basse, Junior*, of Brantry, render their account. *Robᵗ Howard* and *Deacon Samᵘ Bas* made a proposall, that the whole Estate should be at the disposall of *Mary Bas*, wife of said *Samᵘ Bas* Junior, Except the house and Land, in Brantry, with 5 Acres of Land, which house & lands shalbe lett & improved by *Robert Howard* and *Deacon Samᵘ Bas*, which the Court approoved of, 23 April 1657.

---

MARGARET SNOOKE.—Will. I, *Margaret Snook*, of Weymouth, widdow of *James Snooke*, (see Reg. Vol. V. p. 441.) Ordaine my Coussine *Allice Peache*, of Marblehead, my Executoʳ 9.2.60.
Witness, *John Whit Marsh*                             *Marg'ret & Snooke*
    *Nicho Whitmarsh,*
who deposed, 31 May 1660.
[Deacon *John Rogers* was indebted to *Margaret Snooke*, 40ˢ. for a heifer, he bought of her, " In regard yᵗ yʳ is a smale Legacie to be payd to him, I am not willing " she says, " yᵗ it should be taken out of his hand, for pʳsent, if my necessitie Call not for it." She resigns it vp to her Executrix.]
Inventory, taken 9 : 3 : 1660, by *John Rogers, John Vineing.* *Alice Peach*, of Marblehead, deposed 12 July 1660.

---

CHRISTOPHER SMITH.—10 April 1660. I *Christopher Smith*, of Plymouth, in the Countie of Devon, Eng. Carpenter, being sicke, doe make this my last Will. I giue vnto my sister, *Bridget Joel*, £10 ; Coussine *Mary Cook*, £20 ; Coussine *John Joel*, 40ˢ ; Coussine *Elizabeth Joel*, 40ˢ ; Coussine *Margaret Joel*, £5 ; vnto *Willomet Harwood*, 40ˢ ; vnto yᵉ servant maid yᵗ liued with my sister, *Bridget Joel*, (called *Ellenor*,) 40ˢ ; vnto my sister, *Elizabeth Cooke*, all yᵉ rest of my Estate, who I make sole executrix.
Published in yᵉ pʳnce of vs.                             *Christopher Smith.*
*John Clampet, John Holman,*
*John ⋈ Wakefield, William Pearse.*
Item, after yᵉ pʳfecting of this Will, in yᵉ first fforme, I yᵉ said *Christopher*, doe giue vnto my friend *Ann Trenow*, £5, to be payd by my executrix. I giue vnto *Jnᵒ Holma*, wᶜʰ was a servant to me, my sad Colloʳed suite of apparrel, to be Compleated with shirt, stockins & yᵉ rest, to make a suite Compleat, & all my workeing tooles.         *Christ A Smith.*
Witnessed by *George Clampet, Jnᵒ Clampet, William Pease.* *John Clampet, Jnᵒ Holman & Wᵐ Pearse* deposed 25 April, 1660.
25 Aprill 1660. Whereas yᵉ will of *Christopher Smith*, Carpinter of shipp Walsingham, was prooved on Oath at said Court, he depʳting this life on yᵉ tenth of Aprill, aforesaid, & Leaving no friend in trust.
To pʳserue yᵉ Estate in this Will giuen, yᵗ is in the Country, yᵉ Court Ordered yᵗ yᵉ Estate should be Co͞mitted into yᵉ hands of *Mr Abraham*

*Browne*, merchant, to whom y⁰ Cargo of said shipp was Consigned, to pʳserue & Convey to y⁰ pties Concerned, bringing in an Inventory thereof.
Edw. Rawson, Recordʳ.

Inventory given by *Abraham Browne*, who deposed, 8 Feb. 1660. Names mentioned :—William Kennwicke, John Juell, John Archite, Peeter Stutly, Edward Sander, Richard Nicklas, John Tome, E —— Londe, John Hach, John Newman, Christopher Tailor, Gerard Walch, Edward James, Robert Sweet ; *Richard Taprill*, Commander y⁰ ship Wallsingham.

HUMPHRY DAMERILL.—Inventory of the Estate of *Mr Humphery Damerell*, Commander of the Barke Sea Flower, of Boston, apprized by *Richᵈ Gridly, Henry Alline*, 27 Aprill 1654.

*Thomas Jones* and *John Backer* being Intrusted by Mrs. *Sarah Damerell* to prize what the Barke is worth, with all her matterialls, as sailes, Masts, and other Riging, Anchors & Cables, [value the whole at £140. The same value was also put upon it, by *Johṇ Anderson, Jeremiah Cushen*.] *Sarah Damẹrell* deposed 27 Aprill 1654, and the Magistrates did determine that she should give securitie to the Recorder to satisfye her sonne of one hundred marks for his portion out of this Estate.

WILLIAM STEVENS.—His Estate prized by *Thomas Bligh*, 16 May 1657. Amᵗ. £11.08.03. Power of Administration Graunted to *Thomas Blith*, in behalfe of the next kinne.

RICHARD NORTON.—Wee whose names are vnderwritten being desired by *Hugh Williams*, of Boston, Couper, administrator to the Estate of *Richᵈ Norton*, late of Boston, Couper, deceased, & being desired to prize the house, yard, wharfe, & y⁰ pṛiviledges of the Cundit therevnto belonging to the said Norton, doe value the pʳmisses aboue mentioned to the vallew of £160 starling, witnes our hands, 8ᵗʰ Augᵤ 1657, *Joseph Rocke, Henry Alline, John Maynard*.

Due from *George Palmer*, for Rent, &c. *Hugh Williams*, deposed, 21 Aug. 56.

THOMAS HUNT.—Inventory of his Estate, prised by *William Hudson, John Viall*. Amᵗ £84.04.

Desperate debts :—By a bill of one *Brighting*, gone to Jamica ; of one *Will Prichard*, gone to Jamica ; a debt of *Wᵐ King* ; of *Mʳ George Munjoye* ; of good *Brynen*, of Hartford. 13 Aug 1657. *Elizabeth Hunt*, deposed.

HENRY THORNER.—An Inventory of the goods & Estate of *Henry Thorner*, who dyed at Piscataque y⁰ 26ᵗʰ Aug. 1657. Apprized by *Capᵗ. Bryan Pendleton, Capᵗ. Richard Walderne, Tho: Clarke* & *Mr Henry Shrimpton*. Amt. £174.14.04. *Capᵗ. James Garret* & *Edward Thorner*, deposed, 28 Oct. 1657.
Edw. Rawson, Recordʳ.

BARTHOLMEW BARLOW.—Inventory of the Estate of *Bartholmew Barlow*, deceased, 26ᵗʰ Sepᵗ. 57. Apprized by *Richard Croade, Richard Garrett, William Osborne, John Barrell*. Sum Total, £310.06.03½. Power of Administration Graunted to *Thomas Barloe*, his sonn, 15 Oct. 1657, who then deposed.

Memorandum. That *Bartholmew Barloe*, the 25 of Sept. being of a disposeing minde, to our best knowledge, in Answʳ to a Question proposed by vs to him what he would doe with his Estate, he Answered

he would giue or Leave all that he had to his sonne. Being asked
whether he would not giue his servant any thing he had, no not a penny,
he would Leaue all to his Sonne.
Witnes our hands, *Richard Graves, James Phelps.*

------

JOHN STRANGE.—Inventory of the goods of *John Strange*, late of Bos-
ton, deceased, taken by *William Clarke, Robert Williams*, 15 Oct. 1657.
Am^t. £22.18.04. Power of Administration to the Estate Graunted to
*Richard Curtis*, in Right of *Sarah*, his wife. *Richard Curtis*, deposed.

------

WALTER MERRY.—Inventory of his Estate prized by *William Beamsl-
leay*, *Alex. Adams, John Phillips, William Howard*, 20 Dec. 1657.
Debts due :—To men that went to seeke the Corps of the said *Walter
Merry*, 6ˢ; to the men that brought the Corps of the said *Walter Merry*,
10ˢ; *Tho. Anker*, &c. *Mary Merry*, Administratrix to the Estate of
*Walter Merry*, her husband, deposed, 27 Oct. 1657.
It is ordered by the Court that this Estate shalbe equally devided be-
twixt the said *Mary*, the Mother, and *Walter*, the sonne of the said
*Walter*, that the Child should be brought vp out of the profitt of his
portion.              ------

MR NATHANIELL GLOVER, of Dorchester.—Inventory taken by *Roger
Clap, William Clarke*, 5 : 4 : 1657. Am^t. £591.11.08. *Mary Glover*,
relict of *Nathaniel*, deposed, 7 June 1657. [Nathaniel Glover died,
21 : 3 : 57.]              ------

WILLIAM BURNELL, of Pulling point, within yᵉ bounds of Boston.—
Will. I *William Burnell*, doe giue vnto my sonne, *John Burnell*, my
house & ground in Boston, when at age of 21 yeares, provided he is not
Corrupted with that opinion Comonly Called yᵉ Quakers, but, in Case he
should be ledd aside by yᵗ opinion of Quakers, & remaine so, then my
minde is yᵗ he shall haue but £50 ; & thus to be payd vnto him, £5.
when he is at the age of 21 yeares, and so £5. a yeare vntil yᵉ some of
£50 be payd him. In case he dye before he come to yᵉ age of 21 yeares,
then, yᵉ house to remaine my wifes as long as she liueth, and after her
death to be my sonne *Samuells*. My Will is, yᵗ my dau. *Sarah*, haue
£40, as her portion, when 25 yeares old ; and thus to be payd, my moveable goods to be valued, and she to receiue yᵐ, or yᵉ sume as they are
valued vnto, & what is wanting of yᵉ goods to pay yᵉ sume, [to] be payd
out of my farme in Pulling Pointe. I guie vnto my sonne *Samuell*, my
farme in Pulling Pointe, but yᵉ said *Samuell* is not to possesse, nor enter
on it untill the full some of £40 be payd vnto my dau. *Sarah*. My wife
to be my Executrix. *James Bell*, of Pulling Point, and *John Doulittle*,
of Rumney Marsh, to see this my Will fullfilled. 16 : 2 : 1660.
In pʳnce of                                         *William* ⋈ *Burnell.*
*Thomas Laughton, Deane Winthrop.*
*Mr Deane Winthrop*, deposed 12 July 1660.
Inventory of the Estate :—House and Land at Pullin Poynt, vallued at
£100. by Mʳ *Winthrop* & *John Grover ;* house & land in Boston, val-
lewed at £30., & *Henry Boyen* & *Richard Barnard ;* yᵉ Cattle and
other goods, at Pullin Poynt, Vallued at £27, by *James Hill* & *John
Southwicke. Sarah Burnell*, widow of *William*, deposed, 17 May 1661.
Philip Bill, Willm Denison, Barnett Ingolls indebted to the Estate.
William Burnell indebted vnto Goodman Willis, of Boston, & Goodman
Clarke, shoomaker.

# ABSTRACTS FROM THE EARLIEST WILLS ON RECORD IN THE COUNTY OF SUFFOLK, MASS.

[Prepared by Mr. WM. B. TRASK, of Dorchester.]

GEORGE GRIGGS, of Boston. Will. 4: 5 mo. 1655. Being now sicke; make my wife *Alice*, executrix, & doe giue hir my house & ground, with all yᵉ appurᶜᵉˢ, & yᵉ two acres of land at Long Island, be it more or lesse, as also my household stuffe, dureing her life. After yᵉ decease of my wife it is my will yᵗ my sonne, *James Griggs*, shall haue yᵉ house & ground, with the 2 acres of land at Long Island, he paying out of it to my dau. *Anne Joanes*, £5; to my dau. *Mary Brookes*, 40s.; & to my dau. *Sarah King*, £10. I giue vnto *James*, a feather bed & boulster, a blankett & coverlid, yᵗ is greene & white, after his mothᵣˢ decease. I also giue him all my working tools at my pʳsent decease. 4th July 55. Witness to these *George Griggs.*
*Will. Colbron, James Penn.*
*Elder Wm. Colbron* deposed, 3 Aug. 1660.

---

HUMPHERY GRIGGS.—Inventory of the goods and Estate of *Humphery Griggs*, deceased, taken by *Samuell Basse* & *Richard Brackett*, 18ᵗʰ 6 mo. 1657. £109 11.
Power of Administration on the Estate graunted to *Grissell Griggs*, his late wife, 18 Aug. 1657, who deposed the same day. [She was formerly the wife of *Thomas Jewell*, of Braintree. See Reg. Vol. V. pp. 304, 305.] (See pp. 54, 55).

---

THOMAS HAWKINS.—*Mary Fenne*, Administratrix to the Estate of the late *Capᵗ. Thomas Hawkins*, haueing Given an Inventory of the Estate of her said late husband vnto the Court, being in all, as appears, £900. And haueing one sonne, and fower Daughtᵣˢ desire yᵉ Court That *Thomas Hawkins*, sonne of the said deceased, may haue yᵉ Farme at Dorchester, (over the water) prized at £257, he paying £57 to one of his sisters, so rests for his portion. The 4 Dauˢ. £100 p' piece; her selfe the Remainder, which was allowed by the Court, 29: 8: 1657.
Inventory of sᵈ Estate:—taken 26ᵗʰ 5ᵐᵒ. 1654. The Farme at Dorchester, over yᵉ water, [probably on the northeasterly side of the Neponset River,] with a Barne, dwelling house & 180 ackʳˢ of land, £257.; house & land at Dorchester, 50 ackers, £110·; house & land at Boston, £200; ¼ of the Ship Penguin, in England, £75; Cattle in the hands of Mʳ. Robᵗ. Bricke, £60, &c. Total £919. Oweing to *Mrs. Avery* & others, in London, £25.
The Estate of *Capᵗ. Tho: Hawkins* yᵗ lyeth in yᵉ towne of Dorchester, valued by vs. 1: 6: 54. *Humphray Atharton, Nathaniell Patton.*
The house & land of *Mrs Fenns*, lately widdow to *Capᵗ Tho: Hawkins*, wᶜʰ is in the North side of Boston, valued at £205, by *George Davis. Mrs Mary Fenne*, late *Hawkins*, deposed, 29: 8: 57.

---

SAMUEL JEWELL.—An Apprizemᵗ. of the goods of *Samuell Jewell*, late deceased. Amᵗ £5. 3.; prized by Mʳ *William Paine* and *John Sweete*, wᶜʰ are all the goods of *Mary Jewell*, as she saith, only her weareing apparrell. *John Sweete* deposed, 29 Oct. 1657.

JOSEPH TWITCHELL.—An Inventory belonging to *Joseph Twitchell*, late of Dorchester, this 8 : 8ᵐᵒ : 1657 ; apprized by *John Gurnell, John Minott*. Sum total, £43 15.04. " At Mother Brookes, 2 acres, £1. ; one 3ᵈ Division, 4 acres, £1.4ˢ. ; the woode vppon 4 acres of Land, £2. ; " &c. *Timothy Wales* & *Benjamin Twitchell* deposed 26 : 9mo : 1657.

[NOTE.—This name is written Tuchill, Tuchel, and Tuchine, on the Dorchester Records. Francis Tuchill had a grant of land in that town, in 1634 ; Joshua, in 1635. Joseph Tuchel, died 13 : 7 : 57. Mary, dau. of Benjamin Tuchel died 8 : 1 : 58–59.]

THOMAS ALCOCKE.—A true Inventory of the goods and Chattells of *Thomas Alcocke*, prized by *James Johnson, Richᵈ Truesdall*. The sume is £20.07. For debts oweing for a Legacy giuen to two of our Children by *Deacon Allcocke*, deceased, and by vs receiued for them, but wee neuer yet gaue it to them, £4. Power of Administration Granted to *Margery*, his late wife, in behalfe of herselfe & Children. She deposed 30 Jan. 1657. The Court Ordered that this Widdow should haue the Estate, vizᵗ. £16, to bring vp the Children.

THOMAS · DICKERMAN.—An Inventory of the goods and Estate of *Thomas Dickerman*, who deceased the 3 : 11mo : 1657 ; prized by *John Capen Wᵐ Clarke*, 15 : 11ᵐᵒ: 1657. " Land before the house of *Jacob Heṵens ;* house and land at Boston ;" &c. *Ellen Dickerman*, wid. of *Thomas*, deposed, 25 : 11 : 1657.

RICE DAVIS.—An Inventory of the Estate of *Rice Davis*, deceased, £11. 15. 06. ; more a debt due from *Sargᵗ Daniell* to *Rice*, £5. 10ˢ. 8ᵈ. ; ṛoods received, as appears by the *Master Wheatleigh* Oath, £6. 4ˢ. 4ᵈ.

WIDDOW SMEAD.—*Mr. Israell Stoughton*, Administrator to *Mrˢ Judith Smeed*, widdow, deceased, as by Inventory taken yᵉ 18: 3ᵈ: 1639. 3um is £103: 19: 05. Payd to *Batcheller*, of Sallem, wᶜʰ wee apprenended is repayd *Jnᵒ Denman* by him, £13. 06. 08. ; payd to *John Pope*, of Dorchester, wᵗʰ *William Smeed*,* wᶜʰ is repayd into yᵉ Deacons hands, £32. ; to *Mary Denman*, wife to *Clement Maxfield*, £13. 10ˢ. 10ᵈ. ; &c. &c. *Roger Clap, Christopher Gibson, Hopestill Foster* were appointed to examine *Mrs Stoughtons* booke & Inventory concerning *Mrs Judith Smeeds* Estate, who find the balance of the whole Estate to be £85. 07. 11½. ; to be divided among 3 Children. *Jnᵒ Denmans* pte comes to £32 00ˢ. 06ᵈ.; *Mary Denman*, now Clemᵗ. Maxfields wife, £21. 07ˢ.; *Wᵐ*. *Smeeds* pt is £35. 06. The apprisers make a return the 11 of 1mo. 1657-8. Mentions " sister *Visillah, Jnᵒ Scudder, Bro: Knight, Oliver Purchase ;* a tub to sister *Clarke ;* my *Brothʳ Clarke ;* good. *Tomkins ; Bro Kinsly ;* 5 dornix Curtins to *Sumner ;* good. *Jewett* & wife ; a vylett coat to goodman *Oldreges*," &c. &c.

JOHN FRANCKLIN.—An Inventory of goods of *John Franckling*, deceased, pʳsented by *Capᵗ Samuell Scarlett* & *Mr John Freake*, taken 30ᵗʰ June 1658, by *Mr Christopher Clarke* & Seargeant *Alexander Adams*. Amᵗ. £17. 10. 08. *Capᵗ Samuel Scarlet* deposed, 1 July 1658.

WILLIAM FRANKLIN.—The Inventory of such goods & Estate of *Wil-*

---

* William Smead, m. Elizabeth, dau. of widdow Laurence. 31: 10: 58.—*Dorchester Records.*

*liam Francklin,* late of Boston in yᵉ Massachusetts, (who dyed in London) as are to be within yᵉ said Colonie made and apprized, according to yᵉ best judgemᵗ of *Elder James Penn, William Clarke, Benjamin Negus,* & *Robert Howard,* the 28 of July 1658. Sum is £719. 10. besides £28 in England. *Phebe Franckline,* wid. of *William* deposed, 20 Aug. 1658.

EDWARD HOLYOKE. Will made 25 Dec. 1658. As for the holy faith of the holy one, God in trinitie, and of the holy faith of our glorious Lord, the son of God, the Lord Jesus Christ, the second Adam, I haue composed A booke and doe bestowell [?] vpon each of my sonns in law as their best legacy, &c. (Being instructed chiefly by an understanding of the Scriptures) I doubt not to say my booke will giue him A hart of all sound doctrine.

Touching my worldly estate, I dispose the yoke of Oxen and my mare, to my sonn in law, George Keysar, and my mare foale and A Cow, to my sonn *Prenam;* tow kine to my sonn *Andrewes;* A Cow to my dau. *Marten.* These Oxen and kine are in the hands of Goodman *Wilkins,* of Linn; the mare and foale is at Rumney Marsh. I giue to my sonn *Tuttle,* that £4 that yearely hee should haue giuen mee since I put ouer the house at Boston to him. I neuer yet had [a] penney of it; . 40ˢ I gaue him of that, soe theare is yet £6 beehind and theare is £5 mentioned in Goodman *Wilkins* Case that hee oweth mee, I giue to my dau. *Marten,* and 20ˢ. to my kindswoman, *Mary Mansfeild,* and 10ˢ. of it to *John Dolittle,* and 10ˢ. of it to my kindsman *Thomas Morris,* of Newham, and 10ˢ. of it to *Hannah Keasur.* I giue my best Cloake of that Cloth that cam from England to my sonn *Holyoke,* as allsoe my Coate of the same cloth. I giue my other Cloke to my sonn *Keaser,* my best Dublet and breeches to my sonn *Tuttle,* my stuff dublet and my best hat to my sonn *Holyoke;* all the rest of my weareing apparell to my sonn *Keasar.* As touching the whol yeares rent of this yeare 1658, that is Dew mee from Goodman *Wilkins,* of Linn, I owe *Theodore Atkins* 49ˢ.; pay him in what I owe; *John Hull* Aboute 22ˢ., pay him in wheate; pay Mʳ *Russell,* treasurer, 3 bushells of wheate; for *John Andrewes,* 8 bushells of wheate to Mʳ *Wilson,* Paster at Boston, and 8 bushell of Indian. As for my Linell, let all my dauˢ part alike. The 20ˢ Goodman *Page* oweth mee, as my sonn *Tuttle* cann witness, I giue my dau. *Martin.* There is aboute 15ˢ. Capᵗ. *Sauige* oweth mee, intreate him to satisfie my Cosan *Dauis,* and the rest giue to my dau. *Marten.* As for my books and wrightings, I giue my sonn *Holyoke* all the books that are at Linn, as allsoe the Iron Chest, and the bookes I haue in my study that are Mʳ *Beanghans* works I giue him, hee onely cann make vse of them, and likewise I giue all my maniscripts what soeauer, and I giue him that large new testament in folio. with wast papers between euery leafe, allso Mʳ *Answorth* on the 5 books of Moses and the psalmes, and my dixinary and Temellius bible in Latten, and my latten Concent and daniell bound together, and A part of the New testament in Folio, with wast paper betwin euery leafe, and the greate mapps of geneolagy, and that old maniscript called a Synas sight; the rest, for A muskett I gaue of olde to my sonn *Holyoke* : All my land in Linn, and that land and Medow in the Cuntry neere Reding, all was giuen to my sonn *Holyoke,* when hee maried Mʳ *Pynchors* Daughter. Pʳ me. *Edword Holyoke.*

25 June 1660. Power of Administration to the estate of the late Mʳ

*Edward Holyoke* is Graunted to M<sup>r</sup> *Elizur Holyoke*, his only sonn, to performe this Imperfect will of his father as neere as may be.

Inventory of the Estate of M<sup>r</sup> *Edward Hollyoke*, of Lynne, who dyed at Rumney Marsh, the 4th May 1660, taken the 19 June 1660. Prised by *John Tuttle, John Dowlettell.* Amt. £681. "A farme at Lynne, £400 ; 3 acres at Nahant, £6 ; a farme at Bever dame, neare Reading, £150," &c. &c.

*Eleazer Hollyoke* deposed, 25 June 1660.

---

HENRY AMBROSE.—An Inventory of the goods & Estate of *Henry Ambrose*, of Boston, late deceased. P<sup>r</sup> *John Jeffes, John Sunderland.* Sum totall, £337.09. *Susanna Ambrose*, his widow, deposed, 19 Nov. 1658.

---

STEPHEN LINCOLN.—Inventory of the Estate of *Stephen Lincolne*, deceased, made the 18 : 8mo : 1658. £179.10<sup>s</sup>. *Stephen Lincolne*, son of Stephen, deposed, 18 : 9 : 1658.

---

FRANCIS CHICKERING.—Inventory of the Estate of Ensigne *Francis Chickering*, late of Dedham, deceased, made 20 : 8mo: 1658, by *Eleazer Lusher, Henry Chickering, John Haward, Peter Woodward.* Totall £1820. 18. 08.

17 Oct. 1658. *Mrs. Sarah Chickering & Cap<sup>t</sup> Eleazer Lusher* deposed. The Court Considering the good report of the pious and prudent behavio<sup>r</sup> of *Sarah* y<sup>e</sup> Relict of *Francis Chickering*, & bringing vp y<sup>e</sup> Children of the said Francis, &c. doe order that she be allowed out of this Estate as her portion (including the £150. contracted for, before marriage, as a p<sup>t</sup>. thereof) the some of £350. The rest of the houses, lands, debts and goods to be divided betweene the 5 dau<sup>s</sup>. Accompting £100 already payd *Stephen Paine* as part of his wives portion, to be so much of her pte.

---

RICHARD WOODY.—An Inventory of the Estate of *Richard Woody*, Senio<sup>r</sup>, of Roxbury, deceased, prized by *Thomas Weld, Isaac Morrell. Richard Woody* deposed, 16 Dec. 1658.

---

JOTHAN GIBBONS.—Inventory of the Estate of the late M<sup>r</sup> *Jothan Gibbons*, deceased, prized P<sup>r</sup> M<sup>r</sup> *Rob<sup>t</sup> Brecke*, and *John Richards*, 16<sup>th</sup> Dec. 1658. Am<sup>t</sup>. £21. 10. *Susanna Gibbons & Cap<sup>t</sup> Samuell Scarlet* deposed, 16 : 10mo : 1658.

---

MARGARETT GIBBONS.—Inventory of the Estate of the late M<sup>r</sup> *Margarett Gibbons*, Relict of *Major Generall Edward Gibbons*, deceased, as it was taken and Aprized by *John Richards, William Phillips.* Amt. £28. 10. *Susanna Gibbons* and *Cap<sup>t</sup> Samuell Scarlet* deposed.

---

WILLIAM HARVY.—Inventory of the goods & chattells of *William Harvy* prised 18 : 11 : 1658. Amt. £38. 16.

28 April '59, *Martha Harvy* deposed. 29 Aprill 1659. Power of Administration to y<sup>e</sup> Estate of *William Harvy*, deceased granted to *Martha*, his late wife, for her own vse to bring vp her fower young Children.

---

WILLIAM HAYWARD.—Inventory of the goods & lands of *William Hayward*, of Brantree, late deceased, taken 8 July 1659, by *Henry Kingman, John Rogers John French.* Am<sup>t</sup>. £195. 05. 06. 14 June

1659. Power of Administracon granted to *Margery*, his late wife, in behalfe selfe & children. *Margery Heywood* deposed.

---

JOHN MAYNARD.—Inventory of the Estate of *John Maynard*, made by *James Johnson Rich Truesdall*, 7 : 9 : 1658. Am$^t$. £64. 06. 08. " Fowles prized by *John Biggs* & *John Jackson*." 29 July 1659. *Cap$^t$ James Johnson* & *Elizabeth Maynard* deposed.

---

WILLIAM BRIMSMEAD.—21 July. Power of Administracon to the Estate of the late *W$^m$ Brimsmead* is Graunted to *W$^m$ Brimsmead*, his sonne, in behalfe of himselfe & his brother & sisters.

---

CLEMENT BRIGGS.—12 : 23 : 1648. Copie of y$^e$ Estate of *Clement Briggs*. Lands in Weymouth & Plymouth, &c. Sume totall £65. 07. *Elizabeth Briggs* Relict of *Cleoment*, deposed, 28 July 1659.

---

ROBERT GIBSON.—Inventory of the Estate of *M$^r$ Rob$^t$ Gibson*, deceased, Boston 14 : 8 : 1656, prized by *Richard Wooddy, John Skarlett, Rich$^d$ Wayte*. " From *Mr John Richbell*, for wages & wine, £36." &c. 11 Aug 1659. *Benj. Gillam* deposed.

---

THOMAS WALKER.—Inventory of *Thomas Walkers* Estate, late deceased, taken by *Richard Gridley, Samuel Sendall,* & *Edmund Jackson*, who were chosen by *Anne*, the wife of the said Walker, and *Thomas*, his sonne. " In the Killyard of *Samuel Sendall*, hyred by *Thomas Walker*, bricks burnt & raw, with wood & boards, £42," &c. Sume tottall £323. 10. 06. 1 Sept. 1659. Administration Graunted to *Anne*, his late wife, & *Thomas Walker*, in behalfe of themselues & the rest of the Children. *Anne Walker*, deposed.

---

ROBERT RATCHELL.—A Note and Inventory of *Robert Rachell* estate. Amt. £5. 4$^s$. 8$^d$. Power of Administration graunted to *Judah*, his late wife, in behalfe of herselfe & Children. Estate prised by *Jn$^o$ Sweet, Tho: Rallings*. [No date.]

---

RICHARD DENTON.—Inventory of the Estate and Goods of *Richard Denton*, late of Dorchester. Taken by *Abraham How, John Minott*. Amt. £57. 05. *Ruth*, relict of *Richard Denton*, deposed 6 Oct. 1659.
(NOTE.—Richard Denton, of Dorchester, m. Ruth, dau. of Thomas Tilestone, 11 : 10 : 57. Richard Denton died 28 : 10 : 58. Timothy Foster, m. 1$^{st}$ Ruth Denton, 13 Oct. 1663. She d. 5 Dec. 1677. Mr. F. m. 2$^d$ Relief Dous, 9 Mar. 1681. See Reg. Vol. V. p. 399.)

---

MARGARETT PREIST.—Inventory of y$^e$ Goods belonging to *Margarett Preist*, deceased, taken by *Hen: Powning Jn$^o$. Joyliffe*, Constable. Goods in the hands of *Cap$^t$ James Johnson* & *Alexander Becke*. £9 7$^s$. Administration granted to *Alexander Becke*, 22 : 9mo : 59.

---

THOMAS PEAKE.—The testimony of *Thomas Robinson*, aged 25 yeares or there about; of *Jeremiah Miller*, aged 36 yeares or there about; of *John Sawdy*, aged 40 yeares or there about; and *John Clifford*, aged [blank] yeares, concerning the Estate of *Thomas Peake*, (Cooper of the Shipp Edward and Martha whereof *Ellis Else* is Master) dyed at Nevis, and at the time of his decease had aboard the said

167

shipp, as followeth, &c. &c. of the which goods an outcry was made, at the mast, by *Jeremy Miller*, by the Masters Comand, and to those that bought, the master said they must pay money for it; this *Ambrose Cowly* also affirmeth. The said *John Sawdy* and *John Clifford* saith further, that *Thomas Peake* tendered them a faire siluer hat band to sell, which the said *Peake* told the said *Sawdy* the Master bought it of him.

*Thomas Robinson & Ambrose Cowley*, y$^t$ Peake tould y$^m$ y$^t$ w$^t$ goods he had, w$^{ch}$ will not sell at Virginia, he would leaue it with *Andrew Cload*, in Boston, in New England, who was his Country man, & one y$^t$ would send it home for him to his wife, & said he had sent him some what alreddy from Barbadoes.

*Thomas Robinson & Joha Sawdy* deposed, 3 Nov. 1659, when Power of Administration was granted to *Andrew Cload*. *Ellis Else* rendered his account, 4 Nov. 1659. Goods of the deceased were purchased by M$^r$ Jn$^o$ Nowell, Ellis Else, Tho: Robinson, Tho: Horper, Jn$^o$ Peeteete & Jn$^o$ Clifford.

---

HENRY PENNY.—The Estate of *Mr Henry Penny*, deceased, Deb$^r$ vnto *Jacob Sheafe*, as delivered to *Marshall Wayte*. To *Henry Weale*, *Thomas Huckins*, &c. Am$^t$. £49.

12 Oct. 59. Deliuered P$^r$ me, *John Pole*, P$^r$ order of my *M$^{rs}$ Marg$^t$ Sheafe*. Rec$^d$ by me, *Rich$^d$ Wayte*, Adm$^r$. *Richard Wayte* deposed, 22 : 9 : 59.

---

THOMAS READ.—Inventory of the Goods & Chattells of *Thomas Read*, lately deceased, aprized by *Will Cotton*, *Will English*, *John Viall*. Amt. £57. 11. *William Hudson* deposed, 25 : 9mo : 59. Estate indebted te Nath. Renolds, Timothy Prate, Mr Hanniford, &c. Amt, £52. 03. 05. Owned by *Mary Reade*. Witnes *John Ferniside*, *John Viall*.

---

STEPHEN WEEBOW.—16 : 9mo : 1659. An Inventory taken of the Goods & Clothing of *Stephen Weebow*, who deceased Sep$^t$. the last, Administracon graunted to Lieu$^t$ W$^m$ *Phillips*, 25 : 9mo : 1659, who then deposed.

---

HUGH BATTEN.—Inventory of y$^e$ Estate of *Hugh Batten*, deceased [8 : 4 : '59,] taken this 19 : 5mo : 1659. Am$^t$. £144. 04. 07. *Vrsula Batten*, widow of *Hugh*, deposed, 26 : 9mo : 1659. There is also other land & Goods w$^{ch}$ were his, before marrying, as followeth :—House and Land that was *John Grenaways*, father to *Vrselle Batten*, w$^{ch}$ she is to haue during life, w$^{ch}$ is well know, as by deed bearing date 5 : 12 : 1650 it doth fully appeare, &c. &c. Am$^t$. £19. The Estate is indebted to Mr Alcocke, Mr Glouer, Mr Davis, Nath$^{ll}$ Wallis. £6 14$^t$.

---

MRS SARAH PACY.—The Goods of *Mr$^s$ Sarah Pacy*, prized by *Nathaniel Duncan*, *Rich. Gridly*. Cap$^t$ *James Johnson* deposed 26 : 9mo : 1659. The Court allowes the Accompt & Orders the Remainder to be payd to *Mr$^s$ Anne Keayne, Junio$^r$*. & allows *Capt John[son]* 20$^s$ more for his paines.

---

THOMAS WARNER.—Inventory of the Estate of Thcmas Warner, of Boston, fisherman, deceased. Prized by John Baker and John Farnum, 23d April 1660. Amt. £24. 15. 09. Power of Administration granted to Mr Richard Russell & Mr George Corwine

# ABSTRACTS FROM THE EARLIEST WILLS ON RECORD IN THE COUNTY OF SUFFOLK, MASS.

[Prepared by Mr. WILLIAM B. TRASK, of Dorchester.]

SAMUEL BIDFIELD.—Will. 12 : 3 : 1659. I giue vnto my wife my dwelling house and yard with the out house in the yard during hir life, pruided shee stay in this Cuntry and keepe the sayde house in repare, and after her decease or going out of the Cuntrie into England, my will is, saide house shall fall to *Samuell Plumer*, my grandchild, and to his heires. If hee dye with oute issue, it shall goe to the next sonn and his heires, and soe to the rest successiuly. Unto my wife, £40, and halfe the houshould goods ; the other halfe to bee deuided to my tow dau's children, to each of them Alike, that is to say, *Samuell Plumer*, *John Plumer*, *Ephraim Plumer*, *Mary Plumer*, *John Steuens*, *Samuell Steuens*. Also, vnto *John Steuens* and *Samuell Steuens*, £10, to each ; also, my two mares and two horses, after my decease, if non of them bee sold beefore ; and they to receiue this gift at the age of 21 yeares. Vnto my sonn, *Samuell Plumer*, all my wareing Cloths, both linell and wollin. To *Mr Tompson*, £5 ; to *Mr Willson*, 40s. ; to *Mr Norton*, £3 ; to *James Penn*, 40s. ; to *John Seirch*, 20s. ; to *William Dinsdale*, my Joynter, axes, oders, and all my other working tooles, wᵗʰ on coat and a pare of britches. My wife executrix, and *James Penn* and *Samuell Plumer*, ouerseers. It is my will that *James Penn* shall take the £20 I doe giue to my two grandchildren, and keepe it till they come to age.

Witnesses
>    *Nathaniell Williams*
>    *Madott Enges.*

Who deposed 20ᵗʰ Sept. 1660.

Inventory taken 13ᵗʰ 7ᵗʰ mo 1660, by *Richard Dole, Joseph Armitage.* Amt. £512.

*Elizabeth Bidfield*, widow of *Samuel*, deposed.

---

NATHANIEL BARNARD.—Inventory of the Goods and Chattells of *Nathaniel Barnard*, of Boston, deceased, prized by *James Euerill* and *Godfrey Armitage*, 18th Novr. 1659. Amt. £11. 12. 01. Mentions *Thomas Baker*, Smith, and *Thomas Starr*. Power of Administration granted to *Mary*, Relict of *Nathaniel Barnard*, 13th Jan. 1659. She deposed, the same day.

Estate indebted to Zachary Phillips, Nathaniell Adams, Capt. Thomas Savage, James Greene, Richd Bennet, George Nowell, David Showell, John Lewes, Mrs Susanna Gibbins, Esdras Read, Samll Sendall, Elieazer Heaton, Jno Winslow, Jno Meers, Jno Roades, Tho: Baker, Tho Starr, and others.

---

MR. JACOB SHEAFE.—Inventory of the Estate of Mr Jacob Sheafe, deceased, taken by *Anthony Stoddard, Edward Hutchinson, Tho: Brattle, Henry Shrimpton.* Sum Total. £8528. 08. 03. Among the items mentioned, is " a quarter pᵗ of 3 Mills at Roxbery, £173 ; dwelling-house and ground therevnto belonging, £220 ; 50 thousand of sugar, at England and

Barbadoes, at £10 p. thousand, £500; a qʳter pᵗ of yᵉ Ketch Tryall and the Cargo, £155; for yᵉ Sayles of provisions at Newfoundland, pʳ *Mr Croad*, £170. 02. 09. &c. &c. *Mrs Margaret Sheafe*, widow of *Jacob*, deposed, 23: 9 mo: 59.

---

ROBERT SHARP.—24ᵗʰ Aprill 1656. On request of the former widow of *Robert Sharp*, *Thomas Mekins* and *Peeter Aspinwall* are appointed to take the children of the said Sharp's Porcoñ, and to Improve them for the best advantage of the sonne and daughters, defraying all necessary Charges for their Clothes and keeping, by letting the Land and Improoveing the rest of the estate, belonging to the Children, to the best Advantage.

[See Lib. iii. fol. 67. for the Petition of said *Mekins* and *Aspinwall*, in which it is proposed that *Aspinwall* " take yᵉ two daughters and finde them meate, drinke and Apparrell, learne them to read; to knitt, spine and such Houswifery and keepe them either to yˢ day of marriage, or untill yˢ age of eighteene," for which said *Peeter* is to have " yᵉ vse and profitt of yᵉ house and land yᵗ was said Sharps, only yˢ said *Peeter*, besides bringing vp yˢ said daughters, in consideration of yˢ benefit of said house and land, alow yˢ sonne £5 p. Annum, &c. (" *Tho Mekinnes* had the sonne to Bring up to His trade.") Signed, 15 Jan. 1656. Witnessed by *Abigall Clapp*, Relicte and Administratrix to the Estate of the Late *Robert Sharpe*. See also Lib. iv. fol 228, for the Petition of said *Abigaill Clapp*, to the Court, on the 15 April 1665, that said *Meekins* and *Aspinwall* be discharged, having fullfilled their trust. In this Petition it is stated, that *Robert Sharpe* left three Children Behind him in the year 54, one sonne, *John*, and 2 Daughters, *Abigail* and *Mary*. *John* being then, (in 1665) 22 years of age, and married; the eldest dau. about 17 yeares; the youngest, about 12 yeares; &c. &c. Said Petition was witnessed by *John White*, and *Ja. Pemberton*.]
*See Register for July*, 1854: p. 276. (See p. 128).

---

MARGARET JOHNSON.—Inventory of the Estate of Margaret Johnson. Widdow, in the Towne of Hingham, Prized 10ᵗʰ Jan. 1659, by *John Fernig*, *Edmund Hubberd*. Power of Administration to yˢ Estate granted to *John Tucker*, 25 Jan. 59, in behalfe of *Mary Tucker*, his daughter, unless better Clayme appeare. John Tucker deposed, 25: 2 mo: 1660. The Court Considering yˢ Evidence pʳduced by *Mr Hubbard*, in Relatiō to yˢ good will and affection yᵗ *Thomas Johnson*, Late of Hingham, did beare to Mr *Peeter Hubbard*, Minister there, doe order yᵗ yˢ Administrators to yᵗ Estate, pay vnto yˢ said *Mr Peter Hubbard*, £5. out of yᵗ Estate, and yᵉ Dau. of *John Tucker* to have the rest, when yᵉ debts be payd and account thereof Given. Edw. Rawson, Recordʳ.

Wee whose names are underwritten doe testifie vnto yᵉ Honoʳd Court yᵗ about 8 or tenn dayes before *Margaret Johnson*, Widow, dyed, she being in pʳfect memory, I yᵉ said *Thomas Lincoln*, weaver, was at yᵉ dwelling house of *Margaret Johnson*, I fell into discourse with her Concerning yᵗ Estate yᵗ she had, and *Richard Wood* was pʳsent with me, and wee, yᵉ said *Thomas* and *Richard*, heard her say, yᵗ when she dyed, it was her husbands will (he expressed it before he dyed,) yᵗ when he and *Margaret*, his wife, dyed yᵗ yᵗ Estate yᵗ was Left, they would give it to *Mary Tucker*, and as it was my husbands will & minde, so it is mine,

170

y$^t$ all y$^t$ Estate y$^t$ I haue shall be *Mary Tuckers*, and she desired me, y$^e$ said *Thomas Lincolne*, weaver, and *Richard Wood*, to beare witnes y$^t$ it was her will, y$^t$ she should haue it in case she should dye without a written will ; and to this testimony wee set to o$^r$ hands, 10 Jan. 1659. *Thomas Lincoln* and *Richard Wood*, deposed, 25 Jan. 1659.

Margarett Johnson's Estate, late of Hingham, Cred$^r$. To Lycorice and Sugar spent at her burryal, 15s. 4d. ; to the burryall, more, one bushell wheate, 4s. 6d. ; to *Mr Kimball*, of Charles Towne, £2 ; &c. &c. Given in by *Joseph Church*, 30 : 2 mo : 1662.

Whereas the Late *Jno Tucker*, senio$^r$, of Hingham, tooke Administration to the Estate of *Margarett Johnson*, in behalfe of *Mary Tucker*, his Daughter, 25 Jan. 1659. The Court order the said *Jno Tucker*, senio$^r$, to pay *Mr Hubbard*, minister of Hingham, £5., out of the same, the said *Mary Tucker* being marryed to *Joseph Church*, of Hingham. On Request of said *Joseph*, the Court order that the Estate Left in the hands of the Administrator, *Jno Tucker*, senio$^r$, be deliured to said *Church*. Allowed 30 Oct. 1662. Liv. iv. fol. 88.

————

WILLIAM PAINE, of Boston, having binn a long time by the hand of God much exercised with infirmity of body, yet in perfect memory, [do] make my will. Vnto *Hanna*, my wife, £200, and my dwelling house, sittuate in Boston, with all the out houses, archard, gardens, &c. ; allso, my mill, at Watertowne, with the houses, lands, &c. ; allso all my househould stuffe, the vse and Improuement of it for life. Vnto my three grand children, which ware the Children of my dafter, *Hanna Appleton*, deceased, the some of £1500, viz. to *Hanna*, £600, to *Samuell*, £500, and to *Judeth*, £400. And if any of my sayd grandchildren depart this life, Leaueing noe Issue, Then the sayd Legicie or Legicies shall remaine to them that surviue and their heires for euer. If they depart this life leaueing noe Issue, Then my will is, that the sayd £1500, bee repayd back vnto my sonn *John Paine*, to him and his heires. Said Legicies shall bee payd vnto my grandchildren as they shall attaine vnto age, or vppon the day of marridge. I giue to *Hanna Appleton*, my said grand child, all the househould stuff that now standeth in the hall chamber, to remaine to her after my wife depart this life. The rest of my househould stuffe I giue vnto the other of my grandchildren, after my wifes decease. I giue vnto the Children of *Symond Eyers*, sen$^r$. deceased, viz : *Beniamine, Mary, Rebekah, Christian, An*, and *Dorothy*, £5 to each. To *Symond Eyes* the sonn of *Symond Eyes Jn.* deceased, £5 to bee payd when of age. Vnto my *Sister Page*, £3. p$^r$ yeare dewreing life. Vnto my kinsman, *John Page*, which now is in his hands the some of £5. and to the other Children of my sayd *Sister Page*, viz. To *Samuell, Elizabeth, Mary, Pheebee*, £5., to each. Vnto the children of my Sister *Hament*, viz : To *John, Elizabeth*, and *hanna*, £5., to each. To my kinswoman, *Elizabeth House*, dafter to *Samuell* and *Elizabeth House*, £10. Vnto the two dafters of my Cosan, *John Tall*, 40s. to each, when of age. Vnto my sonn in law, *Samuell Appleton*, £10 ; to *William Howard*, £15 ; to *Jerimy Belcher*, 40s. ; vnto *Mr Anthony Stodder*, £10 ; vnto *Christopher Clarke*, £10 ; vnto *Mr Joseph Tainter*, £10 ; vnto *Mr Oliuer Puerchis*, £10 ; vnto *Mary Ingion*, 40s., yearely, dureing life. I giue vnto the free scoole of Ipswitch, the little neck of land at Ipswitch, commonly knowne by the name of Jeferrys neck. The which is to bee, and remaine, to the benifitt of the said scoole of Ipswitch, for euer, as I haue formerly Intended, and therefore the sayd land not to bee sould nor wasted. I giue vnto the Colledg at Cambridge, £20., The which is now payd for that end into the hands of the worshippfull *Mr Thomas Dauenport*, of Cambridge, and shall remaine in the hands of the Committie and president of the Colledge, and by them, for the time beeing, and theire suckcessers after them for euer, Imploy sayd Twenty pounds for the benifitt of the said Colledge. But the sayd Twenty pounds not to bee expended But to remaine as A *stock* to the College for euer. I giue vnto my reuerent freinds, viz : *Mr Norton*, and *Mr Willson*, Paster and teacher of the Church of Boston, 40s. to each. To *Mr Shirman*, Paster of the Church at Water-towne, to *Mr Browne*, paster of the Church at Sudbery, to *Mr Cobbit*, paster of the Church at Ipswitch, to *Mr Fisk*, passter of the Church at Chensford, to *Mr Phillops*, teacher of the Church at Rowley, to *Mr Mayhoo*, paster of the new Church of Boston, 40s. [each.] All the rest of my estate vnto my sonn, *John Paine*. If *John* depart this life, leaue-ing noe Issue, nor Children of sayd Issue, Then my will is that the houses and lands which of right doe beelonge vnto mee, within the bounds of Ipswitch, with the privileges, &c. I giue vnto the Children of my sayd dafter, *Hanna Appleton*, deceased, namely, *Hannah, Judeth*, and *Samuell*, or soe many of them as shall bee then aliue, as Coe heires to the same, to them and their heires for euer, according as there is pᵛvition made in A deede of gift, formerly giuen vnto my sonn, *John Paine*. If *John* de-part this life, leaueing no issue, nor Children of said Issue. Then my will is, that the Children of my sister *Page*, mentioned aboue, shall haue out of my estate the some of £300, to bee equally deuided between them. If my wife should depart out of this life beefore myselfe, Then my will is, that the Children of *Simond Eyers*, sen., deceased, shall haue £5 apeece, A deed to theire former £5 ; and the Children of my sister *Page* and sister *Hanna*, shall haue £5 apeece, aded to their former £5. I doe hereby earnestly request *Mr Olliur Purches*, to be helpefull to my sonne, *John Paine*, concerning the Iron worke and the accounts thereof, whose Abilities and faithfullness I haue had experience of, vnto whose Ceare I doe Commit the sayd accounts. I make my sonn, *John Paine*, my Sonn in Law, *Samuell Appleton*, and *Mr Anthony Stodder*, my executors. And I doe request *Mr Christopher Clarke*, *Mr Joseph Tainter*, and *Mr Olliuer Purches*, to bee my ouerseers and feofess in trust of this my will. My will is, that if my sayd Ouerseeres with my Executors shall see Just Case for some pyous vse and nesessary worke to giue £100., They shall haue power to take it out of my estate.　　　　2 Octʳ 1660.

　　　　　　　　　　　　　　　　　　　　　　　　　Will Paine.

　Postscript.—I giue vnto *Doctter Clarke*, £5 ; and I doe giue to *Capt Thomas Clarke Company*, to bye them *Cullers, the some of fiue pounds*.
　In presence of vs,
　　　*John Mayo, Christopher Clarke,*
　　　*Will: Howard.*
　14 Novʳ 1660. *Mr Samuell Appleton* appeared beefore the Court and declared by reason of his remote living and inability to manage such A trust hee did renounce his excetership to the will. Also, *Anthony Stod-derd*, on Request of *Mr John Payne*, sonn to the late *Mr William Paine*, did renounce his executorship to this will, which was done before the probate of the will.　　　　Edward Rawson Recorder.
　14 Nov. 1660. *Mr John Mayo, Christopher Clarke*, and *William Howard*, deposed.

Inventory of the Estate taken by *Henry Shrimpton, Joshua Scottow, John Richards*, 22 : 8 : 1660. Amt. £4239. 11. 05. *Mr John Paine* deposed, 14 Nov$^r$ 1660.

---

MARTINE SAUNDERS.—Inventory of the Estate of *Martine Saunders*, senior, of Brantrey, deceased, 4th : 6 mo : (58) Amt. £321. 17. Apprizers, *William Allis, Moses Paine, Edmund Quinsey.*

For a full, fynall & Amicable Conclusion & Agreement betweene *John Saund$^r$s, Martine Saund$^r$s, Francis Elliott & Robert Parmenter*, all of Brantrie, sonnes & Sonnes in Law to y$^e$ Late *Martine Saund$^r$s*, of Braintrie. It is agreed vpon, y$^e$ 10th 8 mo. 1658.

That *John Saund$^r$s*, Eldest sonne to the Late *Martine Saund$^r$s*, (the will of y$^e$ said Martine, the father, notwithstanding,) shall haue the house, barne, Cowhouse, together with y$^e$ yards, Orchards, Gardens & a Little piece of meadow lyeing to y$^e$ house, all w$^{ch}$ y$^e$ said *Martine Saund$^r$s* died possessed of, with all y$^e$ liberties, &c.

2. It is agreed vpon, y$^t$ *Francis Elliott*, in right of his wife, shall haue y$^t$ piece of meadow Lying on y$^e$ neck, 6 acres, more or less, to him & to his heirs, &c. And also, with y$^e$ £7 he hath had, haue it made vp out of y$^e$ Estate of *Martine Saund$^r$s*. y$^e$ father, an equall portion with *Martine Saund$^r$s & Robert Parmenter.*

3. It is farther agreed vpon, y$^t$ *Martine Saund$^r$s*, youngest sonne, to y$^e$ late *Martine Saund$^r$s*, shall haue a piece of vpland & meadow, form$^r$ly his fathers, in pumpkin hill, Running from his broth$^r$ *John Saund$^r$s* Lyne of 25 Rodds brooad, till it come to the sea, & shall also haue it made vp an equall p$^r$portion with y$^e$ rest of his sisters, with what he hath had, at his marriage.

4. It is Lastly concluded & agreed, y$^t$ *Robert Parmenter*, in right of his wife, shall haue all y$^e$ Lands Lying in Pumpkin hill, together with y$^e$ meadow thereunto belonging, excepting 4 acres, y$^t$ is *John Saund$^r$s*, as aboue, & y$^e$ vpland & meadow y$^t$ is *Martine Saund$^r$s*, w$^{ch}$ Lyeth at y$^e$ end of *John Saund$^r$s*, as aboue, to y$^e$ sea, & shall also receiue £15, of *John Saund$^r$s*, for his dau. in Law *Rachell's*, vse, & shall also haue it made vp out of y$^e$ Estate Left by y$^e$ said *Martine Saund$^r$s*, y$^e$ father, an equall p portion, with his sister *Elliott*, accounting what his wife had at marriage. Y$^e$ parties aboue mentioned bind ymselues in y$^e$ penall sum of £100. This 10 Oct$^r$. 1658.

In p$^r$sence of vs, *Peter Bracket, William Ellis.*

John Saund$^r$s
Martine Saund$^r$s
Francis Elliott
Robt Parmenter.

Whereas *Francis Elliott*, Sonne In Law to the Late Martine Saund$^r$s, p$^r$senting a will signed by the Late *Martine Saund$^r$s*, bearing date 5th 5 mo. 1658, about w$^{ch}$ y$^r$ was some difference & discontent between y$^e$ sonnes of y$^e$ said Saund$^r$s, w$^{ch}$ y$^e$ Court Considering of, advised y$^e$ Children to Come to a Loueing Agreem$^t$ amongst ymselues, y$^r$ being seuerall objections made against y$^e$ said will. [All things being amicably settled, an inventory was made, and allowed by the Court, 2 Feb. 1659.]

---

LEWIS MARTINE.—Inventory of y$^e$ Goods of *Lewes Martine*, deceased, taken at y$^e$ Request of *Thomas Trapp*, by *John Wiswall, Henry Powning, John Phillips.* Amt. £64. 16. 11$\frac{1}{2}$.

Whereas Administration to y$^e$ Estate of *Lewes Martine*, was giuen, 21

July '59, to *Thomas Trapp*, in behalfe of *Mr John Andrewes*, to whom it was giuen, & yᵉ said *Trapp* failing in giueing securitie to yᵉ Recorder, who, finding yᵉ said *Thomas Trapp* to be Conveying himselfe & yᵉ said Goods out of this Jurisdiccon, to Martin Vineyard, to *Thomas Burchard*, who marryed yᵉ said *Thomas Andrews* mother, yᵉ said *Burchard* hauᵉing wrote to *Mr Elliott* to giue securitie to yᵉ Court for yᵉ said Goods till Order Come from yᵉ said *Andrewes* for yᵉ disposeing thereof, & yᵉ Magistrates finding yᵗ yᵉ said *Trapp* hath vsed £6 of yᵉ said Goods for paying his owne passage & other charges, & being informed of yᵉ great paines yᵉ said *Trapp* tooke with yᵉ said *Lewes Martine*, whiles aliue, & about yᵉ goods, Judge meete yᵗ he be allowed yᵉ said £6.; & whereas, he pʳtends his chest was broken vp & some goods taken out. The Magistrates Judge meete to Order, yᵗ yᵉ Marshall, with yᵉ said *Trapp*, in sight of yᵉ Recordʳ, overhale yᵉ goods now in hand, with yᵉ Inventory thereof, & what is found to Comit into yᵉ hands of *Mr John Elliott*, who is to giue yᵉ Recorder Securitie, &c. 22 Sepᵗ 59.

*Mr Robert Gibbs*, of Boston mʳchant, pʳducing a Lettʳ of Atturney, Signed by *John Andrewes*, of yᵉ Cittie of London, mʳchant Taylor, Impowering to Receiue Goods bequathed vnto him by *Lewis Martine*, deceased, & in Custody of Marshall *Richard Waite*, secured by Order of Court, pʳserued from Imbecelling, It is ordered yᵗ said *Gibbs* Record his power with yᵉ Recorded, & on Receipt of said Goods, to procure a discharge from *John Andrews*, within two years, &c.

[An Invoyce of Goods, found in yᵉ Chest of said *Trapp*, belonging to *Martin's* Estate, on behalfe of said Andrewes, examined by *John Wiswall*, *Henry Powning*, *Richard Waite*, *Thomas Trapp*. 23 Sept 1659. Received by *Robert Gibbs*, 5 May 1660.]

*Thomas Trapp*, aged 20 yeares or thereabouts, saith *Lewis Martine*, of Porley, in Essex, husbandman, to me well knowne, haueing wrought with him seuerall times at harvest time, yᵉ Last yeare, in England, was also with him when he tooke vp a pʳcell of goods, & borrowed seuʳall times money, of *Mr John Andrewes*, of Fanchurch Streete, London, Lynnen drapʳ, & Coming ouer with yᵉ said *Martine*, In yᵉ shipp Exchange, *Capt John Peirce*, Comandʳ, who, falling sicke, on his death bed, called me, *Thomas Trapp* to him, & said, Thomas, I am sicke & weake, & know not how yᵉ Lord will dispose of me, but, if I should dye, I would haue all yᵗ I haue on board, & yᵉ pʳduce of it, goe to yoʳ Coussin, *John Andrewes*, for he is my best friend I haue in yᵉ world; and yᵉ deponent further saith, yᵗ yᵉ said *Lewes Martine*, for seuʳall moneths, Lodged at yᵉ said *John Andrewes*, & had his dyet also free, for what euer he heard. Taken on Oath, before yᵉ Magistrates, 21 July 1659.

pʳ Edw. Rawson Recordʳ.

*Thomas Trapp* indebted to *Thomas Smith*, £6. 04. Power of Administration to yᵉ Estate of *Lewis Martine*, Graunted to *Thomas Trapp*, in behalfe of *Mr John Andrewes*.

THOMAS COLLIER.—March 23, 1659. Inventory of the Estate of the Late *Thomas Collier*, as it was Giuen in to yᵉ Court, 1647, the goods being then Apprized by *Jno Ottis* & *William Hersie*, as in yᵉ file of the Courts may Appeare; yᵉ house & Lands being now Apprized, tho then Giuen in, also, without price, by those whose names are vnderwritten, *George Lane* & *Thomas Hewet*. Amᵗ. £96. *Moses Colier*, son of said *Thomas*, deposed, 22 April 1660. *See Will. Reg.* vol. vii. p, 173. *

*See p. 96.

# ABSTRACTS FROM THE EARLIEST WILLS ON RECORD IN THE COUNTY OF SUFFOLK, MASS.

[Prepared by Mr. WILLIAM B. TRASK, of Dorchester.]

ANNE ORGRAVE.—Inventory of the Goods of *Ann Orgraue*, deceased, apprized 7th May 1660, by *Richard Wayte, Tho. Baker.* Power of Administration to ye Estate, graunted to *Ann Carter*, in behalfe of her selfe & sister, *Dorothy Post. Anne Carter* deposed, that this is a true Inventory of her Late Mother, *Anne Orgraues* Estate. Edw: Rawson, Recordr.

THOMAS BUCKMASTER.—Inventory of the Goods and Estate of *Thomas Buckmaster*, of Boston, Carpinter, deceased, made and approved by *Richard Sanford, Rober[t] Meeres* and *John Starr*, the 15 Decr. 1659. Amt. £39. 16.

1 Feb. 1659.   Administracon to the Estate of *Tho: Buckmaster* Graunted to *Mary*, his Relict, who deposed the same day, Mentions *Richard Knight*, bricklayer.

BRIDGET BUSBY.—Inventory of ye Goods of *Bridgett Busby*, Lately deceased, taken out the 3 July, 1660, by *Edmond Eddenden, Benjamine Negus.* Power of Administration to ye Estate of *Bredgett Busbie*, Granted to *Abraham Busby*, her sonne, 5 July 1660, & to prforme ye deede made & signed by her, 14th May 1651.

MATHEW CUSHIN.—This is to Certify the Honnored Court now Assembled in Boston, That our honnored Father, *Mathew Cushin*, who lately departed this life, on the 30th day of Sept last, being some whiles beefore his decease sensible of his Inabillity, through Age, to make Improuement of his estate for his and his Deare wiues, our honnored Mothers, liuely-hood, did call vs, his sonns & sonne in Law, whose names are heare vnder written, together, And acquainted vs that hee was desirous to set his house in order, and on termes to settle his estate on those his Children, and to giue vs possession of our seuerall portions, that is to say, that all his Cattle and Lands, his dwelling house and orchard, with on Cowe excepted which hee reserued for his owne mother vse, dureing theire naturall liues, with the howse hold goods, after theire death, shuld allsoe fall to vs, and bee deuided Amongst vs in proportion, Following, to *Daniell*, his Eldest sonne, hee gaue all the lands, at present, hee paying out of the same, after A double portion to himselfe was taken out, what shuild make vp A single share to such of his Brothers as had not theire share, or that the Cattle fell short of makeing theire shares ; and for that end valued the Catle and Lands with what was in his sonn in Law, *Mathias Briggs*, his hand, to £155. *Daniell* to haue A duble portion, and the rest, share and share Alike ; and soe, allsoe, after yr mothers decease, the house, orchard, household goods, and Cowe, to bee diuided, *Daniell* to haue the house and land at an equall value, and paying what it Amounted to more then his double part there from, to the rest, thay, allsoe, During his life, paying vnto him, £14, and theire mother after his death, £12 in goods and suitable pay, *Daniell*, £4. 5s. 8d. Jeremiah Cushin, £2. 2s. 10d. and *Mathias Briggs*, his sonn in Law, to pay 25s. 10d. ; which we all ingaged to performe, &c. [They desire that Power of Administration vpon upon the Estate of said *Matthew Cushing* may be given to *Daniell*, his eldest son, their Brother; which request was granted 15 Nov^r. 1660.] This Petition was signed by *Daniell Cushin, Mathew Cushin, John Cushin, Mathias Briggs, Jeremiah Cushin.*

Inventory of the Estate, aprised by *Mathew Cushin* and his sonns, in his life time. Amt. *£155.* Mentions, " a house Lott in Batchalers streete, solt mash bought of *Wakly*, lands bought of *Edward Hubbert* & W^m *Johns*," &c. On the 12^th Nov. 1660, the remainder of the Estate was apprised by *Mathew Hawke* & *Edmond Pitts.* Amt. *£92. Daniell Cushin* deposed, 15 Nov. [An addition was made to this Inventory, and given in to the Court, 30th April, 1662, by *Daniell Cushin.* See Lib. iv. fol. 88.]

----

MRS. MARY GLOVER.—Inventory of y^e Goods & Estate of *Mrs Mary Glover*, y^e wife of *Mr Nath. Glover*, deceased, taken by *Roger Clap*, & *John Gurnell*, the 13 : 12 mo. 1659, by y^e Request of the said *Mrs Glover*. Amt. *£478. 01. 06.* This Inventory was presented to y^e County Court, by *Mr Tho: Hinckley*, on his marriage to *Mary*, y^e Relict of said *Nathl. Glover*. Debts due, to *Quarter Master Smith, Thomas Danford, Samuel Chandler.* On the 31 Aug. 1660, the Court made a Division of the Estate of said *Nathl. Glover;* and the said *Tho. Hinckley*, in right of *Mary*, y^e Relict of said *Nathl. Glover*, now his wife, to have one third of the said *£478. 01. 06.* the other two thirds, to the Children of said *Nathaniel.* The Reversion left by y^e Will of y^e Late *Mr John Glover*, & y^e *£40* due from *Mr Habucucke Glover*, to be devided amongst y^e Children of *Nathl.* & theire mother. *Mr Habuckuck Glover* & *John Gurnell* were by this Court appointed Guardians to y^e said Children; & the Administratrix was required to deliver up the Remainder of the Goods to the value of *£65.*, or thereabouts, with y^e Lands, to said Guardians, in behalfe of y^e Children, they Giueing security to y^e Recorder, for y^e said *£65.*, & the Increase thereof, with y^e Increase of y^e Lands to Runne to y^e benefitt of y^e said Children, *Mrs Anne Glover* & *Mr Habacuck Glover* engageing on their owne charge & account, without Looking for satisfaction from y^e children's Estates, to bring them vp to schoole, & find them meate, drinck, & Cloaths, till they be fitt to be disposed of to good trads. Debts of the Estate of *Mr Nathl Glover*, demanded of the Administratrix, viz. : to *Mr Patten*, for sheepe & sugar; to *Goody Humphreys*, for y^e childrens schooling; to *Goody Tappin*, for y^e Childrens Hatts; to *Goody Dyer*, for Weaving; to *Goody Swift*, for Lyquo^r; to y^e Tucker; to *Mr Greenleife*, for Dying; to y^e Shearman; to *Mr Tyng*, for sundry p^ticul^rs; to *Hannah Tolman*, for wages; to *Sam^ll Jones*, for tanning; to *Sam^ll Chandler*, &c. Amt. *£14. 5. 1.* Said acc^t of Debts presented by *Mr Thomas Hinckley*, 2 Nov. 1660.

----

RICHARD ROCKWOOD.—Inventory of the estate of *Richard Rockwood*, late of Braintry, deceased, the 7: 6: 60. Amt. *£38. 03. 04.* Payd oute of this estate to his Dafter, in yarne, p^t of a Cowe, &c., *£3. 8s.* to *Goodman Belcher*, for rent of Land *£1. 6. 8.*; to *Dormon Dorneing*, for bords, *£1. 5s.*; to *Francis Gold*, 15s.; to *Richard Thayer*, to satisfie for a Cow that was killed, p^r *Jo: Rockwood*, *£4. 13s.* &c. *Elder Kingsly* and *Ann Rockett* deposed, 15 Nov. 1660.

CAPT. THOMAS THORNHILL.—May 4th 1660. Debts oweing by the deseased, amounting to £130. 10. 01. Accounts examined by *Thomas Clarke* & *Edward Tyng*, and the returne accepted by the Court, 31 Oct. 1660. Estate indebted to Thomas Weborne, Capt James Johnson, Edward Cowell, Mr Robeurt Pateshall, John Poades, John Shaw, Capt Nicolas Sharpley; Goodwife George, of Dorchester; Goodman Rogers, Hudson Leuerett, Theodor Atkingson, Josiph More; Thomas Clarke, of Wenese- nitt; John Sunderland, Euen Thomas, Ann Prince, Mr. John Jolliffe, Mr Robert Gibbs, Mr Thomas Kellon, Arther Macon, Goodman Edmons; Goodman Johnson, of Piscataway; Capt Thomas Clarke, Leift William Hudson, Mr Scarlett, George Browne; Francis Gray, of Pascataway; Mary Palsgraue, Christopher Lawson, Mr John Woodmancey; Robeurt Worse, of Dorchester; Leiut Dauis, of Yorke; Nicolas Lawrance, Maior Nicolas Shapley, George Walton, Jonathan Ransford, Good Mettem. Whole Amt. £130. 10. 01. To Funerall charges & his sickness, 17 pr white gloues, £1. 15. 6.; 31½ yds of Corle for scarfes, £3. 10. 10¼.; black & white ribbin; 20 lb. of suger; spice & suger Cakes; 15 Gall. of Wine, £3.; for making his graue, bell ringing and Recording his name at death, 6.; pd Robt Browne, 4s. 6d.; pd Goodman Mesinger, for Coffin and rayles, £1.; &c. &c. Amt. 120. 09. 06½. Estate Creditor by a debt in hands of *Joss More*, wch is good; by a hhd. of Rume and a hhd. mallasses, *Mr John Cutts* reced at Pascataqua. Doubtfull and desperate debts of *Henry Lamperry* & *Jeremiah Belcher*.

Lib. iv. fol. 1 & 2, contains an Inventory of the Estate of the late *Capt. Tho. Thornehill*, taken & appraised by *Thomas Clarke, Joshua Scottow, Chrispin Hooper, John Winslow, John Farnam*, in 1660.

*Mr Thomas Lake, Mr Jno Richards* & *Mr Tho. Leland*, deposed, 31 Oct. 1660.

---

MRS. MARTHA COGGAN.—Inventory of her Estate, taken 29 8 mo. 1660, by *Peeter Oliuer, Thomas Bumsted, Thomas Clarke*. Amt. £1030. 03. *Elder James Penn*, and *Deacon Richard Trusdale*, deposed 31 Oct. 1660. They are also impowered to sell goods & Lumber not fitt to bee kepte & perishable, that damage may be prevented. Mention is made in the In- ventory of "*sister Robinson*," *brother John Coggan & his sisters Mary and Elizabeth*. The farm at Rumly marsh, valued at £450.; ⅓ of ye mill at Charles towne, £40.; 500 Ackers of Land at Ouborne, £10.

5 May 1662. Administration granted vnto *Joseph Rocke*, vpon the Estate of *Mr Jno Coggan*, deceased, wch was in possession of *Elder James Penn*, & *Deacon Richard Trusdall*, being betrusted with ye said Estate by the Court since the death of *Mrs Martha Coggan*, executrix vnto her late husband. Lib. iv. fol. 88. *Joseph Rocke* deposes 19 Aug. 1662, that this is a true Inventory of the late *Mr John* & *Mrs Martha Coggan*, his late father & mother. *Caleb Coggan*, son & heir of *John* & *Martha Coggan*. A bill paid for his schooling; 75 Acres of Land in possession of farmr Greene in Malden.

---

ROBERT BATTILE.—Inventory of his Estate apprized by *Nathaniell Williams*, & *Arther Mason*, 13th Nov. 1660. Debts dew from *Mr Josiph Rock, Mr William Dauis, Mr Mayo*, &c. *Leift Richard Cooke*, deposed, 14 Nov. 1660, to the truth of this Inventory of the Estate of the late *Robeart Battle*.

Lib. iv. fol. 150, contains a list of the Creditors of the said *Robt Battile*, given in 6 : 6 mo. 1663 by *Edward Ting* & *Anth: Stoddard*. Allowed of by the Court, 7 Aug. 1663. The names of the Creditors, were, Mr Henry Bridgham, Mr Ralph King, Mr Jerimy Hutchin, Mr Thomas Wells, Mr Edmund Greenleffe, Mr Edward Lane.

---

JOHN KINGSBURY.—Will of *John Kingsbery*, of Dedham, made 2 : 10 : 1659. Vnto *Mr John Allen*, our pastor, 40s. To my Bro. *Josiph Kingsbury*, of Dedham, one booke, that is allready in his possition, beeing Dr Prestons workes, Called Paules repentence, and one other booke, of Mr Dyke, his worke, called the deceatfullnes of the hart, and allsoe, one other booke, of Mr Cowpers worke vppon Rom : ye 8. I giue vnto *John Kingsbura*, my kinsman, the sonn of my Brother, Aforesayd, my bible and my Psalme booke. I giue vnto *Margrett*, my well bee loued wife, the free vse of all the rest of my estate, both reall and prsonall, during her life. I giue vnto my wife, one halfe of my estate, to her and her heires for euer, [to be at her disposal, & after her decease to be divided into two equal parts, the one pt to be disposed of to the heires of my wife,] the other halfe, to be disposèd as followeth :—vnto *John Kingsbery*, £15, when hee shall obtaine the age of 21 yeares. I giue vnto *Thomas Cooper*, of Seacanque, my kinsman, £5, in consideration of requitall of such paynes as hee may be occationed by this my will. My mind is that after [the] Two Legacies last mentioned are set out, the remainder of halfe of my estate, beeing distinct from that half beefore giuen to my wife, shall bee deuided into soe many equall p'. that my kindsman, *Henry Kingsbery*, of Ipswich, and each of the Children, sonnes and daufters of my Brother, *Josiph Kingsbery*, of Dedham, may haue one equall pt., and that my said brother, *Josiph*, may haue two pts, that is to say, twice soe much as any of the other Legacies in this diuision ; allways to bee vnderstood that I entend such and soe many of them as shall bee then suruiueing when this deuision shall bee made, [to be paid within 6 months after the decease of my wife.] If any of the sonns of my Brother, *Josiph*, at that time shall not attaine the age of 21 yeares, my will is, that my Executors, shall, within the time of 6 months beefore prfixed, deliuer that pt beelonging to the Leegacies vnder age, to my Brother, theire Father, for their vse. I Apointe my two Loueing Frinds and Kinsmen, *Thomas Fuller*, of Dedham, and *Thomas Cooper*, of Seacuqgne, to bee the executors of this my will.

John ⋈ Kingsbury.

Signed & sealed in the prsents of us,
*Eliazer Lusher. John Howard.*

*John Howard* testified before *Eleazer Lusher*, Commissr. 16 : 8 mo : 1660. *Capt Eliazer Lusher* deposed, before Court, 16 Oct. 1660.

Inventory of the Estate, taken the 9 : 8 mo. 1660, by *Thomas Fuller* & *Thomas Cooper* who deposed, before the Magistrates and Recorder, *Eliazer Lusher*, *Henry Chickering*, *John Gay*, *John Howard*, 16 Oct. 1660. Amt. of Inventory, £405. 06. [In addition to Dr·Preston's, Mr Cowper's, Mr Dyke's, & Mr Burrowe's works, is mentioned " 9 other smale bookes, some being very olde." An additional Inventory is recorded, 22 May, 1662. See Lib. iv. fol. 84–87.]

---

MAHALALEEL MUNNINGS. Inventory of Goods of ye Late *Mahalaleel Munnings*, taken & prized by *Capt. Thomas Clarke, Sergeant Nathaniel Williams* & *Jno. Richards*, the 6th of March, 1659–60. The Goods were prized according to their Cost in England, as p^r invoyce, & are bought at 40 p Cent.

Paid to *Mr. Jn^o. Cutts, Richard Cutts*, & others, bills to ye value of £550.

Inventory of the Estate of Mahalaleel Munnings, in Dorchester, taken 23 : 5 : 1659–60, by *Robert Voce*, & *William Robinson. Mr John Wisewall*, Administrator, Mentions in the Inventory, *Henry Gernsey.*

Lib. iv. fol. 93—101, contains a list of Debts of Mahaliell Munnings. Mentions John Phillips, Hannah Bates, James Bates, John Capen, Abraham Dickerman, Robin Wright, Richard Bull, John Blower, William Searge, Henry Douglas, Sam^ll. Chandler, Thomas Andrewes, Rich^d. Mason, sister Vpshall, Mr. Barnet, senior ; my brother Smith, Robin Mason, Nathaniell Robinson, Pollard & Burges, Sam^n Bruet & Sweete, Obediah Ward, Jack, & Sam^ll Clement ; Mr. Barnet & Zechariah ; Nicholas Cady, Syth & Rub ; Adams & Cushing ; Walker, Brickmaker ; John Baker, Mr John Cutts, William Blanton, Thomas Makins, Mary King, Moses Gillman ; Mr. Peter Coffine, Thomas Burd, Mr. Robt Cutts, John Rose, Job Judkins ; "*yo^r. wife Susanna*," Robt Thornton, Thomas Goodwine, Robin Thornton, Rich^d Trusdall, Jn^o Hawthorne, Robine Mason, William Trescott ; Adams, Shipp Carpenter ; Thomas Trewbridge, Thomas Baker, Arthur Mason, Daniell Turrine, John Harrison, Nathaniell Williams, Sam^n Rigby ; little Davy, the Porter ; Stephen Spencer, Sam^ll Arnold, Anthony Checkley, Nicholas Clap, Randell Nichols ; James Knap, of Watertowne ; William Cowell ; Peter Gee, at the Mackrell ; Alexander Adams, John Cole, Nath Fryer, Jn^o. Marshall, Jn^o Lake, Rich^d Woody & George Speere, Mr Joseph Moore, &c, &c.

Creditors :—Mr Eliazer Mather, Mr Eliazar Way, vncle Withington, &c. &c.

28 : 11 : 61. Edward Ting & Anthony Stoddard were appointed to Audit the Accounts of Deacon John Wiswall as Creditor and Administrator to the Estate of Mahalaleel Munnings, who examined said Accounts in the p^rsence of *Hannah*, the Relict of *Mahalaleel*, 1 : 3mo. 1662.—See Reg. vol. vii. p. 273, and vol. viii. p. 75.

[Thus far Abstracts have been made from the Records of Suffolk Wills, to page 352 of vol i., which contains nought but wills. Also, Abstracts *of all the Inventories* contained in vols. ii. and iii., which are made up of Inventories.]

———

HENRY WEBB.—I, Henry Webb, of Boston, merchant, being now in good health, doe make this to be my last will. First, that my debts be payde, in y^e same kinde or specie that I haue, or shall be engaged vnto, at y^e time of my departure ; for present, I owe very little to Any. To my only dau. *Margaret*, y^e late wife of my deare sonne, *Jacob Sheaffe*, £500, which she shall haue, with such further benefitt Accrewing to her by Vertue of her Executrixshipp to this my will, withall that my storehouse, Already built at y^e docke, withall wharfe libertys, And privileges thereto belonging, dureing her widdowhood. But, my will is, that before she enter into a second marriage, shee shall by hir selfe, or by him with whom she Intends marriage, or other sufficient security, giue bond to y^e overseers of this my will, immediately after her death, to pay vnto them, their heires or Assignes, y^e said £500, with the true Vallue of y^e benefit of such surplusage, by virtue of hir Executrixshipp with the said warehouse and land, to be giuen to such Child or Children as shee shall leaue behind hir by a second or other marriage. But, in Case shee haue noe more, or other child or Children then yᵉ Children she had by my deare Sonne, Jacob Sheaffe, then the same in like good specie to be given to it or them. I giue vnto my said dau. dureing hir life, yᵉ vse of my mansion and now dwelling house, with the land Adjoyneing it, soe as shee keepe it in due repayre. Provided also, that shee lett hir dau. *Elizabeth Sheaffe*, my Grand Childe, dureing that tearme, or vntill yᵉ heire male hereafter mentioned shall Come to enjoy it, haue the sole vse and benefit of hir owne now dwelling house and land to it belonging, she keepeing it in good Repayre. I giue vnto my said dau., as a further remembrance of my deare loue to hir, yᵉ two best peeces of Plate I had from Jamaica, with my Couch, And best suite of damaske Table Cloath, napkins, and Cupboard Cloath. I giue vnto my Grandchild, *Elizabeth Sheaffe*, £500, three whereof to be payde her in money or Beavor, yᵉ other two, in good pay equivalent thereto, at yᵉ age of 21 yeares or day of marriage. I giue vnto my said grand childe, my mansion now dwelling house, with yᵉ yard, backe side, Garden and other buildings that shall be thereon at my decease, Imediately after my decease and her marriage, Vnlesse her mother, my dau., shall Chuse to live in it, and Instead. thereof Giue her the sole benefit of yᵉ house and Lands shee liues in, otherwise shee, yᵉ said *Elizabeth*, to Enjoy it, keepeing it in good repayre till yᵉ heire male shall Attayne yᵉ Age of 21, or day of marriage, with consent of his parents, till when, I Alsoe giue vnto my Grandchild all my Garden that Adjoynes to Capt Leueretts land, with all my other lands at fort hill, my third part of A saw mill at Yorke falls, with yᵉ land, timber, Atensills, priviledges, &c., and then I giue my said mansion house, lands at fort hill, third part of saw mill, &c., to yᵉ heires male of my said dau. *Margarett*. [In case neither *Margaret, Elizabeth*, nor *Mehitabel* leave heirs, then, said property to go] to yᵉ President and fellowes of Harvard Colledge, forever, to be Improued for yᵉ best Vse and benefit of yᵉ Fellowes or scholars there, as my overseers, with the Overseers of yᵉ said Colledge, shall determyne, always Provided, that out of yᵉ Rents thereof they bee kept in due repayre, And with yᵉ residue of yᵉ said Annuall Rents, to promote yᵉ best good of yᵉ said Colledge. I further giue to my Grand Child, *Elizabeth Sheaffe*, my ware house now let out to builde, withall libertyes of yarde roome, and the way reserued to it, and free wharfage on yᵉ wharfe; alsoe, yᵉ vse of all my Plate, bedsted, Chayres, stooles, and Table, dureing her life and yᵉ nonage of yᵉ heires male, or in defect thereof, to yᵉ female heires, besides yᵉ plate, for my other househould stuffe, linen, Chests, Trunks, &c., I giue to my Grand Childe, *Elizabeth*, forever. [If Elizabeth or Mehittabell die, before marriage, the survivor shall be the heir to the others portion. If both die, their mother to inherit, vnlesse she haue other children; in that case, they to be heirs to each other.] To my Grandchild, *Mehittabell*, £400, in good special pay, at my decease, to be put out for her best Advantage, till the age of 21, or marriage, by my overseers, takeing good security for yᵉ same. To yᵉ first sonne or dau , as God shall please to bestow on my dau., *Margaret*, by a second or other marriage, £400, to be putt out, as is aboue expressed. Vnto my sister, *Jane*, yᵉ late wife of my brother, *John Webb*, of Titherly, in Hampshire, £20, if shee be aliue at my decease, to be payde vnto hir in England, shee running yᵉ Riscoe of yᵉ sea for yᵉ same, and yᵗ it be donne by £10 a yeare. Vnto *Elizabeth Blackleach*, wife of *John Blackleach*, ouer and aboue yᵉ £100, I promised hir, and A good part thereof Already payd, the summe of £40. more, Provided good security be Giuen to my ouerseers that after y° decease of my said Couzin, *Elizabeth Blackleach*, hir dau. *Elizabeth Blackleach*, shall haue the said £40.; and in case *Elizabeth*, y° dau., dye, then y° sayd legaty, After y° mothers death, remayne to the next childe, y° said *Elizabeth*, y° mother, shall haue by y° said *John Blackeleach*, or other husband ; and, in Case of noe Children, then to y° said *Elizabeth*, forever, said legaty to be payd within two yeares after my decease. To my Couzin, *Francis Grunn*, and hir two Children, *Elizabeth* And *Jone Grunn*, £80. Apeece, to be payde within 12 mounthes after my decease, provided I doe not giue y° whole, or part thereof, before my decease, and that security be taken by my overseers for y° children Legatyes, and that y° mother and Children shall be each others heires. To my late sister, *Elizabeth Sanfords* sonnes, *John* and *Samuell Sandford*, each, £80. apeece, they to be heires each to other ; to be payde in good English goods, or other good pay, within two yeares after my decease, Provided I giue not soe much or part of it to one or other of them before. To my wiues sister, *Barbara Sewell*, y° wife of *Reinold Sewell*, of Salisbury, Joyner, £20., to be payde hir within two yeares by £10. p<sup>r.</sup> Annu<sup>m</sup>, she running y° Risco of y° sea for y° same. Vnto *David Sewell* and *Elizabeth Sewell*, my late deare wiues Couzins, £8. apeece, to be payde within 12 monthe after my decease, Provided, [as before,] and they to be heires each to other, till they be married. Vnto Captayne *Edward Hutchinsons* eldest sonne, that shall be liueing, as a token of my loue to his father, £50. in very good English goods, at merchant prises, remembring y° Cordiall loue and kindnesse of his father towards mee and mine, in the tyme of my troble and afflictions, which I mett with in y° dayes of my Pilgrimage, not to be forgotten of me and mine ; which somme to be payde in 12 monethes after my decease. Vnto my louing friend M<sup>r</sup> *Edward Rawson*, A small token as A gratuity of his Ainecient loue, Viz<sup>t</sup>. that accompt, which is betwixt him and my selfe, as standeth due on my booke of Accompt, at this present day, w<sup>ch</sup> summe I doe Remitt Vnto him, and doe make that Ballance y<sup>e</sup> Vallue of £50. I giue vnto y<sup>e</sup> Towne of Boston, y<sup>e</sup> full Vallue of £100, for A stocke, for y<sup>e</sup> benefit of y<sup>e</sup> poore of y<sup>e</sup> Towne, either to provide Corne, provissions of wood or Coale for y<sup>e</sup> winters season, out of y<sup>e</sup> Increase, or otherwise to build some meet house for y<sup>e</sup> annuall Releife of such as y<sup>e</sup> select men of Boston, from time to time, shall see meete, y<sup>e</sup> whole Towne Engageing To mayntayne y° principle, by reedifying in Case of fier, If before my decease I shall not otherwise bestow y° like somme on y° said some, And Prouided, y° Towne of Boston giue mee, or my Executrixes, firme Assurance of my land I purchased, with my money, 18 yeeres since and Vpwards, on fort hill, which if they refuse to doe, one three monethes after it is desired, my will is, that legacy of £100, shall Cease, and be, with y<sup>e</sup> £20 I lent to M<sup>r</sup> *Stoddard* for y<sup>e</sup> Towne house, be Repayed and Returne to my Executrixes Vse, forever. I giue to my much Honnoured and Respected M<sup>r</sup> *Richard Bellingham*, or to his wife, as a token of my respect and loue, two Jacobus peeces of Gold. I giue vnto Harvard Colledge, Immediately after my decease, my house And land which I lately purchased of *Henry Phillips*, and was y° late house of *Samuell Oliuer*, deceased, with such deed or deeds that Concerne the same, the yearely Rent whereof to be improued, after y° due and necessary Repayres thereof is provided for, to be foreuer, either for y° maintanace of some poore schollars, or otherwise for yᵉ best good of yᵉ Colledge, to be Improued by the Care And discreion of yᵉ President and overseers of yᵉ Colledge, and Approbation of yᵉ overseers of this my will. I further giue vnto yᵉ said Colledge, £50 more, to be payd in speciall good pay within 12 moneth after my decease, to be layd out by yᵉ Approbation of my overseers, and yᵉ overseers of yᵉ Colledge, in some pasture ground, or small house, that may yeeld yearly Rent, to bee Improued, as aforesaid, and that both it, and yᵉ house aboue mentioned, may Continue as A yearly Incombe, for yᵉ ends aforesaid, foreuer. Vnto Mʳ *John Wilson*, our Pastor, if then liueing, as A token of my Respects to him, £5, to be payde in good pay, within 12 monethes after my decease ; to Mʳ *John Norton*, our Teacher, if then liueing, as a token of my Respects, £5 ; vnto Mʳ *Thomas Thatcher*, Pastor of yᵉ Church of Christ in Weimouth, my Antient friend, as a token of my love, £4 ; [each] to be payd as before. I giue vnto Mʳ *Mayo* and Mʳ *Powell*, Elders of yᵉ new Church, as a token of my Respects, £5, or 50s· apeece, if then liueing within 12 monethes after my decease. Vnto Mʳ *Miller*, teacher at Barnstable, if then liueing, as a token of my love, £3, within 12 monethes after my decease. My deare dau., *Margarett Sheaffe*, and my two grandchildren, *Elizabeth* and *Mehittabell Sheaffe*, Executrixes of this my last will, giueing equally vnto them, after yᵉ paymᵗ. [of debts, legacies, & funeral expenses] all my other estate, goods, debts, merchandises, Shipps, Chattles, not formerly given, to be devided Amongst them, part and part like. I giue vnto such servants as shall be with me at yᵉ time of my decease, £5 apeece, to be payd within 12 moneth, in Good pay as before. I Appoynt my Friends, *Edward Rawson, Eldeʳ James Penn*, Mʳ *Anthony Stoddard* and Capᵗ *Edward Hutchinson*, to be overseers of this my last will, and hereby giue vnto each of them, or as many as shall be then here liueing, in English Gold, £5. In Testimony that what is Contayned in yᵉ fiue sheets of paper, hereto Annexed, to yᵉ end of each sheete haueing subscribed my name, is my last Will, I haue sett my hand and seale. 5 Aprill 1660.

In pʳsence of *Thomas Buttolph*,                        Henry Webb.
    *Thomas Scotto, Samuell Robinson.*

*Thomas Buttolph* and *Thomas Scottow* deposed 13ᵗʰ Sepᵗ 1660 ; pʳsent, *Ri. Bellingham*, Depᵗ Gouʳnoᵗ, Majoʳ *Atherton*, Mʳ *Russell*, & Recordʳ. Entered and Recorded 2 Novʳ 1661, Edw Rawson, Recordʳ.

Inventory of the Estate taken 25 Sepᵗ 1660, by *John Cullicke, Henry Shrimpton*, Wᵐ *Davis*. Amt. £7819. 05. 02. Mentions, "Garden by Mʳ⸱ *Richards*, in yᵉ Lane."

*Mrs Margarett Sheaffe* deposed, 29 Octʳ 1662, to this Inventory of yᵉ Estate of yᵉ late *Henry Webb*, her father.

———

Thomas Pigge.—Administration to the estate of the late *Thomas Pigge*, of Dedham, lately deceased, is Graunted to *John Pigge*, his Brother, in behalfe of himselfe & his sisters. An Inventory of the Goods was taken, 5 : 7 mo : 1660. Amᵗ. including debts, due £42. 3s. 8d. as witnessed by *Nathan Aldis* & *Peter Woodard*.

*John Pigg* deposed, 30ᵗʰ Octʳ 1660.

[In the original, on file, the name is written *Pigg, Pigge*, and *Pidge*. See Will of *Thomas Pig*, the father, in the Register, Vol. iii., p. 78.] *

*See p. 20.

# ABSTRACTS FROM THE EARLIEST WILLS ON RECORD IN THE COUNTY OF SUFFOLK, MASS.

[Prepared by Mr. WILLIAM B. TRASK, of Dorchester.]

[In the following abstracts, names and dates do not always correspond, precisely, with those on the record. Such disagreement, however, need not be considered, necessarily, as an evidence of their incorrectness here; for, so far as practicable, the subject-matter has been collated with the originals, on file; the result of which was, that the Probate Records, not infrequently, were found inaccurate. For example, in the will of John Luson, of Dedham, (wrongly labelled "Joseph Layton" on the files,) the name of William Bearstowe, of Scituate, occurs; on the record it is William Brearton. In the same will, the name of Edward Hawes occurs; but it is omitted on the record. Henry Rigby, of Dorchester, reads correctly, *Henry Kibby;* Cary, *Gary;* Powell, *Cowell;* and so on, in many other instances that might be mentioned.—T.]

PHILIP ELLIOT.—Boston 2 Feb. 1660. Power of Administration to the estate of the late *Philipp Elliot*, as it is left by *Elizabeth Elliot*, his relict, is graunted to *Rich. Withington, John Aldis*, and *Jn Smith*, to make division thereof amongst themselues, according to the late will of the said Right of theire wiues.

Dedham 22 : 11 : 1660. An Inventorie of that part of y* Estate sometimes *Philip Elliots*, of Roxbury, deceased, which was in the possession of y* men hereafter named after the death of *Elizabeth Elliot*, y* late wife of y* said Philip, taken by *John Hunting, Eliezar Lusher, Daniel Fisher*. Goods in possession of *John Smith*, of Dedham, *John Aldis*, of Dedham, & *Rich⁴ Withington*, of Dorchester. Mentions land near *Daniell Ainsworth's*, one bill in y* hand of *John Watson*.

*Richard Withington, John Aldis,* & *John Smith* deposed 2 Feb. 1660.

---

JOHN DWIGHT, of Dedham, yeoman, being in pᵣfect health, this 16ᵗʰ June 1658, doe make this my last will. To my wife, *Elizabeth*, that now is, £50 sterling, to be payd her by my Executors, in Currant Country pay, at my now dwelling house, at Dedham, within 3 monethes after my decease, as by Couenant, before our marriage, appeareth ; also all her weareing Apparell, both linen and woollen, alsoe that my said wife shall haue dyet allowed her, at my said dwelling house, in Dedham, dureing y* space of 3 monethes after my decease, if shee shall desire it, that soe shee may y* more Comfortably provide for y* remoueall of hir habitation to some other place. I giue vnto my sonne, *Nathaniell Whiteing*, 20s ; vnto my sonne, *Henrie Philips*, 20s ; vnto my sonne, *Nathaniell Reinolds*, 20s. My will is, that my dwelling house, land, and moveables in yᵉ Towne of Dedham, or elsewhere, which shall be founde to my estate, at my decease, be equally devided into fiue pts, two pts whereof I giue vnto my sonne, *Timothy Dwight*, and one part vnto y* Children of my son, *Nathaniell Whiteing*, and of *Hannah*, his wife, or soe many of them as shall be surviueing at my decease, to be payde by my Executoʳ, as in his discretion will best conduce for their benefitt. I giue vnto my Grand Child, *Eliazar Philips*, sonne of my sonne Henry Philips, and of Mary his wife, my dau., one part of y* fiue ; and if y* said *Eliazar* shall not be surviueing at my decease, then my will is, that my Executoʳ, at his discretion, shall dispose of that one part of y* fiue, vnto y* rest of y* children of my son, *Henry Philips*, and of my dau. *Mary*, his wife. The

183

fifth part remayneing of y⁰ fiue, I giue vnto my dau. *Sarah Reynolds*, or to her child or Children, as my Executor shall see cause to dispose of it. Alsoe, my will is, that my son, *Timothy Dwight*, shall enjoy all that house and land which I gaue him at hir first marriage with *Sarah Sibly*. Alsoe, that my sonne, *Nathaniell Whiteing*, shall enjoy all that 6 Acres of land, be it more or lesse, which lyeth in y⁰ low playne; and y⁰ 2 Acres of meadow lyeing In foule meadow, which I bought of *Lieut. Joshua Fisher*. My will is, that it shall be at my Executors liberty to pay said Legatyes, either in land or Currant Country pay, and to pay them at y⁰ same prise as they were vallued at by y⁰ prises at my decease. Alsoe, my will is, that my Executor shall not be ingaged to pay y⁰ said legatyes to any of ⁻y⁰ said Children, vnder age, vntill they canne legaly giue a discharge for y⁰ receipt of y⁰ same. I Appoynt my son, *Timothy Dwight*, to be Executor of this my last will. *John Dwight.*

In presence of
*Peteer Woodard*
*William Averey.*

*Peter Woodard* deposed, 5 March 1660.

Dedham 8ᵗʰ of 12. 1660. Inventory of the estate taken by *Eliazar Lusher*, *Timothy Dwight*, senʳ, *Peeter Woodward*. Amᵗ £506. 02. 10.

---

ISAACK HEATH.—I giue to my wife, this my dwelling house and orchard, barnes, home lott, with all my land in y⁰ lower Calues pasture, both Vpland meadow and salt marsh, by estimation 27 acres, more or lesse, dureing her life. If my wife thinke this too combersome for her, shee shall be [at] liberty to Choose to haue y⁰ new end of my house, and all roomes appertayneing to it, and £14, a yeare, payde duly vnto her by my sonne *Bowles*, of y⁰ Best that ariseth of y⁰ lands, all these lands and all other lands as they are in y⁰ transcript of Roxbery (except about 6 acres in y⁰ great lott which I haue given my sonne *Bowles*, as long as he liueth, and my part in y⁰ 4000 acres, which I giue to y⁰ schole in Roxbury) I giue to my three Grandchildren, *John Bowles*, *Elizabeth Bowles* and *Mary Bowles*, to them and their heires foreuer, immediately after myne and their grandmothers decease. I giue vnto my sonne, *Bowles*, full power to let, sell, and improue all these lands as they shall come into her hands for y⁰ best education of y⁰ children. My will is, that *John Bowles* shall be mayntayned at Schole and brought vp to learning, in what way I haue dedicated him to God, if it please him to accept him. If my wife Choose y⁰ house and lands, and they be not by due estimation worth 14 ˡᵇ by y⁰ yeare, then my sonne, *Bowles*, shall make vp soe much worth vnto her out of y⁰ rent of my other lands I giue vnto my Cozin *Martha Brand* 2 ˡᵇ; to my kinsman, *Edward Morice*, 2 ˡᵇ; to my sonne, *Bowles*, my searge coat and best hatt; to *Isaacke Heath*, y⁰ rest of my weareing Apparell, my moueable goods, both within doores and without, and debts or state what eueʳ of that kind, I will that they be divided into 4 equal pᵗˢ. betwixt my wife and my three Grand Children. I giue to *Mary Mory*, my kinswoman, 20s. My will is, if there be no provission sufficient to afford my wife what I haue giuen her, and to bring vp *John* to learning, I giue full power to my sonne *Bowles*, with y⁰ advise of my overseers, to sell my pond lot, or woodlot, in y⁰ middle divission for yᵗ supply or both. I request my well beloued brethren, *John Eliot* and *William Park*, to doe y⁰ office of loue to oversee y⁰ fulfilling this my last will, and giue counsell at all tymes as need shall require, to whom I give as a token of my loue, each of them, 20s.  My will is, before my moveables be divided, all my debts be payde, and my houseing conveniently repayred.  I allow my wife convenient firewood out of my nether wood lot, for her life time, and I make my sonne, *Bowles*, sole Executor of this my will, whom I invest with full power to set, let, and Improve y⁵ estate and lands of his three Children, my grand Children, to aske, receiue and order all things till y⁵ time when *Elizabeth Bowles* shall attayne to 18 yeares, or day of marriage, all her pᵗ shall be given her.  I giue to *John Bowles* when hee, cometh to y⁵ age of 21 yeares, besids what falls to him of his share in my goods, a double portion in my land ; to *Mary Bowles*, when shee attaynes to 18 yeares of age, or day of marriage, her pᵗ of my goods and lands. If *Benjamin Mory* duely serue out his time, my will is, that at y⁵ end of his time he shall receiue £5, to be payde him by my executoʳ.

Witnesses this 19ᵗʰ of y⁵ 11ᵗʰ 1660.                                    Isaack Heath.
John Elliot, George Brand, John Stebbins,
    who deposed, 31 Jan. 1660.
Entered and Recorded 2 Novʳ. 1662.

The Inventory of the goods & estate of the said Elder Isaac Heath, taken 25 : 11 : 1660.  Amᵗ. £671. 06. 04.

Mention is made of " Benjamin Mories time," Willm Lyon, Joseph Wise, Daniell Aynsworth, &c.

*Isaac Marrell* and *Thomas Weld* witnesse to an accoᵗᵗ. accepted by the overseers of y⁵ will, before the Inventory was put into y⁵ Court.

*John Bowles* deposed, 14ᵗʰ March 1660.

---

CHARITY WHITE.—Boston, 5 Feb. 1660.  Whereas y⁵ late *Charity White*, a little before hir death, before diverse friends, declared that she gaue hir house and land to the deacons of the Church of Boston,* for y⁵ vse of their Church, on Condicon̄ shee be buried at the Churches charges ; and also, that shee gaue the rest of hir goods and estate to *Deliverance Tearne*, att request therefore of *Miles Tearne*, father to the said *Deliverance*.

Power of Administration to y⁵ Estate of the late *Charity White*, is granted to *Miles Tearne*, y⁵ father, in behalfe of his daughter, in relation to all the goods and estate of said *Charity*, y⁵ house and lands excepted, which is left to their dispose to whom it was left and given.

Inventory taken 1 Feb. 1660, by *Chr : Batt* & *John Marion*.  Amt. £24.  Goods at *Mr Blyes*, &c.

---

DEACON JOHN ROGERS.—8 : 12 : 1660.  Vnto his beloued wife, *Judith Rogers*, his new end of his dwelling house, with one third part of y⁵ Barne, and halfe his orchard and pʳduce thereof, and halfe his pasture, adioyning to y⁵ orchard, to be hers dureing her life.  His will is, that his sonne, *John Rogers*, shall pay vnto his mother, *Judith*, 20 bushells of Corne, yearly, one third in wheate, one third peases, one third in Indian Corne.  If his sonne, *John*, refuse or fayle in paymᵗ of yᵉ said Corne, then his mother shall haue halfe yᵉ land to improue as long as she liues, viz. yᵉ broke vpland.  Hee bequeathes vnto his wife, his feather bed, and all yᵉ furniture thereunto belonging, with halfe of all his househould goods, giueing hir power to bestow it on whom shee please ; provided it be

---

* " Charity White, a singlewoman," admitted to the First Church in Boston, 13 : 4 : 1641.—*First Church Records.*

given to Deacon Rogers Children. Giues his wife, one Cow, and y⁰ use
of y⁰ other Cow y⁰ yeare Insueing, except his sonne, *John*, marry, then
one Cow to be his. Hee giues one heifer to his wife, and halfe his swine
and halfe his Goates and halfe his sheep. It is his will that his sonne,
*John Rogers*, shall keepe one Cow for his mother, and six Goates at
winter, only, as long as shee liues. If *John Rogers* fayle in refuseing,
then it is his will, that his wife, *Judeth*, shall have that part of his meadow adjoyning deacon *Whitmans* meadow, dureing her life. Hee Be-
quathes vnto his dau. *Mary Rane*, his great lott which is 12 Acres,
Bounded by *Deacon Philips* great lot, and further, giues her 40s. ; vnto
his dau., *Liddia Whitte*, six Acres of land lying on y⁰ east necke, or £5.,
which he leaues to his executoᵣs discretion, either to giue her y⁰ land or
y⁰ fiue pound, soe it be donne in one yeares time after his decease. He
giues vnto his dau. *Hannah Pratt*, £5., to be payd two yeeres after his
decease. He giues his dau. *Sarah*, £15.; ten pounds to be payde A
moneth after her marriage, y⁰ other £5, two yeares after marriage. In
case shee marry not, shee is to haue £15; ten pounds at 18 yeares of
age, and fiue pounds at 25 yeeres old. Vnto his sonne, *John Rogers*,
the Remaynder of all his estate, as houseing, Cattle, lands, &c. [said
John paying his sisters out of that part of the estate given to him.] If his
sonne, John, dy without wife or Childe, then his sonne in law, *Joseph
White*, shall haue y⁰ land Adjoyneing *Thomas Dons* house, provoided
*Joseph White* pay out of it to his sonne in law, *John Rane*, £10. It is
his will that his dau. Sarah haue y⁰ Remaynder of his land, houseing and
orchard, in Case his sonne John dye as aboue expressed, viz. that which
belong to his sonne John. And Sarah, shall pay to *John Rane*, £5; and
to *Samuell Pratt*, £8; and to *Joseph White*, £4. Further his will is,
that *William Richard*, his Apprentice, shall serue y⁰ Remaynder of his
Apprentiship with his sonne, John, and that his sonne shall cause y⁰ said
*William Richard* shalbe taught his trade according to Indenture. It is
his will that his wife, Judeth, and his sonne, *John Rogers*, shall be ioynt
Executoᵣs of this his last will; alsoe, that *Thomas White & John Holebrooke* be overseers, and alsoe *Thomas Dier*.

Signed in y⁰ pᵣsence of                               John Rogers.
William Charde, Thomas Dyar,
who deposed 30 April 1661.

Inventory of the estate taken 20 : 12 : 1660, by *John Holbrooke*. Amᵗ.
£275. Mentions " one seᵣvant boy that is apprentice," £10. Judith
Rogers and John Roggers deposed, before Court, that this paper Containes
a true Inventory of y⁰ estate of the late *John Roggers*, of Weimouth, to
the best of his knowledge.

---

ISABELL TURNER.—An Inventory of y⁰ estate of Isabell Turner, wid-
dow, late of Dorchester, taken the 17 day of 10 1660, by *Richard Baker*,
*Nicholas Clapp*, John ⋈ *Gornell*. Amt. £205. 18. 04. Lefᵗ. *Roger
Clap* and Ensigne *Hopestill Foster*, deposed 8 Feb. 1660.

---

ANDREW PITCHER, of Dorchester, being by y⁰ present paynes and
weakenesse vpon mee sensable that my dayes will not be long here, and
willing to dispose of that little estate God hath lent mee, that it may prevent trouble hereafter, hoping ere long I shall be freed from what I now
Vndergoe, and shall be with the Lord, Therefore, after y⁰ buriall of my
body and my debts payde, my will is, my wife, *Margaret*, shall haue all

my estate within Dorchester, dureing life, for her own maintaynance, and to bring vp my Children. My will is, that my Eldest sonne, *Samuell*, shall haue halfe my land that lyes neere goodman *Wods*, behind Medfeilde, and halfe yᵉ meadow belonging to it ; that my sonnes, *John* and *Jonathan*, shall haue yᵉ other halfe of it, with yᵉ other halfe of yᵉ meadow belonging to it ; that after my wifes decease, my sonne, *Nathaniel*, shall haue my houseing and all my lands and Cattle within Dorchester, and shall pay out of it to my eldest dau. *Experience*, £16, within four yeeres [after] he comes to enjoy it, and to my yongest dau. *Ruth*, £12, within six yeeres after he comes to enjoy it. Further, my will is, that what houshould stuffe there* is left after my wifes decease shall be devided equally to all my Children. If any of my Children dye before they come to enjoy theire portion, it shall be devided Amongst the rest, equally, except they leaue Children. I Appoynt my wife, and Eldest son Executoʳ of this my last will. 4 (10) 1660.

In pʳsence of                      Andrew ⋈ Pitcher.
William Robinson, John ⋈ Gill
Samuel Wadsworth.
*John Gill* and *Willm Robbinson* „deposed, 9 3 mo. 1661. Inventory of the Estate taken 19 (1) 1660. Amᵗ. £286. 08s. Debts £20. *Samuel Pitcher* deposed, 9 May 1661.

———

WILLIAM PEACOCKE.—An Inventory of yᵉ estate of *William Peacockes*, prized by *Isaac Morell*, and *Griffen Crofts*, the 22 of Jan. 1660 ; for debts due to him, they do not yet apeare what they be, or whether any thing be oweing him or noe. The summe exprest is £78. 06. 04. The debts demanded of him, besides several charges is, £126. 05.

*Robert Seaver* deposed, 21 Feb. 1660.

On the 30th Jan. 1660, the Court appointed *William Parke*, *Edward Denison* and *Thomas Welde* to enquire into the estate of said Peacocke. They found some difficulty in respect of Trading with the Indians in partnership with *John Curtis* and *Philip Curtis*. A proposition was made by them for an amicable settlement, which was signed by the forenamed partners, 29 : 1 : 1661. The commissioners made a return of debts due from and to the estate, viz : to Arthur Gary, Thomas Smith, John Weld, Henry Powning, John Collins, John Huntley, John Bowles, Henry Bowen, Abraham Busby, Henry Phelph, John Mirriam, Edward Cowell, Mr. Henry Shrimpton, Thomas Hawley, Mr Peter Oliuer, Theophilus Frairy, Isaac Morill, Stephen Hoppin, John Jonsons Executors, Mr John Alcocke, Tobias Bauis, Richard Meades, George Brand, Robert Prentiss, William Linckhorne, Samuel Gore, Joseph Griggs, Robert Seauer, Phillip Curtisse, John Peiropoynt, Joseph Wise, John Stebbins, &c.

———

JOHN LUSON, of Dedham. 15 : 12 : 1660. Age and yᵉ Infirmityes thereof increaseing dayly vpon mee,—doe make this my last will. I did pʳmise *Thomas Battely*, of Dedham, my kinsman, £60, whereof I haue already payde him thirty ; I now giue order, yᵉ other thirty be payde him, within one yeare after my decease. I giue vnto said *Thomas*, and his heyres, my now dwelling house, with my Barne, and all other my buildings thervnto belonging, and all my orchyard, gardens, fences, &c. ; also all my pʳcell of land comonly called the Feild, on yᵉ Backeside, lyeing betwixt my house and orchard aforesaid, and yᵉ Brooke next yᵉ Rockes ; all which houses and lands are given vpon Condicōn that yᵉ said

*Thomas*, his heyres or Assignes, pay £24, vnto *Thomas, Robert* and *Susan*, yᵉ Children of *Robert Luson*, in old England, late deceased, which summe I giue them as a Legaty to be equally devided Amongst them, within 2 yeares after yᵉ decease of *Martha* my wife. I giue vnto *Mary Battely*, my kinswoman, dau. of yᵉ said *Thomas*, £5., to be payde hir, or hir Assignes, at yᵉ time shee shall Attayne yᵉ age of 15 yeeres; vnto *John Batteley*, sonne of *Thomas*, 40s, when [he] come to yᵉ age of 15; both to be payde in Current Country paymᵗ. If John or Mary depart this life before yᵉ age before said, yᵉ surviueing partie shall inherit yᵉ Legacie given to the deceased. To Edward Hawes, of Dedham & his heyres, 40s. Vnto *Mr John Allin*, our deare and Reverend Pastoʳ, as a small declaration of my thankefullness to God and to him for that Good I haue receiued by his ministery, 40s. to be payd in equall sumes, in 4 yeers after yᵉ decease of Martha, my wife. Vnto my wife, for her life, and one yeare after, all my houses & Lands withall yᵉ privileges, &c. to her or her Assignes; alsoe, all yᵉ Remaynder of my estate not disposed of. If my wife shall not surviue me, then I giue vnto *Anne Bearstow*, my kinswoman, yᵉ wife of *William Bearstowe*, of Scittuate, £10, to be payde her or her Assignes, in Dedham, in 5 yeares after yᵉ decease of my selfe or my wife, which of vs shall liue longest; 40s. each yeare. The rest of my estate, giuen to my wife, I giue to *Thomas Batteley* and his heires, foreuʳ; yᵉ said *Thomas Battely* to be my executor, and my very Loueing Friend, Ensigne *Daniell Fisher*, to be overseer.

In the presence of                                  John ⋈ Luson.
Eliezar Lusher, John Kent,
who deposed 25 May 1661.

The Inventory of the Estate was taken by *Henry Chickering* and *Daniell Fisher*, 18 (3) 1661. Amᵗ. £300. 11. 01. *Thomas Battely* deposed, 25 May 1661.

---

CHRISTOPHER BATT, of Boston.—Considering yᵉ fraylty of my nature, that I am at all tymes and in yᵉ most secure places and Imploymᵗˢ subject to many Accidents that might bring me to my End, being now enforced, for the better provoideing for my family to goe a Voyage to Virginia, not being Capable to Expresse myselfe soe fully as I would, yet haueing soe long and large Experience of yᵉ faithfull loue of my deare wife, *Anne Batt*, both to mee and my Children, doe therefore, Appoynt my wife, Executrix of this my last will, and dureing her widdowhood, doe giue vnto her yᵉ Vse [of] my whole estate and power to sell house, lands, Goods, Chattles, &c. and to Improue yᵉ same for yᵉ best Good of her selfe and Children, both one and other which I leaue to her motherly Care and Affection to bestow portions on them, as yᵉ estate will beare, and they need, onely, if in Case shee marry Againe, my desire is, then shee dispose at least of two thirds of my estate to my Children, as shee shall thinke best, but somewhat neer to an equallitie, my Eldest sonne excepted, which I hope shee will thinke on. 19 of [  ] 1656.

In pʳsence of vs                                  Christopher Batt.
Edward Rawson, Rachel
Rawson, Anthony Checkley.

Edward Rawson, Recordʳ., deposed, 19 Sept. 1661.

---

ABIELL EVERELL. Inuentory of yᵉ goods of *Abiell Everell*, deceased, appraised by *John Sunderland* and *John Sanford*, being Chosen therevn-

to by *Mr John Aldin* and *Elizabeth,* his wife, shee being formerly y⁰
wife, and after, the widdow of *Abiell Everell,* before said.   Taken 15 :
12 : 1660.   Amᵗ. £119.   *Jnº Alden* deposed, 22 Feb. 1660.

---

MR. RALPH SMITH.—18ᵗʰ Aprill 1661.   Power of Administration to y⁰
estate of the late *Mr Ralph Smith,* is granted vnto *Nathaniell Masterson,*
his late wiues sonne, that liued A long time with him, and was servicea-
ble to him for y⁰ most part of his time.   Amᵗ. of Inventory taken 16
Aprill (61) £377. 04. 04.   *Nathaniel Masterson* deposed same day,

---

RICHARD LANGER, of Hinghame, being of perfect memory yet very
Aged, doe make this my last will.   To my dau. *Margarets* Eldest sonne,
*Joshua Lincon,* all my land in Hinghame in New England, That is to
say, those two home lotts that I Bought of my sonne in law, *Thomas Lincon,* with my great lott, lyeing neere Glad tidings Rocke, and my lott of
meadow, at Conyhasset, whom I make my Executor.   I giue my Greene
Rugg to my dau. *Margaret,* shee giueing as a gift from mee [to] my
other two dauᵗ. *Dinah,* and *Elizabeth,* 4s. each.   20 Feb. 1659.
Witnes *Nico Baker.*                               Richard ⋈ Langer.
who deposed 2d May 1661.
Inventory of the estate, apprized by *Mathew Hawkes &Thomas Hewet,*
18 Feb. 1660.   Amᵗ. £21. 02s.

---

JOHN WILKIE.—Power of Administration to the Estate of *John Wilkie,*
granted to *Elizabeth Wilkie,* Relict of y⁰ said *John Wilkie,* and *Jeremiah
Cushin,* hir now husband.   Inventory taken 11 March, 1661, by *John
Sunderland,* and *Edward Hutchinson.*  Amᵗ. £102. 1.   *Elizabeth Wilkie*
deposed, the same day.

---

JOHN TUCKER, senior, of Hingham, deceased y⁰ 5ᵗʰ of August 1661.
Being by a Providence of God visited with a sad affliction, yet in his Right
minde, did verbally dispose of his estate as followeth, (viz) I giue vnto my
sonne, *John Tucker,* a·double portion, and my dau., *Mary Tucker,* shall
haue y⁰ Rest, and I would haue yoᵘ to deale righteously by y⁰ mother, and
said that God will deale righteously with you and wished them to remember *Mr Hubberd,* as a minister of Christ, as yoᵘ and your sister shall
thinke fit to bestow, and said *goodwife Jacob* hath beene a mother to me
and mine, remember her, and remember *Goodwife Beals,* God by his
providence did afford me both helpe and Comfort from her.   We whose
names are vnderwritten being at *Joseph Churches* house, A little before
he dyed, heard *goodman Tucker,* senior, speake these words.
An : Bates, Ʊ her marke, Martha Beals, Jane Bates.   Taken vpon
oath, before y⁰ majestrates, 15 Augᵗ. 1661.
Power of Administration to y⁰ estate of y⁰ late John Tucker, of Hinghame, deceased, is graunted to *John Tucker,* his sonne, 7 Augᵗ. 1661.
On the 8ᵗʰ of Augᵗ. on petition of *Anne Tucker,* relict of John, power of
Administration was granted equally to hir as to John, the sonne.   On the
15ᵗʰ, she Renounct hir power of Administration, and gaue vp to John
Tucker, for providing for her till next County Court, before y⁰ Gouᵗnoʳ.
The Inventory of the Estate was prized the 8ᵗʰ of Augᵗ. 1661, by
*John Thaxter,* and *John Ferring.*  Amᵗ. £512. 07. 09.   John Tucker
deposed (9) 1 mo.

WILLIAM BURNELL.—Will. Vnto son John, my house & ground in Boston, at 21 years of age. If he die before he come to age, & my wife living, then, she to haue the use of it during life; after my death it shall be my son Samuel's. Vnto my dau. Sara, £50; [also] two beddes & all the rest of my goods in Part of Payment of the £50., after the death of my wife. [After her death,] the house & land to be let, till the Rent make up the £50, vnto Sara, & then I will it vnto Samuel, & not before. I haue appointed two men to see this will fullfilled,—Namely, *James Bill*, of Pulling Point, & *John Doeletell*, of Rumni Marsh, 5 : 1 : 1660.

[It will be seen from the above abstract of the Will of Wm. Burnell, taken from the files, that it was neither signed nor proved, and that in it he gives his house and land, in Boston, to his son John, when 21 years of age. In less than six weeks afterwards, viz., on the 16 : 2 mo., Mr. B. wrote another Will, in which he gives said property to John on arriving at 21 years of age, provided he be not corrupted with the opinions of the Quakers. Whereas, if he embraces their views, and continues to hold them, he is to receive but £50, to be paid him in instalments of £5 a year.
In the first Will, Sarah is to receive £50, in the second, but £40. James Bill, of Pulling Point, (so written on the files,) is called James Bell and James Hill, on the record. See abstract of the Will and Inventory, in Reg. for 1855, p. 230.] (See p. 162).

---

NATHANIELL WILLIAMS.—22 : 2 : 1661. It is my will after my estate is gathered in, that my wife shall haue yᵉ third part of all my estate, houses, lands, and moveables. To my dau., *Belknap*, beside what I haue given her, I give to her & her two Children that part of yᵉ garden next *Benia. Thwing;* for yᵉ rest of my Children I giue them alike, as my estate shall hould out. My wife sole executrix. I desire *Mr Willm Davis, John Hull*, and *James Penn* to be overseers.

Nathaniel Williams.

Witnesse to this will
*Theoder Atkinson, Henry Powning*, who deposed 1ˢᵗ of August.
Inventory taken of the Goods & Chattells of Nathaniell Williams, Late deceased, upon this 7 : of 3ᵐᵒ 1661 by *Thomas Clarke, Henry Powning, John Wiswall.* Amᵗ. £994. 02. 08.
Debts due to the sume of £520. Estate indebted £700.
*Mary Williams*, Relict of the late Nathaniell, deposed 10. 7. (62.)

---

THOMAS LOREING, of Hull, lately deceased. Inventory prized by *Willm Chamberlyne* and *John Lobdell*, 5 June 1662. Amt. £331. 15. Estate indebted to Abraham Joanes, George Vickre, Nathl. Bosworth, John Prince, Thomas Loreing, John Tucker, &c.; due from John Oates, 10s.
27 June 1661. Thomas Loreing deposed to the Inventory of the estate of his late father, Thomas Loreing.
[See Abstract of the Will of Jane, widow of Thomas Loring, in Bridgman's *Pilgrims of Boston*, p. 352.]

---

RICHARD BROWNE. Inventory of the goods of Richᵈ Browne, deceased, taken by Abraham Browne, and Thomas Clarke. Amᵗ. £80. 18. 02. Mʳ Hezekiah Vsher deposed 19 : 1 : 1661. Mentions Mʳ Mead, Henry Smith, Thomas French.

# ABSTRACTS FROM THE EARLIEST WILLS ON RECORD IN THE COUNTY OF SUFFOLK, MASS.

[Prepared by Mr. William B. Trask, of Dorchester.]

Edmund Heylett, of Deptford, in y⁰ Co. of Kent, Merchant, haue made my wife, *Lyddia Heylett*, to be my lawfull Atturney, to receiue money due vnto mee, also all such sumes as shall by Any meanes grow due as well for wages in yᵉ good ship, Called yᵉ James Bonneyventure, *Jonas Clarke*, Comandʳ, now designed for New England, as for any Goods or Merchandizes as shall be transported in yᵉ aboue said ship, or in any other ship or ships vpon my Accompt. Alsoe to sue for all proprietyes which my Grandfather, *Edmund Heylett*, of yᵉ Citty of Norwich Weauer left me, in his will, and alsoe, after my fathers, *Sumuell Heyletts*, decease, to sue for and recover all such right as I haue in a Messuage or teñement scittuate in beere street, in yᵉ parish of all Sᵗˢ in yᵉ Citty of Norwich, now in yᵉ tenure and occupacōn of my said Father, which tenement wa⁊ given me, by my said father. If it please God to call mee out of this life before my Returne from Sea of this Intended Voyage I doe then by theise pʳsents make my wife executrix.

27 April 1657.                            Edmᵈ Heylett.

In yᵉ presence of vs,

    George Martin, Rebecka ⋈ Martin, who deposed 23 Aug. 1661.

---

Thomas Griffin.—18 July 1661. Power of Administration to yᵉ Estate of *Thomas Griffin*, deceased is granted to *Thomas Parke*.* Inventory of the Estate so far as doth appeare. Impʳᵐⁱˢ. A whom lott, 3 Acres more or lesse Cost, £2. 15: ; an eight part of an old whight mare and a sixt part of her increase, Cost £3. 15. ; in *goodman Shawes* hand, £2 ; in *Thomas Parke*, his hand, due for a musket, 12s. ; in especially vnder Mʳ *Willm Tompsons* hand owned by him dew, £2. ; a payre of bandeleers, 2s. 6d. There is more in Controversy whether his tittle be Right or good, yea or noe, there being many which Chalenge A propriety therein, and it is not yet cleared, to wit, 16 Acres of land, pᵗ of that farme comonly called Peetres farme, when cleared, £30. This is the whole that appeares vnto vs, *George Denison*, *Willm Chesebrough*, Townesmen.

---

John Pears, of Boston.—In Consideracōn of my vnfeigned Love vnto Rebecca, my wife, and also by way of Restoration of what I receiued wᵗʰ her, & have injoyed of her former husbands Estate, I leaue the house & land wee live in, freely, vnto her, & also out of that little, God hath Given mee, my will is, she have in such things as may be, to her Comfort & Content, to the value of £13, in necessaryˢ as bed, Table, chaire, pott, & other household stuffe, as she & my overseers can agree vpon, or the value afore-

---

* There is a Letter, on file, from Thomas Parke to his brother, Mr. William Parke, of Roxbury, in which, he desires his brother to procure for him a letter of Administration upon the estate of *Thomas Griffin*, "who was sumtime a retainer vnto my house." He sends, inclosed, an Inventory of such estate of the deceased as he can find, "as for his clothes, he dying in another jurisdicktion, we cannot reach them." "Intreating you to ackt for me, with the courte, who by reason of my remoatnes cannot ackt for my selfe," &c. he subscribes himself, "your obliged Brother, Thomas Parke." Dated at "Southertowne, [Stonington] July 6ᵗʰ 1661."

said payd her in some convenient time, after my decease. For my owne house & land y<sup>t</sup> I lately purchased in Boston, my will is, that my wife dureing the time of her widowhood, after my decease, shall have one halfe of the yearely rent & profitt of the same, & no longer; y<sup>e</sup> other halfe of the yearely profitt of the aforesaid land I dispose of, for the Education & maintenance of my sonne, Samuell, & after the death or day that my wife shall change her Condition by marriage, that all the said house & land shall be, and Remaine, the Inheritance of my sonne, Samuell, & his heyres foreuer. For my sonne, Nehemiah Pears, I giue him all my working tools & Implements belonging to my Calling, with all the timber & stuffe to worke vpon, be it at home or elsewhere, desireing he may by the helpe of God, be a good husband in the vse of it, & then I hope he may Live like a man. For my dau. [blank] the wife of Jeremiah Rogers, it is my will that whereas her husband stands indebted vnto mee, £20, more or lesse, the same I giue vnto my dau., & her children; also 20ᵉ a peece, vnto his 3 children, after my decease. For my 3 dau⁰. Mary, Mercy & Exercise, I giue vnto them the Remainder of my Estate, be it land, goods, Cattle, &c. be it at Boston, Dorchester or else where; my will is, they haue it equally divided amongst them; & if any dye before age of 18, or marry, there porcons to be divided amongst the survivors. For y⁰ equall Administracon of the pᵣmises I beg y⁰ helpe of my Loving friends, William Killcupp, William Robinson, & John Wisewall; to advise & direct vpon all occasions, according to Law. 16 : 7 : 61. John Pears.

Signed in pᵣnce of
John Wisewall, William Killcupp.

11 Oct 1661. Power of Administration, to the Estate, Granted to Mr. John Wisewall, W<sup>m</sup> Robinson, & W<sup>m</sup> Killcup.

---

HENRY KIBBY.—Power of Administration to y⁰ estate of y⁰ late Henry Kibby, of Dorchester, granted to Gresill Kibby, his Relict, 15 Aug. 1661.

Inventory taken 2 Sep<sup>t</sup>. 1661, by Nathaniell Patten, John Capen. Am<sup>t</sup>. £67.01.10. Grissell Kibby deposed 30 Oct. 61. [Then follows an inventory of the estate which goodwife Kibby brought her husband at marriage, which was then in being, amounting to £71.10.06.]

---

WILLIAM PEIRSE.—Inventory of the goods of William Pierse, marriner, deceased, taken by John Martin, Joseph Webb. Am<sup>t</sup>. £228.5ᵉ. Power of Administration to y⁰ estate granted to his widow, Ester Peirse, 31 Jan. 1661. She deposed the same day.

---

SAMUEL JONES.—Being weake in body, leave this as my last Will, That after my death my Mother haue the vse of £20.; that my father, haue £5, for Cost and Care about me; to brother Eldad, £5; Coussine Samuell Jones, £5; to my 6 Coussins, at Yarmouth, 40ᵉ. a peece. All the rest of my Estate I giue to my Coussine Thankful Rones, & also that thankfull haue what is left of the 20 pounds, after my Mothers death. I desire my father, Kingsley, to see this will truely pᵣformed, That is sole executor & what is of my Estate above what is giuen I Leave to my father, to dispose as he sees good. 28 : 3 : 1661.

Witnes                             By me        Samvell Jones.
Samson Mason, who deposed 7 : 9 : 1661.

---

JOHN ARNOLD.—18 May, 1661. Power of Administration to y⁰ estate of *John Arnold*, is graunted to *Samuell Arnold*, his Brother, he giueing security to £40. value, to Adminster according to law. Inventory of the estate of *John Arnold*, sometymes inhabitant of Boston, taken by said *Samuell Arnold*, of Marshfeild, in Plymouth Jurisdiction, who deposed, 31 July 1661. Mentions " land in yᵉ hand of *John Jackson*, Carpenter, of Boston, lyeing in Boston, prized at £20, by *John Button*, of Boston; the other part of Long Island 1¼ acres prized at £3, by *John Button;* also, 14 acres in yᵉ woods, aboue Braintree, prized at 20ˢ. by *Mr John Hull.*"

---

Major General Humphry Atherton.—[The following is a copy of a letter written by Rev. Richard Mather, of Dorchester, relative to the settlement of the affairs of a distinguished parishioner, Major General Humphry Atherton, who had suddenly deceased. The original is on file.]

These For the right worˡˡ John Endecott Esqʳ & Richard Bellingham Esqʳ Govenor & Deputy Govenoʳ of the Massachusetts.

May it please yoʳ worp·

Some frends having considered & conferred togethʳ about the managemt of oʳ honoured majors estate we haue thought meet to comend to yoʳ worps consideracoñ whethʳ in case the Will wᶜʰ we here send you to pᵉrvse be not legally Valid, it were not meet in such case to comit Administracon to his eldest sonne though for present out of the countrey, & to these 3 sonnes in law who now attend yoʳ worps for that intent. And seth Captayne Hutchinson hath also lands at Naraganset where a considerable part of the majors estate doth lye, & that Liueteñt Clapp & Ensigne Foster were nominated by the major as overseers of his will, we intreat yᵗ if they think not meet to be administratoʳˢ, (though we could much desyre it) that yet they 3 may be be nominated as overseers or Assistants to the Administrators; we doubt not but they will be ready to affoard to them their best advice & direcoñ vpon all occasions; but if they were nōiated herevnto by authority, it might be more pᵉrvalant wᵗʰ, them to affoard it, & more satisfactory to the frends of the deceased. Craving pardon for my boldnesse I comend yoʳ worps in this & all yoʳ weighty Administracoñs to the direcoñ & blessing of the Lord, & rest

Yoʳ. worps in all due observance,

Dorchester this }  Richard Mather.
27ᵗʰ of 7ber 61. }

At a meeteing at the Gouʳnoʳⁱ house, this 27ᵗʰ of September 1661. Power of Administration to yᵉ Estate of yᵉ late Majoʳ. Genⁱⁱ. Humphry Atherton, is Granted to *Jonathan Atherton*, his eldest sonne, and *Timothy Mather, James Trowbridge*, and *Obadiah Swift*, 3 of his sonnes in Law, in behalfe of the widdow, themselves, and rest of the Children, they bringing in an Inventory of that estate to the next County Court, and giueing security to Administer according to Law, which they engaged to doe, in the pᵉrsence of the magistrates, the same time when the Inventory Came in.

6ᵗʰ July 1662. The Court doth order that the estate, amounting to £900, besides a Farme of 700 acres at Woronoco, shall bee deuided in manner following, (i. e.) to the Widdowe, his Late Mansion howse, wᵗʰ the Land adioining, & meaddow att littell necke, & the diuission on this side Naponsett, all vallued at abᵗ. £204, the same to enjoye during life; [all to

193

be kept in good repair, & left so at her decease] ; alsoe, £96.14ˢ out of the Goods Chattells & debts. The remainder of the estate, all iust debts being payed, to be diuided amongst the Children of the said Maior Atherton, to his eldest sonne a double porciõñ, and the rest equaly to be sharers ; & in Like manner the reursion of the howse & Land assigned the widdow, to bee diuided amongst the Children, &c. Major Lusher, Capᵗ Clap, Leift Foster & Mr. Jones, they, or any two of them, to Auditt the Accounts, & the Administrators are to pay such [claims] as shall bee allowed by them, prouided, Major Lusher bee one of the said Auditors.

Inventory of the Estate taken 2 Octʳ 1661, by Roger Clap, Thomas Jones, Hopestill Foster. Mentions his grant of 700 acres layd out at Pechasuk.

Inventory of his Estate at Narraganset, taken 7 Novʳ 1661, by Richard Smith, Edward Hutchinson, William Hudson. Amᵗ. £461.10ˢ.

Timothy Mather deposed 28 : 2ᵐᵒ : 1664.

---

MARGERY ELLIOT.—Will 31 Oct. 1661. Margery Elliott, widdow, doe giue out of my thirds, wᶜʰ is £200, vnto my dau. *Hannah Frary*, £10 ; *Susanna*, £20 ; vnto my dau. *Mehitable*, £20 ; vnto my dau. *Sarah*, & my sonne *Asaph*, £40, a peece ; to my fiue Grand children, £20, to be devided equally vnto them. It is my will that my two sonnes, *Jacob* & *Asaph*, may haue the house & lands, & they to pay the Legacies. My sonne *Jacob* to be executor. Elder *Colbron* & *James Penn* to be overseers. Margery ⋈ Eliot.

Witnesseth, John Wilson senioʳ.

John Wilson senior, Elder William Colebron, & Elder James Penn deposed, 7 Novʳ 1661.

Inventory of her goods, &c. taken 9ᵗʰ Decʳ. 1661, by Robert Walker, John Hull. Amt. £294.19.06. Jacob Eliott deposed 30 Aprill 1662.

Inventory of the stock of Cattle & land of Jacob Eliot senior, deceased, wᶜʰ was designed to pay the portions of severall children, some are already paid. " Thirteen acres of Land about Roxbury gate, £78," &c. &c. Whole Amᵗ. £280. Debts £90. Mentions Edw: Adams, of Medfield, Thomas Dexter, Junior, & others.

---

THOMAS SCOTTOW.—I will that first that my debts be payd, & that my wife, *Sarah Scottow* haue the third of my Estate, according to Law, & what shall be left, to be devided among all my Children equally, my Eldest sonne being brought vp, & the rest being very young, & will therefore stand in need of the more support. I desire my beloved Brother : *Josh: Scottow*, & yᵉ respected Elder *James Penn* to be yᵉ executors of this my Last Will & Testament, made & signed 9 : 3ᵐᵒ.: 1660.

I further giue vnto my aged mother, *Sanford*, to be payd vnto her as her necessitie may call for it. £10. I giue vnto my sonne, *John Scottow*, all my tooles over & above what is expressed above.

Signed in the pʳsence of                                    Thomas Scotto.
John Clark, Thomas Clark.

Sargᵗ. Thomas Clark deposed 18 Decʳ. 1661.

Inventory of the goods & Chattels belonging to Tho: Scottow, late of Boston, deceased, apprised by William Reade, Augustin Lyndon. 18 (10) 1661. Amᵗ. £249.0ˢ.3ᵈ. Elder James Penn & Ensigne Josh: Scottow, deposed.

# ABSTRACTS FROM THE EARLIEST WILLS ON RECORD IN THE COUNTY OF SUFFOLK, MASS.

[Prepared by MR. WILLIAM B. TRASK, of Dorchester.]

JOHN STODDER, senior, of Hingham, being sicke, doe make this my Last will. I giue vnto my dau. *Hannah Wheelocke*, the wife of *Gershom Whelclocke*, £15 starling, to be payd within sixe moneths after my decease by my executo', if my said dau. live till the time of paym' come ; if she die before that time, the money to go to her heir ; [if she leave no heir, then the said *Gershom*, to have one half;] the other half, to the vse of my 3 sonns, *John, Daniell & Samuell Stodder.* Vnto *John Low*, my Grand Child, £7. 10'. to be payd by my executors, when the said *John Low* shall accomplish the age of 18 yeares. Vnto *Elizabeth Low*, my Grand Child, £7. 10', when the said *Elizabeth* shall accomplish the age of 18 yeares. [Provision is made in case of the death of either.] All the rest of my Estate, in Hingham, or elsewhere, shall be devided amongst my three sonnes, my Eldest sonne, *John*, to have a double share. Sonne *John*, executor. 20 Nov. 1661.  John S Stodder.

*Daniell Cushin, Edm: Pitts,* who deposed 31 Jan. 1661.

Inventory of the estate of *John Stodder senior*, of Hingham, who departed this life 19 Dec. 1661, taken by *Daniell Cushin, John Thaxter*. £ Amt. 124. 11. 06.  Debts due £16. 11. 08.

" Land by Waymoth River," " in horkley field," " next to *Moses Colyers* land," " in the plaine Neck," " on the great Playne," " at Cannohasset," " in the waye Necke."

---

ISAAC MORRELL. Will.—Debts payd, the residue of my Estate to my wife. dureing life. After her decease, my will is, that £40 be payd out of my estate vnto these my fower Grand Children (to witt) *John Smith Isaac, Francis & Abraham Smith*, to each, £10. To my Grand Child, *Mary Smith*, my farme between Readding & Andever, being more then 209 Acres. The residue of my Estate, to my two sonnes, *John Smith & Daniell Brewer*, & to my Grand Child, *Sarah Davis*, to be equally devided betweene them ; only to *Sarah Davis*, besides this, the Bed in the parlo'. & all the furniture belonging to it.

My will is, that what I haue given my sonne, *John Smith*, shall be enjoyed by him & his wife, if she outlive him, dureing theire Lives, but after theire decease, my will is, that this estate shall be equally devided betweene all the children the said *John Smith* now hath (which then shall be Living) or hereafter may have by my daughter, *Katherine*, for the accomplishm' whereof, my will is, that this p' of my estate be so disposed of by my Executo', with the advice of my overseers, in the turning of it into Lands, or otherwise, so that the Estate may not be embesselled, & the children disappointed of this, which I have given them.

[Lands to be sold in a judicious manner, for the benefit of his wife, if her needs require it. Said property to be disposed of under the direction of the overseers.]

Sons, *Tobias Davis & Daniell Brewer*, Executors ; *Thomas Weld & Edward Denison*, overseers. 15 : 10 : 1661.  Isaac Morrell.

In the presence of
*Samvell Danforth, Elisha Cooke,*
who deposed at a meeting of the magistrates, at *Leivᵗ Turnᵣˢ*, 23 Jan.
1661. *Mr. Samvel Danforth* also deposed to the first pᵗ of the schedule
annexed :—Wee whose names are vnder written doe testify that wee
heard *Isaac Morrell*, vpon the 19ᵗʰ : 10ᵐᵒ : 1661, declare it to be his will
to give vnto the Church of Roxbury, £3. for the purchasing of a Convenient Carpet, for the Table of the Meeting house, & a Comely & decent
Cushon for the Ministers Deske.
*Samvell Danforth, Edw: Denison, John Smith.*
[*Tobias Davis & Sarah Morrell* testified that they] heard *Isaac Morrell*.
vpon the 19 : 10ᵐᵒ: 1661, declare it to be his mind & will to give vnto
his Coussine, *Isaac Morrell*, his Anvile & all his Smiths Tooles & In-
strum̄ᵗˢ.
[*John Smith, Daniell Brewer & Sarah Morrell* testified that they]
heard *Isaac Morrell* yᵉ day before his death declare it to be his minde &
will to dispose of his wearing apparell, as followeth vizᵗ:—His best Cloake
vnto his Grand Child, *Sarah Davis ;* one of his two best suites to his
Brother *Abraham Morrell*, eithʳ his Leathʳ or his Cloath Suite. The
residue of his Cloathes to be devided betweene his two Sonnes.
Inventory of the estate prised by *Edward Denison, Thomas Welc,
Griffin Craft,* 17 Jan. 1661. Sum total £683. 06ˢ. 04ᵈ. *Tobias Davis,
& Daniell Bruere* deposed 23 Jan. 1661, at a meeting of the Magistrates
at *Lefᵗ Turners.* " Land at Stony River ;" " A parcell called smal
gaines," 1½ acres ; " ground at grauelly point," "in the middle diuision,"
" upon the great Hill," " in the fresh meddow," " in the blacke necke '

MATHEW IRONS, of Boston, being very sicke, maketh his last wil.
Vnto my Eldest sonne *John Irons*, my old dwelling house in Boston
with my barne belonging to the same, with the ground they stand vpon, &
the peece of ground belonging to the said old house which is the Southwarc
division of my Land as it is now fenced in. Vnto my sonne *Thomas Irons.*
the peece of ground, next to good man *Allynes*, belonging to the house nex.
to *Johns*, to the Southard, wᶜʰ was my owne proper Land belonging to
the old house. Vnto my dauˢ. *Elizabeth, & Rebecka Irons*, and likewise
to *Samuell*, my youngest sonne, the Orchard & brew house & the peece
of Land which [was] bought of my brother *Browne*, next to Goodmar.
*Baxters*, & the ground at Muddy River, and at Long Island, and doe de·
sire that the aforesaid pʳcells of land, [&] brewhouse be equally devidec
amongst them all three aforementioned, and if my sonne, *Thomas*, his
portion be not equall with the three aforementioned, I desire that out of
theirs, his portion may be equalized with theirs. For my household stuffe,
I desire it may be equally devided amongst them all. My wearing Clothes
I giue to *John Irons*, my Eldest Sonne. My Cloake I giue to my dau.
*Rebecka.* My fowling peece I giue to Eldest Sonne *John Irons ;* and my
Muskett and Sword, vnto my Sonne, *Thomas Irons*, when his time of
apprenticeship shall be expired. *Leivᵗ. William Hudson* and *Richard
Gridley* executors and overseers. [The sons to receive their portions at
the age of 21, the daughter at 18 years of age. Provision is made in
case of the decease of either, that the property be equally divided among
the survivors.]                                    *Mathew ⋈ Irons.*
Witness *Richᵃrd Knight, John Sanford*,
who deposed 30 Jan. 1661.

Inventory of Mathew Irons' Estate taken by *William Cotton, Thomas Joy & John Viall*, 16 April 1661.

---

NATHANIELL WALES, senior of Boston, weaver.—Debts & funerall expences being payd, my wife shall have my house & Land in Boston, dureing her life, she keeping said house & Land in tenentable repaire, and paying 10ˢ. a yeare rent, vizᵗ. 4ˢ a yeare to my sonne, *Timothy*, 2ˢ. 6ᵈ a yeare to my sonne, *John*, & 2ˢ. 6ᵈ. a yeare to my sonne, *Nathaniell;* and at my wifes decease, I giue my said house & Land to my 3 sonnes, vizt. to my sonne, *Timothy*, one halfe, & the other halfe to my sonne *John* & *Nathaniell*, to be equally divided betweene them. For my Land at Dorchester, which is one pᵣcell. Lately devided, that Lyeth vpon the South east side of Neponset River, I giue to my sonnes *Timothy* & *Nathaniell*, to *Timothy*, 30 accoⁿ. & to *Nathaniell*, twenty : for *John*, I haue giuen him Land equivolent all ready. For the Remainder of my moveable estate I giue the one halfe vnto my Loving wife, she having beene a helpefull & Loveing wife to me in my old age, & the other halfe I giue to my 3 sonnes, *Timothy* haveing a double portion. To my two Servant Maids, *Prisella* & *Sarah*, when their time is out, £5, vizt. 50ˢ. a peece. I doe hereby explain my minde Concerning that pᵗ. of my house I haue giuen my sonne, *Timothy*, yᵗ my Grand Child, *Timothy Walls*, junioʳ, shall be equall sharer wᵗʰ his father, therein. My wife executor, & my Brother in Law, *Humphery Atherton*, overseer.

Dated this 20 : 4ᵐᵒ: 1661.                        *Nathaniell Wales*
Witness hereto, *Humphrey Atherton*.                  *senior.*

Wee whose names are vnderwritten, doe witnes yᵗ yᵉ within written will was read vnto *Nathaniell Wales Senior* who desired it might be soe, because yᵉ Honored *Major Humphrey Atharton* who was yᵉ only wittnes to it was dead, that he might confirme it in our pʳsence, as witnesses. Wee doe wittnes he did owne & confirme it in all points. Adding only this, that he gave his wife, over and aboue what is giuen her in the will, yᵉ bedd in the Little Chamber, with yᵉ furniture thereto.  3 : 10 : 61.

*William Snelling*                 The mᵣke ⋈ of *Nathaniell*
*John Wiswall.*                   *Wales*, Senior, vseing this Expression, there is the beginning Lettᵣs
of name.

*John Wiswall* deposed, 1 Feb. 1661.
Inventory of the Estate taken, 3: 11: 61, by *Edmund Jackson*, *Robert Walker*. Amᵗ. £221. 12. 03. Debts owing from estate £106. 18. *Susan Wales*, relict of said *Nathaniel*, deposed, 1 Feb. 1661.

---

JONAS HUMFREY, [of Dorchester.] Will.—March 12 : 1661-62.—Being weake in body by reason of old age & other infirmities, but of perfect vnderstanding & memory. To my wife, all yᵗ Goods, that is now in being, which she brought with her. Alsoe, a third pᵗ of that foure Ackers of Land, yᵗ lyeth in the great lots, & a third pᵗ of seuen Ackers & a halfe in the 20 Acker lots, and a third pᵗ of two Ackers at the 8 Acker lots, during her life. After her decease, all those parcels of Land to returne to my son, *James Humfrey*. Alsoe, I giue my wife one Cow, on new Chest, on Blanket, one paier of Sheetes, & half yᵉ hempe. I giue my son *Jonas Humfrey*, on bed, on Couerled, & on flocke Bolster. Alsoe my Cloake, and my gray coate. To my Grandchild, *Elizabeth Frie*, £4. & yᵉ Chest yᵗ was her grandmothers. To my dau. *Susanna White*, wife to *Nicholas*

*White*, 10ˢ.  All the rest of my Estate, both Land & goods, to my son, *James Humfrey*, whom I make my whole Executor.  *Jonas Humfrey.*
Witnesses, *Thomas Joans*,
    *William Sumner, Edward Clap.*
*William Sumner* and *Edward Clap.* deposed, 17 April 1662.
Inventory of the estate of *Jonas Humphreys*, who depʳted this life the 19ᵗʰ of March 166⅘, taken by *Thomas Joanes, Edward Clap, William Sumner.*  Amt. £104. 13. 03.  *James Humphreys*, of Dorchester, son to yᵉ late *Jonas*, deposed, 17 April 1662.

[The above abstract of the Will of Jonas Humfrey, was made from a copy, evidently in the hand-writing of Elder James Humfrey, who was the eldest son of Jonas, and, as will be seen, his executor.  This copy is in possession of the family at Dorchester, and is doubtless a *correct transcript of the original.*  There are many errors in the Will, as recorded, in Suffolk Probate Records, Vol. I. p. 382.

Jonas Humfrey was a Constable in Wendover, Co. Bucks, Eng.  He brought to this country a curious copy of Instructions and queries in twelve Articles.  To these questions he was required to give answers in writing, after having faithfully fulfilled the duties incumbent on him as an officer of that borough.  This paper is extant.]

THOMAS BOYDEN.—Bond of *Thomas Boyden*, yeoman, late of Boston, now of Meadfeild, of £180, to *Edward Rawson.* [Said Boyden was] bound for the sum of £300, together with the house, vpland & meadow, [then in ais] possession, lately the inheritance of *Joseph Morse*, late of Meadfield. If said *Boyden* maintain the children of yᵉ late *Joseph Morse* & *Hannah*, ais wife, till the time of their nonage or marriage, or till they choose their guardians, teaching, or Causing yᵉ sonnes of the said *Morse* to write & Read, and, at their seuerall marriages, or days of Age, shall pay unto each of the said children the portions to them assigned by the Court at Boston, in January last, & by the Generall Court approved of, then, this obligation to be void.  18 Octʳ. 1661.  *Thomas Boyden.*
Witnes, *John Ferniside,*
    *Peren Rawson.*
    27 June 1665.

———

Mʀ GEORGE DILL.—Estate of *Mʳ Dill*, Creditor:—to *Mʳ Leader*, on yᵉ Ship Good Fⁱllowes Voyage from Ireland £44; money brought in the Inventory which was soe much left in keepeing by *Mʳ Jeremiah Egginton* £22. 10ˢ.; to *Dʳ Clarke*, for Cureing *Joseph Dills* broken thigh, £5; charged on the Inventorie, for wages due to *Dico Dill* and his three servantes, wᶜʰ could not be recorded, £92. 1ˢ.; *Mʳ John Tinker*, charged, & *Mʳ William Brenton;* *Mʳ Fen* paide £4 to the enlargeing of land belonging to the estate of the deceased Dill; to *Mʳ Lasell*, in Barbadoes for 2500ˡᵇ sugar, £25; to *Thomas Notley* 4800ˡᵇ of sugar, £ 60; a debt from *Amose Richardson*, £1; from *Mʳ Winslow*, at Salisbury, £9; *Capᵗ Clarke* to Accᵗ. of Ship Supply, £3. 5. &c. &c.  Whole Amᵗ. £1569. 4ˢ. 6ᵈ.

———

EVAN THOMAS.—Power of Administration to yᵉ Estate of yeᵉ late *Evan Thomas*, is Granted to *Alice*, his late wife, *Capᵗ Thomas Clarke, Mʳ Thomas Lake, Capᵗ Edw: Hutchinson,* and *Mʳ Thomas Lynes*, of Charles Towne.

Inventory taken by *John Wisewall & James Oliuer*. Amount £719. 13. 06. *Alice Thomas*, the widow, deposed 30 Oct. 1661. An additional sum of three or four pounds was brought in 27 : 11 : 1663, by *James Olliuer* and *John Eucred*, who were chosen to prise seueral goods c. said estate, in 1661.

---

THOMAS BARLOW.—Inventory of the land and goods of *Thomas Barlow* deceased, the 23 of October 1661 ; taken by *John Clarke, John ✗ Andres, Joseph How, Edmund Eddenden*. Am$^t$. £394. 2$^s$. Power of Administration to y$^e$ estate of y$^e$ late *Thomas Barlow*, deceased. is Granted 29 Oct. 1661, to *Elizabeth Barlow*, his relict, who deposed. 27 Feb. 1661, *John Coombe* & his wife, *Elizabeth*, Relict & Administratrix to the Estate of the late *Thomas Barlow*, did bind ouer the house & land, with all the estate formerly *Tho: Barlow*, in the Inuentory, exprest, to *Edward Rawson*, Recorder of the County, to Respond the Judgment of the next County Court in Refference to the diuission of the estate, & brought in *Lef$^t$. Wm Hudson*, with her, who also bound himselfe & heires in the summe of £200, to said Recorder, that the estate shall bee forth coming, & Respond the Judgment of the s$^d$ Court.

---

WALTER PALMER.—Will.—Vnto my sonne *John*, a yoake of three yeare old steares, and a horse ; to my dau. *Grace*, 20$^s$. ; to all my Grand Children, 20$^s$. a peece. To my sonne *Jonas*, halfe the planting Lott at y$^e$ new meadow River, by Seaconcke, & y$^e$ Lott betweene *John Butterwoths*, according to the fower score pound Estate, & the vse of halfe y$^e$ housing, & halfe of the whole Farme for fower yeares. To my sonne *William*, the other halfe of y$^e$ same farme at Seaconck foreuer, and to take *Robert Martine* or some oth$^r$ skill full man & to devide the houseing & the whole farme in two equall p$^r$ts & to take his owne & dispose of it as he pleaseth. I giue him, also, a Mare with her foale, two redd oxen, a paire of Steares of three yeare old a piece, fower Cowes & a Muskett, with all such things as are his owne allready. The other halfe of the farme at Seaconcke I giue to my sonne *Gersham*, for ever, after the ende tearme of fower yeares. All the rest of my Land, goods, and chattell vndesposed I Leave vnto my wife, whome with my sonne, *Elihu*, I make my full executor, to pay my debts, bring vp my Children & pay them theire portions as my Lands and Estate will beare ; but, in case my wife marry againe, before my Children are brought vp, & their portions payd, then, my three sonnes, *Elihu, Nehemiah & Moses* to enter vpon the farme & Estate, and pay vnto their mother 10£. p$^r$ annum dureing hir life, & y$^e$ Land & Estate duely valued to bee equally distributed among my Children, *Elyhu. Nehemia, Moses, Benjamin, Gersham, Hannah & Rebecca* with Consideration of the tenn pound yearely to be payd to theire mother out of y$_e$ Land. But if my wife pay theire portions, according to her discretion, & my three sonnes, *Elihu, Nehemiah & Moses* Possesse the Land, they shall give £20 a piece out of the Land to my sonne, *Benjamine*, besides his mothers portion, in 3 yeares after they are possesst of the Farme.
In the p$^r$nce of                                        *Walter Palmer.*
　　*William Cheesbrough, Sam$^{ll}$ Cheesbrough,*
　　　*Nathaniell Cheesbrough.*
Memorandum.—If *Elihu, Nehemiah or Moses* decease before they have any years, *Benjamine* is to succede in theire p$^t$ of y$^e$ Farme & give to my dau. *Elizabeth*, two Cowes. I give my Executo$^{rs}$ a yeares time for payment of these Legacies.

Testified to, by the three witnesses, on oath, before *George Denison,* Commiss[r].

Approved by the Court on Petition of *Leiut. Richard Cooke,* in behalfe of y[e] *Widow Palmer,* relict of *Walter,* & *Elihu,* their sonne, on the oathes of *W[m].,* *Samuell* & *Nathan[ll] Cheesbrough,* 11 May, 1662.

Inventory of the Goods & Chattells of *Walter Palmer,* now decease[d], at Sothertowne, in the Countie of Suffolke, as it was taken the Last of M[r]ch 1662 by *William Chesbrooke,* & *Thomas Stanton* of the same towne. Am[t]. £1644. 05[s].

One horse, valued at £12, added, by *Elihu Palmer,* as executor, who deposed, 13 May 1662.

---

MARGARET KINGSBURY.—9. 11: 1660.—I, *Margaret Kingsbery,* of Dedham, in the countie of Suffolke in New England, though sickly & Infirme in body, yet whole & sound in memory & vnderstanding, doe make this my Last will. That after my death, my body shall be decently burryed in Christian burryal, at y[e] discretion of my Executor. I giue vnto *Sarah Crosseman,* the wife of *Robert Crosseman,* of Taunton, £5, to be payd by my Executor within three moneths after my decease, in Dedham, in Currant Country paym[t]. I giue vnto *Thomas Fuller,* of Dedham, my Kinseman, as an acknowledgem[t]. of all his Love expended for me, £20.; y[e] remainder of my Estate vnto the children of the said *Thomas Fuller* & of *Hannah,* his wife, my neere kinsewoman, that is to such of them as are at p[r]sent borne & surviveing, to be equally devided amongst them. My will is, that the said Estate shall remaine, in the possession of said *Thomas & Hannah,* for the vse of their said children, & that at y[e] times the sonnes shall attaine y[e] age of 21 yeares, & y[e] daughters shall seu[r]ally come to the age of 18 yeares, theire p[rt] shall be payd them ; y[e] p[rt] of y[e] sonnes & daught[rs] being equall. [If either child die before attaining the age mentioned, the survivors to have, equally, the deceased one's portion.] My loving kinseman, *Thomas Fuller,* sole executor.

In y[e] p[r]nce of vs.                         *Margaret* ✕ *Kingsbery.*
*Samuell May, Eliazer Lusher.*

*Samuell May* deposed, before *Eliazer Lusher,* 20 : 3 : 62.

*Major Lusher* also Affirmed before y[e] Magistrates & Record[r]. 22 May 1662. Present y[e] Gov[r]. Cap[t] Gookin & Record[r].

Ewd: Rawson. Recorder.

---

THOMAS TRAVEGOE.—In y[e] shipp Releife of London, *Robert Clarke* Comand[r]. who dwelleth in Redreif nere London, I make my Last Will, [on board said ship] being visited with sicknes, vpon y[e] coast of Ginnie, 27 Oct[r]. 1661. My wife, *Jone Treaveagoe,* of Dartmouth, in the County of Devon, & *Mary,* My Daughter of the same Towne, my executrixes ; my debts payd, y[e] residue [of the estate] to be devided equall[y] betweene [them] and my friend, *Henrie Ramsay* of Braunton, neare Barnestable, of y[e] same Countie, w[ch] is Gunner of o[r] said shipp Releife, to be true & trustee for the disposing of all that I haue in y[e] shipp, to see my debts payd which I owe in y[e] shipp, & Receiue what is due to me, &c. for this Voyage.                         *Thomas* ✕ *Traveegoe.*

In y[e] p[r]sence of vs.
*Martin Band, James Trew.* Testa me *Henry Ramsey.*

20 Sep[t]. 1662. Martyn Band & James Trew, Mate & Marriner of shipp Releife deposed. The Probate was allowed of, & power of Administration giuen to Henry Ramsey.

# ABSTRACTS FROM THE EARLIEST WILLS ON RECORD IN THE COUNTY OF SUFFOLK, MASS.

[Prepared by MR. WILLIAM B. TRASK, of Dorchester.]

NATHANIEL WALES.—18 May 1662. I, *Nathaniel Wales*, of Boston, shipp Carpinter, being sicke, make my will. The whole Estate, goods, debts, Land & house which I now possesse, or shall be due vnto me, be; (my Executo⁷⁵ in trust) imployed to the best advantage for the bringing vp of my Children in the feare of God, & when they or either of them shall be capable of trades, to be put to Godly masters, and after that all charges is disbursed & payd, the remaineing sume to be devided amongst my Children, whereof my Eldest sonne, *Nathaniell Wales*, to haue a double portion, & the rest Equall portions. I intreate my Loving Brother, *John Wales*, & friend, *John Baker*, executo⁷⁵, in trust, to see this my will prformed.                                     *Nathaniel ⋈ Wales.*

In the prnce of vs,
*John Wales, Susan Wales, William Pearse.*
*William Pearse & Susan Wales*, both of Boston, deposed.
27 May 1662.                              Edw: Rawson Record⁷.
Inventory of the Estate of *Nathaniel Wales*, Praised the 27 day of May 1662, by *Nathaniell Adams & Daniell Turell*, of Boston. Amt. £189.04.ˢ·03.ᵈ· *Jnᵒ Baker*, and *Jnᵒ Wales*, deposed, 27 May, 1662.

---

JOHN LIMBREY.—I, *John Limbrey*, of theᵢ shipp Releife, marriner, whereof *Robert Clarke* is Cōmand⁷, being sicke, make this my Last Will, 28 Dec⁷ 1661. I appointe my Loving friend, *Richard Tuckey*, Coop⁷. of yᵉ said shipᵉ, my sole Executo⁷., And doe Order him to pay Vnto *Wᵐ Perry*, of Limehouse, 56ˢ· sterling, out of salery, in yᵉ said shipp, it be-ing a debt I owe vnto him. The shipps debts being discharged, I give yᵉ remainer of my wages & whatsoeuer is due or aprprtaineing vnto me, in the said shipp, vnto *Richard Tuckey*, my Executor.
                                          *John ⋈ Limbrey.*
Witnes, *Henrie Ramsey,*
*Thomas Webber*, Tho⁵ *Wright.*
19 Aug 1662.—*Henry Ramsey*, Gunner of Shipp Relief, & *Thomas Wright*, Doctor or Chirurgeon of said Shipp, deposed that they did both see *John Limbrey*, marriner of said Shipp, that dyed one the Coasts of Ginney, signe and publish this paper to be his Last Will & Testamᵗ. &c.

---

ROBERT CLARKE.—16 Septᵗ. 1662. I, *Robert Clarke*, of Rederife, in England, Marriner, now resident in Boston, in New England, being sicke, make this my Last will. My debts paid, my will is, that my Estate be equally devided vnto my wife & Children, *John, William, Robert, Mary, Elizabeth*, & that Child wᶜʰ my wife bore vnto me since I came from her. If any of my Children dye, his & theire portions to be devided to those surviving & payd at Age of 21 yeares or marriage. My will is, that my wife shall enjoye said Estate dureing her widowhood, & in case she marry, the Estate to be secured, vnto my Children. My sonne, *John Clarke*, executor. I Intreate my Loving friend, *Jonathan Wilson*, Car-

201

penter, to assist my said sonne, in managing the businesses which he may haue to doe in New England and elsewhere. Collaterally, I will & given vnto my wife & my sonne, *John*, £50, a peece, more then the rest before named. *Robert Clarke.*

In y<sup>e</sup> p<sup>r</sup>sence of vs,
*Thomas Savage*, senior, *Nicholas Page*,
*William Smith, William Pearse* scr, who deposed, 23 Sep<sup>t</sup>. 1662.

For y<sup>e</sup> bett<sup>r</sup> vnderstanding how y<sup>e</sup> state of y<sup>e</sup> s<sup>d</sup> *Robert Clarke* & y<sup>e</sup> own<sup>rs</sup> of Shipp Releife Lyes here in New England, y<sup>e</sup> Magistrates ordered y<sup>t</sup> *Cap<sup>t</sup> Savage, Mr Stoddard & Mr Houchin* be a Comittee to Joyne with *Jonathan Wilson*, Carpenter, & *Mr Nicho: Page*, to procure an Inventory of y<sup>e</sup> ships Estate, and make sale of such things, as may be most Advantagious to y<sup>e</sup> Estate, according to theire best Judgm<sup>ts</sup>. [No such Inventory appears on the records.]

---

JOHN MODESLY.*—29 : 8<sup>mo</sup> : 1661. Power of Administration to y<sup>e</sup> estate of *John Modesly*, deceased, is graunted to *Cicily*, his Relict, in behalfe of her selfe and children.

Inuentory of y<sup>e</sup> estate of *John Modesly*, of Dorchester, taken 4 Oct<sup>r</sup>. 1661, by *Henry Withington* & *Richard Withington*. Amt. £240.3.·8.<sup>d</sup> Cicily Modesly deposed 30 Oct. 1661.

---

SISILLY MODSLY.—28 Nov. 1661. I, *Sisilly Modsly* being of reasonable sence and understanding, though vpon my sick bed, doe dispose of my thirds which fols to mee out of my husbands estate. I give vnto my sonne, *Thomas Modsly*, my part of the house and the home lotte, one fether bed, bolster, coverlit, and a bed ticke, in case he liue or any Child of his ; if he die and leaue no child liueing, then it shall bee equally deuided between my sonne, *John Modsly* and my dau. *Elizabeth.* I giue unto my sonne, *John Modsly*, my halfe of the barne, and my two acres of meddow being at the litle neck. I giue unto my dau. *Elizabeth*, my other fether bed, and all the rest of my moofables, & my cow & my pig. I giue unto my sonne, *Thomas* child, *Mary*, my red coate. All the rest of my wearing apparell, I giue unto my son *Thomas* wife, and to my dau. *Elizabeth*, to be equally devided between them. I make over my letter of administration to *William Pond*, and desire him to administer in my behalfe, if the Lord take me away. This is my last will and Testament. *Sisily Modsly.*

Signed in the presence of us,
*Thomas ⋈ Grant, William Pond.*

---

EDWARD SHRIMPTON.—I, *Edward Shrimpton*, of Bednall Greene, in the Countie of Midlesex, M<sup>r</sup>chant, being weake in Body, declare this my Last Will. Debts and funneral charges discharged, I giue vnto my sonne, *Jonathan Shrimpton*, £650, to be payd him at Boston in New England, p<sup>r</sup>sently after my decease. Vnto my dau. *Mary Shrimpton*, £650, [to

---

* In ancient as well as in modern chirography we sometimes find the letters *l* and *t* written alike, the latter uncrossed. The name Modesly written thus, has led Farmer astray, who says on page 128—" Modesty John, Dorchester, d. 27 Oct., 1661. [MS. copy of records.] The race has probably become extinct." Whereas all of the name of *Moseley*, in Dorchester, it is believed, can trace their lineage to the above John. See a condensed account of him and his family in the Hist. of Dorchester, p. 129, 130. On p. 122 of his Register, Farmer has a brief account of John Maudsley, which is correct. T.

be paid as aforesaid.] I doe require and charge my Sonne *Jonathan* & Dau. *Mary*, that they doe not dispose of theire Portions nor of themselues in Marriage, if God offer an opportunitie, without the knowledge & Advice of my Loving Brother, *Mr Henry Shrimpton*. Vnto my three sonnes, *Ebenezer, Epaphras & Silas Shrimpton*, to each, £400, when they come to the age of one and twenty yeares. Vnto my Dau'. *Elizabeth & Lydia Shrimpton*, to each, £400, at the age of 21 yeares, or day of marriage. My will is that the £2000 giuen to my fiue youngest Children remaine in the hands of my Brother, *Mr Henry Shrimpton*, to be improoved for yᵐ, he allowing my wife, dureing her Widdowhood, a Competent proportion of yᵉ improoovement towards theire Education, & if she happen to Mary so Long as they or any of yᵐ shall continue with her, yᵉ remainder of yᵉ improovement to be added to theire portions. [If either of the five children, last mentioned, die, the deceased one's portion to be divided among the survivors.] Vnto yᵉ Church of Christ, whereof *Mr John Simson* is Pastor, £10 to be distributed to the Poore of the said Church, by the Officers thereof. Vnto *Mr Wentworth Day*, & to *Mr Richard Goodgrome*, to each, £5. to be payd pʳsently after my decease.

Edw: Shrimpton.

I giue vnto yᵉ Church of Christ wᶜʰ vse to meete by Allhallowes by the wall, £10, to be distributed to yᵉ poore of the said Church, by the officers thereof. Vnto my wife, *Elizabeth*, yᵉ remainder of my Estate, as household goods, pale Leases, debts, & all other Chattells, for her owne proper vse.

My Will is, that my Loving friend, Alderman *William Peake* be overseer of this my Will. I make my Brother, *Mr Henry Shrimpton*, sole Executor. 30 Sepᵗ. 1661.    Edward Shrimpton.

In the pʳnce of
*Thomas Norman, William Booker.*

[A Certificate, by Edward Rawson, Recorder, dated 18 Sepᵗ. 1662, informs us, that the Record is a true " Copie of the late Edward Shrimpton' will, wᵗʰ yᵉ Comission out of the prerogatiue Court in England for the probate of wills."

The Commission, from William, Archbishop of Canterbury, in Latin, is recorded. It is directed to *John Norton*, minister ; *Simon Bradstreet, Hezekiah Vsher, William Dauies, Thomas Clarke & Henry Powning*, merchants ; and authorizes Henry Shrimpton to act as Executor to his brother Edward's estate. Dated London, 1 July 1662.

*Simon Rolleston*, Register.

R. *Hoare* pʳ decret wᵗʰ a Great Seale in Red waxe being yᵉ seale of the office appending. Then follows—" The forme of yᵉ Oath to be ministred to yᵉ Executoʳ. Laying his hands vpō yᵉ Bible or New Testament."

" Yoᵘ shall sweare yᵗ yᵉ writing annexed Containeth yᵉ whole effect of yᵉ true & Last Will & Testament, of Edward Shrimpton yoʳ Brothe: late deceased so farr as yoᵘ know or beliue, and yᵗ yoᵘ shall well and truely pʳforme yᵉ same, in paying his debts & Legacies, as farr as his goods, chattells & debts will yʳ vnto extend & as yᵉ Law will charge yoᵘ, & yᵗ you shall make or cause to be made a true & pʳfect inventory of all his sᵈ goods, chattells and debts, whᶜʰ shall or may Come to yoʳ hands, possession or knowledge. And also make a true & pʳfect acco͞mᵗ when yoᵘ shall be there vnto Lawfully required. So helpe yoᵘ God & yᵉ Contents of this Booke."

The Will was proved in Boston, New England, 6 Sep$^t$. 1662. Signed, *W$^m$ Davis, Hezekiah Vsher, Henry Powning.*

SAMUELL HOLLY.*—(Cambridge.) Inventory taken 3 Dec. 1643, by *Edward Jackson, John Jacksone.* Amt. £15. 13. 02.

On the back are the names of *Frances Gould, Will Almey, David Williams, Jo. Barcher.*

WILLIAM BLANTINE.—Will—25 : 2$^d$ mo. 1662. I giue to my Eldest sonne, *William Blantine*, the new house in the Close by the pond, the breadth of y$^e$ Land & house in the front towards the Lane, Containeing 65 foote, beginning at the Corner of the house next vnto the pond, & to goe along in the front, next the Lane towards the South East, and the depth of the Land, with the house before mentioned, to be three score foote along by the pond Syde from the front & so to be layd out in a Square. Also, I giue to my sonne, *William,* the Lott of Land that Lyeth betwixt the Lott of *George Griges* & y$^e$ Land y$^t$ was *Thomas Bells* as it lyeth now fenced in. To my dau. *Pheebe Blantine,* I giue the house next *Joseph Wheeler*, with halfe the Orchard from y$^e$ front downe to the pond, & halfe a little Garden lying betwixt *John Hord* & *Gamaliell Wait*, that halfe next *John Hord,* & she shall haue a high way of sixe footeinto her garden by the pond side. Also, I giue to my dau. *Pheebe,* the Pastor Ground inclosed, next to *Josias Belcher*, being full seven rod wide, next the Streete, & goeing in Length to the beach by the Sea on the South East, & on the East Corner without the fence there is about 11 or 12 foote, & so to runn on a strait line betwixt the towne Land vp to the Streete, with all the fence about the Towne Land is my owne, with the fence next old *Whites* Lott. To my dau. *Mary*, I giue the whole dwelling house I now Live in, with the Shopp next the streete & the other halfe of the Orchard, next *John Hords* house Lott, and the other halfe of the little Garden next to *Gamaliel Wait* & y$^e$ Pastor ground next y$^e$ pond, all of it, when my sonne *Williams* is Layd out, I giue to my dau. *Mary,* as it Lieth inclosed. This my Estate thus bestowed, neither my wife nor my Children shall have pow$^r$ to mortgage or make sale of, neither shall they Let it without the Consent of one another, nor shall any one of them Let this theire inheritance, not for above one yeare. This my Estate thus diuided to my three Children after my wife decease, whome while shee Liue, my will is, she shall enioy all my Estate, to be at her dispose while She Liue, & as for my Share at y$^e$ Iron workes at Taunton, I freely giue to my Wife to Let or sell as her need shall require ; in case she doe not sell it, after her decease, I giue it to my Dau. *Pheebe.* This my Estate, my wife shall enioy without molestation from my Children or from any other whatsoeuer. All my stocke or state in Cattle and household goods I giue to my wife to be at her dispose while she liue & at her death. [Provision is made in case his children die or have any children, or if they die without issue. In the latter case,] all this Estate of mine shall Returne to my Eldest Broth$^r$ *Ralph Blantine* his Children & be equally devided ; & if *Ralph* hath no Children, then it shall be transferred vpon the Children of *John Blantine,* my Second Broth$^r$, and be equally devided ; these two was borne in y$^e$ parish of Vpton vpon Seauerns in Wostershire. My Wife *Pheebe Blantine* executrix.

───────────

* This abstract of the Inventory of Mr. Holly, taken from the Suffolk files, was omitted in its proper place in the Register for January, 1853.　　　T.

The reason why I bestow no more of my Estate vpon my sonne *William* is, because he will not harken to my Counsell, neither had I my Land by or from any predecessors inheritance but from the blessing of God on my endeavour.                                   William W Blantine.
Witnesses,
*Nathaniel Bishope, Benjamin Thurstun,* who deposed 10th July 1662. Inventory of the Estate taken 2d July, 1662. Amt. £498. 6. Witnesses, *Nathaniell Bishop, Henry Rust. Phebe Blanton,* Relict of *William Blanton,* Affirmed 30 July 1662.

THOMAS STREAME.—1st July 1662. Power of Administration to the Estate of the late *Thomas Streame,* of Weymouth, Granted to *Ottis,* his mother, in behalfe of her selfe & Children, she bringing in an Inventory of that Estate to the next Countie Court.          Edw: Rawson Recordr.
Wee, whose names are vnderwritten, being desired to apprize the Goods & Estate that was Left by *Thomas Streame,* of Weymouth, Lately deceased, when wee Came together, wee found that his Estate, his mothers and his Brothr. *Benjamine Streame* were so joyned together that wee could not distinguish it one from anothr. And as wee were Informed, they did all improove theire time & Estates together, & therefore wee thought good to take an Inventory of the whole, out of the wch wee judge all his debts to be payd, and wee thinke one third part of that wch doth Remaine, did belong to him that is deceased. But wee Leave it to ye Honored Court to determine as theire Worships see good.
Signed by *Edward Bate, John Whitman, Thomas Dyar.*
Amt. of Inventory, £431. 12. *Elizabeth Ottis,* Administratrix to ye Estate of *Tho: Streame,* deposed.
Mentions, " 12 Acres of vpland neare *Richd Bolters* house," land " in the Range feild," " in the ferry feild," " at burying Island," " amongst the Great Lotts," " woodland neare *Eldr Bates* Mill," " 24 Accorª nere the pen." &c. &c.
In Lib. iv. fol. 147, date 22 : 5 : 1663, is an Inventory of the Estate of *Eliz. Oates,* liueing, and of her son, *Beniamin Stream,* deceased the 27 : 3m. 1663. Amt. £399.4ª. Power of Administration to one third part of the Inventory, as the right of *Beniamin Streame,* is graunted to *Elizabeth Oates,* formerly *Streame,* his Mother, in Behalfe of her selfe and the Children of the said *Streame.*          Edward Rawson Recordr.

GEORGE PROCTER.—I, *George Procter,* of Dorchester, being very sicke, make my Last Will, 27 Jan. 1661. I giue vnto *Edeth,* my wife, two Cowes, and doe also appoint yt my Sonne, *Samuell,* Shall Lay in winter Stuffe for those two Cowes from yeare to yeare dureing my wife's life. Also, she shall have one halfe of my houseing and halfe the profitts of ye Land, both vpland and meddow dureing her life. Also, my wife shall have fyrewood, brought home by my sonne *Samuell ;* & for the other halfe of my houseing & Land I giue vnto my Sonne *Samuell,* for his owne vse foreuer, & after my wifes death I appointe he shall have the other halfe thereof. I giue vnto my 4 Dauª. vizt. *Sarah, Mary, Hannah & Abigail,* 20ª· a peece, to be payd them by my sonne *Samuell,* within one yeare after my decease, & after my wifes death my will is that my 4 dauª. shall haue £10. a piece, payd them by £10 a yeare betweene them, only my Dau. *Abigail,* Considering that she haue not yet had as much as her sisters. my will is yt in steed of her £10

above expressed, she shall have £12 payd her in fower yeares, after my wife decease, and y$^t$ to be a full discharge of all y$^t$ I have form$^r$ly given her hopes to expect ; & for my stocke of Cattle, vizt. one Mare & two Colts, two oxen, two steers, two Calues, two heifers, 24 sheepe, and sixe swine, these I giue, the one halfe to my wife, & the other halfe vnto my Sonne *Samuell;* & for my other two Cowes, 1 haue giuen those, to my wife ; & for my other Cattle w$^{ch}$ I haue giuen to my wife, my mind is, that if my Sonne *Samuell*, provide winter meate for the Cattle, my wife shall allow my Sonne *Samuell* for her part, and y$^t$ *Samuell* shall haue y$^e$ vse of y$^e$ meddow to Cutt grass for them. And when it shall please God to take away my wife, by death, my will is y$^t$ my sonne *Samuell* shall have all y$^e$ Stocke of Cattle, then in being. All my other Moveable Estate of household goods & such debts as are due to me shall be equally devided betweene [them,] the halfe of such goods and moveables at my wife's disposeing. *George Procter.*
In the p$^r$nce of
    *John Capen, Thomas* ⋈ *Lake.*
I appointe my wife & Sonne *Samuell*, to be Joynt Executors, & desire my Loving friends, *John Capen & Thomas Lake* to be overseers.

*John Capen* and *Thomas Lake* deposed 26 : 12$^{mo}$ : 1661. Inventory of the Estate taken 14$^{th}$ Feb. 1661, by *John Capen* and *Thomas Lake*. Am$^t$. £458.16.09. Mentions land " at y$^e$ neck," 2¼ acres Captins necke, 3 deuissions in the Cow walke, 3 diuissions at Unquety, land in the two last diuissions on both side of Naponset 39 acres & better." &c.

*Samuell Proctor*, deposed to this Inventory of his father's estate, 27 Feb. 1661.

---

WILLIAM COLBRON.—Will. 1 : 6$^{mo}$ : 1662. Debts & funeral expences discharged, I giue vnto the Church of Boston whereof I was a member, £40, to be payd within two yeares after my decease ; to my wife, threescore pounds, for her to dispose of as she will, also, vnto her all my Estate both reall & p$^r$sonall during her life. I make my wife sole Executrix. I giue to my dau. *Sarah Pierce* & her dau. *Sarah Colpit* one fowerth part of my Estate, also, to my dau. *Mary Turand* and her five Children w$^{ch}$ she had by *John Barrell*, as *James, William, John, Mary* & *Hannah*, one halfe of the three fowerths of my Estate. Also, I giue to my dau. *Elizabeth* & her Children w$^{ch}$ she hath, or may haue, by my Sonne *Paine*, the other halfe of the three fowerths of my Estate, to be equally devided betwixt them, to be payd after my wife's decease. I desire Mr. Rainsford & Jacob Eliot to be overseers, & I giue them 20$^s$ a peece. William Colbron.
Wittnes
          the m$^r$ke of
James Penn, Rich:⟩Williams.

Rich$^d$ Williams deposed 29 : 8$^{mo}$ : 1662.
Inventory of the Goods & Chattels of the deceased. Apprized 15 Oct$^r$. 1662, by James Penn, W$^m$ Davis, John Hull. Amt. £895.8.
Mrs Margery Colebron, his widow, deposed, 29 Oct. 1662.

---

JAMES LANE.—Will of *James Lane*, Late of Plymouth, now of Boston in New England, Oct$^r$. 2, 1662. Vnto my Sonne, *Francis*, all my Carpentr$^e$ tooles, with y$^e$ Chest in w$^{ch}$ a p$^{rt}$ of them are, & that he should be brought vp, in y$^e$ trade of a Carpinter & Left with Goodman *Place*, vntill my Sonne *James* Comes over to New England, & in case y^t he Comes not, I Leave him to be desposed on as above said to y^e trade of a Carpenter, p^r y^e discretion of my Executo^rs, vizt. *Mathew Barnard*, Carpinter, goodman *Place* & *Daniell Stone*, Chirurgeon, all of Boston.

My Debts are as followeth :—*Mr Rich^d Cutts* oweth me, Eleven Quentalls 3 q^rters of m^rchantable fish. *Mr Bryant Pembleton* is Debt to me 7^lb. 10^s. in fish, & 50^s. more for work done p^r *Mr Pembletons* order for *Mr Moody* ; *John Pickerine* 15^s. ; *John Hunkins*, A Barrell halfe of Mackrell. My Will is, that what Estate is Left in New England, charges defrayed, be Conveyed to my wife *Delsebelath Lane*.

*James Lane.*

*Alice Place* & *Hannah Talby* deposed 11 : 9^mo : 62.

*Mathew Barnard* deposed in relation to the Inventory 11 : 9^mo : 1662, when it was ordered that *James Lane*, Eldest Sonne of James Lane deceased Coming into this Country, and into this Court, at his request, *Daniell Stone, Mathew Barnard,* & *Peter Place*, executo^rs be discharged, & y^e Estate Comitted to the said *James Lane junior*, in behalfe of his mother & Children, he giving security by *Peter Place*, that what Remaines be sent to his mother in England.

[There is a Bond, on file, from *James Lane*, of Plymouth, in Old England, now resident in Boston, and *Peter Place*, of Boston, yeoman, to *Edward Rawson*, Recorder, in the sum of £20. The Bond bears date 11 Nov. 1662. Conditions :—If said Lane shall convey the estate of the late *James Lane* Sen^r. his father, to *Dousabella Lane*, his mother, &c. then, the obligation to be voyd.

Witnesses, *Jonathan Remington*, & *John Boynton*.

Tools of James Lane, prised by goodman Purchase & Rich: Barnard, Carpenters, 28 Oct. 1662. Signed, *John Purchase, Joseph Bastar, Richard Barnard*. Mentions *Jeams Pickerin*.]

---

WILLIAM BROWNE.—1 : 5 : 1662. I, *Willam Browne*, of Boston, Sope boyler, being sick, make this my last Will. My wife, *Hannah*, executrix, to receiue all Debts due to me, & to pay all debts and duties I owe in right or Conscience to any body. Debts being discharged, the Remainder of my goods & estate I giue vnto my wife. I giue my sixe Children 12^d. a peece ; for my Cowe that is at Billerikey I Leaue to my wife to dispose of her as she shall see meete. I appointe my friends Elder *James Pen, Mr Willam Bartholomew* & *Thomas Buttolph*, of Boston, to be overseers of my will. *Willam Browne.*

In y^e p^rnce of

*Godfrey Armitage, Jonathan Negus*, who deposed 19 Dec^r. 1662.

Inventory of the Estate, prized by *Thomas Butolph*, & *Godfrey Armitage* 17 Dec^r. 1662. *Hannah Browne* deposed 19 Dec^r. 1662.

---

SAMUELL DIXER.—21 Nov^r 1661. Inventory of the estate of *Samuell Dixer*, taken by *John Balch, Isaac Woodberey*. *Willam Dixer* deposed to the Inventory of his son Sam: Dixers estate, 30 Jan. 1661.

---

RICE JONES.—Inventory of the Estate of *Rice Jones*, taken by *Richard Collecutt, John Sunderland*, 30 Jan. 1661. Amt. £206.09.^s06.^d. Mentions the names of *John Hues* and *Beniamin Keden*, servants of Rice Jones. *Anne Jones*, Relict, deposed 1^st Feb. 1661.

# ABSTRACT FROM THE EARLIEST WILLS ON RECORD IN THE COUNTY OF SUFFOLK, MASS.

Prepared by Mr. W. B. Trask, of Dorchester.

EDWARD BRECK. I, *Edward Breck*, of Dorchester, yeoman, being very sicke, make my last Will, 30 Oct. 1662. Debts due to be payd, and my funerall discharged, My will is, that all my dau. *Blak's* Children, shall haue each 40ˢ, out of my Estate in on yeare after my decease. My Sonne, *Robert*, Although he haue had his full portion, yet my will is, yᵗ he shall haue 20ˢ payd him, as a token of my Love and fatherly affection towards him.— *Isabell*, my wife, [to] have one-third part of my moveable Estate, accounting the formeʳ Legacies as pᵗ of the Estate; also, one-third part of my houseing and Lands during her life, she keeping and leaving it in good repaire. The other two third parts of my Estate, both of Land and goods [to] be equally devided vnto my four Children, *John, Mary, Elizabeth* and *Susana*, provided, my Sonne *John* shall have Liberty to reserue the Land to himselfe, and pay his sisters the valuation thereof, vpon a Just apprizement. My will is, that my Sonne *John* shall haue after my wife's death that third pᵗ of house and Land wᶜʰ she in her lifetime is to enjoye, and this to be an Addition to his portion, and to him only, provided, [that if one or more die before they inherit, their portion be divided among the survivors.] I have some Estate at Lancaster, in Land. I Leave it in the Liberty of my wife and other friends, who may be advised with therein, to sell it or not sell it, as shall be thought best. *Isabell* my wife, executrix, with the help and advise of *Edward Clapp* and *John Capen*, Deacons of the Church at Dorchester, with whome she shall Advise and not to act without theire Consent.                                                                  EDWARD BRECKE.

In pʳnce of
*John Capen, Samue Rigbes*, who deposed 11 Decʳ 1662.

Inventory of the Estate of *Edward Brecke*, who depʳted this Life the 2ᵈ of Novʳ 1662, apprized by *Edward Clap, John Capen, Jno. Minott*, 20 Novʳ 1662. Mentions " one *tyde Mill*, with the house over it, and yᵉ Implements belonging to it, and one spare stone, £100."

An Inventory of the house, land and other goods of *Edward Brecke*, belonging to the estate at Lancaster, prised by *John Prescott, James Atherton, Ralph Houghton*, 20 : 9 ᵐᵒ 1662. Amᵗ £81 6ˢ 6ᵈ.
Amount of Estate at Dorchester, £665 5ˢ 9ᵈ. Total sum of Estate, £746 12ˢ 3ᵈ. Debts and legacies to be deducted, £139 12ˢ 2ᵈ.
*Isable Brecke*, Relict and Executrix, deposed 11 : 10 ᵐᵒ 1662.

JOHN CULLICK. Will. I, *John Cullicke*, of Boston, being sicke, I give vnto my sonne *John Cullicke*, £150, of Lawfull money of New England to be payd him at the age of 21 yeares. Vnto my dau. *Mary Cullicke*, [and to] my dau. *Elizabeth Cullicke*, £150 [each] to be payd at the age of 21 years or day of marriage. To my wife, *Elizabeth Cullicke*, my sole executrix, the rest of my Estate. My friends *Capt. John Leverett and James Penn*, both of Boston, overseers. 22 Janʸ 1662.
                                                                  JOHN CULLICK.

Wittness, *Jno. Leverett, James Penn,*
    *Increase Mather*, who deposed 27 Janʸ 1662.

An Inventory of the Estate of Cap$^t$. John Cullicke, taken 10 Febr. 1662, by *Edward Hutchinson, Thos. Brattle.* Am$^t$, £ 972 13$^s$ 08$^d$. Mentions "$\frac{1}{4}$ p$^t$ of a vessell at sea, whereof *Sam'l Gallop* is master." *Mrs. Elizabeth Cullicke,* executrix and Relict of Cap$^t$ John Cullicke, deposed, 19 March 1662.

JANE POPE. I, *Jane Pope,* of Dorchester, widdow, in good health, make my Will, 18 Aprill 1662. Debts payd, and funnerall discharged, my will is, (my Estate being Justly prised) that my dau. *Patience Blake,* shall have £40, at her own disposing, vnto her children, when it shall please God to take her away by death; if she dye before they Come to Age and make noe will or disposall thereof, then my will is that it be equally diuided amongst her Children as they come to the age of 16 years, each Child.— But if my dau. *Patience* Live Longer and at Last make a disposall of it, then it shall be in her power to dispose of it to her Children as she shall Judge meete. For the other part of my Estate over and above this forty pound, my will is y$^t$ it be equally devided amongst the Children of my dau. *Patience,* only *Jane Blake,* her Daughter, shall haue fiue pounds more than any one of the other Children. My will is that *Mary Blake* have my feather Bed and bolster and Bible as p$^t$ of her portion, and my pewter shall be divided betweene *Sarah* and *Jane* as part of their portion. If any of y$^e$ Children dye, those y$^t$ survive shall have it equally betweene them, and at y$^e$ age of 16 years each child have y$^e$ benefitt of theire portion for theire owne Advantage, and in y$^e$ meane time he or they in whose hands this Estate shall remaine shall giue good security for y$^e$ p$^r$formance of the premises. *John Capen* and *John Gornell,* overseers.

My sonne in Law, *Edward Blake,* executor.       JANE POPE.

     In presence of
*John Capen, John Gornell, Mary Capen, Increase* X *Clap. John Capen* and *John Gornell* deposed, 28 Jan$^y$ 1662.

RICHARD DAVIS. *Richard Davis,* of Dorchester, being weake, make my Last Will. Vnto my wife, £20, in such goods as she shall choose, to be foreuer at her disposall. Moreover I give vnto her so much more out of my Estate as will make vp y$^t$ £20, one third p$^{rt}$ of my whole Estate, to haue during life, after her death my will is, y$^t$ all but y$^e$ £20 shall returne to my Children. I giue unto my sonne, *Richard,* two p$^r$ts of the Remainder of my Estate, and to my dau. *Sarah,* one part of my Estate, vnless my wife be with Child, and then my will is, that my sonne *Rich'd* have y$^e$ other halfe of my Estate, and the other two (if so) y$^e$ other halfe of my Estate, and my will is, y$^t$ my whole Estate remaine in y$^e$ hands of my wife for y$^e$ bringing vp of my children, until my dau. Sarah haue attained y$^e$ age of 18 yeares or day of marriage w$^{ch}$ shall first happen, then she shall haue her portion, the rest still to remaine with my wife vntill my sonne, *Richard,* haue attained y$^e$ age of 18 yeares, and then he shall receiue his portion, and my will is, he shall haue all my houseing and lands wheresoeuer they lye, for his portion, he paying to his mother what they come to above his double portion. My will is, y$^t$ if my wife shall marry, and after her marriage my overseers see Cause, for any reason, to take off my children for the said children's good and place them elsewhere, then, in such case, I giue to my overseers full power not only to take off y$^e$ children, but theire portions also to be Imployed at their discretion, for my childrens best good. If either of my Children dye before they Come to receiue theire portions, then the surviving Child shall have the deceased child's portion. My desire to my dear wife is yᵗ she will act nothing off moment without ye advise of my overseers, and in speciall, not to sell any Land without theire approbation, but if they approve of it, and Advise thereto, I give her full power to sell one pᵣcell of Land in Roxbury, being about 20 accres Lying nere some pᵣte of *John Welds* Farme. I make my wife my executrix, and I Intreate my friends, *John Minott* and *Daniell Preston*, to be my overseers. 20ᵗʰ Feb. 1662. RICHARD DAVIS.

In presence of

*Hopestill Foster, Henry Garnesey,* who deposed 19 March 1662.

Inventory of the Goods and Estate of *Rich'd Davis,* who died the 6ᵗʰ of Mʳch 166 ⅔, taken and apprised by *Daniell Preston* and *Tobias Davis,* 13ᵗʰ day of the same month. Amᵗ £346 14ˢ 1ᵈ. Debts due to be payd out of the Estate £22 7ˢ.

*Sarah Davis* deposed 19 March 1662.

6ᵗʰ Sepᵗ 1665. At a Meeting of yᵉ Magistrates and Recorder in Boston. Whereas *Richard Davis,* late of Dorchester, by his Last Will, bearing Date 20ᵗʰ Feb. 1662, appointed *Sarah,* his late wife, to be Executrix to his sᵈ will and provided in case she married, she should only have £20, and the Rest of his Estate in such case should bee to his 3 Children, and whereas, the sᵈ *Sarah Davis* hath not long since intermarried with *Samuel Chandler,* with whom shee Lived not above 35 weeks. The Magistrates and Recordᵣ Judged it meet to Graunt Administration to the Estate of the Late *Richard Davis,* unto Mr. *Jno. Mynott, Daniell Preston,* the two overseers of the Last Will of sᵈ *Richard Davis* and *Tobyas Davis,* his Brother, the sᵈ *Samuel Chandler* having Consented hereunto, bringing a true Inventory of the Estate remaininge, and satisfying said *Chandler* the summe of £20 out of that Estate, and to dispose of the Children of the sᵈ *Richard Davis,* &c.

Inventory of the Goods and Estate of sᵈ Davis as they remayn since the Death of his Relict, *Sarah Chandler,* who Dyed in August 1665, taken 31 (8) 1665, by *John Capen sen.,* and *Thomas Weld.* Amᵗ £291 10ˢ 3ᵈ. Debts due, £5 18ˢ. *John Minott, Tobyas Davis,* and *Daniell Preston.*

*Preston,* deposed, 2 Novᵣ 1665. Mentions *Joseph Wise* and *Robert Seaver,* of Rocksbury, *Enoch Bolton.*

JAMES DAVIS. Power of Administration to the Estate of yᵉ Late James Davis is granted to *Johannah,* his Relict, in behalfe of herselfe and Children.

Inventory of the goods prised by Henrey *Bridgham, John Wiswall,* 25 : 8 : 61. Mentions house and land at sentere hill, and mode [muddy?] river, 6 acres at Spectercell Island, &c. Amᵗ £236 3ˢ.

Inventory of the Estate Allowed *Johannah Davis,* wife of James Davis, 25 : 11 : 1661. Signed by *Josh. Scottow,* and *John Wiswall.*

Johannah Davis deposed 15 Feb. 1661.

Mentions *Jno. Wing,* yᵗ married one of yᵉ daughters of sayd Wm. Davis. Renounct any title to yᵉ estate yᵗ Johanna Davis brought in as belonging to her in trading.

JACOB LEAGER. Will. I, *Jacob Leager,* give to *Anna Leager,* my wife, the third part of my Estate during life ; to my two dauˢ *Bethiah Leager* and *Hannah Leager,* the other two-thirds, to be equally divided betweene them, wᶜʰ they shall possesse at eighteene years of age, or in case of marriage before said terme, they shall possesse at the time of marriage, till which time, it shall be at the disposall of my executors or Administrators to be disposed of for them for theire maintenance, or best Improvem$^t$ for theire Advantage. I will that the third part I give my wife during life, at her death shall be equally divided betweene the children, whether house, Land or moveables. I will that my wife possesse all the moveables till the Children Come to age, provided she give bond that they be forth Coming at said time. If one of my children dye before marriage, the other shall possesse all that was hers. In case they both dye before marriage, halfe of it shall be equally'diuided among my sister *Maries* Children, in England, and of the rest of it, I give to *Jacob Walker* £10 ; to *Joseph Walker* £10 ; to *Elisha Thurstun* £10 ; and that which remaines shall be given to an Alms house. I will that the morter and pestle and two great pewter platters shall be given to my dau. *Bethia*, and the other two great pewter platters shall be given to my dau. *Hannah*, as part of their thirds, and to my second wife's children, I give 12$^d$ a piece to be paid them at their demand. I hereby Impower *Mr. William Parks*, Deacon of Roxbury, and *Robert Walker*, of Boston, to see this will p$^r$formed. Nov$^r$ 10$^{th}$ 1662.

JACOB LEAGER.

Witnesses, *John Drus,*
*Jacob Walker, Benjamin Thurstun.*
The latter two deposed 19 March 1662. Power of Administration granted to Anne his Relict.

Inventory of the Estate of *Jacob Legare*, of Boston, taken 12 March 166$\frac{2}{3}$, by *Thomas Dyon.* Am$^t$ £ 182 05$^s$ 03$^d$. *Anne Leager*, deposed, 19 March 1662.

ROGER WHEELER. 18: 10: 1662. Power of Administration to the estate of the late *Roger Wheeler*, is granted to *Mary Wheeler*, his Widow, in behalfe of herselfe and Children.

Inventory of an estate in the hands of *Mary Wheeler*, widdow, and late wife of *Roger Wheeler,* deceased, the most part of which estate belonged unto the said Widdow *Wheelers* former husband, *John Ston*, who died intested where there was noe lawe, by whom she had one child, which is yet living. Whole summe is £118 18$^s$ 02$^d$. Appraisers, *Francis Hooke, John Phillips, Daniell Turell, Nathaniell Addams.* 2$^d$ May 1662, *Mary Wheeler,* Relict and Administratrix of the estate of the late *Roger Wheeler*, deposed. Mentions *Tho. Ashley, Mounten Rivedon.*

JAMES JEMPSON. 21 : 11 : 1661. Inventory of the goods of *James* Gimson, lately deceased. Am$^t$ £65 17$^s$. Debts due, £10.
Witnesse, *Abell Porter. Henry Alline.* Power of Administration to the estate of the late *James Jempson,* is granted to *Sarah,* his Relict, 1 Feb. 1661, when *Sarah Jempson* deposed.

RICHARD EVANS. Inventory of the Estate of *Richard Evens*, of Dorchester, deceased, taken 11 : 12: 1661, by *Richard Withington, William Pond, John Gornill.* Am$^t$ £170 2$^s$ 6$^d$. Debts due the estate, £5 10$^s$ — from estate, £30 1$^s$ 6$^d$. 20 Feb. 1661 Power of Administration to the estate of Richard Evans, granted to *Richard Evans*, his eldest sonne, in behalfe of himselfe and the rest of his Brothers and sisters. *Richard Evans* deposed.

GEORGE PEARSE. Inventory of the goods of *George Pearse,* deceased, taken by *Edward Raynsford, Daniell Turell, Henry Rust.* Am^t £79 07^s 08^d. Power of Administration to the estate of *George Peirce,* of Boston, Smith, granted to *Mary,* his Relict, in behalfe of his wife and sonne, 29 April 1662, when *Mary Pearse* deposed.

RICHARD HAWES. An Inventory of the estate of *Richard Hawes,* of Dorchester, deceased, taken 27 : 11 : 1656, by *Joan Humfrey* and *Hopestill Foster.* Am^t £ 151.12.08. Mentions meadow in calves pasture about 6 acres, land by *Tolemans,* &c. Debts due to William Billing, Mr. Patten, Sam^{ll} Jones, M^{rs} Stoughton, Richard Baker, Sampson Mason, Ensigne Foster, William Clarke, John Wiswall, Leiftenant Clap, old Nathaniel Wales, George Dier, Theodor Atkinsons, John Farnum, M^r Allcock, Goodn. Vmphrys, Richard Dauis, M^r Holloway, Thomas Swift, Thomas Tolman, Richard Euins, Richard Curtis, Obidiah Hawes, M^r Jones, Goodm: Morrill, William Weekes, Henry Garnsey, Mr. Westman of Waimoth.

At a County Court held at Boston, 29^{th} of Aprill 1662. The Court being informed that Major Atherton and Cap^t Clap as friends to the deceased Richard Hawes of Dorchester took some care about the estate, binding and placing out y^e children, the Major being since dead, Cap^t Clap tendering to give *Obadiah Hawes* sonne to the late Richard Hawes, on account thereof, on request of s^d *Obadiah,* the Court judgeth it meet to grant Administration to the Estate of the late Richard Hawes to *Obadiah Hawes,* his sonne, in behalfe of himselfe and the rest of his Brothers and Sisters. *Obadiah Hawes* deposed same day.

DORMAN MATHUE.—An Inventory of the Goods & Chattells of *Dorman Mahoone.* Appraised by *Rich^d Sanford & James Hawkins,* 12^{th} Aprill, 1661. Amt. £112 01^s. Administration to the estate of *Dorman Mathue,* als. *Mahoone,* granted to *Mary** his Late wife, 17 May 1661.

RICHARD GARRET.—Inventory of the Estate of *Mr. Richard Garret,* who departed this Life, the 29^{th} day of M'ch 1662. Appraised by *Thomas Hatson, John Peas.* Amt. £66 08^s 08^d. *Lydia Garret,* relict of *Richard,* deposed 20^{th} July 1662.

By the Court, *Robert Lord.*

THOMAS FAXON JUN^r.—Brantry 6^{th} : 4^{mo} : 62. Inventory of the Goods & Estate of *Thomas Faxion, Iunior,* deceased 25^{th} : 3^{mo} : [62]. Amt. £225 17^s 6^d. Attested by *Gregory Belshar, William Robinson, Edmund Quincy, Anthony Fisher.* Administration granted to *Thomas Faxon, Senio^r, & Anthony Fisher Iunio^r,* that Marryed one of the Daught^rs of s^d Faxon senio^r. they being Impowered to dispose of s^d fower Children according to theire best judgemen^ts. Giving security, &c.

Anthony Fisher deposed 29 July 1662. Debts due to Roger Billing, Will Pen, M^r Tho: Clarke of Boston, M^{rs} Scott, Goodman Chapen, Rob^t Pond, &c.

JOHN NORTON. I, John Norton, of Boston, at p^rsent in good health, yet not vnmindful of mortalitie, especially being put in remembrance thereof by the Considerations of what changes are Incident, by reason of my

---

* On the original, this is blank, but the record reads Mary.

Call vnto England. In Case God shall take me out of this life, I doe dispose of that outward estate wherewith I am now possessed, as followeth: —Vnto my Brother, M^r *William Norton*, of Ipswich, in New England, I Giue the sixe acre lot, so called, Lying within the Common fence, be it more or lesse, and the three aker lot, so called, lying in the Town be it more or lesse, both which at present, are in his occupation. I giue also vnto him all that house lot containing two acres, more or lesse, which I bought of *Matthew Whipple*, deceased, and is now in the occupation of Goodman *Annable.* Also, vnto my said Brother, *William Norton*, that one hundred pounds due vnto me for my house in Ipswich, which M^r *Cobbett* now dwelleth in; or if that one hundred pounds be not payd vnto him w^th in three monthes space after legall demand made by him, vpon the knowledge of my decease, I then give vnto him the house itself, with the yard, yards, orchard or orchards, and rest of the land lying vnto the house as an house lot or bought since of M^r *Baker.* I meane all that, and only that, which was sold vnto M^r *Cobbet*, conceiving my title therevnto to be good, vpon default of non-payment. Also, vnto said Brother, £10, in currant money of New England, to be payd him within three months after my decease. I giue vnto my euer endeared & Honoured mother £30, of current money of England, to be payd vnto her use in London, at my Brother, M^r *Thomas Nortons* house, within three years following my decease, after the proportion of £10, per annum. To my two sisters, *Mrs. Martha Wood,* and *Mrs. Meary Young*, to each £10, in current money of England, to be payd within one yeare after my decease, at my Brother *Thomas* his house, in London.

I desire my Brother, *Mr. Tho. Norton*, and my sister, *Mrs. Elizabeth Norton*, either of them to Accept of a Gold Ring of 40^s price, for w^ch end I give £4, in Current English money to be paid vnto my Brother Tho: and sister Elizab: by the first opportunity after my decease. I giue, vnto the poore of Boston, £10, to be payd within three moneths after my decease. I intend this ten pounds to the poore of the church in Boston whereto I am an Vnworthy officer. The rest of my estate, except two pounds reserved for two ouerseers, I giue vnto my wife, *Mrs. Mary Norton*, namely, my farm at Ipswich w^th the dwelling house, barne or barnes, outhouses or whatsoeuer belongeth therevnto, also the sixe acre lott which I bought of *Goodman Dane*, also my dwelling house in Boston, w^th all the land be it one acre more or lesse, with whatsoeuer else belongeth therevnto. I Give vnto her, also, all my household stuffe and furniture whether plate, bedding, linnen, pewter, Brasse, Iron, or what kind soeuer. Also I giue vnto her, besides the £340 w^ch I haue in England, three hundred whereof is due vnto hir, during hir life, in the hands of *Captaine John Leveret*, and my Brother, *Mr. Thomas Norton*, or in the hands of whomsoever they, or either of them, according to my order, haue disposed it vnto. I Giue also vnto hir, £117. 10^s of current New England money, now in the hands of *Mr. John Paine*, merchant of Boston, also, what the said *Paine* oweth me vpon the account of 500 acres of land sold vnto him by me, for £50; or, whatsoeuer more is owing to me by *Mr. Epps*, of Ipswich; also, I Giue hir all the money which I left w^th hir in the house, provided, that after the decease of my wife, I give my farme at Ipswich, w^th the dwelling house, [&c] with the sixe acres I bought of *Goodman Dane*, vnto the children of my Brother, *Mr. William Norton*, to be divided equally amongst them, his eldest son having a double portion out of the same, and himself, if he survive my wife, I meane my brother *William*, if he surviue my wife, to Enjoy the same vnto his owne vse during his naturall life, then to be diuided amongst his children as is before sayd. My library I leaue vnto my wife, also, so as if she shall neede and see cause, she may make the best of it for hir owne vse, otherwise my desire by these to hir is, that if any of my brother *William* sonnes be trained vp unto the ministry then to bestow it on him or them so Educated : but this hauing thus farr signified my desire I leaue wholly vnto hirselfe, securing myselfe that she will not be wanting to Answer my true Intent heerein.

I make my wife, *mistris Mary Norton*, sole executrix. I desire my good freinds, *Mr. Rawson* secretary and *Elder Pen* to be my ouerseers, and to accept as a testimony of my thankfulness to them of fiue pounds apiece, which ten pounds my will is shall be payd vnto them, within three moneths after my decease. [Signed] 14th January 1661.

In the p'sence of                                             John Norton.
John Wilson, Junior
James Johnson.
    John Wilson, Jun., deposed 12th June 1662. *James Johnson*, on the 16th April 1663. Will recorded on the 17th.
                          Edward Rawson Recorder.

Inventroy of the Estate of the late Reuerend Mr John Norton, Teacher of the Church of Christ in Boston, taken 24th April 1663, by *John Leverett, Wm. Davis, Hezekiah Vsher.* Amt. £2095. 3ª. " In his study, his library consisting of one hundred fifty nine bookes, in folio, at £187. 19ª," "fiue hundred seaventy Bookes into 4° 8° 12° at 4ª one wth another, £112. 1ª," " fowr pictures, Luthr Beza, fox, & mapp of the world," &c. &c.

DAVID EVANS. 30th June 1663.—I *Dauid Evans*, of Boston, mrchant, make this my last will. Vnto my wife, *Mary Euans*, one third of all my estate, for her owne proper vse, during the time of her widdowhood, and in case she marryes Before the Children Come of age, then I giue her £150. Vnto my eldest son, *Dauid Evans*, my Dwelling house and ground therunto belonging. Vnto my son, *Jonathan Evans*, my warehouse and ground therunto belonginge, and Sixty pound Estate, besides the warehouse. Vnto my dau. *Mary Evans*, £150. Vnto my dau. *Elizabeth Euans*, £150. Vnto my Brother, *John Clark*, as a token of my loue, £5. Vnto my Servant, *Nath : Sellicke*, vpon his faithful discharge of his seruice, £10. Unto *John Mellowes* his Children to be Diuided equally betwixt them, £10. Vnto my maid seruant, *Jane Tucker*, £5. If there be any remaineing of the estate, my will is, it be equally deuided beetwixt my Children. In Case any of the Children dy beefore they come of age, then my will is, yt the Estate shall fall vnto those that remaine, and to be equally Diuided. I leaue all the estate unto my Executrix and Executors for the Education of the Children till they Come of age or are married, and then their Portions to be paid unto them. I giue unto my Executor £10 apece as a token of my loue ; to my ouerseers, £5 apeece as a token of my loue. My wife, *Mary Evans*, my Executrix, and my trustie and well be loued friends, *Mr. Peeter Olliver* and *Mr. John Joyliffe* to be my Executors, and alsoe Disier that *Capt. Jeames Olliuer* and *Capt. Thomas Lake* maye be the Ouerseers of this my will. 13 June 1663.
Witness *Samuell Scarlett*                               Dauid Evans.
    John Freake
    Arthur Mason
    Richard Price.

[*Peter Oliver* and *Richard Price* testify before Court, 30 July 1663, that *Mr. David Evans* gave his wife £150 over and above her thirds, &c. &c. as expressed in the will. The same day, *Peter Oliver, Richard Price,* and *Jno Freake,* deposed.]

Iventory of the Goods & Estate of M<sup>r</sup> Dauid Evans aprized by *Capt. James Johnson & Sergant Thomas Clarke* 10 Aug. 1663. Amt. £860. 6. 3.

A list of Debts hoped Good :—Richard Greene, John Mallowes, Robert Howard, John Thomas, William Peck, Mathew Hawks, Peter Goose, Samuell Linckhorne, Robert Cutt, Cap<sup>t</sup> Jonson Roxbury, John Sampford, Rise Jones, Robert Williams, Joseph Moore, William Ballintyne, Nathaniell Renolds, Antipas Boyce, Goodman Lion, Benjamin Gilliam sen, goodwife Wiatt, Daniell Cushin, Jonathan Raynsford, Abraham Newell, Major Winslowe, John Bushnell, John Pease, Greenleafe y<sup>e</sup> dyer, Robert Hindsall, Robert Gibbs, John Blacklidge, George Vick<sup>r</sup>y : Hull, John Grafton, Capt. Sam : Winthrop, Elijah Corlett, John Sund<sup>r</sup>land, Robert Codman, Robert Nanny, Thomas Andrewes, Joseph Bemis, John Webb, M<sup>r</sup> Mitcheson Cambridge, Cap<sup>t</sup> Clarke, John Gard, Eva<sup>r</sup>ll shoomaker, Nicholas Padge, Insign Phillips, goodwife Shearman, Edward Battey, John Lowell, Maddam Eva<sup>r</sup>d, Ralfe Parker, John Allden, John Hole, Peter Woodward, Elizabeth Pecke, Peter Oliuer, John Benham, John Mellowes, Joseph Peck, William Trobridge, Anthony Ellcocke, James Olliuer, Dauid Sellecke in Barbadose. Whole amt. £643. 3<sup>s</sup> 2<sup>d</sup>.

Debts doubtful.—Deborah Skillinge, Nathaniell Starkye, William Phillips, Thomas Jonson, Eds-all y<sup>e</sup> turner, John Raymond, Samuell Eds-all, Deane Winthrope, William Olford, Jonathan Sellecke, John Payne, Henry Pease, Mordecaye Crevard, Robert Drew, Tho. Davis, John Richbill. Whole am<sup>t</sup> £195. 19. 8½. John Coth<sup>l</sup> Dr. £130.14.1.

[Signed by] Mary Euans, Peter Olliuer, John Jo ·life, who deposed 31 Oct. 1663.

MR. WILLIAM OSBURNE. Inventory of Estate of William Osburne late deceased, prised p<sup>r</sup> *Mr. Richard Milles,* & *Mr. John Cooper,* Apr<sup>ll</sup> 29 : 1662. Suma total is £260.16<sup>s</sup> 01<sup>d</sup>. *James Bishop,* secretary.

Inventory of the house, land, and ¼ p<sup>rt</sup> & of A Catch & Goods, prised 22 Aug. 1662, by *Joseph Rock,* and *John Sunderland.* Am<sup>t</sup> £836.07.05. 110 Acco<sup>r</sup>s at Wenham, 5 Acco<sup>r</sup>s at Dorchester, &c. (See Reg. for 1851, p. 334.)

26 Aug. 1662. Power of Administration to the estate of the late *William Osborne,* of Boston, deceased, Granted to *Freesweed,* his late wife, in behalfe of herselfe and five children.

10 Sep<sup>t</sup> 1662. On the motion of *Mr. Rich'd Collicot* in behalfe of *Freesweed Osborne,* widow, & hir five children, It being alleadged that the Eldest sonne was brought vp in learning & had tooke one degree, & therefore desired that he might haue but a single portion with the rest. The Court ordered, that the widdow shall after all Debts be payd & satisfyed be allowed one cleere third part of the estate, reall & p<sup>r</sup>sonall, and then the rest of the estate to be devided amongst the fiue children, part & part alike, she giving in security to the Recorder to respond the Childrens portions at theire severall ages as the Law directs.

Edw : Rawson Record<sup>r</sup>.

# ABSTRACT FROM THE EARLIEST WILLS ON RECORD IN THE COUNTY OF SUFFOLK, MASS.

ALLICE GREEGSS, of Boston. Will. 20th: 5: 1662. Being now sick, In case my son, *James Greegss,* Come not, my will is that I giue to my grand Child, *William King,* one half of the ground, that half the barnes stands on, by the *Widow plantons* [Blantons?] ground, and my will is, that my dau. *Sarah Burgiss,* shall haue the new end of the house and three rodd broad quite throw the loatt, alsoe the other old end of the house and the rest of all the ground belonging to it. My will is, that it shall be equally giuen to my daughters children; and my dau. *Sarah Burgiss,* shall haue the Cow, & in Case the Cow haue a Calfe the said *Sarah Burgiss,* is to keep him 5 weeks and then to giue it vp to her sister, *Ann Joaness.* And all the rest of the moueables, wich are nott in my husbands will, doe I giue equally to my tow dau⁸ and to their Children, and my dau. *Sarah* is to haue the Better partt wich is to the value of 40ˢ. 20: 5: mo. 1662

Witness to these. *Alice + Greegss.*
*Gamaliell Waite, Richard Price.*
*Richard + Gredle.*

1 May 1663. Power of Administration to the estate of the late *Alice Griggs* is Graunted to *Robert Lattimore,* in right of *Anne,* his wife, & to *Roger Burgis,* in right of *Sarah,* his wife, daughter to yᵉ late *Alice Griggs,* according to the Imperfect will on the other side as their Guide.

Edw. Rawson Recorder.

Inventory of the goods and Chattels of *Alice Greegss,* widdow, deceased 26th 5th mo. 1663, prised by *Rich Gridley, Henry Allen,* 1 May 1663.

At a Meeting of the Magistrates and Recorder in Boston 5ᵗʰ Septᵗ 1665, (present *Fra. Willoughby* Esqʳ Depᵗ Govʳ, *Maj'r Leverett* & Recorder.)
Whereas *George Griggs,* Late of Boston by His Last will and testament gaue unto His sonne, *James Grigges,* his House & Ground about it, with the two acres of Land at Long Island, as also a Feather bed, Bolster, as in that will Date 4 July 1655 & prooued in Court 3 Augᵗ 1660, since when, *Alice Grigges,* His Widdowe, tooke vpon her to Make Her will & therein to make Diuision of the House and Ground amongst Her Daughters & their Children, on which the Courte 1 of May 1663 graunted Administration to the estate of the Late *Alice Grigges* to *Robert Lattimore* in Right of *Anne,* his Wife, & *Roger Burgisse,* in Right of *Sarah,* his wife, ordering the Imperfect Will of said *Alice Grigges* to bee their guide. since when, *Sarah Burgis,* Being Deceased, & *Robert Lattimore.* & *Ann* his Wife. Objecting against the Mothers Diuision and power to Make it, & no Certaine Information of the Death of. the said *James Grigges,* though hee hath Been absent for many yeares, & most probable that hee is Dead, not being heard of for seuerall yeares.
The Magistrates Judged it meet to Graunt administration to the estate of *James Grigges,* to *Robert Lattimore,* in Right of *Anne,* his wife, & the Children of her Bodye, by her former & this Husband, to their use & benefitte, & also to *Roger Burges,* in right of the children of *Sarah,* His

216

late wife, & her former Child, *William King*, and the children he Himselfe had by *Sarah*, His wife, in equall proportions. The House, Lands & goods of the s$^d$ *James Grigges*, to be equally Diuided to the said *Robert Lattimore* & *Roger Burges* in Right & for the Benefitte of their seueral Children as above, they giuing their owne Bonds, to ualue of £80 apeice, & obliging their seuerall Diuisions of Land & Housinge, to the Recorder of this Countye, on Condition that in case *James Grigges* shall euer appear in this Countery & Challenge His Just Right, they shall Respond the same to Him. And it is Desyred that *Ensigne John Hull* & *Richard Gridley* make a Just & equall Diuision of the Houseing, Lands & goods for the ends aforesaid & signifye the same to the Record$^r$ to bee Recorded.

Edward Rawson Record$^r$.

[*Richard Gridlee* and *Henry Rust*, at the request of *Roger Burgisse* and *Anne Latimer*, prized a few articles, Amount £1. 18$^s$, Sep$^t$ 6$^{th}$ 1665. To this inventory *Roger Burgisse* " Deposed on his Corporall Oath," the same day.]

Boston Septemb$^r$ 6$^{th}$, 1665.

Wee whose names are heerunto subscribed, being appointed to Diuide a House & Land & Betwixt *Roger Burgesse*, in Behalfe of the Children of *Sarah*, his Late wife, Deceased, And *Robert Lattimore*, in behalfe of *Anne*, his said Wife & her Children, haue appointed as Followeth (uiz.) That *Roger Burgesse* shall haue for his part, the Dwelling house, & the East part of the Land, being in front to the Towne street, on the north, about 79 Foote. And Likewise Fronting on the towne Common to the East, 162 foot, & on the south, Bounded by the Land set out to s$^d$ *Robert Lattimore* 150 Foote. The said *Robert* hath his p$^r$tion appointed, fronting northward to the towne streete, about 98 foote, And on the west, Bounded by the Land of Widow *Pheebe Blanten*, about 310 foote, And Southward by the towne Lane, about 268 foote, the Easterne & other northern side of the said Land abutteth vpon the Land of the s$^d$ *Roger Burgesse* aboue expressed. All Being by Consent of all the said p$^r$ties, who Haue likewise heervnto subscribed. And for the other small portion of goods being some Few tooles, a bed Blankett, Couerlead & Table, being Formerly all Ualued but at 44$^s$, the said parties concerned haue ordered their parts to their Owne Content, This Being the summe of what seemeth necessarye relating to the premisses, & the trust now Committed unto us by the Honoured Court, Wee make this o$^r$ Returne to y$^r$ Worshippes now sitting in Court.

Resting y$^r$ Humble Servants

{ *John Hull*,<br>{ *Richard* ✕ *Gredlee*.

The two Acres at Long Island is Likewise by Consent to bee Kept Between Both Partyes, not so Meete to Diuide.  }  Consented as { *Robert Lattimore*<br>abous$^d$ p$^r$ us. { *Roger Burgess*.

HENRY BLAGUE. Inventry of the Goods, Chattells & Creditts of *Henry Blague*, of Boston, Brickburner, deceased, praised 2 Aug. 1662 by *Richard Collacott*, *Samuell Sendall*, and *Richard Gridley*. Am$^t$ £464.12.09.

19 Aug. 1662. Power of Administration to the Estate of Henry Blague granted to *Elizabeth*, his Relict, in behalfe of herselfe & seven children. She deposed the same day.

**JOHN JARVIS.** Sep^t 26, 1656. Inventorye of the Estate & wrightings of *Mr. John Jarvis*, deceased, being taken according to order of Co^rt—as also wrightings of other Gentlemen left in his Custody, w^ch after viewing were delivered To the s^d Gentlemen. Imprimis—wrightings of *Mr. Rob't Patteshalls*, viz. Two Journalls, one Invoice booke, Two Ledgers, as also severall other Looss acco^ts & bills of Lading belonging or referring to the s^d bookes, all w^ch were delivered To the s^d *Mr. Rob't Patteshal*, "wompom & pege in the Hands of *Ann Carter*, about Eleven shillings.". Whole am^t of Inventory, £24.14.3½.

"Debtes owing by *Mr. Jno Jarvis*.—To *Wm. Blanten* for Diet 24 Weekes at 7^s p^r weeke," &c. &c. whole am^t of debts, £19.06.09.

**ELIAS PARKMAN.** Inventory of the estate of Elias Parkman supposed to be deceased 28 of July 1662, prised p^r *William Bartholomew, Thomas Rallings,* who deposed 30 : 5 : '62. p^r *Eliazer Lusher.*

Boston 20 Aug. 1662. One Request of *Bridget Parkman*, Relict of *Ellias Parkman*, of Boston, senio^r & her Eldest sonne, as she affirmed, power of Administracon to the Estate of s^d *Ellias Parkman* is granted to *Thomas Rawlings,* in behalfe of the Children & Credito^rs, allowing the widdow her thirds in house & Lands, and the flocke bedd Rugg to value 2^lb 10^s, s^d *Rawlings* Giving security to the Record^r to Administer according to Law. Edw^: Rawson Record^r.

[Rallings bond is on file, dated 25 Aug. 1662. Am^t £32. Witnessed by *Joseph Hills, John Ferniside.*]

**WILLIAM ROBINSON.**—12 Sep^t 1662. Pow^r of Administracon ( "to the Estate of *Wm. Robinson*, Late of Barmudas") is Granted to *Wm. Pearse,* in behalfe of the wife of said Robbinson & theire Children, & for paym^t of his debts, &c.

*William Robinson*, of Barmodos, departed this life the third day of Sep^ber 1662, in Boston in New England, having due to him the one third part of Twenty Barrells of Mackerell in partnership with *Richard Moore* and *Rich'd Toowills,* fishermen, the w^ch share all charges of Boat hier, Salt Caske & bread deducted his partners value at £4.16^s &c. Sum total £8.3^s 2^d.

Estate Deb^r to *Richard Moore* & *Richard Toowill* for money Lent & provisions to him at the Eastward, 5^s 9^d; to *John Bateman,* for Indian dishes w^ch he carryed to Barmodas, 6^s; to said *Bateman* for goods out of his shop, 18^s; to *William Pearse* for dyett; to Phisick to *Mr. Hale* and *Mr. Stone,* to Candle light in time of sickness; to Beere to those that Stretcht him forth; to the Pitman & toleing the Bell; wyne at his burryall, recording his death, money Lent him by *An Pearse,* &c. Whole am^t £4. 13^s 5^d. Remains to ballance £3 09^s 09^d. *William Pearse* bound in the sum of £8 to Administer on the Estate.

**JOHN HAZARD.** Inventory of the Goods of *John Hazard,* who is supposed to be Cast away by shipwracke in *Mr. Hannifords* shipp. Prised y^e 4^th of y^e 7^th (62) by *Richard Gridly,* & *Henry Allen.*

10 ; 7^ber (62.) Administracon to the Estate of *John Hazard* Granted to *Mary,* his Relict, who deposed.

**RICHARD FLOOD.** Inventory of the Estate of *Richard Flood,* deceased, prised 8 : 7^mo 1662 by *Henry Allen,* and *Edward Drinker.* Am^t £26 5^s 6^d.

218

Power of Administracon to the estate of the late *Rich'd Flood* Granted to *Joseph Gridly*, who marryed *Lydia*, the Relict of said *Rich'd Flood*.

The Court also ordered that the s<sup>d</sup> *Joseph Gridly*, for his keeping the 2 Children of *Rich'd Flood* & his p<sup>rt</sup> of the Estate in Right of his wife, the said *Joseph* shall have the house & Land & all ther the Estate, he paying the fower Children of s<sup>d</sup> *Floods* £4 apeece at age of 21 years. Reserving liberty to one or other of the children on theire being at Age to pay the said *Joseph Gridly* £22 in behalfe of himselfe & broth<sup>rs</sup>, the s<sup>d</sup> house to be theirs, otherwise not.

Edw: Rawson Record<sup>r</sup>.

)Then follows a list of "Things that are Left & not seene, but only Judged at from theire reports to vs."(

DAVID KELLY. Power of Administracon to the Estate of the Late *David Kellie* is Granted to *Elizabeth*, his Late wife, in behalfe of her selfe & children.

Inventory of the Estate taken by *Richard Dauenport*, *Elias Maverick*, 22<sup>d</sup> 8<sup>mo</sup> 1662. Am<sup>t</sup> £286 5<sup>s</sup>. *Elizabeth Kelly* Relict, deposed, 23 Oct. 1662.

At a County Court held at Boston 29<sup>th</sup> July 1663, *Elizabeth Kelly* sent in a Copie of hir husbands Invento<sup>r</sup>y & desireing a Just diuision of the estate, the house being burnt & much Goods, the Court on hir request mad y<sup>e</sup> orde<sup>r</sup>.

It being sufficently knowne that the house wherein the said *Elizabeth Kelley* liued tooke fier in the day time & was so furious in its burning, before help Could Come, as consumed at least fifty pounds of the goods in the Inventory Exprest, the which the Court Considering, on the motion of the Widdow for a Just divission of that. Estate. It is ordered that the fifty pounds in Goods mentioned, be deducted from the principle some, & the Widdow be allowed one third part of what Remaines, the rest to be diuided amongst the fiue children, the Eldest sonne to have a double portion, the rest, part & part alike. )Said Elizabeth with the house & land, in Boston, bound, for the security of the children's portion.(

SAMUEL ROBINSON. Inventory of the Chattells & Estate of *Samvell Robinson*, prized by *James Johnson*, & *John Lake*, 29<sup>th</sup> July 1662. Sume is £10 12 10<sup>d</sup>.

Inventory of Goods p<sup>r</sup>sented by *John Robbinson* Administrato<sup>r</sup> to the Estate of *Samuell Robbinson*, prised by *John Wiswall* & *John Lake*, 4: 8<sup>mo</sup> 1662.

*John Robinson* deposed 28 Oct. 1662. )He testified that there was an uncertainty as to the return given in, by reason of some claymes made for what he )Samuel Robinson( traded vpon, being vpon trust from my father and oth's, and also in p<sup>r</sup>tnership, cannot be resolued, vntill accounts be cleared, w<sup>ch</sup> being to be done in England must crave longer time."(

*Mr. Thomas Robbinson* came into the Court and Renounct his being Administrato<sup>r</sup> to the Estate of his late sonne, *Sam'll Robbinson*, w<sup>ch</sup> was accepted of by the Court, & he discharged. 28 Oct<sup>r</sup> 1662.

DANIEL DOVENIES. Inventory of the Goods of *Daniell Dovenies*, deceased being in the keeping of *John Farnam* senio<sup>r</sup>, praised by *Michaell Wills* & *Thomas Watkins*.

19 Dec. 1662. Power of Administration to the Estate of *Daniell Dovenses*

an Irishman, is Granted to *John Farnum* senio^r, in behalfe of the friends of the said *Dovenies*. *Jno Farnum* senio^r deposed. )His bond is on file.(

2 Feb. 1662. )*John Farnum* testifies that, according to his understanding, it was stated " by some that vnd^rtooke to plead *Benjamine Gillams* Case, that *Mr. Benjamine Gillam* by his Acco^tt vnder his hand, owned himselfe possesst of" money belonging to the estate of *Dovenies* which was accordingly entered on the inventory, the same day.(

JOHN MARSHALL. 28 Jan. 1662. Power of Administration to the Estate of the Late *John Marshall,* of Barnstable, in old England, deceased is Granted to *John Sweete,* of Boston, in behalfe of the next of kinn.

An Inventory of the Estate apprised by *Richard Cooke, John Blake.* 18 Aug. 1662. Amt. £60 14 7½. Debts due to *John Sweete,* — (am^t £7 1^s.) who deposed at said time. )There is on file the bond of John Sweete to Edw^d Rawson to the am^t of £73.4.3, together with his house & land to be held for the faithful performance of said obligation. Signed by John Ferniside, W^m Charde. 2d Feb. 1662.(

THOMAS HOUCHINE. 28 Jan. 1662. Pow^r of Administracon to the Estate of *Thomas Houchine,* deceased, Granted to *John Sweete,* of Boston, in behalfe of the next of kinn.

Inventory of Estate apprised by *Richard Cooke,* and *John Blake,* 18 Aug. 1662. Amt. £19.18^s. Debts due the deceased by the Estate of *Moses Row,* by *John Sweet,* from one *Carr* of Road Island. *John Sweete* deposed on the day above said.

MOSES ROW. 28 Jan. 1662. Pow^r of Administracon to the Estate of the Late *Moses Row,* deceased, graunted to *Jno Sweete,* in behalfe of the next of kinn. )John Sweete's bond is on file to the amt of $36 7 9. 2 Feb. 1662.(

Inventory appraised by *Richard Cook* and *John Blake,* 18 Aug. 1662. Amt. £29. 5^s 3^d. Debts due from *John Sweete,* and *Henry Puddiford;* to *Jno Sweete, John Marshall, Thomas Houchine.*

*John Sweete* deposed 28 Jan. 1662.

JOHN SAMUEL. Inventory of the Goods of John Samuel deceased the 8 10^mo 62, prized by *James Johnson, John Morse.*

Mentions " the Ende of a house Joyneing to *William Avery,* £20 "; in *Anthony Newlands* hands, £5; in *Goodman Lovells* hands, £1 3^s ; in *Pr. Peter Oliver's* hands, £3 2^s 9^d.

*Jabesh Eaton* deposed 26 Feb. 1662.

RALPH WOODWARD. Inventory of the estate of *Ralp Woodward* of Hingham, deceased, as it was apprized by *Cap^t. Joshua Hobart & Deacon John Leauett,* of Hingham.

8 Acres of Land lying at a place Commonly called the world's end, £24 ; 4 acres to the east of *John Ferings* house lott, £12 ; 20 acres lying by glad tydings plaine, £20 ; one acre of upland bought of *Clement Bates,* £2 ; 6 acres by waie mouth River next *Thomas Huetts* land, £25 ; 2 acres one Warsall hill next *John Ferings* land, £6 ; salt marsh next *Thomas Linkcolns* land, bought of *Edmund Hobart senior ;* marsh adjoining *John Towers* marsh, &c., &c.

11 April 1663. Power of Administration to the estate of *Ralph Woodward* graunted to *John Smith,* of Hingham, who married *Sarah* the only

Daughter of said *Ralph Woodward*, in hir Right and Right of their Children. At the same time, *John Smith* deposed.

PETER GRAY. Accompt of the Debts of *Peter Gray*, late Deceased, who liued in the town of Brantre, and in the house of *John Basse*. Debts due to M͏ͬ *Allcocke* and others. Administration to the Estate granted to *Deacon Sam^l Basse* in his own & *Sam^l* & other Credito͏ͬˢ behalfe. 28 April 1663. *Deacon Sam Basse* deposed on y^e Daye aboue said.

WIDDOW WILSON. An Inventory of what estate wee *William Alis* and *Francis Eliot* did find in Brantrey to belonge to the widow *Wilson* late of Brantrey.
Money in hands of *David Walsbee*, put out to *John Woord* for 4 years · £4 in hands of *John Gurney*. *Francis Eliot*, of Brantre, deposed 30 April 1663.
The Court accepted the Care and Indeauors of *Francis Eliot & W^m Ellise* & order that y^e Estate in the hands of said *Elliot* be p^d Equally to the Children of said widow *Wilson*, [charges deducted and a due proportion of the £4 allowed them with other creditors to y^e late *John Gurney's* estate.]

JOHN OLIVER. The Estate of M͏ͬ *John Oliver*, deceased, by appraisment amounted in y^e yeare 1646 to £180. Advanced since by Improvement £181 6 4. The Executrix has one third, *John Oliver*, the Eldest Son, a double portion, *Thomas Oliver* [deceased] ⅙ part, *Elizabeth Wiswell*, ⅙ part. The Estate of *Elder Thomas Oliuer* disposed otherwise, soe that nothing Comes to this Estate from thence. The Executrix paid the Eldest son *John*, out of the produce of said Estate.
[A Division of £309 was then made between the executrix and heirs. Signed by *Peter Oliuer* and *James Johnson*. The Court allowed the accompt and Diuision of the Estate, 14 May 1663.]

JOHN.GURNEY, Brantry March 16^th 1663. An Inventory of the Goods and Estate of *John Gurney sen^r*, deceased, taken by *Gregory Belcher, Edmund Quincy, Thomas Faxon.* Am^t £55 14 6. Debts due from Estate to Peter Brackett, Joseph Adams, Francis Nucomb, John Dassit, sen., Goodman King of Waymuth, Goodman Baly, John Mills John Cleverly, Smith, Collins at Boston, &c., &c.
M͏ͬ *Sam. Broadstreet & M͏ͬ Richard Wharton* deposed to the Inventory giuen in to them by the widow or friends of s^d *Gurney* and subscribed by *Gregory Belcher* &c., w^th w^ch they haue added a true Inventory of that Estate to their best knowledge.

JAMES BATHERSTON. 12 Dec. 1663. Pow^r of Administration to y^e Estate of *James Batherston*, late Mariner in y^e Catch Returne, being not heard off for a six years, & supposed to bee dead, is Granted to *W^m Gibson*, his Kinsman, He Going security to Administe^r thereupon According to Law, to Satisfy all debts, & to p^rserve y^e Remaind^r fo^r s^d *Batherson* if ever he Returne, or otherwise, to such as shall Appeare to y^e County Court to have most Rights thereto.
[*James Batherston* was a partner with *Peter Oliver* in the Ketch Returne. *W^m Ballintine* demanded a letter of Atturney, which was granted.] *W^m Gibson* deposed 12 Dec. 1663.
[Bond on file of *W^m Gibson*, of Boston, shoomaker, and *Oliuer Purchase*,

Hamersmith, of Lynn, in the County of Essex. Witness, *Peter Oliuer, Daniell Vernon.*]

ROBERT BILLS. An Inventory of the houshold stuffe & goods pertaineing to *Robert Bills*, who deceased Decemb. 15, 1635.
Mentions, *Goodman Hazard, goodman Kingman, James Clearke.*
A note of Charges attending his sickness and burial signed by *Ralph Sprague, Robert Hale.*
1 8 1638, *Samuell Peirce* affirmed vpon oath, that *John Knowls* married the widow of *Ephraim Davies* & so hee was alowed to administer of the estate of *Robert Bills* marriing his sister.

JOHN COGGAN. *Joseph Rock* bound in the sum of £200 to administer on the estate of *John Coggan*, and *Martha* his wife, 24 Feb. 1662. Witness, *Sam^l Sendall, John Ferniside.*

WILLIAM JOHNS. 11^th June 1663, Powe^r of Administration to the Estate of *William Johns*, of Hingham, deceased, hauing no Relations left in y^e Country as knowne, is Graunted to *W^m Woodcocke*, in behalf of himself & such othe^r's as the Court shall Judge to haue any Right thereto, giuing security to Administer according to lawe. Edw. Rawson Record^r. Inventory of the Estate taken 5 June 1663. Am^t. £65 16 6. *W^m Woodcock* deposed 11 June 1663.

CORNELIUS THAYER. 3 [?] 3 1663. Invoice of the Goods of *Cornilvs Tayer*, deceased taken by *John Holbrook, Thomas White*. Am^t. £34.
25 June 1663. Powe^r of Administration to the Estate of *Cornelius Thaier*, late of Weimouth, is Graunted to *Richard* and *Zackerias Thayer* his brethren in behalf of themselees & the Rest of his brethren & sisters. Estate creditor to the amount of $218 15 1. *Richard Thayer* deposed.
The names of M^r Edward Ting, M^r Brattle, Rich: Wharton, goodman Kingam, goodman Barges, David Randall, goodman Fry, Gregory. Belcher, are mentioned.

# ABSTRACTS FROM THE EARLIEST WILLS ON RECORD IN THE COUNTY OF SUFFOLK, MASS.

[Prepared by Mr. WILLIAM B. TRASK, of Dorchester.]

WILLIAM BLAKE.—The last will* and testament of *William Blake* (being of perfect memory and vnderstanding, the good Lord God be blessed and praised therfore,) made the third day of September, in the yeare one thousand six hundered sixtie and one, as followeth.

Imprmise : my will is, yᵗ my body be desently buried in hope of a ioyfull resurection at the last day. It. I giue and bequeath vnto the towne of Dorchester, twenty shillings, to be bestowed for the repairing of the buring place, soe yᵗ swine and other vermine may not añoy the graues of the saints : prvided it be repaired within one yeare after my decease. The rest of my land, goods, and estate, after my funerall exspenses and debts discharged, my will is, and I doe giue and bequeth vnto my fiue children the one halfe of my lands, goods and estate, to be equally devided amongst them, by equall portions ; not that I disrespect my eldest sone, for he hath ben and is, soe dutifull a child vnto me as any of my Children, but, because he hath least need of it, and he hath noe Charge. The other halfe of my lands, goods and estate I doe giue and bequeth vnto my beloued wife, and doe make her sole executrix of this my last will and testament : And I doe intreat my beloued brethren, brother *Edwarde Clapp*, and *John Capen*, yᵗ they would be pleased to be the ouerseers of this my last will and testament, to se yᵗ it be fullfilled and prformed. Finally, my will is, yᵗ my wife doe not dispose of any of her estate, left her by this my last Will and testament during the time of her life, without the advise and Consent of my ouerseers and my foure sones, or the maior parte of them : yet neverthelesse, in her last will, she may dispose of it vnto whom shee please. In witnes hereof I haue herevnto sett my hand and seale : In the prsence of *John Capen.*

Jnᵒ *Minott,*

who deposed 28 Jan. 1663.

Inventory taken 6th Novr 1663 by *William Sumner, James Humfrey.* Amt. £224. 12.

Mrˢ *Agnes Blake* deposed 29th Jan. 1663, to this estate of her late husband.

---

JOHN MEARES.—Boston: 26 : 7ᵐᵒ· 1663. I, *Jnᵒ Meeres*, lying sick—declare this as my last will, if no other after this doe appeare. I make my dear Vnkell, *James Johnson*, executor of this my last will. I giue to my wife, *Mary*, my dwelling house during her life, & if she marry, her next husband to give to her Child she now goes wᵗʰ, yᵉ said house & ground, & after both her & her childs decease, then, to my two brothers, or yᵉ survivor of them. Moreovr, I giue to my beloved wife, yᵉ bed I now ly on, wᵗʰ all yᵉ furniture thereto belonging, six greene Chairs, a round table, and two paire of sheets, besids them I had with her, with a Long table in the house. To my father *Meares*, my best suit and Cloak, and four Cord of wood, with my Weding hat. To my dear mother

* This is an *entire* copy of the will of William Blake, from the original, on file. T.

*Mears*, my Chest of drawers, two paire of sheets, and bed ticking. To my brother, *Samuell Mears*, a pair of blew Curtains & my 2ᵈ suit and Coat to *James Meers* with my musket and arms ; to my wife, all the rest of my estute.                                         John Meers.

Witness, *James Johnson, James Oliver.*

Moreovʳ wee, *Elizabeth Meers* & *Mercy Meeres*, testify yᵗ he declared this to bee his meaning, yᵗ his child if it liue to yᵉ age of 20 yeares, or att age, it shall injoy ½ yᵉ house during yᵉ Mothers life, & all after her decease ; in case of yᵉ childs death, *Mercy Meers* to have it for her life.

*Capt James Oliver* deposed, 5 March: 63.

Whereas it was desired by *Mrs Sands* & others of yᵉ friends of the dec⬛⬛d *Jno Meares*, that there might be a meeting together Conserning some expretions in his will, ,It was declared by both Capt. *James Johnson* & *Elizabeth Mears*, yᵗ wh⬛⬛as it is expressed yᵗ yᵉ howse is giuen to his wife dureing life and if s⬛ marry, her next husband to giue it her child she now goes with, & after both her & her childes decease, to his two Brothers : yᵉ true words & minde of yᵉ deceased was howeuer not soe clerly exprest, that his wife was to haue the howse dureing her life, & if she should marry an other husband she should not haue power to giue it to any other child she might haue, but it was giuen by this will to the Child yᵗ she went then with, & to yᵉ issue of yᵗ child foreuer, & in case she should liue longer then yᵉ childs coming to age, yᵗ at age he or she was to haue possession of one halfe, but if she dies before yᵉ child comes at age then yᵉ whole benefit to be to yᵉ vse of yᵉ child & his or her issue immediately after yʳ decease.

1 December, 1663.

This was done & expressed in yᵉ presence of *John Wiswall, Edw. Hutchinson, Elizabeth Mears, James Johnson.*

*Capt. James Johnson, Elizabeth Meares* mother, & *Mary Meares* late wife to *Jnᵒ Meares*, deceased, deposed 5ᵗʰ March 1663.

Inventory of the Estate prised 6ᵗʰ : 10 mo : 1663, by *John Lake, Edward Drinker.* Amt. £231. 01. 1. Mentions, " his Wedding Hatt, £1. 10s." " one Hatt Case, 1s. 6d." Captᵗ. James Johnson deposed, 5 March 1663.

---

Tʜᴏᴍᴀs Gᴜʟʟɪᴠᴇʀ.—Power of Administration to the estate of the late *Thomas Gullife*, of Brantrey, deceased, is graunted to *Prudence*, his relict, & *Jonathan*, his elder son, they bringing in an inventory of that Estate, &c.

---

Rᴏʙᴇʀᴛ Lɪɴᴄᴏʟɴᴇ.—Inventory of the Estate of Robert Linchorne late of Winnisemet, within the pʳcincts of Boston, deceased, prised by *Elias Mavericke, Samuell Dauids, Aaron Waye*, 18 : 3 mo : 1663. Amt. £192. 13s. 09d.

*Anne Lincolne* deposed 29 July 1663, to the estate of her late husband.

---

Gᴇᴏʀɢᴇ Dᴏᴅ.—[Mary Dod's petition to the Court is on file. In it she represents that her husband, *George Dod*, " som yeares past departed this life in London, in England, leving with me fouer smale Children to take care for." She states that having made inquiry into his debts and credits, she " finds that his debts far exceed his credits & estate," " his Credits being all desperate debts, lying mostly in Virginia & som in New England, but all of them in such hands as that he in his life time could not get any of them." She therefore desires an allowance out of said estate, &c.

31 July 1663. The Court allow her the best bed boulster, one pillow, one p$^r$ of blanketts, Rugg, bedsteed & Coard, & £5, in money. Administration on the estate was granted to *Richard Way* and *Edward Blake*, who gave a bond, which is on file, to the amount of £40. This obligation is witnessed by *Sarah Wilson* and *Perin Rawson*—date 11 Aug. 1663.]

Inventory of the goods & credits of *George Dod*, of Boston, marriner, deceased, praised by *Thomas Rallings, Richard Way, & Edward Blake*, 26$^{th}$ July 1663. Amt. £23. 13s. 10d. *Mary Dod*, relict of the late George Dod deposed, 31 July 1663.

---

SAMUEL MAVERICK, JR.—14$^{th}$ March 1663. Power of Administration to the estate of the late *Samuell Mauericke Jun$^r$*, of Boston, is Granted to *Rebeckah Mauericke*, his relict, w$^{th}$ *M$^r$ Moses Mauericke, M$^r$ John Wisewall, & M$^r$ Anthony Cheeckley*, in behalf of h:rself & children w$^{th}$ the Credito$^{rs}$ to that estate they bringing in an Inventory of said Estate, &c.

Inventory of said Estate apprised by *Mr John Winslow Senr & Jn$^o$ Farnham*, 28$^{th}$ March $\frac{63}{64}$. Amt. £127. 10. 2$\frac{1}{2}$. *M$^r$ Jn$^o$ Wiswall & M$^r$ W$^m$ Bartholmew* deposed 4$^{th}$ Nov$^r$. 1665.

28 : 5mo. 1665. Vpon Information from *Mr Jonathan Rainsford* that the Chamber Door was Broken up where some goods were left, whereof the Key was lost, &c. [Several articles are then enumerated.] 2 (7) 64. A note was made of what was wanting upon the reueiw of the Inuentory Immediately upon Mrs Mauerickes going out of the House, who was one of the Administrators, formerly. Amount £32. 8s. 4d.

---

ROBERT NANNY, of Boston, being weeke in bodie—make this my last will. 22 Aug. 1663. Debts and funerall Charges be discharged and in particular there being an estate in my hands in partnership betwixt my Vnckle, *Richard Hutchinson*, of London, and my selfe, my will is, that the houses and land I haue at Barbados, as also gouerner *Searle's* bills, of three hundred pounds maye be giuen and made ouer to my Vncle, *Richard Hutchinson*, of London, to ballance all accounts betwixt us, only what is more then will pay him, as I hope there will, the ouerplus to be returned to my executrix. Unto M$^r$ *Maho*, M$^r$ *Madder*, and M$^r$ *Powell*, officers of the new Church in Boston, each 20s. Unto my wife, *Katherine Nanny*, one third of the rest of my estate—the other two thirds to my Children, vizt. son *Samuel*, and dauter *Mary*, and to the Child my wife now goes withall, being yet vnborne, to be equally deuided into fower partes, two partes to my sonne *Samuel*, the other two parts to my other two Children, to be equally deuided. In Case of the death of any of my Children, the Estate of such Child or Children to fall to my wife, who I leaue soll executrix, and desire her care in the bringing vp of my Children, for w$^{ch}$ End I leaue there whole Estates in her hands, and she to haue the use of it for there education and bringing vp, untell they Come to the age of 21 yeares or day of marrage, w$^{th}$ Consent of there mother ; and I request my honered father in law, the Reuerent *Mr John Whelewright*, Pastor of Salseberry, and my louing brother in law, *Mr Sam: Whelewright*, of Wells, to be ouerseeres of this my will, and to assist my Exsequetrix what they Can in her busenes. Robert Nanneye.

*Samuel Hutchinson, John* + *Stones* mark.
*James Mattoek.*

*Samuel Hutchinson* and *James Mattock* deposed 7 mo : 63.
Inventory of the estate of *Robert Nanny*, taken 10ᵗʰ Sept. 1663. Amt.
£1089. 14s. 4¼d. Mentions " dwelling house, warehouse & wharfe, yards
& other privillidges bellonging to the house neare the Draw Bridge, £300 ;
the Red house and land neare to Charlestowne ferry, £200 ; one parcell
of land neere adjoining to the said Red house lately Bought of leut
*Wᵐ. Phillips*, £60."
The property was aprised by *John Joyliffe* and *Robert Pateshall*, 6ᵗʰ
of Oct. 1663. *Katherine Nanny* deposed, 31ˢᵗ Octʳ. 1663.

THOMAS LEADER.—I, *Thomaˢ Leader*, of Boston, 17 Octʳ. 1663, make
my last will. Vnto my wife, *Ales Leader*, the Dwelling house I use to
lett out, ouer Against the house Called *Allcockes* house, with the yard as
it is now fenced, with an Adititon of land to be more layd Vnto itt out of
my Garden & Orchard, that is to say, from the outwardmost post of the
Crosse fence next the lane to Draw a straight line quite Cross the Orchard
through to my Neighbour *Sanfords* ground, I giue all the aboue mentioned, for her life, my son, *Samuell*, to sett and keepe the house and
fencing in good Repayre all time of her life at my son, *Samuells* Cost,
and after her Decease, I giue all the aboue mentioned, vnto my Grand
Child, *Thomas Leader*, the son of my son John, deceased, to him and his
heires for Euer, and to haue it putt Into good Repayre for him by my
said son *Samuell;* further my will is, that my grand Child, *Thomas Leader*,
shall pay out of it a legacie vnto my Grand Child, *Abigal Leader*, his
sister, within one yeare after he posses the aboue mentioned premisses,
the sum of fowre pounds. Vnto my son. *Samuell Leader*, all my now
dwelling house, as also the New house adjoining, with all the appurti-
nances therevnto belonging, with Garden and Orchard and yard therevnto
Bellonging, Excepting that part aboue mentioned wich I giue vnto my
wife & grand Child, with this prouisiall, yᵗ if my son *Samuell* Die without
issue male, to yᵉ next A kind [of kin ?] in Case of Necessity, my son,
*Samuell*, Finishing yᵗ house Adjoyning to yᵉ house I now dwell in. I
give A liberty to sell either that or yᵗ I now dwell in, wᵗʰ halfe yᵉ Ground,
prouided the ground laid to what house yᵗ he doe sell may bee laid out to
as little damage to yᵗ house & ground that shal bee preserved as may
bee. Unto my wife, £4, in Money & goods, to bee payd by my son,
*Samuell*, within A yeare of my departing this world. Vnto *Rebecka*
Leaderʳ, My Grand Child, £6 to bee paid by my son, *Samuell*, in Like
paymᵗ. in money & goods, wᵗʰin [a] yeer after my decease. Vnto my
wife, yᵉ best Shett, yᵉ prouisions left in yᵉ house, & five Cord of Wood.
All my tooles & debts, & otheʳ Estate not Mentioned, I give Vnto my
Son, *Samuell*, he Bestowing A decent Buriall Vpon this poore body of
mine. My son, *Samuell*, sole Executor. My will is, that my executoʳ
should faithfully pay all yᵉ Legacies & what I have in my will Ingaged
him to doe, or else, Vpon not paymᵗ, My wife or Leagices oʳ their Assignes shall Enteʳ Vpon what I have given vnto him till they bee sattisfyed. *Jeames Penn*, yᵉ Ruling Elder of Boston, overseer.
    Wittnesses, *Jer: Howchin.*                          Thomas × Leader.
    *Jo. Endecott, Junior, Samᵘ Wheelwright*, who deposed 3ᵈ Novʳ. 1663.
    Inventory of *Thomas Leader*, prised, 5ᵗʰ Novʳ. 1663, by *John Button,*
*Tho. Mattson, Hugh Drury. Samuel Leader* deposed, 29 Jan. 1663.

## ABSTRACTS FROM THE EARLIEST WILLS ON RECORD IN THE COUNTY OF SUFFOLK, MASS.

[Prepared by Mr. William B. Trask, of Dorchester.]

Edmund Grosse.—I, *Edmund Grosse*, of Boston, giue the bigger halfe of my now Dwelling house to my son, *Isaack*, and the lesser halfe of my house to my wife, Bieing the better p^t thereof, for my wife to Inioy her life time and then to Returne to my daughter, *Susan*. I giue my best suit & cloake to my son, *Isaack ;* my dau. *Susan*, my second Cloake ; my best sease coat to my wife ; my sixe acres of marsh & ten acres of upland that lyeth at Rumney marsh, Equeally to be diuieded bettwene my son, *Isaake*, & my dau. *Susan*. I giue my 50 acres of land that lyeth at mudey Riuer to be equally deuieded betweene my wife and fiue Children, proportionably.

Wittnesses—*Edmund Jackson,*                                Edmond Grosse.
*Francis Hudson, Edward Yeomanes.*

3 May 1655. Power of Administration to the Estate of *Edmund Grosse*, In Behalfe of the widdow & Children, graunted to M^r *Jereny Houchin* & Lefte *James Johnson. Edmund Grosse*, creditor, 29^th April 1655 to *Capt James Oliuer*, & M^r *William Cotton*. In his account he mentions M^r Edmunds, M^r Simeon Kemthorne, John Barnes, Cornelius, Tho: Watkins, M^r Ting, Leuet Bud, M^r Waldrene of Newichaneck, M^r Colchester of London, William Hubborn, " my sister *Mary Grosse*," " my Brother *Edw : Weeden*."

---

John Stone —I, *John Stone*, of Hull, being sick—make this my last will—to my wife, *Jone Stone*, My house & housing, w^th all my Lands, Cattle, boats, debts, & whatsoev^r estate I have, making her my sole executrix. My will is, y^t my wife shall pay out of my estate, £60, to my broth^r *Simon Stones* Children, w^ch some time lived in Cousingtone, in Sumersettsheire, in old England, In consideration of same Acco^t that was betwene him & I, when I Lived in England, w^ch I know not whether it was all paid o^r not, & this £60 to bee p^d to y^e three Children, £20 Apeece ; but if any of them bee dead & leave neither wife nor Children, then to be paid to y^e other, w^thin one yeare after my Decease, Vpon lawfull demands.                                5^th of May 1659.

Witnesse, *Nico : Baker, Nathani ll Bosworth*.          John + Stone

27 Jan. 1663, *Nathaniell Bosworth*, deposed.

Inventory of the Estate of *J hn Stone* who Deceased December 23^d 1663, as apprised p^r us who subscribe, Jan. 13^th, *Nathaniell Bosworth, Nathaniell Backer*. Amt. [£369. 7.] Debts owing by John Stone, " in England," " to our minister," " to Charles Kymball, M^r Lewes, Henry Chamberlaine, Goodwife Dauis, M^r Luke, widow Johnson, Armatage the Taylor, John Tuker, John Faroh, Thomas Dyer. [in all, £70. 14s.] June 8^th 1665, *Joane Stone*, deposed.

[In the appraisement are mentioned 9 Acres of Land at alder point, Sagamore Hill, 12 Acres at petocks pond, Brusters Iland ; a Bill of *John Batmans*, a Bill of *Thomas Joyes*.]

---

Charles Grice.—I, *Charles Grice*, of Braintree, being very weake of Body but of p^rfect Memory, make this my last will. All my goods unto my wife, *Margery Grice*, during her life for A support & sucker to her in her old Age, whom God hath continued w^th mee now this Thirteene yeares to bee help full & servisable to me in my Aged & helplesse Condition. My Will is, that when it shall please God to take my beloved wife out of this wourld that then I give Unto *William Owen* all my lmovable estate, for y^e space of three yeares, as A token of my love for his fillial care & love exprest to me in my Aged condition, in w^ch three yeares my son may prepare & come hither, if he like my Motion. My will is, y^t y^e contents of this my will, be sent into England, to my son, *David Grice*, Vnto whome (after three yeares injoyment of my estate by son in law, *William Owin*) I doe give all my Immovable estate, provided he doe come ov^r to New England for it, w^thin y^e space of three yeares After y^e death of my s^d wife, *Margery*. My will is, y^t if my sone, *David Grice* doe Refuse to Come to New England, that then it bee certified to My Brother *John*, o^r *William Grice*, y^t if one of their sons doe Come ov^r to New England, that then he y^t Cometh over shall Injoy all My imovable estate, But if Neither of My Brothers soñes doe Come, within y^e space of three yeares, after Notise, that then I doe give All My lmovable estate Vnto My son in law, *William Owen*, his heires & Assignes for ever. I doe make my wife, *Margery*, my sole executrix.

9th Novemb^r 1661.

In y^e p^rsence of us,                                  Charles ✕ Grice.
  his mark.
*Peter* ✛ *Brackett*, *Barnabas* ✕ *Dorifield*,
*David* ✕ *Wallsbe*.

12^th of Nov^r 1663, *M^r Henry Flint* and *Peter Brackett* deposed.

Braintry, 9th : 9th : 1663. Inventory of the Goods & Estate of *Charles Grice*, Deceased 10^th of October 1663, attested by *Samuell Bass* and *Edmund Quinsey*. Amt. £92. 13s. 6d.

12 Nov^r 1663, *Margery Grice*, deposed.

---

ROBERT GAMLEN, late of Roxbury, being sicke, make this my last will. Vnto my son, *Benjamin Gamlen*, all my house & Lands in Roxbury to him & heires for ever to possesse Imediately After my decease, vpon y^e Conditions hereafter expressed. I doe heareby Injoyne my sonne to lay into y^e farme yearely so much good hay, at his own charge, as shall sufficiently winter two Cowes, & Also liberty for two Cowes to goe freely into any of y^e s^d Land to pasture, at all such times as is conueniant for feeding, winter & suñer, & also liberiy of housing & yard to keep y^e said Cow for y^e use of my wife, *Elizabeth*, so long as my s^d wife shall live. I injoyne my son to deliuer vnto my said wife, yearely, twelve bushills of good Merchantable wheat, two bushills of pease, & six bushills of Indian Corn, also, to provide & lay down by my dwelling house so much wood as my wife shall need to burn, also my wife to Injoy all y^e dwelling house, except y^e new end of y^e said house, during y^e time of y^e life of my said wife, Also halfe of y^e oarchard. My said son is to pay my son in law, *Isack Chevery*, soe much as one Acre of my salt Medow shalbee valued at. I doe order my said sonn, *Benjamin*, to have my two oxen & my Mare as his owne, w^th this provisall, that my said wife have y^e vse of y^e said Mare to Ride vpon as oft as shee shall need her, this said Mare & oxen to bee praised in y^e Inventory, & my will is, y^t if my wifes necessity should call for y^e value of y^e Mare & oxen, all or parts of it, by y^e advice of mine ov^rseers it shalbee paid vnto my said wife, by my sonn, *Benjamin.* All yᵉ rest of my Moveable goods I give vnto my said wife, *Elizabeth,* whom I make my sole executrix. I request my beloved friends, *William Parke & John Bouls* to bee ovʳseers of this my will. Thus have finished my will, in yᵉ best Manneʳ as I Am Able, this 3 day of August 1663.

In yᵉ pʳsence of *Christopher Peake.*　　　Robert + Gamlin.
*Edward Morris,* who deposed 28 Jan. 1663.

Inventory taken 22 : 9 : 1663, by *William Parke, John Bowles, Robert Searer.* Mentions land " neer yᵉ house of *Abraham Hows,*" " neere *Ed. Bridges* house." *Elizabeth Gamlen* deposed, 28 Jan. 1663.

---

WILLIAM WARDELL.—A Contract made between *William Wardell* on the one pʳte, & *Elizabeth Gillit,* Widdow on the other pʳte, before their ioyning in mariage, being the fourth day of December 1657, is as followeth :—First, that what estate the said *Elizabeth* was possessed of before her mariage was to bee at her disposeing at the time of her death or at the mariage of any of her children, and for the howse and land that now the said *William Wardell & Elizabeth,* his wife, doth posses, it follow by course of law to *Hannah Gillit,* daughter to *John Gillit,* who was the former husband to the abouesaid *Elizabeth,* now the wife of the said *William Wardell.* The said *William Wardell* did then ingage for and in Consideracoñ of the said howse & ground to traine vp the said *Hannah Gillit,* being then about two yeares old, that at the day of her marriage, or at the day of the said *William Wardells* death, to give vnto the said *Hannah* the value of sixteen pounds, which was then to the full vallue of the said howse & ground, the howse beeing much decayed & ready to fall ; this is truth, as witnes our hands.

Witnesse, Seth Perry, John Perry.　　　William + Woodells
3 Nouember 1663.　　　　　　　　　　　Elisebeth + Woodell

The Court allowed of this Couenant only wᵗʰ Consent of *Wᵐ Wardell ;* ordered yᵗ said *Wᵐ Wardell* in full sattisfaction of yᵉ old house, yᵉ Ground of sᵈ *Gillett* to be held & Converted to the vse of said *Wardell* & his heires; ordered that he bring vp *Hannah Gillet* & when she comes to be of age shall pay hir twenty one pounds for the same.

Edw : Rawson Recordeʳ.

---

JEREMIAH STEVENS.—15ᵗʰ of October 1663. At a meeting of the magists. who being Informed by *doctoʳ Clarke* yᵗ yᵉ late *Jeremiah Stevens* desir'd that Administration to his estate might be Graunted to *Sʳ Thomas Temple & Mʳ Jnᵒ Jolyffe* that so they might take Care of his Estate & Convey it to his father. [Administration was Graunted to said individuals.]

Inventory of the Estate of *Jeremiah Stephens* deceased taken in Boston, 17ᵗʰ Octʳ 1663, by *Hezekiah Usher, seinnoʳ, Tho. Lake.* Amt. £72. 4. 11½ ; of this amount, £68. 17. 5. were in books, 122 in number. The names of 38 are given.—*John Joylyffe* deposed, 28ᵗʰ of Octʳ 1663, *Sir Thomas Temple,* 3ᵈ Octʳ 1663.

---

DAVID ABERCROMBY.—5ᵗʰ March 1663. Power of Administration to yᵉ Estate of yᵉ late *Dauid Abercromby* is Graunted to *Amos Richardson,* in behalf of himself & otheʳ Creditoⁿ &c.

ABSTRACTS FROM THE EARLIEST WILLS ON RECORD IN
THE COUNTY OF SUFFOLK, MASS.

[Prepared by MR. WILLIAM B. TRASK, of Dorchester.]

JOHN RUGGLES.—24. 12ᵐᵒ 1657. I, *John Rugles*, of Roxbury, senioʳ,
being att this time in health, yett being old, not knowing yᵉ day of my
death, doe make this my last will. Vnto my wife, *Margery*, one Cow,
which she shall Chuse out of all my Cows, & yᵉ best paiʳ of sheetes vnto
herselfe, to dispose of as she please, yᵉ sheats she brought with her to
me, I Meane yᵉ best pair. Vnto my wife, £4 pʳ yeare, to bee paid by
mine executoʳ in wheat, 30ˢ. in Indian 30ˢ, in barly or Mault 20ˢ, to be pd
quartʳly, if she desire it, in any sort of grain, as is expressed—to bee
paid att yᵉ now dwelling house of yᵉ sᵈ Ruggles. My will is, yᵗ my wife
shall have yᵗ bed wᵗʰ yᵉ furniture about it wᶜʰ we vsually ly vpon, wᵗʰ two
pair of shets, wᶜʰ my wife shall Chuse, these two pair to bee hers as long as
she shall live in this wourld. Vnto my wife, foʳ yᵉ time of her Widdow
Hood, all yᵉ old end of my house wherein I now dwell, provided my son
have libʳty to bake in yᵉ ovens, togetheʳ wᵗʰ halfe yᵉ brass & pewteʳ, old
hodgsheads, tubbs, sets, Chaires, stooles, Chests & such like things, to bee
vsed wᵗʰin dores, togetheʳ wᵗʰ Convenient out housing foʳ hay & Cattle
things foʳ two Cattle, & liberty foʳ hoggs, in season, & foʳ foules to kp
within yᵉ hen house, allwayes provided, yᵗ damage may bee prevented as
much as may bee, togetheʳ wᵗʰ half yᵉ orchard & spott of Meadow my
heire shall divide at, & she shall chuse wᶜʰ part to have, it being by my
heir putt into two parts; also, an Acre & a halfe in bare Marsh, lying
next *Robt. Gamlin*, also halfe an acre of salt marsh lying next *Tho:
Watʳman*, in gravily point, also twenty rod of mudy on hills to sow flax
in, if she desire it, & to have it in yᵉ most convenient place for yᵉ benifitt of them both; also my son to Cul out & bring whom my wife five
load of wood, every year, & to lay it in yᵉ most convenient place we
now lay wood in, & this to be done every yeare in season most fit for hiʳ
Comfort, yᵉ sᵈ Loads of Wood to bee sufficient loads wᵗʰ two good Oxen
& a good Horse; also, my son shall Mow, Make, & bring home all heʳ
hay, every yeare in season, yᵗ grows on heʳ land, & my son shall keepe
all houses in Repair, excepting fire. Also, I give vnto my wife, during yᵉ
time of her Widdowhood, pastoʳ for one Cow in my [underbrush ground?]
at home. All my houses, lands Cattle, monie, not before expressed, vnto
my son, Jnᵒ *Rugles*, whom I make my sole executor. My sᵈ son to enteʳ
vpon emediately afteʳ my decease, to him & his heires foʳ evʳ, vpon these
Conditions. 1: yᵗ my son shall make good my Will in paying all my
debts, leagesies, funerall expenses, & vnto my Wife wt I have injoyned
him to doe for her, but if my sᵈ son shall not, or will not, in season
pʳforme according as is formeʳly expressed, then I impoweʳ my wife, wᵗʰ
Advice of my ovʳseers, to enteʳ vpon my part of my lands, from time to
time to sell & pay my wife what shall bee due to her, wᵗʰ all cost, charge
& trouble about yᵉ same. My will is, yᵗ my servant, *Samuell Pery*, shall
serve out his time accordjng to his Indenture with my sone, *John Rudgles*.
I hereby Injure my sᵈ son, to pʳforme my part of his indenture vnto my
sᵈ servant, hoping my sᵈ son will vse him well vnto yᵉ satisfaction of my
ovʳseers, but if he shall neglect to doe, I give poweʳ vnto my overseers to

place him elce where, so as he may be well used, but if my son keep him out his time, then my will is, yᵗ my son shall Add vnto my sᵈ ser- vant, beside wᵗ I am Ingaged vnto in his Indenture, £3, in Country pay, my meaning is, to make yᵉ 40ˢ expressed in yᵉ Indenture, £5. [Of] yᵉ five load of Wood I Appointed my son to bring my Wife yearely, she shall haue liberty to sell one fifth to heʳ own Charge, two or three more yearly at my wood lott, Answorth hill. I desire my friends, *Isack Heath*, ye Ruling Eldʳ of yᵉ Church of Christ att Roxbury & my Brothʳ in law, *Edw. Bridge, Thomas Weld* & *William Parke*, to bee overseers of this my will [If any difference arise between his son & wife, to be settled by the overseers.] To my wife, one hogg & one pigg, what flax shall bee vpon yᵉ ground or in yᵉ house or cloath vntill ought att my desease, my will is, my wife shall have one halfe & my son yᵉ otheʳ: thus have I finished my will this 26: 4mo: 58.

John Rugles.

Witnesse *William Parke, Edward Bridge*
      who deposed, 30 Jan. 1663.

[Then follows the deposition of *Edward Bridge;* testifying that his brother manifested to him, the said *Bridge*, the intention to add to his will concerning his wife, Margery, that she should be comfortably main- tained out of his estate, &c. This, he thought, should be added to the will.

*William Parke* deposed, that in the year 1658, *Margery*, wife of *John Ruggles*, was " in good health & as active & lively as could be expected to her yeares & ability, but since, she had been disabled by the palsy." For this reason, her late husband told Mr. Parke that he would add to his wife in his will so much as would make her comfortable for life. Mr. P. also was in favor of adding this statement to the will, and proposed that security be given, by the son, to make it good unto his mother-in-law. 30 Jan. 1663.]

Inventory of the Estate of John Rugles Senior taken 16ᵗʰ Octʳ 1663 by *Thomas Weld, Edw: Denison.* Sum £343.1ˢ. Mentions 24 Acres of Land in yᵉ first division, £68; 14 Acres in three divisions, £14; 9 Acres next Dedham, £1.10ˢ; 3 acres fresh meadow, £20; 2½ acres salt meadow, £12. *John Ruggles* Junior, deposed, 30ᵗʰ Jan. 1663.

---

MORDECAI NICHOLS.—1ˢᵗ March 1663. Power of Administration to the estate of the late *Mordecay Nichols*, deceased, is Granted to *Alice*, his wife, in behalfe of hirself & Children, she bringing in a true Inventory, to the next Court, &c.

Inventory of the estate taken 25ᵗʰ of April 1664, by Wᵐ *Bartholmew, Roger Clappe.* Amt. £524. 07ˢ. 03ᵈ. *Alice Nicolls* deposed, 29ᵗʰ April 1664.

[3 Feb. 1664. The Court being informed that since the Inventory of the estate of said Nichols was produced, by losses and debts, the estate had depreciated " to the ualue of two hundred pounds & odd : And the widow being readye to dispose of herselfe, the Court Judged it meete to order that the House & Land mentioned in the Inuentorye at £150, shall bee secured " to *John Nicolls*, his son, as a· parț of his portion, and that his mother *Alice*, the widow, pay unto her said son, £50 more, at the age of 14 years. The house and land to be improved for his use till he come to age—the mother to have the use of the son's portion till that time; " to

Choose his Guardian for his Education, & in the Meanetime His Mother & *Cap' Clap* are appointed his Guardians "—the mother to have all the rest of the estate as her portion—" in case the Child Dye, before he attaine his age, yᵉ Mother to have yᵉ whole."]

---

ALICE SMITH.—*Isack Cullimore, Alex. Adames, Edward Budd* and *Sarah Martin* were desired by *Joseph Baylee* to take a view of such things as were in the chest of *Alis Smith*, late deceased. The above individuals made an appraisement 14th Oct. 1663. Amt. £29. 19ˢ. 3ᵈ·. *John Baulton*, scribb. 9th Octʳ. 1663.

14th Oct. 1663. *Joseph Bayley* desired the persons before mentioned, with *Martha Beamsle*, to prise other goods amounting to £8. 4. 6.; afterward, a few more items were added.

Power of Administration to the Estate of the late widdow *Alice Smith* was Graunted to *Joseph Bayly*, her kinsman, and to *Samuel & Abraham Smith*, two of her sonnes, in behalfe of the Rest of the children, of sᵈ *Alice Smith.*—16 : 8 : 1663. *Joseph Bayly* deposed.

---

ROBERT POND.—[*Mary Pond* relict & Administratrix to the Estate of the late *Robert Pond*, of Milton, deceased, bound herself in the sum of £100 together wᵗʰ the house & 40 acres of land to it belonging, for the payment of £65 due from the estate. Dated 20th of May, 1663. In pʳsence of *Sam: Torrey, Robt. Vose.*]

Inventory of the estate taken 24th of Decʳ. 1662, by *John Gill, James Humphry, William Pond.* Sum total £95. 17. 3. *Mary Pond*, relict of *Robert*, deposed 13th of May 63.

---

JAMES HARROD.—[*John Turell*, of Boston, marriner, & *Daniel Turell*, of said Boston, blacksmith, bound in the sum of £100 to administer on the estate of the late *James Harrod*, sonne of *Wᵐ Harrod*, of Byddifford, in the County of Devon, in old England, they being appointed to administer on said estate. Witnessed by *Thomas Edsell, Thomas Batt*, 28th of April 1663.]

Power of Administration to the estate of the late *James Harrod*, Deceased, is graunted to *John Turel*, of Boston, marriner, in behalfe of the father of the late *James Harrod*, of Biddiforde, or such others to whom it belongs, he giuing securitye, &c. 26th of Aprill 1664.

Inuentorye of the Estate of said Harrod, left by him in the possession of Jnᵒ Turrell at his deposition, out of this Countreye. Amt. £50. 0ˢ. 7½ᵈ. Mentions bill upon *John Connye.* The Inuentorye ueiwed & uallued pʳ *John Sunderland & Daniell Turrell*, 23ᵈ of April 1664. *John Turell* deposed same day.

---

THOMAS EMONS.—20 : 11ᵐᵒ·: 1660. I, *Thomas Emons*, of Boston, in New England, Cordwainer, being sicke, make my last will. [Debts to be paid.] I giue unto my sonne, *Obadia*, sonne *Samuel*, daughter *Hanna Crab*, & daughter *Elizabeth Hincksman*, 5ʳ pʳ peice, to be paid them by my Executrix within a Considerable time after my Decease (Declaring herby that my Children Before named, haue had of my Estate, before the Day of yᵉ Date hereof their parts proportionall with other of my Children heerafter named.) Unto my sonne *Benjamin*, £20, to be paid by my executrix, at or before the end of Fiue yeares after my Deceas, by the ualue therof in good paye. Unto my Gran-sonne *Thomas Emons*, sonne of Obadiah, 40' to be paid to him or to his use within three yeares after my Decease. Unto my Gransonne *Samuell Crab*, 40', to bee paid [as before.] Unto my Kinswoman *Martha Winsor*, 40', to bee paid her on the Day of her Marriage or at her age of 21, which of them shall first happen. Unto my wife, *Martha*, my two Houses in Boston, that is to say, the House I now Dwell in, & my house now in the tenure of *John Andrews*, Cooper; the said Houses & Land to haue & to dispose of as shee shall think good. Unto my wife all the moueable goods within my now Dwelling house. My Wife Martha I make executrix of this my last will.                                             Thomas Emons.

In the presence of us, *John Bateman, William Pearse.*

[There is a memorandum in regard to the " Raze " made in the will by order of the legatee, signed by *Richard Staines* and *William Pearse*, 11th of May 1664.]

17th June 1664. Richard Staines & William Pearse deposed. Present, Ric^d Bellingham Deputy Gouern^r; Mr Tho Danforth, Mr Edward Rawson, Recorder.

Inventory of the Estate of Thomas Emons deceased 11th of May, apprized by *William English, Edmund Jacson.* Amt. £440. 5'. Debts due the deceased to the am^t. of £66. 06. 04.—from y^e deceased, £45. 10. 09.

17 June 1664, *Martha Emmons* deposed to this inventory of the estate of her late husband. ———

JOHN HILL.—Will of *John Hill*, of Dorchester, made 11th of April 1660. I giue unto my Eldest sonne, *John Hill*, that Estate of myne now in his hands, & for a remembrance I giue him 5'. For the Rest of my Estate, house, Land & mooueables I giue unto my wife, *Francis*, During her Life, for her Maintenance & for ·y^e Bringing up of my Children, and at her Death my will is that my whole Estate bee giuen unto my nine youngest Children, or to so many of them as shall be then aliue, alway prouided there be resp'ect had to my sonne, *Samuell*, who hath been helpfull unto mee in my Infirme Dayes. I giue my wife power to dispose of any parte of my estate as shee shall Judge meet, with the Aduise of my Louing Freinds *Tho: Tileston* & *John Minott*. My dau. *Mary*, hauing had her portion according to my abilitye alreadye, I Doe for a Remembrance giue her 5'. And being confident of the Faithfulnes and Care of my beloued Wife I make her my Executrix of this my Last will.

Signed in the presence of                              John X Hill.

*Thomas Tileston, Timothy Tilston, John Minott*, who deposed 30th. 4th. 1664.

Inventory of the estate taken 9th of June 1664, by *Thomas Tileston, Jno. Mynott.* Amt. £281. 1'. *Francis Hill* deposed to this Inventory of the estate ot her Late husband, June 30, 1664.

———

THOMAS MUNT.—Inventory of y^e Goods & chattells of Thomas Munt, deceased, prised by *James Johnson, Robert Sanderson, Edward Raynsford*, 6th of July 1664. Amt. £214. 07½. Mentions " one peece of land lying between *Robert Sanderson* and *John Brackett;*" "one peece of Land lying by *Peter Warren.*"

9th July 1664. Power of Administration to this Estate granted to *Elinor* his late wife in behalf of herselfe and her 3 daughters.

*Elinor Munt* deposed to the inventory of said estate, on the same day.

## ABSTRACTS FROM THE EARLIEST WILLS ON RECORD IN THE COUNTY OF SUFFOLK, MASS.

[Prepared by MR. WILLIAM B. TRASK, of Dorchester.]

MARKE HANDS.—15th July 1661. I, *Mark Hands*, of Boston, being in health & bound on a voyage from the Port of Boston to Barbadoes & elsewhere, make this my Last will. [Debts to be paid.] I giue unto my dau. *Mehitabell Hands* the seuerall p'ticulars in a schedule hereunto annexed, which was Desyred by her Mother, my Deceased wife, to bee giuen her, and my will is that the said p'ticulars shall be prized with the rest of my Estate. Of my whole Estate I giue one third part unto my dau. Mehitabell, & the other two thirds unto my sonne *Jo. Hands*, whom I appoint my executor. My will is that in Case both my Children Dye before they Come to enjoy this my estate and Legacy, that my Kinsman *Joseph Dill* shall haue my Dwelling house & Land in Boston ; out of the ualue therof the s^d Joseph shall paye unto his Mother *Abigaill Hanniford*, £50 if she be then Liuinge, and unto *Samuel Dill* and *Benjamin Dill* £20 apeice, and the rest of my Estate to bee Diuided amongst my Brothers & Sisters Children. If one of my Children dye before he or she come to age my will is that the suruiuor shall enjoy my whole estate. I giue the summe of £5 towards the Building of a schoole house at the North end of the Towne of Boston, to bee paid by my executor, when such a Work shall be began. I giue unto my Louing freinds, *Cap^t Thomas Clarke* & *Mr John Winslow* £3 apiece to buye each of them a Gold Ringe, the which my two Freinds, Clarke and Winslow, I Intreat to bee the Ouerseers of my Children & Estate, to be Imployed for the good and well Bringing up, & Educating of them in Learning & the Fear of the Lord, And that they may be putt into possession of their Legacyes, my sonne when he shall be 21 yeares of age, & my Daughter when she shall be [    ] yeares of age or in Marriage Condition, which of them shall first happen.

In the presence of us                                          Marke Hands.
*John Winslow, John Baker, William Pearse.*

17 June 1664. *M^rJohn Winslow* and *W^m Pearse* deposed.

Inventory of the estate taken by *Peter Brackett* & *Thomas Brattle*, 3^d Nov^r. 1665. Amt. £293. 03. 04. Signed by *Thomas Buttolph, Habbacuk Glouer.*

*M^r Tho: Brattle* & *M^r Peter Brackett* deposed to the Inuentory of the Estate of y^e Late *Marke Hammes*, deceased, excepting the particulars in the Inuoyce annext, which was Lefte in the hands of *Mrs Hanniford* & giuen by the Father & Mother. [Then follows an invoice of goods given *Mehitabell Hands* by her deceased Mother, *Mary Hands*, & Delivered by her father Mark Hands for her use "unto my sister Hannyford & Goodwife *Biggs*, 17^th June 1661," as testifys *Stephen Spencer*. The certificate of Mark Hands and *Abigail Hanniford* of the same date is also given. Testis, *Stephen Spencer*. Certified by *John Wensley*.]

---

THOMAS GATTLIFE.—An appraisement of the Estate of *Thomas Gattlife*,* of Brantrey, deceased, taken by *William Saualls, William Vasty,*

---

* This name is incorrectly given as *Gullife* and *Gulliver*, in Register, vol. xii., page [1] 154. On the Boston Records he is called *Gatline*. See Reg. xi. p. 333.

Farmer says—" Gatline, Thomas, a miller of Braintree 1650, d. 17 May, 1663."

[1] See p. 224.

24th June 1663. Valued at £765. 2ˢ. 4ᵈ. The Estate debtor to Mʳ Habakuck Glouer, Mʳ Symon Lynde, goodwife Nilles, Mrs Bradcott, Mr Olliuer, & others, £113. 11. 7. Mentions in the inventory, lands bought at
Milton, of goodman *Whitt*, of goodwife *Nills*, of *Edward Thomson*, of
*Simon Ray*, of goodman *Foster*, of goodman *Goline*, pease on Nilles lot,
wheat on the Farnes land, Indian corne on *Griches* land, &c. tooles
desposed of to *Joseph Plumbley*, &c. &c.

28th of October '63. *Prudent Gatliefe & Jonathan Gatleife* deposed.

Whereas *Prudent Gatleife*, Relict of *Thomas Gatleife*, of Braintree,
deceased, & *Jonathan Gatliefe*, only son to the late *Thomas Gatliffe* Administratrix and administrator to the said Estate of the late Thomas Gatliffe, bringing in an Inuentory of that Estate which in all amounts to £765.
2ˢ. 4ᵈ. for the setteling whereof to mutuall satisfaction, they haueing
agreed amongst themselues, vizt. the debts of the said Thomas Gatliffe
should be paid out of the whole Estate, which is giuen in by the Inuentory to be £113. 11. 7. and that the household goods shall remaine to the
said Prudence to dispose as she sees cause, and that the said Prudence for
and during hir naturall life for hir owne mentainance and Good Education
of hir two dauthers, Prudent & Mary Gatliffe, till they Come to the age of
20 yeares shall be allowed the full half of the yearly Rent & benefitt of
the whole remaining estate after the deduction for debts & Goods, with
mill house, lands & Cattle, the alloweing and being at one halfe of the
Chardge of Repayres & managing the stock, & that dureing hir Widowhood she shall haue the management thereof, allowing the other halfe of
the yearly benifit & Rent to the sᵈ Jonathan Gatliff, the sone, who, and the
said Prudent, hir altering hir Condition, by marrage or Death, shall Enter
vpon the whole Estate, mill house, lands, cattle, swine &c. & only during
hir life, after marriage to allow Prudent his mother in law, for the Ends
aforesaid, the Cleer halfe of the Rents & profitts & that the said Jonathan
shall pay vnto his said sisters, ouer and besides the Chardge of their Education, as aboue, when they attaine the age of 20 yeares, the sume of
£100 apeece, in English goods, Corne or Cattle for their portions, and
that for the assurance thereof, the said mill house and lands of the ·late
Thomas Gatliffe, shall & is hereby ingaged & bound ouer to the Court at
Boston, &c. Allowed & approved of, by the Court, 29ᵗʰ of Octʳ. 1663,
as a full Conclusion & settlement of the said Estate ; allowed 30 : 8ᵐᵒ:
1663.

---

ROBERT WOODWARD.—Inuentory of the Goods & Chattels of Robert
Woodward, deceased, taken 3ᵈ of March 1653.

Power of Administration to the Estate, graunted to *Rachell Woodward*,
his wife, in Behalfe of hir self and Children.

Rachell Woodward deposed 7ᵗʰ March 63.

An account is given of money disbursed to *Capᵗ Thomas Sauage*, Mʳ
*John Hull*, Mʳ *Theodore Atkinson*, for shingling the house, finishing of a
New End & building of a Leanetow to it, &c. &c. for bringing vp of
three Children, one from 4 yeares, 5 yeares, & 7 yeares, and scooling, to
wright and to Read, and Clothing, that the Honered Court thinks meet to
alowe.

*Rachell Woodward*, late wife to *Robert Woodward*, now wife to *Thomas
Harwood*, comeing into this Court and Desireing that the Estate of the
late Robert Woodward might be deuided, the Eldest sone of the said
Woodward being of age, and others of the Children Drawing neare to

age, the Relicts portion not sett out and an Acount brought in of Debts & Expences laid out by *Thomas Harwood* to value of £53, besides keeping of the 5 Children of said Woodward seuerall yeares, the Court Judgeth it meet to Order the mouebles to bee to satisfie the said Harwood for his Expences and layeing out as aboue, and whereas the house and land valued at £60, is now Judgeth worth £200, this Court doth order that the said *Rachell*, the Relict, be allowed to be at hir dispose the sume of £40, and that the payeing the Eldest son a double portion out of the Remainder, & the other 4 Children as they Come to age, be paid by their Mother their single parts of the remainder & make the best of the whole house and lands to hir owne vse and benefitt, the said *Harwood*, or his wife, Giueing sufficient securitie for payment of the Childrens portions as they grow Due, in good Country pay. Allowed, 3 Nov'. 1663.

---

ROBERT TURNER.—The Last Will and Testament of *Robert Turner*, taken as hee spake it, 9th 5mo: 1664. I giue to my Eldest sonne, *Ephraim Turner*, my new Built house, a part wherof he now Dwelleth in, Reseruing to my Deare wife one roome to herselfe During her life time, either in the new end or the old, at her Owne choyce. Also unto my Sonne, *Ephraim*, my Garden runninge from the House Downe to the Lane, running upon a straight Line home to *Joh. Toppins* Fence. I giue unto my sonne, *John Turner*, all the other part of my now Dwelling house & the Ground below it, Bounded by *M* *Coles* Fence, the other side to bee so lefte as my sonne *Ephraim* may haue passage by the yeard and garden as they two may agree, by aduice of my Freinds heerafter named. Out of this part of my house Bequeathed to my sonne John, my will is, that my sonne *Faireweather*, & my Daughter, shall remayne in the Roomes they now Dwell in, for the time of four yeares next ensuing. To my sonne, *Joseph*, I giue my barne beyond *Dauid Titchburnes* house; also, a parcell of Ground upon the Hill, to be in breadth at the Front [     ] 3 rods and Lye next to my sonne Johns Diuision, and to Runne through up to *M* *Houchyés*. Also I Confirme & Bequeathe unto my sonne, *Faireweather*, the house and land upon the Hill Formerlye Deliuered into his possession. I doe adde unto my s^d sonne, *Faireweather*, a strippe of Ground about 3 Rod in breadth adjoyning unto *M* *Lynes;* also my will is, my sonne, *Ephraim*, shall haue a share of Land upon Center hill next my sonne *Fairweather*, to-be four Rod Broade at the grout & Runne through with the other Diuisions. Also to my sonne, *John Turner*, a portion of the s^d land next to my sonne, *Ephraim*, to be three rods Broad Equall with my sonne, *Joseph*. To my Dear wife, I Bequeathe the thirds of all my houses, Lands and mooueables, and after Debts & Legacyes paid all the Lands abroad, the thirds to my said wife, whom I make the sole Executrix of this my Last will and testament. I Giue to the Church of Boston, wherof through Mercy I haue so Long remained a member, £20, to be paid in such pay as my Estate produceth; to the New Church, £5; £5 to y^e Church of Cambridg; £10 to *M* *Stalham*, of Tarling, in Essex; £10 to *Cap* *Oliuers* Company; £5 to the other three Companyes, to each 50'; all which Legacyes I will to be paid out of the rents or sales of my Lands at Centrye hill or Muddy riuer, & to bee paid by my Dear wife, with the aduice & assistance of my Ouerseers, within Foure yeares next insuing the Date heerof, at the Discretion of my wife & Ouerseers, whose assistance,

236

aduice & Counsell to my wife & Children I Earnestly Intreate, whose names Follow :—*Elder James Penn, Thomas Grubb, William Bartholmew.*                                              Robert Turner.

Test. *John Alcocke.*

24th Aug. 1664. Elder James Penn and Thomas Grubb deposed.

An Inventory of the Estate and Goods of Robert Turner, deceased, apprised Dec. 16th 1664, by *Edward Fletcher, John Hull.* Amt. £1221.17'. Mentions, the Dwelling House and Land thereto belonging, the House Confirmed to Mr Fairweather & Land belonging, the New Frame and all the Land at Centry Hill, the Farme House & Lott at Muddye riuer, & other Land there, Interest in Land & Mineralls at Chelmsford, ¹⁄₃₂ part of the Shippe Supplye, &c. *Penelope Turner* deposed to this Inventory of the estate of her late husband, Jan 31ˢᵗ 1664.

---

ELIZABETH HARDER.—1: 4th: 1664. I *Elizabeth Harder*, of Braintree, doe make this my last will. God hauing giuen mee only one Daughter, which is my only Childe, I doe giue and bequeath my whole estate, mooueable & Immooueable unto her, her heires & assigns foreuer, excepting such legacyes as are heerafter specified, & doe Constitute & ordain her my sole executrix of this my Last will & Testament, & Doe Intreate my Louing Friends, *William Needham* & *Samuel Tomson*, of Brantrye, to be my Ouerseers. I giue unto *Elisabeth Saunders*, my Daughters Child, £20, with my Bed I Lye on, with all belonging to it, to bee paid at the age of 18 yeares, or at the day of marriage, and if shee Dye, if my Daughter haue Farther Issue, I giue it unto the next child, & if not, then to Remaine unto my Daughter. I Giue unto *John Kent* & *Joseph Kent*, 40' apiece to bee paid within two yeares after my Decease. I Giue unto *Joshua Kents* three Daughters, 20' apiece, to bee paid to them when they are 18 yeares old, or at the Day of Marriage. I Giue unto *Benjamin Thomson*, 40', to bee paid unto him within halfe a year after my Decease. I giue unto *John Day*, £5 to be paid unto him when he is 20 yeares old, upon Condition he Liue with my sonne or Daughter till hee be twenty year Old.                                          Elisabeth Harder.

Test. *Samuell Bass, John Basse*, who deposed, Octr 6th 1664.

Inventory of the Estate of *Elizabeth Hardier*, taken Sept 9th 1664, by *Samuell Basse, Richard Brackett, William Needham.* Amt. £268.11'. *Martyn Saunders* deposed, Octr 6th 1664.

---

EDWARD POOLE.—22: 6ᵐᵒ: 1664. The Last will of *Edward Poole*, of Weymouth, Being sicke, but of perfect memorye. [Debts to be paid.] I giue unto my wife, my dwelling house & the Land adjoyning thereunto as long as she doth keepe her selfe a widow, and also the Lott the Towne gaue me, about 8 acres, giuen as aforesaid, and also 2 acres of medow that I Bought of *John Prince*. I giue the aboue said Land, withal the appurtenances therunto Belonging, unto my sonne, *Samuell.* I giue my sonne, *Isaack*, that Lott that was *Weauers*, of 18 acres, & 4 acres of Marsh at Hingham Brook, bought of Lincoll and Nicholls. To my sonne, *Joseph*, all my owne great Lott, & that halfe Lott I Bought of *Stephen French*, near the Cedar swompe plaine ; to my sonne, *Benjamin*, all my Common Lotts and three acres of fresh Marsh giuen me by the towne near the great Pond ; to my sonne, *John*, twenty pounds of my owne goods ; to my daughter, *Sarah*, to my sonne *Jacob* [the same].

If any of these three Dye before they bee of age, hee that Liues shall haue it. It is my will that my wife shall be my sole Executrix, & so to haue the use of three Last Childrens portions to Breed them up & when my Wife Doe marry, & my sonne, *Samuell*, Doe Come to possesse my now Dwelling house and Land, as aboue said, then hee shall giue his Mother, at her surrender, twenty pound starling in good Goods or Cattell.

In the presence of
*Edward Bate, Thomas Dyer*, who deposed, 26 Oct^r 1664.

The mark of
X Edward Poole.

Inventory of the estate taken Sep^t 16^th 1664 by the above individuals. The relict* of Edward Poole deposed Oct^r 26^th 1664. Mentions in the inventory, dwelling house and land, 8 acres at Rockey Swampe, 18 acres of upland, 4 acres of fresh meadow, 24 acres near y^e Cedar Swampe playne, 40 acres of Common Lotts and 3 acres of Marshe in y^e Woods, 2 acres of Medow at the Beauer Dammes, &c.

---

MARGERY LAUER.—I, *Margery Lauer*, of Dorchester, being weake and ill, yet of perfect memory, make my Last will. As for my temporall estate, my Just debts being paid, and Funerall expences Discharged : For Debts few or none will Charg me with any, and for my Funerall 1 would haue that Done Liberally & Comly & Decentlye. And for Legacye & Giftes my will is, that M^r *William Tomson* haue 10*, to M^r *Richard Mather*, 10*, to *John Wiswall*, the youngest of the three, my siluer spoone, to *Daniell Prestons* Children, 5* in siluer, ape[ice], to his Wife a new p^r of Cotton Cardes, to *Jane Gurnet*, 2* for a memorandum. To M^r *John Wiswalls* wife a little peice of Gold ; 3* to *Enoch Wiswalls* wife, & Daughter 20*, to *Goodwife Preston* a half Crowne pe[ice], to *Thomas Wiswall*, in Cambridge, 20*, to M^r *John Wiswall*, £3. For Legacyes I haue now Done after this, & Buriall Discharged. My Further will is, that if it had beene possible that any [friend] of myne in England Could haue had the Rest I would haue [let] them haue it, but I Looke at that, that that Cannot bee. Therefore I would haue what I haue Disposed equally between M^r *John Wiswall, Thomas Wiswall, Daniell Preston* & *Enoch Wiswall. Daniell Preston, Enoch Wiswall*, Executors.

The 4. of the 6: 64.

Margery Lauer.

The will of Margery Lauer
witnessed by W^m *Chaplen, Mary Chaplen*, who deposed 10 (9) 64.

The Estate was apprised by *John Wiswall* and *Thomas Wiswall*, Aug. 30, 1664. *Daniell Preston* and *Enoch Wiswall* deposed Nov^r 10th 1664.

---

JOSHUA KENT.—22. 2. 1664. I, *Joshua Kent*, of Dedham, in the Countye of Suffolke, being of good understandinge and memorye, through the Mercye of God, Make this my Last will. My worldly estate I dispose of as followeth, First, that all my Debts bee paid, and the Remainder of my Estate I Giue unto *Mary*, my Wife, whom I make my sole Executrix.

*Michaell Metcalfe*
*Peter* R *Woodward.*
His   marke.

Joshua Z His Marke.
Kent.

*Michaell Metcalfe* & *Peter Woodward* deposed 14 (9^mo) 1664,
before me, Elea: Lusher.

---

* Name not given.

238

This probate was Owned and accepted of by the County Court 17ᵗʰ 9ᵐᵒ 1664.                                            Edw Rawson Recorder.

An Inuentorye of the Estate taken April 22, 1664, by *Michaell Metcalfe, Wᵐ Auerye, Nathan Aldis.* Amᵗ £156.1ˢ.6ᵈ. Mentions house & land at Dedham, land at Wallumunuppuk.

*Mary,* the Relict & executrix, attested to the truth of the Inuentory, upon Oath, Novʳ 14ᵗʰ 1664, before Eleazer Lusher.

---

JOHN CLARKE.—23[?] of Aug. 1664.  I, *John Clarke,* senior, of Boston, Chirurgion, Being sicke & weake in Body, but of good & perfect memory, make this my last will. [Debts to be paid.]  Vnto my wife, *Martha Clarke,* my Dwelling house, with the Land, Wharfe and appurtenances therunto Belonging, lying in Boston, with the houshold stuffe and Furniture in euery pᵗicular roome therof as it is Furnished at my Decease (with my owne goods) the said house [&c.] to be unto her & her proper use During the time she shall remaine unmarried.  In Case my said Wife be married againe, then my will is: shee shall surrender to my sonne, *John Clarke,* the said House [&c.] at or before the Day of her Marriage.  My will is, that my sᵈ sonne, *John Clarke,* shall pay unto his Mother, my now wife, the ualue of the one third part of the ualue of the said House, land, wharfe, houshold stuffe & furniture aforesaid, the said one third part of the ualue of the premisses my wife to enjoy during her life, and after her decease, the sᵈ part to be repaid by her Executors and Administrators unto my said sonne, *John,* and to my Daughter, *Jemina Drew,* and the Longest Liuer of them.  I giue unto my sonne, *John,* [all the property aforesaid] and to yᵉ Heires male of his Body Lawfully Begotten, to his & their use from yᵉ Day of the Marriage of my now wife, or from the Day of her Death, wᶜʰ shall first happen.  In Case my sᵈ sonne haue no Issue Male, but Daughter or Daughters, then my will is, that my Daughter, *Jeminah Drew,* her Children, *John* and *Elisabeth,* shall haue one third part of the ualue of my estate aforesaid, & my sonne, *John,* his Daughter & Daughters and the Longest Liuer of them the Other two third parts.  I giue unto my wife that Debt which is Due unto mee from Captain *Thomas Lake,* of Boston.  I acquit unto my sonne, *John Clarke,* all manner of Debt or Debts, which he is indebted unto mee, so as that my Executrix, nor any under her, may make any Claim or Demand whatsoeuer for any thing by him from me had before the Day of the Date heerof.  I giue unto my said sonne, *John Clarke,* the one third part of my stock of Horses, Mares & Colts, both in this Colony of the Massachusetts & in Plimouth Colonye.  The other two thirds to the use and propriety of my said Daughter, *Jeminah Drew,* & her Children before named.  I giue unto my sonne, *John Clarke,* all that Debt that shall Justly appeare to be Due to me from [    ] *Boington,* of Rowley, in New England, by Bond, Mortgage, or otherwise howsoeuer. Unto my sonne, *Jnᵒ Clarke,* that Debt which is Due unto mee from the Executᵐ & Administratᵐ of the Deceased *Major Anthony [Humphery] Autherton,* of Dorchester; unto my sonne, *John,* all my Books, Instruments & Materialls, whatsoeuer I haue at the time of my Decease, belonging to the arts of Physicke & Chirurgery.  Prouided that in Case my sonne, *John Clarke,* be married & Doe Dye without Issue, that then my will is, that his widow shall enjoy the sᵈ Dwelling house & Land, wharfe with the appurtenances together with the Implements of houshold stuffe

239

& Furniture, in such roome as aforesaid During her Widowhood, & in case she be married againe, or die in her widowhood, which of them shall first happen. That then my will & meaning is, that that estate mentioned in this prouiso the one third part thereof shall bee unto my said Daughter, *Jeminah Drew*, for her Life, and the other two third parts shall be unto her Children before named. And after their Mothers Decease then y⁰ said Children & the Longest Liuer of them to Enjoy the whole. I ordain *Martha*, my wife, sole Executrix, & as for ouerseers I Leave her to her Liberty to make choice & use of such pᵣsons as she shall Judge most able to Councel her. John Clark.

In the presence of
*John Search, Daniel Turell, William Pearse* ser.

Daniell Turell & Wᵐ Pearse deposed Nov 23ᵈ 1664.

The Goods & Chattells of *Mr John Clarke*, of Boston, Deceased, apprised pʳ *Mʳ John Wiswall* & *Mʳ Amos Richardson*, Jan. 24ᵗʰ 1664. Amt. £1295.6ᵣ. *Elizabeth Clarke* deposed Feb. 3, 1664 to this Inventory of her Late Husband, *Mr John Clarke* His Estate. Mentions in the inventory 3 Stoues,* valued at £3.

---

* In the Massachusetts Records, vol. iii. p. 283, vol. iv. part 1, p. 104 (printed volumes), under date of October 19th, 1652, is the following vote on the subject of " Fireworks to save fuel : "—

" Mr Clarke['s] invention "—" Mr Clarkes monopolie." " Itt is ordered by this Courte, that no person shall for the space of three yeeres next ensuing, make vse of Mr John Clarks invention for saving of fire wood and warming of roomes with little cost and charges, by whicH meanes great bennefitt is like to be to the countie, especially to theise populous places ; and if any family or other person doe, by the consent and direction of the said Mr John Clarke, or wᵗʰout, improove or vse the said experiment, they shall pay tenn shillings to the said Mr Clarke, for which the said Mr. Clarke may sue or implead any person before any comissioner for the same, as the cawse shall require."—*Oct.* 19, 1652.

In 1656, the above grant, having by limitation expired, the General Court confirmed the order to Mr. Clarke " for the terme of his life."—*Records*, vol. iii. p. 401, vol. iv. part 1, p. 260.

# ABSTRACTS FROM THE EARLIEST WILLS ON RECORD IN THE COUNTY OF SUFFOLK, MASS.

[Prepared by WILLIAM B. TRASK, of Dorchester.]

JOHN HANNIFORD.—I, *John Hanniford*, of Boston, Marriner, being in health, make this my will. Unto my wife, & to *Sarah*, or Daughter to they as Joint, the one third part of all my Es[t]ate, being in Goods, Money & Household stuffe. Unto my sonne, *Samuell Hanniford*, the Land & the Housing theron (lying as the Deed makes mention of upon Record) sctuate [in] Boston, Lately purchased by me of my Father in Law, *John Button*, of Boston. Unto my sonne, *Samuell*, my siluer porringer, two siluer spoones, my Gold Ringe & all my wearing apparrell & one third part of all such goods as shall exceede the ualue of the said Bequeathed house. Unto my Daughter, *Hannah Hanniford*, that House and Land wrin I sometime Liued, Joining to the Lands abouementioned, & bequeathed to my sonne, *Samuell*, now in the Occupation of Mr *Richard Hickes*, in Boston. To my Daughter, *Hannah*, one siluer Beer bole & 2 siluer spoones, all the Linninne which appertained to mee, one Feather Bed & Rugge, and whatsoeuer is myne in ye Custodye of my Father in Law, *John Button*, & one third part of all such goods as shall make the portion equal unto her as I haue giuen to my sonne, *Samuell*. My will is, that my sonne, *Samuell*, and my Daughter, *Hannah*, or their executors, administrators of the one & of the other & of them Both, shall pay unto my Daughter, *Sarah*, £20 sterling, each of them, at such time as said *Samuell* & *Hannah* shall bee of age. My will is that if either my sonne or daughter dye single persons & unmarried, that then the Longest liuer of them shall haue ye half of the estate to him or her so bequeathed, & the other Halfe unto my Daughter, *Sarah*, all the aboue mentioned Legacyes unto they & their heires foreuer. In Cause that my sonne Dye without an heir, or my Daughter *Hannah*, or my Daughter *Sarah*, that then the Lands to bee the one halfe unto the Children of my sister, *Mary French*, equally & the other half unto the children of my sister, *Rose Morrish*, equally, and halfe the goods or money to them appertaining, the other halfe of the goods & money unto the three sonnes of my Wife, had by *George Dill*. In Case my Louing wife happen to be with Childe at my Departure from her then my will is, that thc Ouerseers of my Estate take a proportionable part from the before mentioned Children, that is, from *Samuell* & *Hannah*, & £10 from *Sarahs*, £40 & giue it that Childe. My will Conserning my wife is, that shee shall haue the one third part of whatsoeuer my estate shall amount unto. And I Intreat my Louing Freinds, *Deacon Marshall*, *Michaell Wills*, and *Christopher Gibson*, to Joyne with my Father in Law, *John Button*, to see this my will performed. In token of my Loue unto either of them, I will that my Louing wife, my executrix, Deliuer unto euery of them, £3 starling to buy each of them a Ringe. As Concerning the Estate of my Predecessor, *George Dill*, my Desire is, yt the Honoured Court of Boston would be pleased to Order unto my Wife that part unto her Due, as also the parts Due unto the three sonnes of him. My Desyre is, Farther, that the Estate of my predecessor, & the Estate properly to mee Belonging, may not be intermixt, & that the affaires of both ye Estates may bee so

Ordered, as that their may bee no Cause of strife Between Brethren. Dec. 26th, 1657.                                                    *John Hanniford.*
In the presence of
    *George Mountjoy, William Pearse.*
This will was produced in Court 5ᵗʰ Feb. 1660, to be proved by the executrix, she to bring in an exact accompt of the estate of the Late *George Dill*, in relation to the Inventory she formerly Brought into the Court of that Estate.                               *Edward Rawson*, Recorder.
    12. 9ᵐᵒ 1664, *Wᵐ Pearse* Deposed.
Memorandum, the 5ᵗʰ Feb. 1660, the *Widow Hanniford*, in open Court, Demanded a Bond that Goodman *Burton* had giuen to *Mʳ Hanniford* about securing the thirds of yᵉ House & Lands by him sold. *Wᵐ Pearse* acknowledged that he had such a Bond Committed unto his Custodye by Mʳ Hanniford.                              *Edw Rawson*, Recorder.
    An Inventory of Mʳ Hanniford's estate was taken by *John Anderson* and *James Euerell*, 15 April 1661. Amt. £1064. 01. 06. Mentions a dwelling house and wharfe with the land thereto belonging where his wife now lieueth as now it is. £200; one negro boy servant, £20; yᵉ house wherein *Timothy Pratt* liues and *Samuell Norden* keepes shopp, £280; yᵉ house wherin *Mʳ Hickes* liueth; creditors, Stephen Ford, Leiftenant William Phillips, Thomas Warner, William Avorie, John Laddehorne, Thomas Swift, Henery Lampery, Mʳ Mayre, Mʳˢ Mader, James Everel, John Matson, Edward Page, Mʳ Greeneleffe. Estate indebted to Father Button, Mʳ Peake of London, Marke Hands, Goodman Biggs, to paymᵗ for *Samuel Hanniford* at schoole, £2. 4s.; to John Convey, Humphrey Milom, Capᵗ Clarke, &c.
    When I married yᵉ within named, *John Hanniford*, he tould mee he had an estate of £900 or thereaboutes of wᶜʰ hee disbursed £380, for a house to his Father in Law, *Button*. When he went last away he carried wᵗʰ him £500 or vpwards he tould me he had in Portingall a debt of £100, but in whose hands it is, I know not, neither is there any Accᵗ of it pʳ booke or bill; he reced in part of it a Butt and a hoghead of wine. He shipᵗ from Barbados for England to pay debts thereaboutes, a hundred pounds worth of sugar, as my Brother, *Hands*, tould me, which was lost, yᵉ ship was taken. He had a pᵗcell of Wines which came to him from Barbadoes, by wᶜʰ he lost a £100[?] neere of yᵉ principle. Seuerall debts are due to him in Barbadoes of which there is noe probability to receiue any of it, as my Brother, *Marke Hands*, tells mee.
    This is the best Acct. that Can be given of yᵉ estate of this said *John Hanniford* by mee, *Abigael Hanniford*.
    [Then follows the inventory of the estate of *Mʳ George Dill* the former husband of *Mrs Hanniford*. The estate is mentioned as Creditor among other things, " by an Irish maydo, £10."]

----

WIDOW HEATH.—Jan. 1ˢᵗ 1664. I. *Elizabeth Heath*, of Roxbury, widow, weake in body, make this my last will. I giue unto my sister; *Burnett & Martha Band*, my two Cowes, heer at home, after my Death, my sister to take her Choice, & my will is, they Bee kept this winter of my Hay, without any Charge to them. I giue to *Isaack Burnet*, Lately gone to sea, my young sow if he either Come Back or send before yᵉ next summer, else my will is, that his mother, my sister, shall have her, & that she [be] kept at my Charge untill then. I giue unto *Jacob Newells* wife 20s. to be paid her within one month after my Death, halfe in

money, the Rest in corne. I giue unto *Isaack Jones* his Daughter, that
he had by *Hannah Heath*, 15s. fiue in money, the rest in Corne, p^d her
within a Month after my Death. To *Mary Heath*, 20s. & to *Nicholas
Williams* as much, to be p^d to either of y^m within one month after my
Death. To *Thomas Morry*, 10s. to bee paid him a litle before his time
of seruice now Come out, & as much to his Mother that now is, to bee
paid her within a moneth after my Decease. I giue to my Cousinne
*Garry*, the Old man, 20s., & to *Goodman Fruysell*, that married *Goodman
Busketh* Daughter, as much, to be p^d each of them within one moneth
after my Death. I will & appoint that my Cousinne, *Cap^t Johnson*, shall
haue the First yeares increase of my two Cowes at *Isaack Williams*.
I giue to my Grand Children, my three Cowes, two Being at *Isaack
Williams*, & that I Lett to *Goodman Bush.* My Minde and will is, that
my Sister, *Waterman*, shall haue the use of my Mare, During her Life,
& I giue her unto *John Bowels*, my Grandchild, & my wearing apparrell
I giue Between my sister *Burnett* & *Waterman*. I appoint my sonne in
Law, *Bowels*, Executor of this will.

19^th Jan. 1664. Power of Administration to the Estate of *Elizabeth
Heath*, Widow, is Graunted to *John Boules*, to perform the Imperfect will
abouewritten, as neer as may bee, Bringing in an Inuentory of the Estate
to the next Court.                              *Edw. Rawson*, Recorder.

Inuentorye of the estate of Widow Heath, at Roxbury, prised p^r us,
Jan. 31, 1664, *William Parke, Thomas Welld*.

Debts owing to the Estate from M^r William Crowne, John Palmeter,
Robert Pepper, Jonathan Peak, Hugh Thomas, Arthur Garye, M^m Maeder,
Jn° Polly, Joseph Wise.

The Estate Debtor to George Branne, to her sister Burnum, to M^r
Jones Daughter, Jacob Newells wife, Thomas Morry & His mother,
James Frissell, Mary Heath, Nicholas Williams, Edward Morris, Arthur
Garye, Isaack Burnop ; Goodman Griffinne for Worke, for Coffinne &
Rayles, wine at her Buriall ; to Edward Morrisse for worke, Joshua
Lamb for worke, to Goodwife Tellar for nursing Her, to Thomas
Hanley, &c. Her Inuentory & Debts, £53.13s.09d. Legacies &
Debts owing, £46.18s.03d. Resteth Due, £6.15s.06d.

Feb. 8^th 1664. Jn° Bowles Deposed to the truth of the Inuentorye of
the Estate of the Widow Heath, his Late Mother in Lawe.
                              *Edward Rawson*, Recorder.

---

JAMES PENNYMAN.—The Last Will and Testament of me, *James Pennyman,* of Braintree, the 18th of the 10^th month 1664. My Debts being
discharged, and the Charge of my Funerall, which being Done, my
moueable Estate I thus Dispose of Halfe my uplands, halfe my Meadows,
halfe my Orchard, halfe my Barnes & outhousing, aad all my Dwelling
house, I doe giue unto my Beloued wife, for her support, & my Lesser
Children with her. The other halfe I giue unto my sonne, *Joseph*, & if
he thinke good, to Improoue it all for his Mothers Comfort, upon such
termes as his Mother & hee may agree. I thinke it will be Best, if hee
marry & build neer my wife, shee shall Lett him haue which part of the
Orchard she pleaseth. My moueable Estate I also giue wholy to my
wife, for her support & the Education of my Lesser Children. And
Because God hath blessed me with many Children I doe Commit it to
my wife's Discretion to Doe good unto them all, in as neer a proportion
as shee Canne, & to be most helpfull to them that haue most need, and

when she finisheth her life w$^t$ remaineth in her hands, either of my Lands or goods she shall, by y$^e$ Best aduice she can, proportion out unto my Children, so as to make them as equal sharers as shee Canne. My first borne, *James*, hauing been educated into such a way of liuinge as hee is hauing already had a portion I trust in the Lord it will bee such a Blessing as will answer his Double portion. To my youngest sonne, *Samuell*, & my 3 youngest Daughters, I giue £20 apeice, if it bee to bee had at my Wifes Decease, or afore, if need bee, & such as are married, to be made up to such a sum, if it be to be had.

Witnesse, *Richard Brackett*,                    *James Pennyman.*
*Robert Parmanter, Joseph Adames, Benjamin Thomson.*

31 Jan. 1664. *Richard Brackett* & *Joseph Adams* deposed [adding] that they heard James Penniman before he Dyed, while he was in good memory, Declare it as his Last will, that hee added to his will, that hee gaue his sonne, *James*, the wood of Fifteen acre in Great Feild.

*Edward Rawson*, Recorder.

Power of Administration, the same day, granted to the Estate of the Late *James Pennyman*, to *Lydia*, his wife to performe the Imperfect will aboue written, as neer as she Canne.          *Edward Rawson*, Recorder.

Inventory of the Estate taken 27th of Sept. 1664, by *Moses Paine*, *Joseph Adams*, Amt. £505.03s. Mentions, " his part of his Lease of M$^r$ Hoffes Necke," dwelling house, barne, stable, old house & orchard, 30 acres of Land or thereabout lying neer y$^e$ Mill pond, £70; 15 acres neer Knights necke, £30; about 18 acres nigh Weym° Ferrye, £55; 3 acres by Goodman Parmenters, £15, &c. &c.

Jan. 31, 1664. Lydia Penniman deposed to the Inventory of this Estate of her Late husband, James Penniman.

---

EDWARD CLAPP.—The last Will & Testament of M$^r$ *Edward Clappe*, of Dorchester, made this 3$^d$ day of January 1664—being weak in Body. My Funeral being Discharged & Just debts paid, I giue unto my wife, £20, in what goods she shall Desire it, and my will is, that shee Enjoye all my Housing, Land, orchard, planting Land and Meadow, together with y$^e$ two neerest Diuisions of woodland (except what is heerafter expressed) During her widowhood, except my sonne, *Nehemiah*, shall first Marry or attaine the age of 21 yeares, then, in such a Case, he shall haue such part as is heerafter expressed, also my wife shall enjoy one quarter of the tide Mill, untill Nehemiahs age afores$^d$, but if my wife marry, then my will is, that all my Land shall Returne unto my two sonnes as is heerafter expressed, & then my will is, that my wife·shall haue fourescore pounds more added to the first twenty, to bee hers foreuer. As for my children, my will is, that *Ezra*, shall haue as much as my Daughters, & that my four Daughters shall haue an equall portion, my sonne, *Nehemiah*, £20 more than my Daughters, I Canne set no summe, because I know not w$^t$ it will Come to, but my meaning is, they shall haue equall portions with what they that are married haue already receiued, it being £30 apiece, which is to be part of their portions. I will & appoint that *Ezra*, my Eldest sonne, shall haue my Land Lying at Milton, in the 12$^{th}$ Lott upon apprisement, & all my Lands lying on that side Naponsett Riuer, also a parcell of Medow at Dorchester necke, near pow-wow point, & another small parcell of Meadow at or near pine neck, at that Land on y$^e$ plaine at neck towards pow-wow point, & a quarter of the tide Mill, all

244

to bee prized & he receiuing paying as is Due by the aprointment of my Ouerseers, unto whom I giue full power to Order as they shall Judge most conducing to the good of my wife & of all my Children, keeping as near as may bee to this my will.  I Giue unto my sonne, *Nehemiah*, at marriage or age, one halfe of the Housing, Land, orchard Meadow, wood land, one quarter of the Mill, all to be prised, & he to pay his sisters their portion, to bee paid at the appointment of the Ouerseers.  [Unto his Daughters, *Susanna* and *Esther*, he gives equal single portions to be paid by his Executors, at the appointment of the Overseers.]  I appoint my wife & my sonne, *Ezra Clappe*, to bee my Executors, and Intreat my Louing Brethren, *Captaine Roger Clappe*, Ensighns *John Capen* & *Nicholas Clapp* to bee my Ouerseers.

[No Signatures.]

The testimony of *Roger Clapp*, aged 55 yeares or thereabout, & *Jnº Capen*, aged 51 yeares, & *Nicholas Clap*, aged 52 or thereabouts. Wee euery one of us being present at the House of *Edward Clappe*, on the 3ᵈ day of January 1664, did hear the writing now presented read unto the said *Edward Clap*, now Deceased, & he approued of it to be his will, & hee Caused it to bee read againe, in the hearing of his wife, to see if shee had any exception to make & then appointed it to be writ fairly out againe, which accordingly was forthwith Done, & wee Coming to the Intent to haue it perfected, were informed that he was asleepe & therefore were not willing to trouble him, it being Late in the night, went away & forbore at that present, & afterward it was neglected to bee presented, so nothing elce was done, concerning setling his Estate that we know of. Taken upon oath the 1ˢᵗ of February 1664, as the probate of the will hereto annext, yᵉ wife & sonne, Execut ͬˢ therein, accepting therof, the wife by her Letter & the sonne in Court by the 3 p ͬties aboue written, as attests,                                        *Edward Rawson*, Recorder.

Inventory of the Estate of *Edward Clappe*, of Dorchester who Departed this Life the 8th Jan. 1664, apprised by *Hopestill Foster*, *William Sumner*, Feb. 17th 1664.  Amt £794.15.3. including debts due the estate.  The Estate debtor to the amt. of £113.02.07.  Mentions land at seuerall places, at the litle & great necke, in the Cow walke at Milton, by Mr Stoughtons Farme, &c. &c.  Halfe the Mill valued at £50.

*Susanna Clapp* deposed, March 30, 1665 to this Inventory of the Estate of her late Husband, *Edward Clappe*.

---

SUSANNAH COMPTON.—The Last will and Testament of *Susannah Compton*, being in good health, widow of the Long since Departed, *John Compton*.  I Desyre that after the Lord hath taken me out of this Life & my Bodye Layed in the graue my few goods heerafter mentioned 1 giue & bequeath unto my Litle Grandchild, *Joseph Brisco* (uizᵗ) 1 Featherbed, 2 Feather Bolsters, 2 pͬ of Blanketts, 1 yearne Couerlead, three sheetes, 4 striped Curtaines, 2 pillow coates, 3 table Clothes, six napkinnes, 2 towells, foure pewter platters, three litle pewter Dishes, one porringer, 1 Bason, one Brasse skellet, 1 Iron pott, 1 scummer, 1 warmingpan, 2 Brasse Candlesticks & likewise 23s. in money, or what shall be unexpended by mee of the same during life.

12 (9 mo.) 1664.  Administration to the Estate graunted to *Abraham Busby*, in Right of *Joseph Brisco*, her Grandchild, to perform the Imperfect will aboue written.                    pͬ *Edward Rawson*, Recorder.

It was also Ordered that the Estate left by the said widdow *Compton*, amounting as p$^r$ Inuentory, £16.16, bee thus diuided, *Abraham Busby* to haue one halfe for Bringing up the s$^d$ *Joseph Brisco* & that hee pay £8.8s. for the other halfe in uery good pay, to s$^d$ *Joseph*, at twenty one yeares of age.                                   p$^r$ *Ed: Rawson*, Recorder.

The Inventory of the Estate taken by *Robert Saunderson, Edman Eddendon. Tho. Stedman senior* indebted to the estate, £1.17s. Nov$^r$. 12. 1664. *Abraham Busbye* deposed.

---

ROBERT PEARSE.—I, *Robert Pearse*, weak in body, knowing that this fraile Life will not Continue Long, doe desire, as Faithfully as I Canne, to Leaue that Little which God hath giuen mee of the things of this Life, so that it may be enjoyed after my Decease, by my survivors, with Comfort and peace. My debts paid, I giue unto my wife, *Anne Pearse*, the one halfe of all my Housing & Land in Dorchester, and the one halfe of all my Householde goods, and halfe of whatsoeuer is myne, and this houshold goods to be at her Disposing at her Death, but my Land and Housing to return to my sonne, *Thomas Pearse*, at her Death. My will is, that my wife shall haue power to sell any part of my Land (if need Doe require) for her maintenance, but not else, and I hope she will not need to doe it : I giue unto my sonne, *Thomas Pearse*, the other halfe of my housing & Land, to bee his at my Death, with the one halfe of my houshold goods, & whateuer is myne, to bee equally diuided between his mother & him, at my Death. My will is, that at the deeease of his mother, my sonne, *Thomas Pearse*, shall haue the other halfe of the Housing & Land his Mother had during her life. I giue to my Daughter, *Mary*, the wife of *Thomas Hearin*, of Dedham, £20, to bee her portion with that which I haue already giuen her. To her 5 Children, my Grandchildren, £10, to be equally diuided amongst them. [The two legacies of £30, to be paid by *Thomas Pearse*, within 3 years after the decease of his mother.] And now my Dear Child, a Fathers Blessing I Bequeath unto you both & yours, bee tender & Louing to your mother, Louing and Kind one unto another, stand up in your places for God and for his Ordinances while you Liue, then hee will bee for you & Blesse you. I appoint my wife, *Ann Pearse*, together with my sonne, *Thomas Pearse*. to be my Executors.  13 : 8$^{mo}$ : 1664.

Test *William Robinson,*                                   *Robert* ℳ *Pearse*
    *Elizabeth Arye*                                              his marke

2$^d$ March 1664.  *William Robinson* deposed.

Inuentorye of the Estate of *Robert Pearse*, who deceased Jan. 6$^{th}$ 1664, apprised Jan 28, 1664, by *Thomas Tilestone, William Robinson*. Mentions One necke of Land commonly called prime [pine] necke about 20 acres, £50 ; one House, barne & home Lott Cont. 6 acres, £40 ; 5 Acres of Meadow, £25 ; 36 acres of Common Land, £20, &c. &c. Whole amt. £181.  *Thomas Pearse* deposed, March 2$^d$ 1664, to this Estate of *Robert Pearse* his late father.

---

JOSHUA CARWITHY.—Inuentory of the Goods & Estate of *Joshua Carwithy*, late of Boston, mariner, deceased, taken by *Nathaniell Adams senior* & *William Pearse*, Sep$^t$. 1$^{st}$ 1663.  Amt. £70.11.7.

Mentions one parcell of land lying at the North end of the Town of Boston.

Power of Administration to the Estate graunted to *Elizabeth*, Relict of the late *Joshua Carwithy*, Oct.ʳ 27th. 1663.

The Court on request of the said *Elizabeth*, Relict of the said *Carwithy*, with her Consent, Ordered that she being married to one *Edmund Mumford*, shall bring vp the Child of yᵉ said *Joshua Carwithy* till it Come to the age of 18 or Daie of marriage, and also that the Child haue the one half of yᵉ Estate in the Inuentory expressed payd vnto it as its portion—£35.5s.10.                              *Edw : Rawson*, Recorder.

---

THOMAS GROCER.—I, *Thomas Grocer*, of London, in Old England, now Residing in Roxberry, in New England, & being by the prouidence of God, sicke & weak & not knowing how the Lord will dispose of mee, Doe make this my Last Will and Testament. For what Estate I haue in New England, which may amount to the ualue of £250, at the ualue of New England Money, out of which goods my will is that all my debts bee paid according to Couenant, also that the remainder therof, according as it is prized, be sent for Old England, that is when the goods doe Returne from Barbadose, and that to be done by the first opportunity by my Brother in Law, *John Goodall*, in such goods as shall be most profitable to send according to the wisedome & discretion of my ouerseers, the said Goods to be deliuered unto my mother in Law, *Sarah Goodall*, to bee disposed of by her according to her discretion. But if shee bee dead, then to be deliured to my Brother, *Jnᵒ Grocer*, in the County of Suffolke in Walson by the Wallowes. My mother Liues in London, in Mary Magdalens Court yard at the bottom of Barnabees Streete in Southwàrk, if my Mother be dead, my will is that my Brother shall diuide that goods that shall Come to him from New England equally amongst my Children. Mʳ *Edward Denicon*, of Rocksbery & my Brother in Law, *Jnᵒ Goodall*, aforesaid, to bee my executors, & I Intreat *Reuerend Mʳ Danforth*, of Rocksberye, & *Mʳ Robt Gibs*, Merchant of Boston, to bee ouerseers, that my will may bee performed, without whose Councell and allowance the Executors shall haue no power to act. Being sencible what I doe, 29ᵗʰ Jan. 1664.                              *Thomas Grocer.*

Witnesse, *John Swinerton*

        his
    *William h Cleaues*
      marke

Mʳ *Edward Denicon* came publickly into the Court Renounct his executorshippe to this will.                              *Edward Rawson*, Recorder.

This will on the other side exprest, being writ in Haste, & not accordinge to true forme, I therefore by these presents giue unto *John Swinerton*, now at Rocksbery, Full power to make a will for mee, in true forme, according to the Law of New England, & the true Intent of my will Expressed on the other side of this paper, 29ᵗʰ Jan. 1664.

Wit. *William ∩ Cleaues*                              *Thomas Grocer.*
     marke
*Elisabeth ⋈ Parkers*
    marke

8th Feb. 1664. *Wᵐ Cleaues & Elisabeth Parker* deposed.

An Inuentorye of Mʳ Thomas Grocers goods, at *Goodwife Parmeters* House, at Roxburye, this 5ᵗʰ Febr. 1664.

Goods Belonging to his Estate at Boston, taken pʳ *James Oliuer & John Saffan*, Feb. 6ᵗʰ 1664. Furthermore a Considerable number of

Bookes, of seuerall sortes, which time will not permitt to apprise in p'ticular and 'therefore ualued at a guess or Lumpe according to estimation to the summe of £56.

Debts due the Estate from *M* *Parker*, *M* *John Paine*, *Coll. Searle*, *Mr John Wilson*, *Capt James Oliuer*, *John Lowell*, *M* *Ratcliffe*, *Mr Phillippe Wharton*. Summe totall, £243.11.9.

Debts due to *Doctor Alcocke*; *M* *Daniell Weld* for Cakes for his Buriall ; to *Gm. Parmiter* for wine & Beer ; *Jn°* *Chandler* Digging the graue ; to *Samuell Gore* for Coffinne & Raile ; to *W* *Crawes*, *M* *Atkinson*, *M* *Chaplin*, &c. &c.

This part of the estate apprised by *John Swinerton*, and *Thomas Weld*, being desyred therunto by *John Goodale*, who is Brother to the Deceased.

Feb. 8th 1664. *Jn°* *Goodall* Came into the Court and made choice of *Richard Way* to bee his Guardian, which the Court allowed of. The said *John Goodall* deposed to this inuentorye.

5th Feb. 1664. An Inuentorye of seuerall Books Belonging to *Thomas Grocers* Estate, deceased, which were found in his Warehouse. 160 volumes, many of them mentioned by name, besides 410 Bookes in 8°, 12°, 24°, 120 sticht Bookes at 2*d* p* each, 384 Books at 18*d.* Whole am* of books apprised, £66. 10. 06.

(12) 3. 65. *Hezekiah Vsher.*

----

WILLIAM HOLLOWAY, of Boston, being sicke, Doth make his Last will. First, Debts to be paid. Unto my sonne, *Timothy Holloway*, 5*s*. [to his sons, *Nehemiah*, *Elisha*, *Mallachey*, and dau. *Esther Holloway*, 5*s.* each.] Unto *Elizabeth*, my wife, my House & Orchard which I now possesse, in the Town of Boston, with all my Household goods, Debts & Estate, not before giuen, with all such portions of Land as now Belong or shall heerafter fall to me in New England or in Old England, shee to haue the sole Dispose of all after my Decease, whom I make sole executrix of this my will, 9th May, 1664. *William Holloway.*

Witness heerunto,
   *Sarah Sandford, John Sandford,*
      *John Sandford*, deposed, 6th of April 1665.

Inuentory of his Estate taken by *Henry Allinne*, *Edward Drinker*. Amt. £289. 9. 9. Mentions 2 Chaires & a pillion, &c.

*Elizabeth Holloway.* Relict & Executrix, deposed April 6th 1665.

----

JOHN GILLET.—Inventory of *Jn°* *Gilletts* Estate, testified to by *William Wardell* and *Elizabeth* his wife. *William Wardell* deposed, November 3, 1663.

(See Register, Vol. XII., page 275.) (See p. 229).

----

BARTHOLOMEW CAD.—Inuentorye of the Estate of *M* *Bartholmew Cad*, Deceased, Apprised by *John Wiswall*, *Daniell Turell*, June 14, 1665. Amt. £482.09.06. Mentions, A House & Land by the new meeting House, £120 ; ⅓ part in the pinke patience, at sea, £100 ; a parcell of Land about Casco baye, Cost £30, &c. &c. Mary Cadd, Relicte of the Late Bartholmew Cadd, Deposed, June 16th. 1665, to the Inuentorye of the Estate of the said Bartholmew, her late Husband.

# ABSTRACTS FROM THE EARLIEST WILLS ON RECORD IN THE COUNTY OF SUFFOLK, MASS.

[Prepared by WILLIAM B. TRASK, of Dorchester.]

BARBARA CHADWELL.—25th March 1665. I, *Barbara Chadwell*, wife of *Thomas Chadwell*, of Boston in New England, Shipwright, being sick, make this my Last will. As for such worldly Estate as it hath pleased God to blesse me with, & according to ye power reserued to my selfe before my marriage with my now Husband, *Thomas Chadwell*, & that with his approbation (before marriage obtained) Do desire that the will & Legacies of my first Husband, *Georg Dauis*, be fully fulfilled towards his Children, *Samuell & John Dauis* & that their Respectiue Legacies be paid to them according to the tenor of ye sd will (uizt) to *Samuel Dauis*, £100, & to *Jnᵒ Dauis*, £60. And as for that Estate I haue in my owne power reserued, as aforesaid, I giue to my said two sonnes, to be equally diuided between them when they shall attaine to the age of 21, each of them, & in case of death of either, the suruiuor to haue the whole, & in the mean time, till they shall accomplishe that age, I Desire my Louing Freinds, *John Baker & Daniel Turell*, to take the Care & ouersight of my said Children, & in Conuenient time to place them forth as they shall see may bee for the good of the Children, & my sd Ouerseers to take sd Estate wholie into their Custodye & to improoue it as may bee for the benefit of my Children, And thereout also to supplye them with what they or either of them shall stand in need of, in the time, before they are placed forth.

Barbara ⋈ Chadwell.

In the presence of *Alexander Adams, William Pearse, sen.ʳ* who deposed, 30th March 1665.

Power of Administration to said Estate Granted, the same day, to *Daniell Turell & Jnᵒ Baker* Ouerseers by her appointed to performe the Imperfect will of hers.      *Edw. Rawson*, Recorder.

*John Phillips* and *John Sunderland* were chosen by the above named overseers to make an Inventory of said Estate. Amt. £361. 5. 9¼. Mentions Land pr the new Burying place, &c. *Daniell Turell & John Baker* both of Boston, Blacksmiths, deposed, March 31, 1665.

---

JOHN FEARING.—I, *John Fearing*, of Hingham, being sicke, make this my Last will. I giue unto *Margrett Fearing*, my wife, the new End of my Dwelling house, both Lower & upper Roomes, during her Life. I giue unto *Margrett*, my wife, the Bed as it now stands in the parlour, furnished with one Fetherbed, one Fether Bolster, two feather pillows with pillowbeers, two pair of sheetes, the Best Couering & blankett with the Curtaines, wᶜʰ said Bed and Furniture, together with the wearing apparrell of my said wife, both of Woollen & Lining, she shall haue Liberty to dispose of unto whom she please after her Decease. I giue unto my wife, £30 to take it out of what part of my Estate shee please, & also the one halfe of the Orchard & the summer keeping of two Cowes in the Home pasture, which said thirty pounds Estate, if my wife Doe not spend it During her life, shall be Diuided amongst my Children, as my other Estate is, after her Decease. Unto my Children, the rest of my Estate, my eldest sonne a double portion, the Rest of my Children equall shares, & they shall pay unto their mother, *Margret Fearing*, eighteen pence upon the pound, yearly, During her life, according to what portion of my Estate each Child possesseth, the s^d pay to be paid unto their Mother, shall bee two thirds in wheate & Barley, & one third in Indyan Corne. Unto my two sonnes, *John Fearing* & *Israell Fearing*, all my Lands, both upland & meadow, & they shall pay unto their sisters, *Mary Fearing* & *Sarah Fearing*, their portion of my Estate within one year after my Decease, their portions to bee paid them, the one halfe in Corn & the other halfe in Cow Cattle, and my Lands shall bee Diuided unto my sonnes as Followeth, to my sonne, *John Fearing*, the other part of my Dwelling house, and also y^e new end of my Dwelling house after the Decease of my wife, also the Barne with y^e other out houses, together with the Home Lott that was Formerly *Henry Tuttills*, & halfe the Home Lott which was Formerly *Edmond Hubbards*, together with all the Fencing belonging thereunto, and all my Land upon Squirrill hill & three planting Lotts upon weiryall Hill, one Formerly the Lott of *Ralph Woodward*, one Formerly the Lott of *Edmond Pitts*, one Formerly the Lott of *Henry Rust*, & my planting Lott near Weymouth Riuer & my salt Meadow at Weymouth riuer & the one halfe of my Woodlotts at the weare. I giue unto my sonne, *Israell Fearing*, the Home Lott that was Formerly *Ralph Woodwards*, halfe the home Lott that was Formerly *Edmond Hubberts*, my Land at the Old planters hill, Formerly *John Towars*, a Lott upon weryill hill, formerly *Jn° Beales sen^r*., my great Lott upon the great playne, all my meadow at Connyhasset, & halfe my wood Lotts at the weare. I appoint my two sonnes, *John Fearing* & *Israel Fearing*, Joint Executors. 11^th May 1665.

It is to be understood that my will is, that when my sonne, *John*, possesseth the new end of my house then as it shall be ualued to be worth, he shall pay y^e other of my children there shares of it as my other estate is Diuided. *John Fearing.*

In y^e presence of

*Mathew Hawkes*, *John Thaxter*, who deposed, 15^th June 1665.

Inventory of the Estate of *John Fearing* taken May 26, 1665, by *Mathew Hawkes*, *John Thaxter*, *Thomas Lincorne.* Amt. £331. 4^s. Among the lands enumerated, was a planting Lott formerly *Austens.*. Mentions, A prentice Boye, valued at £6. *John Ferringe*, sonne of the Late *John Ferring*, deposed June 15^th 1665.

---

WILLIAM FEILD.—Inventory of William Feild presented by Jn° Sweete. Mentions " a noat from M^r Richard Prise." 27 July 1664, administration on the estate is granted to Jn° Sweete, in behalfe of y^e mother of y^e said Feild or other his neerest freinds, giving security to administer according to lawe. Jn° Sweete deposed before the court that Edward Rawson Recorder has a true Inuentory of y^e late W^m Feild to his best knowledge &c. July 28, 1664.

---

HENRY BISHOP.—Inventory of y^e Goods & Chattells of Henry Bishop late of Boston, deceased. Signed by John Hull, July 19, 1664.

24^th Aug. 1664. Power of Administration to the estate granted to Elizabeth, relict of Henry Bishop.

---

SAMUEL MAYO.—April 26, 1664. Power of Administration to the Estate of the Late Samuell Mayoh, Marriner, Deceased, is graunted to M^r John Mayo, his Father, the Widow of the said Sam Mayo refusinge to take Administration in the Behalfe of the Creditors & Children of the said Sammuell so farr as the Estate will Reache unto.

Inventorye of the Estate taken Apl. 25, 1664. Amt. £21. 8. 10. Apprised pr Christopher Gibson, Michaell Wills. Mr John Maio deposed, 26 April 1664, to the Inventory of the Late Samuell Mayo, his sonne.

---

ANDREW CLOADE.—Inuentorye of the Estate of Andrew Cloade, Deceased, apprised by Thomas Brattle, John Andrus, William Tillye, 4th of Aprill 1664. Amt. £417. 15. Elizabeth Cloade deposed to this Inuentorye of the Estate of her Late Husband, Andrew Cloade, Apl 30th 1664. Sundrye payments made pr Elizabeth Cloade since her Husbands Decease. Debt to Capt. Alleis, Cooper; to the Ministers at the New Church; to Richard Price; for Neglect of Training, 5s.; to Godfrye Armitage, &c. Amt. £18. 4. 6.

---

ANNE ROCKWOOD.—Power of Administration to the Estate of the Late Anne Rockwood is graunted to John Taylor, that Married Phœbe, Daughter to said Anne Rockwood, in Behalfe of His Wife & such others it may Concerne.

Inuentorye of what goods was found Lefte by ye Widow Rockwood, Late of Braintree, at her Decease, March 1, 1664. Amt. 21. 12. 06.

Apprised pr Frauncis Elliott, Caleb Hubberd. John Tailor deposed 29th Apl. '64.

---

JOHN NEWGATE,* of Boston.—25 of Nov 1664. Debts being paid and funeralls discharged, I give vnto my wife, *Ann Newgate*, my farme at Rumly Marsh, with all my lands belonging there vnto, and my house at Charles towne, with the orchard there vnto belonging, and my house in which I now dwell, with the appurtenances thereto belonging, and the house in which my sonne in lawe, *Simon Linde*, now dwells in, with all the ground thereto belonging, during her naturall life, she the said *Ann* continueing in the state of widdowhoode, payeing vnto the Colledge in Cambridge, the sume of five pounds pr ann. during the said tyme of her widdowhoode, for the security of which payment my said farme is already bound and ingaged.† But if my said wife should happen to marry againe, then my will and mind is, That she shall haue onely the thirds of all my said houses and lands in Boston and of my said farme at Rumly Marsh, but not the thirds of my said house and land at Charles towne, for that the said annuall pay to the Colledge is after such marriage of her, the said Ann, to bee paid by others. I give vnto my sonn, *Nathaniell Newgate*, my said farme, with all the lands there vnto belonging, and my house and

---

*Newgate, John, a merchant, selectman and constable of Boston, was admitted freeman in 1635, and elected representative at the March and Sept. sessions, 1638. He d. in 1665, leaving several children. Nathaniel, Boston, son of the preceding, was member of the artillery company in 1646. He had one son, Nathaniel, whose children were, Isabel; Lewis, b. 1697; John, b. 1703; some of whom wrote the name *Newdigate.—Farmer*.

†Thomas Greenough, in a letter to Shute Shrimpton Yeamans, dated May 1, 1767, writes thus, "By the will of John Newgate, who owned the Chelsea farm, who died in the year 1665 [he] gave £5 p. ann. forever to Harvard College in Cambridge, and subjected the farm to pay said sum, and your great grandfather, Col. Saml. Shrimpton, purchased this farm of Jno. Newgate's son Nathaniel, with this incumbrance of £5; he gave £350 sterling for said farm, as appears by the deed."—*Sumner's East Boston*, p. 358.

In 1779, it was leased to Henry Howell Williams for £300 a year; on the 8th of April, 1793, it was purchased by Mr. Williams.—*Ibid.*, p. 324.

ground at Charlestowne, for him, his heires and assignes, to possesse and enioy them, next and ymmediately after such marriage of her, the said *Ann*, as is aforesaid, or otherwise next and ymmediately after her decease, if she continue in the state of widdowhoode, he my said sonn, *Nathaniell*, his heires and assignes payeing the said annuall payment of £5 to the Colledge, next and ymmediately after he shall possesse and enioy the said farme, in lew of which annuall payment I giue him my said house and ground at Charlstowne, also yeilding and payeing vnto my said wife one third part of the rent of the said farme, during her life, after such marriage as aforesaid. I giue vnto my said sonne in law, *Simon Lind*, my said house in Boston, in which I now dwell, with the appurtenances thereto belonging, and my said house in which he the said *Lind* now dwells, with all the ground thereto belonging, for him, his heiers and assigns, to possess and enioy next & ymmediately after the decease of *Ann*, my wife, or otherwise after such marriage of the said *Ann*, yeilding and payeing vnto her during her life a third part of the annuall rents or proffitts thereof. Also £220 within six moneths after hee shall possesse said houses and lands, videlt £110 to my sonn in law, *Peeter Olliver*, that married with my daughter *Sarah*, and the other £110 vnto my sonn in law, *Edward Jackson*, that married with my daughter Elizabeth. And if, either my said sonne *Jackson*, or my said sonn *Olliver*, shall depart this life before their said legacies shalbe payable, as aforesaid, then my will and mind is, that the £110 shalbe equally divided betweene the children of the said *Elizabeth*, and the other £110, betweene the Children of the said *Sarah*. I giue vnto my grand Children, *John Olliver* and *Thomas Olliver*, sonnes of *John Olliver*, deceased, £20, [£10 to each] To bee paid them when they shall accomplish their severall ages of 20 yeares, And in case either of them depart this life before he hath accomplished his said age, Then that sonne which survive shall haue the others portion. I giue to all the Children now liveing that my daughter, *Elizabeth*, had by the said *Edward Jackson*, her now husband, £10 a peece, to bee paid vnto the said *Edward*, their father, or *Elizabeth*, their Moother, which of them shalby then liveing, within one yeare after my decease, and they to ymprove it for their said Children, vntill they shall accomplish their severall ages of 18 yeares, or dayes of marriage, which shall first happen, And in case any of them shall depart this life before they attayne their severall ages of 18 or dayes of marriage, then those Children which survive shall haue the others portion proportionably divided amongst them. I giue to all the Children now liveing, that my daughter, *Sarah*, had by the said *Peeter Olliver*, her now husband, £10 a peece, [conditionally given as to the other children, and contingencies provided for.] vnto all the children, now liveing, that my daughter, *Hanna* had by my sonn in law, *Simon Lynd*, £10 a peece [on like conditions with the other grand children] To the child, now liveing, of my sonne, *Nathaniell Newgate*, £10 to bee paid twoe yeare after my decease, hee to improve the same for his said childs vse, vntill he accomplish the age of 18 yeares, or day of marriage. To my brother in law, *Thomas Townsin*, of Lin, £10 to be paid him within 3 yeares after my decease. Vnto my wifes sister, that married with *Willinam Newgate*, my Vnckls sonn, liveing in London, £5, to be paid within one yeare after my decease. To *Jonathan Jackson*, sonn of the said *Edward Jackson*, £5, within halfe a yeare after my decease. Vnto the free Schoole of the towne of Boston, to bee ymproved towards the yearely mayntenance thereof, £10, to be paid within 3 moneths after

my decease. To *Mr. John Wilson*, Pastor of the Church of Boston, £8, to bee paid within 3 moneths after my decease. Vnto such Ministers within this Jurisdiction as ar Consionable in their places, and yet haue but small Mayntenance, £30, to be paid to the said *Mr. John Wilson* and he to dispose thereof as he shall see meete, to the intent aforesaid ; to be paid within 3 moneths after my decease. Vnto the poore of the Church of Boston, £10, to be disposed of by the deacons of the said Church, as they shall see neede. To my said daughter, *Jackson*, a gilt Salt and a gilt wine cup. To my said daughter, *Olliver*, a silver beere boule and a silver wine cupp. To my said daughter, *Linde*, a silver porringer and three silver spoones. The rest of my plate I leaue to my wife, to dispose thereof as she please. I will that whatsoever goods of myne there shall appeare to bee more then is bequeathed as aforesaid, be equally divided between my wife and my fower children, namely, *Nathaniell, Elizabeth, Sarah* and *Hanna*. And hopeing of the faithfulness of my said sonnes in law, *Edward Jackson* and *Simon Linde*, to prforme the trust herein committed vnto them, I make them executors of this my last will, and also my said sonn in law, *Peeter Olliver*, my overseer of this my will, and doe giue him, for his care and oversight thereof, £10, over and aboue what is before vnto him bequeathed.                          *John Newgate.*
In prsence of *Robert Howard.* Not. publ.
& *Mary Howard*, who deposed 11th Sept 1665.
   Codicil.—Whereas in my bequest to my sonne in law, *Simon Lynde*, it is thus expressed (And the said house in which he now dwels with all the ground thereto belonging) my intent and meaneing is, That inclosed land lyeing next aboue that land late in the possession of *Governor Indecott*, together with the house the said *Lind* lives in, with the orchard & rest of the ground about the same house, all which contayneth fower acres, more or lesse. Further my will is, that *Thomas Townsin*, of Lin, haue his leagacy aboue mentioned, within one yeare after my decease. And that bequest of £10, to the free Scoole in Boston, I, doe hereby make void whatsoever is aboue written, to the Contrary thereof notwithstanding. 8th of May 1665.
   *Robert Howard* Not. publ.                          *John Newgate.*
   *Elizabeth Baker*
   11th Sept 1665   Mr. Robert Howard, notary publick, & *Elizabeth Baker*, deposed.
   Inventorye of the Goods and Estate of M*r*. *John Newgate*, deceased, taken the 8th September 1665, by *James Pen, Tho: Brattle, Tho. Buttolph*, Amt. £2496, 13. 11.
   26th Oct. 1665. M*r*. *Edward Jackson*, and M*r*. *Simon Lynde*, deposed. Addition made by M*r*. *Simon Lynd* one of ye Executors vpon ye original Inventory to ye sume of £173. 16. 10.


THOMAS THAYER.   I, *Thomas Tayer** of Brantrey, in Suffolke, in the Massachusetts Colonie, of New England, Shoemaker, 24th June 1664,

---

*"Old Thomas Thayer dyed 2d. 4 mo. 1665. Margery Thayer dyed 11 d. 12 mo. 1672."—*Thayer's Family Memorial*, from Braintree Records.
   Children :—*Thomas*[2] *Thayer, Jr.*, was probably married in England, to Hannah or Anna ——. They had eight children, viz: Thomas, Elizabeth, Isaac, John, Experience, Isaac, Ebenezer, Deborah. He died Aug. 9, 1663, at the age of more than 70; his wife, Anna, deceased Feb. 7, 1698, a. about 73. *Ferdinando*[2] second son of Thomas[1] and Margery Thayer, m. Huldah Hayward, of Braintree, Jan. 14, 1652. "He lived in Braintree, until after his father's death," says Dr. Thayer, "when he removed to

253

doe make this my last will. Vnto my wife, *Margery*, that now is, all my lands, goods and estate in Brantrey, duing the tyme of her life, and after her decease I giue vnto my sonne, *Thomas Tayer*, his heiers & assigns all my ground, being over Monotoquot River, within the limmitts of Brantrey, with the tymber and other wood growing or fallen vppon the same, with the other the appurtenances, part of which ground he hath allready in his possession. Vnto *Fardinando Tayer*, my sonne, his heiers and assignes (ymmediately after the decease of *Margery*, my wife) my house and orchard therevnto belonging, lyeing in Braintrey, with all the planting ground and pasture lyeing betweene y⁰ high way and the River, called Montoquot River, aforesaid, And on the other side of the high way from the south sid of the barne to the end of the lotte. Further my will is, that the said *Fardinando*, shall haue free liberty to cut fale and Carry away fier wood for his and his now wifes owne burning, of and from my lott called Twenty acre Lotte, during his and his said wifes life. Vnto my sonne, *Sidrache Tayer*, his heiers and assignes, ymmediately after the decease of *Margery*, my wife, a parcel of ground in Brantrey, which shall begin at the corner of the barne next his dwelling house and shall run with a straight line to the vpper end of the lott. I giue twenty acres of land more vnto the said *Sidrach*, his heiers and assignes [as before] land in Brantrey, next vnto the ground of *Henry Neale*, provided he, his heiers and assignes, pʳmit my sonne, *Fardinando*, & his now wife, to take wood thereof for their owne burneing during their naturall lives, as before éxpressed. I giue all my goods and Chattells vnto my grand Children, to be equally divided amongst them. If any of my said Children shall appeare to be discontented & murmur at this my last will and testament, Then my will and minde is, That any such child, one or more of them, shall haue but five shillings for their portion, and the portion or portions of any such Child or Children so murmoring and discontented, as aforesaid, shall be equally divided amongst the rest of my Children and Grand children. I appoint my wife, *Margery*, & sonne, *Fardinando*, executors of this my last will and testament. *Thomas ⋈ Thayer.*
*Sarah ⋈ Sauill, Ruth ⋈ Basse, Margery Flint.*
13 Sepᵗ 1665. *Sarah Sauill & Ruth Basse* deposed.
[On the other side of the original will, is the following, which is not on record :]—" Wee, *Ferdinando, Thomas,* and *Sydrach Thayer,* children of *Thomas Thayer,* deceased, That is to say upon Aduice & counsell, The Abouesayd *Ferdinando,* who by his fathers will is made executor [of] his fathers last Will and Testament seeing some Inequality, especially in the behalfe of his elder brother, with some litell to *Sydrach,* in consideration that brotherly loue may continue, Doth grant to his beloued brethren all the land aboue the highway excepting Two acres, which two acres is bounded on the line running from the highway from the south side of the land where the barne stood and so upon a streight line to the south corner

---

Mendon, Mass. with a colony from Braintree and Weymouth, where many of his descendants are living at this day.'' Ferdinando and Huldah Thayer had 12 children, five or six born in Braintree, the others in Mendon. The names of the children were Sarah, Huldah, Jonathan, David, Naomi, David, Thomas, Samuel, Isaac, Josiah, Ebenezer, Benjamin. Huldah died at Mendon, Sept. 1, 1690; Ferdinando d. March 28, 1713. *Shadrach*² youngest son of Thomas¹ and Margery, m. Mary Barrett, 1, 11, 1654, and settled in Braintree. Shadrach² and Mary had two children, Rachel and Tryall. She died 2. 2. 1658. The second wife of Shadrach² was Deliverance Priest. By this connection he had seven children, viz: Freelove, Mary, Timothy, Samuel, Ephraim, Hannah, William. He died Oct. 19, 1678. Deliverance, his widow, d. Jan. 17, 1723, a. about 79 years.—*Thayer's Family Memorial,* pp. 136–153.

of goodman *Prays* line; all on the south side of this, to bee to *Sydrach*, to him & his heires for euer, and the said *Ferdinandoes* to come Inward towardes *Thomas* from that line seuen rods [    ] broad towards *Thomas*, and the rest to bee to *Thomas*, to his heires execqutors and assignes for-euer. This being a full and unanimous agreement betweene the three brethren. And wee, the Aboue said *Thomas, Ferdinando* & *Sydrach* doe heerby engage ourselues, Joyntly and seuerally, for himselfe, neuer to make any disturbance, either of other any expression in our fathers will notwithstanding.

Witnesse our hands this fhirtieth of June one Thousand six hundred sixty fiue.                                                    [No signatures.]

Inventory of the estate of Thomas Thayer sen^r of Braintree Late deceased, taken by *Francis Elliott, John French, Samuell Tomson*, 7th June, 1665. 13th Sept. 1665. *Ferdinando Thayer* deposed.

---

LAWRENCE SMITH.—The testimony of *William Stoughton* & *Mary Manfield*, of Dorchester, concerning the last will & Testament of *Lawrence Smith*,* late of Dorchester, who did decease there upon 3 (8) 1665 is, That the sayd *Lawrence Smith* upon the 29 (7) foure dayes before his decease, being of good understanding, & very apprehensive of his approaching end, did, in the presence of his wife & children & the persons above mentioned, Expresse and declare, That as to his Temporal estate his will was, that it should bee divided between his wife & children, ac-cording to the Law of this Jurisdictiõ in that case provided, only unto his wife hee gave, over & above her thirds, his Land wch lyes upon Dorchester Neck, And of this his Last will & Testament he did constitute his wife his sole executrix.

31 Jan. 1665.   *Mr W^m Staughton* & *Mary Mansfeild* deposed.
                                              *Edw. Rawson*, Record^r.

Inventory of Estate taken 28 (9) 1665, by *Hopestill Foster, John Minott, Clement Maxfilld.* Amount £485. 18. Mentions 6½ acres land on Dorchester neck—£26; two lots on the north side of Naponset River, the other on the south side, contains 15 acres, £5, &c., &c. Bought of John Wilcock, 5¼ acres, 32 rod. 31 Jan. 1665, *Mary Smith* deposed.

---

PHILIP EDWARDS.—Boston 9ber 9th 1664. Power of Administration to the Estate of the Late *Philip Edwards*, who was found Drowned, is Graunted to *William Trescott*, in Behalfe of his wife, or the neerest of Kinne or others Concerned, Giuing securitye, &c. Goods prised, by *Thomas Jones, Henry Garnsey*, at £14.15.01. Mentions Goodman *Gurnill, Clem. Maxfeild, Tho. Bird, Lawrence Smithe, Goodman Garnsey, Captain Clappe, Robert Walker, Mr Greenleife.*

*W^m Trescott* deposed.

---

NATHANIEL HEATON.—Boston, Feb. 1st 1664. In Answer to the petition of *Nathaniell Heaton*, of Dedham, & *Elisabeth Heaton*, of Boston, Power of Administration to the Estate of *Nathaniell Heaton*, Long since Deceased, is graunted to M^r *W^m Parkes* & Ensighne *Daniell Fisher.*

---

* Blake, in his Annals of Dorchester, under date of 1665, says :—" This year Died Lawrence Smith, often Selectman, &c." We do not find him mentioned as holding that office, in the lists given by Blake from year to year. John Smith, who, it is conjectured, was his father, was one of the Selectmen of Dorchester in 1650. In 1657 Lawrence Smith was a "Bayliff," and in 1663, one of the three Raters in the town. He died on the 3d of October, 1665.

Inuentorye of the Estate prised by *Edward Ransford, Jacob Elliott, Theophilus Frary*. Amt. £139.17.02. Giuen to *Cornelius Fisher Wife Leah*, £10.

M*r* *W*m *Parkes*, of Roxburye, & *Ensighne Daniell Fisher*, of Dedham, deposed, Feb. 1st, 1664.

For the setlinge of the abouesaid estate, Betweene the Widow of the said Heaton & Her Children by the said Heaton, The Court Doth order that the Widow shall haue one full third part of the whole, & that the Eldest sonne shall haue a Double portion of the remainder, & the Rest of the Children shall haue the remainder equally Departed among them; & In Case that any persons possessed of any part of the said Estate refuse to render the same to the order of the courte, the Administrators are Impowered to make Legall proceeds against the with Holders.

*Edward Rawson*, Recorder.

_____

PHILIP RICE.—Inuentorye of *Phillipe Rice* His estate apprised by *Gamaliell Waite* & *Simon Rogers*.

Feb. 3, 1664. Administration to the Estate graunted unto *Deacon Richard Trusdall* & *Richard Tailor*, who deposed.

# ABSTRACTS FROM THE EARLIEST WILLS ON RECORD IN THE COUNTY OF SUFFOLK, MASS.

[Prepared by MR. WILLIAM B. TRASK of Dorchester.]

WILLIAM ASTWICKE.—Being in my perfect understanding & memorye Doe make this my Last will & Testament. My soul I giue unto the Lord Jesus my Redeemer, & my Body to my friends to be Decently Interred by them. Debts due me in this Countrey, as far as may bee, Improued for the payment of my debts, so far as it will amount unto, & lest that should fall short, my will is that my executor, Mr. John Swinerton, be impowered, in case there lack any thing for the Defraying of Charges, that then my will is y^t Mr. John Swinerton bee, and is by these presents fully & absolutely in power to aske, receiue, Demaund & recouer for mee the full and just summe of £20 in the hands of my Loueing [      ] in North Hampton, there in old England, that what remaynes, all Charges being Defraied heer, that the residue Mr. Swinerton being honestly satisfyed. My Executor is my Louing Friend, Mr. John Swinerton, & my Ouerseers, p^r my request, is Mr. Danforth & John Palmeter Jr, July 31, 1665.

Witnesse, *Edward Denicon*                                    *William Astwicke.*
            *John Goodall*

My great Coate, with silver lace & Doublet & Breeches to it, of Broad Cloth, I by this will give to Mr. John Swinerton.

14 Feb. 1665. Mr. Edward Denison deposed.

Inventory of the Estate taken by *Edward Denicon, John Stebbinnes.* Mentions, *James Hophton, Nathan Bradley, Jn^o Blackman, Thomas Green Jr.,* of Malden ; *Peter Addams, Th^o. Holman, M^r. Allcocke, G^m. Parmenter.*

*John Swinerton,* deposed, Feb. 14, 1665 to the estate of *W^m Astwicke,* late of Aundle, in North hampton, that Dyed in Rocksburye.

---

ROBERT BLOTT.—I, *Robert Blott*, Being in perfect memorye, Doe Make this my Last will and testament. I make *Edward Ellis*, my sonne in Law, Husband to *Sarah*, my Daughter, my Executor, and giue unto him my House and the lot belonging thereunto, with all the appurtenances. Also my will is, that he pay my Daughters Children, whose names was *Woodford*, of Conniticott, £3. My will is, that my sonne *Edward Ellis*, shall giue to my dau. Tosiors children, £7, and 3 bushells of wheate, & two of Indyan Corne, besides, to her Eldest sonne, *John Green*, Cloth to make him a Coate. My will is that the said Edward shall giue to my dau. *Lovetts* Children, of Braintree, £7, and 3 bushells of wheat, and 2 bushells of Indyan, also to my sonne in Law, *Danil Turins* Children, £8 ;—that my dau. *Tosior*, & my dau. *Louet* shall haue halfe the house hold stuffe equally Diuided betweene them, and the other halfe to my dau. *Ellis*, also 3 bushells of Maulte to be Diuided Between my three Daughters. Also to Daniel Louett my sonne in Law I giue my Best Coate, in Witnesse whereof I haue sett to my hand this 27^th of the third Month called May 1662.

257

I, Edward Ellis by god's helpe shall pay these Legacies, without Fraud or guile at or before twelue months after yᵉ Death of my Father in Lawe.

Robert Hall and Robert Walker, Ouer eers.

Robert † Blott.

Witnesse, Robert Saunderson
Alexander Baker.

Boston yᵉ 27ᵗʰ of March 1665. Whereas since the time specified in my will on the other side I haue through gods Fauor & patience liued to expend the Corne of seueral Kinds then giuen by Legacye, my will is therefore that the aforesaid Legacies so far as Related to the Corn, Do Cease and Determine. Also my will is that Daniel Louetts eldest sonne haue a remnant of Clothe, that I haue by mee, besides that Cloth before mentioned. And further my will is that sicknesse & Funeral charges be paid for out of my Houshold stuffe, and the Rest to bee as before is said to bee Diuided. Lastly my will is that whereas I haue giuen my house and Ground unto my sonne Ellis, my meaning & will is herein only this, that it is for the good & Benefit of my Dau. Sara & the children of my sonne Ellis by her During their Liues or the suruiver of them; but my meaning is not that it shall at all goe from him otherwise then for their Benefitt, & thereby of him in them. I also make my sonne & dau. Ellis Executoʳ of this my whole will & heer unto put my hand being through Fauour of competent understanding & memorye.

Witnesse herunto          The marke of R Robert Blott.
John Hull, Alexander Baker.
Feb. 2, 1665. Mr. Jnᵒ Hull, Robert Saunderson & Alexander Baker Deposed.          [Liber i. fol. 460.]
Inventory of the estate taken Aug. 22, 1665, by Alexander Baker, William Parson, Theophilus Frarye.          [Liber 4, fol. 257.]
1 Feb. 1665 Edward Ellis deposed.

---

PETER HUBBARD.—8th June 1665. I, *Peter Hubberd* now resident in the Island of Barbadoes, Marriner, being sick of Body, but of sound and perfect minde and memorye, Doe make this my Last will.  *   *   *   *
Debts to be paid. Unto my wife, *Susanna Hubberd*, and to her heires, foreuer, all yᵗ parcell of Land, Conteining by estimation 100 Acres, Ly-ing in Hingham, near Coad Pond in New England, wᶜʰ was formerly giuen mee by my Father, *Capᵗ. Joshuah Hubbard*. Unto my said wife, my House and ground in Boston. In case my said wife should be with Childe and the said Child should liue to yeares of understanding, then my minde is, that from & after the Decease of my said Wife *Susanna*, the the said Childe shall haue and enjoy my said house and Ground in Bos-ton aforesaid to him or her & his or her heires foreuer. Unto my said wife, the remaining part of my estate, both Reall and personall, as also all my Debts, Horses, Mares, Catle, houshold stuffe, goods & chattells, my debts, Legacyes & Funerall expenses being First paid. And my further will is, that my wife haue and enjoye all such part & portion of Estate as shall fall to mee out of my Father's estate. I appoint my wife Executrix of this my Last Will, and my Father *Capᵗ. Joshua Hubberd*, of Hingham, *Ensighne John Hull*, of Boston, and my Brother, *Jacob Elliot*, to be Executors in Truste of this my Will, Desyring them, as they will Answer the same before the Judgment seat of Almighty God, to see

this my Last will and Testament performed, according to the true meaning thereof, as before is Declared. I Likewise Desyre my said wife in consideration of the Care & paines which my Executors may haue & take upon them in her Behalfe, to giue unto each of them & the rest of my Friends and kindred such seuerall Legacyes and summes of Money in Remembrance of my Loue as shee, in her Discretion, shall thinke fitt and Conuenient. *Peter Hubberd.*
In presence of *Nath. Hathorne, Nathan Rainsford,*
*Beniman Bram.*

*Nathan Ransford*, aged 24 yeares or thereabouts, sworne, saith that he being in the Barbadoes, in the Beginning of June last, uisiting *Peter Hubberd*, Late of Boston, then Lying sicke there, he heard yᵉ sᵈ *Peter Hubberd* Desire *Edward Hunt*, of said Barbadoes, to write his will, for he sayd I Know I shall Dye ; & when the sᵈ *Hunt* had writt three or foure Lynes from him he caused him to read it to Him, and so did till all was written & reade ouer, and then Caused yᵉ sᵈ *Hunt* to read ouer all the whole, which he Liked, & Declared that that was his will, Desiring him to get it fairly transcribed, & when hee Did this, hee was in his good & perfect understanding to the Deponents best Knowledge & Discretion, only adds that two Dayes after, when it was brought to the said *Peter Hubberd*, Fairly written ; & hee desired to sighne & seale the same. Hee was then present, being not aboue twenty foure houres before his Death, & saw him sighne & seale the same, but did not Judge him at yᵗ. Instant to bee Composmentis.
Sworne by the sᵈ. *Nathan Rainsford*, 21ᵗ Nouember, 1665.
Edward Rawson Recorder.

*Nathaniel Hathorne*, aged twenty sixe yeares, & *Benja. Bran*, aged 25 yeares or thereabouts, Deposed, that hauing subscribed yʳ. names to the fourth sheete of paper which the Late *Peter Hubbard* Did sighne & seale as his Last will, They were present & did so doe, but at that Instant they Judged him not to be Compos Mentis. Taken upon Oath yᵉ 21ᵗ Nouember 1665. Edward Rawson Recorder.

May it please the Honoured Court, wee, whose names are underwritten, Doe humblye Conceiue that the written will of the Late *Peter Hubberd*, which was brought from Barbadoes, was the true mind and will of the said *Peter*. First, because it is testified by one that was present with him in his Sicknesse, that when he was in good memory and understanding he Desired that his will might be written, & did Dictate to yᵉ scriuener what he should write, & Caused the seuerall sentences therein to be read to him, wᶜʰ he did owne & expresse that it was his will, and although through the uiolence of his Disease, infirmitie so farr preuailed on him, that at that time, when hee Did sighne & seale the same, hee was not thought to be Compos mentis, yet we are perswaded to beleiue that it was his Reall Will, because there is particular mention of such things as wee suppose none there but himselfe knew of. And the substance of the written will is the same with wᵗ he had before expressed to us.
These Deponents say, that the Late *Peter Hubberd*, at his going away to Barbadoes, he Desired us to take notice that if god should take him away by Death that he should not haue time to write his will. His will was that his wife, *Susanna Hubberd*, should enjoy all that estate he had

in this world, or that should bee Coming to him from his Father, *Capt. Joshua Hubberd.* To the truth of this expressed, as spoken to us by the abouesaid *Peter Hubbard*, wee are readye to be Deposed if the honoured Court shall see cause.

John Hull

January 31, 1665.                                     Jacob Elliot

Theoph. Frayre.

*Jacob Elliot* & *Theophilus Frayre* deposed from the beginning of the Interlyne (These Deponents &c.)          Edward Rawson Recorder,

[Will allowed and approved of by the Court.]

Inventory of the Estate taken by *John Thaxter*, *Thomas Linkhorne.* Am*t.* £197 08.

*Susanna Hubbert*, Relict of the Late *Peter Hubberd*, deposed, 27th Aprill 1666.

———

RALPH ROOTE.—The Deposition of *Jacob Elliot*, aged 33 years or thereabouts, testifieth & saith, that I, being sent for by *Ralph Roote*, a few Dayes before his Death, in February Last, I went to him & *Goodman Salter* was with him, & he Did Desyre both of us to take notice that Considering he had binn Long weake and had experience of the Loue Care & Charge of his sonne & Daughter *Balston*, with whom he liued, therefore, this was his will for the Dispose of his Estate, to giue unto them his sonne & Daughter *Balston*, all that was his, excepting ten shillings to his Daughter *Jeanne Buttell*, and fiue shillings to his Daughter at Linn, & the Rest whatsoeuer to his sonne & Daughter *Balston.* Taken upon Oath before the Gouernour & Major Generall & Recorder the 29th of March 1666, as Attests          Edward Rawson Recorder.

Power of Administration to the Estate of Ralph Roote, is graunted to *James Balston*, to performe this nuncupative will as neer as may be.

Edward Rawson Recorder.

Inventory of the Estate of *Ralph Roote*, Deceased, taken 27 : 1 m° 1666, by *Jacob Elliott*, *Theophilus Frayre.*   Am*t* £21·19·6.   March 29, 1666.   *James Balston* deposed to the estate of his Late Father in Lawe, *Ralph Roote.*   ———

JANE WOODCOCK, widow, declare this to be my Last will.  As for those temporall goods that God hath bestowed upon me, my minde is, that my sonne, *Wm. Dey*, shall be possessed of them, and in Case he bee dead, my will is that his heires bee possessed of them, & in Case in fiue yeares there be no newes Concerning him, neither by Letter nor Coming, then my mind and will is, that my Execut*rs* & Ouerseers shall haue it.  I appoint my Friend, *John Cleuerly*, of Braintree, in the County of Suffolke, in New England, to be my Execut*r*. & *Richard Barnam* & *Joseph Webb*, of Boston, in the same County, to be Ouerseers.

16th March 1665–6.                         Jane  X  Woodcock.

I giue one shilling to *Richard Brook.*

Sighned, sealed, in the presence of us,

William Read,   Franers Franersco.

8th May 1666.   *William Read*, Deposed.

———

HENRY SHRIMPTON.*—I, *Henry Shrimpton*, Brasier, of Boston, weake in Body, but in perfect memory & understanding, declare this to be my

———

* See an extended account of the Shrimpton family in Sumner's History of East Boston

Last Will. My Just debts both in Old England & and New, & funerall Charges be first Discharged.  My Will is, that my Cousinne, *Mary Shrimpton* daughter of my Late Brother *Edward Shrimpton*, Deceased, be paid the remainder of her portion according to her Father's will, with Interest at sixe in the Hundred.  My Will is, that the two thousand pound giuen by my fore mentioned Brother, *Ed*ʷ. *Shrimptons* [to his] fiue youngest Children, that is to say, *Ebenezer, Epafras, Silas, Elisabeth & Lidya Shrimpton*, be put out to Interest, and good Security taken for it, and they to be allowed for their Maintenance out of the produce of it according to Contract with my Sister, their Mother.  To my wife, *Mary Shrimpton*, £40 pʳ. an, in New England Mony, yearly, during her Life.  I haue freely allowed her all the Estate she had before shee was my Wife, the wᶜʰ she haue had the Disposall of untill this Day, whither it bee Houses or Lands, goods or Chattels; neither do I allow any of my heires to Molest her in any part therof.  To my sonne *Samuell Shrimpton*, £500 & my now Dwelling House, & all the outhouses & woodyeards belong[ing] therunto, together with all my tools for pewter & Brasse, with my Warehouse situated in the Lane below the House of *Capᵗ. James Oliuer ;* also, I giue him my pasture in the Northe End of the town, Scituated Between *Goodman Bennet & Goodman Bernard*, to him and his heires foreuer.  But in Case he shall dye without heires, then the sᵈ Dwelling house with warehouse & pasture are to be sold & equally Diuided between my four Daughters, *Sarah Shrimpton, Abigail, Bethiah & Elisabeth Shrimpton*, or as many of them that shall suruive with their heires, for I haue giuen my sonne, *Samuel Shrimpton*, already £500, with Household stuffe, since he haue been Marryed, wᶜʰ is the Reason yᵗ I giue him no more in this my Will.  I farther will that my sonne, *Samuell*, shall haue £1000, wherby he may be Enabled to pay the forty pounds a year that l haue giuen to my Wife, to be paid her During her Life, after which, my Sonne, *Samuell*, shall enjoy the whole thousand pounds to himselfe & his heires ; but, in Case hee be dead & without heires, then the thousand pounds shall bee equally Divided between his four sisters & their heires that doth suruive ; I mean, all the heires of one of the Sisters shall haue but the part of one of the sisters.  I giue to my four Daughters, £1000 apiece, for their portion to be Disposed of & Improved at the Discretion of my Ourseers, vntill they come to the age of 20 yeares or their Day of Marriage.  I giue unto my dau. *Sarah Shrimpton*, the House Called formerly the states armes, with all the outhouses, yards stabls & all the priuiledges belong[ing] therunto, to her and her heires foreuer ; but, in case shee Dye without Heires, then it shall be sold & Diuided equally between the Brothers & Sisters & their heires that shall suruiue.  To my dau. *Abigail Shrimpton*, my Garden & Garden house & all the appurtenances, & £300 to build a House.  To my dau. *Bethiah Shrimpton*, £400, to buy her a peice of ground & to build her a House.  [To his dau. *Elisabeth*, the same as to *Bethiah*.  Provision is made in regard to all his dauᵐ that if either dye without heires their property shall be sold and equally divided between the brother & sisters & and their heires that shall suruiue.]  In case either of my dauᵐ marry Contrary to the good Liking of my Ouerseers, then I Impower them to Distribute the aforesaid £1000, giuen for her portion to the Rest of my Children, then Liuing, equally to be diuided.  But this power shall not reach to Depriue any of them of their Interest in their Executrixshippe, or of any other Legacies, the wᶜʰ I shall further giue unto them in this my Last will.  I further giue unto my 4 dauᵐ all my Household goods, to be equally Diuided

261

among them, or to as many of them as shall bee aliue at my Death. I appoint my 5 children, Executor & executrixes of this my Last will, & giue unto them equally to be Diuided between them all the ouerplus of my Estate after all Debts & Legacies shall bee paid ; & in Case any shall be dead afore they come to the age of 21 yeares or be Marryed, then the share of the Deceased shall be equally Diuided among those that suruiue. I giue to my sister, *Elizabeth Shrimpton*, wife to my Brother, *Edward Shrimpton*, Deceased, £10, as also to the seven Children of my late Brother, *Edward Shrimpton* (that is to say, *Jonathan Shrimpton, Mary Shrimpton, Ebenezer, Epafras, Silas, Elisabeth & Lydya Shrimpton*, £10 apiece, all to be paid heer, in New England money ; & my Desyre is, that if there shall appear any error or mistake in y^e accompts of my aforsd. sister or her Children, that it may bee made good unto them. I giue to the Church of Boston, wherof I am a mẽber, £50 in money or goods at Money price ; & to the town of Boston, £50 in the like pay, prouided that they will giue leaue that I may be buried in the tombe wherin my former wife, *Ellenor Shrimpton*, was buried, otherwise I giue nothing. To my Bro. & Sister *Fletcher*, £20 apiece, & to *Mr. Jn^o Wilson*, pastor, now of y^e church of Boston, £10, if hee bee then a Liue, also, I giue to *Mr. Powell*, ruling Elder of the other Church, £10, if he be then Liuing. To my Seruant, *Mary East*, if then liuing with me, £10, as also to her sister, *Elisabeth*, £5 ; to my servant W^m *Mumford*, £5 ; [that sum to each, if then living with him.] To my Seruant, *Crechly*, 50 shillings. I giue to the Society of Christians that doth now Meet at Nodles Island, of w^ch is *Gold & Osborn*, and the rest, ten pound as a token of my Loue, as also £5, apiece, to my Friends, *Mrs. Elisabeth Scott*, & *M^rs. Sandys*, Widowes, as also to *Sister Blanchett*, widow, £5. In case it shall fall out that my estate shall be lesñed by the prouidence of God, either by fire, or by any Disaster at Sea, and therby shall not reach to the full performance of this my will, then my Will is, that euery Legacye Contained therin shall be abated accordingly. I Request & appoint my Louing Brother, *Edw. Fletcher*, *Mr. Hezekiah Usher*, and *M^r Thomas Lake*, with *Mr. Peter Oliuer*, to be Ouerseers of this my Last will & testament, and do Intreat them to take the Care of my children & of their estates, and to Improue them for y^eir Best advantage, as also that they Dispose of my Children for their Education either to their Aunt *Fletcher* or some other godly Family, where they may bee Brought vp in the fear of the Lord ; & I also desyre their assistance in all other Matters that are concerning this my will, & doe giue them as a token of my Loue, £20 apiece, to be pd. in Money or goods at Money price, within one year after my Decease, and do giue them as full & ample power in all things as any Ouerseers by Law Canne be Capable of. Witnesse my Hand & Seal, 17th 5^mo 1666. *Henry Shrimpton.*

Witnesse *Jn^o Alcocke, Edmond Eddenden, Thomas Bumstead.*

Aug^t 4, 1666. *Edmond Eddenden & Tho. Bumstead*, deposed.

Inventory of the estate taken 24th July 1666 [Lib. v. fol. 15, sixteen pages,] by *Anthony Stoddard, William Dauis, Thomas Bumstead.* Amt. £11979 2 4¾. Estate indebted, £5743 19 7. Funeral charges, £134 5s. 6d.

6th Feb. 1666. *Mr. Samuel Shrimpton* deposed to his father's inventory.

# ABSTRACTS FROM THE EARLIEST WILLS ON RECORD IN THE COUNTY OF SUFFOLK, MASS.

[Prepared by Mr. William B. Trask of Dorchester.]

Thomas Robinson.—17th March 1665. My just debts & Funeral Expenses paid, my will is, that the Remainder bee Disposed of as followeth ; Goods & Chattells in Boston to my Children, *Thomas, James, Joseph & Mary Robinson.* I appoint my sonne, *Jn°. Robinson,* (supposed to be in England) *M*ʳ *Peter Oliuer, Thomas Buttolph, senior,* & my Brother, *M*ʳ *Joseph Rocke,* my Executors ; unto each 40 shillings. Though my Wife hath not Carryed her self as a wife should haue done towards mee, but, Contrary to the Law of God & Man, hath withdrawn her selfe from Liuing with mee as she ought to Doe, yet prouided shee will accept of ten pounds from my Executors out of my Estate, & Make no more Claymes and Demaunds, I freely giue it to her as a token of my Loue. But, if she Refuse to accept of it, then I wholy make voyd this Legacye & Leaue it to the Discretion of my Executors. If any of the Legatees dye, then the Estate shall be equally Diuided among the Rest.
In the presence of us. *Thomas Robinson.*
*Thomas Grubb, Richard Graues, John Ferniside.*
*Thomas Grubb* & *Jn° Ferniside,* deposed, April 27, 1666.
Inventory of the Estate of *M*ʳ *Thomas Robinson,* Late of Boston, deceased March 23, 166⅔, prised by *Thomas Grubb, Jn° Lake.* Amᵗ. £340. 19. 3. Debts due from the Estate, £69, 10s. Mentions Houses & Lands in Boston, Lying between the House of *Tho. Miller* & the House that was *M*ʳ *Houghes,* £310.
*Thomas Buttolph* & *Joseph Rocke,* deposed, April 27, 1666.

---

William Manning, senior.—I, *William Manning,* of Boston, being weake of Bodye but of perfect memorie, do make this my Last Testament. Debts and Funerall Expences paid, I giue my Wife all my Estate, during her Life, & at her Decease, my Will is, that of what shall be then left of my Estate, which was my own before my Last Marriage, I Dispose of it as followeth, For as much as my Louing sonne, *Wᵐ Manning,* haue through the prouidence of God a good Estate, I therefore giue unto Him but one third part of that which shall Bee Lefte, of what was my owne Before this Last Marriage, & the other two thirds I giue unto my Grand childe, *Samuel Walsbie,* & my desire is, that this grandchild might bee putt to a trade according to the Discretion of my Executrix & ouerseers. I make my wife sole Executrix, and desire *Robert Walker, Jacob Eliot* & *Theophilus Frary,* to bee my Ouerseers. 17th Feb. 1665.
*William* × *Manning.*
In presence of *John Tapping, Edward Porter,* who deposed, April 28, 1666.

---

Sampson Lane.—Feb. 3, 1665. I, *Samson Lane,* being Sick in Body but of perfect Memory, doe make this my last will. I Impower my friend, *Ensigne Jn° Lane,* of the Island of Sᵗ Christophers, Gentleman, to be Executor of all my estate, the one part Lying in Slegoe in Ireland, which amounteth to the Value of some £1400 or £1600 starling, the Deeds of which Estate Lyes in *M*ʳ *William Hunters* Keeping. I Be-

263

queath unto the Daughter of *Thomas Jones,* whom is my God Daughter, £50 Starling, therof to her own proper use ; & as also there is in *Thomas Jones* his hand, Copies of deeds & bonds to the value of the summe aforesaid in M^r *William Hunters* Hands.          *Sampson Lane.*

In the presence of *Walter Hinckson, Nehemiah Stockwell,* who deposed in Court, Feb. 6, 1665, before mee,          *Will. Watts.*

Administration granted to *John Lane.*

Boston in New England, Aug. 15^th 1666.   This Day personally appeared before mee, *Ezekiell Canveath,* & made Oath that the aboue written will was proued before *Coll. W^m Watts,* Gouern^r [of] the Island S^t Xtophers, by the Oaths of the abouenamed Witness in the presence of this Depon^t, being then Secretary of the said Island.

*Walter Hinckson* appeared the same time and deposed.

> *Ri. Bellingham* Gov^r, *Fr. Willoughbye,* Dep^t Gov^r.
> *John Leueret* Assistant.

Entered & Recorded the 24th of Aug. 1666, word for word Agreeing w^th the originall, at Request of M^r *John Lane,* late of S^t Christophers Island, now in Boston, in this booke of Records, as Attests, Edw. Rawson Record^r.

---

JOHN BAKER.—I, *John Baker,* of Boston, in New England, in America, Smith, being weake in Body, yet in full, perfect & disposing memorie, doe declare this to be my Last will.   I giue unto my wife, *Thankfull,* that portion of Estate that she had with her w^ch was to the ualue of £50, to bee paid in Quality as I Receiued it.   I giue unto her a parcell of Land lying at Dorchester neck, which I purchased of her uncle *Bates,* being thirteen acres or thereabout, be it more or Lesse.   I giue unto her my part or Interest that I haue in the Shippe Hercules, M^r *Jn^o Winge,* being now M^r and Commander as also my part & interest in the shipp Mary, M^r *Joseph Cock* being at present M^r & Commander of her, and also my part and Interest in that Boate which *Richard Eggleton* goes in, all which I Freely giue unto her to be at her owne Dispose, if she accordingly accept therof, but if not, then she shall haue the third part of my whole Estate for her use during her Life, prouided it be not Sold nor no way Embezeld, but after her decease, to Returne, unto my Children, accordingly as shall be after Expressed.   I appoynt that the Income of my Estate, either y^e whole or two thirds, shal be improued for the mayntenance of my Children in their minoritye, only the Housing to be kept in repair out of the same.   I giue unto my sonne, *Thomas Baker,* my Best bed, with Furniture, and my second best Kettle, as also that Land that was his grandfather *Swifts,* Lying at Dorchester neck, and the third part of my Estate that remaynes both of Housing, Land & Houshold goods, to be surrendred unto him when hee Comes to be 19 yeares of age, if he Liue therunto.   Unto my dau. *Elizabeth Baker,* my second best bed, with furniture therunto belonging, and my Best Kettle, as also a third part of my estate that remaines, both of Housing, Land & Houshold Goods, to possesse when shee Comes to be 18 yeares of age, or at the day of her Marriage, if it be before, if she Liue thereunto.

More ouer, whereas my wife is now with Child, if it Liue, my will is, that be it sonne or Daughter, it shall haue a third part of my Estate that remaines, both of Houses Land & Houshold goods, if it Liue till it Come to age or otherwise to Returne to my sonne, *Thomas,* & daughter *Elisabeth,* equally.   More ouer, if my sonne, *Thomas* dye before he Come to the age aboue specified, then his portion to Remaine unto His Sister, *Elizabeth*, & if his sister, *Elizabeth*, dye before she receiues her portion then that to remaine to Her Brother *Thomas*, & if both of them dye before, it shall remaine unto the youngest. But if they should all dye before any one of them Comes to age then the whole estate to Remain to my wife.

I giue unto my Sister, *Katharine Johnson*, as a Legacy, y$^t$ debt y$^t$ is due unto me from her Husband. Of this my last will, I ordaine my wife, *Thankfull*, my sonne *Thomas*, & Daughter *Elizabeth*, Executor & Executrixes. My welbeloved Friends, my Father, *Hopestill Foster*, my Uncle, *Richard Baker*, & my Cousinne, *W$^m$ Ireland*, my Ourseers, Desiring them to see this my Will truly Executed and performed to all Intents therin Expressed & to giue their Best & faithfull aduise & Counsell unto my said Children.

26 March 1665–6.                                    John Baker.

In the presence of *Aron* + *Way*

*W$^m$ Ireland*, both of whom deposed July 5, 1666.

Inventory of the estate of John Baker, Smith, of Boston, taken July 3, 1666, by *Christopher Gibson*, *John Phillips*, *Dan: Turrell*. Amt *£*798. 19. Mentions ⅛ of the Ketch William & Mary, M$^r$ *Read*, master, *£*30 ; halfe the boate of *Igledens*, *£*20 ; $\frac{1}{16}$ of the Ketch Mary & Joseph, *Coxes*, at sea, *£*16 ; 13 Acres of Land at Dorchester neck bought of *James Date*, bee it more or less, *£*40 ; 6 Acres more or less at Dorchester neck, of *Father Swift*, *£*18 ; a yong mare of *William Augers*, at Maulden, *£*4. 10. Debts due the estate—from James Nash, M$^r$ W$^m$ Steuens, Thomas Chadwell, Peter Goodhouse, John Paine, &c. *Thankfull Baker* deposed, Nov. 1, 1666.

The following Petition is on file :—

To the Honoured County Court assembled in Boston this 31 of July 1666 the [petition] of Thankfull Baker widow to the late John Baker, of Boston, Smith, deceased.

Humbly sheweth, that wheras my dear husband, after a long time of affliction and weakness of body which was noe small affliction to mee also, and then leaving mee an afflicted widow and also great with child, near unto the time of my travell, and now delivered : yet out of his love did give mee a portion out of his estate, as by his will doth appear, Which said portion is like to be much less then hee intended mee if not some releif by this honoured Court. First, in regard that the one half of that part of the vessell he had in M$^r$ *Joseph Cocks*, he sold before his death, intending that it should bee laid out on something more certain for mee, and as for that part which by his will he gave mee in the ship of which M$^r$ *Wing* was M$^r$ that also was lost and taken before his death, and he not having oppertunity to alter his will Which if he had I doubt not but hee Would have bequathed something in the stead of it, yet notwithstanding being acquainted with M$^r$ *Wings* loss by a freind of his, he did express that It should.be made up to his wife out of the rest of his estate, wherefore, consider the mind of my deceased husband and the equity and Justness of the thing and that estate soe considerable as may well bear it and I being but weak, and his housing and most substantiall estate reserved for his children.

My Humble request is, therefore, to this honoured Court, that you would be pleased to order that that part of the estate given by my husband in his will to mee and lost in M$^r$ *John Wing*, and also that part sold in M$^r$ *Joseph Cocks* vessell, might be made good to me out of the rest of the estate, It being but a small portion, and so fleeting and hazardable, also which I hope you will see good reason to grant unto your petitioner, who also as shee is Bound in duty shall Pray &c.

CHRISTOPHER PEAKE.—2. 2 mo. 1666.  I, *Christopher Peake*, of Rocksbury, doe make this my Last will.  My wife, *Dorcas*, sole Executrix. M* Edward Denison* & M* Thomas Weld*, both of Roxsburye, Ouerseers— to Order all my Estate & guide my wife in all such [ways] as may be for Gods Honour & my wifes & Childrens [best] good.  Debts paid out of mine Estate.  I giue use & Rents of my House Lands & mooueables to my wife, she maintaining tbe reparation of y* the whole time of her Life, excepting a Litle pasture where I intend to make a tan yard, if God please to Lett me Liue.  My will is, that Little pasture, being about two acres of ground, and what soeuer buildings I shall set upon that ground, shall be my three sonnes, *Jonathan, Joseph,* & *Ephraim,* & it shall be diuided equally between them, for them, their heires or assignes.  And further, that my two daughters, at the day of Marriag, if God so dispose of them, both *Dorcas* and *Sarah*, shall haue ten pounds, each, out of the mooueable goods.  My will is, that the pasture or tan yard, that I giue my sonnes, shall not be alienated or sold by them, or any of them, but each to the other, Prouided my other Estate will pay my debts.  After my wife's decease, I bequeathe my Goods unto my Children, *Jonathan, Dorcas, Joseph, Ephraim,* and *Sarah*, to them & to their heires foreuer, to be diuided between them as Followeth, my Eldest sonne, to haue a double portion, the Rest of my Children to haue a part alike.  My sonne, *Jonathan,* hath already receiued four acres of Land, by the great pond, w^ch shall be accounted as a part of his double portion, with a Cow, which shall be Counted to Him also, and further, that if my Children shall receiue what is abouementioned (that is to say) My sonnes the pasture, or my daughters ten pound apiece, that shall be accounted to them as part of their portion also.  It shall be Lawfull for my wife, if need, to Make sale of Chattell or Lands for the payment of my debts, with the aduice of the ouerseers, and my Children to Enjoy the Remainder, and no more, accordingly as I haue formerly mentioned.

*Edward* ⋈ *Bridge*
His Marke

*Christopher Peake.*

*Edward Morris*, both of whom deposed Aug. 2, 1666.
Inventory of the Estate taken, June 8, 1666, by *Edw. Denicon, Tho: Weld, Daniel Bruer*.  Amt. £109. 13. 05.  Mentions. lands " about Gambling End," " neer grauely point," " in the 1000 acres neer Dedham," " at Bare Marsh," " neer Rockye swampe" " where he intended to set up Tanfatts," &c.
*Dorcas Peak* deposed to the Inventory of her late husband, Aug. 2, 1666.

JOHN ENDICOTT.—The last will & Testament of *John Endicott sen'*, late of Salem, now of Boston, made 2^d: 3 mo. called May 1659.  Being in health & of sound memory.  To my wife, *Elizabeth*, all that my farme, called Orchard, lying within the bounds of Salem, together with the dwelling house out houses, barnes, stables, Cow houses & all other buildings & Appurtenances thereto belonging, & all the Orchards, nurseries or fruitt Trees, Garden fences, meadow & salt marsh theretu Appertaininge, & all the feeding Ground & Arable & planting Ground there, both that which is broken vp, and that which is yet to breake vp ; as also all the Timber Trees & other Trees for wood or other vses, together w<sup>th</sup> all the swamps thereunto belonging or Appertaininge, during her life. Unto my wife, all my mouable goods which are at Boston In the House I dwell in vizt. All my beds, bedsteads, bolsters, pillowes, Couerletts, blanketts, Ruggs, Curtaines, & vallence, & all furniture belonging to them, And all my Carpets, Cushions & all goods of that nature. I Giue vnto her, all my table boards, Table lining, cubberds, cubbard clothes, chaires, stooles, Truncks, chests, or any other goods now in my Possession, vizt. pewter, brass, Iron, Andirons, spitts ; also, all my siluer plate & spoones of one kind & another, & all my linnen of what sort soeuer. Also, all my Ruther [Rother, i. e. horned] Cattle, my sheepe & all my wearing Clothes which shee may bestow on my Children as shee shall see good. I giue vnto her all my bookes, whereof shee may bestow on my Two sonns such of them as they are Capable to make vse of, & the rest to bee sold to helpe pay my debts. I Giue vnto her, my Houses at Salem & the ground belonging vnto them & all the goods there which [I haue,] leauing to my wife full power to dispose of them, whether Houses or goods, as shee shall see good. Also, all such debts as are due or shall bee due unto mee at the day of my departure, either from the Country or from any Person or persons inhabiting in this County or in England or Elsewhere. I Giue vnto her, Catta Island, at Salem, which the Generall Court gaue mee, during her life, & after her decease to my two soons, *John* & *Zerobabel* or to the longest liuer of them.

I giue to *John Endicott*, my Eldest sonne, the farme which I bought of *Henry Chickering*, of Dedham, (which I formerly bestowed on him, lying within the boundes of Salem,) & all Houses or Lands whether meadow, Pasture or Arable Land as it is Conveyed vnto mee, in an Indenture bearing date, 4th 8th mo. 1648, and the said Indenture to bee deliuered vnto him & the said Land with the Appurtenances to him & to his heires foreuer.

I Giue to him & to my yonger sonne, *Zerubabel*, the whole Farm, called Orchard, to bee parted indifferently betweene them after the decease of my wife. I Giue vnto *Zerubabel*, a farme out of the farme lying vpon Ipswich Riuer, Containing 300 Acres, whereof 40 Acres is meadow, lying along the plane by the Riuers side, next to *Zacheus Gould* his Land, which lyeth by the Brooke side that runneth into Ipswich Riuer at the farthest End of the plaine. To my wife, my Eldest mare, which shee was wont to ride on, & hir Eldest mare foale. Vnto my sonn, *John Endicott*, the horse Colt that now runns with the mare. My wife sole Executrix. Doe desire that Elder Penn & Elder Coleborne will be the Ouerseers of this my last will, & if God should take either of them out of the world, that the longest liuer of them hath hereby libertie, with my wiues Consent, to Choose another Ouerseer vnto him. And Whereas the Generall Court hath giuen vnto mee the fowrth p<sup>t</sup> of Block Island, I doe hereby bequeath it vnto my wife to helpe pay debts withall if I dispose not otherwise of it before I dye. I Giue vnto my two sonns, *John* & *Zerubabel*, the two Farmes I bought, the one of *Capt Trask*, the other of *Captaine Hawthorne*, lying vpon Ipswich Riuer, next adjoyning to my farme vpon the said Riuer. I Giue all the rest of my Land belonging to my Farme vpon the said Riuer, which is not disposed of, to my two sonns, *John* & *Zerubabel*, my Eldest sonn to haue a double Portion thereof. Vnto *John* & *Zerubabel*, all the Land that was giuen mee by the two sachems of Quinnebaug, my Eldest sonn to haue a double Portion thereof. To my Grand child, *John Endecott*, *Zerubabel* his sonn, £10, to bee payd him when hee is 21 years of Age. Also that the Land I haue bequeathed vnto my two sonns, in one place or another, my will is, that the longest liuer of them shall Enjoy the whole, Except the Lord send them children to inherit it, after them. To M$^r$ Norrice, Teacher of the Church at Salem, 50s.; to M$^r$ Wilson, Pastor of Boston, 40s.; to M$^r$ Norton, Teacher, 40s. To the poore of Boston, £4, to bee disposed of by the deacons of the Church. John Endicott.

From the Files in Suffolk Probate Office :—
The County Court last at Boston having presented to them this Instrument & finding that the difference betweene the mother & the Eldest sonne about the probate thereof to be such as their determination would not be rested in, transferred it & what both of them Could say & produce thereabouts to the Generall Courts determination. The magis$^ts$ hauing duely pervsed this Instrument as the Last will & testament of the late Honoured Gouerno$^r$ written, signed & sealed by his owne hand (apparently knowne so to be) together w$^{th}$ the testimony of W$^m$ Salter attesting that it was made in the time of his health & memory, & that it was shewne vnto him in the forme as now it is, and also pervsed what hath binn tendered by M$^r$ Houchin to Invalidate the same. The Magtsts. Judge it meete to declare that they doe allow & approove of this Instrument to be the last will & testament of the said late John Endecot Esq$^r$ their brethren the deputies hereto Consenting. Edw. Rawson Secretary.

This was Voted by y$^e$ magists. instead of what is aboue written.

| | |
|---|---|
| The Deputyes Consent not with o$^r$ Hono$^{rd}$ magists. in approueing of this Instrument as a Will.<br><br>William Torrey Cleric.<br><br>3 : 6 : 65. | The Deputies Judge meete to referre the Issue of this Case to the next session in October & y$^t$ all p$^r$sons Concerned attend the same reffering to the Consent of o$^r$ Hon$^{rd}$ magists. hereto.<br>William Torrey cleric. |

Voted by the whole Court together that they doe not approoue of this Instrument to be the last will & testament of the late John Endecott Esq$^r$ Gouerno$^r$: 17 October 1665.         pr Edw: Rawson Secrety.

Inventory of the Goods & Chattells* prized by John Wiswall, & Peter Bracket, S1: 5. 1665. Am$^t$. £224. 07. 07. Mentions—"a prentice boy, £10, a small bed for him, £10." Mrs. Elizabeth Endicott deposed at a County Court held at Boston, Feb. 13, 1666.

Salem: 27 : 2$^d$ : 1665. Estate of John Endicott Esq$^r$ the late Gou$^r$ of the Massachusetts, prized by John Porter, Thomas Putman. Amt. £815. besides Lands, cattle, &c. enumerated in another list, " to be uallued." Of the real estate mentioned, is, the home farme together with the Housing Orchards & fences, 550 Acres, £550 ; 250 Acres at a farme lying vpon Ipswich Riuer, being parte of a farme giuen by the Country, together with the meadow to it, 80 acres, £80 ; a house at the Towne with 3 Acres of Land to it, £100 ; 250 Acres of the Farm in Topsfield ; 2 Farmes in the Country purchased of Major Haythorne & Capt. Trask, giuen them by the Country, £500 ; Catta Island.

---

* From the Records of the Colony of the Massachusetts Bay in New England, Vol. iv, Part 2, p. 289.
Oct. 11, 1665. " In answer to the peticon of M$^r$ John Endecot for the setlinge of his Fathers estate, the Court judgeth it meete, that administration to the estate of the late Jn$^o$ Endecot, Esq. be granted to M$^{rs}$ Elisabeth Endecott & hir two sonnes, John & Zerubbabel, & that an inventory of the said estate be given in to the next County Court at Boston, & they to dispose of the same as the lawe in that case directs."—See more in relation to the estate on pp. 311, 312, of the same volume.

# ABSTRACTS FROM THE EARLIEST WILLS ON RECORD IN THE COUNTY OF SUFFOLK, MASS.

[Prepared by Mr. WILLIAM B. TRASK of Dorchester.]

ANNE CLARKE.—The last will of *Ann Clarke*, Widdow. That which I leaue after my Death, I leaue it all w^th *Robert Miller*, in whose House I liue, first to see my Body buryed. I Giue to *Elizabeth Gold*, my Gold Ring & my Bible, a black Scarfe & an Elle of Holland. To *Rob^t. Millers* child *Lydia*, a siluer pine, a braslet & two hoodes. To *Francis Cooper*, all my Linnen Except a shirt & a shift for *Rob^t. Millers* wife, & a shirt for *William Copp*, the shift is for *Ruth Copp ;* to ould goodwife Copp my sarge Wastcoate ; the rest of my Estate is all for Rob^t. Miller, Excepted a bill for 21^s· due from *Elizabeth Tomson*, which I giue vnto *Francis Cooper*, all this in my perfect memory, & hereto I set my hand & seale this 19 day of October 1666.                    *Ann* ⋈ *Clarke*.

Wittnesses, *Robert Sanford, George Broughton*, who deposed Dec. 27, 1666.

Power of Administration to the Estate granted to *Rob^t Miller*.

Inventory of the Estate taken by *George Broughton, Rob^t. Sanford*, Dec. 24, 1666. *Rob^t. Miller* deposed Dec. 27, 1666.    Lib. V. fol. 5.

---

JOHN BACKWAY.—Aboard the Ketch Speedwell at Sea : 17 : 8 ber : 1666. John Backwaves last will & Testament, And hee hath Appoynted *John Sweate* & *John Bracket* to bee his Executors to dispose of his Estate as followeth :—To the poore of Boston, £5 ; to *Thomas Berry*, £10 ; to the seamen now belonging to the Ketch, £1 ; to the boy, *Joseph Gobner*, one barrell of molasses, aboard that is in the Ketch houlde ; to *Margaret Cleffland*, in England, what money shee hath in her hand of mine, which is about £35. And I shall intreat you whose names are aboue written to dispose of my part of the Ketch, & what fraight is due to mee, with two Hogsheads of sugar, that I haue aboard of my owne, with one mare at Bastabell about Three yeares old in *John Tomsons* hand, & one mare & one Coalt one yeare old & something more, and one Coalt something under one yeare old, only to pay for marking of them in *Tristram* Hulls hands with what money & bills & other things that is in my Landlord *Sweate* hands, all these to be disposed of to the best advantage. And after those things paid aboue mentioned & your selfe sattisfyed for your paines, to returne the remainder vnto my Father & Mother in the parrys of Cill-Hampton* in the County of Cornwall in the Hundred of Stratton, if either of them aliue, if not to bee disposed Equally amongst my Six Brothers & Sisters, and my Bro. Walter not to haue any thing.

Wittness, *Thomas Thacher* jun^r.                    John ⋈ Backway.
*John Chantrell*

At a meeting of the Gou^r & magistrates in Boston, Oct. 15, 1666, *Thomas Thacher junio^r* & *John Chantrell* deposed.

An inuentory of the Estate of John Backaway late deceased at sea, about the 20^th of Nouember 1666, taken by *Richard Collacott, Joseph*

---

* This is undoubtedly Kilkhampton, in the Co. of Cornwall, 5 miles N. E. of the town of Stratton, which gives the name to its hundred. The churchyard of Kilkhampton was the scene of Hervey's "Meditations among the Tombs," the author having made an excursion to this place during his residence in Devonshire. This work was published in Feb. 1745-6.

*Cock*, Feb. 9, 1666. Amt. £123. 6. 8. Mentions the names of John Sweet, John Bracket, John Hayman, Nicko: Dauis, Thomas Berry. John Sweet deposed to the truth of the Inventory of the Estate of the late John Barkaway, Feb. 12, 1666.

ARTHUR GARY.—Hauing formerly disposed of my Housing, my Orchard, & my Home Lott & seuerall of my mouables to my sonn, *Samuell Gary*, & seuerall other of my mouables & goods vnto him & to my other two sonns (to witt) *William Gary & Nathaniell*, as Appeares by my deed of guift made to him & the writting giuen vnder my hands vnto him & them according to the tearmes as are in those writtings Expressed, The Lord being pleased to vissitt mee with much infirmity & weakness yet hauing the perfect use of my vnderstanding & memory, doe make this my Last will. My soul I giue vp into the hands of my most mercifull Sauiour Jesus Christ, & my body I leaue to my deare wife & Louing children to bee decently interred; and for all the rest of my Worldly goods which I die possessed of, whether it bee housing, Lands, Cattle, Corne, mouables, or whatseuer else, I dispose of it as followeth :— That my funerall Charges shall bee sattisfyed & all other debts discharged. My will is, my deare wife, *Frances Gary*, shall haue the vse of my Housing & Lands, & my whole Estate during her life, Excepting as before. After my wiues decease, my will is, that all my Lands & whole Estate, as is before Expressed, bee Equally deuided betweene my three sonns, *William*, *Nathaniell* & *Samuell Gary*. Euery one of them to haue their proportion of Land, soe as may bee neerest, most Conuenient, & bennificiall for Euery of them. My will is, that my sonn, *Samuell Gary*, shall haue that Land, which lyeth next vnto my dwelling House, hee paying vnto his other two Brethren, *William* & *Nathaniell Gary*, in Case that Land amounts to more than the said Sam[uel's] proportion, what is due to make them Equall with him, In Case that Land fall short of his Proportion, then Samuel shall haue the residue Ells where, according to what is before Expressed. And for the Equalnes of the Apprizall & diuission of the said Estate after my wiues decease, my will is, that if it cann bee that my said sonns Louingly agree amongst themselues (which I most desire) but in Case that Cannot bee attaned to mutuall sattisfaction of them all, then my will is, that my Three sonns choose Each of them one man, who shall either all of them or any two of them, haue full power to determine & set downe Conserning the Apprizall & diuission of the said Estate aforesd in Case that they together with my sonns Cannot come to a louinge Agreement in a way of Councill & perswasion. My will is, that in case my wife should, either by way of sickness or any other Casualty, bee brought to stand in need of more than what is aboue Expressed in this my will, for her Comfortable supply, that then shee shall haue liberty with the aduice of her Children, to sell either goods, Cattle or any of the Lands for her Comfortable reliefe, always Provided, that first such Lands as is most remote & least benneficiall should bee sold to make the supply aforesaid. My will is, that my Louing sonn, *William Gary*, bee sole Executor of this my last will, requesting my Louing Freinds, *Edward Denison* & *Edward Bridge*, to bee my Ouerseers of this my will. Nouember: 18th: 64. *Arthur Gary*. Witness, *Robert Seauer*, & *Robt. Pepper*, who deposed Jan. 30, 1666.

Dec. 31, 1666. An inuentory of the Goods & Estate of *Arthur Gary*, late of Roxbury, deceased, taken by *Wm. Parke*. Amt. £123.06. Men-

tions lands " neere Grauily point," " wood Land vpon the Great hill,"
" broake Ground adjoyning to the Land of *Rob¹. Seauer*," " broake vp
Land vpon pond hill," " vpon the Pond plaine," " in middle diuision,"
&c.  *William Gary* deposed, Jan. 30, 1666.

---

SAMUEL COLE.—I, *Samuell Cole* of Boston in New England, in America, being in full, perfect & disposing memory though otherwise weake in
in Body through many weaknesses that doe attend mee, doe hereby declare this to bee my last will. ✱ ✱ ✱ ✱ ✱ ✱
I giue vnto my daughter, *Elizabeth Weeden*, that Land of mine at
Rumney marsh, which at pʳ sent her husband and shee liues vpon, &
haue done for some years past, which is the sixth part of my land, the
residue where of I sold to *Cornet Hassey*, as appeareth by the deed made
vnto him, as also, all the marsh ground that I haue at Hogg Island, which
is six Acres or thereabouts, bee it more or less, all which Land my said
daughter & her Husband shall Enjoy during their life, and my will is,
that after their decease, it shall bee Equally diuided amongst all their
Children.  I Giue to my Daughter, *Maryes* Children, which shee had by
*Edmund Jackson*, viz¹. Elisha & Elizabeth, a House lott in Boston neere
the Brickkills, butting vpon the street bounded vpon the north by *George
Nowells* Lott & on the south side by *John Scenter & Elizabeth Grose* their
Houses & Lotts.  To my grandchild, *Sarah Scenter*, a Coult wᶜʰ is now
in the possession of her Husband, *John Scenter*. I Giue besides what for-
merly is Exprest, vnto my dau. *Elizabeth Weeden*, the sume of £20, which
is due vnto mee from *John Scenter*, to bee layd out towards the building
of a new house, vpon that Land formerly Exprest, at Rumney Marsh.
Vnto my sonn *John Coles* Children, £10, to be Equally diuided Amongst
them, & vnto my dau. *Elizabeth Weedens* Children, £10 also, to bee also
Equally diuided Amongst them, which £20 is due vnto me by *Elizabeth
Gross*. I giue my Land at Monaticott bought of *Clement Cole* & giuen him
by the Towne, how much and where it lyes the deed Expresseth, vnto my
Grand child, *Samuell Cole*, the Eldest sonn of my sonn, *John Cole*. Vnto
my old servant, *Elizabeth Ward*, that Cowe that I haue in the keeping of my
sonn in Lawe, *Edward Weeden*, as long as shee liueth to Enjoy the benefitt thereof & afterwards to remaine to my dau. *Elizabeth Weeden*. My
old greene Coat I Giue vnto the said *Elizabeth Ward*. To the Old Church
of Boston, 20ˢ.  Whereas I promised to giue 20ˢ to Harvard Colledge &
some part of it paid in Wooden ware by *Elzer* to Mʳ. *Danforth* & what
else I know not, my will is, that the residue bee duly paid, together with
20ˢ more, which I giue to the said Colledge.  For the remainder of my
Estate at my decease, whether in Household Goods, debts due, wearinge
Apparrell or otherwise, I giue to my sonn, *John Cole* & my dau. *Elizabeth
Weeden*, Equally, to bee diuided betwixt them, the which *John & Elizabeth*
I make joynt Execuroˢ of this my last will & Testament.  But if my said
sonn, *John Cole*, shall refuse to bee an Executoʳ to my said will & vpon
any pretence whatsoeuer shall wrangle with his said Sister & not agree
peaceably according to the true intent & meaning of this my will, then,
that my dau. *Elizabeth* shall bee sole Executrix, and I giue only to my
sonn, *John Cole*, a legacy of 20ˢ.  I giue to my Grandchild, *Samuell
Royall*, 40ˢ. as a legacy towards building of a house which sᵈ haue bin formerly Exprest.  I confirme the deed of guift made my sonn, *John Cole*,
for the one halfe of my House at Boston, which is mine in possession till
my decease.

This will was taken from the mouth of the aforesaid Testator & read before him, who Owned it to bee his last will & Testament, Dec. 21, 1666, in the pʳsence of vs whose names are underwritten. This also the Testator further desired at the same time, namely, that *James Euerell* & *Goodman Search* the weauer would bee pleased to bee Ouerseers, & giues either of them 20ˢ. *Samuell Cole.*

*Elias Mauericke, Aron* ⋈ *Way, John Senter.*

Feb. 13, 1666. *Elias Mauerick & Aaron Way* deposed.

An Inuentory of the Estate at Winnesimet, of *Mʳ. Samuell Cole* deceased, taken by *Elias Mauerick, Aaron Way, William Ireland.* Amt. £156.15.02.

May, 2, 1666. *John Cole & Elizabeth Weeden* deposed.

---

JOHN BRACKET.—*John Bracket*, sick in Body but of a sound & perfect memory doe make my last will. Bequeathing my soule to Jesus Christ & my body to decent burial, making my Father *Bracket* & Father *Stedman* my Executoʳ. I Giue vnto the Old Church at Boston £10; vnto the poore at Boston, £5; vnto my sister, *Vpham*, £10; vnto *Brother Cooke*, £10; vnto mother *Williams'* her Fiue children, £5 a peece; vnto Brother *Twelues*, £10; vnto Bro. *Nathaniell Renolds*, £10; vnto Bro. *Nathaniell Bracket*, £10; vnto sister, *Sarah Bracket*, £10; vnto my Executoʳˢ £10 a peece; vnto *Lydia Dickson* 20ˢ. Prouided, my will is, that if my Estate at sea should miscarry & that which is in debts, then the legacies of £10 to bee abridged vnto £5 a peece at my Executoʳ discretion; the rest of my Estate, the legacies aboue mentioned, my funerall Expences & debts being discharged, I Giue one third vnto the child my wife now goes withall, if it liue to marriage Estate & marry, if not, then my wife to haue all my Estate whatsoeuer, mouable & imouables. 12: 10: 1666.

Wittnes whereof *John Bracket.*

*John Wiswall senʳ., Thomas Clarke.*

Boston, Jan 30, 1666. *John Wisewall & Thomas Clarke* deposed.

Inventory of the Goods and Estate taken Feb. 22, 1666, by *James Penn, Anthony Stoddard*, Amt. 1021.04.4. Mentions, " the sale of ¼ pt of *Bureys* Ketch—in money, £110;" " a fourth pt. of the ship Endeavour, apprized by *John Wing & Mʳ Clements*, £ 250;" " cash in the hands of *Mʳ John Clemens* of London, by *Edward Clements*, £15.11.10; by £50 in *Mʳ Humphrey Dauies* hands by order of *Mʳ Crisp* for 2000 Royall plates"; " 5000ˡᵇ of Sugar in Barbados in the hands of *Abraham Hawkins*, desperate; " a quarter part of 100ˡᵇ. Cargo from London to Barbados, in the hands yet of *Mʳ Johnson* of Barbados, a good debt.

March 20, 1667. *Mʳ John Stedman*, of Cambridge, & *Mʳ Peter Bracket*, of Boston Executoʳ to the will, deposed.

---

NICHOLAS UPSALL. 9: 6ᵗʰ mo: 1666. I, *Nicholas Vpsall*, of Boston, Inholder, being weake in Body but of perfect memory, doe make this my last will. I make my wife, *Dorothy Vpsall*, to be my whole Executrix of all my Lands, Houses & goods. I Giue to my dau. *Elizabeth*, the wife of *William Greenough*, the one halfe of my Land, vizt. That halfe which is next to *John Farnhams* Land, from the middle of the wharfe to the south side of my Entry, & from thence to the midst of the higher End of my Garden vpon a straight line with the Houses vpon that Land. Vnto my dau. *Susanna*, the wife of *Joseph Cock*, the other halfe of my

Wharfe & Land vpon the south west, next to *John Sweets*, to the End of my Garden with the Houses vpon the Land, Prouided that my wife shall keepe & Enjoy the Houses & Lands during her life & after her decease to remaine vnto my Two Daughters, during their liues, and after the death of them or either of them to their respectiue children, and in case their are noe children, then to their Respectiue Husbands. I Giue to my dau. *Dorothy Greenough*, £20; to my Grand dau. *Elizabeth Greenough*, £20; to my Grand sonn, *Nicholas Cock*, £20; to bee payd to them respectiuely at their Age of 14 yeares, by my Executrix. I Giue to & for the vse of such servants of the Lord as are Commonly termed quaker, my new Feather bed, bolster & pillowes, with a good paier of sheets & a paier of blankets, with the new Rugg & a bedstead fitted w$^{th}$ Rope matt & Curtins to it, in that little Roome within my house called the Parlor, or in the Chamber ouer that Parlor, duringe the life of my said wife, And after her decease to bee there Continued by my dau. *Cock*, within whose line that part of the House falleth. I Giue to the said Society of Quakers, my Chest, with all my books & Papers, therein lying, with a small Table in the Roome. I Giue my great Coate to the Children of *John Chamberlin*, to Cloth them.

Prouided & my will is, if my Executrix or my dau. *Cock*, see meet to set vp a House on any part of my Land for the vse of Quakers, that then it shall bee built foure & Twenty foot in length & Eighteen foot wide, with a Chimney, & the said bedstead, beding & Table in it, & it shall bee for their Company & it shall stand with my will.  *Nicholas Vpsall.*

In the presence of vs,
*William Greenough*, *Thomas Bill*, *William Pearse* sen$^r$.

Oct. 31, 1666.  *Thomas Bill & William Pearse*, deposed.

Inventory of the Estate of *Nicholas Vpsall*, of Boston, who deceased the 20 of the 6 mo : 1666, taken & apprized, 3: 7: 1666, by *James Euerell*, *John Search*, *John Sweete*, Amt. £543, 10. [after deducting debts due and the Goods to be delivered to the Quakers.]

Oct. 31, 1666.  *Dorothy Vpsall*, deposed.

ROBERT HAWES.—Being sick in body but hauing the p$^r$sent vse of my memory & vnderstanding, I doe make this as my last will & Testament. [Debts to be paid.] * * * * My will is, that my sonn, *Thomas Hawes*, shall bee paid out of my Estate within a month after my decease, £10 in such Cattle as may be best spared according to the aduice of my ouerseers. For the rest of my Cattle that remaines after the £10 is paid to my sonn *Thomas*, my will is, that they bee then Equally deuided betweene my sonn, *John Hawes*, & my dau. *Mary Hawes*, to bee Carefully & wisely improued by the Council & with the aduice of my Ouerseers for their only vse & benifitt, only reseruing two Cowes for the vse & profit of my wife, vnto whom I bequeath the vse & benifitt of all the residue of my Estate, Lands, mouables or what else during hir life, Prouided shee marry noe other man, but in Case shee should marry, or, in case of her death, whether of these times shall first come, that then the whole Estate left in her hands, by my will as aforesayd, shall bee Equally diuided betweene my sonn, *John Hawes* & my dau. *Mary Hawes*, Always to bee soe vnderstood that in case the Lord by his prouidence should soe dispose either by sickness or any other way as that the vse & profitts of the Estate will not Comfortably maintaine my wife, then my will is, that with & according to the Council & aduise of the ouerseers, saile may bee made of the

273

mouables as may bee least damage for her Comfortable supply. [lf the children by sickness or otherwise stand in need of help before their Estate come into their hands, they are to be supplyed out of the Estate. In case *John* or *Mary* die before what is given them by will is due, or by marriage, that the suriuo', shall Enjoy the whole Estate giuen to both ; if both die, what is bequeathed to them to be giuen to *Thomas*.] I make my sonn, *Humphrey Barritt*, Executor of this my will, requesting my kind Brother, *John Perpont* & my Louinge Friend, *Edward Dennison*, to bee Ouerseers. Feb. 5, 1663.                                         *Robert Hawes.*
Witness, *Samuell Ruggles, John Clarke.*
Jan. 18, 1666  *Samuell Ruggles* & *John Clarke,* deposed.
Inuentory of the Estate taken by *Griffin Craft* & *Hugh Clarke,* Jan. 3, 1666.  Amt. £123, 14, besides, some debts due to and from the Estate.
*Humphrey Barret,* deposed, Jan. 18, 1666.

---

JOHN BIGGS.—The last will & Testament of *John Biggs* being in perfect memory, 19. 4. 1666.  My debts & funerall Expences being discharged, I Giue vnto my wife, my House & Land belonging to it; all my Land & Marsh in Boston; all my Land & marsh at Muddy Riuer, & all that I now possess.  Doe Constitute my wife my sole Executrix, and appoint my *Father Dosset,* Ouerseer.  I desire [to have] *Elder Penn* & *Peter Bracket* my Ouerseers.                                        the marke of
Witness hereunto                                                         John ⋈ Biggs.
*Theodor Atkinson, William Salter,* who deposed Oct. 19, 1666.
Inventory of the Goods & Chattles of John Biggs, of Boston, lately deceased, taken July 11, 1666, by *Tho: Bumsted, Theo: Atkinson,* Amt. £623. 1.  Debts due, £31.
Oct. 19, 1666.  *Mary Biggs* Relict & Executrix to the late *John Biggs,* deposed. ———

WILLIAM GARRETT.—Feb. 4, 1664.  Power of administration to the Estate of the Late *Wm. Garrett,* of London, Marriner, is graunted unto *John Farnham,* in Behalfe of the Wife of the said *Garrett* & his Children.
Inventory of the apparrell & Goods of William Garrett, of London, seaman, who while he was in Boston in New England, sojourned with John Farnham of Boston, & at his going forthe in the Widow Nicholls her Barque, Left in the Custodye of the said John Farnham senior [articles enumerated—including a debt due s^d Garrett from s^d Farnham—to the amount of £14. 7.]  The said Garrett Dr. to Farnham for 3 weekes Dyet at 6'=18 shillings.  Appraisers, *John Phillippes, Nathaniel Addams.*
*John Farnham* deposed. ———

EDMOND BROWNE.*—Edmond Browne Departed this Life in the Countrey of Serrenam, about Michillmas Last, beinge in the yeere of our Lord 1665, w^thout Isue, & his wife, *Elizabeth,* he gaue all his' estate to her to pay his debets and for her liuelyhood ; and he haueinge Left some estate in this Country of New England & ould Engld. she humble pray the honoured Maiestrates to grant her letters of Administracoñ to his estate here and in England, and as in duty bound shall praye &c. and when she can finde any she shall bringe in an Inventory of the particulars vpon oath.
Administration granted to *Elizabeth Browne,* relict, &c.  Boston, 11 October 1666.

---

* From the files.

274

# ABSTRACTS FROM THE EARLIEST WILLS ON RECORD IN THE COUNTY OF SUFFOLK, MASS.

[Prepared by MR. WILLIAM B. TRASK of Dorchester.]

MARTHA EMONS.—March 30, 1666. I, *Martha Emons*, of Boston, widow,* being sicke & weake in body, but of p⟮r⟯fect memory, make this my last will. Debts to be paid. I give vnto my sone, *Obadiah Emons*, all that my messuage tenem⟮t⟯. or dwelling house, with the land thereto belonging, wherein he now dwelleth, being in Boston. Vnto my sone, *Samuel Emons*, my dwelling house wherein I now live, w⟮th⟯. the land thereto belonging, situate in Boston. Vnto my sone, *Joseph Emons*, £20, to be paid him by my execuȯt⟮rs⟯, at such times as the oꝛseers to this my will shall judg meet, (that is to say) when he doth take such good corses as to live orderly & to follow the Trade of a Cordwaine⟮r⟯. & is clear of such debts as he now owes by following the imploy he now hath taken up. Vnto my Sone, *Benjamin Emons*, Foure score pounds, to be paid him by my execuȯt⟮rs⟯, as followeth, £60 thereof in such pay as will p⟮r⟯duce him lether & other things w⟮ch⟯ he may need. I will that the £20 given my Sone, *Benjamin*, by his fathers will, be paid to him, in the moneth of June, w⟮ch⟯ shall be in the year 1667, by my execuȯto⟮rs⟯; & for the £60 aforesaid, to be paid unto him £40, by my sone, *Obadiah*, out of the value of the house I have hereby bequeathed him, & £20 by my sone, *Samuel*, out of the value of the house I have bequeathed him, & £20 by *Obadiah*, & £10 by *Samuel*, to pay the said *Benjamin* in June 1668; the other £30 to be paid in specie in the moneth of June thence next ensuing; the other £20 to be paid my sone, *Benjamin*, to make up the sume of Fourscore pounds to be paid vnto him by the value thereof, of my goods, viz. that Fether bed w⟮ch⟯ he best liketh, with the Bolster & pillow, the new Couꝛled, a paire of Blankets, Curtins, hangings, the bedstead I now ly on, Two paier of my best sheets, a paire of pillow beers, my Silver Beker & Silver Spoon; & of other my goods, as pewter, Brasse & old bedding, to make up the value of £20; said goods to be paid him when he receives the legacie of £20, aforesaid, given him by the will of his father or soone⟮r⟯ if his occasions cale for it, & the plate & bedding immedyatly after my Decease. Vnto my son, *Samuel*, my Cloth Gound to make him a sute, & to his wife my best cloth petticote. To my dau. *Alice Emons*, my Turkey moehaire coate & my finest paire of new pillowbers. Vnto my grandsone, *Thomas*, 40ˢ; vnto my Grand Dau. *Martha Emons*, my Gold ring & my silue⟮r⟯ bodkin; to my grandson, *Samuel*, my Silver wine cup & Dram cup; vnto my grand dau. *Mary*, 20ˢ, to be paid her in pewter; to my grand dau. *Elizabeth* 10ˢ to buy her a silue⟮r⟯ spoon. Vnto my grandson, *Samuel Crab*, £18, to be paid him by my execuȯto⟮rs⟯ when he shall be 20 years of age; vnto my Kinswoman, *Martha Winsor*, £8, to be paid vnto her at her age of 21, or day of Marriage, w⟮ch⟯ of them shall first be, & my hire Calliminco gound, & my old Moehaire petticoate & a red taminy petticoate & a new cloth wastcoate, w⟮ch⟯ lyeth in my chest, & a sute of my linning complete, (except a white Apron) & my bible & box. To Goodman *Prat*, of Charlestowne, 10ˢ; vnto my Kinswoman, *Hannah Winsor*, Two platters to be paid her at her

---

* See abstract of the will of *Thomas Emons*, her husband; will proved in 1664. *Reg.* xii. 345. (See p. 232).

Marriage. Vnto Goodwife, *Cop*, & goodwife, *Goold*, 10ˢ apeece ; vnto my loving neighboʳˢ Goodwife *Stanes* & goodwife *Winsor*, each of them, a dresing of my best, after that my dau. *Alice* hath take her choice. My will is, that such of my waring lining not disposed of, my dauʳˢ to Devid between them. My will is, that my Sone, *Samuel*, shall have the refuse of such implemᵗˢ in my house wᶜʰ he shall desier, paying for it as it is prized. Vnto my sons, *Obadiah* & *Samuel*, all my goods, Debts & estate not hereby bequethed, to be devided between them, whom I make joint executoʳˢ of this my last will & testament. I intreat my loving friends, Mʳ *John Wiswell* & Mʳ *William Engⁱish* to be overseers, whom I do hereby also impower, that in case my executoʳˢ be remisse in pʳforming this my will, that then, upon such neglect, they shall have power over the before. bequeathed dwelling houses to dispose of them for time, till my debts & legacies be paid, anything before expressed to the Contrary there of notwithstanding. Vnto my before named friends, Mʳ *Wiswell* & Mʳ *English*, 40ˢ a peece for theire paines. I have here vnto set my hand & seale the second day of April in the year above written. In Case my houshold goods & debts will not amount to pay my debts & legacies hereby ordered & bequeathed, then the same shall be made up & paid by my executoʳˢ out of the Value of the houses respectively, hereby to them bequeathed, *Obadyah* paying two parts & *Samuel* one part thereof.

In the pʳsence of us                                           *Martha Emons.*
*John Wiswall, William Inglish, William*
    *Pearse* Sʳ.

[On the back of the will, it is added, that a parcel of goods to the value of £20, which were her son *Hincksmans*, being then at her dispose, her will was, that if her son *Hincksman* should pay £20 to her executors within some convenient time after her decease, he shall have the goods in kind, otherwise, the executors to have them. Unto her son *Joseph Emons*, £20 more than is given in the will, to be paid him, £10 at a time " vpon the          of Mʳ *William Brenton* for his vse, whom I humbly desire to haue a Care ouer & to see he walkᵉ as he ought to doe." Signed 1 : 7 mo. 1666, by *Martha Emons.* Witnessed by *John Wiswall* senior, *William Inglish.*] Will recorded—Book I. page 499.

18 Feb. 1666. Wᵐ *English* and Wᵐ *Pearse*, deposed.
Inventory of the estate of *Martha Emons* taken by *Edmond Jacklin* & *Richard Stanes*, 18 Dec. 1666. Amt. £417. 17. Mentions " a share in the Conduit, £14 ;" debts from *John Hincksman*, &c. *Obadiah Emons* & *Samuel Emons* deposed, May 7, 1667.

———

ROBERT HULL.—I, *Robert Hull*, being in good memory of body and mind doe giue to sonne, *John Hull*,* my part of this house which was first bylt, and the orchard or garden, with all opporttynances to yᵗ., and on lotte at muddye riuer, of thurty Accores, which I promised to him at his marridge to giue at my death, and doe make him my full executores of all oether goods, cattells after my death, and to see this my will to be performed, that is to saye, I giue to my sonne, *Edmund Quinney*, [Quincy] that porsson which is due to me by my wife, that £20 in goods and corne, be yᵗ more or less, and to his sonne, *John Quiney*, on lote at brantrye which was my sonne, *Richard Storer ;* to the oether childrens, 12 pence a peece. To *Richard Storer*, £9, to be payed before or after my death,

---

* The celebrated master of the mint  See *Drake's Boston*, pp. 449–453, for an account of the family, with interesting extracts from the Diary of John Hull.

and to sonne, *Edward Hull,* that peece of ground at the water mile and three[s]core poundes in money or goods.          *Robert Hull.*
20 of 3 present, 1657. [Recorded—Book I. folio 511.

[In the same file is a deed of gift, endorsed " *Rob*ᵗ *Hull :* my fathʳˢ deed of Gifte vnto me 12 febr. 66." His son, *John Hull,* "being now upon his marriage, being about the one and twentieth yeare of his age," his father gives him as follows :—" My dwelling House & garden, with all the fruit trees and Appurtenances, bounded one the north, with the land of *Job Judkin ;* on the south, with the land of *John Hurd ;* one the east, with the Land of *Gamaliel Waite ;* one the north west, with the high way. As also my Lott of ground at mudy river, given to me by the towne of Boston,* of about 36 or 38 ackras, bounded with Cambridg line one the North; vpon the south, with the Land of *Edward Belsher ;* one the East, pᵗly: with the Land of *Robert Turner ;* one the west, with the Lotts of *Thomas Wheeler, Thomas Scottow* & *Isack Perry.* As also A Lott of 21 ackras, given by the towne of Boston vnto my sonn, *Richard Storer,* & by me purchased off him, Lieing at Brantree, by Manatticott river, betweene *Mʳ Francis Loyall* & *Mʳ Ting.* Said property, *Robert Hull* gave to his son, *John,* reserving to himself during his life, the full enjoyment of it.
Dated Dec. 15, 1646.          *Robert Hull.*]

Feb. 12, 1666. Power of Administration given to *John Hull* to administer on the estate of his father, *Robert Hull,* John being " his Eldest & now only sonn."

Inventory of the estate taken, 4 : 6 : 1666, by *Edw. Raynsford, Rob*ᵗ *Sanderson, Rob*ᵗ *Walker.*

---

THOMAS MAKEPEACE.—June 30, 1666. I, *Thomas Makepeace,* being weake in body but of Competent & good memory, doe by this my Last will, dispose of my temporal estate in manner following. Vnto *Thomas Makepeace,* mine eldest sonne, (beyond yᵉ seas) & to his heyrs for euer, the debt of £50, which hee oweth mee (for which end I have torne off the seale of his bill) & no more, because I haue giuen him his portion formerly, vizᵗ. yᵉ house & land in England (he being the heyre to it) which he hath longe possessed. Unto my sone, *William Makepeace,* yᵗ my house in Boston, wherein my sonne in Law, *Lawrence Willis,* now dwelleth, wᵗʰ yᵗ peece of Land as I haue now staked out to it, I say, I giue the same to him, my sd sonne *W*ᵐ & to his heyres foreuer, hee to enter upon the same at the death of my dau. *Mary Willis,* & not before; besides this, I freely giue vnto my said sonne, *William,* a debt due to mee from *Thomas Terry,* of Blocke Island, being three pound odd money. Vnto *Hannah,* mine eldest dau., the wiffe of *Stephen Hoppin,* of Thomsons Island, & to her heires foreuer, £5, to be payed her, or her order, wᵗʰ In one yeare affter my death. Vnto my dau. *Mary,* the wife of *Lawrance Willis* of Boston, that house in Boston wherein shee wᵗʰ her sd Husband now dwells, during her life only. And at her death, her brother, *William,* shall haue yᵉ same. Also, unto my dau. *Mary,* & to her heires foreuer one debt owing to mee from *Jn*ᵒ *Willis.* of Bridgewatter, senioʳ, & also one debt due to me from his sonne, *Jn*ᵒ *Willis,* of yᵉ same towne aforesᵈ, Junior. Vnto my dau. *Hester,* yᵉ wife of *John Browne,* of Malborrough, & to her heyrs foreuer, £5, to bee pd wᵗʰin one yeare affter my decease, also to her & her heyrs, yᵗ debt her sd husband owes me.

---

* In 1636. See *Drake's Boston,* p. 196.

Vnto my dau. *Waytawhile*, the wiffe of *Josiah Cooper*, of Boston, £5, [to be pd, as before.] Vnto my Grand Children, *Delieurance, Jn°. Stephen, Hannah, Sarah, Thomas, Oppertunity, Joseph & Benjamen Hoppin*, '(they being the nine children) of my Dau. *Hannah*, the wife of *Stephen Hoppin*, aboue sayed, to each, £10, which sayed Legacies the male Children shall receiue as they come to the age of 21, & the females, at 18, or day of marriage, which shall happen first, with this exception, Relating to *Stephen*, only, That if my Executo<sup>rs</sup> shall, when he comes to 21 yeares of age, Find him to persist on in his wild & wastfull courses, then they shall pay him (of his sd Legacy of £10) Only 10 shillings p<sup>r</sup> Anumm till hee be well reformed, & then, & not before, they shall pay him the residue he hath not receaued of the sayed tenne pounds. Vnto my Grand Children, viz<sup>t</sup>. *Elizabeth, Joseph, Sarah, Mary, & John Browne*, they being the fiue Children of my dau. *Hester*, y<sup>e</sup> wife of *Jn°. Browne*, vnto each £10, males at 21, females at 18 or day of marriage. Vnto my Grand Children, *Elizabeth & Thomas Cooper*, the two Children of my daughter *Waitawhile*, the wife of *Josiah Cooper*, £10, to be paid them as all the other my Grand Children aboue mentioned. It hath pleased God to take away *Thomas Cooper*, one of y<sup>e</sup> children aboue named, my will is, y<sup>t</sup> if shee be now w<sup>th</sup> child, that child to injoy y<sup>e</sup> ten pound. If any of my Grandchildren dye before the age & time afforesd, theire Legacies shall bee pd. by an equall deuision amongst all their bretheren & systers as they from time to time come to the Age & time abouesd. Vnto my kinswoman, *Mary*, the wife of *Jn°. Pearce*, of Rhoad Island & to her heires foreuer, £3, to bee payd in one yeare affter my death.

Vnto my wiues three dau<sup>s</sup>. vizt. *Mary*, y<sup>e</sup> wife of *James Dennis*, of Boston; to *Martha*, y<sup>e</sup> wife of *Joseph Walters*, of Milford; vnto *Mary*, y<sup>e</sup> wife of *Emanuell Sprinckfeild*, in old England, vnto each, & theire heires 50<sup>s</sup>. to bee payd in one yeare affter my death. I also Freely Giue them such debts as any of theire respective husbands oweth mee. I Appoynt *Elizabeth*, my wife, & my sonne in Law, *Josiah Cooper*, of Boston, & my dau. *Waiteawhile*, his wife, (or the surviuors of them) to bee my Executo<sup>rs</sup> & Executrexes, to pay sd. Legacies, either by selling my houses & Lands or any other waies as they in theire best discretion shall see to bee most Conduceable to all ends & purposes beforesd. All debts due mee being Receaued & all debts owing by mee being payed, my wiues third pt of the whole being deducted, and the Afforesd Legacies being pd or secured, my will is, that the Remainde<sup>r</sup> of my estate bee deiuded into three equall parts or shares to y<sup>e</sup> propper vse of my executo<sup>r</sup>s, viz<sup>t</sup>. one third p<sup>t</sup> thereof to bee *Elizabeths*, my wiues, the other two third p<sup>ts</sup>. to bee *Waitawhile*, my Daughter, & *Josiah Cooper*, her husband. If any of the Exeutors shall dye, theire shares giuen them of the remainde<sup>r</sup> of my estate shall Fall into the hands of the Surviueo<sup>r</sup>s or Surviueo<sup>r</sup> of my sd Executo<sup>r</sup>s to bee his or hers and his or her heires foreuer. I giue vnto my sonne in Law, *Abell Langly*, 50<sup>s.</sup> to be pd him as y<sup>e</sup> like legacies Abousayed.                                        *Thomas Makepeace*.

Signed & Sealed in the presence of us,
*William Bartholmew, John Cleare, Joseph Bartholmew.*
   March 8, 1666–7. *W<sup>m</sup> Bartholmew & John Cleare* deposed.
[Recorded, Book I. folio 518.
   Inventory of the Estate of *Thomas Makepeace* taken March 2, 1666–7, by *John Phillipes, Daniel Turell*. Amt. £291. 07. 01.
   March 8, 1666–7. *Elisabeth Makepeace & Josiah Cooper* deposed.
[Recorded, Book V. folio 31.

JAMES MATTOCKE.—Jan. 21, 1666. I, *James Mattock*, of Boston, Cooper, being of perfect memory, do make this my last will. Debts to be paid. I Giue to my Sone, *Samuel Mattock*, 20ˢ; to my dau. *Alice*, now the wife of *John Lewes*, 20ˢ; to my dau. *Mary*, now the wife of *Samuell Browne*, 20ˢ. I ordain my wife, *Mary Mattock*, to be my exec-utrix. Inasmuch as my Children respectively have had portions of my estate, if any or either of my Children Do make any Sute, Demand, to the trouble & vexation of my wife, for any part of my estate in land, goods or debts otherwise then according to this my Will, That then either of them so Doing shall clearly loose such legacy by me given, & that my bequeath to him or her shall be clearly void as if the same had never been to him or her given or made. Jan 28, in the yeare above written.
In the presence of                                    *James Mattocke.*
*Richard Collacott, William Pearse* scr.
*Wᵐ Pearse* deposed, Aug. 1st, '67. [Recorded, Book I. folio 541.
Inventory of the estate taken 12 : 4 : 1667, by *Thomas Lake, Joseph How.* Amt. £277. 15. 05. *Mary Mattox* [so written on the inventory] deposed Aug. 15, 1667. [Recorded, Book V. folio 48.

---

THOMAS JONES.—I, *Thomas Jones*, of Dorchester, doe make this my Last will. Debts to be paid & receaved. Unto my wife, two Cowes, to bee hers absolutely & to bee taken at her own choyce. Vnto my dau. *Hannah*, £50, to bee paid to her in good pay within one twelve month after my decease. And for the Remainder of my Estate, my will is, that my wife shall have the income & use thereof during her life, that is to say, she shall possesse & enjoy my present dwelling House, wᵗʰ the Barn & out Housing, my Areable & Pasture Land & Meadow together wᵗʰ necessary firewood & Timber for all repaires from any wood lot & the use of all my Household stuffe, Provided that she at all tymes keep in sufficient repair the foresaid dwelling House, Barn & out Housing & the fences belonging to the Land, & make no wast of firewood or Timber. After the decease of my wife, I give unto my Grandchildren as followes, to my Granchild, *Isaack Jones*, if then living, £5 ; to his Sister, *Hannah*, £5 ; provided, that if eyther of them dy before Age, their legacy shall then return to bee divided amongst the Rest of my Grandchildren then Living. To the Eldest child of each of my daughters, £5 ; to *Henry, Richard & Elizabeth Way* 50ˢ apeece ; to *James & Thomas Green*, 50ˢ apeece. My will is, that the Remainder of my estate shall bee equally divided between my son & Daughters, provided that if any of them shall dy before my wife then His or Her part that shall so dy, shall come equally to his or her children that shall bee surviving. My will is, that my son, *Isaack Jones*, or his sons, shall have the liberty, in case of sale made at any tyme, to purchase My dwelling House or any of my Lands, of the Rest of my children or Grandchildren that shall bee minded to sell & Alien their proportions therein, before any other, giving the worth ac-cording as then it may bee. I Appoint my wife Sole Executrix ; & my sons, *Isaack Jones, Richard Way, James Green*, too bee overseers. March 26, 1667.                                    *Thomas ⋈ Jones.*
In the presence of us,
*William Stoughton, James Minott*, who deposed Jan 15, 1667.
[Recorded, Book I. folio 517.
An Inuentory of the Goods & Estate of the late *Mʳ Thomas Jones*, of Dorchester, who deceased this life 13 : 9 : 1667, taken & apprized by

*Hopestill Foster*, *James Humphery*, *John Minott*, Dec. 11, 1667. Amt. £555. *M*<sup>rs</sup> *Ellin Jones*, Executrix, deposed, Jan. 15, 1667, to the inventory of her late husband's Estate. [Recorded, Book V. folio 75.

HUMPHERY MILAM.—Feb. 14, 1666. I, *Humphry Mylam*, of Boston, Cooper, being sick but of sound memory, do make this my last Will. Debts to be paid. Vnto my wife, *Mary Mylam*, my now dwelling house with the Shop & the building thereto adjoining & the land where on it standeth, & £30 in money. To my dau. *Mary Mylam*, £30 in money & the value of £10 of my goods & a fether bed & bolster, a Rugg, a Blankett, Two paier of Sheets & a Silver Spoon. To my dau. *Constance Mylam*, £30 in money & the value of £10 in goods & a fether bed & bolster, a Rugg, a Blankett, Two paier of Sheets & a Silver Spoon. To my dau. *Sarah Mylam*, £20 in money & £10 value in goods & a bed & bolster, a Rugg, Two paier of Sheets & a Blanket. To my dau. *Abigail Mylam*, my mpiety or halfe in that ware house our against my dwelling house & the wharf thereto belonging & my Silver Taster. Vnto my dau. *Hannah Mylam*, £20 in money & that peece of ground behind the yard behind my dwelling howse, w<sup>th</sup> the priviledg of way & passe there from & to foreu<sup>r</sup>. on the wharfe at the Southwesterly end of my dwelling house from & to it into the street. My will is that the before mentioned legacies to my Daughto<sup>rs</sup> shall be paid them respectively when they shall be of the Age of 19 or at theire Marriage w<sup>ch</sup> shall first be, p<sup>r</sup>vided each of them marry w<sup>th</sup> the app<sup>r</sup>bation of theire mother, & in her absence w<sup>th</sup> the App<sup>r</sup>bation of my friends here after named, any or either of them, whom I intreat to be theire ou<sup>r</sup>seers. If any of my Children die before she come to the age aforesaid or be married, then, the survivo<sup>rs</sup> shall have such part epually divided amongst them. My meaning is, that my wife shall have my abovesaid dwelling house but during her life & after her decease to her & my Children together to be divided equally amongst them. Vnto my wife all my goods, debts, Chattells, not hereby before disposed of & the term of yeares yet to com & vnexpired at the time of my decease in my Apprentize *Nath: Claddis*. I ordain my wife sole executrix, most heartily beseeching her that as she hath showed her selfe faithfull & louing to me whilest we have lived together so she will continue a naturall mother towards my Children as my trust in her is she will be. I intreat my friends, *Cap*<sup>t</sup>. *Thomas Lake*, my Cozen, *M*<sup>r</sup> *Jeremiah Cushen* & *M*<sup>r</sup> *Joseph How*, to be ou<sup>r</sup>seers of this my will. I have here vnto subscribed my name y<sup>e</sup> 15<sup>th</sup> 12<sup>th</sup> moneth in y<sup>e</sup> yeare above written.

Signed & sealed in the p<sup>r</sup>sence of us: *Humphrey Milam*.
*Will: Turner, William Pearse scr*.

3 May, 1667. *W*<sup>m</sup> *Turner* deposed. *William Pearse* took like oath in open Court 6 May 67. [Recorded, Book I. folio 523.

Inventory of the Estate of the late *Humphery Milam*, deceased, prized by *John Conney*, *William Turner*, May 1, 1667. The net state resting, £700. 06. 01. *Mary Mylam*, Relict of *Humphery Mylam* deposed, May 3, 1667. [Recorded, Book V. folio 39.

## ABSTRACTS FROM THE EARLIEST WILLS ON RECORD AND ON THE FILES IN THE COUNTY OF SUFFOLK, MASS.

[Prepared by WILLIAM B. TRASK of Dorchester.]

ELKANAH GLADMAN.—Inventory of the Estate of *Elkanah Gladman*, apprised by *Hezekiah Usher, Thomas Snawsell*, Nov. 23, 1664. Amt. £211.10.11½.

Inventorye of Debts Due to the Estate of Mr Elkanah Gladman as they were found in His Book at His Death. From Capt. Thomas Bredon, Goodwife Cutler of Charlestowne, John Holliday of Boston, Nurse Greene, Mrs Trarice, Mrs Roades, Mr George Saunders, Mr John Blake, Mr Edward Nailor, Samuel Mattox, Goodwife Farnham, Alexander Steward, Sarah Potterton, Mrs.. Mary Johnson, Mr John Gifford, Mrs Susan Jacklin, Thaddeus Mackartye, Mr Wollaston, Anne Carter, Lawrence Smithe, Zacheus Sedgwicke, Mr Stephen Goodieur, Mrs Eieres, Edward Page, Goodwife Baxter, Edward Lillye, Serjant Wm. Cotton, Mr Job Sayres, Mrs Allice Thomas. Total, £139.05.01¼. Out of which is to bee paid, [specified sums] to Mr Thomas Lake, Jno. Watts, Benj. Gillam senior, Mr Tho. Deane.

Feb. 8, 1664. *Capt. Thomas Bredon & Capt. Thomas Lake*, deposed.

[On page 261 of vol. I, is a recital of the doings of the Court in regard to the estate of Elkanah Gladman. It is stated that the Administrators, *Capt. Thomas Bredon* and *Capt. Thomas Lake*, brought into Court an inventory of said Estate, producing also "a Letter from Mr Elkanah Gladman, Father to the late *Elkanah Gladman* Deceased March 21st 1664 in which it appears that the sd Elkanah Gladman Desyres & orders that one hundred pounds of his Late sonnes Estate, with halfe his Bookes shall bee & goe to Mrs Lydia Goodyear, who was the Contracted Wife of the Late Elkanah Gladman Junor, the which the Court allowes & approues of, and orders that the Administrators Remit the Rest of the sd Elkanah Gladmans estate, to Mr Elkanah Gladman the Father, as in & by his Letter may appear to bee his Desyre, which this Court orders to be Recorded & kept on File. And on a Certificate from Mr Elkanah Gladman senior that he Doth Allow & approue of this Order, by sufficient Witnesses Coming into these parts, or on testimonye of some knowne publick Notarye to his said state, this Court shall approue of the Administrators Accompt and Giue them a Discharge from their Administration.

At a County Court 16th June 1665. EDWARD RAWSON Recorder."]

———

DANIEL WELD.—July 1, 1666. I, *Daniell Weld*, of Roxbury, Yeoman, hauing the perfect vse of my vnderstanding & memory, make this to bee my last will. * * * * * I giue my House where I now dwell, in Roxbury, my barne, Orchards, Gardens & home Lott, all my Cowes, Heiffers & Hogs, my mare & bees, all my Household stuffe bedding, brass, pewter, linnen & wollen. And furthermore I giue

281

my orchard & parcell of Pasture thereto adjoyning, lying neare
Stony Riuer bridge, purchased of *John Watson.* Also twelue Acres
of plowed Land & Pasture, lying vpon the great Hill in Roxbury
neare Muddy Riuer, which I purchased of *Hugh Clarke.* All debts
due to mee, All my personal Estate, I doe giue to *Ann Weld,* my
wife, to bee Enjoyed by her soe long as shee shall remaine my widdow, but in Case it please God soe to dispose, that my deare wife
change her Condition, And marry another man, then my will is, that
shee should Enjoy the thirds of my Estate, for the tearme of hir life.
And my will is, that nothing bee sold of my Estate, Except there
bee great necessity for the maintenance of my wife & children, And
that not without the Council and aduice of my Ouerseers, vnless it
should appeare clearly to my Executor & to my Ouerseers, that it
should bee much for the bennifitt of my wife and children to sell all
here in Roxbury & purchase Housing & Lands in some other place
to the full worth of it, where it might bee plainly for their advantage.
For my deare sonn, *M<sup>r</sup> Daniell Weld,* in England, whether hee be
liuinge or noe I know not, yet out of my tender respect I haue to him,
although the Portion hee hath already receiued hath bin as much as
my whole Estate now remaining, yet out of my Fatherly affection to
him at my decease, I can doe noe less than giue vnto him, by this
my will, 20ˢ, out of my Estate, as a small Token of my great loue.
For the rest of my children, my will is, that after the marriage of
my wife (in Case shee marry) that two thirds of my Estate bee deuided by Equall Portions, betweene them, that is, mine & my wiues
children, namely, *Joseph Weld, Bethiah Weld,* & *Timothy Hide,* And
after my wifes decease, the other third part of my Estate, or in case
shee marry not, then the whole Estate to bee Equally divided betweene them, Prouided always that in Case the Lord soe dispose that
any of my said children should marry before my wifes marriage vnto
any other man, or whilst shee remaines my widdow, then my will is,
that there should bee due Encouragment allowed to them or any
such of them out of the Estate, with the Consent of my Executrix, &
by & with the aduice of my Ouerseers, according as they shall judge
Expedient, all things Considered, which proportion of the Estate is
to bee taken notice of soe as to bee allowed for by them who shall
receive it, vnto the rest, at the time or times of the diuission of the
Estate, to make Each proportion Equall according to the will. And
in Case the Lord should take away any of the three children before
Expressed, before the time or times of the diuission, then my will is,
that the Estate shall bee Equally diuided betweene them & Enjoyed
by the suruiou<sup>rs</sup>. As for my dau. *Mary Hide,* shee hath had her Portion already, And my will is, my wife should haue libertie at her
death to giue her sonn some small token of her loue to remember her
by, with & According to the aduice of my Ouerseers. I appoint *Ann
Weld,* my wife, to bee my sole Executrix & I doe most hartily request
my deare & faithfull Couzens, *M<sup>r</sup> Edward Denison, M<sup>r</sup> Thomas Weld,*
& *M<sup>r</sup> John Weld* to bee the Ouerseers of this my will, praying them
to see this in trust Carefully performed, And to haue a Care of my
poore wife, whome I leaue into the hands of the Lord & to you my
deare Couzens to Council & direct her.                     DANIEL WELD.
   Wittnes,
      *John Weld, John Stebbins,* who deposed, Nov. 3, 1666.

Inventory of the Estate of M<sup>r</sup> Daniel Weld, taken Aug. 1, 1666, by *Edward Denison, John Weld, Thomas Weld, John Stebins.*
M<sup>rs</sup> *Ann Weld,* Relict & Executrix to the last will & Testament of the late *M<sup>r</sup> Daniel Weld,* deposed, 3: 9ber: 1666.

———

DAVID HOMES.—To my Eldest sonn, *Dauid,* I leave £10; to the other two yonger, £5 a peece; if in Case they bee put forth to printiss for time, such as take them shall take their Portions with them, Learne them to Read & write, & dubble their Portions to them at the End of their time; if in Case such as take the Children are vnwilling soe to doe I leaue this £20, in the hands & to the disposing of *Stephen Kinsley,* & for want of life to his sonn, *John Kinsley,* & to *Thomas Hollman* & they to putt it to the best improuement & for the vse & bennifitt of the Children & to bee payd to them when at age of 21, in such pay as they receiued. If any of the children die, their mother shall haue their Estate, if shee die, they shall haue hers amongst them Equally. My will is, also, that my dau. *Margaret,* shall haue £5, to bee paid at Age or day of marriage if shee liue, if not, to bee at her mothers disposing. The rest of my Estate I leaue to my wife to pay my debts & to improue to her best advantage, & to see my body Lawfully Buried.
Nov. 15, 1666. Power of Administration to the Estate of *Dauid Holmes* is granted to *Jane,* his Relict, shee bringing in an Inventory of that Estate & performing this imperfect will as neere as may bee.
EDW. RAWSON Record<sup>r</sup>.

This is to sattisfie that I, *Henry Crane,* doth testifie this to be the will of *Dauid Homes;* p<sup>r</sup> mee, *Henry Crane,* this 15<sup>th</sup> of the 9: month 1666.
Inventory of the Estate of Dauid Homes deceased the 2<sup>d</sup> of Nov. 1666. Prisers, *Gregory Belcher, William Daniell.* Amt. £73.13.7.
Nov. 15, 1666. *Jane Holmes,* Relict of *Dauid Homes,* deposed.

[On the back of the original document on file, James Humphry & W<sup>m</sup> Weekes stand bound in 20<sup>s</sup> apiece to y<sup>e</sup> Treasurer "on this Condition that Francis Crabtree shall be of good behauiour till y<sup>e</sup> next County court & shall then appeare & so from court to court till her case be ended." Signed by EDW. RAWSON, Record<sup>r</sup>.]

———

HENRY WITHINGTON.—8: 11: 1664. I, *Henry Withington,* of Dorchester, in New England, being about the Age of 76 yeares or vpon 77: being in perfect memory doe make my last will. * * * My will is, That my sonn, *Richard Withington,* one of my Executo<sup>rs</sup>, shall well & truly performe vnto my wife, *Margerie,* all such Agreements as are Expressed in a writting made & sealed before our marriage, bearing date, 25: 4: 1662: witnessed by M<sup>r</sup> *John Eliott* & M<sup>r</sup> *Samuell Danforth,* And then soe doing I giue vnto him all the rest of my Houses & Orchard & Lands that I haue in Dorchester, Except Tenn Acres in the Twenty Acres Lotts, which Tenn Acres I Giue to my dau. *Batte,* & I Except also my devision of Land which is about 30

Acres, lying neere Dedam mill, which if it bee not sold before my death, my will is, that it shall bee sould & come in as part of my Estate, And álso I Except all my Land that is mine, about *Sensions* House, which Land I Giue to my dau. *Batte*, to bee hers foreuer, And her Husband shall haue noe power to dispose of it without her free Consent. But all my Land Except these parcells Excepted I Giue to my sonn *Richard* to bee his foreuer. And for my goods, my debts & buriall being discharged out of the whole, I Giue as followeth, namly, to my Beloued wife, *Margerie*, £10, ouer & besides that £10, I promised her before our marriage which is sett downe in a writing, aforesayd, And to my sonn, *Richard*, £10, & to his fowre sonns, *John, Ebenezer, Henry & Phillip*, each, £5; to M^r *Mather*, £5; M^r *Tompson*, £5; And towards the maintenance of an able ministrie in Dorchester, which they haue or may chuse, I Give £20 to bee improved by the Deacons then in being, And the bennifitt thereof shall bee brought in yearely to the Select men, then in being, to bee giuen to the vse aforesaid. And £10 more I Giue vnto the poorest inhabitants in Dorchester, And the said £10 shall bee disposed at & by the discresion of the Deacons, then in being. I Giue vnto *John Baker*, £5, *Samuell Batte*, £5, *Samuell Paull*, £5, *Samuell Danforth*, £5. To all the Childeren I am Grandfather vnto, Except *Mary Robinson*, & such Children as I haue herein giuen legacies vnto, I giue each of them, 40^s. For the rest of my goods, legacies being discharged, shall bee Equally diuided among my 3 dau^s namly, *Faith Baker, Mary Danforth*, and *Anna Batte* And for that Fiue Acres of Land that I latly bought of *James Batte* at the south End of his Lott, next the High way, which Cost mee, £16, it is my will that she, I meane my dau. *Batte*, shall haue that Fiue Acres, & shée shall dispose of it for her good & for her Children, but her Husband shall haue no power to sell it away, without her Consent, nor any Land that I haue giuen her Else where. And further it is my meaninge, that this £16, which the Land Cost mee, though the Land Returne her as aforesayd, yet it shall bee reconed as part of that Portion which I leaue with hir other Sisters. For my Executo^rs, I Appoint my sonn, *Richard Withington*, & my sonn, *Richard Baker ;* for my Ouerseers, my sonn, M^r *Thomas Danforth*, & my sonn, *James Batte*. The legacies [to be paid] one halfe within a yeare after my death & the other halfe the next yeare after, if it may bee well had & done.                                HENRY WITHINGTON.
    Wittnes hereof
        *Enoch Wiswall, Samuell Paull.*

    [In a codicil, Mr Withington states, that he has given to his son, *Richard*, the £10 expressed in his will, also delivered to him the £5 for *John Withington*, his Eldest son. "For the Tenn Acres of Land I gaue to my daughter *Batte*, lying in the Twenty Acre Lott I haue sold that, since, to *Samuell Clap* & haue deliuered & giuen to her & her Husband all my Land at *Sensions* house." All which is acknowledged by *Richard Withington. Samuel Paul*, acknowledges "that I haue reeeiued from my *Father Withington*, that Fiue pounds which is Expressed in his will, to bee Giuen me. 23: 9: 1666."]
    15 Feb. 1666. *Enoch Wiswell & Samuel Paule*, deposed.
    An Inventory of the Estate of Elder Henry Withington, of Dor-

284

chester, who deceased this life Feb. 2, 1666, taken & apprised by *John Capen senr & William Sumner*, March 6, 1666–7. Amt. £850.17.3. Due from the Estate, £14.4.6. Mentions, $\frac{1}{16}$ pt. of three Ketches; ½ of a warehouse at Boston; two shares in the iron works at Tanton.
*Richard Baker & Richard Withington*, deposed to this inventory, May 2, 1667.

———

RICHARD WOODCOCK.*—An Inventorye of the Estate of Richard Woodcock Deceased Nouember 22th 1662, as apprised by *Edward Fletcher, Michaell Wills.* Amt. £38.9.5. " Also seuerall armes of other mens, as we are Informed, in yᵉ shoppe (uizᵗ.) 8 swordes, 10 pistolls, 39 gunnes with stockes, 23 fyre Lockes," &c. Sworne in Court Dec. 19, 1662, by *Richard Wayte & Thomas Matson.*
[The Administrators of said estate were ordered by the Court, to deliver to *Capᵗ Davenport*, of the Castle, *Mʳ Rosewell* & *Mʳ Daiues* man & such other their seuerall gunnes " they Making proofe by Oath before any Commissioner in Boston, or on yᵉ Acknowledgment of the wife, or Late apprentice of the said *Woodcocke* to bee theires.
EDWARD RAWSON Recorder.

———

GEORGE DAVIS.—I, *George Davis*, beinge bound for Cape Feare, doe now dispose my outward estate as followeth, in case I die before I come againe or shall hear after make any other will; being in health, My whole estate, that I leaue in New England, I do bestow vppon my wife and Children, and doe make my wife executrix, and my son, *Benjamin*, executor Joyntly. My estate to be diuided into fiue parts, two parts I giue to my wife and my son *Benjamine* equaly, the other three parts I giue to my fiue dauˢ to be diuided equaly, and to be paid vnto them when they come to age, or when they may, as their mother shall Judg best, and their mothers part she has power to dispose it to her she dies to those or to all of my Children, soe it be to my Children, that are most Louing and dutifull vnto her. My house and land I do dispose to my wife and my sone *Benjamine*, pro-uided my daughters haue theire portions, though it be in other things. To my sone, *Joseph*, I giue all that I haue now in the shipp, and that we cary with vs to Cape Feare, with the weauers loome; but in Case it does Miscary before it come ther, and he com agen to new Eng-land, my executors out of the whole estate shall pay him ten pound farther, becaus my Daughters, som of them, are young, and to be brought vpp in the feare of God and well educated, is my desire, which I hope my wife will not be wanting in, therfor their portions shalbe responsable for theire bringinge vpp and left to the discresion of my wife what to pay them when they come to age, or when she

* The following is from the files. See Will of Jane Woodcock, *Reg.*, vol. xv. 76.**
"*William Day*, sonne of yᵉ late *Hugh Day* & *Jane* his wife, yᵗ married to yᵉ late *Richard Woodcocke* & *Richard Brooke*, of Boston, Gunn smith," were bound to Ed-ward Rawson, Recorder, in the sum of £50, Aug 10, 1666, " by virtue of hir said last will bearing date 16th March 1665," to the performance of the conditions as administrators of said will. Signed by *William Day* and *Richard Brooke*, with seals, bearing impressions of coats of arms. Witnessed by *John Clauerle, Recompence Os-borne.*
**See p. 260.
¹ *For* dispose it to her as she dies *read* dispose it when she dies.

dies. I haue chosen for one ouerseer of this my last will, my brother, *William Clark*, of linn, and doe you chuse another whome you think fit, and giue them 40ˢ apeece, and trust to their faithfullnes and care for my poor Chilldren. Dec. 7, 1664. GEORG DAVIS.
Wittnes,
*William Killcupp, Grace ✗ Killcupp.*

My son, *Joseph Coult*, I doe desire my sone, *Benjamine*, to haue Care of him till he doe take farther order about him. GEO: DAVIS.

*William Kilcup, & Grace Kilcupp* his wife, deposed, Sepᵗ 30, 1667. Recorded, Book I, fol. 522.
Inventory of the goods of *Georg Davis*, leatly desesed at cape faier, taken by *John Gould, William ✗ Clark.* Amt. £355.01.
*Benjamin Daius* deposed, Oct. 29, 1667. Recorded, Book V, fol. 63.

---

ROBERT WOODMANSEY.*—The Last Will And testament of *Mʳ Robᵗ Woodmansey*, being weake of Body but off A disposing mind and having before me the thoughts of my departure out off this world. Concerning my little estate I have left vnto me, wᶜʰ lyeth in monyes, debts & Household stuff, and is speicified in An Inventorie, I dispose off it to my wife, *Margarett*, And my two dauˢ *Martha* and *Bathia.* I make my wife, *Margarett*, sole executrix. As vnto Any Proportion I bequeath one halfe to my sᵈ Two daughters, the rest vnto my wife, excepting some Perticulers which I have caused to be putt into writing & to be disposed off by my sᵈ Executrix according to my sᵈ desire therein. That this is my will I acknowledge by my hand seale herevnto Put, this 5ᵗʰ day of July 1667. ROBT WOODMANSEY.
Wittnesse herevnto,
*John Hull, Gregory Clement.*

*John Hull* deposed, Nov. 15. Recorded, Book I, fol. 523.
An Inuentory of the Goods & Estate of *Mʳ Robᵗ Woodmansey*, late shoolemaster of Boston, deceased, taken by vs, *Richard Gridley & Edmond Eddenden*, Sept 18, 1667. Amt. £196.07.2. Added, £3.3.
*Mrs. Margaret Woodmansey* deposed, Nov. 15, 1667.

---

* Mr. Woodmansey was one of the early school-teachers in Boston. His name is on the records April 11th, 1650. March 12th, 1666, Mr. Daniel Henchman was engaged "to assist Mr. Woodmansey in the Grammar School and teach children to write." The successor of Mr. W. was the celebrated Benjamin Tompson, "a man of great learning and wit, well acquainted with the Roman and Greek writers, and a good poet." (See *Register*, XIV, 54, 141; XV, 113, 116.) He was chosen, Aug. 26th, 1667, and with Mr. Henchman, appears to have continued in the employ of the town, until Jan. 3, 1671, when the noted Ezekiel Cheever took the principal charge of the school. The immediate predecessor of Mr. Woodmansey was probably a Mr. Woodbridge, mentioned Dec. 2, 1644. Previous to this, in August, 1636, Mr. Daniel Maude was chosen to the office of "free school master." He was a minister, and removed to Dover, N. H., where he settled in 1642, and died in 1655. Johnson, in his *Wonder Working Providence*, says: he was "both godly and diligent in the work" of a pastor. But the probable pioneer in the Boston "free school," was *Philemon Pormortt*, who on the 13th of April, 1635, according to the *Town Records* was "intreated to become a schoolmaster for teaching and nurturing of children with us." Whether this office was accepted, we know not. He was dismissed Jan 6, 1639, as appears by the church record, "to join Mr. Wheelwright and others at Piscatuqua."

JASPER RAWLINS.—17: 11th mo: 1665. I give vnto my wif, *Mary Rawlins*, my now Dwelling howse wᵗʰ all the moveable goods in it, as also all my Debts and Demands, for her vse and Despose after my decease, and doe hereby Constitute my deare wife to be my sole executrix, where vnto I doe set my hand. And in case any of my children should come over to settle here, I do give a peece of ground where the clay doth ly to build him an howse, if not, to be left to my wif for her dispose; witnes my hand.

The mark of × JASPER RAWLINS.

Witnes herevnto this 17, of 11th mo. 1665.

*Joseph Knight.*

The mark ᴼᶠ
*John* ∃ *Skinner.*

13th June, 1667. *Joseph Knight & Jnᵒ Skinner* deposed.

———

HUMPHERY MILAM.—Feb. 14, 1666. I, *Humphry Mylam*, of Boston, Cooper, being sick but of sound memory, do make this my last Will. Debts to be paid. Vnto my wife, *Mary Mylam*, my now dwelling house with the Shop & the building thereto adjoining & the land wheré on it standeth, & £30 in money. To my dau. *Mary Mylam*, £30 in money & the value of £10 of my goods & a fether bed & bolster, a Rugg, a Blankett, Two paier of Sheets & a Silver Spoon. To my dau. *Constance Mylam*, £30 in money & the value of £10 in goods & a fether bed & bolster, a Rugg, a Blankett, Two paier of Sheets & a Silver Spoon. To my dau. *Sarah Mylam*, £20 in money & £10 value in goods & a bed & bolster, a Rugg, Two paier of Sheets & a Blanket. To my dau. *Abigail Mylam*, my moiety or halfe in that ware house our against my dwelling house & the wharf thereto belonging & my Silver Taster. Vnto my dau. *Hannah Mylam*, £20 in money & that peece of ground behind the yard behind my dwelling howse, wᵗʰ the priviledg of way & passe there from & to foreuʳ on the wharfe at the South-westerly end of my dwelling house from & to it into the street. My will is that the before mentioned legacies to my Daughtoʳˢ shall be paid them respectively when they shall be of the Age of 19 or at theire Marriage wᶜʰ shall first be, pʳvided each of them marry wᵗʰ the·appʳbation of theire mother & in her absence wᵗʰ the Appʳbation of my friends here after named, any or either of them, whom I intreat to be theire ouʳseers. If any of my Children die before she come to the age aforesaid or be married, then, the Survivoʳˢ shall haue such part equally divided amongst them. My meaning is that my wife shall have my abovesaid dwelling house but during her life & after her decease to her & my Children together to be divided equally amongst them. Vnto my wife all my goods, debts, Chattells, not hereby before disposed of, & the term of yeares yet to com & vn-expired at the time of my decease in my Apprentize *Nath: Claddis*. I ordain my wife sole executrix, most heartily beseeching her that as she hath showed her selfe faithfull & louing to me whilest we have lived together so she will continue a naturall mother towards my Children as my trust in her is she will be. I Intreat my friends, *Capᵗ Thomas Lake*, my Cozen, *Mʳ Jeremiah Cushen* & *Mʳ Joseph How* to be ou<sup>r</sup>seers of this my will. I have here vnto subscribed my name ye 15<sup>th</sup> 12<sup>th</sup> moneth in y<sup>e</sup> yeare above written.     HUMPHREY MILAM.

Signed & sealed in the p<sup>r</sup>sence of us:
> *Will: Turner, William Pearse scr.*

3 May 1667, *W<sup>m</sup> Turner* deposed.   *William Pearse* took like oath in open Court 6 May 67.   Recorded, Book 1, fol. 523.

Inventory of the Estate of the late *Humphery Milam*, deceased, prized by *John Conney, William Turner*, May 1, 1667.   The net state resting, £700.06.01.   *Mary Mylam*, Relict of *Humphery Mylam* deposed, May 3, 1667.   Recorded, Book V, fol. 39.

———

JOHN ALCOCKE.—I, *John Alcocke*, of Roxbury, hauing had more then ordinary occasions & oppertunitys duely to weigh & Consider the Incertainty of this life, being in a peculiar manner by my Calling excersised for the few yeares I haue hitherto liued, being helpfull as God Enabled to othe<sup>rs</sup> & knowing the decree is Certaine that he only is the great & only phisition, in whose hands my times are, according to his mind & will & my duty, being in my good and sound vnderstanding & memory, tho' weake in body, doe make this my last will.  I Giue my soule into the hands of him that Gaue it, and my body I Comitt vnto the Earth to be buried as neere my beloued wife y<sup>t</sup> was.  Debts to be payd.  I Giue my dear wiues Apparrell & what did belong to hir & was in hir Custody to my daughte<sup>rs</sup> & children as she Gaue it, as I was Informed by nurse *Clarke* whose testimony I allow & will to be sufficient for y<sup>t</sup> end.  I bequeath all my Estate in houses, lands, plate, goods, debts, Catle, horses, mares & other estate whatsoeuer in & out of this Jurisdiction to my 8 children, *George, John, Pagraue* [Palgrave], *Anna, Sarah, Mary, Elisabeth & Joanna*, my eldest to haue a double portion & the Rest part & part alike; only as my wife desired so I doe bequeath my farme at Assabath Riuer of 1000 acres w<sup>th</sup> the stok & Vttensills now vpon it to my three daughte<sup>rs</sup> *Anna, Sarah & Mary* as their portions, at least on a due value to be Recconed to them as p<sup>rte</sup> thereof, if the Estate will hold out & Reach to be better; and my mind & will is, that my lands what may be mine, be kept Intire w<sup>th</sup> the wood from any spoyle or wast, at least as litle as may be, & that my bookes & manuscripts may be kept for my sonnes those two that are desireus to be scholers, & my estate or favo<sup>r</sup> of my friends will procure them so to be, only my books & manuscripts a true Inventory of them being taken by my executo<sup>rs</sup> & oue<sup>r</sup>seers I will to be left w<sup>th</sup> *M<sup>r</sup> Mihills*, till he shall *  alter his Condition and then to be Returned to my executor<sup>s</sup> custody to be kept for my two sonnes that shall proue scholers; & my will is, that each of my children shall during their being und<sup>r</sup> age be heires each to othe<sup>r</sup> in Case of death to be divided amongst them, part & part alike.  My mind is, & as a furthe<sup>r</sup> & due manifestation of my deare loue & respect w<sup>ch</sup> I owe my deare mother *Pagraue*, I giue hir those three peeces of plate w<sup>ch</sup> my wife gaue vnto hir & she hath had in hir possession.  I further will & order hir £5 a yeare to be payd vnto hir during hir life & desire hir faithfull motherly Counsell & Advice may be w<sup>th</sup> hir Inspection oue<sup>r</sup> my children.  I

*Mihills *should be* Mitchell.

288

make my children executo<sup>rs</sup> & executrixes of this my last will & because they are Vnder Age I desire *M<sup>r</sup> Sam: Danforth*, & *M<sup>r</sup> Edward
Dennison* to be execu<sub></sub>to<sup>rs</sup> in trust in their behalfe, And desire *Major
Generall Jn<sup>o</sup> Leueret, Cap<sup>t</sup> W<sup>m</sup> Dauis, M<sup>r</sup> John Hull,* to be my ouerseers, & desire their Acceptance of 40<sup>s</sup> a peece a smale token of my
loue as a remembrance to them, & £4 a peece to my executo<sup>rs</sup>; to
*M<sup>r</sup> Mihills*, 40<sup>s</sup> to buy him a Ring to weare for my sake and desire*
his greatest Care to gett in my debts for w<sup>ch</sup> I will him twelve pence
in the pound for what he Getts in.  In Testimoney whereof I haue
hereunto sett my hand & seale this 10th May 1666.

I giue to y<sup>e</sup> church of X<sup>t</sup> in Roxbury £3 to buy them a good wine
boule.                                                    JOHN ALCOCKE.

In p<sup>r</sup>sence of
    *William Parke, Elisha Cooke.*

May 2, 1667.  *M<sup>r</sup> Samuell Danforth* came into Court & discharged
his power of Executorship.

May 22, 1667.  *M<sup>r</sup> Edward Dennison* came into the Generall Court
before the Gove<sup>r</sup>no<sup>r</sup> & magist. & did disclaime any right and powe<sup>r</sup>
of executo<sup>r</sup>ship in y<sup>e</sup> will.

May 4, 1667.  *Deacon William Parkes* & *M<sup>r</sup> Elisha Cooke* deposed.
Recorded, Book I, fol. 526.

*Mihills *should be* Mitchell.

# ABSTRACTS FROM THE EARLIEST WILLS ON RECORD AND ON THE FILES IN THE COUNTY OF SUFFOLK, MASS.

[Prepared by W. B. TRASK of Dorchester.]

THOMAS BUTTOLPH.—25: 3: 67. I, *Thomas Buttolph*, of Boston, Glouer, being weake in body, but in perfect memory, make this my Last will. For my outward estate that the Lord hath Lent me, I giue as followeth: Vnto *Anna Butolph*, my wife, the dwelling house wherein I now Liue, together with the yards, stable, Barne, and other housing belonging to the same, during her Life, and after her decease to my sonn *Thomas* and his Heyrs. Also, my meaning is, that the garden shal belong to my new house, to my wife; and my will is, that my wife shall haue all my Linnin, woollen, Beding, Pewter & brass, wearing aparill and mony, to be at her disposs for euer, she defraying my funerall charges & debts. Also, my will is, that my wife shall haue the one halfe of Centry Feilde, & one halfe of the furder Garden, soe called, next plantans,* during her life. My will is that my wife haue one Cow, which my wife shall choose. I giue vnto my son, *Thomas Butolph*, the house where he now Liueth, Called the old house, with the Breadth of the house from the house downe to the [ † ] hill place duringe the Life of my wife his mother, and after my wiues decease, I giue the old house to vnto my sonn *John Butolph* and his heyres for euer. My will is that my sonn *Thomas*, shall haue that halfe of Centry feild that Lyeth from *Mr. Brattles Close*, and my sonn *John*, shall haue the halfe next to *Mr. Bratle* for him and his heyrs for euer, after his mothers decease, that is, the one halfe of the meadow in Centry feild where the watering is. Also, I giue to my sonn, *John Butolph*, and his heyrs, for euer, the whole parcell of Land called the furder garden, next vnto plantons, and he to haue the one halfe of it during the Life of his mother, after my decease. My will is, that my dau. *Abigall*, shall haue £40, to bee paid vnto her after the decease of her mother my wife. I giue vnto my dau. *Mehitebell*, that spott of Land yᵗ Lyeth front upon the highway, abutting vpon *Mr. Brattle, Mr. John Endecot & Francis Dowse* & £50 there is in the hands of *John Parker*, my kinsman, with £3 [ ]. All the interest vntil the said £50 be demanded after my decease. My wife *Anna*, & son *Thomas*, executors, and what Lether, Silke and other Vtensells yᵗ are belonging to my calling, in my possession, at my decease, or any other estate whatsoeuer doth belong vnto mee, shall bee diuided betwixt my wife & children in equall proportions. Also, my will is, that my Louinge Freinds, my *Brother Henry Bridgham, Henery Ensigne Philips, Edmond Edendon & John Parker* bee my

---

*Probably *William Blantaine*.

†I am not entirely satisfied as to the correctness of the record which reads: "dung hill place." The most of the letters are gone from the word on the original document —T.

290

Ouerseers to this my Last will; and I giue vnto them 40ˢ apeece, to be payd by my executors after my decease.     THOMAS × BUTOLPH.

Signed, sealed & delivered in the presence of *Theodoer Atkinson, James Hill.*

18 June, 1667, *Theodoer Atkinson,* senioʳ, deposed.

7: 6: 1667, *James Hill* deposed.     EDWARD RAWSON, Recordʳ.

---

BUTTOLPH—FRARYE—HARDINGE.—The Petition of *Tho. Buttolph, Jo. & Elizabeth Frarye & Jo. Hardinge.*

May it please the Honoured Court these are to Informe that *John Frarye, Junioʳ,* by Couenants of Marriage with *Elisabeth Hardinge,* the Relict of *Abraham Hardinge,*[*] Deceased, haue possessed the Estate left in the Hands of the aboue sᵈ *Elizabeth,* & haue through Gods Blessing Comfortablye Brought up foure Children, & now the Eldest sonne *John Hardinge,* is 21 yeares of age, & according to his fathers will is to haue a double portion. They haue therefore agreed yᵗ *John Harding,* shall haue all his Fathers Lands & Housinge, as they are specified in the Inuentorye; & what other graunts of Land haue since fallen to the whole Estate they are Jointly agreed upon a Diuision of seuerall parcels, to their Mutuall Satisfaction, which Estate of House & Lands, with £19 of other Estate doe amounte to £172, which is *John Hardinges* Double portion, & the portion of 2 of the other Children, which *John,* Being willing to take into His Hand, & giue such securitye as the Court shall thinke Meete for the payment of their portions as they shall Come of age to Receiue. It is therefore yᵉ Humble petition of *Thomas Buttolph,* seniʳ., & *John Frary & Elizabeth* his wife, & *Jŏ. Hardinge,* that they might haue the approbation of this Honouʳᵈ Court for the Confirmation of this their agreement, so as may bee to the Discharge of that Bond wherin *Thomas Buttell & Elizabeth,* now the wife of *John Frarye,* are Bound for securitye to the whole Estate; so your humble petitioners shall Rest yours in all Dutye as God shall enable.     THOMAS BUTTOLPH,
                                                  JNᵒ. FRARYE,
                                                  ELIZABETH FRARYE.
The 1st of October, 1665.     JNᵒ. HARDINGE.

The Court approues of this agreement for the Eldest sonne *Jnᵒ. Mary & Abraham,* the sᵈ *John* Giuing his owne Bond, together with his Engagement of his Land for the two Childrens portions till they Come to Age to Choose their Owne Guardians.
                                        EDWARD RAWSON Recordeʳ.

---

At the same time the Court Ordered that *John Frarye* on Request of *Elizabeth Hardinge* testifyed by her Mother & Brother *Jnᵒ. Hardinge* shall bee guardian to the sᵈ *Elisabeth,* the Daughter, giuing securitye to Respond her portion of Forty three pounds, & the Former securitye is Discharged.     EDW. RAWSON, Recordʳ.

---

[*] See will of Abraham Harding in the Register for Jan., 1855, page 35. (See p. 141).

THOMAS BIRD.—I, *Thomas Bird, Seni^r*, of Dorchester, in y^e County of Suffolk in New England, Tanner, being by y^e p'udence of God not well in my body, yet through y^e mercy of God in p'fit memory, make my last will & Testament vnless I shall see Cause heerafter to alter it.  My will is, that all my Just depts be paid & funerall discharged.  My will is, that *Ann*, my wife, haue one Third p't of all my housing & land duering her life.  For y^e rest of my Estate I giue one third p^t thereoff vnto my wife wholly to be at her owne dispossall as God shall moue her hart.  My will is y^t y^e other two third p^ts of my Estate be deuided as Followeth, viz:  Wheeras I p'mised my sonne *Thomas*, at his marrige fifty pounds, of w^ch a good p^t is paid, as by my booke will appeare, then (that fifty pounds being accounted as p^t of y^e Estate) y^e estate shalbe equally deuided to my Fower Children, viz: *Thomas, John, James & Sarah*, only my Sonne, *Thomas*, shall haue ten pounds added to his p^t more then any one of y^e rest of my Children.  For that third p^t of my houseing & land w^ch I leaue in my wiues hands duering her life, my will is, that when it shall please God to put an end vnto her days that then that houseing & land shal be equally deuided vnto my three sonns; but if either of them dy & leaue not Isue, then this p^t shall goe equally to those that doe suruiue.  I appoint *Anne*, my wife, to be execetrix of my wholl Estate.  I appoint my loving freinds *Liftenant Hopestill Foster & Ensigne John Capen* to be ouerseers.  12th July, 1666.

THOMAS BIRD.

In p'sence of vs, viz: *John Capen, Senr., Jasper Rush.*

Boston 17th of July, 1667.  *John Capen, Senr., & Jasper Rush* deposed.

An Inventory of y^e Estate of *Thomas Bird, senr.* of Dorchester, who departed this life y^e 8th day of June, 1667, taken & apprized by *John Capen, Senr., William Sumner, James Humfrey.*  Amt. £997, 11: 5, including debts due the estate.  Debts due from the Estate, £61: 14: 10.  Mentions the names of *John Blackman & John Davenport.*  "The p'rsons y^t prized y^e stock in tanning, *John Gurnell, Henry Bridgham.*"

17th July, 1667, *Ann Bird*, relict of *Thomas Bird*, deposed.

THOMAS BIRCH.—At a Countye Court held at Boston Jan. 31, 1664, *John Gornel & Jno. Mynott* administrators to the Estate of y^e Late *Thomas Birch,** came into y^e Court & presented y^e Eldest sonne *Joseph Birch*, as of age, to the Court, together with his request for this Courts making ouer the whole remainder of the Estate unto the s^d *Joseph Birch*, six acres of Land remote only excepted, which is referred as part of *Jonathans* portion, at twelue pounds; the said *Joseph* Declaring that hee was willing to allow each of his Brothers & Sisters; instead of twentye foure pounds apece, thirty pounds apece, as they shall Come to age, in Corne & Cattell, & Bound ouer the House & Land as giuen into this Court in the Inuentorye to the Record^r of the Countrey & his successors.  For the performance thereof, the Guardian of the second sonne Consenting heerunto.  The Court allowed of this agreement, on which the s^d *Joseph Birch* did accordingly Bind ouer,

---

＊See Will of Thomas Birch of Dorchester, in the *Register*, vol. VIII, p. 281. (See p. 133).

in open Court, his House & Land for the performance of this Order, to the Recorder & His successors.

By the Court.                              EDW: RAWSON, Recorder.

There is paid out of *Thomas Birches* Estate for repairing the fences & Housing, Clothing for some of the Children & other charges, £17: 02:11.

The Estate Cr. by 1s: 2d to bee added to the Inuentorye & seuerall debts of Rent £21: 6s: 5d which makes the Inuentorye, £191: 18: 4d out of which is paid to the Eldest Daughter £24. This Accompt was Brought into the Court Jan. 31st, 1664, by *John Gurnell* & *Jŏ. Minott* & addition, & is accepted; & *Jonathan Birch* Came into the Court & made Choyce of *Thomas Tilestone* to bee his Guardian, which the Court approued of.                              EDWARD RAWSON, Recorder.

———

THOMAS MUNT*.—According to an Ord$^r$ from the Honoured Gouern$^r$ and Major Leuerett to us, whose names hear und$^r$ written, for the diuisions of the Estate of Thomas Munt deceased, Between *Tho. Hill* the Husband of the Relict of *Thomas Munt* & his three Children is as followeth: The whole Estate amounted vnto £216: 4: 3. To *Thomas Hill* the one Halfe, £108: 2: 1½.

To *Clement Short*, Husband to *Faith Munt*, Imp. a piece of Land Lyeing nigh the Mill dam between *Robert Sanderson* and *Jno. Bracket*, £30; 2½ acres of Land at Spectacle Island, £3; for *Thomas Hill* in goods 6s: 8½, &c. &c. Amt. £36: 00: 8½.

To *Thomas Kingston*, Husband to *Mary Munt*—To a peice of Land Lying at the upper end of *Tho: Hills* Lot fronting upon the Common, £16; to 2 acres of Land at Long Island, £2, &c., &c. Amt. £36:-00: 00½.

To *Patience Munt*, 2 peic of Land lying by *Peter Warrens*, £20; a debt w$^{ch}$ *Wm. Hersy* of Hingham, owes, &c., &c. Amt. £36.

| | |
|---|---|
| EDWARD RAINSFORD, | THOMAS KINSTON, |
| ROBRT SANDERSON, | THO. DUER pro. CLEMENT SHORT. |
| HENRY ALLINNE, | his |
| | THOMAS X HILL, |
| | mark |
| | EDWARD RAWSON, Guardian to |
| | PATIENCE MUNT. |

April 28th, 1666, The Court allowes & approues of the Returne & the Diuision of the Estate therin.                    EDWARD RAWSON, Record$^r$.

———

THOMAS ETHRINGTON.—At a meeting of the Magistrates and Recorder, at Boston, the 8th September, 1665. P$^r$sent Gouerno$^r$, Deputy Gournor, M$^r$ *Danforth* & Recorder. Whereas, *Thomas Ethrington* of Newichewannok, perished with His wife in the sea, Coming for Boston. The County Court being then Informed thereof, & that *Zechariah Gillam* had his Chest & seuerall goods in his Custody, the Court, on his Motion, appointed Marshall *Richard Wayte* & *Thomas Fitche*, Late Constable, to take into their Hands the said Chest & Goods & Bring

———

* See abstract of the inventory of Thomas Munt in the *Register*, vol. XII, p. 346.
(See p. 233).

a true Inuentorye thereof into Court, & giue the s<sup>d</sup> *Zechariah Gillam*
a Discharge for the same, they Keeping the s<sup>d</sup> goods in specie, to
Respond the Order of the Court for such as shall appeare to haue
most Right. And *Wm. Spencer*, the sonne of *Thomas Spencer*, & Brother
in Law to the said *Thomas Ethrington*, appearing Before the Magistrates & Recorder, desiring administration to y<sup>e</sup> Estate of said Late
*Thomas Ethrington* as it Lyeth heere, & in Yorkshire. The Magistrates
Judge it meete to graunt him, the s<sup>d</sup> *Wm. Spencer*, Administration to
the Estate of *Thomas Ethrington*, both there & heer, hee giuing in a
true Inuentorye of that Estate that Lyeth in Yorkshire, & giuing his
personall Bond to double ualue of the whole to the Recorder to Respond the Judgment of the County & the Court, & to Administer
according to Lawe, in Behalfe of the children of the Late *Thomas
Ethrington*, & Engaging his House and Land in Yorkeshire to the
Recorder for that end; which, when Done, the Marshall, *Richo. Wayte*,
is ordered with *Thomas Fitche*, to Deliuer up the Goods in specie
in the<sup>r</sup> Custodye to the s<sup>d</sup> *Tho. Spencer*, he satisfiing them for their
paines, & answering the ordinary Charges, sixe shillings apeice, to the
trustees, & 12d apeice to the apprisers.

EDWARD RAWSON, Recorder.

The Inuentorye of the goods of *Thomas Ethrington*, Deceased-
rec'd of *Mr. Zachariah Gillam* the 14 of (9 mo.) 1664. Appraised by
*Edw. Fletcher, Habbacuk Glouer, Thomas Blighe*, who deposed at
Boston 17 (9 mo) 1664.
A true Inuentorye & exact Accompt taken of the Houses, Lands &
Goods with all the Implements thereunto Belonging of *Thomas Eth-
erington*, Deceased, sometime Inhabitant of the Town of Kittrye, at
Newitchewanneck, whom with his Wife was Cast away in *John Coles*
Lighter in Nouember 1664; taken by *Humphrey Chadborne, Richard
Nason*. Amt. £94: 18.
*William Spencer* deposed Sept. 9, 1665.

———

THOMAS MARSHALL.—An Inuentory of some Clothes of *Thomas Marshalls*, Lately Deceased, taken by *James Euerill*, & *William Englishe*,
3:6: 1665. Mentions—Deacon *Richard Trusdall*.
October 31st, 1665, *James Pemberton* deposed.

[*James Pemberton* rendered his accompt as administrator to the;
Estate of *Thomas Marshall*, deceased, late of Boston. Amt. £49:7:6:]
The estate was indebted to *Doctor Alcock* for Physick; to *Theod<sup>e</sup>.
Atkinson;* to *Gm. Clear;* to *Mr. Bradstreet* for Physick; to *Mr. Rawson;*
to *Lieft. Tho. Clarke;* to *Goodwife Topping*, of Boston; to legacies paid
to *James Pemberton* and to *Joseph Howe*. Accompt allowed by the
Court Jan. 31, 1665. *James Pemberton* deposed.

———

GABRIEL MEAD.—I, *Gabriell Mead*, of Dorchester, being aged &
Infirme in body, yet of perfect Remembrance, doe make this my last
will & testament. My will is, that *Joanna* my wife be my sole execu-
tix & have y<sup>e</sup> full dispose of all my estate for her owne comfort &

helping to bring vp my children while shee lives, & after her disease my will is, yᵗ my sonne, *Israell*, shall haue yᵉ house I now dwell in, with yᵉ orchard & apurtenance therevnto belonging. I giue vnto my sonne, *Dauid*, my old house and that orchard or garden thervnto adjoyning, & also my plott of land being in yᵉ field neer the buriall place. I giue vnto my dau. *Lidia*, 30ˢ, to be paid as my wife shal be able, within two yeres after my desease. I giue vnto my daus. *Experience, Sarah* and *Patience,* 30ˢ apiece, to be paid them within one year after they shalbe maried, if they liue soe to bee; and it is my mind that if either of my sonns dye before they come to enjoy that before giuen them, or either of them, that then yᵉ same to bee equally deuided. after my wifes disease to yᵉ rest of my children; also it is my mind & will, that if my wife shall by nessesity be forced to sell either part or yᵉ whole for maintenants of her selfe or children, while she is a widdow, yᵗ she shall haue powre soe to doe with yᵉ aduise off my friends after named; and In case shee should marry, then my mind is, that my sonns shall enjoy yᵈ former gifts when they shall attaine the age of one & twentye yeares. I intreat my louing Freinds, *Deacon Clap & ensigne Foster*, to be ouerseers and to asist and aduise my wife & children as need may require. Jan. 15, 1654.
witnes hervnto                                                    GABRELL MEADE.
    *Hopestill Foster.*

Boston 17th of July 1667, *Capt. Hopestill Foster* deposed.
                                            EDW. RAWSON, Recorder.

———

WILLIAM CHEINEY.—Being sick in body, & of perfect understanding & memory according to my measure, I make this my last will & testament. My will is, that my deare & afflicted wife, *Margaret Cheiney,* be carfully & sufficiently prouided for during the time of her life, & to that end my will is, that she haue all the rents & proffitts yearely, & euery yeare, during the aforesayd tearms, of all my houses, lands, & orchards, that I die possessed of, either in Roxbury, Boston, or els where, except such part of my lands or estate which I shall here after in this my will dispose of to my children or otherwise, which estate bequeathed by me unto my sayd wife, it is my will, that she enter upon & be possessed of immediately after my decease (to witt) the present cropp upon all the land & the use of all my household stuffe & goods, my debtts & funerall expences being in the first place with all conuenient speed fully discharged; & for my wifes more comfortable being, my desire is, that one of my executors may liue in my house in Roxbury, with her, to inioy the housing & lands by the yeare which I haue as is aforesayd giuen unto my wife, upon such equall tearmes as my other executor & ouerseers shall agree with him for; but in case both my executors see cause to refuse to accept of this motion in answer to my desire herein, then my will is, that it be let outt by my executors & ouerseers to the best advantage for my wife [s] comfortable maintenance. When all my debts & Legacies are discharged out of my stock & husbandry utensills, as cartts, plows & such like, what remaines of my stock afterwards, my will is, it be let out or disposed of for my wifes use by my executors, with the aduice of my ouerseers; And my will is, that all my moueables

be for my wifes use during her life, except what is before disposed.
And in case what is aboue expressed be not sufficient for the comfortable maintenance of my wife, then my will is, that the house at
Boston be sold & improved for her further & better supply. I
bequeath unto my sonne, *John Cheiney*, all that land both Aeirable &
pasture lying on the east side of the great lotts, being with in the
great lotts, being twenty accres, more or lesse, being nowe in the possession of the sayd *John*. Allso, I giue to my sayd sonne, a percell
of meadow in the fresh meades being two accres, be the same more
or lesse, as it lyeth on the south of a ditch made to dreîne the sayd
meadow. Also I giue unto him one accre of salt marsh, be it more
or lesse, as it lyeth bounded with a creeke next the marsh of *John
Bowles*, formerly *Isaack Heaths*. Also I giue unto him eight accres of
land, more or lesse, lying neare the house of *William Hopkinns*, All
& euery of these percells of lands my will is, that my sayd sonne
*John*, be possessed of imediately after my decease. I giue to my
sonne, *William Cheiney*, all my land lying in Medfeild, lately in the possession of my sayd sonne, upon this condition or promise, that he & his
wife, *Deborah*, be reconsiled & liue together in Meedfeild or ells where
to the satisfaction of *John Wiswall*, of Boston, & *Deacon Parke* of
Roxbury, but not in Prouidence or that Jurisdiction; prouided allso,
that what either my selfe or Deacon *William Parke* haue allready
payd, or doe stand ingaged for unto the Court in his behalfe, be first
repayd & fully discharged by him, his heires, or assignes; but otherwise, if my sayd sonne neglect or refuse to accept it with these pro-
uisoes, then my will is, that twenty pounds be payd to *John Wiswall*,
of Boston, out of my estate. To my sonne, *Joseph Cheiney*, £60 (to witt)
my land lying in the third deuission, being thirty seauen accres, more
or lesse, & twenty pounds to be payd to my sayd sonne, *Joseph*, out of
my stock. My will is, that my three daughters (to witt) *Ellin, Margret* & *Mehitobell*, haue each of them £10 payd to them out of my
stock. After my wifes decease, my will is, first that all my houses &
lands in Roxbury undisposed of before by this will, I doe giue unto
two sonnes of my eldest sonne, *Thomas Cheiney* (to witt) his sonne,
*Thomas*, & his sonne, *William*, to be improued for their benifitt by
ther father untill they are 21 yeares old, then to be inioyed by them.
What remaines of my estate after my wifes decease either in stock or
otherwise, in housing or lands (in any other towne) or estate in any
kind undisposed of by this my will, My will is, that one halfe of it
be giuen to my sonne, *Joseph Cheiney*, & for the other halfe therof,
my will is, that it be Deuided into fowr equall parts, & so dispose of
it to my sonne, *John Cheiney*, & to my three aforesayd daughters, to
each of them an equall portion thereof. I make my two sonnes,
*Thomas Cheiney* & *Thomas Hasting*, the executors of this my will,
requesting my friends *Mr. John Eliot, Deacon William Parke,* & *Edward Denison* to be ouerseors. Aprill the last, sixty seauen.

Witnesse,                                         William X Cheiney.

*John Newell, Samuell Scarborow,* who deposed July 30, 1667.

Inventory of the estate taken by *Edward Denison, Thomas Weld,*
July 10, 1667.   Amt. £886:11:4.

296

[The original of the above will of William Cheney, as the name is now written, appears to be in the handwriting of the " Apostle Eliot," so called, who was one of the overseers.].

———

WILLIAM STARR.—At a meeting of the Gouernour, Maj^r. Generall Leverett & Recorder, in Boston, 12th Feb., 1665. Power of Administration to the Estate of the Late *Wm. Starr*, of [      ] in Deuonshire Marriner & Late sojorner in Boston, who Departed this Life in his Going to Salem on 6th Instant, is Graunted to *Robert Starre* of Salem, in behalfe of such as shall appeare to have most right to it, he giuing securitye to Administer according to Lawe.

EDWARD RAWSON, Recorder.

Inventory of the estate prised by *John Fuller, Christopher Skinner, Nathaniel Adams.* Amt. £9:6:8. *Robert Starr* deposed Feb. 12, 1665.

297

## ABSTRACTS FROM THE EARLIEST WILLS ON RECORD AND ON THE FILES IN THE COUNTY OF SUFFOLK, MASS.

[Prepared by W. B. Trask of Dorchester.]

Henry Kingman.—The last will and testament of *Henry Kingman,* of Waymoth, aged 74 yeares or theirabout, being weake of boddy but of perfect memmory. Debts payed, all the rest of my worldly goods I dispose of as folow. To my sonn, *Edward Kingman,* my dwelling house with all my housing perteining their vnto, and my orchords with all the appurtinantes therto belonging, and I doe giue him as much land a Joyning ther to as will make it 25 acors. I giue him two third partes of myne own comon lot. I giue to my son, *Edward,* that peece of meddo that was *John Alines,* and more meddo I doe giue him, one acor nearest to my house, of that which was *Mr. Jeners.* To my son, *Edward,* my fether bed that I ly on and all the furniture theirto belonging. To my son, *Thomas Kingman,* half the rest of the land that I haue aioyning to my house, except it be two acors which I shall here after Express. I giue to my son, *Thomas,* the other two acors of meddo which I haue, that was *Mr. Jeners.* To my son, *Thomas,* 25 acres of vpland that lyeth near and aboue *Samuell Whites* house. To my son, *Thomas,* one third parte of my own comon lot. I giue my son, *Thomas,* that fether bed which he lyeth on and all that doth belong their vnto. To my son, *John Kingman,* the two acores of land that I aboue reserued, and it shall be near his house from his barne to his planting lot as conuenient as it may be. I giue to my son, *John,* the other half of my land at home. To my son, *John,* the two acors of meddoe that I haue which was *William Richards,* and lyeth near the tyed mill; and my son, *John,* shall haue one acor of vpland that lyeth along by the meddo to make medoe of if he will. To my son, *John,* half the comon that did belong to owld *Brother Holbrook,* which I had of him. To my son, *John,* the cow that hee hath of myne in his hand allreddy. To my dau *Holbrook,* £12. I giue to my dau. *Holbrook,* the chest that standes at my beds feet. To my dau. *Dauis,* £10; to the chilldren of my dau. *Barnard,* £10, they be now fiue, they shall be payed when they com to be of age, the sons at 20 years old and the dau. at 18; and if Either of them dy before, his portion shall be deuided to the rest. I appoint my three sons aboue Expresed, to be my Exccutors and to fullfill all my will as above written and to diuide the rest of my Estate among them Equaly; and hear vnto I haue set my hand and Seall, 24th of May 1667.

H

The mark of
Signed sealed and delivered            Henry Kingman.
in the presents of vs
    *Edward Sale, Thomas Dyer.*
    31 July 67.   *Edw. Sale & Thomas Dyar,* deposed.
                              Edw. Rawson Record<sup>r</sup>.

Inuentory of the Goods & Chattles of *Henry Kingman*, that deceased in Weymouth the 5th of the 4th month 1667, taken by *Leift. John
Holbrook, Thomas Dyar*, the 9th of 4rh month.
31st July 1667. *Edward Kingman & John Kingman* deposed. Whereas I, *Thomas Kingman*, of Weymouth, sonn of *Henrey Kingman*, of
Weymouth, lately deceased, am by my father made a joynt Executor
with my two Brothers, *Edward & John*, in my Fathers last will &
Testament, doe hereby signify my acceptance of Executorship with
my brothers, & Consent to the will, & also my desire that the will
may bee rattifyed according to Law.  Thomas T Kingman.

his marke

wittnes my hand,
Weymouth July: the 29th: 1667.

———

Henry Douglas.—I giue to my wife, *Judea Dugles*, £100 of my
estate so longe as shee contino a wido.  To my eldeste sonn, a du-
bell porshon of the Reste of my estate, and the other parte of my
estate to be equally devided between my other toe children, only to
my granchild, *Samuell Hett*, I giue 25 shillings sheare of lande at
cape feare; and in case my wife mary a gaine, shee then to take the
thurds of my estate during hure life, provided the ouerplush of the
hundred pound be euequally deuided to my chilldren that ear liuing,
and when my wife dye that thurd parte of the estate to be devided
betwexte my children that ear living; and if eany of my chilldren dye
not being mared then that estate that I giue them to be eaquelly to
be deuided a mongest the Reste of my chilldren and grandchilldren,
prouided all my dates be payed and my funerall discharged.  My
wife and my sonn, *John*, to be my admenistraters and *Mr. John Senderlin*, sener, *John farnum*, sener, and *Richard Woodde*, to be my ouer-
sers of this my laste will and testament, the 9th of february 1662—as
Witnes my hand and seale.  Henry Douglas.
  Boston.  Wittnes
    *Richard Woodde, Isaack Woodde.*

31 July 1667.  *Rich. Wooddy & Isack Wooddy* deposed.
At the same time power of Administration to the Estate of the
late *Henry Douglas* is granted to *Judeth Douglas*, Relict of ye said
*Henry*, to p'forme the Imperfect will of the said *Henry Douglas* as
neer as maybe.  E. R. R.

This Paper was brought by *sergeant Woody*, sealed up & declared
that it was left by *Henry Dvglas* wth him as subscribed by him his
last will to be kept by him, the said *Ri. Woody*, vntill he cald for it
or his death; this given to *Thomas Dvglas*, in the presence his brother
*Hett*, the 17 May 1667.  before  J. L.

An Inuentory of all singular the Goods & Chattles of *Hennery Dowglas*, deceased, taken the 9th of July 1667, by *James Euerell, Joseph
How*.  Mentions—the old building Containing 4 lower roomes & the
roomes aboue with the chimney, belonging to the said house, & all
the Ground from Eighteene ynches beyond the Ground sill of the

same house southward, & all the Land soe farr as the Ground of *Goody Jameson* northward, £40.

31 July 1667. *Judeth Douglas* Administratrix, to the imperfect will of *Henery Douglas*, her late husband, deposed.

———

HENRY POWNING.—An Inuentorye of the goods & chattels Belonging to *Henry Powning*, deceased, taken by *James Penn, John Wiswall, Edward Hutchinson.* Amt. £585.15.01. Debts owing pᵣ the Estate, to seucrall persons Heer in New England Knowne—£358.08.01. More owing *Mᵣ Rouck*, in England, not yet Knowne.

July 27ᵗʰ 1665. *Elizabeth Powning* deposed.

EDWARD RAWSON Secretarye.

Added by *Elizᵃ. Powning*, yᵉ 16 July 1684. Six acres of Land lying at Kittery.

———

HENRY BISHOP.—An Inuentory of the Goods & Chattells of *Henry Bishop*, Late of Boston, Deceased. Taken by *John Wiswall, John Hull.* Amt. £359.15.03. Mentions 2 Horses at New Hauen; Debts at Barbadoes 11500 lb. sugars, £169. Debts due from the Estate amounts to £370.

6ᵗʰ Nouember 1665. Pʳsent the Gouernour, *Majᵣ. Gen. Leuret, Mr Lusher.* *Nath. Bishop* deposed to the Inuentory of the Estate of the Late *Henry Bishop*, His Brother.    EDWARD RAWSON, Recorder.

Boston 1665. A true Inuentorye of the apparrell & some other small things of *Elizabeth Bishoppe*, Widow, Late wife of *Henry Bishop*, Both Deceased, prised by *Thomas Grubb, John Lake*, at Boston, Oct. 4, '65. Amt. £13.13.7.

16 Nouember 1665, speciall Court, *Nathaniell Bishop*, deposed.

EDWARD RAWSON, Recorder.

———

JAMES WHITE—Boston In New England 1666. I, *James White*, of Barbados, mʳchant, Infirme of body but of sound & perfect memory, ordaine this my last will and testament. As to my worldly estate in Barbados or elsewhere I bequeath as followeth: Vnto yᵉ parish of Horne church, in yᵉ County of Essex, & to yᵉ parishes of Sᵗ. Johns & Sᵗ. Michalls in Barbados, to each of them, a peace of plate of tenn pounds for value to yᵉ seruice of yᵉ Comunion table, for ever. To yᵉ said parish of Horne church, being yᵉ place of my Natiuity, one thousand pounds, for yᵉ Erecting or buying of an Almes house yᵗ may Cont: sixe poore men which Cannot [    ] otherwise, & to be pᵈ on euery fifth of Nouember sixe pound str. to each of them, & a new gound; & yᵉ ministers of yᵗ parish to haue forty shillings for A sermon for euer; yᵉ aforesaid monys I doe will shall be paid within twelve months after all my Just debts are pᵈ & to [be] disposed of in purchase at yᵉ Discretion of my suruiueing executors, in trust, with yᵉ aduise of the next two Justises in yᵗ parish of Horne church, or Adjacent theirto; but in case my Es[tate] amount not to tenn thousand pounds str: my debts pᵈ, then I giue but fiue hundred pounds str: to yᵉ Vse & behalfe aforesaid, & to be disposed of as aboue men-

tioned. I giue vnto *M*ʳ. *William Leisly* & [          ] *Johns* [          ] ministers in Barbados, to each a Ring of ten pounds sterlin in Value; to
*M*ʳ. *John Bowden, M*ʳ. *Rich: Seawell M*ʳ. *Chr. Jason, M*ʳ. *Job Browne*,
to each of them Rings of 20ˢ value. I giue vnto yᵉ parish of sᵗ.
michalls, in Barbados, one tenth part of yᵉ neate Value or rent Raised
by my houses & Land in yᵉ said towne & parish; & in case my Executors, in trust, shall sell & dispose of all or any p't thereof, then I
will & ordaine yᵗ one tenth pᵗ of the produce or p'veneiw shall bee to
yᵉ Vse of yᵉ said parish for yᵉ building, buying of a worke house, or
yᵉ setting of poore people at worke, at yᵉ discretion of any of executors in trust with yᵉ advise of yᵉ Justices in q'ter sessions of yᵗ place;
this is to be after my debts are pᵈ vzt. in 12 months after. I giue
Vnto *Ann Gallop, Ralph* & *Catherin Trutle*, to each of them £50 str.;
& to *William Trutle*, £100 str. to be pᵈ two yeares after my debts
are pᵈ; but in case my estate be not valued at £10,000 str. at my
decease, then I giue but halfe yᵉ sumes to be pᵈ as aboue mentioned.
I giue vnto yᵉ children of my well beloued Brother, *Will*ᵐ *White*,
Late of London, in old England, vzt. *John, Will*ᵐ, *Ann, Dorothy*, &
yᵉ rest, Equaly, Except *Josiah* & *Jeames*, £700 to purchase of their
father yᵉ free hold of yᵉ farme of Fethes, alias fethes, in yᵉ County of
Essex, by Chensford, yᵉ which farme so purchased, I giue vnto his
sonn, *Josiah White*, student in Oxon, & to his heires for euer, which
if he haue of his owne, if not, then of his Relation, I desire him to bestow it yᵗ their may neuer want one of yᵉ name to serue at yᵉ Alter,
Vntill Christs second Comeing in glory. I meane £700 str: amongst
them; not to each.                                             JEAMES WHITE.

 I giue vnto my wife, *Katherine White*, £100 str. to buy her a Ring
in Remembrance of mee, with my Jewells, plate, household stuffe
for euer, & yᵉ vse of my dwelling house on my plantⁿ & yᵉ prouis-
sion, stock, Vntill her mariadge, Besides yᵉ bond giuen her by fea-
feas in trust, for which she is to release all claime of thirds or other
interest in or to any part of my estate, & not other wise, this Legacy
being in full of her Dower. I giue to yᵉ Child she now goeth with
[          ] pounds starling, to be pᵈ after my debts or [          ] my
Executors besides yᵉ bond giuen & made to feafees in trust, for his
portion, yᵉ which bonds I leaue be [aring] date wᵗʰ this my will in
yᵉ hands of *Coll. Daniell Sirle*. I giue vnto yᵉ Eldest child of *M*ʳ
*Edward Bowdon*, deputy secretary of Barbados, & to *Elizabeth More*,
Late Daughter of *Thomas More*, to each of them, £100 str. to be paid
at each, of their day of Mariadge ; my debts being pᵈ, this to *Eliza-
beth More* Desire speedily. To my Broⁿ. *John* & *Will*ᵐ *White* & [their]
wiues, to each of them, Rings of £10 str. in Value, wᵗʰ mourneing.
Vnto my Nephew, *Jeames White* my Brother, *Will*ᵐ *White*, of
London, all my [estate] Reall & p'sonall, hereby constituteing yᵉ
said *James*, my sole heire & execut'ʳ of this my Last will & testament.
Appointing *Coll. Henry Hawly, Edw : Py Esq, Jeames Beake, Esq :
Will*ᵐ *Bate Esq.* my Brother, *Will*ᵐ *White* & *Jeramiah Egings* march'ts:
Execut'ʳˢ in trust of this my Will, in behalfe of my said Nephew,
*James*, or any two of them, & yᵉ suruiuer, desireing them to follow
the aduise of my said Bro : *Will*ᵐ, his Guardian, to yᵉ be[st] ad-

uantage of my Nephew, his son, Giueing my sa[id] Execut$^{rs}$ in trust, or any two of them, full power to buy more Lands, stock or other necessaryes for my plant$^n$, &c, or to sell, Lease, or to farme, Let, any [or] all my estate, reall or p$^r$sonall, as in their discretion may seeme most for y$^e$ profit of my said Nephew & heire, desireing them to doe by him, As they desire others may doe for theirs, in y$^e$ Like case. I giue vnto M$^{rs}$ *Elizabeth Hawley*, (Long since maried) dau. of *George Hawley*, march$^t$, in Gracious Streate, London, £300 str: to bee p$^d$ three yeares after my debts are p$^d$, & in case of her death, without Ishue, then to y$^e$ meanest of relicts of y$^e$ Children of y$^e$ said *George Hawly*, at ye discretion of my Execut$^{rs}$ in trust. I hereby revoke & declare voyde, y$^e$ will & bonds Left with *John Harris*, to giue *M$^r$ Job Browne*, at my Comeing from Barbados Last, & all other wills or papers tending theireto, p$^r$vided this & y$^e$ bonds Come safe to hand ; & to my Execut$^{rs}$ y$^t$ Come & appeare in trust for my Nephew, to each of them, I giue a Ring of tenn pounds ; & if my Brother, *Will$^m$*, Come not ouer, I giue y$^t$ Execut$^r$, or any two, one, y$^t$ will take sume p$^r$ticular charge therof. To *Coll. Daniell Sirle*, I giue a Ring of fiue pounds ; to *Thomas Grey, Jeames Cluterbooke*, to each of them, two thousand of musCo: sugar, vzt, to *John Harris & George Fryar* three thousand pounds each of them.

10 Sept. 1666. JEAMES WHITE.

Indorst.
Acknowledgd by *James White* to bee his Last Will & by him signed, sealed and deliuered in these words In y$^e$ presentes of vs, with y$^e$ Adition vnder written. GEORGE FRYER.

Te$^t$. *John Goble, Fra. Punchard, Richard Gregorie.*

Boston In New England. Att a meeting of y$^e$ *Gouernor. Richard Bellingham Esq$^r$, John Leueret Esq$^r$, Major Generall, & Edward Rawson, Record$^r$,* in Boston, 28th of March 1667.

*John Goble*, aged forty three yeares or thereabouts, *Frances Punchard*, aged thirty eight yeares or thereabouts, *Richard Gregorie*, aged twenty foure yeares or thereabouts, & *George Fryer*, seruant to y$^e$ late *Capt James White*, of Barbados, aged twenty three yeares or thereabouts, on theire Corporall oathes, deposed, y$^t$ on y$^e$ 15$^{th}$ of this Instant march, being present w$^{th}$ y$^e$ s$^d$. Late *Jeames White*, at his lodging in Boston, on his request, & did heare the s$^d$ *Jeames White* acknowledge & publish these two sheets of paper to be his Last will & testament, y$^e$ w$^{ch}$ he had formerly according to y$^e$ date therof so signed & sealed; & on y$^e$ s$^d$ fifteenth Instant, they did see y$^e$ said *James* White put also on & take his seale therefrom, saying, I deliuer this as my act, [&c. The words—" *Richard Gregorie*, aged twenty four yeares " was interlined; and *John Goble* affirmed, " y$^t$ he set his hand, as a Wittnesse, some day in March, but before the fifteenth."]

An adition to my Will.—Whereas I am advised of a great fire in London, to my Brother *Will$^m$*. *White* great [loss] as well as others, I hauing invited him ouer, his wife & children, I will declare & giue him my household stuffe, being in more want thereof then my wife, whose bond I doe giue her to make Void her Dower, & debare her

all therds or clames or other Interest in any of yᵉ Estate, reall or pʳsonall, belonging vnto me, or any thing to yᵉ Contrary before exprest.                                                                JEAMES WHITE.
Boston Oct. 12ᵗʰ 1666.

Test: *Richard Gregorie, Fra. Punchard, George Fryer*, who deposed to the above, March 28, 1666.

Boston 1666.—Instructions to my Executors, in trust, nominated in my Last will, bearing Date wᵗʰ these pʳsents, being the 10th Oct. 1666.
As to my wife, *Ka : White*, I haue wrote her Letter, which I desire you, H. Hawley, or some other, to pʳvse & be verry priuate in it ; then seale & deliuer it at your owne time, I doubt not but I shall recouer yᵉ £4000 of *Mʳ Bantly*, £2000 may be secured to her & her child, either by morgage or to let it ly in a Judgment to yᵉ payment of her child £150 pʳ annᵐ, or if M. B. bee not willing to keep it, Let it be deuided, & she to take her £1000 to her new husband, but Let it not goe wᵗʰout securing a Joynture Vpon her ; if she be Kind to yᵉ Child, let her haue £40 pʳ ann. out of yᵉ interest of his £1000, for I would haue yᵗ £1000 be let out to M. B. at 4 pʳ Cᵗ Vntill yᵉ Child be 17, & if A boy that he be fitted for a marchᵗ, & bound out, yᵗ hee wᶜʰ hath yᵉ mony shall advance £200 to binde him out, and Keep yᵉ mony fiue yeares gratis ; this is but by way of aduise, I leaue it to yʳ care & Discretion, as in all things elsc. As to those two great debts I owe, you will find pʳtiall Instructions herewᵗʰ, & another Copy in yᵉ hands of *Mʳ Browne* or *John Harris*. If my wife is not Contented wᵗʰ her Legacy, vzt. my bond which I giue her in full of her therds, Dower, & all other claime to my Estate, reall & pʳsonall, then wᵗʰhold yᵉ present yearely allowance mentioned in my will, for she deserues no Kindnesse from mee.          Yoʳ seruant
Boston Oct. 10, 1666.                                                     JEAMES WHITE.

Test : *John Goble, Geo. Fryer, Fra : Punchard, Richard Gregorie*, who deposed March 28, 1666.                        EDWARD RAWSON, Recordʳ.

Boston the 30ᵗʰ 1ᵐ : 1667. Inuentory of the Estate of the late *Capt. James White*, deceased, as it was shewen vnto vs, the subscribers, by *George Fryer*, his domestique seruant. Signed by *Rich: Cooke, Josh: Scottow*. Amt. £178.12.5. Debts the deceased oweth, to *Josuah Scottow, Mʳ Atwater, Mʳ Lynes, Edward Lilly, Deacon Trusdall, Mʳ Ruddock, Mʳ Lidget, Leift: Cooke, Arthur Mason, Ben: Gillam, John Lake, Mʳ Bendall, Goodman Felch ;* to *George Fryer*, for his Sallery, in pᵗ whereof hee hath £6.11.06 paid in 69 gall. of Rum & a bill. " *Colonell Searles* hath tooke the negro boy* as in pᵗ of the funerall Expence." Amt. of debts : £184.11.
*George Fryar*, deposed, April 1, 1667.

———

EDWARD FLETCHER.—Feb. 20, 1659. I, *Edward Fletcher*, now of Badgeden, in the County of Gloucester, Clerke, being in health of body, doe make this my last will. I giue all that my messuage or tenement wᵗʰ the appurtenances, scituate and being neere the Little

---

* The negro was valued at £25.

303

Cloisters, within the precincts of the Colledge, in the Citty of Gloucester, and the rents, issues & profit thereof, vnto *Mary*, my wife, during the terme of her life, she keeping the same in repaire, & also giving free & full liberty to *Mr James Forbes*, of Gloster, and such other Christians w[th] him as he shall allow of, to meete and assemble themselues together, from time to time, in the great Hall of the said Messuage or tencment, for the worship of God only, and to haue free liberty of ingresse, egresse, and regresse, to & from the same, thorough all vsuall wayes, at their will, & pleasures, paying 40[s] p[r] ann. rent, for the same, during my wifes life; and imediately after my wifes decease, I giue said messuage or tenement w[th] the appurtenances, vnto my sister, *Elizabeth Hooper*, for the tearme of her life, shee keeping the same in repaire. And vpon this further condicon, y[t] my said sister, *Elizabeth*, her executo[rs], Admin[rs]: or assignes, pay to my Cozen, *Margarett Ellis*, now of the Citty of Gloucester, Spinster, out of the rents, issues and proffits of the said Messuage or tenement, £10 of Lawfull English Money, within Fower yeares after my said wifes decease, in Case my said sister shall liue and enjoy the said house, messuage & premises soe long. And my will is, that from & after my wifes decease, the said *Mr James Forbes* & such other Christians as hee shall allow of, may, if they desire it, have the vse of the said great Hall for the vses aboue mencōned, during my Sisters life [with rights and privileges as before expressed,] w[th]out giuing any rent for the same during my said sisters life. I giue the Reuercōn and inheritance of said Messuage or tenement, w[th] the appurtenances expectant vpon & after the death of my wife or my sister Elizabeth & either of them longest [Liuing,] vnto my well beloued Freinds, *Mr James Forbes*, of the Citty of Gloucester, Clerke, *William Sheppard*, the younger, of the [same] Citty, gent, *Thomas Cole*, of the same Citty, scriuener, *Thomas Henning*, of the same Citty, joyner, *Thomas Shipton* of Ba[rn]wood, and *John Badger*, of St. Bridge in the County of the same Citty, yeoman, & their heires foreuer, vpon trust and confidence, neuer the lesse to the intent & purpose y[t] they the s[d] *Forbes, Sheppard, Cole, Henning, Shipton & Badger* & the surviuo[rs] or suruivor & the heires or assignes of such surviuor shall and [may dis]pose of the rents, issues & proffits thereof to & for the relief of such godly poore and needy people as they shall judge meete, and to beę distributed by them in such sort & manner as they in their discretion shall thinck convenient, All [need] full charges in reparacōns and otherwise being allowed & defaulked out of the rent, from time to time, as it shall grow due & payable. All the rest of my goods, chattells and personall estate whatsoeuer, [all] my debts pay[d] & funcrall expences discharged, I giue to my wife, *Mary Fletcher*, whome I make sole executrix of this my last will & testament.

EDW: FLETCHER.

Sealed and published in y[e] presents of
 *Tho: Browne, Ridge Van, Susana Rogers.*

An Inuentory of the Goods & Estate of *Edward Fletcher*, lately deceased, in Boston, & Apprized by *Thomas Bumstead, William Kilcup*, Dec. 31, 1666.

Boston 12th Feb. 1666. Power of administration to the estate of the late M. *Edw: Fletcher*, deceased, is granted unto *Mary*, his relict. *Mrs. Mary Fletcher* deposed.

---

CAPT. RICHARD DAVENPORT.—30th Octob[r]. 1665. Power of Administration to the Estate of the Late *Cap[t].* *Richard Dauenport*, on Request of *Elizabeth*, his Relict, testifyed p[r]. her sonnes, is graunted to *M[r] W[m] Staughton, M[r] Nathaniel Dauenport & M[r] Stephen Minott*, they giuing securitye to Administer according to Lawe & bring in a Just & true Inuentorye therof to the County Court.      EDW. RAWSON Recorder.

Inuentorye of the Estate taken Oct 9, 1665, p[r] *Roger Clapp, Hopestill Foster, John Minott,* Amt. £917.4. *M[r] W[m] Stoughton, M[r] Nathaniell Dauenport, & M[r] Stephen Minott* Administrat[rs] deposed, Oct 30, 1665.

---

NICHOLAS BADDITIER.—An Inuentory of the Estate of *Nicholas Badditier*, of Datsum,* neer Dartmouth, in England, that Departed this Life, in June last, at *Edw: Barkers* House. Taken by *John Search, Edward Ellis, John Sweete,* Amt. £3.15.11.

Oct 31, 1665. *Edward Barker* deposed.

---

ARTHUR CLARKE.—Oct 31, 1665. Power of Administration to the Estate of the Late *Arthur Clarke* is Graunted to *Sarah*, his Relict, in Behalfe of Her selfe & sonne.

Inventory of the Estate taken by *Thomas Matson.* The gallie pots prised by *M[r] Jn[o] Endecot & M[r] Daniel Stone.* Amt of inventory, £71.19.6. *Sarah Clarke* deposed.

---

305

## ABSTRACTS FROM THE EARLIEST WILLS ON RECORD AND ON THE FILES IN THE COUNTY OF SUFFOLK, MASS.

[Prepared by WILLIAM B. TRASK of Dorchester.]

STEPHEN SPICER.—Dec. 24, 1664. I, *Stephen Spicer*, of the Island of Barbados, merchant, being weake in Body but of good & perfect memory, doe make this my last will. My body I commit to the Earth to bee decently buryed w$^{th}$ such Charges & such place as my deare wife *Dionisa* shall thinck good; & touching the distribution of my mortall Goods I dispose of the same as followeth: I will that all such debts & duties which I shall Owe vnto any person or Persons at the time of my decease, Either by Law or Consience, bee well & truly Contented & payd within Conuenient time. Whereas I am indebted to the Estate of *M$^r$ John Williams* as by my Ledger & Jornall N°: A: more planely Appeares, & Whereas I haue recouered by Law seuerall judgments in seuerall Courts of this Island against seuerall Persons debtors to the said Estate, for their seuerall debts by them Respectiuely due & Owing, now my will is, that all such debts, soe Recouered, when receiued, shall bee with all Conuenient speed Remitted for London vnto *M Edward Micho*, merchant, for the Account afore sayd, And that before remittance of the full ballance due to the said Estate Ample acquittances & discharges bee demanded & taken of & from the Person or Persons interested & Lawfully Capacitated to make & giue such Ample acquittance & discharges as aforesaid. Whereas there is remaning in my hands a Certaine parcell of salt unsould, I doe hereby Acknowledge & declare that one halfe part thereof is the proper Goods of *M Phillip Crossing*, merchant, And one fourth part thereof, belongs to *M$^r$ Rob Nutt*, merchant, And that I my selfe had interest in the other Fourth part thereof. Debts paid, or Ordaned to bee paid, I Giue vnto my mother, *M$^{rs}$ Jane Spicer*, of Topsham, in the Countie of Deauon, Widdow, £20 of Currant English money, which I will shall bee payd vnto her by my Executrix hereafter named within Twelue monthes next after my decease if my sayd mother shall soe long liue. I giue vnto my Brother, *John Spicer*, of Topsham, marriner, And to my sister, *Elizabeth*, Wife of *William Taylor*, of Topsham, aforesayd, marriner, to each of them £10 of like Currant English money, a peece, to bee paid to them respectiuely in manner as aforesaid. I Giue to my Vnckle, *George Sannders & Margaret*, his wife, or to the suruiuor of them, £5 Currant English money payable as aforesaid. I giue vnto & Amongst the poore people of the Towne of Topsham, £5, which I will bee distributed or ordered to bee distributed amongst them within Twelue monthes after my decease, According to the discretion of my Executors. I Giue to *Josiah Helmon* the sume of T [    ] thousand pounds of muscouado sugar. I give vnto *John Cooper*, now liuinge in my imployment, besides his yearely sallery, the sume of Two Thousand pounds of muscouado sugar, vpon Condition that hee

306

shall bee Ayding & assisting vnto my Executrix, in the Recouering of my debts to mee [due ?] & Owing & perfecting my accounts, wherein he is [    ] vtmost Care & dilligence during the tearme of [    ] monthes next after my decease, or longer if need bee. I giue vnto Euery of my Freinds hereafter named, vizt. *Hen* [    ] Esq[r]. & his now wife, *M[r] Richard Barrett* & his wife, [    ] *Nutt*, & to *M[r] William Byrdall sen[r]* & *William Byrdall* [    ] a mourning Ring, Each Ring to bee of the uallue of 20[s]. starling. I ordaine my wife, *Dionisa*, Executrix of this my last will, And my Louing Father in Law, *M[r] Henry Quintin*, I make Ouerseer, And I giue vnto him & my mother in Law, *Mary Quintin*, his now wife, Each of them a new suite of mourning Apparrell & a mourning Ring a peece, Each Ring to bee of the same uallue as before, in Consideration of his paines to bee taken in the Ouersee [ing] thereof. STEPHEN SPICER.

Witnesses,
  *John, Cooper, Jos: Hilman, Rich: Glascock scr.*

Barbados—By the Dep[ty] Governour.

This 2[d] October 1665. Personally Appeared before mee, *M[r] Rich: Glascock* & *M[r] John Cooper*, & made Oath that they did see the within named *Stephen Spicer*, signe, seale, declare & deliuer the within written, being two sheets of Paper, whereunto his hand Is subscribed as his last will & testament.

Sworne before mee,
  *Hen: Willoughby.*

This is a true Copie of the Records in the Secretaries office, Attested this 5[th] of October 1665.

Attested by mee:
  *Edward Bowden*, Dep[ty] Secry.

Barbados—By the Dep[ty] Governour.

Know yee, that on the second of October, in the yeare of our Lord one Thousand six Hundred Sixty & Fiue, before mee, the last will & Testament of *Stephen Spicer*, late of this Island, merchant, deceased, was proued, Approued & allowed & therefore *M[rs] Dionisa Spicer*, Relict of the said deceased, & full & whole Executrix in the said Will, nominated, is admitted to take into her Custody & Possession, & to Administer on all the goods, chattles, debts, dues, Accompts, & all other the Estate of the defunct, which I hereby publish & make knowne, to all Judges, Justices, clerkes, marshalls, & Bayliffs whatsoeuer, the said *M[rs] Dionisa Spicer* hauinge benn sworne, to bring into the secretaries within fowreteene days next Ensuing the date hereof, a true & perfect Inuentory of all & Euery the said deceaseds Estate which hath, shall, or may, Come to her hands, possession or knowledge, there to bee Recorded, & to pay the just debts & legacies, & perform such other things, as an Executrix ought to doe.

Giuen vnder my hand the day & yeare first aboue written.
                                        HEN: WILLOUGHBY.

To all whome these p[r]sence shall or may Concerne.

Endorst—The within written is a true Copie of the Originall Attested the 5[th] of October 1665.     p[r] mee  EDWARD BOWDEN,
                                                              Dep[ty] Secry.

[M<sup>r</sup> John Jolliffe & M<sup>r</sup> Thomas Brattle appeared in Court Feb. 1, 1665, & produced the probate of the last will of the late M<sup>r</sup> Stephen Spicer, vnder the Certificate of the Dep<sup>ty</sup> Gov<sup>r</sup> of Barbados, Henry Willoughby Esq<sup>r</sup> with the Certificate of Edward Bowden, Secretary there, that M<sup>rs</sup> Dionisa Spicer, his Relict, is sole Executrix of the last will of said Spicer, and said Jolliffe & Brattle desire to be discharged of their Bonds giuen by them to the Court in behalfe of the said Dionisa Spicer, and the Court cancelled the Bond.

Then follows the discharge of John Gibbs & Dennis Gibbs, his then wife, Executrix to the Estate of Stephen Spicer, deceased, discharge the County Court of Boston in new England from all Claymes by Reason of an Inuentory giuen into said Court of the Estate of said Spicer, deceased. " Wee doe Acknowledge to haue Transported all the Effects thereof into this Island of Barbados." May 15, 1666.

In the p<sup>r</sup>sence of
Jeremiah Quishin, Rich : Price,
Joseph Grafton jun<sup>r.</sup> ]

JOHN GIBBS.
DENNIS GIBBS.

M<sup>r.</sup> Richard Price deposed in Court Aug. 3, 1666, that he did see & heare John Gibbs & Dennis, his wife, signe, seale & deliuer the discharge as their act & deed. EDW: RAWSON, Record<sup>r</sup>.

M<sup>r</sup> Jeremiah Quishion, deposed the same day.

An Inuentorye of the Goods, Debts & Estate of M<sup>r</sup> Stephen Spicer, in New England, who Dyed in Boston June 10<sup>th</sup> 1665, taken by Jn<sup>o</sup> Joyliffe, Tho: Brattle. Amt. £373, 17.04. Mentions M<sup>r</sup> Nathaniell Fryer, M<sup>r</sup> James Russel. M<sup>rs</sup> Denise Spicer deposed. June 16, 1665. Administration granted to M<sup>rs</sup> Denise Spicer, Relict of Stephen Spicer, Late of Barbados, to that part of her late husband's estate that is in this Country.

———

SAMUEL HUTCHINSON.—Boston, 7th Aprill, 1667. I, Samuel Hutchinson, of Boston, in New England, being in perfect health & memory, doe make my last will. Just debts & funerall Expences first paid. I giue vnto Samuell Wheelwright, Eldest sonn to my sister Wheelwright, two mares & six Ewe sheepe; to Elizabeth Person, Katherine Naylor, Mary Loyd, Rebecca Mauerick, Hannah Chickley & Sarah Wheelwright, the six daughters of my sister Wheelewright, to Each of them a mare & six Ewe sheep; vnto Edward Rushworth, one mare & six Ewe sheepe; vnto Elifall Hatton, six Ewe sheepe; vnto [     ], Thomas, Ephraim, [     ] Mary & Dine Sauage & Hannah Gillam the seuen Children of my Cozen, Faith Sauage, deceased, 20<sup>s</sup> a peece, to be paid to them in a [     ] or other stock that my Executo<sup>r</sup> shall Appoint. I giue vnto my Couzen, Peleg Sanford, my Orchard, lying in Portsmouth, in Rhoad Island, with the twenty Acres of Land adjoyning vpon it, bee it more or less, & all my Land in the north feild & Common fence & Calfe pasture, with the marsh called musceto marsh, to him & his heires foreuer, yet paying for my life halfe the rent hee shall make of it Euery yeare, putting mee to noe Charge about it & at my decease or within one yeare after, paying also £50, in siluer to my sister Wheel-wrights Children, namely, to Samuell Wheel-

*wright*, Eldest sonn to *my sister Wheelewright*, £10; to *Edward Rushworth*, Eldest sonn to *my sister Rushworth*, £10; to *Katherine Naylor*, £10; to *Hannah Chickley*, £10; to *Sarah Wheelewright*, £10, & if any of them dye before they shall come to haue their legacies due out of this £50, the legacy or legacies to bee diuided amongst the suruiuou<sup>rs</sup>. I Giue vnto *Elizabeth Person, Mary Loyd, Rebecca Mauerick, & Elizabeth Hudchinson*, the Eldest daughter of my Cozen, *Elizabeth Hutchinson*, my Orchard & Land adjoyning vpon or Ouer against *Theodor Atkinson* Warehouse, neere to M<sup>r</sup> *Peter Olliuers* house, to them & their heires foreuer, being about one Acre of Land, bee it more or less, to bee Equally deuided to them, or one Hundred Pounds in siluer, which *Peter Olliuer* is to pay, for it six monthes after my decease, or at my decease to them. I Giue vnto *Elizabeth Hutchinson*, one mare & six Ewe sheep. I Giue vnto *Restram, William & Ezbon & Elisha Sanford*, 20<sup>s</sup> a peece, to bee paid out of my stock; to *Elisha Hutchinson*, Eldest sonn to my Cozen, *Edward Hutchinson*, my Two Hundred Acres of Land, bee it more or less, that lyeth at Segnest, vpon Rhoad Island, that was of late in the occupation of *Bartholomew West*, as also I Giue vnto him one mare & six Ewe sheepe to him & his heires foreuer; vnto *Elizabeth Hutchinson, Ann Diar & Susan Hutchinson*, or soe many of them as shall bee liuing at my death, my neck of Land together with mackpila, as also that six Acres of meadow Ouer against mackpila, which is in the occupation of *Edward Fisher*, which lyeth in Portsmouth, in Rhoad Island, to them & their heires foreuer, Excepting twenty Acres in the neck, next the Ferry place, which my Brother, *Edward Hutchinson*, is to haue, in lew of Forty Ewes which I [promised?] him, to him & his heires foreuer. Vnto *Ann Dyar & Susan Hutchinson*, Each of them, one mare & six Ewe sheepe. Vnto *Edward, Katherine & Hannah Hutchinson* [      ] other children of my Couzen, *Edward Hutchinson*, to Each of them Fiue Ewe sheepe; vnto my Couzen, *Susan Cole*, one mare & six Ewe [sheepe]; vnto my Cozen, *Bridget Willis*, 40<sup>s</sup>; vnto *Abigall, Sarah & Samuell Bath* [      ] them two Ewes; vnto *Sarah Langdon*, the wife of *John Langdon*, [      ] great bible. I giue vnto my Couzen, *Edward Hutchinsons* [      ]. For my neck of Land & mackpelon my will is, that the [      ] Tenn pounds in Siluer to bee disposed as followeth [      ] *Powell*, 40<sup>s</sup>; to *Elefall Stratton*, 40<sup>s</sup>; my *Couzen Willis*, of Bridgwater, 40<sup>s</sup>; the other Fowre pounds to bee deliuered vp into the [      ] the Elder & Deacons, to bee disposed on to Eight poore [      ] whome they shall thinck most needfull, Euery one [      ] shillings vpon the sale of the neck of Land & the re [      ] money for it. Notwithstanding what is aboue exprest, if I haue not soe many mares at my decease, but haue Horses, my will is that my E [      ] shall giue some of them Horses in roome of the mares. I Giue vnto my Couzen, *Edward Hutchinson senio<sup>r</sup>* of [      ] in New England whome I make my sole Executo<sup>r</sup> all the rest of my Goods, Lands & chattles [not] disposed of in this my will: hereby cutting off all others [      ] from any clayme to any part of my Estate, And doe Order him to take into his possession immeadiatly after [my] decease all the seuerall legacies giuen by my will, & to [pay on] or about the 29: of September next after my decease, all the legacies giuen by this my will, as being a time most conu[eni-

309

ent] for taking off Lambs from the Ewes, & foles from their mares [    ] Except those to his owne children, which hee is to haue the vse of during their minority; & what sheepe I haue disposed of in this my will, or mares, I leaue to my Executo<sup>r</sup> to Appoint Each party where he shall receiue them. And the parties to whome I haue giuen any legacies vnto, though they should not bee of full Age, yet their receipt shall bee a full discharge to my Executo<sup>r</sup>; & for those that are in their minority, their mother or Fathers receipt shall bee a full discharge for the vse of their children, & shall bee a full discharge also to him. I request my Couzen, *Eliakim Hutchinson*, to bee an ouerseer of this my will, for which I giue him Forty shillings to buy him a ring. 17 April 1667.            SAMUEL HUTCHINSON.
      In the presence of
            *Thomas Vnderwood, William Kilcupp.*
who deposed July 16, 1667.

———

SAMUEL MAVERICK, Jr. (*ante*, XII, 155).—Inuentorye of the Estate of *Samuell Mauerick*, apprised p<sup>r</sup> M<sup>r</sup> John Winslow Sn<sup>r</sup> & Jn<sup>o</sup> *Farnham*, March 28: $\frac{63}{64}$.   Amt. £127.10.2$\frac{1}{2}$.
      Nov. 4, 1665, M<sub>r</sub> Jn<sup>o</sup> Wiswall & M<sup>r</sup> W<sup>m</sup> Bartholomew Deposed to the Inventory of the Estate of the Late *Samuel Mauerick*, the Bill of Particulars on the other side taken away, alwayes excepted, & a Bill, in *Cap<sup>t</sup> Sauages* Hand, not yet Brought into them, on which *Cap<sup>t</sup> Sauage* sued.
      28: 5<sup>mo</sup>: 1665. Vpon Information from M<sup>r</sup> Jonathan Rainsford, that the Chamber Door was Broken up, where some goods were lefte, whereof the Keye was Lost, we understand as Followes. [Articles enumerated.]
      2: 7: 64. A note of what was Wanting upon the reuiew of the Inuentorye Immediately upon M<sup>rs</sup> Mauerickes going out of the House, who was one of the Administrat<sup>rs</sup> Formerlye.   Amt. £32.8.4.

———

JOHN ENDICOTT.—Jan. 27, 1667. I, John Endicott of Boston, in new England, Eldest sonn to the late John Endicott Esq<sup>r</sup>, & late Gouernor of the Massachusetts Colony, being sick of a sore throate & other distempers of body, but as well & perfect in mind & memory as Euer I was when I was in my best health, & greatest strength, God bee praysed, doe make this my last will.
      Wher[as I for?]sooke all other women & joyned my selfe in marriage vnto [my] deare wife & wee twaine became one flesh, And shee hath Carryed her selfe a louinge, helpfull, & painefull wife vnto mee. [I] giue vnto her all my Estate. I giue vnto my wife my house in Boston, joyning to *George Bates* on the west, with Appurtenances thereto belonging. I giue vnto my wife, all Lands within [    ] of Salem, the whole farme called Chickrells farme, to her & assignes foreuer. I giue vnto *Elizabeth*, my said wife, all Chattles within & without dores, wheresoeuer they shall [    ] all other Estate that belongs to mee both in reuersion [    ] to bee disposed by her foreuer. I Appoint *Elizabeth*, my wife, sole Executrix of this my last will.                                   JOHN ENDECOTT.
      I make my Father in Lawe, M<sup>r</sup> Jeremiah Howchin, & [    ] Saffin, Ouerseers of this my will.

310

In the presence of
>Jeremiah *Howchin, Nathaniell Greene, Rob,* Bradford, *Moses*
Bradford.

24th Feb. 1667. *Jeremiah Howchin, Rob<sup>t</sup> Bradford & Moses Brad-*
*ford* deposed.

———

JOHN HILL.—July 7, 1665. Whereas *John Hill,* Late of Barbadose,
Uintner, on his Uoyage From Barbadoes to New England, & on the
Coasts of this Countrey, departing this life, Hauing, as *M<sup>r</sup> John*
*Winslow,* of Boston, affirmed, made his will in Barbadoes & left it
there, in the Hands of *M<sup>r</sup> Phillippe Herbery* of said Barbadose, one of
His executors, who since the said Hils departure from Barbadoes
wrote to the said Winslow in Case of the Death of said John Hill, to
take the said Hills goods that hee Brought with Him into His Custo-
dye to preserue & Respond the Will of the said Hill, Therefore,
Power of Administration to the Estate of the Late M<sup>r</sup> John Hill, as
it is in this Jurisdiction, is Graunted to the said M<sup>r</sup> John Winslow,
of Boston, Merchant, hee Bringing in a true Inuentorye of the Estate.
Inuentory of the Estate prised by *Thomas Lake, John Winslow,* Boston, July 18, 1665. Amt. £26.4.
More prised p<sup>r</sup> *Thomas Bredon & Rich. Waye.* Amt. £27.11; p<sup>r</sup>
*Antipas Boyer & Tho. Kellond.* Amt. £68.5.
*M<sup>r</sup> John Winslow* deposed, July 26, 1665.

The account rendered, July 18, 1665, by *John Winsley.* The whole
charge of his burial was £26.4.6, including 36 p<sup>r</sup> of gloues, 20 gall.
Malego wine, 3 gall. Canary, scarfes, a post & rayle, &c. Mentions
*W<sup>m</sup> Jones; M<sup>r</sup> Fickes,* in Barbadoes.

———

MR. JOHN PAINE.—Oct. 17, 1665. Power of Administration to the
Estate of the Late *M<sup>r</sup> John Paine,* Granted to *Agnes,* his Relict. In-
ventory of the Estate prised by *Abraham Browne, Jo<sup>n</sup> Woodmanseye,*
Oct. 11, 1665. Amt. £135.12. Debts due to *M<sup>r</sup> Hezekiah Usher,*
*M<sup>r</sup> John Joyliffe, M<sup>r</sup> Tho. Kellond, M<sup>r</sup> Peter Oliuer, M<sup>r</sup> Symond Lyndes,*
*M<sup>r</sup> Peter Lidgett, M<sup>r</sup> Hudson Leauerett, M<sup>r</sup> Nicholas Redwood, John*
*Paine Jun<sup>r</sup>., William Smith.* Amt. £160.4.8.
Boston, Oct. 31, 1665. *M<sup>rs</sup> Agnes Paine* deposed in Court. Or-
dered that the Recorder Issue out an Order for *M<sup>r</sup> Edward Tinge &*
*M<sup>r</sup> Stoddard,* as auditors & Commission<sup>rs</sup>, to examine all Credito<sup>rs</sup>,
Debts, & accompts, & make their Returne to the Court. [As the
Estate was "more indebted then it will Reach to paye," *M<sup>r</sup> Edward*
*Tinge & M<sup>r</sup> Anthony Stoddard,* as Auditors & Commissioners, were
authorised to pay the creditors their just proportion of debts, proved
within a twelve month, the widow being allowed the bed & furniture
as y<sup>e</sup> Law prouides.                        EDWARD RAWSON, Recorder.

———

ROBERT PRENTICE.—Inuentory of the Goods & estate of *Robert Pren-*
*tise,* apprised by *W<sup>m</sup> Parke, Edward Denicon,* 7 (12) 1665. Amt.
£174.16.5. Mentions a house bought of *Samuell & Jn<sub>o</sub> Perry,* salt
marsh in the island; salt marsh at grauely point; fresh meadow near

Dorchester sheepe penn; 29 acres in the thousand acres next Dedham, &c; *Father Palmeter, Cap_t Isaack Johnson, Robert Pierpoint; Gilburt,* of Boston; *Lewis,* of Nashaway; *Peter Gardner.*

Debts due or demanded from the Estate: Feb. 2, 1665: From *John Stebbin, Thomas Haly, 'Robert Seauer, Tobyas Dauis, Shubaell Seauer, Deacon Park, M^r Peacock; M^r Alcocke,* for physicke; *John Weld; M^r Bracket,* of Boston; *M^r Rawson, W^m Curtis, Robert Pepper.*

*Cap^t Thomas Prentice* deposed in Court April 26, 1666.

EDW. RAWSON, Record<sup>r</sup>.

---

JOSEPH CHANDLER.—An Inuentory of the Estate of *Joseph Chandler* who deceased 20th June 1666, was prised by *Richard Gridley, Theophilus Frarye.* Amt. £29.10.6.

*Hannah Chandler* deposed to the inuentorye of her late husband, Aug. 3, 1666.

---

EDMUND BROWNE.—Whereas *Elizabeth,* the wife of *Edmund Browne,* of Boston, lately deceased, hath left two children, the said *Edmund Browne* hauing absented himselfe for seuerall yeares & none left [to] looke to his Estate remaining, & left by his wife, nor Prouision for the said Children, that the Children may duly bee prouided for, & what Estate is left of the said *Edmund Brownes* may bee preserued as much as may bee & what is due to the said *Edmund Browne* may bee gott in, This Court judgeth it meet to Order & impowre, *Mary,* the relict of the Late *Robert Bouchier,* alias *Garret,* Grandmother to the said Children, & *Benjamin Ward,* shipwright, as feofees in trust, not only to take a true Inuentory of the Estate of the said *Edmund Browne,* but out of the same to prouide for the children, & to gett in by all legall wayes & meanes what is due to the said *Edmund Browne,* or they shall find to bee due from one or other, giuing this Court an Account thereof by the next Court in Aprill, & security soe to doe in the meane time, & bringing into the Inuentory of what they find by the next Court:—the 2d Nouember 1666.

p<sup>r</sup> the Court: EDW: RAWSON, Record<sup>r</sup>.

28: 11 mo. 1667. An Inuentory of the Goods & chattles of *Edmund Browne* of Boston, deceased, taken by *Henry Olliue, Gamaliel Wayte, Abell Porter.* Amt. £216.3. Mentions *Nicholas Baxter ;* land at Muddy river, land at Long Island; *Peter Till, Edmund Stockden,* of new Castell, in old England.

Jan. 29, 1667. *Elizabeth Browne* deposed.

---

MRS. ALICE LISLE.—Boston, Nov. 1, 1666. Power of Administration to the Estate of the late *M^rs Alice Lisle,* granted to *M^r Freegrace Bendall,* in behalfe of *Mary,* his wife, daughter to the sd. *Alice Lisle,* & *Francis* her husband, together w^th *Joseph,* their sonn. (Lib. iv. fol. 275.)

(Lib. v. fol. 125.) Boston 3: 3: 1667. Inuentory of the visible Estate of *Ann Lilse,* Widdow, deceased the 30<sup>th</sup> of the 3<sup>d</sup> month 1666.

312

Estemed p[r] *John Freake, Rich: Williams.* £24.10. Mentions land at Braintry.

The 9[th] of May, 1667. *M[r] Hope for Bendall* deposed before the Gouernor, *major Generall Leuerett* & Recorder, to the Inuentory of the Estate of the late *Allice Lisle,* his mother in Lawes Estate.

EDW. RAWSON, Record[r].

[In vol. II, of the *Register,* for Jan. 1848, p. 102, was commenced* by Mr. Drake, the abstracts of Suffolk wills, which were continued to vol. V, p. 297; 82 wills and inventories being furnished by him. From thence, to the present time, the abstracts have been made by the writer of this paragraph. In a note, vol. IV, p. 53, Mr. D. remarks** in regard to the first volume of the Record of Wills, "There are in the volume 542 pages foolscap, and we hope to be enabled to continue our labors through it." That labor, with the present issue, is completed by his successor. In addition thereto, abstracts of the most important parts of all the inventories contained in volumes II, III and IV, have been made. These three books contain 664 pages, making in all, with the first volume, 1206 pages of the records. Besides this, in vol. VII, of the *Register,* are abstracts of 106 wills and inventories from the files, which are not on the records. Abstracts of 704 wills and inventories have been contributed by the writer, which, added to those given by Mr. Drake, make a total of 786.

It may be well in this connection, to remark what has been stated before in substance, that in the abstracts of wills and inventories prepared for the *Register,* names and expressions do not always correspond with those on the record, there being occasionally mistakes in the latter. In many instances the record has been compared with the original, in other cases the abstracts have been made from the originals, on file. Our aim and endeavor has been correctness or conformity to the originals, when they can be found, rather than uniformity with the records. Thus much it seems proper to state in justification of the transcriber, so that errors may not be imputed to him, unwarrantably. See note on the subject in *Register,* vol. X, p. 263.

It has been the aim, throughout, to make faithful abstracts of the wills, giving all *facts, names* and *dates,* retaining the phraseology of the originals; tautological or superfluous matter, only, being omitted.

W. B. T.]

*See p. 1.
**See p. 35.

## ABSTRACTS FROM THE EARLIEST WILLS ON RECORD AND ON THE FILES IN THE COUNTY OF SUFFOLK, MASS.

[Prepared by WILLIAM B. TRASK, Esq., of Dorchester.]

[In vol. xvi, of the *Register*, p. 336, was completed the abstracts of the Suffolk|* wills, as contained in vol. i, of the Records. The succeeding volumes ii, iii, iv, v, of the Probate Records are occupied with inventories, so that vol. vi (1667–1686), contains the wills, in continuation from vol. i, of the Records. The abstracts of inventories, in the present number are continued from vol. v.]

JOHN WILSON.—I, *John Wilson*, senior, Pastor of the Church of Christ, at Boston in New England, being now aged and many weaknesses attending of me, yet of sound judgment and memory, do hereby declare my last will.

My body I commit to the earth to be decently interred in the same tomb where is now lying the body of my beloved wife, *Elizabeth*, in Boston. Just debts and funeral expences being paid, I dispose of the remainder as followeth: To *John Wilson, Jun.*, the son of my son, *Edmond Wilson*, Doctor of Physick, late of London, deceased, I bequeath £233 6s. 8d. to be paid to his lawful Guardian, within two years after my decease, in Boston, in New England, in Merchantable Goods, either for the Indies or for England at the currant prices with the Merchants, on the receipt whereof sufficient security shall be given by such Guardian or Attorney, that the said Estate shall be to the use of my said Grand child and duly paid to him the said *John Wilson*, his heires or assignes when he shall come to one and twenty years of age, or in default thereof to remain in the hands of my Executors until he, the said *John Wilson*, shall arrive to that age. To my Grand child, *Bridget Prideaux*, the dau. of the above said *Edmond Wilson*, decd. the now wife of *Nicholas Prideaux*, Merchant in Barbadoes, I bequeath £100, to be paid him, the said *Nicholas Prideaux*, or his lawful Attorney in Boston, within two years next after my decease. To my son, *John Wilson*, Pastor of the Church at Medfield, & to my dau. *Mary Danforth*, wife of *Samuel Danforth*, of Roxbury, Pastor of that Church, to whome I have by Deed made & signed the same day with the said presents given and granted all my houses and Lands whereof I am now seized together with all other my estate real & personal, I do confirm the same to them. I ordain my two sons, *John Wilson* & *Samuel Danforth*, joint executors of this my last Will and Testament. To *Sarah, Elizabeth, John* and *Susanna*: my Grand Children by my son, *John Wilson*, I give £25 apiece to each of them, as also to such children my dau. his wife, may beare within the space of two years next following after my decease. To my Grand Children, *John, Mary, Elizabeth* and *Samuel*, children of my dau. *Mary Danforth*, £25 apiece, as also to such children as my said dau. shall beare within the space of two years next after my decease. To my son, *John Wilson*, I give all my old Bookes and my new Bookes lately bought of *Mr. Usher* or of any others in New England, to be di-

*See p. 313.

314

vided between my son, *John Wilson* and my dau. *Mary Danforth*, two third parts to my s<sup>d</sup> son, *John*, and one third part to her my s<sup>d</sup> daughter. To my beloved cousin, *Edward Rawson*, at Boston, I give £100. To *Mrs. Anna Paige*, my Kinswoman, £20. To my brother, *John Mansfield* and his children, I give £10, vizt. to him and his wife £5, and the other £5 to be equally divided between his children. To my dear cousen, *Mrs. Sarah Higginson*, I give £5. To the church over whome I am an overseer, as aforesaid, £10. To my beloved Brother and fellow Elder over the same Church, *Mr. James Penn*, I give £3. To my beloved Brethren *Capt. James Johnson, Mr. Richard Truesdale, Mr. Jacob Eliot,* Deacons of the same Church, 40s. apiece. To my ancient and good friend, *Mrs. Norton*, as a small expression of my affectionate love to her, I give 20s. To my faithful and good Friends, *Gaudy James* and *Ann* his wife, I give £5, as a testimony of my thankfulness to them for their love and service done unto me. To my Cousen, *Benjamin Brisco*, I give 40s. To my Cousen *William Smith*, I give 40s. To my reverend and beloved Brethren and fellow labourers in the worke of the Ministery, *Mr. Richard Mather* of Dorchester, *Mr. John Alline*, of Dedham, *Mr. Zechariah Symes* senior of Charlestown, *Mr. John Sherman* of Watertown, *Mr. Jonathan Mitchel*, of Cambridge, *Mr. Thomas Shepheard*, of Charlestown, and *Mr. Michael Wigglesworth*, I give 10s. apiece. All these Legacies to be paid within two years next after my decease. In case the Estate by me given to my sons, *John Wilson, Samuel Danforth* & *Mary*, his wife do not amount to the full sum of £666 13s. 4d. all these above Legacies being paid, that then all the above said Legatees shall abate proportionably, excepting onely the Legacies given to my Grand Children, the Children of my son *Edmond Wilson*, of whose Legacies my will is, there shall be no abatement. I give to my Grand Children, *John Wilson*, son of *Edmond Wilson*, a silver Goblet, and to his sister *Prideaux*, the cover thereof. To my son, *John Wilson*, I give the gold Ring with the Seal. To my dau. *Mary Danforth*, an Enameled gold Ring. I appoint my Honored Friends, *Mr. Thomas Danforth*, of Cambridge, and my Loveing Kinsman, *Mr. Edward Rawson*, overseers of this my last will & Testament, & bequeath to the said *Mr. Thomas Danforth*, 40s. 31 May, 1667.

In presence of us,                      *John Wilson, senior.*
    *Daniel Dennison,*
    *John Leuerett.*

Proved Aug. 21, 1667, *Daniel Dennison & Major Generall John Leuerett*, deposed.

Inventory of the Estate taken Aug. 14, 1667, by *John Hull, Tho. Bumstead*. Amt. £419 14s. 6d. *Lib. v. fol.* 53. [*Richard Bracket* and *Edmond Quinsey*, being desired to put a just estimate on the farme wherein *Thomas Faxon* doe now dwell, appertaining to the Estate of *Rev. John Wilson*, deceased, judge said farme, containing one dwelling house & barne with about 700 acres of land, as also 10 cowes & a mare, to bee deliuered by said *Faxon* at the end of his tearme, the whole doe ualue at £1300 in Currant payment of the Country.]

315

ROBERT MEERES.—I, *Robert Meere*, of Boston, being aged, Appoint this to bee my last will & Testament. After my funerall charges, I Giue vnto my wife *Elizabeth Meeres*, my whole Estate, till the day of her death, to bee soly at her disposell, & if need require to sell any part thereof to supply her necessity, & after her decease to bee disposed of as followeth: I haue bequeathed to my sonn *John*, who is deceased, for himself & his heires foreuer, his Estate before his decease, and what I haue both giuen & lent vnto my said sonn, I giue to his heirs foreuer, neuer to bee molested by mee nor my heires. I bequeath to my Grandchild, *John Meeres*, aboue mentioned, [*sic*] a Chest of Drawers, which Chest of drawers is to remaine in the hands of my sonn, *Samuell Meers*, or his till the day of my said Grandchilds marriage. And if my said Grandchild should dye before hee come to bee married, then the said *Samuell Meers* is to haue the said Chest of Drawers. To my aboue said Grand child, to be paid at his marriage, 40s. in money, & the said moneyes to bee paid by my two sonnes, *Samuell & James Meers*. To my sonn, *Samuell Meers*, the House which I now dwell in, & halfe the Orchard, & halfe the peece of Ground aboue the Orchard. &'the way that goes into the Orchard, which is at the south End, the said house adjoyning the Grounds of the late Esq$^r$ Gover [Endicott]. Also vnto my sonn, *Samuell*, that halfe of the hither Pasture that joynes to *Mr. Richard Parker*, Pasture, lying betweene *Mr. Parker* & Goodman *Hawkins*, & the highway on the west side. And to haue halfe of that pasture that lyeth betweene *Mr. Tarne*, late of Boston, deceased, & Goodman *Bates*, & *Mr. James Johnson*, & the high way & the aboue sayd Pastures to bee Equally diuided betweene my two sonns, *Samuell & James*, soe that Each of them shall haue his Land butt to the high way Proportionably, soe that one may haue as much of his Land butt to the high way as the other. I giue vnto my sonn, *James Meeres*, my other dwelling House, that is within my yard, which House fronts towards the late Esq$^r$ Gou$^r$, *John Endecott*, with one End facing to the street, & another End facing the Land of *Mr. Lynes*, & the other End to the Orchard. I giue to my sonn, *James Meeres*, the one halfe of my Orchard next to his House, & halfe the Land aboue the Orchard. And that halfe of the hither Pasture that lyes next to the great gate, going into the feilds, with halfe the further pasture. And further, the well that is now in the said yard, I bequeath it to them both, *Samuell & James*, to bee as much vse full to one as to the other. I bequeath to my sonn *James*, a highway into the Orchard, at the north west End of the House I now dwell in. I giue vnto my sonn, *Samuel Meeres*. his first borne Child, & to my sonn, *James Meers*, his first borne, 40s. apeece to bee paid them out of my Estate at the day of their marriage. After my wife is deceased, all the rest of my Estate to bee Equally diuided betweene my two sonns, *Samuell & James Meers*. I appoint my beloved wife, my sole Executrix of this my last will & Testament. I doe also make my beloued Brother, *James Johnson* and Mr. *Thomas Wilder*, Ouerseers of this my last will. 20th Feb. 1666.

his
*Robert* × *Meers.*
marke.

316

Signed & sealed in the
  presence of vs:
    *Samuell Keyes, John Williames.*
  *Samuell Keyes* & *John Williams*, deposed, Sept. 10. 1667. Present,
*Symon Willard, Eliazer Lusher*, Esq<sup>rs</sup>. & Recorder.
  Inventory of the house, Land, goods & Estate belonging formerly to
*Robt. Meers*, now deceased, taken by *Jeremiah Howchin, James Oliver,
James Johnson.* Amt. £349 1s. *Elizabeth Meers*, widow of *Robert
Meers*, deposed, Nov. 13, 1667. Lib. v, fol. 67.

  WILLIAM HARDING.—Power of Administration to the Estate of the
late Mr. *William Harding*, of Fyall, merchant, deceased, is granted to
Mr. *Robert Gibbs*, of Boston, merchant, Oct. 29, 1667.

---

## ABSTRACTS FROM THE EARLIEST WILLS ON RECORD AND
## ON THE FILES IN THE COUNTY OF SUFFOLK, MASS.

[Prepared by WILLIAM B. TRASK, of Dorchester.]

  NATHANIEL ROBINSON. I giue vnto Goodman *Greenleafe* & Goodman
*Shaw* & each of their wines a pr. of gloues. Also to *Thomas Sauage*
his wife & children, each, a pare of Gloues, to M<sup>rs</sup>. [        ]
& each of her children a pare of Gloues, to Mr. *Hez : Vsher* &
Capt. *William Dauis* & each of their wiues a pare of Gloues ; to each
of the bearers of my Corps a pr. of Gloues ; to Mr. *John Wilson*, to
*John Gilbert* & his wife, Each a pare of Gloues. To my bro. *Jonathan*
& sister *Mary*, Each, a ring of tenn shillings price, to bee sent to Mr.
*Henry Barton* if they bee yet living. I make my freind *Thomas Sauage* Ouerseer of this my will, & what shall remaine aboue the debts
& funerall charges & legacies aboue mentioned, I giue vnto him
the said *Sauage*, with thankfulness for all his loue, with what comes
from England also in returne of trases sent thither by Mr. *Forwell* to
sell for mee. 2d day of March 1667.          *Nathaniell Robinson.*
  Wittnes hereunto
  *Thomas Sauage,*
  *John Greenleafe.*

  25 July 1667. Capt. *Thomas Sauage* Appearinge before the Gour.
& Major Generall &c. declaring that hee did refuse to haue to doe,
with the imperfect will on the other side, that the Creditors of the
late *Nathaniell Robinson* may haue their just dues soe far as the Estate
will reach.

317

Power of Administration to the Estate of the late Nathaniell Robinson deceased granted to *John Gilbert* in whose House hee died, hee bringing an Inuentory of that Estate, & giuing security to Administer according to Law. *Edw : Rawson*, Record[r].

Inventory of the Goods & Estate as is found in the possession of *John Gilbert*, Tanner, of *Nathaniel Robinson* deceased, the 15th of June 1667, taken by *Nathaniell Bishop, Henry Rust. John Gilbert* deposed 25 July 1667.

[Prefixed to this will is "A noate of Goods in my chest," consisting of clothing, &c.; "a parcel of bookes at M[r]. *Atlifes* amounting to 4[s] ;" "a booke at Goodman *Carrington* at 14[s] price ;" "As for the bookes aboue mentioned I had of M[r]. *Forwell* & I sent pay for the bookes by the said *Forwell*, which was trases to bee sold in London, the bookes were about 8[s]. worth, & what hee had of mee about 20[s] worth soe much in London." "I owe as followeth—To M[r]. *Atwater* 24[s] ; To Goodman *Collemore* 3[s] ; To M[rs]. *Tilly* 2[s] ; To a woman of Charstow[n] 4[s] ; To Goodman *Greenleafe* 4[s] ; To Capt. *Clarke* about 50[s].]

THOMAS PAINE. 29 July 1667. Power of Administration to the Estate of the late M[r]. *Thomas Paine*, marriner, is granted to *Hannah*, his Relict she bringing a trne Inuentory of that Estate to the next Countie Court, & giuing security to Administer thereupon according to Law. p[r] Order. *Edw. Rawson*, Record[r].

BENJAMIN WARD. 26 Dec. 1666. Att a meeting of the Gou[r]. Major Generall & Record[r]. Power of Administration to the Estate of the late *Benjamin Ward*, shipwright, deceased, is granted to *Mary* his Relict, shee bringing in an Inuentory of that Estate to the next County Court & giving security to Administer thereupon according to Law. *Edw. Rawson*, Record[r].

Inventory of the Estate of *Benjamin Ward*, taken 26 Jan. 1666, by *Peter Olliuer, Henry Allen*. Amt. £940. *Mary Ward*, Relict, deposed, Feb. 15, 1666. Book 188, page 188.

MARY WARD.—PETITION. To the Honorable the Generall Court now Assembled. The Humble Petition of *Mary Ward*, Widdow— Humbly Sheweth :

That it hath pleased God lately to take to himselfe the late *Benjamin Ward*, youre Petitione[rs] deare Husband, before hee did or could settle that Estate, which God hath bestowed on him, by his & youre Petitione[rs] labor & Care for about Forty & fiue yeares, wherein they liued together with the Constant & faithful Seruice of *Stephen Butler*, sonn to the Petition[r] by a former Husband, who was very deare to youre Petition[rs] late Husband Ward, who alwayes told youre Petition[r]. that hee resolued to manifest his loue & affection to her said sonn Butler, as to his owne that God had giuen to themsclues, as a reward of all his faithfull & dilligent seruice both before & after hee was for himselfe, but hee dying intestate & youre Petitioner uery aged & weake, & vnfit to mannage what is Left & being desirous that the Estate of her late Husband may bee diuided & settled on herselfe & her three grand-children which is all the issue that God hath pleased to spare the Petitioner & her late Husband, the one halfe thereof to youre Petitioner & her dispose whereby shee may bee Enabled to liue in some measure Comfortably the remainder of her life, but also leaue behind her some Testimony of her loue to her sonn Butler & his children to whome her Husband intended soe well. And the other halfe of the whole to her said Grand-Children, to bee giuen to them at the day of marriage, & youre Petition[r] as in duty bound shall pray.

In answer to the Petition of Mary Ward, Widdow, the Court on perusall of the Petition declare that the Cognizance thereof belongs to the County Court of Suffolke to whome it is referred.

Edw. Rawson, Secrety.

At a County Court held at Boston 31 July 1667 :

The Court on due perusall of the late Mary Ward's Petition to the Gennerall Court in May last, & the Court's Answer thereunto, with the Euidences of *Richard Gridley* & *Henry Allen*, together with the last will & Testament of the said Mary Ward, now Also proued in this Court by sufficient Euidences to bee her last will & Testament, consideringe her Equall minde & due Care to her Children both by first & second Husband, doe allow & Confirme the said will to bee a fynall issue for the settling of the Estate betweene the Children, ordering that her Petition & Evidences therewith bee Recorded with that her will.

Edw. Rawson, Record[r].

MARY WARD.—WILL.—I, Mary Ward, Relict of the late *Benjamin Ward* of Boston, being weake of body, but of perfect vnderstanding, Considering the trouble I haue mett with & benn put vnto, by Reason Sicknes came soe on & death soe suddenly issuing, taking my Husband out of this world before hee setled his Estate, & knowing that hee often declared vnto mee, that hauing from a Child brought vp my sonn *Stephen Butler*, that I had by a former Husband, that hee found soe dutifull, hopefull, & seruiceable to him as if hee had been his owne, hee alwayes telling mee hee minded to giue him a Considerable part of his Land & Estate, that had soe great a hand & helping to gett it, least after my decease my deare Husbands mind should not bee vnderstood, I hauing alwayes a hand also in getting of the Estate, judge it for peace sake, that my sonn & sonn in Lawe & grand-children may liue in loue & peace, necessary to make this my last will & Testament, being sole Administratrix to my said late Husbands Estate, hereby anulling any late or former will of mine. I Giue to my Reuerend Pastor Mr. *John Wilson* 40s ; to Mr. *Thatcher* & Mr. *Allen* 40s a peece ; to the poore of the Church of Boston Fowre pounds. To my sonn in lawe *William Holloway* Tenn pounds. Unto my much Honored Freinds Major Generall *John Leueret* & Mr. *Peter Olliuer* my Ancient & neere neighbors alwayes helpfull to mee Thee [Three] pounds a peece, to buy them a Ring. I bequeath all the rest of my Estate, hoth Reall & personall, in Houses, Lands, wharfes, goods & Household stuffe & whatsoeuer my Husband left & now I possess, the one halfe thereof, that is of all the Houses, Lands & goods to my Three grand-children, *Mary Holloway* whome my Husband and I brought vp, *William Holloway* & *Benjamin Holloway*, to bee divided Equally betweene them when they come to bee of Age, and that they bee heires Each to other. And in Case of their de-

cease, the one halfe to their Father *William Holloway* & the other halfe to *Stephen Butler*, my sonn and his heires. I giue the other halfe of the Houses, Lands & goods to my beloued sonn *Stephen Butler* & his Children hee hauing soe industriously laboured with & for my Husband, & in Case of his & all his Childrens decease, before my grand-children being of Age, in such Case what I giue to them, my mind & will is it should goe to my Grand children or the longer liuer of them. My will is, that my sonn in Law *William Holloway* shall giue security to my Executor to Render it vp what I haue giuen to my grand-children, that during their non-Age he shall have the ben- nifit & improuement thereof. I Appoint my sonn *Stephen Butler* to bee sole Executor of this my last will & Testament & desire my Honnored Freinds Major Generall *John Leuerett* & M^r. *Peter Olliuer* to bee ouerseers of the same. 4 July 1667.          *Mary* × *Ward.*
In presence of vs,
*William Salter, Henry Allen, John Prince, John Saunders.*
21 July 1667.   *William Salter* & *Henry Allen* deposed.

The Testimony of *Henry Allen* aged 47 yeares or thereabouts, Tes- tifyeth & saith that hauing conference with Brother Ward, deceased, not long before his death, Concerning the disposall of his Estate, & to my best remembrance that hee did Answer mee that it should be di- uided amongst them, & that his sonns did Carry on the worke to- gether as wittnes my hand.
Deposed in County Court 31 July 1667 : by *Henry Allen*, as Attests.
          *Edw. Rawson*, Record^r.

The Testimony of *Richard Gridley* aged 65 yeares, Testifyeth & saith that hauing had Conference with Brother Ward, deceased, about 2 yeares since, hearing of him Complaine of the trouble hee had with his servants, I did ask of him, how hee did Carry on his work now. And hee did Answer mee that hee was Eased of his trouble by his two sonns, for they did Carry on the worke Comfortably & that they did agree very well & then I did ask of him, how hee did thinck to dispose of his Estate lying as it did abroad & at home, hee did tell mee that they did the better it should bee for them, for it should bee diuided together, for they did Each one the worke to his great Com- fort.                    his marke
          *Richard* × *Gridley.*
Sworne to in Court by *Richard Gridley*, 1 Aug^st 1667.
          *Edw. Rawson*, Record^r.

Inventory of the Estate of Mary Ward, widdow, deceased, taken 19 : 5 mo. 1667. by *Richard Woodde, Henry Allen.* Mentions twelue Acres of land at Muddy ryver, £24 ; two parsell of land at Billerica at 12^d an acre, £4. Amt. £46. 10.
31 July 1667.   *Stephen Butler* deposed.   Book V, page 193.

R̲ICHARD C̲ARTER. Boston, 28 Feb. 1667. Power of Administration to the Estate of the late *Richard Carter* is granted to *Ann*, his Relict.

E̲LIZABETH R̲OBINSON.—21 Aug. 1666. I, *Elizabeth Robinson*, being in a weake Condition of Body, yet of competent vnderstanding & memory, concerning such Estate as it hath pleased God to leaue to my disposing I doe Order & bequeath as followeth. That the Estate

320

Giuen by the last will & Testament of my former Husband, *Richard Shearman,* I doe hereby will & desire that it may bee performed accordingly & for the Ouerplus of what the House & Land shall yeald I doe out of the same giue vnto *John Browne,* sonn of *Edmond Browne* of Dorchester, £5. To *Samuell Deman,* sonn of *John Deaman* of Redding, 40ˢ. To *Elizabeth Spaule,* dau. of *Thomas Spall* of Boston, 40ˢ. To my sister *Bridget Locks* children of Faucet in England, if liuing, to Each of them £5, Prouided that if the Ouerplus aboue mentioned shall fall short of these legacies aboue written, that then they are to haue proportionably as it shall fall, the which I referr to my Executoᵣˢ hereafter named. I giue to my kinsman, *John Greenleafe,* my Orchard, to him & his heires foreuer, Prouided hee pay to his sister *Mary Greenleafe,* £20 within six months after my decease, the which I doe hereby giue & bequeath to my said kinswoman. To my said kinsman, *John Greenleafe,* one bedstead in the Chamber with the furniture to it. Vnto *Mary Spall,* dau. of the said Spall aforesaid, one feather bed, boulster & pillow. I giue vnto *Mary Greenleafe,* one feather bed & bedstead with furniture belonging to it as it now standeth in the Parlor, together with one Table, Fowre Stooles & fowre Quishions. And whereas there is due vnto mee the sume of £50, from the Estate lately of my Husband *Thomas Robinson* as by Couenant vpon marriage, I doe referr the whole or what shall bee recouered of the same to bee disposed the one halfe of it among my Husband *Shearman's* children or Grand children, according to the discretion of my Executoᵣˢ, the rest of the said sume & other mouables after my debts funerall & other necessary charges paid to bee disposed of at the discression of Deacon *John Wisewall* & Mᵣ. *William Bartholomew,* whome I Appoint Executoᵣˢ of this my last will.

In presence of            *Elizabeth* ✕ *Robinson.*

*Nathaniell Bishop, Joseph Bartholomew.*

16 Nov. 1667. *John Dammon* appeared in Court, with *Thomas Spall, Edmond Browne* & *Joseph Knight* & Acknowledged themselues to bee agreed with Deacon *John Wiswall* Executor to Elizabeth Robinsons will, & was willing it should bee proued, the said Deacon Wisewell presenting *Joseph Bartholomew* & Mᵣ. *William Bartholomew* Euidences. Taken before Mᵣ. *Edward Tyng,* which the Court Orders to bee Recorded with the will & approved of them as a probate of the same. As Attests,  *Edw. Rawson,* Recordᵣ.

The Testimony of *Joseph Bartholomew,* Aged 29 yeares or thereabouts, Concerning the last will & Testament of *Elizabeth Robinson,* bearing date, 21 Aug. 1666, now deceased, this deponent Testifyeth that the said *Elizabeth* came diuers times to this deponants Fathers house uery earnestly desiring to haue her will drawne, as not willing to haue her former Will stand, but to alter it. And after many times comming, the Father of this deponant, on a day brought a Coppie drawne as from her, & written to my best Remembrance, hee said by Mᵣ. *Wiswall* & himselfe, the which this deponant wrought out & meeting with the Widdow Robinson afterwards shee Exprest her selfe uery joyfull that it was done & uery well sattisfyed with it & Owned it as her will & Testament, after goodman *Bishops* hand was at it ; soe when shee had soe Owned it, to bee her Act & deed I set to my hand also, at which time I tooke her to bee of a disposing mind, only shee had a great defect in vttering her mind, vntil shee had tyme to make her mind knowne by degrees, & further saith not.

Taken upon Oath Aug^st 21, 1667.

Before mee,        Edward Tyng, Commiss^r.

The Testimony of *William Bartholomew*, Concerning the last will & Testament of *Elizabeth Robinson* deceased saith, that the said *Elizabeth* came often to the House of this deponant, diuers times weeping to him, to get her will formerly drawne to bee Altered & to bee, new drawne. My business being more then Ordinary, I could not in some Weekes attend it, but sometime before the date of her last will, went to M^r. Wiswall at her request, and wee together tooke this her last will from her Owne mouth, wording of it as meetly as wee might, but in nothing altering the sence of her mind Expressed to vs. I doe not remember wee dictated any thing to her of it, but only when shee was speaking of some bequeathed to her kindred in England wee wished her to insert that clause, vizt. if the Estate might afford; & whereas shee had drawne two formes of wills before, I doe account this will the most rationall of them all, & the Reasons shee gaue for altering her former will, were upon rationall grounds, & I doe affirme to my best vnderstanding, that at the drawing & at the signing & sealing of this her last will & Testament shee was of a Composed & disposing mind, also shee declared her selfe seuerall times to this deponant, after the will was signed & finished, to bee well.sattisfyed & quieted in her mind, who indeed seemed restless till it was done; further this deponant testifyeth, that hee this deponant meeting her the Euening before shee sickned, going from her House, it being a uery cold Euening, asked her why shee would hazard her health soe, as to goe forth in soe cold an Euening, shee Answered mee, that shee was going to a priuate meeting. And to my best Remembrance I then asked her as I had done vpon occation at times before, whether shee heard with vnderstanding at the meetings & shee said yea, shee praysed God for it.

Taken vpon Oath the 29^th of the 7: 1667.

Before Edw. Tyng, Commiss^r.

EDWARD YARD. 25^th March, 1668. Power of Administration to the Estate of the late *Edward Yard*, Fisherman of neere Dartmouth In the County of Deuon, in old England, deceased, is granted to M^r. *Peter Olliuer* of Boston, merchant, in behalfe of himselfe & other Creditor^s with such others as are neerest of kinne to the said Yard, hee bringing in a true Inventory of the Estate to the next Countie Court, & givinge bonds to Administer thereupon according to Lawe :

By Order, Edw. Rawson, Record^r.

## ABSTRACTS FROM THE EARLIEST WILLS ON RECORD AND ON THE FILES IN THE COUNTY OF SUFFOLK, MASS.

[Prepared by WILLIAM B. TRASK, Esq.]

THOMAS RUCK. 7 Dec.·1662. I, *Thomas Ruck* of Boston, being sick & weake in Body but of perfect memory doe make this my last will. That my wife, *Elizabeth Ruck*, shall haue all my Estate in Lands, House, debts, goods & mouables of what quallity & quantity soeuer, for life. After the decease of my said wife, my will is, that the said Estate be equally diuided by my three Children, *John Ruck, Samuell Ruck, & Joane*, the wife of *Henry Farnham*, amonge themselues, & my will is, that my dau. *Joane Farnhams* third part shall bee Enjoyed by her during her life, and after her decease I Giue vnto her sonn, *Thomas Swan*. All debts I Owe in

323

right or Conscience to any Person or Persons whatsoeuer, within Conuenient time after my decease, be paid.        *Thomas Ruck.*
In the presence of
    *Sam: Ruck, William Pearse.*

1st May 1668.   *William Pearse* deposed.   Power of Administration to the Estate of the late *Thomas Ruck*, Sen^r. deceased, is granted to *Elizabeth Ruck*, his Relict. (Lib vi, 11.)

Inuentory of the Goods of *Thomas Ruck*, deceased, taken by M^r. *Edward Collicott* & Goodman *Deaken*.   *Elizabeth Ruck*, Relict of the late *Thomas Ruck* Sen^r. deposed. (Lib. v, 133.)

EDWARD DENNISON.—I, *Edward Dennison*, of Roxbury, being weake & sick & Expecting my great change, but at p^rsent of sound judgment & memory, doe declare my last will. Just debts & funeral Expences paid.   My will is that my wife, *Elizabeth Dennison*, during her Widdowhood, shall according to her best skill & the Council & aduice of her Christian Friends manage my whole Estate, for the maintenance of her self & of my children, and that shee shall not sell any of the Land except meere necessity require for the payment of my debts & the releife of the family, nor sell any of the Timber but for repair of the Houses, & fences.   If my wife, *Elizabeth*, marry againe, my will is, that halfe of the Estate bee at her dispose duringe her life, and that shee see to it that due Care bee taken, that the other halfe bee put into Faithfull hands & improued for the Comfort of my children.   After the decease of my wife, my will is, that the whole Estate remaining, bee diuided into two Equall parts, & that my sonn, *William*, shall haue the one halfe thereof for his Portion, and that the other halfe bee equally diuided betweene my daughters, wherein they shall haue share & share alike, without any Consideration what I haue formerly giuen any of them.   In Case any of my Children marry, before my wiues decease, my will is, that such children should haue Forty pounds allowed them, out of my Estate, for their present inCouragment, and that after my wiues decease that Summe bee abated out of the whole proportion.   I desire my brother, *John Weld*, & my beloued Kinsman, M^r *Thomas Weld*, to bee my Ouerseers, & ordaine my wife, *Elizabeth*, solé Executrix, and giue her power to dispose of £100 of the Estate at her decease, prouided that shee giue vnto my daughter, *Mary*, in regard of her weakness, not less than £20, more than the rest.   25^th April, 1668.        *Edw: Dennison.*
In the presence of
    *Samuel Danforth, John Stebins.*

On the day of the date hereof the said M^r *Edward Dennison* did declare it to bee his mind & Earnest desire that his sonn, *William*, should bee brought up in good literature, according as the improuement of his Estate will beare, this wee Attest.
                                *Samuell Danforth, John Stebins.*

28^th May 1668.   M^r *Samuel Danforth & John Stebins* deposed (Lib VI. 12.)

Inventory of the Estate of M^r *Edward Dennison* taken by *Thomas Weld, John Bowles, John Stebins*, 13 May 1668. apprised at £1257. 5. [including dwelling house, home lott, two orchards, 9 Acres "as you goe towards Boston," £100; 24 Acres of wood Land neere the great pond, £80; 12 Acres of marsh & vpland toward muddy River, £80; 7 Acres of wood land neere dead swamp, £40; 9 Acres of vpland neere the heirs of *Isaac Heath*, £70; 5 Acres of Salt marsh in Lower calfe pasture, £40; 12 Acres of salt marsh in the Lower Calfe pasture £70; 4 Acres more or lesse Commonly called Pine Island, £40; 60 Acres of Common wood land in the second Diuission, £150; 7 Acres more or less wood land neere *Hopkins*, £15.]

28th May 1668. Mrs *Elizabeth Dennison* deposed. (Lib V. 92.) Added by Mrs *Dennison*, 16 March 1684. 55 acres ¼ of wood-land lying at Jamaica end in Roxbury.

JOHN TAYLOR. The last will of *John Taylor* senior, of Weighmouth, now lying sick & weake of Body but of Rational vnderstanding. My debts honnestly paid. To my wife, *Rebecca Taylor*, my bed & all that belongs to it & my Household Stuffe to her disposing, & House roome soe long as shee doth liue. To my sonn, *John Taylor*, all my House & Lott adjoyning to 'it, & seauenteene Acres of my Common Lotts, to him & his heires foreuer .To my dau. *Rebecca Gurney*, Seauen Acres of my Common Lotts. I Giue Eight shillings to my dau. *Gurney*. I appoint my sonn, *John Taylor*, to bee my Executor. 6: 11 mo.: 1667.

*John* X *Taylor.*
his mark.

In the presence of

*Obadiah Whitman, John Dyer,* who deposed, 22 May 1668. (Lib VI. 13.)

Inventory of the goods & Estate of *John Taylor*, of Weighmouth, lately deceased, apprized by *Thomas Dyar, John Holbrook.* Amt. £22.

*John Taylor* deposed 22 May 1668, to the inventory of his late father, *John Taylor's* Estate. Mentions a house & 6 Acres of land, £10; 24 Acres of land in the woods, £5. (Lib. V. 130.,

ROBERT GARRETT.—The last will & Testament of *Rob.t Garrett*, of Boston, being of perfect judgment & sound memory for the disposing of my Outward Estate, being now vpon a voyage to the Barbados. I give to my wife, *Mary*, my House in Boston wherein shee now dwells, for her life, & after her decease I giue the said House, with the Appurtenances, vnto my fowre Children, *John Garret, Rob.t Garret, Mary Garrett & Sarah Garrett,* to bee Equally Diuided Amongst them, & soe many of them as shall bee liuinge, & haue any child or children liuinge, & to their heires seuerally foreuer; and for all my Goods & Catle [chattells] I Giue & bequeath to my said wife, *Mary*, whome I make Executrix of this my last will, dated Nouember 27: 1660.

*Robert* X *Garret.*
his marke.

Wittnes

*Penelop Bellingham, Joseph* X *Fowlers* marke,
*Richard Bellingham.*

*Joseph Fowler* deposed 1st August 1668. (Lib. VI. 13.)

HENRY FLINT.*—24: 11 mo: 1652. Concerning my children & Estate. 1. vntill my wife or any of the children marry I leaue all my Estate in the power & to the Wisdome & discretion of my wife for her Comfort & bringing vp of the children. 2. If shee should bee called away by death, before the Children bee growne to take some

---

* The will of Rev. Henry Flint is here given entire.

Care of themselues & of one another, then I leaue it to her Wisdome to make choyce of the next person to whom shee may Commit the Care of Children & Estate vnto. 3ly. To my sonn, *Josias,* I giue my Dwelling House, with those two Lotts it stands vpon, which I bought of *Richard Wright, & M^r Moses Paine,* deceased, together w^th all that Land of mine, now in the Occupation of *William Vezie,* after the decease of his mother. 4ly. I Giue to my sonn *Seth,\** my great Lott & halfe my bookes, if it please God to make him a Scholler; if hee bee brought vp to some other Course of life, then his brother *Josias†* to haue them all, & to allow him for halfe in some pay Sutable to his Condition. 6ly. to my daughters I appoint Each of them an Hundred pounds, if my Estate will reach it. 7ly. if any of my Children marry whilst my wife doth liue & and Continueth vnmarried I leaue it to her Wisdome what Portion to giue at p^rsent, though I intend that finally all my yong Children should bee made Equall. 8ly. for the p^rseut I know not what Porsion of my Estate to assign to my wife in Case God call her to marriage, otherwise then as the Law of the Country doth prouide in that Case, accounting all that I haue to little for her; if I had nothing else to bestow vpon my children.

*Richard Bracket,* aged 56 yeares or there abouts deposed saith, that about Fowre dayes before the late M^r *Henry Flint* departed this life, himself, & M^rs *Joanna Quinsey* being with him, they heard him say hee had made & written his will, which being now produced, vnder M^r *Flints* owne hand writting, which they well known to bee soe, & the sume & substance thereof hee himselfe repeated to them, only said that his sonn, *Josiah,* being growne vp, should bee his Executo^r, with his wife Executrix.

Taken vpon Oath by the said *Richard Bracket,* before the Gou^r., Capt. *Gookin* & Record^r. 2 July 1668, who allowed of the will hereby proued.          *Edw : Rawson Record^r*

An Inuentory of the Estate of M^r *Henery Flint,* Teacher of the Church of Christ at Braintry, as it was apprized by Capt *Richard Brackett,* Goodman *Gregory Belcher* & M^r *Moses Paine.* Mentions—the dwelling house & barne, the orchard & homestall, the feeding in the burying place & the Land in the stony feild, together with a small peece of vpland & flatts, lying in the great Knights neck, which was part of *Buttons* Lott, & about 7 Acres of marsh with vpland belonging to it, lying betweene *Speares* farme & Catt Island, £395; L and & little Knigbts neck, about 5 Acres, £15; vpland & meadow about 28 Acres in great Kuights neck, £140; a meadow at the holes with Islands of Creeke lying by it, £20; the farme at Smelt Brooke, £200.

2^d July 1668. M^rs *Margery* deposed that this paper contains a true Inuentury of the Estate of the late M^r *Henry Flint,* her late husband, to her best knowledge, &c (Lib. V. 95.)

JANE HUMPHERY.—I, *Jane Humphery,* being weake in Body, & not knowinge how soone the Lord may take mee hence, doe this 29^th of the Eleanenth month 1666, declare how I would haue my goods disposed of after my decease. I give to my sonn *Williams* wife,

---

\* Seth died at Dedham, May 12, 1673, in his second year at Harvard College, and in the 21st year of his age.

† Josiah, the eldest son of Henry, was Pastor of the church at Dorchester, where he died Sept. 15, 1680, aged 35 years. See the inscription on his tombstone, in *Register* ii, page 382.

ye jump * which was my sister *Sarah Caps*, [*Clap's*,] Also my best Redd Kersey petticoate & sad gray Kersey Wascoate, my blemmish Searge Petticoate & my best hatt, my white fustian Wascott, a wrought napkin with noe lace about it, a black sike† neck-cloath, a quart glass Bottle, a handkerchife, a blew Apron, a plaine black quoife without lace, a white Holland apron with a small lace at the bottome. I Giue to my sonn *Amiells* wife, a redd Searge Petticoate & a blackish Searge Petticoate, a green Searge Wascoate, & my hood & muffe. Also my greene Linsey woolsey petticoate, my whittle‡ that is fringed & my jump; my blew short coate, a wrought napkin with noe lace about it; a handkerchife, a blew Apron, my best black quife with a lace, a black Stuffe neckcloath, a white Holland Apron with two breathes in it, Six yards of Redd cloath, if it will hold out after all things bee discharged; a greene vnder Coate. I Giue to my daughter, *Jane*, my staning kersey Coate & my murry Wascoate, my Cloake & my blew Wascoate, a pare of fine sheets, a holland Table cloath, halfe a duzzen of napkins, my best white Apron, my wrought platter; a pare of pillow beers; my best shift, one napkin wrought about & laced; my little chest & one of my best neck-cloaths, one of my best plane quiues, my best holland square cloath with a little lace & one Callico vnder neck-cloath, a stone jugg, a yard of Holand that is hemmed & marked with an J, a siluer spoone & my wedding Ring. I Giue to my sonn, *Joseph Weekes*, my great old chest, my best brass pann, two platters a bigger & a lesser, & a Couerlide; my booke of Mr. Burrowes Gospell Worship, a sheet of Cotton & linnen, also a Tablecloath. I Giue to my Grandchild, *Amiell Weekes*, my bed & chafe boulster & my Rugg. To my Grandchild, *Ebenezer*, my Feather Boulster & a pare of new blanckets. To my Grandchild, *Thanckfull*, two pillows, two old Pillow beers & my skillet. To my Grandchild *Elizabeth*, *Amiels* Daughter, my new great Chest, my spinning wheele, my little brass pan & my little Bible; Also I giue vnto *Thanckfull*, the biggest of my small boxes. To my grandchild, *Jane Weekes*, one of my best platters. To my Grandchild, *Renue*,§ my lesser small Box. To my sonn, *Amiell*, my Great Bible. To my sonn *Amiell & William* Tenn pounds of hemp yarne & Cotton to be put vpon it, to be Equally deuided betweene them. I giue to my sonn, *Amiell*, Mr. Borrowes Booke of Gospell Conuersation & my psalme booke, Also my Cowe. I Giue to my soun, *William*, my booke of Mr. Shepards workes, also 15 shillings. I giue tenn shillings to my Grandchild, *John Weekes*, & to Each of the other of my sonn *Williams* Children, Fiue shillings, if there bee soe much remaininge when things bee discharged. I Giue to to my sonn in Law, *Benjamin Bate*, Mr. Taylors Booke on the 32 psalme. I Giue to my sister, *Jone Clap*, a fine thine neck-cloath & a Square cloath with a little lace vpon it. I Give to my sister, *Susannah Clap*, the next best neck-cloath to that of Sister *Jones*, & square Cloath. I Giue to my Couzen, *Hannah Clap*, my next best neck-cloath & the next best Square Cloath

---

* *Jump.*—A short coat, or a sort of bodice for women.
† A country word, signifying a quillet or furrow. *Silk* may be intended.
‡ *Whittle.*—A white dress for a woman; a double blanket worn by west country-women in England, over the shoulders, like a cloak.
§ Renew Weeks, dau. of William Weeks, b. 12 Aug., 1760; m. Benj. Carpenter.

& whatsoeuer Else I haue I Giue to my Sonn, *Amiell*, whome I make my Executo$^r$. I Giue my best greene Apron to *Mary Atherton*. This being my last will & Testament, 1 wittnes my hand in p$^r$sence of vs.

The marke of *Jane* × *Humphery*.

*Roger Clap*
*Samuell Paull*.

19 Nov. 1668. Capt. *Roger Clap & Samuell Paule* deposed.

An Inuentory of the Goods of *Jane Humphery, Widdow*, late of Dorchester, deceased, taken the 20 Oct. 1668, by *Roger Clap, James Humphery*. Amt. £39.12.04. Debts owing, £1.3.09.

19 Nov. 1668. *Amiell Weekes* deposed to the Inuentory of the Estate of the late *Jane Humphery*, Widdow, his late mother. (Lib. V. 108.)

[Jane Humphrey, as the name was usually written, was the widow of Jonas Humphrey, of Dorchester, who died 19 March, 1662. Jane was his second wife, and Mr. Humphrey was her second husband. Her maiden name was Jane Clap, sister of Capt. Roger Clap. She m. 1st, George Weeks, by whom she had sons Amiel, Joseph and William. Mr. Weeks died in Dorchester, Oct. 27, 1659.]


## ABSTRACTS FROM THE EARLIEST WILLS ON RECORD AND ON THE FILES IN THE COUNTY OF SUFFOLK, MASS.

[Prepared by WILLIAM B. TRASK.]

JONATHAN FAREBANCK. June 1, 1668. I, *Jonathan Farebanck*, of Dedham, in the Countie of Suffolke, senior, being sick and weake, and expecting that the day of my dissolution is drawing nigh, make this my last will. I Giue vnto *Grace*, my wife, all and Euery part and parcell of my whole mouable Estate whatsoeuer, as well within dores as without, namly, all my household stuffe, also, my Cattle, all my Corne, carts, plowes, working tooles and vtensells of Husbandry, all debts due to mee, and whatsoever Else come within the denomination of mouable Estate. All vnto my said wife, to dispose of when and to whome shee shall at any time see meete. I Giue to my said wife, an annuety of £8 p' Ann. to bee paid to her or her assignes to her vse yearely, in two equall parts, that is to say, at the end of Euery halfe yeare, fowre pounds, during her life. To my said wife, the vse of all my Houses, yards and yard room, for her selfe and her cattle, her assignes and all her occations, for the space of fowre monthes next after my decease. To *George Farebanck*, my second son, and to his heires, forever, £16, the one halfe to bee paid him within the yeare next Ensuing after the decease of my wife. Whereas I haue already giuen and doe hereby Confirme to my sonn *George*, all that my part in the Generall diuident already layd out neere Meadfield, and some working tools, and such like small things, my will is, that the said parcell of Land and shop, tooles and other small things, soe giuen, shall bee all indifferently and Equally apprized, and if they shall together amount. to the uallue of £8, then it shall bee accounted for his first payment. And then my mind is, that my dau. *Mary*, shall haue her first payment within the first yeare of my wiues decease, otherwise shee is to

328

tarry till the second yeare. 1 giue my dau. *Mary*, the wife of *Chris-topher Smith*, the sume of £16, which I giue to my said dau. distinct from her Husband's Estate, and to bee alwayes at her dispose; this, to bee paid in two Equall sumes, Eight pounds, in case my sonn *George* bee paid, within the space of one yeare after my wiues decease, and in case *George* bee not paid soe much, then shee is to bee paid her first payment within two yeares after my wiues decease. I giue to my said dau. £3, to purchas her a suite of apparrell with, to bee paid within the space of Three monthes next after my decease. To *Jonas Farebanck*, my third sonn, and to his heires foreuer, the like sume of £16, to bee also paid in two Equal sumes, the first £8 to bee paid the next yeare after his sister *Mary* haue receiued her first payment. Vnto *Jonathan Farebanck*, my yongest sonne, and his heires, the like sume of £16, to bee paid also in two Equall sumes, the first halfe to bee paid in the yeare next Ensuing, after his brother *Jonas* is paid his first halfe. Whereas I haue already giuen, and doe hereby Confirm to my sonn *Jonathan*, one parcell of Land, uallued at £5, my mind is, that hee shall haue the same in part of his first payment aforesaid, and also what debt shall appeare then to bee due from him to mee, shall bee reconed vpon the same account. My will is, that when all my sonns and my daus. aforesaid, shall haue and receiued their first pay ment in manner and time successiuely as is before Expressed, that then my sonn *George* shall bee paid his second £8 ; and then my dau. and soe in the same order. *Jonas* and *Jonathan* shall bee paid to them their heires or assignes, their second £8 Each, one yeare after another, vntill they bee all paid their full legacies. I Giue to *Sarah*, the Eldest dau. of my sonn *John Farebanck*, one yong beast betweene one and 2 yeares of age. And more, three pounds to be paid by my Executor when shee shall attain Lawfull Age. The yong beast before mentioned, I reserue out of the Cattle bequeathed to *Grace*, my wife. To my sonn in Law, *Ralph Day*, 40s., to bee paid with-in six monthes after my wiues decease. I Giue to Each of the fowre Children of the said *Ralph*, which hee had by my dau. *Susan*, his late wife, 40s., to be paid them seuerally, as they shall attain Lawfull Age, prouided all my other Legacies to my Three sonns and my dau. bee first paid, in manner as is above exprest. My will is, that all these my legacies, aboue bequeathed, the specie or kind of pay-ment whereof is not named, shall bee all paid in Currant Country pay-ment, at price the Current, in Deadham. To *John Farebanck*, my Eldest sonn, all my Houses and Lands whatsoeuer and not being for-merly aboue in this my will disposed of, together with all my Com-mon Rights and Towne priueledges whatsoeuer, to him and his heires foreuer, to enter vpon all my Lands forthwith after my decease. And all my houses and yards, at the End of 4 monthes next Ensuing the same. I ordain *John Farebanck*, my Eldest sonn, to bee my sole Ex-ecutor. I entreat my uery Louing freinds, Mr. *Eliazer Lusher* and *Peter Woodward* senior to be Ouerseers.

In the presence of      JONATHAN ᴎ FAREBANCK sen'r.
*William Auery, Thomas Medcalfe,*
who deposed, Jan. 26, 1668.        (Book vi. page 15.)

Inventory of the Estate taken 16 : 10 : 1668, by *Eliazer Lusher, Daniell Fisher, Peter Woodward.* Mentions—The home Lott, with the Addition of Land in the Wigwam plane, the Orchard and all the buildings thereupon, £150; 8 Cow Commons, £16; 6 Acres of meadow in broad meadow, £15; 2 Acres of fowle meadow and Common meadow there, £6; 22 Acres of meadow in Purgatory plane, £22; 4 Acres in the Low plane, £8; in Natick Divident, 24 Acres, £10; Land in the clap board Trees, £2; Swamp in the great Sedar swamp neere the saw mills, £4; at Wallumnappeage,* and Cow Commons, £8; right at Paucumtack,† £3. (Book v. page 112.)

ROBERT BELLOW. I, *Robt. Bellow*, som time of Rhoad Island,‡ in New England — uery sick and weake, and in perfect memory. I Giue vnto my wife, *Susannah Bellow*, all my Worldly Estate in one Case or other, in debts or goods, to bee at her owne disposing, only to my two daus. and sonn, 12d. a peece, desiring my wife to haue a Care of my Grand-children and also my Couzen *William* and *Henry*, and not to bee vnmindfull of them. Making her my Executor and Administrator of my whole Estate, I shall Constitute Mr. *Wm. Brenton*, Esq., Mr. *Nicholas Eson* [*Easton*], deputy Gou'r, and also my sonn in Lawe, *George Gardener*, and my well beloued Freind, Mr. *William Vauhan*, to bee Ouerseers, for mee, ouer my wife and Children. This being my last will and Testament, I leaue you all to the Protection of Almighty God, dated 2d June, 1668.

Wittnes—*Samuell King, Jacob Browne, John Cleasby.*

18 June 1668, *Samuell King* and *Jacob Browne* deposed. It was read audibly to him, [*Robert Bellow*], on the day of the date of it, and hee declared hee vnderstood it, and that hee did not know it necessary to set his hand to it, and that hee was of a sound disposing mind to their best knowledge when hee soe declared.

*Edw. Rawson*, Record'r.

An Inuentory of the Goods of *Rob't Bellow*, which hee left in the hands of *Jacob Browne*, at his decease. Am't £1 16s. Prized by *William Pell, Miles Farne, Jacob Browne*, deposed June 20, 1668. (Book v. page 103.)

JOHN FISHER. 26 : 4 : 1668. I, *John Fisher*, of Meadfield, in the Countie of Suffolke, in New England, being weake of body, yet sound in memory and vnderstanding, doe ordaine this my last will and Testament. I Giue to *Mary*, my wife, all that Estate, whatsoeuer that I had with her, that is soe much as is now in being, and more, one Feather bed vpon which wee ordinarily lodge, with all the bedding, furniture belonging thereto, Except that furniture about it that Came by my former wife *Elizabeth*,§ and also the free vse of that part of the House, wherein I now dwell, with free liberty of water and Conuenient yard roome for wood and other her necessary occations, with free Egres and

---

* Wollonopauge or Wollonspaug, incorporated as the town of Wrentham, 1673.
† Or, Pecomptuck, now Deerfield. See Mather's *Relation*, Drake's ed., p. 158.
‡ At a town meeting in Portsmouth, R. I., Oct. 5, 1643, it was ordered, " that the lot laid out to Robert Bellow at the first brook, he shall enjoy it; he using his trade for the benefit of the towne." Mention is also made in 1664 of " Robert Ballow's brooke." See *Rhode Island Colony Records*, transcribed and edited by John Russell Bartlett, Secretary of State. Vol. i. pages 77, 83.
§ According to Savage, his wife Elizabeth, whom he married in April, 1658, was the dau. of Thomas Boylston, of Watertown, and his wife, Mary, was probably dau. of Nathaniel Treadway.

regrese for her selfe, her seruants and assignes, duringe all the time shee shall remaine a widdow and vnmarryed. Prouided, that shee at noe time take in any other dweller with her into the said House, or any roome or roomes therein, besides her child or children, and necessary seruants. I also giue to *Mary*, my said wife, her right of the thirds or dower according to the Lawe in that Case prouided. All which aboue bequeathed, I giue as aforesaid, vnto my wife, towards her Owne supply and maintenance, and the Education and bringing vp of that child or children which the Lord hath or may yet giue mee by her. Vnto my wife, one halfe of the Prouisions that shall bee in my House, when the Inuentory is taken. My will is, that after my decease, a true Inuentory bee made of my whole Estate, Whereof I giue to *John Fisher*, my Eldest sonn, a dubble Portion, that is twice soe much thereof as any one of my other children, to whome, that is to say, to my sonn *Jonathan Fisher*, and my dau. *Elizabeth Fisher*, and to that child that *Mary*, my said wife, may now be Conceiued with, to Each of them, an Equall Portion to bee paid Each of them, at that time as they shall seuerally attaine lawfull Age or day of marriage, which soeuer shall come first, only their parts in my said wiues thirds Excepted, which they are not to Enter vpon vntill after her decease. I giue vnto my sonn *John*, those Curtaines and uallance and bed and bedding thereto belonging that came by my first wife. Vnto my dau. *Elizabeth*, all her own mother's wearing cloathes, both wollen and linnen, silkes, &c. Also the Cubbert that stands in the House, I giue to my sonn *John*; and all other things that Came by my former wife, that are not in Common vse shall bee deuided between those my two Children, *John* and *Elizabeth*, and for that Estate or legacie that may yet come to my children by the guift of their Grandfathers Vnckle in England, my will is, it shall bee paid only to my two Eldest children last above named, my sonn *John* to haue a dubble portion therein because it come to them in their owne mother's right. If it please God by death to take away Either of my two children, *John* or *Elizabeth* before they attaine Lawfull Age, or marriage, then their portion shall goe, one third of it to the suruiour of them two, one third part to my Child or Children that I haue or may haue by *Mary*, my wife, the other third part to goe to the Children of my Brother *Joshua Fisher* and the children of my sister *Mary Batle*, two thirds of it to my Brother's children, one third of it to my sister's children to be diuided Amongst them, at the discretion of their Fathers or Parents. And according to that Proportion the Estate to bee diuided, if God please to take away any of my Children before they come to Lawfull Age or marriage. I ordaine my Brother, *Josuah Fisher* of Deadham, and Couzen Ensigne *Daniell Fisher*, of that Towne, to bee my Executors. I will that my mother, *Ann Fisher*, may Enjoy that part of the House my Father and shee liue in, instead of that End that now I liue in, which shee is to haue during her life, with one row of Apple Trees, as is expressed in my deed from my Father to mee. But my will is, shee should haue free Egress and regress for water, yard rome, &c. for her necessary occations if shee should rather Choose that End then the part of the House shee now liue in, which is my desire shee should Enjoy, with the benifit of halfe the orchard, I meane that part of the house wherein now shee liue. I intreat our Reverend Pastor, Mr. *John Wilson*, and my Father, *Josuah Fisher*, both of Meadfield, to bee

Ouerseers to this my will, and to be assisting to my Executors about the disposing of my two Eldest Children, to whose care and trust I Commit them to bee placed, And to provide for in Education and otherwise as the greater number shall see best for the said Children from time to time. As for that Child God hath giuen mee by Mary my wife, I leaue to her Care to prouide for, and dispose of as shee shall see best.                                                JOHN FISHER.

In presence of
*John Wilson, Samuell Bullen*, who deposed July 28, 1668.

[The two Executors having deceased, power of administration to the Estate was given to *John Fisher*, eldest son of the testator, March 4, 1683–4.]

Inventory of the estate taken by Capt. *George Barber, William Auery, Peter Woodward, Thomas Wight*, and *Henry Adams*, 9 : 5 : 1668. Am't, £344 12 5. Left. *Josuah Fisher* and Ensigne *Daniell Fisher* deposed July 28, 1668. Estate Creditor, £56 15 11½; debtor, £40. In the smith's shop, wherein the deceased was owner of one halfe in the tooles by his fathers gift, am't £20 19 6. The dwelling House and one Lento against the barne, £30 ; 4 Acres of Arable land at home, £16 ; 6½ Acres of meadow at Stop Riuer, £16 ; 5½ Acres meadow at North meadow, £16 ; 2 Acres in broad meadow, £8 ; 4 Acres of vpland in bridge street plane, £6 ; 60 Acres of Land in the new grant, £6 ; 3 Acres of Land ouer Hop Riuer, £1 10s.; 10 Acres of Swamp, £3 ; 9 Acres of Land in the new plane, £3 ; 2¼ Acres of Land by Bagestowe, £2 ; Course meadow vp-streame, £2 ; the reuersion of Houses and Lands after his father's decease, £100.

                                                (Book v. page 134–136.)

NICHOLAS ELLIN.    16 Nov. 1667.    Vnto all Concerned and also to whome they may necessarily come, grace and peace as to all the Israell of God. I, Nicholas Ellin being in present weakness of body, but in enjoyment of vnderstanding. Debts paid, my will is, that my wife, *Mary Ellin*, shall have the vse of my House and halfe the Land and Cattle and all other mouables during the term of her Widdowhood, to bring vp my youngest Children borne of her, and if shee marry, then to take Care only of that which now shee is thought to Goe with. My will is, that my wife then shall haue, mainly, when she marryes, £10 paid her and soe to remoue. My will is, that my Eldest sonn, *Daniel Ellin*, shall haue the vse of the other halfe of my House and Land and mouables together with my wife during the time of her Widdowhood. When my wife shall remoue by death or bee marryed, then her Dowry of £10 being paid, and 5s. to *Martha Pond*, and 5s. to *Mary Pond* my wiues dau. which my will is to giue to them as a Remembrance of my loue to them, then the Risidue of my Estate bee prized and Equally diuided Among them all, namely, my Children, only my Eldest sonn, *Daniel Ellin*, to haue that swamp lying at the West End of my barne, which I haue began to cleere, and his [        ] which my will that hee shall haue more then rest, and if my wife shall marry before that Child bee growne vp to get its owne liuinge, which shee is Conceiued now to bee with child of, then my will is, that shee shall haue 30s. more then the rest, and that 30s. to be paid to my wife. It is to bee vnderstood that when my Louinge wife is

332

Either marryed or Else by God's Prouidence remoued by death, that my sonn, *Daniell*, shall haue the refusing house and Land, paying the rest of my children their Equall Portions in Currant pay ; and for as much as hee is to haue the present vse of one halfe of my House and land, therefore, my will is, that halfe the portions of the Rest of the Children shall bee paid as they come to Age, by my Eldest sonn, although my wife Continue in the possession of the rest. My will is, that my wife, *Mary Ellin*, and my eldest sonn, *Daniel Ellin*, bee Executor and Executrix of this my last will. I desire my Friends *Thomas Swift* and *Samuell Wadsworth* bee Ouerseers.

NICHOLAS ⋈ ELLIN.<br>his marke.

In presence of
*William Robinson, Samuell Robinson*, who deposed May 29, 1668.

The Vissable Estate of *Nicholas Ellin*, late of Dorchester, now deceased, Esteemed by vs whose names are heere subscribed at £187 11 6. Owing about £20. Signed by *William Robinson* and *James Wadsworth*, 24 : 10 : '67. Dwelling house, barne, vpland, meadow, £117. *Daniel Ellin* and *Mary Ellin* deposed May 29, 1668.

(Book v. page 98.)

JOSEPH BUCKMINSTER. 24 Nov. 1668. Administration granted to *Elizabeth Buckminster*, relict of the late *Joseph Buckminster*, and to *Hugh Clarke*, her Father, in her behalfe, and behalfe of the children of the said *Buckminster*, the said *Hugh Clarke* giuing sufficient security, to performe the Couenants betweene the said *Joseph Buckminster* and his mother, the late *Johannah Buckminster*, now *Garfield*, and that shee haue all her Rights and dues.

## ABSTRACTS FROM THE EARLIEST WILLS ON RECORD AND ON THE FILES IN THE COUNTY OF SUFFOLK, MASS.

(Prepared by WILLIAM B. TRASK.)

RICHARD CHURCH. I, *Richard Church*, of Hingham, hauing perfect vnderstanding, yet visited by sicknes of body, order this my last will. Debts payd, then my will is, that my wife, *Elizabeth Church*, shall enjoy the Remainder during her life. And when it shall please God that shee shall leaue this life my will is, that what Estate I shall leaue to her that shall not bee necessarily Expended for her maintenance shall then bee Equally diuided amongst my children, only my sonn *Joseph* to have a dubble Portion, that is twice soe much as any of the rest of my children, by reason of the lamnes of his hand, whereby hee is disinabled above the rest of my children for the getting of a liuelihood. I ordaine my sonn *Joseph* to bee my sole Executo[r]. 25 Dec., 1668.          RICHARD ⋈ CHURCH.

In the presence of vs,
*Josuah Fisher, John Farebanck,* sen[r]*., John Farebanck,* jun[r].

26 Jan., 1668. *Josuah Fisher* and *John Farebanck*, senio[r], deposed.

Inventory of the estate, apprized by *John Thaxter*, and *Matthew Cushin*, Jan. 1, 1668. Amt. £365.14.

Mentions—dwelling house with the barne, orchard and house £110. Lott, containing six Acres, £110; halfe a tide mill, £110; his share of the iron worke at Taunton, £50; 2 Acres of Land Lying by the mill, £10.

*Joseph Church* deposed.

[The above Richard Church was father of the celebrated Benjamin Church, so distinguished by his exploits in the Indian wars.]

EDWARD BUGBY. I, Edward Bugby, being stricken in yeares and but ill in my body, not knowing how short my day may bee, in sound mind, make this my last will. Debts paid, my sonn *Joseph* shall Enjoy my Housing and Land, barne and Orchard, all that is mine, on the right hand of the Way leading to the great Lotts, and Eight Acres of Swamp and vpland, bee it more or less, lying by M[r]. *Elliots* Land, on the left hand of the way aboue said. And a Lott of Eleuen Acres, lying by *Nathaniell Brewers*, at Wake hill, and one Acre of fresh meadow, bee it more or less, lying in the Towne great meads, Two Acres of salt marsh, lying by Goodman *Watermans* marsh, in that which is called grauell point; eight Acres of vpland, lying vpon the Pond Hill, lying by the Land of *William Lyon* and *Samuell Gary*. Also, two Cowes, one Coult, and two Hoggs, that I have heretofore giuen him, and that bedding and household stuff that I have already giuen him. My will is, that my sonn, *Joseph*, shall haue this for his Portion, and he shall haue noe more of my Estate. My Will is, that

334

my dau. *Sarah*, shall haue my Tenn Acre Lott, in the first diuission and sixteene Acres lying by it, that I bought of *Edward Pason*, and twelue Acres in the Thousand Acres, and one Acree and a halfe of salt marsh lying in grauely point, by Goodman *Finçh*. My will is, that my dau. *Sarah*, shall haue that bedding and household stuffe and those Cattle that I shall leaue at my decease, and also my money and Euery thing that is mine, which I have not giuen to my sonn *Joseph* as is above expressed. My will is, that out of that which I haue giuen my dau. *Sarah*, there shall be payd my sonn in law, *Chamberlin*, the Husband of my daughter, £18 in Corne or Cattle, to two of my Grand children *Mary* and *Rebecca Chamberlin*, the one halfe of the £18 to *Mary Chamberlin*, and the other halfe to *Rebecca*. I Appoint my sonn in lawe, *Chamberlin*, my Executor. *Robert Harris, Nathaniell Bruer, John Bridge*, ouerseers. Nouember 26 : 1668.

In the p'sence of vs, EDWARD ⋈ BUGBY.

*Robt. Harris, John Bridge, Nathaniell Bruer, John Whitney.*

30 Jan., 1668. *John Bridge* and *Nathaniell Bruer* deposed.

The Estate belonging to *Edward Boogby*, of Roxbury, deceased, prized by *Robert Eares, John Bride, Benjamin Cludd*, Jan. 29, 1668. Amt. £336.06.06. 30 Jan., 1668. *Richard Chamberlaine* deposed.

JOHN SNELL. Nov. 25, 1668. I, *John Snell*, of Boston, Shipwright, being sicke but of good memory, ordaine this my last will. For my Estate in Land, House and Household stuffe, my will is, that my wife shall haue the one third part of the whole, the other two third Parts to bee diuided amongst my Fowre children, that is to say, my [?] to haue a dubble Portion, and to the rest of my Children part and part alike. As for my sonn, *John Snell*, him I doe bequeath to my Father in Lawe and mother in Lawe *James Smith* and *Jone Smith*, to bee by them Educated and brought vp in good nurture, and when Capable of a trade to bee put to, bee instructed in some honnest calling. My dau. *Susanna*, I bequeath vnto my wife. My dau. *Hannah*, I bequeath vnto my master and mⁿ. Mʳ. *Timothy Prout*, senioʳ, and *Margaret* his wife, by them and Either of them to bee Educated and brought vp in the Feare of the Lord till shee bee of full Age or marriageable which shall first happen ; and I doe intreat my said master *Timothy Prout* to demand and receiue that debt which is due to my Brother, from Mr. *Eleana Cooke*, merchant in Barbados, and by mee left in his hands, as my said master doth know of, and by my said master to bee sent home to England to my Brother *Symon Snell*. I make *Hannah Snell*, my wife, sole Executrix.

Collaterially and before signing and sealing hereof, it is hereunto added that out of my whole Estate my wife shall take Tenn pounds towards the bringing vp of my yongest daughter, *Jane Snell*; and in Case shee or Either of my before named Children dye, the portion belonging to the party or parties deceased to bee to the party suruiuing.

In p'sence of JOHN SNELL and a seale.

*Timothy Prout*, junʳ., *John King, William Pearse*, ser.

27 Jan. 1668. Mʳ. *Timothy Prout* and Mʳ. *William Pearse* deposed.

An inventory of the Estate of *John Snell*, late of Boston, Ship Carpenter, who deceased 27ᵗʰ Nov., 1668, as presented by *Hannah Snell*, Relict and Executrix. Apprised Dec. 5, 1668, by Capt. *Thomas Savage* and M$^r$. *Benjamin Gibbs* of Boston. Estate indebted to *John Farnam, Edward Mumford*, M$^r$. *Walker, Samson Shoare, Jeremiah Morrell, Symon Snell* of London. Amt. £46.06. *Hannah Snell* deposed Oct. 15, 1669.

DANIEL DOUINES. The Account of the Estate of Daniel Douines, giuen in by John Farnham, senio$^r$, Administrato$^r$ to the said Estate. Debtor, £43.17.02. Creditor £44.00.06. 3 : February, 1668. John Farnham senio$^r$ deposed.

As Attests EWD. RAWSON, *Recorder.*
The bond was Cancelled accordingly ; vide file bonds : 1662.

# ABSTRACTS FROM THE EARLIEST WILLS ON RECORD AND ON THE FILES IN THE COUNTY OF SUFFOLK, MASS.

[Prepared by WILLIAM B. TRASK.]

ANNA PALSGRAUE.—The last will and Testament of *Anna Palsgraue*, of Roxbury, Relict of *Richard Palsgraue*, formerly of Charles : Towne, made the Eleuenth of March, 1668. Whereas my late sonn *Alcock* did take into his Owne possession the two Hundred Acres of Land formerly granted by the Generall Court, vnto my late Husband, *Richard Palsgraue*, and for that my said sonn did obtaine a grant thereof from the Generall Court, which hee hath thereupon layd out with his other Lands, and the Generall Court hauing Confirmed the same vnto him, my sayd sonn, and his heires, with which I am well pleased and sattisfyed, is to preuent all future trouble thereabouts, I doe hereby giue the same vnto the heires of my sonn *Alcock*, according as hee hath disposed thereof in his will to them and their heires foreuer, they paying for the same, that is to say, I doe hereby will and appoint that those children of my said sonn *Alcocks* to whom hee hath giuen the said Two Hundred Acres shall proportionally, according to their parts thereof, pay as a legacy and token of my loue, vnto my Eldest daughter, *Mary*, the wife of *Roger Willington*, £15, to bee paid vnto her owne hands and to bee at her only dispose, and her acquittance shall bee a full discharge for the same to the Children of my sonn *Alcock*, the pay to bee made in some good pay in one or two yeares after my death. I Giue vnto my said daughter, *Mary*, my best Gowne and best Petticoate and best hood and the lace I had of Mr. *Rawson*. I also Giue vnto *Mary*, the wife of *John Maddox*, my black Gowne, all which Garments shall bee deliuered them within Three monthes after my death. I Giue vnto *Anna Alcock*, Eldest daughter of my late sonn and daughter *Alcock*, my dwelling House and Land in Boston, with all my mouables, shee paying the seauen pounds debt due from mee to *John Pattison*, in old England, and out of the same the legacy heereunder mentioned to *John Heylet*, I also hereby order to bee paid, in manner as followeth. I Giue unto *John Heylet*, Eldest sonn of my daughter *Lydia*, £20, to bee paid out of the rent of my House and Land at Boston, giuen vnto *Anna Alcock* at 40ˢ pʳ Ann. during his minority and 40ˢ more shall if my Executoʳˢ see Cause, bee also Annually paid for and towards his maintenance and keeping at schoole, yea if need requires at the judgment of my Executoʳˢ hereafter named, the full rent of the said house shall bee Expended for his Education and keeping, till hee shall bee one and twenty yeares of Age, during which time my will is, that if my truly Louinge Friend Deacon *Robt. Sanderson*, bee willing hee bee Committed vnto his Charge and Custody or otherwise at the discretion of my Executoʳ soe as hee bee brought vp to soe much Learning as that if Possible he may bee Capable for practice in Phissick. I Giue him also my medicens and instruments and all my bookes. I nominate and appoint my Honnored Friends Mᶠ. *Edward Rawson,* and Mᶠ. *John Hull,* of Boston, my Executoʳˢ, and to bestow as they shall judge best out of my Estate vpon my funerall, and any small Token of my loue not Exceeding 5ˢ. Each vnto any other of my Grandchildren or speciall Friend that shall attend the same. I nominate Deacon *Robt. Sanderson* and Deacon *Henry Allen,* both of Boston, to be Ouerseers of this my will. March 11, 1668–9. ANNA PALSGRAUE. *Samuel Danforth, John Greene,* who deposed May 13, 1669.

ANTIPAS BOYSE. I, *Antipas Boyse,* merchant, of Boston, hauing been for a long time Exercised with a lingering sicknes and much weaknes being thereby put daly in mind of my duty, make this my last will. I Commit my fraile body, after its departure to the graue, to bee decently buryed, as neere as may be, to my beloued wife. My will is, that my just debts be discharged by my freinds hereafter named, to whose faithfull loue and Care I haue Committed the Ouersight and dispose of my only sonn and beloued *Antipas Boyse,* as in this will shall bee further declared, shall bee sattisfyed and paid in the most just manner as may bee, not doubting and Earnestly desiring my said hereafter mentioned Louinge Freinds to take their best Care and with their vtmost skill and diligence to search soe into my bookes, accounts, bills, and debts owing or pretended to bee by mee owing, that my sonn *Antipas* may not in the last thereby bee injured or defrauded.

I Give vnto my servant and late well beloued wiues brother, *Samuel Hill,* as a further testimony of my loue to him, the sume of £50, to bee paid to him at the End of his time, leauinge him to my choyce and Louing Friends, to procure him a good and sutable master, to serue his remainder of time, that soe hee may not altogether loose my paines and charge I haue benn at with him, and that hee vse his vtmost Endeauʳˢ to assist my Friends in what hee may or cann, about getting in or otherwise furthering my debts owing to mee, to bee brought in and paid for the good of my Estate. I giue vnto my negro seruant, *Janemet,* next after two yeares bee Expired after my decease, hee in the meane time faithfully assisting and seruing my choyce freinds for the best Comfort and bennifit of my beloued sonn *Antipas* and his Estate, the sume of £5, and at the End of that time, freely and fully discharging him his seruitude and set him free for himselfe. I Giue for the vse and towards the building of a meeting house now a building for the new Church of Christ in Boston, the sume of £10. Vnto my Friend, Mᶠ. *Thomas Gwin,* as a Testimony of my loue for his Care and paines hee hath benn at with mee since hee came last hither, the sume of £10, in money, within one month after my decease, to bee paid by my Freinds to him, noe way doubting of his fidelity to performe his faithfull promise to satisfy his just debts to my heire or freinds, for his vse, when as God Enables him.

I Giue to my sonn, *Antipas,* my Fatherly blessing, leauing him to the Father and God of all Grace and mercy to follow him with his choysest blessing, and charge him as hee growes in yeares to looke vpon my choyce freinds hereafter named, as in my stead, to bee guided by them, and of that Estate in house, Lands, household goods, plate, money, parts of Ketches as of *Gidney* and *Offeild* and what Else debts or otherwise any way due to mee. I Giue the whole, Except ᵥₕₐₜ in this my will shall bee bequeathed, to Enjoy to him and his heires fur-

338

euer, making him sole Executor, and both him and his Estate to bee at the whole dispose of my Freinds, Capt. *William Dauis*, Mᴿ. *Thomas Brattle*, Mᴿ. *John Joylife*, my Couzen *John Rowe* and *Edward Rawson* during the time of his minority, for his best Education, good and Comfort, whilst hee is in this Country, i. e. two yeares after my decease. And then if my vnckle, Mᴿ. *Robt. Row*, of Ratlife, neere London, merchant bee aliue, and Continue his Louinge desire to haue and Entertaine my sonn, *Antipas*, for his bringing vp and good Education, my said sonn io bee sent to him. And my said Freinds are hereby fully impowred as Ouerseers to this my last will, or the major part of them, agreeing to sell my said House and Lands, parts of 'uessels and Else making the most of them in ready money, soe that it may by bills of Exchange, or otherwise, in the best manner returned to their Order in England, to bee deliuered vnto my said Vnckle, as my said sonn, *Antipas*, his Portion, on my said vnckles giuing them or their Order sufficient security for the improuement and management of the said Estate during the minority, and when hee is of Age to surrender vp the same to them or their Order for the deliuery thereof to my sonn, from whom they and himselfe may receiue a full discharge ; and in Case it should please the Lord to take away my sonn before hee attaine to full Age of Twenty one yeares or day of marriage, with the Consent of his and my freinds then alive, then I bequeath vnto my Couzen, *John Rowe*, what Euer may then bee Comminge due to my sonn had hee liued, &c. to Enjoy to him, the said *John Rowe* and his heires foreuer. In Case of *John Rows* decease before hee come to the Enjoyment thereof, then I Giue all that his Brother John Rowe should haue had, to my Couzen *Robt. Rowe* and his heires, and in Case of his death to my Couzen *Jesop Rowe* and his heires. [He gives £5 a piece to the overseers of his will. The charge of his burial is not to exceed £60.] I Giue vnto my noble freind, major Generall *John Leuerett*, a Gold ring of 20s. to weare for my sake, as a small Testimony of my Thanckful Acknowledgment of his Loue. 3d July, 1669.

In the presence of Aɴᴛɪᴘᴀs Bᴏʏsᴇ.
*Thomas Smith, James Hill, John Saunders.*

18 August, 1669. *James Hill* and *Thomas Smith* deposed.

Capt. *Wm. Dauis, John Joylife*, Mᴿ. *John Rowe* and *Edward Rawson*, appearing in Court, declared their acceptance of the trust reposed on them. *Edw : Rawson*, Recordᴿ.

Inventory of the Estate taken by Capᵗ. *Thomas Sauage*, Mᴿ. *Hezekiah Vsher*, Mᴿ. *Peter Oliuer*, Aug. 4, 1669. Amt. £1708 10 03.

Among his " siluer peeces of plate," one Cawdell Cup and Porringer, 2 Lilly Pots with Couers, Large whissell, Currall and chaine with 7 bells, &c.


Rɪᴄʜᴀʀᴅ Cʜᴀᴘᴍᴀɴ. The last will and Testament of *Richard Chapman*, senioʳ, being in his perfect vnderstanding and scnce liuely, I doe will and bequeath vnto my sonn *Richard Chapman*, junioʳ and his Children, after my decease and my wiues, all my whole Estate for his owne proper vse and the vse of his Children foreuer, whereunto I set my hand this 9: 1: 1668: 69. Rɪᴄʜᴀʀᴅ ᴍ Cʜᴀᴘᴍᴀɴ

In the pʳsence of vs his marke.
*Allexander Plumb, Joseph Arnold.*

26 Aug., 1669. *Allexander Plumb* deposed to the above will of *Richard Chapman*, late of Braintry.

Power of Adminstration granted to *Joane*, his Relict, and *Richard*, his sonn, to performe the imperfect will aboue written.

*Edw: Rawson*, Record<sup>r</sup>.

Inventory of the Estate taken 9 : 6 : 1669. Testified by *Francis Elliott, John French*. Amt. £32 01 06.

22 Aug., 1669. *Joane Chapman*, Relict, and *Richard Chapman*, junior, deposed.

SAMUEL ALLEN. August 2, 1669. The last will and Testament of *Samuel Allen*, of Braintry, in the County of Suffolke in New England, being uery weake in Body, yet of perfect memory and vnderstanding. What debts I owe, be paid with as much speed as may bee conuenient. I Giue vnto my sonn, *Samuell Allen*, £20, to bee paid him or his out of my Estate, £10 within one yeare after my decease, and £10 within three yeares after the first payment bee made. Vnto my sonn *James Allen*, £5, to be paid him or his within three yeares after my decease. Vnto my sonn-in-law, *Josiah Standish*, £10, to bee paid him or his, £5 within one yeare after my decease, and the other £5 within two yeares after the first payment bee made. Vnto my sonn-in-law *Nathaniel Greenwood*, £5, to bee paid him or his within three yeares after my decease. Vnto my dau. *Abigall*, £30, to bee paid vnto her when shee shall bee at the Age of 21 yeares. The rest of my Estate, as House and land and what Else remains, I leave betweene my beloved wife and my sonn, *Joseph Allen*, that is to say, that my wife shall haue halfe the bennifit of House and land and what Euer Estate may bee left after the discharge of the legacies, during her life, and the other halfe to my sonn *Joseph*. Prouided they both joyne together in what is necessary for the support of such as are left in the family. My will is, that if my sonn *Joseph* shall marry where his thoughts haue first binn, that what Estate hee hath shall remaine to his Children. If it please God hee die without issue, his Estate, after his wiues Death, shall returne to my Children. My will is, that my wife shall haue liberty to Giue vnto any of her Children to the whole uallue of £10, where she shall see need. I make my wife, and my sonn *Joseph*, my Executrix and Executo<sup>r</sup> of this my will—wittnes the hand of

SAMUEL ALLEN.

Wittnes : *Francis Elliot, Thomas Holbrook, John French*.

16 Sept., 1669. *Francis Elliot* and *John French* deposed.

Inventory of the Estate taken 6th mo. 27th day, 1669, by *Francis Elliott, John French*. Amt. £228 12 09.

16 September, 1669. *Margaret Allen* Executrix, and *Joseph Allen* the eldest sonn, Executor to the last will of *Samuel Allen*, deposed.

TOBIAS PAINE. Will No. 4. What I haue heere in money or Goods, what shall come in from any other place as debts and Aduentures, what is due from mee being first made good and moderate, funerall Expences discharged, I doe hereby Giue vnto youre daughter my wife and to our little sonn, to whose Care, Charge and Education I leaue him, Enjoyning her in Case shee marries againe that hee may not bee abused or wronged, but duly taken Care for, which I hope also you will mind if it happens during your life.

21 Sept., 1669. M[r]. *John Winslow* deposed, that hee heard his late sonn-in-Lawe, M[r]. *Tobias Paine*, on the 11th instant, to declare it to bee his mind and last will, and that hee was of a sound disposing mind ; hee departed this life the 12 instant.

As Attests, *Edw. Rawson*, Record[r].

This is a true Copie of the late *Tobias Payne*, his 24[th] instruction, to which M[r]. *John Winslow* deposed, as is aboue, and Annext to his Administration, and this left in stead of the Originall. As attests,

EDWARD RAWSON, Recorder.

21 Sept., 1669. Power of Administration to the Estate of the late M[r]. *Tobias Paine*, deceased, is Granted to *Sarah Paine*, his relict, in behalfe of her selfe and the sonn of the said *Tobias* and *Sarah* (*William Paine*), to performe the imperfect will of the said *Tobias*, as it is truly transcribed out of the Originall, and Annext out of the Originall, wherein hee left instructions for his Father-in-Law, and that shee giue security to Administer thereupon according to Law, bringing in a true Inventory of that Estate into the Court.

By Order : *Edw. Rawson*, Record[r].

ABSTRACTS FROM THE EARLIEST WILLS ON RECORD AND ON THE FILES IN THE COUNTY OF SUFFOLK, MASS.

[Prepared by WILLIAM B. TRASK.]

ELIZABETH BITFEILD. The last will and Testament of *Elizabeth Bitfeild*, Widdow,* being in her right and perfect memory, this 13th of the 11th month, 1663. To my sister *Crowne*, £20 ; to my sister *Mar-*

---

* Savage says Samuel Bitfield, constable, Boston, in 1652, died 1 Sept. 1660, leaving widow Elizabeth. In *Drake's* Boston, p. 250, we find, that Feb. 24, 1640, 20 acres of land were allotted Samuel Bitfield, for 5 heads.

*garet Parker*, £20. If either of my sisters die first, the last suruiuo[r] shall Receiue the other £20. In case both my sisters die before mee, then my will is, that £20 of it shall goe to *Ann Jeffryes* Children that bee not Quakers. The other £20 to my Cozen, *Katherine Darke*, her children. This to bee paid to them within seauen yeares after my death, if they send for it within that time specifyed after their first intelligence after my death. Vnto M[r]. *Thomson*, £5; vnto M[r]. *Flint*, I give £5 in money. To the Church of Boston, £10; vnto *John Steuens and Samuell Steuens*, £5 between them; vnto *William Titcomes* children, £5 to bee Equally diuided Amongst them; to *Samuell Plummer's* children, £10, to bee Equally diuided amongst them. To Deacon *Marshall*, 50s.; to *William Dinsdall*, 50 shillings. Elder *James Penn*, of Boston, to bee my Executo[r], *John Sunderland* and *Godfrey Armitage*, Ouerseers, and as a token of my loue doe Giue them 50s. apeece. To my dau. *Mary Plummer*, £10; to my dau. *Elizabeth Titcomb*, £10, to bee paid in money; to *James Mattock*, £3; to M[r]. *Wilford*, £5; to M[r]. Allen, £5; to *Sam: Armitage*, 20 shillings.

ELIZABETH BITFEILD.

Wittnes hereunto—*Thomas Cox, Joseph Pease,* [*sic.*]

Proved—Sept. 23, 1669. *Joseph Pearse* deposed.

Inventory of the Goods of Widdow Bitfeild deceased the 30[th] of the 7[th] month, 1669, and what shee gaue away by word of mouth on her death bed since her will was made. Taken by *John Search* and *William Read*, 20[th]: 7: 1669.

23 Sept., 1669. Elder *James Penn* deposed.

THOMAS WOODWARD. 15 Aprill, 1669. M[r]. *Henry Taylor* Appeared before the magistrates and Recorder and Acquainted them that the late M[r]. *Thomas Woodward*, of Neuis, deceased, as Appeares by the letter of *Walter Symonds*, of the said Neuis, dated the 10[th] of December, 1668, and produced a bill of Lading, Containing Certaine Goods of the said Woodwards, and an account of the said Goods vnder his hands, said *Taylor* desiring it, Power of Administration to the Estate of the said *Thomas Woodward*, as it lyes and is within the Jurisdiction of this Court, is granted to the said *Henry Taylor*, to sattisfy what just debts shall Appeare to the Court that the said *Thomas Woodward*, or his late wife, Contracted in these parts, and in behalfe of such as shall Appeare to have most right to the said Estate, bringing. in a true Inuentory of the said Estate into this Court, and giuing security to Administer hereupon according to Law.

EDW: RAWSON, Record[r].

THOMAS SNOW. The last Will and Testament of *Thomas Snow*, of Boston, although weake in Body, yet of perfect memory, my Will is, that I leaue all my Estate, after my debts are paid, to my beloued wife, *Milcha Snow*, to bee disposed of according to her discretion, soe long as shee liues to haue the vse of, and after her decease that which is left to bee disposed of according to her discretion amongst my children, and my will further is, that my wife shall be my sole Executrix. My desire is, that my beloued Brethren, M[r]. *Edward Belcher, Edward Rainsford, Theophilus Frary,* and *Jacob Elliott* be the Ouerseers of this my last will and Testament. Wittnes my hand the 10[th] day of November, 1668. The marke of THOMAS T SNOW.

Wittnes: *Mary Lane, Timothy Harkman,* who deposed April 28, 1669.

Inventory of the Goods and Chattles of the late *Thomas Snow,* of Boston, deceased, taken the 13: March, 1668–9, by *William Davis, Peter Olliuer.*

The new and old dwelling House and all the Land belonging thereto, £200. Whole amt. of Inventory £239 4.

An Inventory of Debts to be paid cut of the Estate to M$^r$. *Samuell Shrimpton,* in money, £100 ; to Goodman *Swift,* of Dorchester, for malt, £3 05 ; to *Edward Crowell,* for boards, £1 16 ; Goodman *Howard,* of Deadham, for hoops, £1 ; to Ensign *Dauis,* of Roxbury, for wood, £1 12 ; to *Timothy Horton,* for seruis, £2 ; to M$^r$. *Belcher,* 5s. ; *Samuell Mason,* 7s. ; M$^r$. *Stoddard,* 6s. 6d. ; M$^r$. *Holloway,* 9s. To Excise, which is yet owing out of my husbands Estate, and our Custome not affoarding it must be pd. out of stock w$^{cb}$ is more then Cann be done, about £7.

*Milca Snow* deposed, 28 Aprill, 1669.

Samuell Poole. *Edward Bates,* aged sixty Three yeares or there-abouts, and *Mary Raines,* aged about Twenty-eight yeares, sworne, say that being present with *Samuell Poole,* of Weymouth, when hee lay vpon his death bed, hee did declare, being of a disposing mind, vnto vs as followeth : That his will was, that his wife should haue all his Estate Reall, and Personall, vntill his daughter *Mary* came of Age or was married. That at the time of Age or marriage his dau. should haue halfe of the whole aforesaid Estate, and at the death of her mother shee should haue the whole. In Case the dau. dye before Age or marriage, his will was, his wife should Pay his Brother, *Benjamin Poole,* £3.

Aprill 30, 1669. Elder *Edward Bates* and *Mary Raines* deposed.

Inventory of the Estate taken by *Edw: Bate, John Holbrooke,* 29 : 1 mo., 1669. Amt. £74 12. Mentions the dwelling house and the out-housing with the Land adjoyning to it, £50 ; 2 acres fresh marsh, £3. &c. &c.

30 Aprill, 1669. Power of Administration to the Estate of the late *Samuell Poole* is granted to *Mary Poole,* his Relict, in behalfe of hir selfe and Child to perform the non-Cupative will now proued in Court.

*Mary Poole* deposed. Ewd: Rawson, Record$^r$.

Richard Mather. The will of Rev. Richard Mather, of Dorchester, is given entire in this number.

Boniface Burton. I, *Boniface Burton,* being in some indisposition of Body, but through the Lord's mercy in good memory and vnder-standing, declare this to bee my last will. My body to bee decently interred by my wife, *Francis Burton,* whome I make sole Executrix. To M$^r$. *Increase Mather,* 10s. ; to my neece, wife to *Samuell Bennett,* one shilling ; to her Husband, *Samuell Bennet* and to Every one of his Children, Foure pence, Each one of them, the which legacies are to bee paid within one month after my departure. The rest of my Estate I Giue to my wife, *Francis Burton.*

his marke.

21 Feb., 1666–7.    her marke.    Bonniface ✛ Burton.

Wittnes : *Henry Phillips, Sarah* ✛ *Shelly.*

24$^{th}$ June, 1669. *Henry Phillips* and *Sarah Shelly* deposed.

[In the *Register*, Vol. xvi. page 367, we gave copies of two Wills of Richard Fitch, of Boston, from the originals in possession of the Society. They were published partly as a matter of curiosity, both being on the same sheet of paper, and bearing dates within thirteen days of each other, and in part to settle the fact, that Richard was brother to James Fitch, of Muddy River. Mr. Savage says he was "perhaps brother of James," that James had "Elizabeth, bapt. 15 May, 1636 ; and I find no more of him, but that he was of Muddy river, 1638." The second will, above referred to, says, "I giue to *Elizabeth Fitch*, y° onely daughter of my brother *James Fitch*, deceased [this was 29th, 12 mo., 1645], the sixteene acres of land (be it more or lesse) W$^{ch}$ I haue at Muddy River." We have no evidence that either of the wills was acted upon, neither do we find them recorded.

But the chief object of these paragraphs is to draw attention to the fact, that both the wills of Richard Fitch were witnessed by Boniface Burton, in his own hand writing. Was he the farmer of Lynn, who died June 13, 1669, according to Sewall, at the age of 113 years ? If so, he must have been about 90 years of age when he signed his name, and the signature is remarkably good for a person of that age. See Mr. Savage's remarks in his *Dictionary*, under Burton ; Lewis's *Lynn*, pp. 59, 63 ; Drake's *Hist. of Boston*, p. 386 ; Diary of John Hull in the Transactions of American Antiq. Soc. iii. 229. According to the latter authority, Mr. Burton was, at his decease, 115 years old. The other age mentioned would make him in his 80th year when made freeman, in 1635.

In the list of early settlers of Reading and South Reading, Mass., from 1640 to 1700, printed in the *Register*, Vol. ii. p. 46, is Boniface Burton. Lewis, in his History of Lynn (p. 109), under date of Sept. 7, 1639, says, "Another grant of land was made to the town by the General Court," on "petition of the inhabitants of Lynn, for a place for an inland plantation," "4 miles square," "at the head of their bounds." "The settlement thus begun was called Lynn Village, and included Reading, South Reading, and North Reading."]

# ABSTRACTS OF THE EARLIEST WILLS ON RECORD, OR ON THE FILES IN THE COUNTY OF SUFFOLK, MASSACHUSETTS.

Prepared by WILLIAM B. TRASK, Esq., of Boston.

THIS series of abstracts was commenced by the late SAMUEL G. DRAKE, A.M., in the first number of the REGISTER edited by him (January, 1848, vol. ii. p. 102), and was continued by Mr. D. to July, 1851 (vol. v. p. |297). The writer began his abstracts of wills, inventories, &c., with the will of James Bate, of Dorchester, printed on the last named page. The volume of the REGISTER for 1853 (vii.) contains more than thirty-one pages devoted to unrecorded wills and inventories, being upwards of a hundred in number, which were taken from the Suffolk files. The abstracts in all the other volumes before and after the above date, with, it may be, one or two exceptions, are from the records, but occasionally corrected by the files. An attempt was made in the year above mentioned to copy these papers from the files, chronologically, but they were then in a very disordered state, a difference occurring, sometimes, of a century or so in the same bundle. Often the wills and inventories belonging to one estate were separated from each other, as though they had no family connection. Not unfrequently they were wrongly labelled, and the names written on the backs in some cases were as far from the real names given on the documents inside as can well be imagined. Under these circumstances it was considered too great a labor to carry out the plan as contemplated, consequently it was only in part fulfilled. But recently these files, down to a late date, have been carefully arranged, and the good work is still in progress. The papers have been placed in tin boxes, sometimes a hundred or more files in a box, suitably enveloped, labelled and numbered. Indices and dockets have been made, evidently with great care, and the volumes containing them have been substantially bound. The facilities, therefore, now afforded for consulting these documents are of the best kind, creditable alike to the city and county, and to those who arranged and carried out the work.

We have accordingly recommenced giving abstracts, and in some instances copies of the entire papers from these early files, omitted in 1853, being matter not on record, unless so stated.

OLIVER MELLOWES.[1]—Inventory of the outward Estate of Mr Olyvar Mellowes deceased, taken y⁸ 12th day of y⁸ 9ᵗʰ Month Called November 1638.

Elizabeth Mellowes was granted administration 5ᵗʰ 10th 1638.

[1] Oliver Mellowes and wife Elizabeth admitted to the Church in Boston, July 20, 1634. He was made freeman on the 3d of Sept. following; was one of the 59 Boston men who were disarmed in 1637, as "opinionists," or supporters of Wheelwright. See Court Records, i. 211.
His widow, Elizabeth, m. Thomas Makepeace of Dorchester. She was his second wife. On the Records of the First Church, Boston, according to the "*Makepeace Family*," page 11, is the following entry.—" The 25th day of yᵉ 5th Mon. 1641, Mrs. Elizabeth Makepeace, lately called Mrs. Elizabeth Mellowes, but now yᵉ wife of Mr. Makepeace, of Dorchester, was granted l're of Recommendation thether."

*See p. 1.
**See p. 47.

Mentions dwelling house, garding, & ground about it, 50℔; 6 acres of planting ground on the necke, 25℔; 5 acres of wood land & 8 acres of marsh att Hogg island, 4℔; Lott att Mount Woollystone conteyning 80 Acres, 20℔. Whole amount of inventory 190.19ˢ. Signed by Atherton Haughe, Tho Leueritt, Will Colbron. More in Corne 20℔. Deposed by said Elizabeth, 17th, 12th mo. 1638. before vs, Jo: Winthrop Gou', Increase Nowell. (File No. 9, Suffolk Wills.)

JOHN LOVERING.[1]—Will. October the 4, 1638, that John loueren of water towne being sicke in boody did mak his will as folloeth. first I giue to my wif Ann lovern all my hoole Estat of goods and all that I haue and my mynd is that thar shall be payd ought of my Estat After my wifes death twenty poundes to the Church of watertowne to Remayn for a stoak and one hundered pounds to my brother in England which hath childeren.

   witnes
     Edward Howe,
     Margret How.

The 24th of the 9ᵗʰ m° 1638 Edward & Margaret How appeared before mee Incr: Nowell & tooke their oaths that this is a true Coppey of the will of John Loveren.     witnes my hand,     pᵣ Increase Nowe ll.
(File No. 13. The above is a copy of the paper entire.)

JUDITH SMEAD.[2]—An Inventory of the goods of the weadow Smead deseassed, taken the 18ᵗʰ day of the 3 mounth 1639. "My selfe had as followeth"—(various utensils, household goods, produce, &c., mentioned), "I haue had for Commones of Mʳ Joanes, £4.; of goodman Bird for the house & lot & Corne, £30; for Necke of land of Mr Joanes, £5.5." The names introduced, to whom various household articles were given, are those of John Pope, Sumner, Gibson, goodman Tomkins,[3] Mʳ Payne, Brother Knight,[4] sister vrsilah, Johnson, Joanes, goodman Juets[5] wife; vyolette coat

---

[1] John Lovering, of Watertown, was made freeman, May 25, 1636'; according to Savage was from Dedham, Co. Essex, Eng.; a selectman in 1636 and·7, a grantee of 9 lots in Watertown, all large in proportion to most others. His homestall, of 40 acres, was bounded S. by the river; E. by E. Child; W. by J. Benjamin; N. by highway. After Mr. Lovering's death, his widow, Anna, became the wife of the Rev. Edmund Browne, the first minister of Sudbury. She was probably a sister of John Barnard, Sen., of Watertown. He is doubtless the Loverell of Watertown, who was allowed by the General Court, in 1637-8, to sell in W. "wine and strong water made in the country, and no other strong water is to bee sould.'" See the testimony of Elizabeth Child and others, REGISTER, iii. 79, in regard to the will * and effects of "John Lovran," or "Loveran," as he is there and elsewhere called.—*Bond's Watertown, Barry's Framingham, Court Records.*
See also abstracts of papers on file at East Cambridge, relative to Thomas Loverin, of Watertown, in the REGISTER for October, 1864, *ante* xviii. 338.
[2] Judith Smead joined the church in Dorchester about the year 1636; had 20 acres of land granted her below the burying place in D. in 1638. It is stated by Savage, that she was a sister to Israel Stoughton. Although she died in or before the year 1639, her estate was not settled until March, 1657-8. Israel Stoughton, Administrator. See REGISTER, ix. 344. **
[3] Ralph Tompkins, of Dorchester, freeman May 2, 1638, removed to Salem some nine or ten years afterwards. Inventory of his estate taken there, Nov. 12, 1666.
[4] John Knight, in September, 1634, with eight or nine others, had a grant of land from the town of Dorchester of 3 acres each upon the Neponset river. Also in November of the same year, "John Knite" had 6 acres allotted him, with 12 others, for "their small and great lotts at Naponset betwixt the Indian feild and the mill," Stoughton's mill. See REGISTER, xxi. 274, 276.
In 1642 he was proprietor of lands in Watertown, and in 1651-2, with his wife Mary, sold to Thomas Underwood, late of Dorchester, ten parcels of land in Watertown. See *Bond's Watertown*, 328.
[5] Joseph Jewett, of Dorchester, had wife Mary; removed to Rowley; was freeman May 22, 1639, representative 1651-4 and '60; died Feb. 26, 1660. His second wife was Ann, widow of Bozoan Allen, whom he married in May, 1653.
*See p. 21.
**See p. 164.

to goodman Oldreges;[1] Swift, bro. Kinslie,[2] Mr. Newman,[3] White, sister Clarke, Oliver Purchase, Butler, Thomas Bird, brother Clarke, Mr. Mathers maide, Mr Palsgraue, John Dorman for stockines and shoos, clothes to his master, to goe forth with him, £13.06.08; payd goodman Pope with the boy,[4] £32; payed towards clothing of Mary, £1.10.03; payed John Scudder, 10[s]; payed for bloodding, 1[s]; payed for other charges of wine & cake, £1. Articles to the amount of £8.15.10 are given as "Things I know not who had as they are still in being." "debts payed by me on my sisters Account," &c. (File No. 15.)

RICHARD CRUSE.[5]—This is a true a cont or in ventory of the estate of Richard Cruse [which consisted chiefly of wearing apparel. Mentions, also, one cheste, one bybel, &c.] Amt. £1. 4. Signed by Simmon Rogers, the marke of Richard × grigley. 29. 2. 1640. (File No. 18.)

ROBERT HUNT.[6]—Will. The last will and Testament of Robert Hunt, late of Sudbury in the County of Hampton,[7] Yeoman, &c. As followeth. Imprimis I Comit and comend my Soule into the hands of Allmighty God my Creato', And my body to bee buryed in a deacent and comely maner.

Itm. I doe by this my last will and Testament make Constitute and ordeine Susana my deare and welbeloved wife, my sole executor For possessing inioying and improueing of all my Estate Temporallse Lands Howses Tenements Chatells debts or goods moueable or immoueable For the sol vse benifit and Subsistance of her my sd wiffe and all my Children to bee at her disposall dureing the time of her widdowhoode or single estate.

Itm. my will is That if the sd Susan my wiffe shall not Continue her widdows estate but Marry and therby allter her condicon That then my Estate be deuided equally into Fowre parts the one of w[ch] parts thus deuided shall belong vnto her my sd wiffe as her proper estate and Legacy and the other Three parts of my sd Estate to bee deuided equally among my Children then liuieng unmaryed or vnder age.

[1] George Aldrich, or Aldridge, had wife Catherine; freeman Dec. 7, 1636; was afterwards of Braintree, and in 1663 became one of the first settlers of Mendon.

[2] John Kinsley, or Kingsley, was in Dorchester before the arrival of Richard Mather; had a grant of land in 1635; was one of the seven signers of the covenant in 1636, when the church was newly organized and Mr. Mather became pastor. Mr. Kinsley married Alice, widow of Richard Jones, of Dorchester. The latter died in 1641.

[3] The celebrated Rev. Samuel Newman, author of the Concordance, subsequently of Weymouth, then of Rehoboth, where he died July 5, 1663, aged 61 years. See abstract of his will, REGISTER, vi. 96.

[4] This was William Smead, her son, who is spoken of in John Pope's will (12: 2: 1646), as "my Littell boy" to whom Mr. Pope leaves his "Lomes, and such Tackling as do belong vnto them, which is to the vallew of 3lb. provided he be willing to dwell with my wife after his time is out, also provided he be willing to Learn my Trad, and that there be a comfortable Agreement mad betweene the[m] Afterward. See REGISTER, vii. 229. *

[5] The name of Cruse may be found in Paver's list of Matches or Alliances, Yorkshire pedigrees, REGISTER, xi. 265. See Burke's Encyclopedia of Heraldry for description of Coats of Arms of the Devonshire and other Cruse families.

[6] Robert Hunt, of Sudbury, was admitted an inhabitant of Charlestown, 1638. An inventory of Mrs. Susan Hunt, of Soodherie, probably his widow, taken 24: 9: 1642, is given in REGISTER, vii. 32. **

[7] John Hunt, of Sudburowe, Northamptonshire, England, husbandman. Will dated Sept 1, 1623; proved Oct. 6, 1623. Sister Alice, wife of Thomas Hunt, of Islip. Sister Helen, wife of John Fowler. Sons-in-law James Hornby, Thomas Carrington and Thomas Foster. Brother-in-law Robert Simpson. (See Hunt genealogy, by Thomas B. Wyman, pages 5, 137.)

*Sudborough,* *Sudborow,* or as it is called in Domesday Book, *Sutburge,* is in the Hundred of Huxlow or Huxloe, sometimes Hocheslaw, and Hochesland, in Northamptonshire, England. It is 4½ miles northwest from Thrapstone. The church is dedicated to All Saints. (See Lewis's *Topographical Dictionary of England.*)

*See p. 102.

**See p. 87.

Itm. I doe will and declare that if any of my sd Children shall in the meane time (dureing the widdowhoode or single estate of my sd wiffe) ateine to the age of Twenty and one yeares or shall hapen to Marry That then at the time of theire age of Twenty and one yeares or vppon theire day of marriage which of them first shall happen: my estate: that is to say Three parts of the aforesd Fowre be equally deuided by estemacōn among the Children then liueing and that a part proportionable thervnto bee giuen in preasent possession vnto that Child as his or her property dowry and portion and For their proper vse and benifit.

Itm. I doe will and ordeine my trusty and well beloued Friends [blank] Sedgwick and [blank] Lyne of Charles Towne in New England my ouerseers For the due performance and execution of this my last will and Testament giueing them Full power and authoryty as I my selfe to ouerveiue and see the well ordering and manageing and improueing of all my afforsd estate to preuent the vnlawfull Embezelling or makeing of it away from the vse and benifit of my wife and Children: allsoe vppon the seuerall times seasons and occations aboue specifyed to deuide and alot vnto eatch person theire seuerall porsions, as allsoe if my sd wife shall depart this preasent life or allter her Condicon by mariage to take soe many of my Children as are liueing vnder age and so dispose of them seueraly wᵗʰ their portions as feofeers in trust, and my will is that what soeuer Charge or paines they are at shalbe made good vnto them by my estate to theire Full satisfacon: and this doe I confirme by my hand and seale the second day of October in the yeare of Lord one Thousand Six Hundred and Forty.

Witnessed by               pr me ROBERT HUNT.
Ro. Fordham
John Tinker           (File No. 20. The above Will given entire.)
Thomas Bacon

SAMUEL HOLLY.—An abstract of the will of Samuel Holly is printed in the REGISTER, ii. 385, from the Record, page 30. He gives to his son one * "Black Stuffe suit," instead of blue, as mentioned in the REGISTER. Samuell Hollye makes his mark, and the name of Renolt bvsh, between the names of John Jackson and Edward Jackson, is given as a witness to the original will. From the inventory we learn that he died "in yᵉ bounds of Cambridge." On the back of the instrument are the names of Frances Gould, Will Almey, David Williams, Jo. Barcher. (File No. 26.)

DANIEL SHEPERDSON.[1]—Inventory of the Howsing, Lands, Goods,[1] Cattell and Chattells that belonged vnto Daniell Shepherdson, deceased in Charltowne, which inventory was taken the 25ᵗʰ of the 3ᵈ Moneth 1647. Amt £49. 17. 00.
     Witnesses and prisers.
     John Greene
     Faithfull Rouse[2]
Other articles enumerated to which John Greene deposed 27 : 3 : 1647.
                         INCREASE NOWELL, Sec.
                         (File No. 28.)

---

[1] Abstract of his Will in REGISTER, vii. 32. (See p. 87).
[2] Faithfull Rouse and his wife Suretrust joined the church in Charlestown, the wife in 1642, and the husband the year after. He died May 18, 1664, aged 75.
*See p. 17.

# ABSTRACTS OF THE EARLIEST WILLS ON RECORD, OR ON THE FILES IN THE COUNTY OF SUFFOLK, MASSACHUSETTS.

Prepared by William B. Trask, Esq., of Boston.

Richard Barbour.[1]—Inventory of the house, lands and goods of Richard Barbour deceased taken and apprised by Henry Chickering, Samuell Morse and Nathan Aldous,[2] 15. 1mo. 1644. The house and lands, £18. Amount of inventory, £30. 03. 09. See abstract of the Will of Richard Barbour, Register, iii. 178. (See p. 26). (File No. 33.)

Jeffery Stapell.—A True Inuentory of the goods of Jeffery Stapell latte deseased valewed By Eaderd Batts [Bates] and John vppame,[3] in the fyrst month 1647. On house with 8 ackers of land. 12. 0. 0 ; wearinge aparell, Bedinge, Brass vesells, puttor, Iron, workinge Toolls, Earthen vesels, woodene things, goatts and a Callf, Debts Dew, swyne. Sume is, 34. 7. 2. Edward Bate, John vppame. (File No. 58½.)

[Jeffrey Staples, or Staple, of Weymouth, had Martha, buried Feb. 17, 1640. *Savage.*]

Thomas Lechford.—An in ventory of the goods of Tho: Leatchford,[4] deceased, valued by Robert hull and James Johnson acording to theire best Judgment & Consience.

| | | | | | |
|---|---|---|---|---|---|
| 3 day | Imp^r 4 paire sheetes one p' | | 01 | 10 | 00 |
| 3 mo. | | 2 paire | 01 | 00 | 00 |
| 1648. | | 3 paire | 00 | 16 | 00 |
| | | 4 paire | 0 | 10 | 00 |
| | It. foure paire of pillow beares | | 0 | 13 | 06 |
| | It 4 table cloathes | | 00 | 07 | 06 |
| | It 14 table napkines | | 00 | 07 | 06 |
| | It 6 old towels | | 00 | 01 | 04 |
| | It two old cloathes | | 00 | 00 | 06 |
| | It one glass | | 00 | 01 | 00 |
| | It one Pillow | | 00 | 04 | 00 |
| | It an old cloake badge & seuerall small things in it, but all valued at | | 00 | 06 | 00 |
| | It A cap 8' & a bible 6' | | 0 | 14 | 00 |
| | It A chest | | 00 | 02 | 06 |
| | | | 06 | 13 | 10 |

lett^s ad colligendum bona defuncti are granted to Rob^t Hull

Robert Hull
James Johnson.

[1] Richard Barbour, or Barber, of Dedham, was freeman May 13, 1640. He was one of the 68 original proprietors of Lands in Dedham, to whom was granted 6. 12mo. 1642, "upland ground fit for improvement with the plough." He died June 18, 1644, leaving probably no near connections, as he gives his house, lands and goods in Dedham to his executors, Henry Brock and his son John Brock.
[2] Nathan Aldis, one of the first two deacons of the church in Dedham.
[3] John Upham removed from Weymouth to Malden about 1650.
[4] Incorrectly *Fratchford*, Register, vii. 175. (See p. 98).

M<sup>r</sup> Samu: Wilbore did depose that when he married the widow of Tho: Lechford late of Boston scriv. deceased, he never received or had any of the Widow or other estate of the s<sup>d</sup> Lechford no not so muche as his s<sup>d</sup> wiues wearinge apparell, taken vpon Oath before the Court   Incr. Nowell, Sec<sup>ry</sup>
2 (3) 48          (File No. 71.)

NOTE.—The Hon. J. Hammond Trumbull, of Hartford, Conn., who so ably edited and annotated an edition of Lechford's "Plaine Dealing: or, News from New-England," in 1867, has the following in his introduction to that work (page xviii.), relative to the wife of Lechford. "His wife is mentioned in 1639 and afterwards; and, as no evidence has been discovered of his marriage on this side of the water, we infer that she accompanied him from England; but he nowhere gives any information of her family, nor even introduces her Christian name. In July, 1640, he writes: 'I have not yet here an house of my owne to put my head in, or any stock going.' He lived in a house, or part of a house, hired of Nathaniel Micklethwaite of Boston, who was, I think, the agent or factor in New-England of Richard Hutchinson of London, and perhaps of Edward and William Hutchinson after their removal to Rhode Island. It appears that he paid his rent, until August, 1639, to Samuel Hutchinson, and subsequently to Mr. Micklethwaite, whose signature appears, on a page of the journal, to the lease of 'the chamber, etc.,' at £5 per year, from Sept. 1, 1639." He borrowed from Mr. Story, as we learn from the journal, in 1639, two and a half pounds "of the best suger," at 2 shillings a pound, received "of Mr. Keayne for a silver laced coate and a gold wrought cap, £2. 10s.," had also "of Mr. George Story" some holland for his wife's waistcoat, etc. He mentions his wife again in 1640, and also in 1641. He embarked from Boston for England, and sailed on the 3d of August of that year, in company with John Winthrop, Jr., Hugh Peters, Thomas Welde, William Hibbins and others. There were forty passengers, according to Gov. Winthrop, in all. The preface to his book was written from "Clements Inne, Jan. 17, 1641," that is 1641-2, and the work, itself, was printed in London in 1642. Rev. John Cotton, in his *Way of Congregational Churches cleared*, pt. 1, p. 71, says, "When he came to England, the Bishops were falling, so that he lost his friends, and hopes, both in Old England and New : yet put out his Book (such as it is) and soon after dyed." Such was the finale of "*the first Boston lawyer.*" But some of his personal effects remained, and they are enumerated and prised in the above inventory, made by two prominent men in the colony.

Having recently seen this inventory of Lechford, among the files at the Suffolk Probate Office, I at once communicated to Mr. Trumbull the fact relative to Lechford's widow. In his reply, dated Jan. 26, 1876, he makes the following suggestion and remarks with regard to Lechford. "Probably he was too poor to pay his wife's passage, with himself, to England in 1641, and left her to follow him when he could provide means. He was in intimate relations with all the banished Wheelwright men, and the 'Antinomians' generally, and acted as the attorney of several of them for the care of the property they left in Boston."

As regards the marriage of Samuel Wilbor to the widow, it must have been prior to Nov. 29, 1645, for on that day, according to the records of the First Church in Boston, Elizabeth Wilbor was admitted to the church. She was his second wife, for it appears that he had previously married Ann, daughter of Thomas Bradford of Doncaster in the south part of the county of Yorkshire, as in his will of March 1, 1607, is shown, as Savage says. Wilbor was an esteemed merchant in Boston. He was disarmed and banished for his known sympathy with the opinions of Wheelwright. In company with Coddington and others, he purchased Aquidneck, afterwards returned to Taunton and Boston, where he had possessions. In his will, dated April 30, 1656, he states that he is "of tanton, in plimouth patten," but gives to his wife Elizabeth, "all y<sup>e</sup> moueable goods y<sup>t</sup> is or shalbee in my house in Boston, where at present I doe inhabit at y<sup>e</sup> time of my decease." His property seems to have been in various other places, as in Dorchester, Braintree, Rhode Island, Bridgewater and Taunton. He died Sept. 29, 1656, and his will was proved the 6th of November following. An abstract of said will from the original record, Suffolk Probate office, Vol. i. page 281, is printed in the REGISTER, vi. 290. A copy was ordered to be made for the county of Plymouth. A brief abstract of it, from the Plymouth Probate records, was published in the REGISTER, v. 385. *

HENRY PEASE.—The last Will & testam<sup>t</sup> of Henery Pease Senior. This preasent writeing testifyeth that I, Henery Pease, being verey weake in bodey but in p'fect memorey, haue giuen and granted and by thes preasents doe giue and grant vnto my beloued wife her dwelleing in that p't of my dwelleing howse w<sup>ch</sup> I now dwell in, vntill my two Sonns haue finished my howse w<sup>ch</sup> standeth next the streette. I doe giue her also all the moueables in the said howse, w<sup>th</sup> the wood and garden stuff and hay. I doe giue her also my Kow and Swyne, w<sup>th</sup> fowre pownds of the 24<sup>l</sup> w<sup>ch</sup> is in the hands of Richard Tare [Thayer] of brantry. I doe also giue her my aforsaid

*See p. 79.

howse next the streett (w[ch] howse my 2 Sonns ar to finish for hor so soone as conveniently may be) w[th] the ground therunto belonging, w[ch] is all the ground betwixt Thomas Matsons[1] and Arthur Clarke,[2] w[th] all the convenyensyes & easm[ts] therto belongeing, so long as shee liueth, and at her desece shee shall giue it to one or more of my posterity whom shee pleaseth & to noe other. I doe also giue her my aker of ground, be it more or lesse, lying at Blackstons poynt,[3] so long as shee liueth. I doe also herby giue and grant vnto my Sonn John Pease,[4] The South west p't of my dwelleing howse, w[th] halfe the ground now belongeing to the whole howse, for him and his heires foreuer. I doe giue him, also, Eight pounds and ten shillings of the 24[l] w[ch] is in the hands of Richard Tare, of Brantry. I doe also giue him halfe my aker of Grounde at Blackstons poynt, after my wifes desece. I doe giue him also one of my greate bibles. I doe further by thes presents giue and grant vnto my sonn, Henrey Pease, (when my wifes howse is finished) the North east end of my dwelleing howse, w[th] halfe the ground Now belonging to the whole howse, the ground is to be deuided by the Execitor and Superuisers. I doe also giue him Eyght pounds and ten shillings of the 24[l] y[t] is in the hands of Richard Tare, of [Brantry]. I doe also giue him halfe my aker of ground at Blackstons poynt, after my desece. I giue him also one of my greate bibles, as also all my wearing cloathes.

I doe also giue vnto my Daughter, Susaña Jacklin, three pounds of the 24[l] y[t] is in the hands of Richard Tare, of Brantrey, and from her to her 2 Children, that is to say, forty shillings to the Soñn, and Twenty shillings to her daughter.

I doe Further make Thomas Matson Exec'tor, and Franses Dowse[5] and Robert Bradford[6] sup'visers. And to this last my last will & testam[t] I haue sett my hand this 3 of August, 1648.

The mark **H** of
Henry Pease

Confermed in the presense
    of Arthur Clarke
      William Ludken[7]
Witnes my hand, henery Pease.


Testifyed by Arthur Clarke & W[m] Ludkin, before the Court, that this was the last will & test. of Henry Pease, & that he was of a disposeing mind. Sworne 26(11)48 in Court. WILLIAM ASPINWALL, Recorder.

At a County Court sitting in Boston,
    by Adjournm[t] 6° February A° 1683.
The Court being informed that the wife of the above named Testato[r]

---

[1] Thomas Matson, a church member and freeman, was one of the disarmed men; a friend of Wheelwright. He moved to Braintree, where he had children born to him. He subsequently became a military officer; died after 1666.

[2] Arthur Clarke was of Hampton and Salem, removed to Boston in 1643, wife Sarah, children Sarah and Samuel; died probably in 1665.

[3] Blackstone's Point, Mr. Drake thinks, "was that afterwards called Barton's Point, now near the northern termination of Leveret street and the Depot of the Lowell Rail Road." See *Drake's Boston*, p. 97.

[4] Savage makes no mention of John and Henry Pease, sons of Henry, Sen., nor of his daughter, Susanna Jacklin. The latter was probably the wife of Edmund Jacklin of Boston. whose will was proved in Sept. 1681.

[5] Francis Dowse lived in Boston, afterward removed to Charlestown, had wife Catharine and several children.

[6] Robert Bradford was of Boston, had wife Martha and children, afterwards wife Margaret; will dated Nov. 16, 1677.

[7] William Ludkin, of Boston and Hingham, was a member of the artillery company.

dyed without makeing a will or disposeing of the house and ground within bequeathed to her for life, with power to give the same to one or more of his posterity as shee should please at her decease, Did therefore grant Power of Administration, de bonis non Administratis of the Testato[r], unto his surviveing son, Henry Pease, And hee hath given Security to Administer the same according to law, and to bee accountable and responsable for the same and his Adm[con] thereof unto the Court for the County of Suffolke when lawfully required and called thereunto.

Attest p[r] Is[a] Addington, Clre

Administrator's Bond.—Know all men by these pnt[s] that wee Henry Pease, Obadiah Wakefield[1] Joyner, & Grimstone Bowd[2] Cordwainer, all of Boston in the County of Suffolke in New England, are holden and stand firmly bound & obliged unto M[r] John Hubbard, of Boston, Treasurer for the s[d] County, his successors in s[d] office or assignes, in the Sume of two hundred pounds currant money of New England, To the true payment of which Sume wee do binde and oblige our selves, our heirs Exec[rs] and Am[rs] jointly and severally, firmly by these presents. Sealed with our Seales. Dated in Boston the Seventh day of February Ann[o] Dom[1] 1683.

The Condicoñ of this present obliga[con] is such that whereas Henry Pease, formerly of Boston dece[d] did make and ordein his last will and Testam[t] and thereby gave a certain p[t] of his Estate unto his wife during her life, impowering her to make her will concerning the same and dispose thereof at her death to some of his posterity, but shee makeing no disposition thereof, Power of adm[con] de bonis non Administratris of the s[d] Henry Pease was grant[d] unto his surviving son Henry Pease to bee annexed to y[e] will of his said Father. If therefore the above bounden Henry Pease shall and do exhibit unto y[e] County Court for Suffolke a just and true Inventory upon oath of all such goods and Estate left by his s[d] Father as are yet unadministered, and shall well and truely Administer y[e] same according to law, And bee accountable and responsible for the same and his Adm[con] thereof unto y[e] Court for s[d] County of Suffolke when lawfully required & called thereunto, Then this above written obligation to bee void & of none Effect, Or else to abide and remain in full force and virtue.

Sealed and Deliu[rd]  
in y[e] presence of  
    Samuell Beighton[3]  
    Is[a] Addington Clre.

HENRY PEASE.  
OBEDIAH WAKEFEILD.  
GRIMSTONE BOWDE.

(File No. 78.)

[The Will of Henry Pease is not on record. It is now printed in full from the files.]

THOMAS SATELL.—This to be the last will and Testament of my servant Thomas Satell lately deceased w[th] much comfort in the Lord. I John Wilson can & will (if called therevnto) Attest vpon my oath w[ch] he expressed to me, betweene him & me Alone, being not willing as he sayd that any

---

[1] Obadiah Wakefield is not mentioned by Savage. Mr. Drake in his Boston history, page 427, has this name on the list of 129 "Handy craftsmen," who petitioned. in 1677, for protection in their several callings.  
[2] Not found in Savage, but among the inhabitants of Boston, 1687.—*Dunton's Letters*, p. 325.  
[3] Samuel Beighton, of Boston, by wife Ann, had children. He died about 1692.

other should be privy thervnto saue my self vntlll he was dead (saue that he declared the same or most of it to his brother when he came to visitt him) having Expressed the same to me a former time but After he had spoken to him, he called for me again And declared the same over againe w^th this addition, y^t my daughter Mary should have 20^s for a legacy as hauing been much beholding to her (so as is in his will expressed). The w^ch will of his, laying aside what I wrote before, I did presently sett downe in writing, (according as is in this paper on the other side) setting my name ther vnto. 18. 9. 1651.                                    JOHN WILSON.

[The above statement and the nuncupative will of Thomas Satell—an abstract of which is given in the REGISTER, iv. 286—are in the hand-writing * of the first minister of Boston, who deposed in Court on the presentation of the will, at the date above given.]                    (File No. 111.)

MARGERY ELLIOT.—To the Honno^rd County Court now sitting at Boston
The petition of Margery Elliott Relict of the late Jacob Elliot,[1]

Humbly sheweth

That wheareas yo^r petitioners late husband made his last will & testament bearing date 28 2m° 1651 appointing Elder Willyam Colebron & James Penn to be y^e overseers of the sayd will, but on due pervsall thereof finds y^t neither executor nor executrix is named therein yett the minde of the Testator in relation to his Eldest sonne & Eldest daughter is fully expressed; And the rest of the children in relation to their portions left with the death of yo^r petitioner or alteration of her Conditōn. And whereas yo^r petitioner by the Advise of the Elders aforesaid hath married two of hir daughters, & deliuered the some of fifty pounds apeece to their husbands in order to their portions, yo^r petitioner finding It lyes not in hir power or theirs to devide y^r estate, And y^t Its but necessary for the prevention of future troubles & Inconveniences y^t may arise betweene hir children that due order be observed In order wherevnto hir Request (hir children therevnto consenting & concurring) to this Honno^rd Court is that Administration to the estate of hir late husband be Graunted vnto yo^r petitioner and an order for the stateing of each of the childrens parts, y^r Eldest sonne & daughter being appointed by the said Testator & left at their libertys to make & take necessary exchange and satisfaction for their parts as the sayd Administrator & Elders and themselves shall agree for the same as also such part for hir self by y^e said order Assigned to hir as this Court sees meet & just, y^t so when God Calls hir out of the world shee maye dispose thereof to such & all of hirs as shee judgeth meete & their neede may be, and that if what shee hath payd allready should exceed their parts due provission in the same order may be made for the Repayment of so much as this Court shall determine and yo^r petitioner shall pray, &c.

                                                    marke
                              MARGERIE  +  ELIOTT.

This petition of o^r honnored mother we whose names are vnder writt: doe declare y^t wee doe allow & approve thereof as just & necessary & w^t

---

[1] Jacob Elliot was an elder brother of the Rev. John Eliot, "the Apostle." An abstract ** of his will is printed in the REGISTER, iv. 53, proved 20. 9. 1651. His widow, Margery died Oct. 30, 1661.
*See p. 38.
**See p. 35.

order y[r] Hono[rd] shall make therein wee shall gladly rest in the same

Jacob Elliot[1]
Theophilus Frary for my selfe & wife [Hannah.]
Susanna Elliot
Mehetabel Elliot

Att a County Court held at Boston the 9[th] of May 1661. In Ans[r] to this petition the Court graunted y[e] say[d] Margery Administration to the estate of the late Jacob Elliot to performe the Imperfect will as neere as she may: as this Court shall order. EDW. RAWSON, Recorder.

Seth Perry of Boston, Taylor, & Mehittable, Daughter to y[e] late Jacob Eliot & Margery his wife, now wife to y[e] s[d] Seth Perry, consideration, fifty pounds w[th] such other somes as legacies given vnto y[e] said Mehittable by hir late father Jacob Eliot & Margery his wife by wills now payd vnto vs by Jacob Eliot o[r] eldest brother & executor to y[e] last will of y[e] late Margery Eliot o[r] mother of all which wee acknowledge o[r]selves fully satisfied, do discharge s[d] Jacob Eliot, from all due vnto vs by virtue of y[e] last will of y[e] late Jacob Eliot & Margery o[r] father & Mother or by any other way or meaning w[t]soeuer 14[th] 8[mo] 1662. SETH PERRY.

MEHETABELL PERRY

Witness herevnto Willm Colbrou
James Penn

[The above acquittance of Seth Perry was copied from the *Massachusetts Archives*, Book 15 B, page 94.]

Decemb[r] 9, 1661.—An Inventorie of the remaining stock of Cattle & Land of Jacob Eliot· senio[r] formerly deceased w[ch] was designed to pay the portions of severall children, some are allready p[d].

Thirteen Acres of Land about Roxbury Gate, £78; one old house, £08; five Cowes, one yearling, £23; Twenty sheep, £08; Mares & horses at Rehoboth, £38; Att Medefeild one Mare & half off a Colt, £14; one Mare at Sudbury, £12; debtes To the s[d] stock Edw[d] Adams of Medefeild, £05. 10s; Tho: Dexter Junio[r], £13; Goodman Puffer, £5; Jacob Eliott, Junio[r], £1. 10s; M[r] Pett[r] Oliv[r], £8; Theoph. Frary, £44; Mares & colts at Brantrey with Francis Eliot, £22. Whole amount, £280.

(File No 113.)

WILLIAM FROTHINGHAM.—An Inventory of the estate of William Frothingham of Charlestown, who departed this life 18[th] of the 8[th] m[o] 1651. Dwelling house & orchard & 7 acres of lande, more or lesse in the east feild, £71; 4 acres at Newtowne line, £08; 14½ acres beyond wenotomies & a house there, £30; 7 acres by goodman Lothrops house, £4; 6½ cow comons; £13; 2 hay lots on misticke side, £4; 2 hay lots in the high Feild on this side, £6; 60 acres at Wooburn bounds, 2s. p[r] acre, £6; a bible & doct[r] Prestons worke, 15s. etc. etc. Whole amount of inventory, £308. 09s. 9d. (File No. 119.)

---

[1] Jacob Eliot, son of Jacob, his brother-in-law Theophilus Frary, and Seth Perry, were three of the twenty-nine original members of the Third, or Old South Church in Boston, which was formed at Charlestown in May, 1669.

# ABSTRACTS OF THE EARLIEST WILLS ON RECORD, OR ON THE FILES IN THE COUNTY OF SUFFOLK, MASSACHUSETTS.

Prepared by WILLIAM B. TRASK, Esq., of Boston.

Capt. WILLIAM TYNG.[1]—Inventory of the Goods and Chattells of Capt William Tyng, made 25. 3. 1653. See REGISTER, vol. viii. p. 62. Houses, warehouses, etc. cattle at the Farme at Brantree called Salters Farme, at Goodman Mattocks, at George Speres Farme; 600 Akers of land at Rockstones Farme, 48 Akers land at Brantree, and Marsh in the possession of John Gurney; 80 Akers of land at Monoctecott, £16; 30 Akers at Winchester's Neck, 4; 26 Akers vpon the Plaine, £13; 20 Akers of Marsh in Knight Neck, £40. Whole amᵗ of lands, cattle, furniture, etc. 2774–14–04. Appraised by Natha: Duncan, Anthony Stoddard, Wm. Dauis. Plate afterwards mentioned.

*Bookes, in folio.*—Bookes of Martyrs in 3 volumes, Books of Statutes at Large, The Survey of London, Speeds Chronicle, Camdens Brittania, Ainsworth on Moses and Psalmes, Mʳ Harris'[2] Workes, Dʳ Sibs Saints Cordiall, Marchants Accompts, Gecords Herball.[3]

*In Quarto.*—A Concordance, Prestones Workes 2 of them, Dʳ Vsher against Jesuitt, Barriffe, The Soules implantation, Treatise of Magistracy Two, Childe of light in darknes, goodwin; Enonimous Tresure, Apeale to Parliament, Janua Linguarum, Ans. to Mʳ Dauenport, Parralells Censures observations, Dod & cleauer on Sacraments, defence of the Wach-Word, Sibbs on faith, Mʳ Barnard against Seperatists, the Discouerer, Ecclesiastical cannons. Complainte euill doers, Interest States & kingdomes, Bloody Tenent, Forbes 4 sermons, Axe at the roote, Popish Idollatry, Experience of light & health, Circkle of Comerse, Mary Pope, Edward Renolds, Minester against briges ; Doctrine of the Saboth, the still destroyer ; a Vindication bf mʳ Burrowes, a Duch Worke, An apollogy of Brownists, Doctrinall & Morrall instructions, Reformations obseruations, Censure on Anabaptists Answer, abridgmᵗ of Camden, Tolloration Justifyed, Burrowes gospell Conversation, Moses Choice, Gospell Worship, Churches Resurrection Cott, Childrens Baptisme, 7 vialls 3 Congregationall churches, Singin Psalemes.

---

[1] Capt. Tyng died Jan. 18, 1652. " leaving larger estate," says Savage, " than any in the country of that day." This is the earliest extended list of books to be found among the estates in the Suffolk Probate Office. One of a prior date, that of John Benjamin, of Watertown, 12 (4) 1645, contains about twenty volumes.

[2] Probably Robert.

[3] Doubtless "The Herball or Generall Historie of Plantes, Gathered by John Gerarde of London." The first edition was imprinted by John Norton, London, in 1597, pages 1392. The address to the reader is, " From my House in Holborn within the Suburbs of London, this first of December, 1597." The second edition was printed by Adam Islip, Joice Norton and Richard Whitaker, London, Anno 1633. To the Reader—" From my house on Snow-hill, Octob. 22, 1633, Thomas Johnson," who, it appears, edited this edition ; pages 1630, besides the indices. Both these volumes are in folio, illustrated with many hundred wood-cuts. It is " ornamented with a more numerous set of figures," says Pulteney, " than had ever accompanied any work of the kind in this kingdom." A second edition of this rare work is in the library of the Mass. Horticultural Society. Allibone mentions two other editions as having been published, one in 1636, fol., and another in 1744, 8vo.

*In Octavo.*—Excellency of a gratious spirit, office of executors, pentisia Indicaria, christians Engagement, Imposts & customes, Concordance, logick & Rethoricke, Christians dayly Walke, duch testaments & psalmes, An arrow against Idollotry ; 16 Ciceroas orations.     (File, No. 128.)

JOSEPH MORSE.—Thomas Boyden, late of Boston, now of meadfeild, co. Suffolk, in New England, yeoman : bond £300, together with the house, vpland & meadow now in my possession, lately the Inheritance of Joseph Morse, late of Meadfeild, w^th all libe^rtyes, etc. to the same belonging, to pay unto Edward Rawson, Recorder, or his successo^rs, the some of one hundred & eighty pounds, etc.
Oct. 18, 1661.

The Condicoñ of this obligation is such, that if the aboue bounden Thomas Boyden shall by himselfe, or his heires, executors, etc. keepe and mainteine the seuerall children of y^e late Joseph Morse & Hannah his now wife during the time of theire Nonage o^r Unmarried Condicoñ, or till they choose theire Guardians, teaching or Causing y^e sonnes of the said Morse to write & Read and at theire seuerall marriages o^r days of Age, shall pay unto each of the said Morse his children, the seuerall portions to them Assigned by the County Court at Boston In January last & by the Generall Court Approved of as in s^d County Courts order so Allowed by the Generall Court in May 1661, Then this obligation to be voyd, etc.

THOMAS BOYDEN.

In the presence of vs 27 June 1665.
John Ferniside                                     (File, No. 149.)
peren rawson

See abstract of the inventory of the estate of Joseph Morse, REGISTER, viii. 277.

JOHN HARBOR, Senior.[1]—I, Jn° Harbor Sen^r of Braintrie in New England, yeoman, doe acknowledge myself bound to Edward Rawson Recorder for y^e County of Suffolk, in the some of fiuety pounds, etc.   Boston, Aug. 10. 1654.

The Condicoñ of this obligation is such that if the said Jn° Harbor Sen^r etc. pay or cause to be paid the seuerall portions determined by the magists. to be paid to the seuerall children of Benjamin Scott according to the times p^rfixed in ye determinacoñ, then this obligation to be voyd, else to stand, etc.

JOHN HARBOR.

Signed Sealed & deliu^rd in p^rsence of vs,
     Edward Rawson Jvn:
     William needom.

A Trew Invitori of the Goods And Chattells of the Widow Scott, the late wife of Benjamen Scott, of brantri, deceased, and now the Wife of John Harber, of brantri, married 21 7 month 47.
     Amount of inventory, £86. 14^s.   Debts 3. 6. 0.
                    Steuen kinsley, Samuel bas, William needom.

Power of Administration to y^e estate of Benjamin Scott is granted to Jn° Harbor and Hannah his wife, late wife to Benjamin Scott, in behalf of hirself & the children.                          EDW. RAWSON, Record^r.
13 July 1654.
present y^e Gou^rn^r, m^r Nowell, m^r Hibbins, Cap^t Gookin & Cap^t Atherton.

[1] Neither John Harbor, senior, nor John Harbor, junior, are mentioned by Mr. Savage.

Present y<sup>e</sup> Gou'ner, m<sup>r</sup> Nowell, Cap<sup>t</sup> Atherton & Recorder. The magistrates on the 10<sup>th</sup> of August determined y<sup>e</sup> estate should be thus divided, the wife to have one third p'te viz. twenty five pounds, Benjamine the Eldest sonne fowerteene pounds, the other [illegible] children seven pounds apeece : to be paid vnto them at the day of marriage or at their ages of fowerteene yeeres, the s<sup>d</sup> Jn° Harbor givinge in securitye to pay the said persons accordingly, education of the children being allowed for.     EDWARD RAWSON.

(File, 150.)

## ABSTRACTS OF THE EARLIEST WILLS ON RECORD, OR ON THE FILES IN THE COUNTY OF SUFFOLK, MASSACHUSETTS.

Prepared by WILLIAM B. TRASK, Esq., of Boston.

JOHN AVERY.—Bond of William Follett of Oyster River on Pi[scattoway] to Edward Rawson, 19 Sept. 1654, to Administer on the estate of John Avery, deceased; in behalfe of Laur[ence Avery, his brother] ; witnessed by Rachel Awbrey, margaret Rawson.  See Administration, REGISTER, viii. 354.                                        (File, No. 151.)

ARTHUR GILL.—I, John Sweete, of Boston, acknowledge myself Indebted to Edward Rawson Recorder for the County of Suffolke in New England, some, 180<sup>lbs</sup>.  Jan. 16, 1654.

357

The above bounden John Sweete shall Administer to the estate of Arthur Gill, in behalfe of y⁰ children of y⁰ said Arthur & payment of his Just debts, and from time to time shall give a Just and true Accompt thereof to the County Court of Boston, etc.

Teste, John Gill

William Awbrey

Jₙ° + Sweete

yᵉ bond was Cancelled by order of Court, March 28, 1656. E. R. R. (See abstract of the inventory, Register, viii. 356.)\* (File, No. 152.)

Robert Sharp.—I, John Sharp, sonne of the late Robert Sharp, of muddy Riuer, in the p'ecints of Boston, bound to Edward Rawson, some 56 pounds; for the payment whereof I bind myself, wᵗʰ my now dwelling house & land formerly yᵉ dwelling house & land of my late father, in the some of one hundred and twenty pounds. Aprill 25, 1665.

If the above John Sharp pay vnto Abigaile & Mary Sharpe, his two sisters, the sume of 28 pounds apeece, as they shall attaine their seuerall ages as the Law prescribes, & also pay & sattisfy vnto them or their guardians yearely duringe their minority the some of 50 shillings a peece, then this obligation to be voyd, etc.

JOHN SHARP.

In p'esence of vs
  Richard Peacocke
  Paul Batt

See inventory of the estate of Robert Sharp; petition of his relict and administratrix, Abigail Clapp, who subsequently became the second wife of Nicholas Clapp, of Dorchester, etc. See Register, viii. 276; x. 84. (File, No. 153.)\*\*

Ellinor Trusler.¹—Salem dated 15ᵗʰ february 1654. I, Ellinor Trusler, being vppon my sick bed, but of perfect memory, appoint my sonns Henry & Nicholas Joynt Executo'rs of this my last will & testament. I bequeath my Farme to my sonns Henry & Nicholas, with the houseing; my tenn acre Lott in the North feild to Henry. My house & ground at the towne to my son Edward. My househould goods I bequeath in this manner: One bead to Henry, and the other to Nicholas, the sad Collored cloake to Edward & the other Cloake to Henry, the old brass pott, the least of the brass pans, two deep pewter platters, one broad one, a Couerled, a blanket, with one pʳ of sheetes to my son Edward; my Wascote, Safegard & Goune to goe together, my best pettecoate, with the rest of my wearing Cloathes to goe together, & my daughters to have them; the rest of my wearing linen to my two daughters, & the other linnen to the executoⁿ. To John Phelps, my Grand Child, two oxen & cheyne, with one ewe. To my Grand daughter, Elizabeth, one ewe. The other two ewes to Nicholas his two children. To my Grand children Samuell & Edward, I giue either of them a yearling Calfe. The rest of my goods & cattell to be left with my executoⁿ to pay my debts, & the legacy bequeathed by my late husband to his daughter in England, to witt the summe of ten pounds.

Robert Moulton² Senyʳ
George Gardner³

The marke of
ELLINOR + TRUSLER

¹ Thomas Tresler or Trusler, Salem, was admitted to the church Dec. 15, 1639, freeman Dec. 27, 1642, d. March 5, 1654. His wife was Elinor, and he had a daughter who married Henry Phelps. He was clerk in 1650 of the market.—See *Savage's Dictionary.*
² Robert Moulton came to Salem with Higginson; was one of the first selectmen in Charlestown whither he removed; was also a representative from C. to the first court in 1634, and for Salem, to which place he had removed in 1637. In the latter year his name is found among those who were disarmed as adherents and friends of John Wheelwright. He left a son Robert who was a witness with his father to the above will of Mrs. Trusler.
³ In 1658, Elizabeth, the wife of George Gardner of Salem, was indicted for favoring the quakers.

\*See p. 140.

\*\*See pp. 128, 170.

Robert Moulton Juny[r] test.
This is a true copy compared with its originall, taken out of the Records
of Salem Court, p[r] me,                                   HILLIARD VEREN Cleric.
                                                             (File, No. 154.)

REBECCA WEBB.—Peter Oliuer, Thomas Buttolph and Godfry Armitage,
of Boston, bound in the some of 180 pounds to giue a true Accompt of the
estate of Rebeckha Webb deceased, by hir late will and Approbation of the
County Court of Boston comitted to theire hands, as in the Inventory given
Into the s[d] County Court Appeares.  Signed Peter Olliuer, Thomas Buttolph, Godfrey [mrke]A Armitage.  In p[r]sence of John Kingsley, William
Awbrey.                                                      (File, No. 155.)

See Will and Inventory of Rebecca Webb, REGISTER, v. 303; viii. 356.[*]

GEORGE BURDEN.[1]—[Memorandum on the back of the original will.]
  Bought of M[r] Foster a chist of Seuger containeing
    6 hundereth                                                    19.10
  Bought of William of the Wist Einges one hoghed
    contaneing 500                                                 15.00
  bought of William a small nashe of sueger                         4.17
  bought of M[r] Hahones 2 hoghedes                                25.17
  bought of William Stranges[2] 5 hoghedes of Tobaccoe
  Bought of George Maning fore hoghedes
    of suger and a berell giner                                   65.06  0
                                                             (File, No. 157.)

WILLIAM STEVENS.[3]—Bond of Thomas Bligh,[4] of Boston, to Edward
Rawson; sum twelve pounds, to administer on the estate of Wm. Stevens.
July 24, 1657.
In the presence of                                           THOMAS BLIGH.
Moses Noyes,[5] Margarett Rawson.                            (File, No. 159.)
See REGISTER, ix. 229. (See p. 161).

JOHN GORE, of Roxbury.—Bond of John Gore, Samuel Scarborough,
and Richard Hall,[6] all of Roxbury unto William Stoughton Esq. sum Two
hundred & Fifty pounds, Oct. 26, 1693, to Administer on the goods &c. of
John Gore Gent, left unadministered by Rhoda his Relict and sole Executrix, and make a true inventory, on or before Oct. 26, 1694.  John Gore,
Samuell Scarbrough, Richard Hall.  In presence of Is[a] Addington, Reg[r],
Edward Turfrey.                                              (File, No. 162.)

Abstract of Will of John Gore, REGISTER, viii. 282. (See p. 134).

[1] George Burden came in the Abigail, in 1635, aged 20 years, admitted to the church in
1637, made freeman in May; was disarmed in November.  The maiden name of his wife
Ann may have been *Soulsby*, or Silsbee, as he mentions "my father *Soulsby*" in his will.
There is an intimation that he was about to visit England, when his will was signed in
October, 1652, as he says—"if my wife & children Stay in England, but if wee Returne to
New England," &c.  This document was proved in Boston less than five years afterwards,
namely, in April, 1657.  See abstract of it, REGISTER, viii. 277.                     [**]
[2] Not mentioned by Savage, unless William Stranguage or Strangeways of Boston, 1651,
a mariner, be the man.
[3] Who was this William Stevens?
[4] Was this the Thomas Bligh, of Boston, mentioned by Hutchinson, and Hazard, who
served in the expedition under Willard in 1654, for bringing Ninicraft to submission?
[5] Moses Noyes, who was he?
[6] Probably son of Richard, of Dorchester.
[*]See pp. 53, 140.
[**]See p. 129.

359

ROBERT KEAYNE.[1]—Jan. 29, 1683–4. Petition of Cap$^t$. Nickolas Paige of Boston & Anna his wife, Grandaughter & sole heir vnto Cap$^t$. Robert Keayne, some times of Boston, Deceased. Humbly sheweth, That Wheras the s$^d$ Cap$^t$ Keayne by his Last Will & Testament, in writing, ordained his only son, Maj$^r$ Benj. Keayne his sole Executor of his s$^d$ Will, who deceased before the s$^d$ Testator, & further the s$^d$ Cap$^t$ Keayne prouided by his s$^d$ Will, in such Case, that his Relict should be Executrix only dureing her Widdowhod, who is also some times since deceased, soe that there is Noe other p'sons now Liueing that of Right ought to adminester vpon the Estate & fulfill the will of the s$^d$ Testator more then your Pettioners. Humbly pray that Administration may be granted to y$^r$ Pettioners to Administer on the Estate of the s$^d$ Cap$^t$ Robert Keayne, &c.   NICHO: PAIGE, ANNA PAIGE.

Administration granted.                                   Is$^a$ ADDINGTON Cl$^re$.

Bond of Nicholas Paige, of Boston, and Anna his wife, unto M$^r$ John Hubbard of Boston, Treasurer, in the sume of one thousand pounds. Feb. 9, 1683.   Nicho: Paige, Anna Paige.   In the presence of John Joyliffe, Josiah Torrey, Is$^a$ Addington Clre.      (File, No. 171.)

RICE DAVIS.—Learnard Wheatleigh[2] m[aister      ] wherein and when Rice Daues Died affermeth, that the sayd Rice on his death bed, gaue him the clothes he had with him, and all estate besides (he being buried decently), he gaue to M$^r$ Euan Thomas and William Tilly, ioyntly, he also affirmeth, that Rice being at the same time demaunded of him what he did owe to any, Rice affirmed that he owed nothing to any man, except a small matter, to the aforesayd M$^r$ Thomas.   Farther he affirmeth, that he found his estate as is specified and not more to his remembrance.

Item, 1 barrell of tobacco and a littell p'cell of leafe.
"     in wages du to him.   £10. 10sh.
Farther he affirmeth, that he hath disbursed in goods to him and on his burial fiue pound ten and 8s.
There is more, an old chest, two small pap$^r$ bookes, a broken Jacob staffe, and a scale.   There was moreouer a remainder of a debt due to Rice from sergeant Daniel, w$^{ch}$ was also expended vppon his buriall, besides the £5. 10s. 8d.

                    Taken vpon oath 3. 2. 1658, before me,
                         RI. BELLINGHAM Dep$^t$ Gov$^r$.

Power of administration granted to Evan Thomas and William Tilly, Ap$^l$ 1$^{st}$, 1658.   The conditions attending the administration of the estate of Rice Davis, was signed by Evan Thomas and William Tilly of Boston, April 13, 1658, in p'esence of Beniamen Brisco, Elkanah Cooke, Evan Thomas & William Tilly deposed before Ri. Bellingham Dep$^t$ Gov$^r$, 22 of Aprill 1658.                         (File, No. 181.)

RICHARD HARDIER.—Bond of Elizabeth Hardier, of Braintry, widdow, & Martin Saunder's, of Braintry, yeoman, bound in the sum of 60 pounds

---

[1] A brief abstract of the lengthy Will of Capt. Robert Keayne may be found in REGISTER, vi. 89, 152. This will, written with his own hand, begun by him August the 1st, 1653, was finished, as he says, Nov. 15th, with an addition, Dec. 15, 1653. It was proved May 2, 1656. The original will, which occupies 158 pages folio, vol. i. Suffolk Records, is the most curious document we ever saw.
[2] Neither Davis nor Wheatleigh mentioned by Savage. See abstract of the Will of *William Weare*, REGISTER, viii. 353, and inventory of Rice Davis, ix. 344. **
\* See pp. 65, 69.
\*\* See pp. 137, 164.

to Edward Rawson, Recorder to the County of Suffolke, to performe the will of hir late husband, Richard Hardier, according to lawe.

Elizabeth + Hardier, Martin Sanders.   In presence of Richard Peacocke, Caleb Peacocke, September 24, 1658.

The names of Richard Brackett & William Allis (which do not appear on the record) are signed to the inventory, dated 25. 2. 1657. [See abstract of the will of Richard Hardier, REGISTER, viii. 352.*  Martin Saunders, above, married his daughter, Lydia, April 1, 1651.]

(File, No. 183.)

JOHN COGGAN.[1]—Whereas there appears sundry difficulties in reference to y⁰ Execucɔ̃n of the last Will and Testamᵗ of Mʳ John Coggan, deceased, and two of y⁰ Executoꞌs therein nominated disclaimeing the proving thereof, so yᵗ it now resteth wholly vpon Mⁿ Coggan his relict widow & Executrix to vndertake a buissines of so troublesome a nature as y⁰ Execucɔ̃n thereof is likely to prove, or otherwise the will of the deceased must be wholly frustrate; for the pꞌvention whereof, the Overseers of the said Will taking the matter in to their Serious Consideracɔ̃n, together with seuꞌall Queries propounded by the widow & her freinds to be resolved before shee proceed to prove the Will, as 1ᵘ In case yᵗ her sonne Caleb should depꞌt this life before he attaineth vnto the age of 21 years, Whether shee, as Executrix to her Husbands Will, or otherwise, shalbe liable to give any accᵒ of the pꞌfits & revenews of the porcɔ̃n & estate bequeathed vnto the said Caleb by the said Will, shee haveing had his sole Educacɔ̃n & clearly discharged the same.

The overseers do Judge meet, as their finall conclusion thereof, to resolve this question on the Negative.

Also, whereas vpon pꞌsent veiw of the estate, compared wᵗʰ knowne debts & legacies to be sattisfied acccording to the mind of the deceased, there doth not appear where there wilbe any thing left for the discharge of the said Caleb's Educaccion for four or five of the first years at least, and if more debts should happen to appeare, then for a longer time.

The 2ᵈ Quest. is, in what way the Executrix shalbe sattisfied for the charge of her sons Educacɔ̃n.

The overseers haveing considered the weight & difficulty of this question do Judge meet to resolve, that Whether the said Caleb Coggan shall live or dy, in case that the revenews of his estate do not fully discharge all his expences, that then y⁰ Executrix shalbe repayd for all her paynes, care & disbursemᵗˢ for his Educacɔ̃n, by sale of any of the houses to him the said

---

[1] John Coggan was first of Dorchester, 1632, freeman 1633.  The next summer, July, 1634, his wife Ann joined the church at Boston.  "Another wife, Mary," says Savage, "died Jan. 14, 1652, but he soon found consolation in marrying 10 March following, with Martha, widow of Gov. Winthrop, who before had been widow of Thomas Coytemore." He died in 1658.  "Of his widow, a letter of Rev. John Davenport, printed in 3 Mass. Hist. Coll., x. 45, contains a story of unusual interest."

John Coggan opened the first shop for merchandise in Boston, of which we have any account, in 1634, and Samuel Cole the first tavern.  John Capen, of Dorchester, July 1, 1647,—writing to his "Sweete-hart," Mary Bass, of Braintree, whom he afterwards married, and from whom all of the name of Capen, in this country, probably descended,— mentions that "whill I was wᵗʰ you at Brantrey Sister Swift bᵉing at Boston wᵗʰ Sister Vpsall they boath being at y⁰ hatters shop did thinke vppon you for a hat and Chose out y⁰ comlyest fashon hatt yᵗ they could find: (avₒyding fantastick fashons) & caused y⁰ man to set it by vntell this first day thinking we should speak wᵗʰ some of yqu this day; Y⁰ hat was a demecaster, the priz was 24ˢ; y⁰ shop was y⁰ corner shop over againsⁱ Mʳ Coggings on y⁰ right hand as on goe up to Mʳ Cottens house."  See Hist. Dorchester, page 45.

*See p. 136.

Caleb Coggan given & bequeathed by his father beforenamed, in case y$^t$ other agreem$^t$ be not made with y$^e$ executrix by y$^e$ said Caleb, when he shall come of age to receive his estate into his owne hands, or any other his successo$^r$s, by virtue of the said will in case of his decease, before he arive to y$^e$ age of 21 years.

Also for p'venting of future differences, the overseers do Judge meet to declare, that twenty pounds p' Annu. dureing the time that the said Caleb Coggan shalbe brought vp at English or Gram$^r$ schooles, and thirty pounds p' Annu. dureing the time that he shalbe at the Colledge, in such payments as is made by the farm or of .the Houses & lands, shalbe accounted a meet recompence to the Executrix, with allowance for w$^t$ shee shall lay out for his bookes, & Extreordnary Expences for phisicke etc. & allowance for forbearance of her estate.

provided always in case of his decease before he come of age, the said Executrix shall not be accountable for any of the revenews of his estate except in case of her owne demands for non satisfac$\tilde{o}$n of her expences for y$^e$ said Caleb Coggan.                                   JOHN NORTON.
                                                          THOMAS DANFORTH.

M$^r$ Thomas Danforth Appeared in the County Court, 3$^d$ August 1658, & declared this paper to be the declaration of M$^r$ Norton & himself in Reference to the Interp$^r$ta$\tilde{o}$n of so much of M$^r$ Cogans will as it refers unto, & y$^t$ he signed y$^e$ same.                           EDW. RAWSON Recorder.

Att a meeting of the magists. 24$^{th}$ of October 1660, present dep$^t$ Gov$^r$ maje$^r$ Atherton & Recorder. The magists. having binn Informed of M$^{rs}$ Coggan, y$^e$ Relict of y$^e$ late M$^r$ John Coggan, sudaine death, y$^t$ not w$^{th}$out suspistion of poison, Ordered y$^t$ y$^e$ Recorde$^r$ Issue out warrant to y$^e$ Constables of Boston, to sumon & Impanell a Jury of Inquest for the Inquiry how shee Came to hir end. And also Judged it meete for y$^e$ preservation of y$^e$ estate left by hir behind hir y$^t$ it may not be Imbezled but preserved), to Appoint Eld$^r$ James Penne & Deacon Richard Truesdall, Administrato$^r$s to the estate of y$^e$ late M$^{rs}$ Martha Coggan, Impowring them forthwith to take into theire Custody the keyes plate, &c. of y$^e$ s$^d$ M$^{rs}$ Coggan & secure y$^e$ same, taking a true Inventory of that estate, & bringing it into y$^e$ next County Court, & Providing for hir decent Interment.           E. R. R.

Joseph Rocke,[1] of Boston, bound in the some of 400 pounds to Edward Rawson Recorder, Feb. 24, 1662, to administer on the estate of the late John Coggan & Martha his wife. Signed, Joseph Rock, in the presence of

his marke
Samuel S Sendall, John Ferniside.                      (File, No. 185.)

Abstract of the Will of John Cogan or Coggan, inventory, settlement of his estate & that of his widow Martha, REGISTER, ix. 36; x. 175. *

JOHN FRANCKLYN.— Jonathan Negus,[2] of Boston, bound, Aug. 20, 1658, to Administer on the estate of Jn$^o$ Francklyn, deceased. Signed, Jonathan Negus. Witnessed by Henry Webb & Ed. Hutchinson Jr. See his inventory, REGISTER, ix. 344.| (See p. 164).           (File, No. 187.)

[1] Joseph Rock married Elizabeth, daughter of John Coggan.
[2] Jonathan Negus was a faithful clerk of the writs in Boston, 1651, & after; had wife Jane. His sister, Grace, married Barnabas Fawer, of Dorchester.
*See pp. 142, 177.

# ABSTRACTS OF THE EARLIEST WILLS ON RECORD, OR ON THE FILES IN THE COUNTY OF SUFFOLK, MASSACHUSETTS.

Prepared by WILLIAM B. TRASK, Esq., of Boston.

JOHN MAYNARD.—An Inuentory of what debts is oweing frō the Estate of John Miner [sic] this 25. 9ᵐᵒ 1659.
Impˢ to Henery Brigam, 17.15.5; Mʳ Rocke, 03.00.9; Samˡ Sendal, 01.06.0; Elisabeth Eaton, 04.10.0; Mʳ Walker, 01.06.6; William Poland, 00.08.0; Eliaser Eaton, laid out at funeral, 00.09.0; goodwife Rouse, 00.08.0; Zacre Phillips, 02.00.0; goodman Armitage, 01.04.0; goodman Peede, 00.07.4; mʳ Atwater, 00.10.0; Elder Penne, 00.03.0; John Bigs, 00.08.0; decon Trusdaile, 00.05.0; Robrt Walker, 00.06.4; William Browne, 00.03.0; mʳ Nugaite, 00.02.7; William Corser, 00.03.0; Mary Jay, 00.01.0; Sergt. Cotton, 00.05.0; Beniamin Thohinge [Thwing?], 00.15.0; goodman Crichley, 00.02.0; mʳ John Euered, 01.08.1; goodman Robinson, 00.04.0; Left Turner, 00.07.0; mʳ Stare Senʳ, 00.11.2; Thomas Starre, 06.00.0; William English, 00.10.0; Ed. Cowel, 00.07.0; Ed. Hutchinson, 00.08.10½. [Total] 45.15.00½.

Wee whose names ar vnderwritten haueing examined the debts due from the estate of John Maynard deceased by vertue of an order of the County Court doe find the estate debeter forty fiue pounds fiftene shillings and on half pennie as by the p'ticulars aboue mentioned

ANTHONY STODDARD, JER: HOUCHIN.

See REGISTER ix. 347, for a prior inventory    (File, No. 214.)
of the estate of John Maynard.*

THOMAS CROMWELL.—Inuentory of yᵉ Estate of Thomas Cromwell Deceased, April 1687. Dweling house & aboute Eighteen poles £42; a bed at Jonathan Pickrins (Esteemed att) £2. &c. &c. Apprised as Money pʳ Robᵗ Kitchen, Benjᵃ Marston, 69.08.00. Ann Cromwell Administratrix of the Estate of Thomas Crumwell decᵈ appearing 12 May 1687 made oath. Daniel Allin Cler. Recᵈ 6s. 6.    (File, No. 81.)

CAPT. THOMAS THORNHILL.—A list of what is due to capᵗ Thomas Thornehill as it was taken from his mouth, by his desire, March 10ᵗʰ 16⁵⁸⁄₅₉. Due from mʳˢ Gunnison of Puscataque about nine pounds in fish; from mʳ Henry Lampory, for wᶜʰ one wᵐ Rogers is Security, about 17ˡᵇ. Due from Jeremy Belcher of Ipswich on 2 bills, there rests due about 12ˡᵇ; from Majoʳ Shapley forty shillings, & yᵉ taylor in his house 30ˢ.
What is due from the sᵈ Thornehill to severall p'sons as follows. Mʳ Thomas Kellond, mʳ Wosley, capᵗ Johnson, mʳ Robᵗ Gibbs, Theodor Atkinson, mʳ Jollife, capᵗ Clarke, mʳ Joseph More, Arthur Mason, the sadler, Goodm. Rogers; mʳˢ Scarlett for dyett, lodgeing &c. in her house from Jan. 8. 58, whereof about six pound paid; to Geo. Broome the Taylor 7 or 8ˢ, who hath a cloake & suite yᵗ must be caled for; to Goodm. Edmunds sen., Hudson Leverett, Johnson of Puscatoque; Anne Prince, the maid in money 20ˢ.

*See p. 167.

M$^r$ Thomas Lake, m$^r$ Thomas Kellond, & John Richards, this is to request, & desire yo$^u$ (in case god take me away in this sicknes) that yo$^u$ will use yo$^r$ endeavo$^r$ in procureing the aboue said soñes due to [me] or what else may appeare by any bills or writeings yo$^u$ may meet w$^{th}$ & when received, pray satisfy what yo$^u$ finde Justly due from me, mentioned aboue or else. The charges of Sicknes & buriall being first defrayed. I should also further entreat, that yo$^u$ would enquire after any letters or goods comeing from Barbadoes &c. & to receive any consignm$^{ts}$ vnto me, & make Sale thereof, returneing the produce to my Brother coll. Timothy Thornhill, my just debts here being first paid as is aboue desired.

Boston March 10$^{th}$ 16$\frac{59}{60}$.           THOMAS THORNHILL.

Witnesses—Hudson Leuerett, Isaack Addington, who deposed 20$^{th}$ March 1659-60. Edw. Rawson. Commission$^r$ power.

At A meeting of the magīsẗs 20$^{th}$ march 1659, at y$^e$ Gōuno$^{rs}$ house present y$^e$ Gou$^r$no$^r$ dep Gouno$^r$ & Recorder. Power of Administration to the estate of y$^e$ late Cap$^t$ Thomas Thornehill, late of barbadoe$^s$, according to his Request aboue mentioned is Graunted to m$^r$ Thomas Lake, m$^r$ Thomas Kellond & m$^r$ John Richards, they bringing in an Invento$^r$y of y$^t$ estate to the next County Court, and Giving security to Administer according to lawe as farre as what of his shall Come to theire hands will reach vnto.

EDWARD RAWSON Recorde$^r$

Inventory of the estate of the late Cap$^{ne}$ Tho. Thornehill taken and appraised by vs the subscribers, Tho: Clarke, Josh: Scottow, Chrispin Hooper. Am$^t$ 26.02.03.

A horse & bridle & saddle apprised at twelue pounds by vs,

John Winslow, Jn$^o$ P$^{his marke}$ farnum.

Goods Consigned to y$^e$ said Tho. Thornhill on his peaper and Came Since his death to our hands, John Winslow, John Scottow, Am$^t$ 66.4.3. Att Court. 31 October 1660, Mr Tho. Lake, m$^r$ Jn$^o$ Richards & m$^r$ Tho Kelond deposed. Good debts, Joseph More, 01.05.0. Bad & doubtful debts, Jeremy Belcher, 01.1.9. Henry Lempry, 17.0.0. (File, No. 235. REGISTER, x. 175, contains a list of creditors additional to the above.)*

THOMAS GRIFFIN.—Administration granted July 18. 1661. [Private Letter on file relating to this estate from Thomas Parke to his brother William Parke.] To His loving and mvche Respacktad brother m$^r$ williame Parke at his Hovs in Roxberey this presant I pray.

Louing Brother
                        after due respects presented vnto youre selfe and yours, this are to intreat you to doe me the faviour as to procure for me as spiedylye as you can a letter of administratian from the Courte, acording vnto law, wherby I may be Impoured to dispose of the estate of Thomas Griffin (who is deseased) for the sattisfying of his Creaditors so Farr as the Estate will goe, thar being severall that Challang debts, and none that will administer, nether can his creditors com at the Estate for thar owne satisfacktion, whearfor I am willing for his sake who is dead, who was sumtime a retainer vnto my howse, I say I am willing to take the paines as to improue the Estate (which is but small) so farr as it will goe for the satisfacktion of his creaditors provided care may be taken, that I may not suffer tharby in my owne estate and the truth is such was the Clamers of one of his creditors that to prevent further truble, I haue payd vpon that acoumbt betwene

*See p. 177.

eleuen and twellue pounde, Confideing in your loue and Care, and the Courts readines to answer my request in a Case so Honest : I haue sent in Closed an inventory of all the Estate that we can finde, and the state of it, as for his Clothes, he dyeing in another Jurisdicktion we cannot reach them, supposeing also that the Charge of his sicknes may amount neare vnto a ballance, thus haue I aquainted you with my desires intreateing you to ackt for me with the Courte who by reason of my remoatnes cannot ackt for my self, and tharby you shall further ingadge him who allreadye ownes himselfe

    southertowne                your oblidged Brother Thomas Parke.

July the 6ᵗʰ 1661. (File, No. 270. Register, x. 359, gives an abstract [1] of the inventory, power of administration, and a reference to the letter.)

John Gore.—Inventory of that part of the Estate of Mʳ John Gore, late of Roxbury deceased which was Left unadministred at the death of Rhoda his relict widow, and sole Executrix of his last will and Testamᵗ. Taken and apprized by us whose names are under written, as it was presented to us by John Gore Administratoʳ upon the same and other relations then present 15 November 1693. The dwelling house being not worth repaireing, £10. The Barne (in the same condition) with a sider mill in it, £5. About two acres of land on which the sᵈ houseing stand consisting of Orchard yard and arable land, £23 ; halfe the wight Pasture, being about 5½ acres, £16 ; one acre salt marsh at Muddy River, £10 ; A great Bible and other Books in the house & lent out, £1.10 etc. etc. Total £101.3.

               Henry Bowen,      Nathanael Holmes.

By the Honᵇˡᵉ William Stoughton Esqʳ. John Gore admʳ presented this Inventory and made Oath, etc. Aprill 4ᵗʰ 1694.

                 Jurat Cor. William Stoughton.

                      (File, No. 162.)

(Abstract of Will in Register, viii. 282. Bond, present volume, p. 104.) [2]

Ralph Smith.—Inventory of goods of Ralph Smith taken by William Cotton, William Inglish, April 16, 1661. Amount 37.04.04. not 377.04.04, as expressed in the Register, x. 269. More found since in bookes to [3] value of 16ˢ & a watch clocke or alarum at mʳ Clarks at 20ˢ & 3 other booke at 13ˢ 4ᵈ & a little Hammer.          (File, No. 263.)

Deacon John Rogers, of Weymouth.    Inuoice of the Estate, 20 : 12 : 1660.    See Register, x. 265, for Will and Inventory, the landed [4] property not given there. One Dwelling House Barne out house & orchard 60.00.0 ; Meadow, 26.00.0 ; Broake land ten ackers, 25.00.0 ; Pasture Land ten ackers, 20.00.0 ; Swamp Land 3 ackers 01.10.0 ; Halfe one Great Lot 15 ackors, 05.00.0 ; one Great Lot 12 ackors, 04.00.0 ; one Lot more of 3 ackors, 04.00.0 ; one Lot of the Diuision of Comons 56 ackors, 08.00.0. Sume Totall as formerly mentioned £275.        (File, No. 264.)

Andrew Pitcher, of Dorchester.—19 : 1 : ⁶⁰⁄₈₄. Inventory of real estate. (See Register, x. 266, for Will and Inventory.) A dwelling house, barne [5] house Lot and Orchard, 100.00.0 ; three acres of meadowe 12.00.0 ; two hundred acres of vpland & meadowe Lyinge in or neare vnto mead Feild, 110.00.0.                    (File, No. 265.)

[1] See p. 191.          [3] See p. 189.          [5] See p. 186.
[2] See pp. 134, 359.      [4] See p. 185.

JOHN WILKIE.—11 March, 1660–61. Power of Administration on estate & inventory given, REGISTER, x. 269. One item or two of interest not[1] there enumerated. 5 siluer spons w^ch my husband gaue to ech of his 4 children one & y^e fift to me his wife, 1.10.0 ; the halfe howse & ground 60.00.0. (File, No. 267.)

CHARITY WHITE.—Feb. 1, 1660. Inventory, power of administration, etc. REGISTER, x. 265. House and ground £7. (File, No. 256.) [2]

ISABELL TURNER, widdow, Dorchester. Inventory, 17. 10. 1660. See REGISTER, x. 266. House, barne, orchard home lott in the feild In twd[3] parcells prized at 75.00.0 ; 3 akers meddow In calues pasture, 06.00.0 ; 12 akers In gr^t lotts at, 30.00.0 ; land in the 3 deuisions, 05.00.0 ; out comons uallewed at, 05.00.0.

RICHARD LANGER, of Hingham. Inventory of the estate taken Feb. [4] 18, 1660. Abstract of Will and Inventory, REGISTER, x. 269. Four acres of land giuen for two house Lotts, 08.00.0 ; A greate lott of tenn acres, 04.00.0 ; one acre & halfe of meadow lyeing at Cony hassett, 01.10.0. (File, No. 258.)

ABIELL EVERELL.—Inventory, REGISTER, x. 268. The dwelling house :[5] w^th all the priviledges of it that is seler and back yard 33 futt Long and 18 : brode, 80.00.0. (File, No. 260.)

JOHN DWIGHT, of Dedham.—See Will, REGISTER, x. 263, also, Inven-[6] tory. The latter, dated, 8. 12, 1660. The dwelling house, bake house, home barne & his p't in the vpper barne & all the home Lands west of the mille Creek, 150.00.0 ; all the Lands in Roxbery playne : broken : vnbroken & meadow, 30.0.0 ; 6 Acres of vpland in the great playne, 06.00.00 ; 6 Acres of meadowe called the Iland meadowe, 15.00.0 ; 10 acres at Fowle meadowe, 20.00.0 ; all Comon Towne Rights swamps woodelands & p'iueledges, 10.0.0 (File, No. 261.)

JOHN LUSON, of Dedham.—See Will, REGISTER, x. 267. The Invent-[7] ory (268) taken 18 (3) 1661. Dwelling house, Barne, orchyard garden & yard rome, 60.00.0 ; the p'cell enclosed behind the house, 03.00.0 ; the woodey p't of the lott & the swampe, there by lyeing. vnenclosed, 06.00.0 ; the planting Lott before the house, 27.10.0 ; one Acre ½ mead. by the Causey in Broad mead, 05.00.0 ; 2 p'cells at Foule meadowe, 15.00.0 ; 2 Acres of Ceader Swampe neere South playne, 04.00.0 ; one p'cell at Rocke meadowe & one smale p'cell at Rose mary Meadowe, 01.10.0 ; one p'cell amonge the woodland deuisions & all other deuidents, Comon Town Rights and p'iueledges, 15.00.0. (File, No. 268.)

NATHANIEL WILLIAMS.—Will, REGISTER, x. 270. Also, Inventory,[8] taken 7. 3. 1661. The howse & ground, 300.00.0 ; the howse & land y^t was m^r Blackstons, 150.00.00 ; a mare w^th francis litlefeild at weld, 14.00.0. Goods in the shop. (File, No. 271.)

JOHN TUCKER, senior, of Hingham.—Will, REGISTER, x. 269, and In-[9] ventory, the last dated Aug. 8, 1661. Dwelling house & a home lott &

[1] For all references on this page see p. 367.

barne & other housing, 90.00.0; 4 acors of pastor land lying at broad Coavo, 25.00.0 ; Salt meadow lying at broad Coave, 21.00.0 ; 8 acors of land lying in broad Cove feild, 24.00.0 ; 3 great lotts lying nigh vnto Waymouth river amounting to 50 acors or there abouts, 60.00.0 ; 3 acors of land lying in the necke among the home lotts, 05.00.0 ; two acres of land at Squirrill hill, 05.00.0 ; 3 planting lotts at yᵉ worlds end containing 13 acors, 22.00.0 ; a great lott at the great plaine containing 14 acres, 03.00.0 ; a 12 acor lott lying at the great plaine, 02.10.0 ; 2 acors 3 quarters of fresh meadow at Conahavset, 02.00.0.                                    (File, No. 272.)

¹ See p. 189.
² See p. 185.
³ See p. 186.
⁴ See p. 189.
⁵ See p. 188.
⁶ See p. 183.
⁷ See p. 187.
⁸ See p. 190.
⁹ See p. 189.

# ABSTRACTS OF THE EARLIEST WILLS ON RECORD, OR ON THE FILES IN THE COUNTY OF SUFFOLK, MASSACHUSETTS.

Prepared by WILLIAM B. TRASK, Esq., of Boston.

WILLIAM PADDY.—Leonard Dowden* and Thomas Paddy, both of Boston, principalls, in the Sume of two hundred pounds, and Benjamin Davis and Daniel Turill, jun'., of Boston, Sureties, in one hundred pounds apiece, bound unto Edward Tyng, Esq., Treasuro'. for the County of Suffolke, in New England, July 19, 1680, to administer on the remaining estate of M' William Paddy, their Father, Dece'. (formerly under y' charge of Cap'". Tho: Willett and Cap'". W'" Davis Executo'' of y' last will of s' m' Paddy) according to Law, &c. [Signed by the above parties and witnessed by Is'. Addington Cler.]

See abstract of the Will of William Paddy and the inventory of his estate, REGISTER, viii. 355; vii. 339. (See pp. 139, 114).                    (File, No. 189.)

GEORGE RUGGLES.—[Petition of his widow.] I wolde desier the honered Courte that thay wolde be pleased to take in to Consideration my youngest sonn, as touching his fathers desier Conserning the hauing of the one side of his fathers house which was well knowen to be his minde, and all the Rest haue had somthing alredy and he is now unprouided for in Respect he is a yong man and must be w'th mee to helpe mee, and John nuten lifing in the house with vs while my husband was yet lifing Cane testifi that it was hise desier it sholde so be, and Elizebeth Ellis liveing by one of ouer naibers Can also testifi [to] the same.

The Testimony of Elizebeth Ellis, ageed about Twenty four yeers, this deponant sayth, that shee heard Gorg Rugels say, about Two or Three yeers since, that his Son Samuell should haue his house, and firther sayeth not.

Taken vppon Oath this 27 July 1669,

before                    JER: HOWCHIN Comiss.
                              (File, No. 194.)

LEWIS MARTYN.—[Power of Attorney.] Bee It knowne vnto all men by these pn'ts, That on the Second day of the month of December in the yeare of our Lord one thousand six hundred fifty and nyne, Before me, John Daniell, notary and tabellioy publick, dwelling in this Citty of London, admitted and sworne, and in the presence of the witnesses here after named personally appeared, John Andrews, Cittizen and marchantailor of London, principall Legatary of the Estate of Late Lewis Martin, deceased, in his life time of London, marchant, who dyed in his voyage goeing to New england, The which appearer hath in the best manner and forme unto him possible made, ordained, constituted, and appointed, and by these presents in his stead and place doth make, ordaine, constitute, and appointe M' Robert Gibbs, marchant, at present resideing in New England, his true and Lawfull Atturny, Giueing and by these presents graunting, vnto his said Atturny, full power and authority for him Constituant, and in his name, and to His

---

* Leonard Dowden married Mercy, daughter of William Paddy. He died in 1682, and his widow died March 11, 1694.

vse, to aske, demannd, recouuer, and receaue, of whatsoeuer person or persons as of right shall appertaine, all Summe and Summes of monny, goods, Estate, Lands, houses, Chattell, Cattell, and other things what soeuer which are bequeathed, deuised, giuen, or Legated vnto the said John Andrewes by the said Lewis Martin, deceased. And of the recoueryes and receipts to giue acquitances or other Sufficient discharges, which shall bee soe firme and uallid as if hee, Constituant, himselfe had made and passed the same. And if neede bee, by reason of the premisses, to appeare in any Court of Justice there to Sue, Implead, arrest, Seaze, Sequester, attache, imprison and to Condemne, and out of prison againe to deliuer, And generally in and Concerning the premisses to doe all things which hee, Constituant, himselfe, might or Could doe, beeing personnally present, with power to substitute one or more Atturnyes vnder him, with like or Limmitted power, and the Same againe to reuoake, And hee, Constituant, doth promise to rattify, confirme, and hold for vallid, all & what soeuer his Said Atturny and his Substitutes shall lawfully doe, or cause to bee donne, in & about the premisses by these p'nts. In witnesse where of, the said Constituant hath Signed, Sealed and deliuered, these p'nts, Thus donne and passed in this said Citty of London, in the presence of the persons vnder written, witnesses hereunto Called and required.                                          JOHN ANDREWS.

John Winder
P. Whetcomb                          Quodatt escor
Francis Parson                       rogatus et Requisitus
Wᵐ Allen
    1659
James Whetcombe                      Ioᴱˢ. DANIELL, Not. Pubᶜᵘˢ
                                     1659.        (File, No. 211.)

See inventory of the Goods of Lewis Martine, deposition of Thomas Trapp, &c., REGISTER, x. 87.| (See p. 173).

## ABSTRACTS OF THE EARLIEST WILLS ON RECORD, OR ON THE FILES IN THE COUNTY OF SUFFOLK, MASSACHUSETTS.

Prepared by WILLIAM B. TRASK, Esq., of Boston.

HUMPHREY ATHERTON.—Humphrey Atherton was appointed by His Excellency Joseph Dudley, Esq$^r$ Gov$^r$ &c., Administrator on the estate of his grandfather, Major Humphrey Atherton,* of Dorchester, deceased, Oct. 27, 1715.

We, Humphrey Atherton Husbandman & Ebenezer Withington, husbandman, both of Dorchester & Edward Weaver Gent. of Boston & all in the County of Suffolk, are bound in the sum of Two hundred Pounds, Oct. 27, 1715. The Conditions of this Obligation is such, That if the above bounden Humphrey Atherton Admitted Adm$^r$ to the Estate of his Grandfather Humphrey Atherton, late of Dorchester, Yeoman, decd. in behalf of him self & the rest of the Grand Children & heirs of the said deced., do make a true Inventory of all the Goods, Chattels, Rights and Credits of the said Deceased, &c. &c. then the obligation to be void.

<table>
<tr><td>Sealed and Delivered<br>in Presence of<br>Samuel Tyley Jun$^r$<br>Timothy Mather</td><td>HUMPHREY ATHERTON,<br>EBENEZER WITHINGTON,<br>EDWARD WEAVER.</td></tr>
</table>

Dorchester October 1, 1716.—Received of Humpry Atherton, the some of fourtene shillngs, for two days work at subdiuidiug and shewing the Lines of his Lots of Ceder swamp Medow and upland by me, by me,

EBEN$^r$ MAWDSLEY.

June 6, 1717. An Inuintorey of my granfather Atherton, Comon Rightes in Dorchester, It being all that I Can find of his.—To a Lot in the 12 deuisons in dorchester New grant Con taining 198 acres, prised a fiue shiling and six penc per acre, 54. 09. 00 ; In the Ceder swamp, the 2 Lot,

* The following deed is on record at Boston :

Capt. Humphrey Atherton, of dorchester (for and in consideration of fyve shillings the Acre by him in hand received) granted vnto Eleazar Lusher, of dedham, all that his meadowe as well that sixty Acres already laid out, as also all that which belongs to him the sd. Humphrey by Cõmon rights, by him purchased, wch. sd. meadow is scituat in Fowle meadow, provided that if within the space of thirty yeares next after the date hereof, the Inhabitants of dorchester towne or village erected & set vp in that place neere the Blue hills where formerly it was intended, & yt all the charges disbursed by the sd. Eleazar, his heires & assignes, for purchase, measureing, or other improvements, whereby the meadow is meaded† & made better, be againe repaid them, and if the sd. Humphrey, his heires & Assignes, make demand thereof, then the possession quietly to be d'd within the space of one whole yeare after such demand made : otherwise the former bargaine to stand in force. Date 20 (9) 1646.

<table>
<tr><td>Sealed & d'd in p'nce of<br>William Aspinwall,<br>Matthew Boyes.</td><td>HUMPHREY ATHERTON & a seale.<br>Recorded. 4. 5. 1650. Suffolk Registry of Deeds,<br>vol. i. p. 120.</td></tr>
</table>

† According to Bailey's Dictionary, the noun *meadow* is derived from an Anglo-Saxon word meaning *to mow*. Perhaps the verb *to mead*, evidently from the same root, which we do not find in any dictionary to which we have had access, means to render better adapted for mowing.

370

6.¼acr, it is layd out in Bear Swamp in dorchester, new grant, it being pore, sum alowance is giuen in henshaws Shwamp ; The 34 Lot on the meadows Botom, Laid out to my grandfather in Dorchester new grant, 7. 2. 0.; In the upland in Dorchester new grant is Laid out to my grandfather, 125 acres, and abut 12 years ago Reseued of the selectmen one my granfathers A Compt, one pound one shiling or their aboutes, 01. 01. 00.

July 22, 1717.  We whose Names are under written haue Received of Mʳ Humphry Atherton, the day of yᵉ Date herof, for three days Service, horse & Man, to vew & apprize yᵉ Remaining part of humphry Athertons Estate deces'd. the Sum of Twenty shillings to Each of us, we say Receivᵈ by us, £3. 0. 0. James Blake, Junʳ, Thomas Tilestone, Phillip Withington.

Messrs. Thomas Tilestone, Philip Withington, Blacksmith, and James Blake Junʳ, Yeaman, ordered to make an apprizement of the estate, July 16 or 19, 1717, signed, Samuel Sewall.  Apprized by them, 198 acres of upland in yᵉ Twelve Divisions in Dorchester, at six shillings pʳ acre, £59. 8. 00 ; six acres & a quarter in yᵉ 2ᵈ lot in yᵉ Cedar swamps in Dorchester at Ten shillings pʳ acre, £3. 2. 6. ; Seven acres & half of Meadow bottom, it being part of yᵉ 34ᵗʰ Lot of Meadow bottom in Dorchester, at fiveteen shillings pʳ Acre, £5. 12. 6.; One Hundred twenty & five Acres of Upland in yᵉ Twenty fiue Divisions of Land in Dorchester, it being part of yᵉ 35ᵗʰ Lot, at four shillings & six pence pʳ Acre, £28. 2. 6.  Totel £96. 5. 6. [Another inventory, sworn to before Samuel Sewall, June 24, 1717, varies slightly from the above ; it mentions, also, Pidgeon Swamp. Signed by Philip Withington, Thomas Tileston.]

The Administrator's account was rendered and approved Sept. 26, 1717. Amt. £10. 5.  Among the items—" To Mr Meriam for Recording Do. &c. [that is, the inventory] 8s."

Humphrey Atherton gives bonds, with Ebenezer Williams and Benjamin Cheny, in presence of Jonathan Willis and John Boydell, Oct. 9, 1717, to pay the heirs their portions.

The Deposition of William Royall and of Mary His Wife, both of full Age, Testifyeth and Sayeth, yᵗ we, yᵉ Deponents, living near the Burying Place in Dorchester, do Know yᵗ about 14 years agoe Major Athertons Tomb was fallen all down, and lay in a shamefull manner, and was built up again by His Grandson Humphrey Atherton, and it now Stands in a Decent manner.  March 3. 1717–18.*

| Witnesse our Sign Manuall | | his | |
| WILLIAM | × | ROYALL |
| | mark. | |
| | her | |
| MARY | × | ROYALL |
| | mark. | |

Suffolk Ss :

William and Mary Royall being Personally Examined affirmed The Truth of yᵉ aboue written Testimony, Upon their Certain knowledge and Remembrance, & made Oath thereof.

Before me,  ELIJAH DANFORTH,
Dorchester    Pacis Justiciario in Comitatu Prædicto.
March 3, 1717–18.

* The well-known inscription on the tomb of Maj.-General Humphrey Atherton is printed, REGISTER, ii. 382.  A representation of a drawn sword, 3 feet and 11 inches in length, is cut into the freestone over the inscription on the horizontal tablet.  This stone, by measurement, is 6 feet in length; 3 feet 2 inches wide; and 3½ inches in thickness.  It rests on a brick base, 2 feet 6½ inches in height.  The slab projects about 3½ inches over the sides and ends of the base.

To the Hon^ble Samuel Sewall Esq.^r Judge of Probate, &c. The Me-morial of Humphrey Atherton. Humbly Sheweth, That the Memoriall of Humphrey Atherton of Dorchester Admin^r De bonis non &c. of his Grand-father Maj^r Humphrey Atherton deceased humbly sheweth That your Memorial^st having received Letters of Administration from your Hon^r is ready to give in a true and just Inventory of the said Estate yet remaining excepting nine Acres of Meadow at Burnt Swamp in Dorchester New Grant, which tho' the Numerous descendants of my said Grand Father would have brought into said Inventory, I humbly conceive it would be to my own wrong to insert therein for the reasons following. About 14 years ago the Tomb of my Grandfather being much out of Repair Samuel Wales and others of the selectmen of Dorchester since deceased, represented to me, that my said Grandfather having been a Major General and in his day a Person of Considerable Figure and Repute, It was a shame his Tomb should ly in so ruinous a Condition, and Moved that his heirs would repair the same. Whereupon I applyed myself to several of them to joyn with me therein, but their answer was that I being the next heir and the only Person who bore up his name, it belonged of right to me to do it. Upon their refusal I soon made the said Reparation at my sole Cost and Charge. Upon my representing thereof to the selectmen, I obtained a proprietors vote at a Publick Meeting October 1704 that the said Nine Acres of Mea-dow, which had like to have been lost for want of Looking After in time and which on 2 former Applications had been denied me, should be now laid out upon Account of the Charge I had been at for repair of the Tomb to me in right of my said Grandfather which I humbly conceive Do's vest the Right in me Personally. I have possessed it ever since, Cleared and Improved it, And therefore humbly pray your Hon^r would allow me to make out the Inventory exclusive of that Article that so Persons may be Appointed and Sworn to make Apprizement of the Lands mentioned in said Inventory; and I may be put into a Capacity to pay off the other Descendants their respective shares. Your Hon^r humble Servant

HUMPHREY ATHERTON.

Suffolk Ss. By the Hon^ble Samuel Sewall, Esq^r Judge of Probate, &c.

The aforegoing Petition being presented by Humphrey Atherton the subscriber, I do hereby Settle upon him and his Heirs forever The Nine Acres of Meadow at Burnt Swamp within mentioned for the Reasons men-tioned in the said Petition.

Boston March 3^d, 1717.            SAMUEL SEWALL.
Examined p^r John Boydell Reg^r.

For his Worship Samuell Sewell, Boston.
May it Please y^r Worship,
                            I beg y^r worships favor in heareing me in one word or two, in answer to y^e peice of writing you some time since show'd me, tuching somthing of the Inventory, which I suppose is Con-cerning y^e swamp, which swamp has been allowed me as I Can Prove by y^e Judge of Probates & in form of Law, besides this I Can shew by Proper account y^t I haue paid more than y^e whole Land was at y^t time valued at. I beg you to Consider y^t at y^e Divisions from y^e setling y^e town to this very day were Laid out in my granfathers name, but this is Laid out to me in name and person. If you please to Remember about twelve months since I were Examined before y^e Governor & Counsill Concerning

372

my Grandfathers Chilldren and at yᵉ same time they all acknowledged my self to be yᵉ true heir to my granfathers Estate.

I have advanced for my Granfather, since his Disceas, £5, but neither of these Children would Contribute one farthing to yᵗ, although the Expence may be Easy Proued to be a pure act of Charity Performed by me, as shall be made appear if Required, by yᵉ Cheif men of yᵉ town.

Further yʳ humbell Petitioner sayeth not but desireth yʳ Honer to Consider yᵉ Case. I am & shall Remain yʳ Honers most humble & Obediant serᵛⁿᵗ　HUMPHREY ATHERTON.

Recd 8ʳ 1. 1717.

Suffolk Ss.

By the Honᵇˡᵉ Samuel Sewall Esq. Judge of Probate &c.

Whereas, Application was made to me, by Humphry Atherton, Administrator of the Remaining Estate of his Grandfather, Humphry Atherton, heretofore of Dorchester, in the County of Suffolk, Gent. deceased, To have what remains of his Estate and Lands Apprized, in Order that the Heires of the said Humphry Atherton, deceased, may have their just shares of the said Estate, According to the Apprized value thereof (the same being incapable of a Division among them, without great prejudice thereto, whereupon Thomas Tilestone, Philip Witherington, and James Blake Junʳ. Yeomen, & Freeholders within the said County, were Impowered, and sworn, to make a due Apprizement of the said Deceaseds remaining Real Estate, who, accordingly, on the twenty ninth day of July last, valued the same, upon Oath, at the sum of ninety six pounds, five shillings and six pence ; And Whereas the said Humphry Atherton, the Administrator and Eldest son of Consider Atherton, deceased, who was the Second Son of the said Humphry Atherton, deceased, hath accepted of the said Estate, at the Apprized value thereof, The Heirs of Jonathan Atherton, deceased, who was the Eldest son of the deceased Humphry Atherton, who hath the refusal by Law, declining to take the said Estate at the Estimaçõn made of the same, Pursuant therefore to an Act or Law of this Province, Entituled, An Act for the Settlement and Distribution of Estates of Intestates and the direction, power, and Authority to me therein given, I Do by these presents Order and Assign the said .Remaining Real Estate, of the said Humphry Atherton, deceased (whereof he made no disposition) unto the said Grandson, Humphry Atherton, To hold & Enjoy the same with the members and Appurtenances thereof, unto him the said Humphry Atherton, his Heirs & assigns, forever, he or they paying unto the Heirs or Assigns of the said Humphry Atherton, deceased, their Ratable parts and Shares of the apprized value thereof (after the sum of Ten pounds five shillings is Defaulted and allowed out of the said Estate to the Administrator, for his Expences, time, trouble and Charges of Administration, their being no personal Estate to be found to satisfie the same) That is to say, To the Heirs or assigns of Jonathan Atherton, deceased, the sum of fourteen pounds six shillings and nine pence [as their double portion] To the Heirs of Hopestill* Atherton, deceased, seven pounds three shillings and four pence half penny [To the Heirs or assigns of Watching† Atherton, Elizabeth Mather, Rest Swift, Margret Trobridge,

---

* This name is generally written Hope. See the fac-simile of his signature with a sketch of his life, in the History of Dorchester, p. 490. He was minister of Hatfield. Rev. Hope Atherton died June 8, 1677.

† On one of the documents the name is Waiting, instead of Watching. The latter is

Isabel Wales, Mary Weeks, Patience Humphrey, all deceased, and to Thankfull Bird, the only surviving daughter of the said Humphry Atherton deceased, to each of those, thus enumerated, £7. 3s. 4½d. apiece] to Compleat their respective shares in said Estate, to be paid within one year, with Interest till paid, at the rate of five p<sup>r</sup> Cent p<sup>r</sup> Ann. Each Party to whom a share is allotted to give Bond with Suretys (in Case debts be hereafter made to appear), to pay back to the Administrator aforesaid their Respective Parts of all such Debts, and of the Administrators Charges.

Oct. 9, 1717.                    SAMUEL SEWALL.

John Boydell, Reg<sup>r</sup>.

Suffolk Ss.

To the Hono<sup>ble</sup> Samuel Sewall Esq<sup>r</sup> Judge of Probate, &c.

The Petition of Benjamin Bird, son of Thankful Bird, one of the Daughters and Heirs of Major Humphrey Atherton, late of Dorchester, decd., Intestate, & also Assign of y<sup>e</sup> s<sup>d</sup> Thankfull,

Sheweth, That Humphrey Atherton, Grandson and Administrator of the Remaining Estate of the said Major Humphrey Atherton, hath Omitted, In the Inventory thereof Exhibited to your Honour, to Include One hundred & Twenty five Acres of Upland, which was given as an Addition to the same quantity of Upland in the Twenty five Divisions of Land in Dorchester, it being part of the 35<sup>th</sup> Lott and given by the Committee who

doubtless correct. He married, Jan. 23, 1677-8, Elizabeth, daughter of Samuel Rigby. The names of the husbands of the seven daughters mentioned above, are as follows: Timothy Mather, Obadiah Swift, James Trowbridge, Nathaniel Wales, Jr., Joseph Weeks, Isaac Humphrey, Thomas Bird, Jr. There were twelve children in all. Besides the ten above enumerated, he had a son *Consider*, who married, Dec. 19, 1661, Ann Annable, and Increase, bapt. Jan. 2, 1641, who "died at sea," says the History of Dorchester, page 105.

We have taken especial pains to learn the number and names of the children of Humphrey Atherton. Heretofore there has been much perplexity attending the attempt. We are satisfied as to the correctness of our list so far as names are concerned, though not so sure, in the absence of some of the births or baptisms of the children, that they are all placed in precise genealogical order. Savage mentions a daughter "Catharine, sometimes called Elizabeth." We have seen no evidence, after much research, that the Major General ever had a daughter named Catharine, though we think his grandson Humphrey had a Katharine. He had a daughter Isabel, it is clear, who married Nathaniel Wales, Jr., as above stated, and a wife Mary, perhaps the mother of all his children, who died his widow about ten years after him. Neither of these two are mentioned by Mr. Savage.

Mary Atherton, of Dorchester [widow of Major Humphrey Atherton], will made Feb. 21, 1671. Mentions daughters Patience and Mary; daughters Mather, Swifte, Bird; sons Watching, Consider, Hope; grandchildren Mary Walls, Mary Weeks, Elizabeth Throwbridge, Katherine Mather, Rest Swifte, Thankfull Bird. Witnessed by William Prescott and John Gurnell, who deposed Oct. 3, 1672. (Probate Records, vol. vii. pages 245, 246.)

Inventory of the estate of the late Increase Atherton, of Dorchester, to the 13th pt. of £471. 2s. 6d. in the hands of the Children of ye late Major Generall Atherton, as by the Audit & Determination of Capt. Hopestill Foster and Wm. Parks of the Diuision of ye sd 13 pt. being £33. 14s. 00d. Mr Jonathan Atherton deposed Aug. 15, 1673. (Probate Records, vii. 319.)

Inventory of the estate of Humphrey Atherton, of Stoughton [grandson, as we understand it, of Major Humphrey Atherton of Dorchester], April 10, 1749. Elizabeth Atherton, widow, Administratrix. Mentions Cuffee, a Negro Man, £300; Land by the Way that Goeth to the Calves Pasture, £1050; 6 acres of Land on the Great Neck, butting on the road leading to Castle William, £660; 10 acres of Meadow pt English & pt salt that lyeth between the Little Crossing going on the Great Neck & the old Harbour so called, £640; two acres of upland lying on the Neck by the Way to Castle William, £240; 2 Acres of salt meadow joyning to the old Harbour, £80; 10 Acres of Pasture Land lying in the 3 Divisions, £200. Total old Tenor £2878. Taken by Joseph Bass, Zebadiah Williams, Preserved Capen. Elizabeth Atherton, widow of Humphrey, deposed May 23, 1749. There was an agreement made March 18, 1772, in the division of the land of Humphrey Atherton, deceased, among the five children, viz. Humphrey Atherton, of Dorchester; Elizabeth, who married Ebenezer Moseley; John, yeoman; Consider, Gentleman; and Anna, who married Edward Belcher, she and her husband both dead, her son John represents her in the agreement. Witnessed by David Clap and Thomas Moseley. (Probate Records, vol. 42, page 398.)

laid the whole 250 acres out in consideration of the badness of the Land, and y' pet' further saith, That the said Humphrey Atherton, Adm' as afore-s⁴, Hath neglected to Inventory Five Acres, three Quarters, and 17 Rod of Meadow Land in Dorchester, whereof the said Major Atherton dyed seized; and he, the said Humphrey Atherton, yᵉ Adm' claims and holds the said Lands not Inventoryed, under pretence that your Hon' hath settled the same upon him. And further, your Petit' saith, That the s⁴ Adm' received Twenty Two shillings of Samuel Wales, which he received for lands sold, left of the six Divisions of Dorchester, belonging to the said Major Ather-ton, And yet hath Given his Estate no Credit in his Accompt of his Admin-istration for the said Twenty two shillings, To the Damage of your Pet' and other of the Grand Children of the s⁴ Major Atherton.

Your Petitioner, therefore, for himself, and also on their behalf, humbly Prays your Honour, That the said Humphrey Atherton, as Adm' afores⁴, may be forthwith Cited to Appear before your Honour to Answer to the Premisses, and that such Order may be taken therein for the Relief of your Petit' and others Concerned, as to your Honour in your great Wisdom and Justice shall seem Right and Equitable.

And your Pet' shall Pray &c.                    BENJ^A BIRD.

[Citation was issued for s⁴ Administrator to appear before the Hon^ble Samuel Sewall Esq. Judge of the Probate of Wills &c. at his Dwelling House in Boston, on Monday, June 9ᵗʰ, at 10 o'Clock in the forenoon, to answer to above Petition. Dated Boston, May 17, 1718. John Boydell Reg'.]

Endorsed : " a cording to the with in sitaon I haue sited humfri Arin-ton to apeare at the plase with in this sitaon. Jerijah Wales."

In yᵉ additional Lots to the 25 Division In Dorchester New Grant, so Called,—No. 62. Maj' Atherton 301A. 2q. 10r. part in yᵉ 26ᵗʰ Range & part in yᵉ 27ᵗʰ, next to Wrentham, by great Meadow. A true Copy from the Pro^trs Book in Dorch^tr.          Attest SAM^ll PAUL Pro^trs Clerk.
the Return made to the Record, Jan^ry 11ᵗʰ 1720–1.

Suffolk Ss. To Humphrey Atherton, of Dorchester, in the County afore-said, Husbandman, Adm' of the remainder of Estate of Major Atherton Deceased.

Whereas you have hitherto Neglected to Exhibit a true & perfect Inven-tory of the said Deceaseds Estate contrary to Law,

These are therefore to Cite you to Appear before the Hon^ble Samuel Sewall Esq. Judge of Probate &c. at his dwelling House in Boston, on this day fortnight, at 10 oClock in the morning, in order to bring in the Deceaseds Estate not already settled, & to prevent your Administration bond being put in Suit.

Hereof you are not to fail,
Dated in Boston the 30ᵗʰ day of November, 1724.

1724, Decemb' 14ᵗʰ Continued to
3 a Clock p.m. on Thursday next.                    JOHN BOYDELL Reg'.
Names on the back—Maj' Thoˢ Tileston,          p' order of s⁴ Judge.
James Blake Jun', Robert Spur Jun'.

Endorsed—                    Dorchester, Dec. 7ᵗʰ 1724.
By Virtue of the within Citation, I have summoned the within named Atherton to meet at time and place as within Directed, by
EBENEZER WILLIAMS.

We, the subscribers, Being appointed and sworn by the Judge of Probate for the County of Suffolk, to prize the Remaining Estate of Major Atherton, of Dorchester, Deces<sup>d</sup>, have accordingly on the day of y<sup>e</sup> date hereof, prized it as followeth (viz)

Laid out to Maj<sup>r</sup> Atherton, in the 25 Division, in Dorchester, one Lott N° 62 : 30lacr 2qr 10rd—225 15

THO<sup>s</sup> TILESTON,   ROBERT SPUR Jun<sup>r</sup>
Dorchester Feb<sup>r</sup> 1<sup>st</sup> 1724–5.         JAMES BLAKE Jun<sup>r</sup>.

Humphry Atherton, Administrator, made Oath that this is a true and perfect additional Inventory of the estate of Major Humphry Atherton, of Dorchester, deceased, so far as is come to his knowledge, and that if more hereafter appear he will Cause it to be added.     THO<sup>s</sup> TILESTON

Feb. 11<sup>th</sup> 1724–5.   SAMUEL SEWALL J. prob<sup>t</sup>.   ROBERT SPUR Ju<sup>r</sup>
                                               JAMES BLAKE Jun<sup>r</sup>


[Benjamin Bird, Yeoman, Obadiah Swift, Blacksmith, & Richard Withington, Yeoman, all of Dorchester in the County of Suffolk, gave bonds unto the Hon<sup>ble</sup> Josiah Willard Esq. Judge of the Probate of wills, in the sum of Five hundred pounds Currant money in New England. Oct. 26, 1730.]

The Condition of this Present Obligation is such, that Whereas the Remaining Real Estate of Humphry Atherton, late of Dorchester, in the County of Suffolk, Gent. deceased, Intestate, not admiting of a Division among all his Heirs, & the said Estate having been Apprized at the sum of Two hundred Twenty five Pounds & fifteen shillings is assigned unto the within bounden Benjamin Bird [one of the sons of Thankfull Bird, one of the daughters of the said Humphrey Atherton deceased] he paying thereout to the Heirs & Representatives of the said Deceased their Reatable Parts and shares of the Apprized value thereof to Compleat their Respective Shares of and in the said Remaining Estate (after the aforesaid sum of Thirteen Pounds & fifteen shillings is Subducted & allowed thereout) which sums are to be paid within one year with Interest for the same all paid, at the rate of six p<sup>r</sup> Cent p<sup>r</sup> annum. Now if therefore the said Benjamin Bird fulfill the Decree of the s<sup>d</sup> Judge of Probate by paying the aforesaid sum of Money with Interest, then this Obligation to be void, otherwise to remain in full force.

Signed sealed & Delivered          BENJ<sup>a</sup>. BIRD
In presence of us                OBADIAH SWIFT
Geo : Thornton                  RICHARD WITHINGTON.
John Boydell Reg<sup>r</sup>.

The Accompt of Humphrey Atherton, Adminis<sup>r</sup> de bonis non, &c. on the Estate of Grand Father Humphrey Atherton, late of Dorchester, Gent. deceased.

The said Accomptant Chargeth himself with all & singular the Rights of the said Deceased specifyed in an Inventory by him Exhibited on the 1<sup>st</sup> of Feb. 1724, Amounting to £225. 15. And the s<sup>d</sup> Accomptant prays allowance [for sundries mentioned, Amt. £13. 15]. Humphrey Atherton, Admin<sup>r</sup> presented the foregoing & made Oath that it contains a just & true Accompt of his Administration on the Remaining Estate of his Grand Father, Humphrey Atherton, deceased, so far as he hath proceeded therein ; which I Do Accordingly allow & Approve of, Benj⁺ Bird, one of the Heirs of the Deceased, being present & was Consenting thereto.

J. WILLARD.

Boston Octob' 1730.

[File, 275. Probate Records, new arrangement, xviii. 512 ; xix. 343 ; xx. 6, 22, 63, 295 ; xxiii. 530 ; xxviii. 203, 204.]

See REGISTER, vol. x. p. 361, for administration on estate of Major General Humphrey Atherton, in 1661, as also for a copy of a letter from the Rev. Richard Mather, written at Dorchester, Sept. 27th of the same year, directed to John Endicott, Esq., and Richard Bellingham, Esq., Governor and Deputy Governor of the Massachusetts, relative to the settlement of the estate of the said deceased.

It would seem as if the maiden name of the wife of Humphrey Atherton was Mary Wales, as Nathaniel Wales, Sen', in his will, dated June 20, 1661, says, "my Brother in Law, Humphrey Atherton." Atherton, who was appointed overseer to the will, and was the only witness, died about four and a half months previous to the death of the testator, Nathaniel Wales, Sen. The day before the death of Wales, which occurred Dec. 4, 1661, his written will was read to him, "who desired it might be soe." This was witnessed by William Snelling and John Wiswall.

In this connection it may be well to mention that Mr. Savage says that Nathaniel Wales, Sen' "had wife Isabel, who outlived him but two weeks," whereas Isabel was the wife of Nathaniel Wales, Jun'. Her death is recorded in Boston—where the father, son, and son's wife died,—thus : "Isabel, wife"—not widow—"of Nathaniel Wales, died Dec. 18, 1661. "Nathaniel Wales"—that is the junior—"died May 20, 1662." The widow of Nathaniel Wales, Sen., was Susan, or Susannah, whose maiden name was Grenaway, daughter of John and Mary Grenaway of Dorchester. [See this volume of the REGISTER, page 56.]

## ABSTRACTS OF THE EARLIEST WILLS ON RECORD, OR ON THE FILES IN THE COUNTY OF SUFFOLK, MASSACHUSETTS.

Prepared by WILLIAM B. TRASK, Esq., of Boston.

MARTINE STEBBINS.* An Inventory of y⁺ Household Goods of y⁺ Late deceased Martine Stebbins, prized £34. 04. 01. More the booke Debts.

* 2 (10) 1650. Martin Stebbin, of Boston, granted vnto Richard Gardner, of Roxbury, his house, barne, orchyard & three roodes of land in Roxbury, bounded with the lands of John Levins his heires vppon the South, the highway west, & the lands of Wᵐ Cheiney North & east, & this was by an absolute deed dated 29 (7) 1648.

Sealed and dd in　　　　　　　　　　　　　　MARTIN STEBBINS & a seale.
　　p'nce of
Wᵐ Parke, John Stow, Wᵐ Aspinwall.

Martin Stebbins of Boston granted vnto Tho: Gardner, of Roxbury, 13 acres & 20 rods

At A Countie Court held at Boston 23: 9: 59. John Stebbins Acknowledged on his Oath that this is a true Inventory of the Estate of Martine Stebbins to his best knowledge, that while he knowes more he will discover it.

A list of debts due to the late deceased Martine Stebbins victualler, Anno 1657, 1658, 1659. [These are in amounts from 5 pence to four pounds 2 shillings 6 pence.] John Comer; Thomas Watkins; James Pearose; Zacharie Buckmaster; Good. Hawkes, of Hingham; Nicholas Whitmarsh; The Stoddrs, of Hingham; Mr Chard, of Weymouth; Phillip Long, Tobacco man; Goodman Bunne, of Hull; Goodman Emans, shooemaker; Henry Curtis, seaman; Thomas Andrews, of Hingham; Jonathan Webb, of Maulden; Nathaniell Huñe; Elder Bates, of Weymouth; Nicholas Morton, of Weymouth; Symon Lapdell, of Hartford; Goodman Lincolne; William Harvie; Widdow Johnson, of Hingham; John Ripley, of Hingham; Richard Fellowes, of Springfield; Isaac Walker; Hen: Peas, fisherman; Robert Cademan; William Furnel, seaman; David Wheeler; John Love, of Hingham; Rich^d Holeman, of Plymouth; Goodman Baker, of Dorchester; Goodman Francis, of Brantree; Roger Spencer; Goodman Largine; John Pole, m^r Sheafes man; Mr Atkinson; Gilbert Dundee; John Davis, Sawyer; M^r Peirpoint; Goodman Cheney; Phillip Beale; William Risby; Mr Hickes, of Boston; Goodman Drinsdall, Coup'.; Symon Roberts; Daniell Bacon, of Woburne; Thomas Hull, Coup.'; Nath Boswith; Goodman Pitts, of Hingham; M^r Fish; Goodman Shedwell; Goodman Sterns, of Watertowne; Thomas Lambert; Stephen Barret; William Ford; John Goram, of Bastable; Henry Adams, Shipwright; Nicholas Badiford; Daniell Lincolne, of Hingham; Thomas Gill, of Hingham; Goodman Williams, of Nawset; Jeremy Beales, of Hingham; Giles Elby; M^r Anthony Crosby; Rich^d Kent; Joseph Bates, of Hingham; John Finch; Math: Coy; Tristram Hull, of Bastable; M^r Edzer, the turner; Joseph Greene, of Weymouth; James Ware, fisherman; Goodman Ward, of Scittuate; Philip Wharton; Benjamine Boswith; Thomas Filbrooke, of Hampton; Rice Jones, fisherman; John Clough, Hatter; John Tuckerman; Thomas Withhead, seaman; Thomas Fitch; M^r Lindon; John Pentecost, seaman; Will. Ockinton; Will. Woodcocke; Goodman Midge, of Mauldine; Edward Bedwell; Goodman Baker, of Hull; Thomas Cohowne, of Hull; Goodman Rawlins, housewright; Goodman Bird, of Scittuate; Goodman Benson, of Hull; John Gent, fisherman; Cap^t Johnson; Goodman Gridley; Goodman Hagburne; Thomas Wilson, Smith; Math: Abda; M^r Anderson; Robert Sanford, Carter; Goodman Sonart, Seaman; Robert Peirce, of Ipswich; David Hitchborne; Tho Wilshier; Harbart of Brantrey; Goodman Sprage, of Hingham; Will. Peacocke; M^r Buncker; M^r Wilson; M^rs Keayne; M^r Breaden, m^rchant; M^r Tilly; Richard Woodies, fisherman; M^r Davis; Rayment, of Salem; John Towers, of Hingham; Barlow, fisherman; Sam^ll Hancocke; John

of land in Roxbury, wood & pasture land, 20 (9) 1649. Witnessed by John Stowe, John Pierpont, William Aspinwall. And another lot to the same person of 20 acres, in Roxbury 5 (10) 1649, bounded on the southwest w^th m^r Blackstone or his heirs, betweene him & W^m Courser, northwest vppon M^r Leveret, being there on the North side of the Hogscott hill.

15. 10. 1653. Martyn Stebens, of Boston, brewer, sold unto Wm. Bartholmew, of Ipswich, & to his Assigns, the Copper now being in his brewhouse, together w^th all the brewing vessels in y^e said brewhouse. If said Stebins pay said Bartholmew, 6 pounds 10 shillings in money, Corne or english goods to content the said Bartholmew or his assigns, this obligation to be voyd.

Witnessed by Nathaniell Dixer, Mather U Clarke.
his
mark

378

Keen, Seaman; Robert Nash; John Lowel, Carp.; Benjamin Negus; Joshua Scottow; Goodman Belcheere, of Brantree; Goodman Euerill; Sam[ll] Lincolne; Rob[t] Tayler, fisherman; Thomas Joanes, of Hull; Job Juttkins; Cap[t] Olliver; M[r] Bridgham; Will. Norcutt; John Thompson, of Newhaven; M[r] Woodcocke, Gunnsmith; Rob[t] Wier; Thomas Smith, seaman; Goodman Goodall; Doctor Stone; Georg. Hallsall; Will. Waters, senio[r]; Thomas Barlo, fisherman; Andrew Cload; Goodman Bosten; Ambrose Phillips; Josiah Eaton; Edward Messinger; M[r] Graves; James Robison; Sarg[t] Woody; James Filbrooke; Sam[ll] Sherman; Josep Wise; Goodman Myrrick, of Springfeild; Ambrose Leech; M[r] Clarke, of Virginia; John Stone, of Hull; Edward Powell, seaman; Goodman Tabutt; Edward Gould, of Boston; John Barber; Goodman Howard, of Weymouth; Samu[ll] Bucknell; Gabrill Collins; John Lewis, welchman; William Wardell; Sam[ll] Jutkins; M[r] Barnes, of Plymouth, Doctor Alcocke.

Debts Chalenged from y[e] deceased Estate. [From 7s. to 4 pounds.] M[r] Lynd; Tho Bradbery; M[r] Sheafe; Goodman Baker, of Dorchester; Mr. Cursome; Goodman Stubes, of Hull; Will. Chamberline, of Hull; Goodman Belcher, of Brantrey; To Harbert, of Brantrey; Marshall Wayt; Goodman Euerill; Ellias Parkman; Georg. Bran; William Hambleton; Mathew Irnes; Robert Sandford; John Lowell; Goodwife Davis; Ellihar Far; By a woman of Charlestowne; M Bunker; Ben Thwing; M[r] Glover; Tho: Wiborne; by a man of Redding; M[r] Olford; Thomas Waterman; Daniell Hancock; Goodman Douce; M[r] Alcocke; John Stebbins. 83. 19. 07.

WILLIAM PEIRCE.* Agreement of Widow Peirse & her Children.— Whereas William Peirce, marriner, formerly of Boston, died Intestate & left but a small Estate besides an house & some land on y[e] back side thereof as by the Inventory doth appear [see REGISTER, x. 360], & leaving* four sons & one daughter, most of them being very small, Administraçõ. to the Estate was granted unto Esther Peirce, the Relict of y[e] s[d] W[m] Peirse, & nothing else done by y[e] Court about dividing the Estate. The Children now being growne up, twc of y[e] sonnes being in age, & two of y[e] Children more having chosen theire Guardians, w[ch] Guardians were accepted by y[e] Court, & y[e] County Court having appointed a Guardian for y[e] youngest Child, & advising them to make an agreement amongst themselves, they have accordingly met, considered & agreed, as followeth.

First. That in Consideraçõ. of the great paines, care, diligence & cost of the mother in Educating & bringing up of all these Children, & hath

* William Pearse, of Boston, seaman, and Hester his now wife, in Consideration of £38.16.8. sterling, to vs payd, by John Euered, alias Webb, of Boston, merchant, sell vnto the said John Euered alias Webb, land on the north side of the streete or markett place, in Boston, betwixt the land of M[r] Jacob Sheafe on the west side, and the lands of the said William Pearse on the east side, the lands now or late in the tenure of M[r] John Blackleach on the north, and facing on the markett place, southerly, conteining vpon the said front Thirty and seuen foote in breadth Southerly, and thirty two foote and a halfe in breadth at the Northerly End, and threescore foote in length whereon the said John Euered, alias Webb, hath built a dwelling house, a shop, and a cellar (and is now in his tenure), To Haue and to Hold, &c. March 18, 1653. William Pearse, Hester Pearse. In the presence of James Oliuer, Tho. Bratle, John Richards, Nathaniell Anther, Not[y] Pub[le]. Possession given same day. Suffolk Registry of Deeds, Vol. 3, pp. 144, 145.

Hester Peirse, of Boston, Spinster, in consideration of £40 paid by Nathaniel Peirse, of Boston, do sell the s[d] Nathaniel Peirse land in Boston, bounded on the south with the common Alley or passage leading into the land of Esther Peirse the Elder, containing 35½ foote, a little more or less, on the North with the land of Samuel Plumer, 32½ foote, on the East with the Land of Ebenezer Peirse 45½ foote. To have and to hold, &c. Oct. 30, 1679.
Suffolk Deeds, Vol. 11, page 251.

*See p. 192.

379

not wasted but bettered the Estate by adding to the building & otherwaies, she shall haue the movables that yet remaine, to her one disposing, & alsoe, the now dwelling house & Leaneto adjoining to it as farre as y$^e$ middle of the Chimny's, together w$^{th}$ y$^e$ Land behinde the house, being twenty four foote & three inches Northward from y$^e$ Leanto, & twenty three foote & a halfe from y$^e$ Northwest corner of Cap$^t$ Walden's Land.

Secondly. William Peirse, her Eldest Sonne, is to haue the aforesaide house & Land, after the death of his mother, for his double portiō. hee paying when it comes into his hand to the other four Children ten pounds in mony, to bee Equally divided to them.

Thirdly. Nathaniell Peirse, her Second Sonne, who is alsoe in age & acts for himselfe, shall haue in his present possession that parcell of Land on the west side of the foresaide house & land, bounded on the East w$^{th}$ the foresaide house & land (provided that although Nathaniells part reach to the middle of the Chimnies on the South part alsoe, as well as on the North, yet that part on the South of the Chimnies shall remain for the use of the now dwelling house, during the continuance of the same) on the South w$^{th}$ the great Streete, on the west w$^{th}$ M$^r$ Thomas Deane's Land, on the North w$^{th}$ the Land laide out for Esther Peirse his sister, he Leaving an Entry or passadge way on the west side, & on the North End through the whole Length and breadth thereof, five foote wide, to bee a passadge way for his Mother's & Esther's Land, but hee may build over the Entry provided it bee not Less then Seven foote high. It is agreed alsoe, because his Land is far better then the other parts in Vallew; espetially Esther's, that hee shall pay unto his sister Esther ten pounds, in mony, when she shall attaine to the age of one & twenty yeares, & ten pounds more, when she shall attaine to the age of 23 yeares. But if God take her away by death before the money be dew, she may, by will, dispose of it to whom she please to receiue the said Suffies in these yeares of the Lord in which she might haue received it if she had lived, alsoe, the saide Nathaniell shall pay ten pounds more in mony to his mother at her demand.

Fourthly. Moses Peirce, unto whome Cap$^t$ Roger Clap is Guardian, hee being under age, is to haue (when hee comes to age), that parcell of land which is bounded on the East with that Lane that goes down towards Clement Grosses on the North, with saide Grosses Land on the West, w$^{th}$ the Land of Saffiuel Pluffier on the South, w$^{th}$ Ebenezar's land, fronting to the lane, forty foote more or less, North Thirty Seven & a halfe, on the west Thirty Nine, on the South Thirty Seven and a halfe.

Fifthly. Ebenezar Peirse, unto whome Joseph Webb is Guardian, is to haue, w$^n$ hee comes to age, that peice of Land which is bounded on the East with the Lane going downe to Clement Grosses, on the North with the Land of Moses Peirce, on the west w$^{th}$ his Sister Esther, on the South with the Land of Cap$^t$ Walden & the Land belonging to the now dwelling house, fronting to the lane, thirty Eight foote, North Thirty Seven foote, West forty fiue, South thirty Seven & a halfe.

Esther Peirse, unto whome Phineas Vpham is Guardian, is to haue (w$^n$ she attaines the age of one & twenty years, or marriage w$^{ch}$ shall first happen), that parcell of Land bounded on the South w$^{th}$ the Common Alley or passage, on the west w$^{th}$ the Land of M$^r$ Tho: Deane, on the North w$^{th}$ the Land of Saffiuell Pluffier, on the East w$^{th}$ the Land of Ebenezar, it being forty fiue foote on y$^e$ East, on the South thirty fiue and a halfe, on the west forty Eight foote and a halfe, on the North thirty two foot & a halfe.

It is alsoe agreed, that the Well shallbee for the vse of the now dwelling house & for Nathaniell & Esther, they all bearing equal shares in the reparation of the s^d well, & the priviledge of the well to remaine to them & theire Successors.

Finally, it is mutually Agreed, & by these p'sents wee doe binde o'selues, that if any of us bee minded to sell o^r houses or Land thus laide out to us, we will first profer it to o^r Brethren or theire heires & they shall haue the refusall of it at another price, to buy the same, either jointly or seuerally, as may bee most sutable for those that sell. The Estate thus divided, as is herein Expressed, is the mutuall Agreement of the Widow and Children that are in age, and the Guardians to the younger Children that are under age. As Witnes o^r hands & Seals. June 3, 1672. Esther Peirse, William Peirse, Nathaniell Peirse, Roger Clap as Guardian to Moses Peirse, Joseph Webb as Guardian to Ebenezer Peirse, Phineas Vpham Guardian to Esther Peirse. Brought into Court, 14. 4^mo 1672. As Attests Free Grace Bendall Cler.

Recorded & compared, June 28, 1672. As Attests Isaac Addington, Cler.                                          (Book 7, pp. 215–217.)

NATHANIEL WALES.* Samuel Sewall Esq^r Commissioned by his Excellency Sam^l Shute Captain General and Gouernour in Chief in and over his Majestys Province of the Massachusetts Bay in New England by and with the advice and Consent of the Council to be Judge of the Probate of Wills, and for granting Letters of Administration on the Estates of Persons Deceased, having Goods, Chattels, Rights or Credits in the County of Suffolk within the Province aforesaid To Jerijah Wales of Dorchester in the County of Suffolk Yeoman Greeting. Whereas Nathaniel Wales heretofore of Boston Weaver Deceased in his last Will and Testament made his Wife Susannah Wales Executrix, who is since deceased, without having fully Administered on the Estate of the said Nathaniell Wales, I Commit unto you full power to Administer his Remaining Goods, left Unadministered by his Executrix, at the time of her Decease. And to make a true Inventory, on or before the sixth day of October next ensuing. July 6, 1719.             SAMUEL SEWALL.             JOHN BOYDELL, Reg^r.
                                (Book 21, page 430.)

Jerijah Wales and Ebenezer Holmes of Dorchester yeomen, and Thomas Wales of Braintry Blacksmith, all in the County of Suffolk, gave bond in the sum of £200, July 6, 1719. In presence of David Webb, John Boydell.
                                (File 292.)

An Inventory of the Remaining part of the Estate of Nathaniel Wales Deceased, of Dorchester, as it was apprized us, Dec^r 21, 1719.

His Lot in the 12 Divisions in Dorchester, 51 Acres at 12s. p' acre, 30. 12.; In the Cedar Swamps 3 Acres & 20 Rods at 30 p' acre 4. 13. 9 ; In the Meadow Bottom 3 Acres & 3 q^m at 20s. p^r acre, 3. 15 ; In the 25 Divisions

---

* Oct. 16, 1654. Nathaniel Wales, late of Dorchester, webster, of the one partie, & Thomas Toleman, whelewright, of Dorchester, of the other partie. Said Nathaniel Wales, in consideration of £18 paid, do sell said Thomas Tolman, land in Dorchester, in the Great lotts, Contayning by estimation 8 accres, more or lesse, Bounded w^th a Creeke & the lands of Richard Leeds on the east, the land of M^r Richard Mather on the North, the land of John Pearse on the south, the great lott fence on the west of the same, To Haue and to Hold, &c.
    In the p^resence of                         NATHANIEL WALES w^th a scale.·
Nathaniell Patten, Edmond Bowker.
Acknowledged by Nathaniel Wales and his wife, 1 (2) 1657, before me,
    Recorded May 14, 1657.                         HUMPHREY ATHERTON.
        (Suffolk Deeds, Book 3, p. 18.)

62 Acres & 2 q$^{rs}$ at 7s. p' acre, 21.17.6 ; In the Additional Lots not yet laid out 43¾ at 4s. p' acre, 8. 15. Total, £69. 13. 3. Thomas Lyon, James Blake jun$^r$, Jerijah Wales Admin$^r$ presented the above, and made oath, Dec. 28, 1719. ( Book 21, page 582.)

Tho$^s$ Tileston, Robert Spur, Jun$^r$, appointed by the Judge of Probate to prize the remaining Estate of Nathaniel Wales, of Dorchester, Deceased. Laid out to Nathaniel Wales in the 25 Divisions in Dorchester part of a Lott No. 80, 43A. 3q. at 10s. p' acre, £21. 17. 6. Jerijah Wales Admin$^r$ made oath that it contains a true Inventory on the Estate of Nathaniel Wales late of Dorchester, Husbandman, Deceased. March 8, 1724.

( Book 23, page 545.)

See abstract of the will of Nathaniel Wales, senior, REGISTER, xi. 37. *

*See p. 197.

## ABSTRACTS OF EARLY WILLS ON RECORD, OR ON FILE
## IN THE COUNTY OF SUFFOLK, MASSACHUSETTS.

Prepared by WALTER K. WATKINS, Esq., of Boston.

NOTE.—The number prefixed before the abstract is that of the number on the present docket. The reference following is that of the volume and page of the records. Many instances occur where the original is not on file, and others where they are not recorded.

No. 500.—JACOB FRENCH of Weymouth, deceased, intestate, 12 April, 1669. Inventory of lands and personal effects appraised by Thomas Dor and William Holbrock, 17 July, 1669.

Administration granted to Stephen French, sen., in behalf of himself and his sisters. Vol. v., p. 163.—(See Savage's Genealogical Dictionary.)

No. 501.—WILLIAM SAVEL, sen<sup>r</sup>, will, 19 Feb. 1668-9. Wife Sarah, house and half the orchard during life. Son Benjamin, heir of house, may give her twenty shillings towards hiring a chamber where she please, and if she live in town, sons John, Samuel and Benjamin shall provide four loads of wood yearly, also three fat swine, eighty weight, twenty bushels corn, all this if she bear his name. Her land in Bridgewater to be hers.

Son John to have house and barn, shop and tools, &c., pertaining to his trade, also three acres of land that was brother Bass.

Sons Samuel, Benjamin and William to have farm land equally; three eldest shall pay remainder of debt on Salter farm equally. John and Benjamin shall have equal share of stock and land in Bridgewater, and Quinipauge, and pay therefrom their sisters' portions.

Daughter Hannah, land and money; daughter Sarah, when twenty-one; other bequests of land to sons.

Son John and brother Samuel Bass to be executors. Son William to be apprenticed with John. Edward Bass and Edward Quinsey witnesses. Thomas Faxon, sen., and William Needham overseers.

Articles of Agreement between John, Samuel, and Benjamin Savel, and Sarah, relict of William Savel:

1. She being dissatisfied, they agree she shall have her whole estate she brought their father for her whole use.

2. Instead twenty bushels corn, they engaged to pay three bushels wheat, three of rye, six of malt, eight of Indian.

3. If she marry, to have four pounds yearly, twenty shillings in pork three pounds in corn, for which she promises to be satisfied. 14 June, 1669. Vol. vi., p. 36.—(See Savage, Boston and Braintree records, and Suffolk Deeds.)

No. 502.—WILLIAM WOODWARD of Dedham, his inventory, by Eleazer Lusher, William Avery and Robert Hinsdell.

Administration granted to Peter Woodward, juni, his brother. 31 July, 1669.—(See Savage.)

No. 503.—JONATHAN BRAGG, administration granted on the estate of, who died 19 June, 1669, at "the Castell," to Capt. Roger Clap in behalf of his mother or other friends that have right therein. Inventory, apprized by Nicholas Baxter and Eliazer Hawes, gives a pair of looms, cloth, &c.

No. 505.—MICHAEL WILLIS, will, Boston, 21 June, 1669. Wife Mildred executor. Two sons, Experience and Michael, shall have free use of shop and tools, utensils, &c., paying rent to their mother, and, on her decease, enjoy dwelling honse, with yard, garden and warehouse, the same to go to their male heirs. Daughter Temperance, if unmarried and obedient to her mother, fifteen pounds. Grandchild Joseph Phillips, when he comes to discretion, twenty shillings. Married daughters five shillings apiece, grand children two shillings apiece. Cousin Jabesh Salmon of Roxbury five shillings, sons to be partners in business.
William Alford, Richard Cooke and Elisha Cooke, witnesses. Inventory by Thomas Bumsted and John Odlin. Vol. vi., p. 38.—(See Savage and Morse's Willis Family.)

No. 506.—FRANCIS CROCUM, Joan Crocum, relict and administratrix on the estate of, Boston, giving bond for same. Witnesses, William and John Saunders. 29 Oct. 1669.
26 July, 1694, John Leach, laborer, John Vicars, fisherman, gave bond as administrators on the estate of Francis Crocum, left unadministered by Joane Crocum, with John Hill, cordwainer, and Alexander Bulman, baker, on the bond as sureties. Vols. v., pp. 176–7; xiii., p. 469.—(See Savage, under Croakham.)

No. 508.—HEZEKIAH GAY, son of John Gay of Dedham, deceased, being about 27 or 28 years, expressed his mind in reference to disposing of his estate, 25 Oct. 1669, as is here testified.
Deposition of Mary Wilson, age about 54, and Hannah Hunting, age about 28 years: We being with Hezekiah Gay in time of his sickness, he being then of sound mind, declared what he intended to have done, said: I give my brother John Bord (*sic*) my cloth cloak that I have at my father's for a suit, with the trimming, bands and linen.
To my brother Nathaniel Gay my pair of bullocks; my father my mare, and my brother John my one year old colt; brother Jonathan Gay the first colt of the mare.
The testator was then interrupted by pain and lay still awhile, his mother then told him he had forgotten his brother Samuel. He said: I give brother Samuel that which I have in my pocket; whereupon his mother felt in his pocket, and not finding anything, said to him, is it in this pocket? he said no, it is in my other pocket; and we heard no more of that. Then he said: give my mother, Mr. Burrowe's Book and my sister Whiting that new book concerning Thomas Savage. To my sisters, Abigail and Judith, five shillings apiece, and to good wife Wilson five shillings; and then extremity of pain again interrupting him, he only said to his mother who was by him, there are other things of mine that I pray father dispose of as you see cause, and these words he spake twice.                HANNAH HUNTING.
Mary Wilson further said: she heard him pray his father that every one of his brothers and sisters might have some thing of his, though he had forgotten them.                Before ELEAZER LUSHER, Assistant.
Administration granted to John, the father, and Nathaniel Gay, brother, 11 Nov. 1669. Vols. v. 176, and vi. 43.—(See REG. xxxiii., p. 45.)

No. 510.—RICHARD MILES, will, by parole, 8 Jan. 1669-70, was attested 3 Feb. 1669-70.

Inventory: 200 acres beyond Chelmsford granted by General Court to Mr. Collicut, and other effects.  394£ 14. 00.  Appraised by

WILL BARTHOLOMEW.
JAMES EVERILL.

Whereas RICHARD MILES being taken sick on board the Endeavor, being in perfect sense, we, whose names are hereunto subscribed, attest that it was his will and desire his estate be committed to his wife, &c.

RICHARD SPRAGUE.
WIll SINGLETON.

House and ground at New Haven given by his father upon a covenant of marriage.  Widow Experience Miles.  Vol. vii. 57.—(See Savage, under Miles and Collicot.)

No. 511.—ABRAHAM CHIVERS, late of Boston, administration, 12 Nov. 1669, to Mr. Jno. Atwater, in behalf of himself and rest of the creditors; his brother, Benjamin Chivers, renouncing the same.

Inventory of personal effects apprized by Jno. Odlin & Richard Gridlie.

Caleb Jones and Free Grace Bendall on a bond as sureties.  Vol. vii. p. 3.

No. 512.—TOBIAS DOBLE of Dedham died about the latter end of November or beginning of December, 1669, and no body appears to administer according to law, Joshua Fisher being " Clark of the Writs att Dedham," informs the honoured court thereof the 26 of Jan. 1669-70, signed Joshua Fisher, and administration was granted him.

Inventory of estate was made by Nathanel Colburn and Timothy Dwight 24 Feb. 1669-70, and one appraised by John Gay, Thomas Battelle, and Isaac Bullard.  Vol. vii. p. 58.

No. 515.—JOHN MINOT, of Dorchester, will, 15 July, 1669.

Provides for the necessity of his father.

Wife to dwell in his house and have fifty pounds.  Son John one hundred pounds over an equal dividend with rest of the children.  Daughter Martha, as a particular remembrance of her mother, all her mother's clothes and linen.  Son James to be kept at learning.  Son Stephen to be placed at some convenient trade.  Son Samuel to be brought up as a husbandman, and have his portion in land.  The estate not to be divided till James is twenty-one.  Other provisions for division.  Martha to be under mother's care, and James, Samuel and Stephen under the executor's care.  Father Minot, brother Stephen and son John to be executors.  Witnesses, Thomas Wilson and Timothy Foster.

Inventory, 28 Jan. 1669-70, by John Gurnell, Thomas Tileston, Roger Billing.  Vol. vi. p. 40.  (See REG. i., Minot Family.)

GEORGE BRAN, administration to his widow Martha.

Inventory, 13 Aug. 1669, by Peter Oliver and Edward Morris, giving list of household effects.  Vol. v. p. 166.

No. 513.—HUGH BROWN, inventory found in the hands of John Swett of Boston; prized by Peter Peace and Benjamin Sanderson, and one by Thomas White and Peter Frothingham; sworn to by Richard Lowden and William Browne, 27 Jan. 1669-70.  Vol. vii. p. 13.

No. 516.—WILLIAM BALLANTYNE, cooper, County of Suffolk, New England, will.

Wife Hannah one third of his estate for life. Children John, David, Elizabeth, Hannah, William, Susanna and Jonathan. Rest of estate equally divided, except twenty pounds to David on account of lameness.

Wife Hannah executrix; friends Joseph How and Thomas Dewer overseers and witnesses.

Inventory, mostly of cloths, linen, &c., and small wares. Apprized by John Bateman and Nicholas Stones, 17 Dec. 1667. Vol. vii. p. 4.—(See Savage.)

No. 517.—THOMAS MILLARD, of Boston, administration, 4 Feb. 1669–70.

Bond of John Miller of Rehoboth, with John Lake and Thomas Bligh of Boston.

Testimonies of

William Hudson of Boston, aged 57 years or thereabouts, in regard to land lying by Centry Hill; the testator said he would give it to his kinsman at Seaconk who hath many children.

Peter Oliver of Boston, aged 52 years or thereabouts, saith that about seven years ago he said to the testator that if he would give him his house lot he would build a fair house for his maintainance; but he said he had a kinsman in y$^e$ country to whom he intended to give it.

John Jackson, aged about 60 years; about twelve months ago Thomas Millard said he would give his estate to his cousin Millard, because he was brought up at his father's house. Abigail Jackson, age about 60 years, testified to the same effect.

John Waite, aged 26 or thereabouts, being at the house of Mr. John Lake where was then Thomas Miller very ill near death, stated he intended cousin Miller should have good part of his estate, and said, I have no other kindred in the country nor certainly do know that any other is alive.

John Lake, aged fifty-one years or thereabouts, spoke to Thomas Millard about an hour or two before his death about his estate; he said he intended his cousin have a good part of it.

Inventory apprized by John Wiswall & Richard Cooke. Vol. vii. p. 18.

No. 518.—CLEMENT GROSS, Jr., Bond of Clement Gross with James Oliver and Richard Collicott as administrator on the estate of his son, Clement Gross, jun., 5 Feb. 1669. Witnesses, Thomas Weld and Free Grace Bendall.

No. 519.—MARY JONSON, will, 11 Feb. 1669. To son Samuel Jonson fore part of house, and after his death to his eldest son, if he have one, if not, to eldest son of either daughters. To daughter Rebeckah Allen the back part, and on her death to her son, &c.

Daughter Hannah Liscomb and her son John Liscomb, her daughter's husband, John Liscomb, money owing by William Allen. Son Samuel Jonson, Rebeckah Allen and Hannah Liscomb, executors.

Debts to be paid out of goods in shop. Henry Bridgham and Nathaniel Bishop, overseers.

Witnesses, James F. Jonson and Nathaniel Bishop.

Inventory by John Wiswall, sen., & Thomas Clarke. Vol. vii. pp. 21, 23, 40.

No. 520.—John and Isaac Woody, Bond of Richard and Isaac Woode, to administer on the estate of John and Isaac Woody, 20 Apr. 1670, for next of Kin.

Witnesses, John Walley and Free Grace Bendall.

Inventory, John Woodie's house in Boston.

7% per annum from 25 Mch. 1653, to date, when he would have reached 21 years. Isaac Woodie's portion given by his father, John Woodie, dec'd, his will, which fell to first mentioned John Woodie as being longest lived, evidently settlement of John Woodie of Roxbury's estate. Vol. vii. pp. 23, 90. (See Reg., Vol. vii. pp. 338–339.) (See pp. 113-114).

ERRATA.—Page 325, lines 15 and 16, *for* 12 Nov. 1669 *read* 12 : 11 mo. 1669–70; l. 16, *for* John Atwater *read* Joshua Atwater; l. 17, *for* Benjamin Chivers *read* Bartholomew Chivers.

ERRATA.—Page 325, No. 511, Abraham Chiver's brother should be Bartholomew instead of Benjamin, and John should be Joshua Atwater, the date 12 Jan. 1669–70 instead of 12 Nov. 1669. The abstract was correctly taken from the records as the files were being transferred recently, and could not be consulted.

# ABSTRACTS OF EARLY WILLS ON RECORD, OR ON FILE IN THE COUNTY OF SUFFOLK, MASSACHUSETTS.

Prepared by WALTER K. WATKINS, Esq., of Boston.

No. 521.—Nicholas Wood, will, 16 Jan. 1669–70. At his farm in Natick; some time under the inflicting hand of God. To Anna his now loving wife one third of all houses and lands at his farm which he bought of Mr. Parker, with all her wearing Clothes &c, and 17£ a year out of the farm produce, until son Jonathan comes to twenty one years, for bringing up two youngest children. To Jonathan all lands &c bought of Mr. Parker which he now lives on; other lands and cattle &c.

Son Eleazer lands bought of Lieut. Fisher of Dedham; cattle &c. Daughter Mehitabel Wood land in Milton and cattle.

Daughter Abigail Wood land in Roxbury and cattle. Daughter Beththya houses and land in Watertown which he had by his last wife (after her decease); cattle &c.

If son Jonathan die before twenty one unmarried son Eleazer to be heir to his portion giving ten pounds apiece to sisters living (among them sister Mary Thurston).

If Eleazer die Jonathan to be his heir on like conditions. To grand child Abraham Harding son of daughter Hannah Harding deceased 5£ at twenty one.

Residue of estate to be divided between two sons and six daughters when Jonathan is twenty one.

If any child shall contest, they shall lose their share. Wife Anna, Jno. Thurston. sen. and Thos. Bass, sons in law executors, friend George Barber of Medfield supervisor.

Witnesses Henry Laland and Hopestill Laland.

Probated 2 June, 1670.

Nicholas Wood of Bogastow in Natick. Inventory apprized by Henry Adames, Henry Laland and John Thurston, sen.
Bond of John Thurston and Thomas Bass with Edward Shippen and Free Grace Bendall as witnesses. Vol. vii. pp. 24, 26, 29, 49 (See Savage).

No. 522.—MR JOHN DAVENPORT, late pastor of the First Church of Christ in Boston. Inventory 22 July 1670 taken by James Penn, Anthony Stoddard and Thomas Clarke. Mr. Jno. Davenport made oath that it was a true inventory of the estate of his father. Vol. vii. pp. 49, 83.

No. 523.—JNO. PEPPER, Roxbury, will, 3 Mch. 1669–70. Being weak and infirm, his body left to his father, mother, brethren and sisters to bury.
Mother-in-law's sister shall have twenty-seven pounds due him by his father-in-law's gift, on marriage with his daughter, in profits of the land.
Twenty four pounds to four natural brothers and three natural sisters, eldest brother Joseph to have a double portion, father Robert Pepper rest of estate and to be sole executor. Uncle Isaac Johnson and friend William Gary overseers, witnesses John Watson and David Richards.
Inventory 22 Mar. 1669–70 by Timothy Dwight and Nathaniel Stearns, and one by William Gary and John Humfries. Vol. vii. p. 29, 30.

No. 524.—JOSEPH HOLDSWORTH, administration.
Deposition 13 April, 1670, of George May, Thomas Wheeler, Thomas Bollon and Job Hawkinges that Joseph Holdsworth deceased owned Joshua Holdsworth to be his brother.
Bond of Joshua Holdsworth as principal and John Harrison and George May as sureties.
Inventory 10 June, 1670, 51 pieces of eight and 3 reals, one spanish shirt and one old trunk, estate held by the deceased in Jamaica. Vol. vii. pp. 49, 58.

No. 525.—WILLIAM WARDELL, will probated 18 April, 1670.
To wife Elizabeth one-half of dwelling house in Boston during life, also movables.
To daughter Rachel Wardell 25 pounds paid in furniture. To wife's daughter Hannah Gillet 21 pounds paid in household stuff on day of marriage or at eighteen years. To wife's daughter Deborah 20 pounds.
Eldest son Uzall Wardell other half of dwelling &c., son Elihu Wardell.
Daughter Leah, wife to William Tower, 10 shillings; daughter Meribah, wife to Francis Littlefield of Wells, 10 shillings; daughter Mary, wife to Nathaniel Rust, 10 shillings.
Son Uzall, executor. James Everell and William Bartholmew, overseers. Witnesses, Ambrose Dawes, Joseph Wheeler, Wm. Bartholmew, James Everell.
Inventory, 30 April, 1670, appraised by Isaack Walker, Richard Woodde, William Parson. Vol. vii. pp. 35, 36, 94, 95, 96.

No. 526.—JOSEPH MOOR, mariner, Boston.
Inventory 9 Feb. 1669–70, of estate by Hannah Moor, giving list of sundry persons to whom debts are owed, appraised by John Lake and William Ingraham.
Richard Sharpe and John Lake of Boston on the bond of Hannah Moor to administer on estate of the late Joseph Moor. Witnesses John Temple and Free Grace Bendall. 1 April, 1670. Vol. vii. p. 19.

No.527.—WILLIAM COPP, Boston, cordwainer, will, 31 Oct. 1662, probated.

To wife Gooddeth house they live in.

Daughter Tewxsbery to live in the house where son David lives on her death to grand child William Harvey he to give his brothers Thomas and John Harvey ten pounds apiece and sister Mary ten pounds.

Son Jonathan house after his wife's decease, he to pay ten pounds to daughter Ruth, ten to daughter Lidia and to grand children John & Sarah Atwood five pounds apiece, grand children Sarah Norden and Mary Harvey five pounds each.

100 acres beyond Braintree 30 to David, 20 to Jonathan, 10 to daughter Lidia, 10 to daughter Ruth, 10 to John Atwood, 10 to grand child Samuel Norden, 10 to grand child William Harvey.

Son David executor. Witnesses Richard Croad and John nathan (*sic*) Copp.

Inventory 15 Mch. 1669–70 by John Larch and James Everell. Vol. vii. pp. 32, 33 (see REGISTER, x. p. 369).

No. 528.—JOHN MATTHEWS, taylor, Boston, will.

Wife Elizabeth to enjoy his dwelling house, son John, daughter Hannah Wigeer living in Dartmouth, old England.

Witnesses Ez. Gary [?] of Roxbury, tailor, and Thomas Swan, Boston, barber. Inventory 11 Apr. 1670, by Thomas Grubb and Nathaniel Bishop. Widow Elizabeth administratrix. Vol. vii. pp. 50–54.

No. 529.—ANTHONY FISHER, late of Dorchester deceased. Inventory 7 Apr. 1670, by Joane Fisher, apprized by Peter Woodward and John Gay.

Josiah Fisher's bond as administrator on estate of his father, Anthony Fisher late of Dedham, farmer, unadministered by Joane Fisher, late of Dedham, widow, deceased.

James Fales and Joseph Ellis sureties. 10 June, 1723. Vol. vii. p. 50. (See Dedham Historical Register, Vol. 3, p. 191.)

No. 530.—JOHN FRAIRY, junior, of Medfield. Will.

Wife Elizabeth and own two daughters, when youngest comes to fourteen years the estate to be divided in three equal parts, paying 5£ to Abraham Harding wife's son and 40 shillings to Mary Harding, her daughter.

To son John Harding one half certain land in Medfield. Wife Elizabeth, brother Theophilus and Thomas Thurston of Medfield to be executors. Witnesses George Barbur and Henry Adams, dated 27 March, 1670.

Inventory 19 Apr. 1670, by Thomas Wight sen Henry Adams and George Barbur. Vol. vii. pp. 44, 45.

No. 531.—ELNATHAN DUNCKLE, Dedham. Inventory apprized by Henry Chickering, Nathan Aldis, Daniel Fisher.

Widow, Silence Dunckles. 29 Apr. 1670. Vol. vii. p. 57.

No. 532.—EDMUND GROSE, inventory of the estate of Edmund, son of Clement Grose of Boston.

Money received from his (Edmund's) father Clement Grose. Given by Clement Grose (his mark) 27 Apr. 1670.

No. 533.—JOHN MAY's will. "We whose names are here underwritten being sent for upon the Sabbath morning being the 24[th] of Aprill 1670 to come unto y[e] House of Jno. Mays now deceased hee then being sick yet of a perfect Understanding hee said to Us" he wished to dispose of his estate to prevent trouble &c between his two sons & his wife.

Son John to have all his tools &c, half a lot of land on east side of stony river.

A brass pan to his eldest grandchild.

Rest of land &c to son Samuel.

Household goods divided equally between two sons after death of his wife.

Edward Bridge and Edward Morris to be his overseers, sons John and Samuel executors.　　　　　　　　　　　(Attest)　WILLIAM PARKE.
29 Apr. 1670.　　　　　　　　　　　　　　　　EDWARD MORRIS.

Inventory apprized by Edward Bridge, Edward Morris, Robert Seaver. Vol. vii. 56, 57, 122.

No. 534.—NICHOLAS PHILLIPS. Inventory. Deceased Thursday 15 Mch. 1669–70, prized Tuesday 24 April, 1670. Prized by John Bateman and Joseph Hobb. Vol. vii. pp. 37–39.

No. 535.—JAMES HAWKINS will.

Son James Hawkins half of pasture at end of orchard at one and twenty.

Wife all land house & cattle not disposed of. Five daughters, Mary, Ruth, Damarus, Elizabeth and Sarah.

To ten grandchildren each a bible at twelve years of age. Wife Mary sole executrix, and friends William Davis and Thomas Lake overseers 25 June, 1699. Witnesses William Dawes Samuel Hayward and Thos Lake. Probated 30 April, 1670.

Inventory James Hawkins sen of Boston.

Apprized 1 Apr. 1670, by Peter Brackett, John Morse. Vol. vii. pp. 42, 43.

No. 536.—RICHARD CRAZE will. Thomas Wiborne aged about 32 years and Jabez Heaton aged about 36 years doe testify that upon the twenty fourth day of Aprill in this present year 1670 wee the Deponents being called to the house of William Baker Pump-Maker in Boston in New England to be witnesses of the disposal of the whole estate of Richard Craze now deceased then lying at the house of the said W[m] Baker having formerly seen and known him he declared it to be his will that all the estate should be delivered to said Baker that he should pay testator's debts & that he should pay a legacy given by sd. Craze to the eldest son of John Lovell a tanner living at Rehoboth of ten pounds, the remainder he gave to sd Baker and his eldest son John Baker deposed 28 April, 1670.

Bond of William Baker pumpmaker and Symon Rogers shoemaker both of Boston.

Witness Edward Shippen. Vol. vii. pp. 59, 67, 68. (See REGISTER, xxx., 80.) (See p. 347).

# INDEX

(?), Alice 12
(?), Angola 73
(?), Anna 7
(?), Casarmakine 111
(?), Daniel (Sgt.) 360
(?), Davy 179
(?), Edee 129
(?), Elizabeth 129
(?), Elzer 271
(?), Grace 73
(?), Hen 307
(?), Henry (I) (Kng.) 6
(?), Henry (IV) (Kng.) 6
(?), Henry (VIII) (Kng.)
   6
(?), Janemet 338
(?), Jeremy 28
(?), John 3
(?), Mary 7
(?), Nathaniel 12
(?), Prisella 197
(?), Richard 73, 133
(?), Sarah 197
(?), Speedgood 63
(?), Symon 31
(?), William 359
(?), William (Rev.) 203
(?), cuffee 374
(?), margery 50
Abbot, Georg 143
Abda, Math. 378
Abdie, Math. 120
Abdy, Mathew 149
   Tabitha (Mrs.) 149
Abercromby, Dauid 229
   David 229
Abet, Georg 143
Acres, Thomas 109
Adames, Alex. 143, 232
   Allex 143
   George 90
   Henry 388
   Joseph 244
Adams, (?) 179
   Alex. 162
   Alexander 140, 143,
      157, 179, 249
   Alexander (Sgt.) 164
   Allexander 160
   Edw. 194
   Edward 90
   Edwd. 354
   Henry 15, 90, 119,
      122, 332, 378, 389
   John 90
   Joseph 90, 221, 244
   Nathaniel 297
   Nathaniell 169, 201
   Nathaniell (Sr.) 246
   Nathll. 111
   Peter 90, 141
   Samuel 90
   Vrsula 90
Addam, (?) 97
Addams, Nathaniel 274

Addams (cont.)
   Nathaniell 211
   Peter 257
   Wm. 98
Addington, Ann (Mrs.)
   126
   Isa. 352, 359, 360,
      368, 370
   Isaac 381
   Isaack 364
   Isacke 36
   Jsa. 75
Addis, (?) 97
Adington, Isacke 126
Adkins, Mary 99
   Theoder 99
Adkinson, (?) 97
Ainger, John 122
Ainsworth, Daniell 183
Aires, (?) 28, 98
Albe, Benjamin 14
Albie, Beniamin 119
Alby, Hannah 141
Alcock, (?) 122, 337
   (?) (Dr.) 294
   Anna 337
   Carwithy 3
   Chandler 3
   George 3, 86
   John 3
   Samuell 3
   Thomas 3
Alcocke, (?) 168, 312,
   379
   (?) (Dr.) 248, 379
   Anna 288
   Elisabeth 288
   George 3, 288
   Jno. 262
   Joanna 288
   John 127, 157, 187,
      237, 288, 289
   Margery (Mrs.) 164
   Mary 288
   Pagraue 288
   Palgrave 288
   Sarah 288
   Thom 3
   Thomas 3, 164
Alcocks, (?) 337
Alden, Jno. 189
Aldin, Elizabeth (Mrs.)
   189
   John 189
Aldis, (?) 133
   John 183
   Nath. 133
   Nathan 182, 239, 349,
      389
   Nathaniell 40
   Sarah (Mrs.) 133
Aldous, Nathan 349
Aldrich, Catherine
   (Mrs.) 347
   George 347

Aldridge, Catherine
   (Mrs.) 347
   George 347
   Henery 132
Aleborne, Daniell 156
Alford, (?) 93, 98, 122
   William 127, 215, 384
   Willm. 120
Alines, John 298
Alis, William 221
All, (?) (Cpt.) 120
All be, Beniamin 90
All cocke, (?) 113
Allam, Grace 106
Allcock, (?) 212
Allcocke, (?) 147, 164,
   221, 257
Allcockes, (?) 147, 226
Allden, John 215
Alleis, (?) (Cpt.) 251
Allen, (?) 104, 319, 342
   (?) (Cpt.) 122
   Abigall 340
   Ann (Mrs.) 346
   Anne (Mrs.) 123
   Bezoun 49
   Bezoune 49
   Bozoan 346
   Bozone (Cpt.) 121
   Bozoone (Cpt.) 120
   Edward 5
   George 122
   Henry 216, 218, 318,
      319, 320
   Henry (Deacon) 338
   Hope 150
   James 340
   Jo. 22
   John 93, 120, 178
   Joseph 340
   Margaret (Mrs.) 340
   Nicho 111
   Rebeckah (Mrs.) 386
   Samuel 340
   Samuell 340
   Thomas 110
   William 10, 386
   Wm. 369
Allestree, Paul 127
Alley, Phillip 150
   Susanna (Mrs.) 150
Alleyne, Edward 16
Allibone, (?) 355
Allin, Bozoone 119
   Daniel 363
   Hen 136
   Henry 136, 137
   John 144
   John (Rev.) 188
Alline, Henry 137, 161,
   211
   John 315
Allinne, Henry 248, 293
Allis, William 98, 136,
   154, 173, 361

Allynes, (?) 196
Almey, Will 204, 348
Altherton, (?) (Maj.) 59
Amadowne, Roger 102
Ambrose, Henry 118, 166
  Susanna (Mrs.) 166
Ames, (?) (Dr.) 88
  Hannah (Mrs.) 154
  William 154
  Wm. 99, 154
Amsden, Isacke 99
Amydowne, Roger 123
Anderson, (?) 26, 378
  David 12
  John 59, 161, 242
Andras, Jo. 121
Andres, John 199
  Richard 110
Andrewes, Dorothy 112
  John 138, 165, 174,
    369
  Mary 140
  Thomas 179, 215
Andrews, John 174, 233,
    368, 369
  Tho 111
  Thomas 174, 378
Andros, E. (Sir) 34
Andrus, John 251
Anger, Andrew 160
  Edmund 159
  Samson 102
Angier, Besaliel 99
  Edmund 98
  John 43
Angire, Sam. 99
Anker, Tho. 162
Annable, (?) 213
Answorth, (?) 165
Anther, Nathaniell 379
Apleton, (?) 99
Appleton, Hanna 171
  Hanna (Mrs.) 172
  Hannah 172
  Judeth 171, 172
  Samuell 171, 172
Appleyard, Sarah 32
Archer, Isaac 50
  John 50
  Rachell 50
  Samuell 122
  Theophilos 50
  henery 50
Archite, John 161
Ardell, (?) (Widow) 151
Ares, (?) 110
Arinton, humfri 375
Armatage, (?) 227
Armettage, Godfree 112
Armitage, (?) 121, 363
  Godfrey 53, 138, 140,
    147, 169, 207, 342
  Godfry 359
  Godfrye 251
  Joseph 37, 128, 149,
    169
  Rebecca 53
  Sam. 342
Arnald, Edward 120
  William 127
Arnall, Edw 122
Arnell, (?) 97
Arnold, John 192, 193
  Joseph 339
  Samll 179
  Samuell 193
Arye, Elizabeth 246
Ashley, Tho. 211

Aspenholl, (?) 98
Aspinuall, Peter 128
Aspinwall, Elizabeth 64
  Peeter 170
  William 92, 94, 95,
    97, 98, 101, 102,
    103, 105, 106, 107,
    110, 117, 351, 370,
    378
  Wm 64
  Wm. 51, 89, 90, 92,
    110, 377
Astod, James 123
Astwicke, William 257
  Wm. 257
Astwood, (?) 122
  James 112, 127, 136,
    146
  John 112
  Joseph 112
  Sara 112
  Sara (Mrs.) 112
  Sarah (Mrs.) 112
Atharton, (?) (Maj.)
    134, 149
  Humphray 163
  Humphrey 108, 136
  Humphrey (Maj.) 197
  Humprey 103
Atherton, (?) 80, 370
  (?) (Cpt.) 56, 85,
    356, 357
  (?) (Gen.) 374
  (?) (Maj.) 57, 58, 60,
    64, 75, 77, 83, 114,
    182, 194, 212, 362,
    375, 376
  Ann Annable 374
  Anna 374
  Bird 374
  Catharine 374
  Consider 374
  Elizabeth 374
  Elizabeth (Mrs.) 374
  Hope 373, 374
  Hope (Rev.) 373
  Hopestill 373
  Humfrey (Cpt.) 93
  Humphery 197
  Humphery (Cpt.) 82
  Humphrey 56, 197, 370,
    371, 372, 373, 374,
    375, 376, 377, 381
  Humphrey (Cpt.) 123,
    370
  Humphrey (Gen.) 371,
    377
  Humphrey (Maj.) 150,
    370, 372, 374
  Humphry 371, 373, 374,
    376
  Humphry (Gen.) 193
  Humpry 370
  Increase 374
  Isabel 374
  James 208
  John 374
  Jonathan 193, 373, 374
  Katharine 374
  Mary 328
  Mary (Mrs.) 374
  Mather 374
  Patience 374
  Swifte 374
  Waiting 373
  Watching 373, 374
Athertons, (?) (Maj.)

Athertons (cont.)
  371
  humphry 371
Atkingson, Theodor 177
Atkins, Theodore 165
  Walter K. 383
Atkinson, (?) 122, 248,
    378
  Susan (Mrs.) 118
  Theo. 274
  Theode 294
  Theoder 190
  Theodoer 291
  Theodoer (Sr.) 291
  Theodor 107, 274, 309,
    363
  Theodore 129, 146, 235
  Thomas 118
Atkinsons, Theodor 212
Atlifes, (?) 318
Atwater, (?) 303, 318,
    363
  Jno. 385
  John 387
  Joshua 387
Atwood, Ann (Mrs.) 118
  Hermon 118
  John 389
  Sarah 389
Auberry, (?) 121
Audley, Thomas (Ld.) 6
Auerill, James 147
Auery, William 329, 332
Auerye, Wm. 239
Augers, William 265
Auldine, (?) (Sr.) 156
Austen, Jonas 81
Austens, (?) 250
Autherton, Anthony
    (Maj.) 239
  Humphery (Maj.) 239
Averell, Abiell 188, 189
Averey, William 184
Avery, (?) 127
  (?) (Mrs.) 163
  John 138, 357
  Laur(ence) 357
  Laurence 138
  William 220, 383
Avorie, William 242
Awbrey, Rachel 113, 357
  William 113, 358, 359
Awstin, Jonas 122
Axtell, Mary (Mrs.) 23
  Thomas 23
Ayger, Andrew 140
Aymes, John 156
Aynsworth, Daniell 185
Babcocke, Robert 154
Babington, Richard 18
Bacers, John 123
Backer, John 161
  Nathaniell 227
Backland, Willm. 122
Backwaves, John 269
Backway, John 269
Bacon, Daniell 103, 104,
    378
  John 103, 104
  Michaell 104
  Michall 103
  Nathaniell 7
  Rebecca 85
  Sarah 104
  Thomas 348
Badcock, James 79
Badcocke, George 83
Badditier, Nicholas 305

Badger, John 304
Badiford, Nicholas 378
Bagnley, Tho. 17
  Thomas 10, 116
Bagnly, Tho. 10
  Thomas 10
  Thos 10
Bailey, (?) 370
Baily, Thomas 17
Bairstow, Nich. 97
Baker, (?) 127, 156,
  213, 378, 379
  Alexander 36, 258
  Daniell 111
  Elizabeth 253, 264,
  265
  Elizabeth (Mrs.) 36
  Faith (Mrs.) 284
  Jno. 201, 249
  John 72, 121, 168,
  179, 201, 234, 249,
  264, 265, 284, 390
  Lauce 120
  Nath 54
  Nath. 99
  Nathaniell 122
  Nicho 84
  Nicholas 97, 122
  Nico 97, 105, 189
  Nico. 227
  Nicolas 105
  Richard 56, 83, 103,
  186, 212, 265, 284,
  285
  Sarah 72
  Thankfull (Mrs.) 264,
  265
  Tho. 169, 175
  Thomas 122, 169, 179,
  264, 265
  William 390
  Wm. 390
Balch, John 207
Balden, Jno 111
Ball, John 102, 120
  Mathew 39
  Mathewe 39
Ballantyne, David 386
  Elizabeth 386
  Hannah 386
  Hannah (Mrs.) 386
  John 386
  Jonathan 386
  Susanna 386
  William 386
Ballard, Sarah (Mrs.) 8
  William 8
  Willm 8
Ballintine, Wm. 221
Ballintyne, William 215
Ballow, Robert 330
Balls, John (Jr.) 122
Balston, (?) (Mrs.) 260
  James 260
Baly, (?) 221
Bancroft, Roger 93
  Thomas 104
Band, Burnett 242
  Martha (Mrs.) 242
  Martin 200
  Martyn 200
Bantly, (?) 303
Barachew, Richard 58
Barber, Georg 153
  George 129, 387
  George (Cpt.) 332
  Jeremy 2
  John 9, 379

Barber (cont.)
  Richard 26, 349
  Zac. 9
  Zechariah 9
Barbore, Edward 9
  George 9
  John 9
  Richard 9
  William 9
Barbour, Richard 349
Barbur, George 389
Barcher, Jo. 204, 348
Barges, (?) 222
Barkaway, John 270
Barker, Edward 305
  Joseph 41
  Ruth (Mrs.) 41
  ffrancis 10
Barkers, Edw. 305
Barlo, Thomas 379
Barloe, Bartholmew 98,
  161
  Thomas 161
Barlow, (?) 378
  Bartholmew 61, 106,
  161
  Elizabeth (Mrs.) 199
  Tho. 199
  Thomas 199
Barlowe, Bartho. 122
  Bartholl 110
Barnam, Richard 260
Barnard, (?) 355
  (?) (Mrs.) 129, 298
  Anna 346
  John (Sr.) 346
  Mary (Mrs.) 169
  Mathew 207
  Nathaniel 169
  Rich. 207
  Richard 162, 207
Barnes, (?) 111, 379
  Jno. 149
  John 227
  Mathew 147
  Richard 31, 42
  Sarah 97
Barnet, (?) 179
  (?) (Sr.) 179
  Mathew 154
Barrell, Anne 16
  Anne (Mrs.) 15, 16
  Geo. 11C
  George 15, 116
  Hannah 206
  Iohn 42
  James 16, 206
  Jno. 124
  John 15, 16, 42, 138,
  158, 161, 206
  Mary 206
  Mary (Mrs.) 138
  Thomas 15
  William 15, 206
Barret, Humphrey 274
  Stephen 378
Barrett, Mary 254
  Richard 307
  Robt 120
Barritt, Humphrey 274
Barrowes, (?) 131
Barry, (?) 9, 80, 346
  (?) (Rev.) 19
Bartholmew, Joseph 278
  William 159, 237, 278,
  388
  Wm. 225, 231, 278,
  378, 388

Bartholomow, Joseph 321
  Will 385
  William 207, 218, 321,
  322
  Wm. 310
Bartlett, John Russell
  330
Barton, Henry 317
Bas, Mary (Mrs.) 160
  Samll. 160
  Samll. (Jr.) 160
  Samuel 356
Bass, Edward 383
  Joseph 374
  Mary 361
  Mary (Mrs.) 123
  Saml. 123
  Samuel 383
  Samuell 123, 228, 237
  Thomas 388
  Thos. 387
Basse, John 221, 237
  Ruth 254
  Sam (Deacon) 221
  Saml. 54
  Saml. (Deacon) 221
  Samm well 85
  Samuell 163, 237
  Samuell (Jr.) 160
  samm well 84
Basset, Will 111
Bassitt, Willm 121
Bastar, Joseph 58, 207
Bastarr, Joseph 149
Basto, Mihel 99
Bastor, Joseph 119
Batcheller, (?) 164
Bate, Allice 48
  Allice (Mrs.) 48
  Benjamin 327
  Edw. 343
  Edward 90, 205, 238,
  349
  Gibson 48
  James 47, 48, 151, 345
  Jas 48
  Margret 48
  Mary 48
  Richard 47
  Richd. 48
  Saml. 48
  Willm. 301
Bateman, John 218, 233,
  386, 390
Batemans, (?) 111
Bates, (?) 137, 205,
  264, 316, 378
  An. 189
  Clement 220
  Eaderd 349
  Edward 95, 343
  George 310
  Hannah 179
  James 48, 179
  Jane 189
  Joseph 378
Bath, Abigall 309
  Samuell 309
  Sarah 309
Batherson, James 221
Batherston, James 221
Batis, Edward 17
Batle, Mary (Mrs.) 331
Batmans, John 227
Batt, (?) 121
  Anne (Mrs.) 188
  Chr. 185
  Christopher 188

Batt (cont.)
Paul 358
Thomas 232
Batte, (?) (Mrs.) 283,
284
Anna (Mrs.) 284
Clement 50
Edward 14
James 284
James (Jr.) 50
James (Sr.) 50
Rachell 50
Samuell 284
Batteley, John 188
Thomas 188
Battelle, Thomas 385
Battely, Mary 188
Thomas 187, 188
Batten, Hugh 168
Vrselle (Mrs.) 168
Vrsilla 156
Vrsula (Mrs.) 168
Battey, Edward 215
Battile, Robert 177
Robt 177
Battle, Robeart 177
Batts, (?) 106
Eaderd 349
Edward 13
Baughtons, (?) 122
Bauis, Tobias 187
Baulton, John 232
Baxstar, Bethia 148
Deareing 148
Dearing 148
Gregory 148
John 148
John Adam 148
Joseph 148
Joseph Adams 148
Baxter, (?) (Mrs.) 281
Gregory 149
John 149
Margaret (Mrs.) 149
Margarett 140
Nicholas 312, 384
Baxters, (?) 196
Baxtor, Gregory 149
Bayle, Oades 21
Oads 21
Oates 21
Baylee, Joseph 232
Bayley, Joseph 232
Otis 21
Bayly, John 118
Joseph 232
Thomas 17, 147, 159
Baytes, George.101
Beach, (?) (Rev.) 76
Beake, Jeames 301
Beale, Nathll. 145
Philip 378
Tho 98
Beales, Edmond 144
Jeremiah 49, 145
Jeremy 81, 378
Jno. 81
Jno. (Sr.) 250
John 123, 144, 145
John (Sr.) 145
Nath. 120, 122
Nathaniel 81
Nathanyell 145
Nathll. 145
Rebecca (Mrs.) 145
Beall, Thos 50
Beals, (?) (Mrs.) 189
Martha 189

Beamesley, Willm 120
Beamsle, Martha 232
Beamsley, Anne 143
Elizabeth 143
Grace 143
Hannah 143
Mary 143
Mercy 143
Willi 101
William 143
Beamslleay, William 162
Beamsly, Martha (Mrs.)
143
William 143
Wm. 143
Beanghans, (?) 165
Beard, Tho. 44
Beares, Anthony 117
Bearesto, John 117
Bearstow, Anne (Mrs.)
188
William 188
Bearstowe, William 183
Beatts, Thos. 50
Beck, Alexander 116
Becke, Alexander 167
Beckett, John 120
Bedwell, Edward 378
Bee, Jno. 149
Beecher, Thomas 85
Beedeman, John 119
Beellaze, Will 6
Beeres, Rich. 117
Beighton, Ann (Mrs.) 352
Samuell 352
Belcheere, (?) 127, 379
Belcher, (?) 99, 176,
343, 379
Edward 342, 374
Gregory 125, 221, 222,
283, 326
Jeremiah 177
Jeremy 363, 364
Jerimy 171
John 374
Josias 204
Bell, (?) 89
Ann (Mrs.) 146
James 162, 190
Thomas 146
Bellantine, William 137
Bellcher, Andrew 111
Bellingham, (?) 40, 74,
101, 107, 121
Penelop 325
Ri. 31, 128, 182
Ri. (Gov.) 264, 360
Ricd. 233
Rich. 9
Richard 31, 34, 36,
47, 181, 193, 325,
377
Richard (Gov.) 76, 302
Bellow, Henry 330
Rob't 330
Robert 330
Robt. 330
Susannah (Mrs.) 330
William 330
Bells, Thomas 204
Belshar, Gregory 212
Belsher, Edward 277
Bemis, Joseph 215
Bendall, (?) 303
Free Grace 385, 386,
387, 388
Freegrace 312
Grace 97, 381

Bendall (cont.)
Mary (Mrs.) 312
Benet, George 34, 111
Richard 110
Benham, John 129, 215
Sarah 129
Benit, Richard 34, 124
Benitt, (?) (Mrs.) 124
Benjamin, J. 346
John 25, 99, 121, 355
Mary 26
Bennet, (?) 261
Alice (Mrs.) 154
Francis 154
Richd 169
Bennett, (?) (Mrs.) 123
Adey (Mrs.) 119
Andrey (Mrs.) 119
George 119
Jo. 121
Richard 127, 149
Samuell 149, 343
Bennit, (?) 99
Bennitt, George 64
Richard 64
Benson, (?) 378
Bent, Agnes 31
John 31
Peter 122
Berbor, Edward 9
George 9
John 9
Richard 9
Bernard, (?) 261
John 121
Berry, Ambrose 120
Thomas 269, 270
Wm. 97
Bersto, John 122
Beten, Richard 17
Betfield, Samuell 147
Betscomb, Richard 84
Bettle, Joseph 156
Betts, (?) 98
Bicknall, John 137
Joseph 53
Bidfield, Elizabeth
(Mrs.) 169
Samuel 169
Bigg, Rachell (Mrs.) 50,
51
Biggs, (?) 242
(?) (Mrs.) 234
John 167, 274
Mary (Mrs.) 274
Biglaw, John 129
Bigs, John 363
Bill, James 190
Philip 162
Thomas 273
Billing, Roger 212, 385
William 212
Billings, Roger 136
Bills, James 128
Robert 222
Biram, Nicholas 5
Birch, Jeremiah 133
Jonathan 293
Jonathans 292
Joseph 133, 134, 292
Mary 133
Thomas 133, 292
Birches, Thom. 108
Thomas 293
Bird, (?) 346, 378
Ann (Mrs.) 292
Benja. 375, 376, 377
Benjamin 374, 376

Dird (cont.)
James 292
John 292
Sarah 292
Thankful 374
Thankfull 374, 376
Tho. 255
Thomas 292, 347
Thomas (Jr.) 374
Thomas (Sr.) 292
Bishop, Elizabeth (Mrs.)
250, 300
Henry 250, 300
James 215
Nath. 151, 300
Nathaniel 386, 389
Nathaniell 150, 151,
205, 300, 318, 321
Bishope, Nathaniel 205
Nathaniell 79
Bishoppe, Elizabeth
(Mrs.) 300
Henry 300
Bishops, (?) 321
Bitfeild, Elizabeth 342
Elizabeth (Mrs.) 341,
342
Mary 342
Bitfeld, Samuel 26
Bitfield, Elizabeth
(Mrs.) 341
Samuel 341
Bittlestone, Elisabeth
(Mrs.) 14
Elizabeth 14
Thomas 14
Bitts, James 75
Blacke, Henry 121
Blackeleach, Elizabeth
181
John 181
Blackleach, (?) 123
Elizabeth 181
Elizabeth (Mrs.) 180,
181
John 180, 379
Blackleich, (?) 110
Blackley, Edward 84
Blacklidge, John 215
Blackman, Jno. 257
John 292
Blackstone, (?) 378
Blackstons, (?) 366
Blague, Elizabeth (Mrs.)
217
Henry 217
Blainfeeld, Tho. 116
Blak, (?) (Mrs.) 208
Blake, (?) 24, 108, 255
Agnes (Mrs.) 223
Edward 209, 225
James (Jr.) 371, 373,
375, 376, 382
Jane 209
Jo. 108
John 220, 281
Mary 209
Mary (Mrs.) 137
Patience (Mrs.) 209
Richard 159
Sarah 209
William 134, 223
Willm 158
Blanch, (?) 97
Blanchard, Anne (Mrs.)
42
Hanna 41
Hannah 41

Blanchard (cont.)
Hannah (Mrs.) 41, 42
John 41
William 41, 123
Willm 42
Willm. 123
Blancher, Thomas 31
Wm 111
Blanchett, (?) (Mrs.)
262
Blandfeild, Elizabeth 3
Blantaine, William 290
Blanten, Pheebe (Widow)
217
Wm. 218
Blantine, John 204
Mary 204
Pheebe 204
Pheebe (Mrs.) 204
Ralph 204
William 204, 205
Williams 204
Blanton, Phebe (Mrs.)
205
William 179, 205
Willm 107
Willm. 127
Blasden, (?) 102
Blaxton, William 60
Bligh, Thomas 161, 359,
386
Blighe, Thomas 294
Blith, Evan Thomas (?)
58
Thomas 161
Bloffe, ffrances 93
Blogget, Daniel 10, 11
Samuel 11
Susan (Mrs.) 10
Susanna 11
Thomas 10, 11
Bloghead, Daniel 10
Ruth 10
Bloors, (?) 151
Blot, Robert 79
Blott, Robert 106, 257,
258
Sarah 257, 258
Blower, John 179
Blyes, (?) 185
Boarne, Nehemiah 37
Bodey, Ferdinando 111
Bodman, John 121
Bodry, fferdjnyndo 37
Boington, (?) 239
Bolden, Richard 127
Bollon, Thomas 388
Bolters, Richd. 205
Bolton, Enoch 210
Bomstead, (?) 141
Bond, (?) 346
Jno 111
Boner, George 146
Bonson, (?) 122
Boogby, Edward 335
Booker, William 203
Boords, (?) 158
Booth, (?) 127, 146, 158
Bord, John 384
Borne, (?) 102
John 156
Borrell, (?) 111
Boseworth, Benj. 121
Nathaniell 122
Zachey 123
Bosten, (?) 379
Bosveile, Godfrey 7
Boswith, Benjamine 378

Boswith (cont.)
Nath 378
Bosworth, (?) 129
Ann (Mrs.) 59
Elizabeth 59
John 103
Nathani-ll 227
Nathaniell 227
Nathl. 190
Samuell 59
Zacheus 59
Bouchier, Mary (Mrs.)
312
Robert 312
Boules, John 81, 243
Bouls, John 127, 229
Boultons, (?) 150
Bourne, Nehemiah 18
Bournes, (?) 108
Boutaile, John 99
Boutle, John 2
Bowd, Grimstone 352
Bowde, Grimstone 352
Bowden, Edward 307, 308
John 301
Bowdon, Edward 301
Bowels, John 243
Bowen, Henry 187, 365
Tho. 120
Bowker, Edmond 381
Bowles, (?) 184, 185,
243
Elizabeth 184, 185
Jno. 243
John 146, 184, 185,
187, 229, 296, 324
Mary 184, 185
Bowlles, Jno. 149
Bowman, (?) 111
Nathl. 89
Bowstred, Elizabeth 17
William 17
Wm. 17
Bowstree, William 17
Bowyer, (?) (Mrs.) 147
Boyce, Antipas 215
Math 111
Boydell, John 371, 372,
374, 375, 376, 381
Boyden, (?) 117
Tho. 122, 153
Thomas 198, 356
Boyen, Henry 162
Boyer, Antipas 311
Boyers, Symon 138
Boyes, Matthew 370
Thom 108
Boylston, Elizabeth 330
Mary (Mrs.) 330
Tho. 22
Thomas 330
Boynton, John 207
William 22
Boyse, Antipas 338, 339
Brackelbery, (?) 111
Brackenbury, (?) 22
William 23
Brackenburye, (?) 22
Will 22
Bracket, (?) 272, 312
Jno. 293
John 269, 270, 272
Nathaniell 272
Peter 173, 268, 272,
274
Richard 123, 315, 326
Sarah 272
Brackett, John 233

Brackett (cont.)
  Peeter 160
  Peter 221, 228, 234
  Rich. 116
  Richard 15, 87, 90,
    116, 136, 148, 163,
    237, 244, 361
  Richard (Cpt.) 148,
    326
Bradbery, Tho. 379
Bradcott, (?) (Mrs.) 235
Bradford, Alexander 23,
    24
  Ann 350
  John 24
  Margaret (Mrs.) 351
  Martha (Mrs.) 351
  Moses 311
  Robert 351
  Robt 122
  Robt. 311
  Sarah (Mrs.) 24
  Thomas 350
  Willm 105
Bradish, Hannah 157
  James 157
  John 157
  Joseph 157
  Mary 157
  Robert 157
  Vashty (Mrs.) 157
  Vastie (Mrs.) 157
Bradley, John 10, 87
  Nathan 257
  Richard 114
Bradly, Jno. 111
  Richard 114
Bradstreet, (?) 294
  Simon 203
  Symon 75
Bradstreete, (?) 123
  (?) (Mrs.) 46
Bragg, Jonathan 384
Brakenbury, Anthony 22
Brakinbury, Richard 22
Bram, Beniman 259
Bran, Benja. 259
  Georg. 379
  George 385
  Martha (Mrs.) 385
Branch, John 8
  Peter 8
Brand, Georg 30
  George 127, 185, 187
  Martha 184
Brandon, Hanah 95
  Mary 95
  Mary (Mrs.) 95
  Sarah 95
  Thomas 95
  William 90, 95
Branne, Geore 243
Brasier, Edw. 98
Bratle, (?) 290
  Tho. 379
Brattle, (?) 222, 290
  Tho. 169, 234, 253,
    308
  Thomas 234, 251, 308,
    339
  Thos. 209
Brawton, Tho. 125
Bray, Osomant 101
Breaden, (?) 378
Brearton, William 183
Breck, Edward 208
  Elizabeth 208
  Isabell (Mrs.) 208

Breck (cont.)
  John 208
  Mary 208
  Robert 208
  Susana 208
Brecke, Edward 208
  Isable (Mrs.) 208
  Robt. 166
Breckett, Peter 390
Bredon, Thomas 311
  Thomas (Cpt.) 281
Breedon, (?) (Cpt.) 123
Brenton, William 58,
    198, 276
  Wm. 51, 138, 150, 153,
    330
Brettle, (?) 123
Brewer, Ann 94
  Daniel 12, 93, 94
  Daniell 93, 94, 195,
    196
  Joanna 94
  Joanna (Mrs.) 93
  Sarah 94
  daniell 81
Brewers, Nathaniell 334
Brewster, (?) 14
  Jonathan (Jr.) 156
Brick, Robrt. 111
Bricke, Robt. 163
Bride, John 335
Bridg, Edward 94
Bridgam, Henry 157
Bridge, Edw. 231
  Edward 94, 231, 266,
    270, 390
  John 6, 7, 8, 93, 152,
    335
  Margery (Mrs.) 231
Bridges, (?) 122
  (?) (Cpt.) 75, 110,
    122
  Ed. 229
  Matt 111
Bridgham, (?) 379
  Henny 107
  Henrey 210
  Henry 178, 290, 292,
    386
Brigam, Henery 363
Brige, Clement 106, 107
  Clemt. 107
  Dauid 107
  John 107
  Jonathan 106, 107
  Remond 107
  Thom 106
  Thom. 107
  Thomas 106
Briges, Mathias 122, 149
Briggs, Clement 167
  Cleoment 167
  Elizabeth (Mrs.) 167
  Mathias 175, 176
  Willm 120
Brighams, Tho. 99
Bright, Henrie 97
  Math. 111
Brighting, (?) 161
Brimblecome, John 56
Brimsmead, William 167
  Wm. 167
Brinsmead, Wnj. 30
Brinsmeade, Alexander
    30, 31
  Ebbet 30
  Mary 30
  William 30

Brinsmeade (cont.)
  Wnj. 31
Brinsmeads, (?) 31
Brisco, Beniamen 360
  Benj. 137
  Benjamin 107, 315
  Benjamine 157
  Joseph 245, 246
Briscoe, Beniamin 107
Brittaine, Richd. 50
Bucke, (?) 99, 111, 128
Buckley, (?) (Sr.) 75
Buckman, Wm. 99
Buckmaster, (?) 110
  Elisabeth 26
  Elizabeth 80
  Jabesh 80
  Joanna (Mrs.) 80
  Joseph 80
  Lawrence 26, 27, 80
  Mary 27, 80
  Mary (Mrs.) 175
  Sarah 80
  Tho. 175
  Thomas 80, 175
  Zacharie 378
  Zachary 27
  Zackery 80
  Zackry 80
  dorkas 80
Buckminster, Elizabeth
    (Mrs.) 333
  Johannah (Mrs.) 333
  Joseph 333
Bucknell, Samll. 379
Bud, (?) 120
  (?) (Lt.) 227
Budd, Edward 232
Budman, John 127
Buers, Francis 138
Bugby, Edward 334, 335
  Joseph 334, 335
  Sarah 335
Bukly, John 98
Bull, Henry 79, 102
  Richard 179
  Wm. 99
Bullard, Isaac 385
  Will 6
Bullen, Samuell 332
Bullin, Mary (Mrs.) 49
  Samuell 49
Bullock, Edward 82, 83
Bullocke, Edward 83
  Edwd. 83
Bulman, Alexander 384
Bumstead, (?) 107
  Tho. 262, 315
  Thomas 262, 304
Bumsted, Tho. 274
  Thomas 177, 384
Bumsteed, (?) 99
  Thomas 59, 142, 147
Buncker, (?) 378
Bunker, M. 379
Bunne, (?) 378
Burch, Thomas 83, 134
Burcham, Eliz. (Mrs.) 49
Burchard, Thomas 174
Burchill, Jno. 83
Burd, John 146
  Thomas 179
Burden, Anne (Mrs.) 129
  George 129, 130, 359
  Robert 149
  Soulsby 130
  Timothy 130
Bureys, (?) 272

Burge, John 17
Burges, (?) 179
  James 127
  Roger 216, 217
  Sarah (Mrs.) 216
  Tho 110
Burgess, Roger 217
Burgesse, Roger 217
  Sarah (Mrs.) 217
Burgis, Roger 216
  Sarah (Mrs.) 216
Burgiss, Sarah (Mrs.) 216
Burgisse, Roger 216, 217
  Sarah (Mrs.) 216
Burke, (?) 347
  (?) (Mrs.) 6
Burmop, Robert 149
Burnel, John 134
Burnell, John 162, 164, 190, 293
  Samuel 190
  Samuells 162
  Sara 190
  Sarah 162, 190
  Sarah (Mrs.) 162
  William 162, 190
  Wm. 190
Burnet, Isaack 242
Burnett, (?) 243
Burnop, Isaack 243
Burnum, (?) 243
Burrel, John 81
Burrell, John 80
  Sarah 80, 81
  Sarah (Mrs.) 80, 81
Burridge, Jo 22
Burrowe, (?) 178, 384
Burrowes, (?) 327, 355
  Jeremiah 122
Burt, (?) 122
  Edward 146, 156
Burton, (?) 129, 147, 242, 344
  (?) (Mrs.) 119
  Boniface 343, 344
  Bonniface 150, 343
  Francis (Mrs.) 343
  Margaret (Mrs.) 131
Busbie, Bredgett (Mrs.) 175
Busby, (?) 123
  Abraham 130, 131, 175, 187, 245, 246
  Anne 131
  Bridget (Mrs.) 175
  Bridgett (Mrs.) 175
  John 131
  Joseph 131
  Katherine 131
  Nicholas 130, 131
  Sarah 131
Busbye, Abraham 246
Bush, (?) 243
Bushe, John 120
Bushell, James 61
Bushenell, John 120
Bushnell, (?) 122
  Edward 143
  Glazier 151
  John 215
Busketh, (?) 243
Buswell, (?) 112
Butcher, (?) 127
Butland, Thomas 154
  William 154
Butler, (?) 347
  Stephen 318, 319, 320

Butler (cont.)
  William 119
Butolph, Thomas 53, 157, 207, 291
  Thomas (Sr.) 53
Buttell, Jeanne (Mrs.) 260
  Thomas 291
Butten, John 138
Butter, John 147
Butterwoths, John 199
Buttler, Stephen 153
Buttolph, (?) 291
  Abigall 290
  Anna (Mrs.) 290
  John 290
  Mehitebell 290
  Tho. 253, 291
  Thomas 140, 158, 182, 207, 234, 263, 290, 291, 359
  Thomas (Sr.) 263, 291
Buttolphe, Tho. 129
Button, (?) 98, 242
  Abigall 109
  Abigall (Mrs.) 109
  Hannah 109
  John 138, 193, 226, 241
  Robert 109, 120, 121
  Robt. 121
  Samuel 109
  Sarah 109
Buttons, (?) 326
Byles, Mather 62, 63
Byom, Nathaniell 112
Byram, Nicholas 5, 53
Byrdall, William 307
  William (Sr.) 307
Byrome, Nicho. 137
Byshopp, Townsend 84
Cad, Bartholomew 248
Cadd, Bartholomew 248
  Mary (Mrs.) 248
Cademan, Robert 378
Cady, Nicholas 179
Call, Tho. 156
Callycott, (?) 102
Caltor, (?) 99
Cambridge, Mitcheson 215
Cane, Cristo. 99
Cantleburry, Cornelius 81
Cantlebury, Cornelius 123
Canveath, Ezekiell 264
Capen, (?) 47
  John 59, 164, 179, 192, 206, 208, 209, 223, 245, 292, 361
  John (Sr.) 210, 285, 292
  Mary 209
  Preserved 374
Caps, Sarah (Mrs.) 327
Carley, (?) 120
Carltons, (?) 32
Carpenter, Benj. 327
  Dauid 99
Carr, (?) 220
Carrey, John 156
Carrington, (?) 318
  Hannah 19
  Stoctdell 19
  Thomas 347
Carter, (?) 129, 147
  Ann 218
  Ann (Mrs.) 175, 320

Carter (cont.)
  Anne 281
  Anne (Mrs.) 175
  Richard 320
  Thomas 88
  Thomas (Rev.) 95
Caruer, Tho 127
Carver, Elizabeth 13
  Grace (Mrs.) 13
  Richard 13
  Susanna 13
Carwithe, Dickery 126
Carwithen, Samll 110
Carwithy, Elizabeth (Mrs.) 247
  Joshua 246, 247
Cary, (?) 183
Casarmakine, (?) 111
Cauliffe, Henery 151
Cave, Ezra 113
Cawards, John 133
Chadborne, Humphrey 294
Chadwell, Barbara (Mrs.) 249
  Tho. 160
  Thomas 140, 249, 265
Chafey, Mathew 139
Chafine, Matthew 101
Chamberlaine, Henry 227
  Richard 335
Chamberlin, (?) 335
  Hen 111
  John 273
  Mary 335
  Rebecca 335
  Tho 111
  Tho. 114
Chamberline, Will. 379
Chamberlyne, Willm 190
Chambers, Thomas 120
Champnies, Rich. 98
Champny, (?) 93
Champroune, Frauncis (Cpt.) 37
Chandler, (?) 99
  Hannah (Mrs.) 312
  Jno. 248
  Joseph 312
  Samll 176
  Samll. 179
  Samuel 176, 210
  Sarah (Mrs.) 210
Chantrell, John 269
Chapen, (?) 212
Chaplen, Mary 238
  Wm. 238
Chaplin, (?) 248
  Henr. 110
Chapman, (?) 127, 146
  Joane (Mrs.) 340
  Richard 339, 340
  Richard (Jr.) 339, 340
  ffaithfull 99
Chard, (?) 378
  Richard 149
Charde, William 186
  Wm. 220
Chayneies, John 138
Checkley, Anthony 179, 188
Cheeckley, Anthony 225
Cheesbrooke, G. 108
Cheesbrough, Mathanll 200
  Nathaniell 199
  Samll. 199
  Samuell 200
  William 199

Cheesbrough (cont.)
  Wm. 200
Cheesholand, Tho. 14
  Thomas 14
Cheesholme, Thomas 14
Cheever, Bartholmew 126
  Ezekiel 286
Cheiney, Deborah (Mrs.)
    296
  Ellin 296
  John 296
  Joseph 296
  Margaret (Mrs.) 295
  Margret 296
  Mehitobell 296
  Thomas 296
  William 295, 296
Chelney, Wm. 377
Cheney, (?) 378
  William 297
Chenney, (?) 122
Cheny, Benjamin 371
Chesbrooke, William 200
Chesebrough, Willm 191
Chesholme, Tho. 98, 99
Chever, Bartholomew 28
Chevers, (?) 55, 129
Chevery, Isack 228
Chickerin, Francis 130
Chickering, (?) 123
  Francis 125, 166
  Henery 57
  Henry 40, 144, 166,
    178, 188, 267, 349,
    389
  John 156
  Sarah (Mrs.) 166
Chickley, Hannah (Mrs.)
    308
  John 123
Chickrin, Francis 130
  Henry 119
Child, Benjamine 149
  E. 346
  Elisabeth 20, 21
  Elizabeth 21, 26, 346
  Eph 117
  Ephraim 117, 121, 127
Childs, (?) 89
Chittenden, William 14
Chivers, Abraham 387
  Bartholomew 387
  Benjamin 385, 387
Chrichley, Richard 99
Church, Benjamin 334
  Daniell 122
  Elizabeth (Mrs.) 334
  Joseph 171, 334
  Richard 334
Churches, Joseph 189
Churchill, Hannah 140
Claddis, Nath. 280, 287
Clampet, George 160
  Jno. 160
  John 160
Clap, (?) 150, 151
  (?) (Cpt.) 194, 212,
    232
  (?) (Deacon) 295
  (?) (Lt.) 151, 212
  Ambros 59
  Barbara 89
  David 374
  Ebenezer 59
  Edward 59, 83, 109,
    128, 198, 245
  Elizabeth 59
  Elizabeth Prudence 59

Clap (cont.)
  Ezra 59
  Hannah 59, 327
  Increase 209
  Jane 328
  John 59
  Jone 59, 327
  Nathaniell 59
  Nehemiah 59
  Nich. 108
  Nicholas 59, 179, 245
  Nicholis 59
  Prudence 59
  Richard 59
  Roger 47, 48, 59, 83,
    85, 109, 114, 151,
    162, 164, 176, 186,
    194, 328
  Roger (Cpt.) 328, 380,
    384
  Roger (Lt.) 56, 150
  Samuell 59, 284
  Sarah 59
  Sarah (Mrs.) 327
  Susannah 59, 327
  Thomas 59
  deborah 59
Clapp, (?) (Lt.) 193
  Abigail (Mrs.) 358
  Abigaill (Mrs.) 170
  Abigall (Mrs.) 170
  Edward 59, 89, 208,
    244, 245
  Edwarde 223
  Edwd. 83
  Joan 151
  John 59
  Jone (Mrs.) 59
  Nicho 48, 111
  Nicholas 59, 186, 358
  Roger 59, 111, 245,
    305
  Susanna (Mrs.) 245
Clappe, (?) (Cpt.) 255
  (?) (Lt.) 85
  Edward 244, 245
  Esther 245
  Ezra 244, 245
  Nehemiah 244, 245
  Nicholas 245
  Roger 231
  Roger (Cpt.) 245
  Susanna 245
  Susanna (Mrs.) 245
Clark, Jeminah 240
  John 32, 104, 109,
    194, 214, 240
  Penuis 18
  Samuel 14
  Tho. 143
  Thomas 113, 128, 194
  William 286
Clarke, (?) 66, 122,
    154, 158, 162, 164,
    240, 288, 347, 379
  (?) (Cpt.) 102, 154,
    198, 215, 242, 318,
    363
  (?) (Dr.) 172, 198,
    229
  (?) (Mrs.) 164
  Ann (Mrs.) 269
  Anne (Mrs.) 269
  Arthur 121, 127, 305,
    351
  Christo. 111
  Christopher 164, 171,
    172

Clarke (cont.)
  Edward 121
  Elizabeth 43, 201
  Elizabeth (Mrs.) 240
  Emanuell 120
  George 156
  Heugh 102
  Hugh 152, 274, 282,
    333
  Jemina 239
  Jeminah 239
  Jno. 239
  John 53, 109, 126,
    146, 199, 201, 202,
    239, 240, 274
  John (Sr.) 239
  Jonas 63, 191
  Mannell 120
  Martha 240
  Martha (Mrs.) 239
  Mary 201
  Mather 378
  Richard 149
  Robert 200, 201, 202
  Samuel 351
  Sarah 351
  Sarah (Mrs.) 305, 351
  Tho 110
  Tho (Cpt.) 153, 154
  Tho. 34, 127, 128,
    140, 161, 212, 364
  Tho. (Cpt.) 120
  Tho. (Lt.) 294
  Thomas 20, 34, 58, 90,
    96, 110, 116, 125,
    143, 177, 190, 203,
    272, 386, 388
  Thomas (Cpt.) 58, 76,
    112, 121, 172, 177,
    178, 198, 234
  Thomas (Sgt.) 215
  Will 91
  William 162, 165, 201,
    212
  Wm. 128, 156, 164
Clarkes, (?) 109
Clarks, John 240
Clear, Gm. 294
Cleare, John 278
Clearke, Anna (Mrs.) 18
  James 222
  Vennis 18
Cleasby, John 330
Cleaues, William 247
Cleffland, Margaret 269
Clemens, Augustine 82,
    83
  Austine 83
  John 49, 153, 272
  Mary 49
Clement, (?) 272
  Augustine 153
  Gregory 286
  Jack 179
  Samll. 179
Clements, Edward 272
  Job 44
Clemons, John 153
Clerck, Joseph 9
Clerke, John 109
Cletherly, Richd. 49
Cleuerle, John 285
Cleuerly, John 260
Cleues, Wm. 247
Cleverly, John 221
Clifford, Jno. 168
  John 167, 168
Cload, Andrew 168, 379

Cloade, Andrew 251
  Elizabeth (Mrs.) 251
Close, Brattles 290
Clough, John 378
Cludd, Benjamin 335
Cluterbooke, Jeames 302
Coachman, Thomas 140
Cobbet, (?) 213
Cobbett, (?) 213
Cobbit, (?) (Rev.) 172
Cobit, (?) 73
Cock, (?) (Mrs.) 273
  Joseph 264, 269, 270,
    272
  Nicholas 273
  Susanna (Mrs.) 272
Cocks, Joseph 265
Coddington, (?) 350
  Emm (Mrs.) 148
  John 148
Codington, John 37
Codman, (?) 121
  Robert 215
Codogen, Rice 102
Coe, Math 120
Coffine, Peter 179
Cogan, John 107, 142,
    362
  Martha (Mrs.) 362
Cogans, (?) 362
Coggan, (?) 114, 117
  (?) (Mrs.) 361, 362
  Ann (Mrs.) 361
  Caleb 141, 142, 143,
    177, 361, 362
  Elizabeth 177, 362
  Humphery 142
  Jno 177
  John 141, 142, 177,
    222, 361, 362
  Martha (Mrs.) 141,
    142, 177, 222, 362
  Mary 177
  Mary (Mrs.) 361
Coggans, (?) 131
Coggings, (?) 361
Cogins, (?) 66
Cohowne, Thomas 378
Coker, (?) 160
Coking, John 51
Colborne, (?) 72
  william 85
Colbornes, (?) 86
Colbron, (?) 194
  Elizabeth (Mrs.) 206
  Mary 206
  Paine 206
  Sarah 206
  Will 107, 346
  Will. 137, 163
  William 36, 78, 107,
    159, 206
  Willm 79, 354
  Wm 75
  Wm. 35, 36, 55, 78,
    163
Colbrvn, (?) 128
Colburn, Nathanel 385
  Willm. 124
Colchester, (?) 227
Colcord, Edward 138
Cole, (?) 73, 123, 147
  (?) (Jr.) 122
  Anna 73
  Anne (Mrs.) 73
  Clement 271
  Elizabeth 271
  John 179, 271, 272

Cole (cont.)
  Mary 271
  Ryse 22
  Same. 127
  Samuel 271, 361
  Samuell 271, 272
  Susan 309
  Thomas 304
  Willm 101
Colear, Moses 96
  Susan 96
  Susan (Mrs.) 96
  Tho 97
  Tho. 96
Coleborne, (?) 267
Colebron, Margery (Mrs.)
    206
  William 194
  Willyam 353
Coleman, Edward 120
Coles, (?) 236
  John 156, 294
  Rice 88
Coliar, Tho 97
Colier, Moses 97, 174
  Thomas 174
Collacott, Richard 217,
    269, 279
Collecot, (?) 122
Collecutt, Richard 207
Collemore, (?) 318
  Isaack 61
Collens, Jno. 111
Collicot, (?) 385
  Rich'd 215
Collicott, Edward 324
  Rich'd 41
  Rich. 44, 121
  Richard 41, 137, 138,
    386
Collicut, (?) 385
Collier, Moses 97, 139
  Susan (Mrs.) 97
  Susannah 97
  Thomas 96, 97, 174
Colliers, Moses 139
Collins, (?) 120, 221
  Edward 85
  Edwd. 127
  Gabrill 379
  John 122, 156, 187
  Robert 120
Collocott, Richard 44
Collymore, Isack 153
Colpit, Sarah (Mrs.) 206
Colthl., John 215
Colyer, Moyses 122
Colyers, Moses 195
Coman, Rich. 120
Come, (?) 99
Comer, John 120, 378
Compton, (?) (Mrs.) 245
  John 50, 245
  Susannah (Mrs.) 245
Comstock, John 14
Coney, (?) 43
  John 43
  Mary (Mrs.) 43
Conney, John 280, 288
Connye, John 232
Convars, Edward 95, 96
Convers, Edward 95
  Edwd. 22
Converse, Edward 95, 116
Convey, John 242
Cooe, marke (Cpt.) 77
Coogine, (?) (Cpt.) 99
Cook, Mary 160

Cook (cont.)
  Richard 220
  Richard (Lt.) 127
Cooke, (?) 98, 111, 121,
    129, 272
  (?) (Lt.) 59, 303
  Eleana 335
  Elisha 59, 196, 289,
    384
  Elizabeth (Mrs.) 160
  Elkanah 137, 360
  Elkenah 129
  Joseph 99
  Philip 99
  Rich 38, 116
  Rich. 303
  Richard 97, 129, 138,
    146, 147, 220, 384,
    386
  Richard (Lt.) 177, 200
  Thomas 89
Coolage, John 95
Cooledge, (?) 23
Coolidge, (?) 2
  John 23, 117
Coombe, Elizabeth (Mrs.)
    199
  John 199
Coop, Anthony 84
Cooper, Benj. 84
  Benjamin 84
  Elizabeth 278
  Ester 84
  Francis 269
  Jno. 99
  John 53, 123, 215,
    306, 307
  Josiah 278
  Laurence 84
  Rebeka 84
  Thomas 122, 178, 278
  Waiteawhile (Mrs.) 278
  Waytawhile (Mrs.) 278
Cop, (?) (Mrs.) 276
Copp, David 389
  Gooddeth (Mrs.) 389
  John nathan 389
  Jonathan 389
  Lidia 389
  Ruth 269, 389
  Tewxsbery 389
  William 269, 389
Coppen, (?) 102
Corben, dorkas (Mrs.) 80
Corington, (?) 116
Corlett, Elijah 215
Cornelius, (?) 227
Correll, (?) 28
Corser, William 363
Corwine, (?) 108
  George 168
Corwithie, Caleb 121
Cossen, Tho 110
Cotten, (?) 101
  John 101
Cottens, (?) 361
Cotton, (?) 37, 38, 44,
    111, 112, 138
  (?) (Mrs.) 72
  (?) (Sgt.) 363
  Jno. 78
  John 34, 36, 43, 53,
    78, 106, 110, 124
  John (Rev.) 72, 78,
    350
  Marja 78
  Mary 43
  Sara (Mrs.) 43

Cotton (cont.)
  Sarah 34, 78
  Sarah (Mrs.) 78, 124
  Seaborn 44
  Seaborne 43, 53
  Will 168
  William 197, 227, 365
  Willm 121
  Wm. 53
  Wm. (Sgt.) 281
Coult, Benjamine 286
  Joseph 286
Courser, Wm. 378
Cousens, Isacke 98
Couzens, Edward 154
Cowdell, (?) 97
Cowdery, willm. 13
Cowel, Ed. 363
Cowell, (?) 183
  (?) (Mrs.) 129
  Ed. 120
  Edward 28, 177, 187
  William 179
Cowley, Ambrose 168
Cowly, Ambrose 168
Cowper, (?) 178
Cowpers, (?) 178
Cox, Thomas 342
Coxes, (?) 265
Coy, Math. 378
  Mathew 154
  Matthew 27
Coytemore, Martha (Mrs.) 361
  Thomas 361
Coytmoor, Thomas 87
Coytmor, Katherin (Mrs.) 87
  Thomas 87
Coytmore, Thomas 118
Crab, Hanna (Mrs.) 232
  Samuel 275
  Samuell 233
Crabb, Henery 137
Crabtree, Francis 283
  John 120
Crackbone, (?) 2
  Gilbert 99
Crackborne, Gilbert 23
Craft, (?) 110
  Griffin 117, 196, 274
  Griffine 127, 133
  Griffine (Lt.) 151
  Serat. 122
Crafts, John 152
Crandell, Jno. 111
Crane, Henry 283
Cranwetts, John 35
Crawes, Wm. 248
Craze, Richard 390
Crazewill, Richard 390
Crechly, (?) 262
Crevard, Mordecaye 215
Crichley, (?) 363
Crisp, (?) 272
Croad, (?) 170
  Richard 389
Croade, John 139
  Ri. 139
  Richard 139, 161
Croakham, (?) 384
Crocum, Francis 384
  Joan (Mrs.) 384
  Joane (Mrs.) 384
Crofts, Griffen 187
  William 45
Cromwell, Ann (Mrs.) 363
  Anne (Mrs.) 32

Cromwell (cont.)
  Elisabeth 32
  Thomas 32, 363
Crosby, Anthony 378
Crosseman, Robert 200
  Sarah (Mrs.) 200
Crossing, Phillip 306
Crowell, Edward 343
Crowes, Samuel 26
Crowne, (?) (Mrs.) 341
  William 243
Crumwell, Ann (Mrs.) 363
  Thomas 363
Cruse, (?) 347
  Richard 347
Cuddington, (?) 89
Cudworth, James 108
Cuenfeild, John 118
Cuke, (?) 124
Cullemore, Isaac 48, 49
  Isaack 153
  Isack 49
  Isacke 61
Cullen, Zachary 45
Cullet, (?) 137
Cullick, John 208
Cullicke, Elizabeth 208
  Elizabeth (Mrs.) 208, 209
  John 182, 208
  John (Cpt.) 209
  Mary 208
Cullimore, Isack 232
Culliner, John 120
Culluer, Edward 104
Cuminges, Richard 109
Cursome, (?) 379
Curtis, Henry 378
  John 187
  Philip 187
  Phillip 51
  Richard 162, 212
  Sarah (Mrs.) 162
  Wm. 312
Curtisse, Phillip 187
Cushen, Jeremiah 161, 280, 287
  Mathew 81
  Sarah (Mrs.) 132
Cushin, Daniell 175, 176, 195, 215
  Jeremiah 175, 176, 189
  John 176
  Mathew 82, 175, 176
  Matthew 334
Cushing, (?) 179
  Daniell 176
  Matthew 176
Cushion, (?) (Col.) 123
  Daniell 122
  Mathew (Jr.) 122
  Mathew (Sr.) 122
Cutler, (?) 88, 97
  (?) (Mrs.) 281
Cutt, Robert 215
Cutter, (?) 97
  Barbara 14
  Rich. 99
  Richard 14, 127
  William 14
  Wm. 14, 99
Cutting, (?) 122
Cuttler, James 95, 117
Cutts, (?) 44
  Jno. 179
  John 149, 156, 177, 179
  Richard 179

Cutts (cont.)
  Richd. 207
  Robt 179
Daiues, (?) 285
Daius, Benjamin 286
Dale, (?) 22
Damerell, Humphery 161
  Sarah (Mrs.) 161
Damerill, Humphry 161
Damine, Abigail (Mrs.) 159
Dammant, John 144
Dammon, John 321
Dane, (?) 213
  Anic (Mrs.) 143
  Elizabeth 143
  Frances 143
  Francis 143
  Jno. 143
  John 103, 127, 143
Danford, (?) (Cpt.) 127
  Thomas 176
Danforth, (?) 105, 257, 271, 293
  (?) (Rev.) 247
  Elijah 371
  Elizabeth 314
  John 314
  Jonathan 99
  Mary 314
  Mary (Mrs.) 284, 314, 315
  Sam. 148, 289
  Saml1 60
  Samll. 148
  Samuel 47, 314, 315, 324, 338
  Samuel (Rev.) 314
  Samuell 283, 284, 289, 324
  Samull 46
  Samvell 196
  Tho 99, 233
  Thomas 60, 142, 143, 148, 284, 362
Daniel, (?) (Sgt.) 360
  Robert 98
Daniell, (?) (Sgt.) 164
  Ioes. 369
  John 368
  William 283
Darbey, Henerye 7
Darke, Katherine (Mrs.) 342
Darvell, Robert 111
Dassit, John (Sr.) 221
Date, James 265
Dauenport, (?) 44, 123, 355
  (?) (Cpt.) 122
  (?) (Mrs.) 53
  Elizabeth (Mrs.) 305
  Nathaniel 305
  Nathaniell 305
  Richard 219
  Richard (Cpt.) 305
  Thomas 172
Daues, Rice 360
Dauids, Samuell 224
Dauies, Humphrey 272
  William 203
Dauis, (?) 165, 343
  (?) (Lt.) 177
  (?) (Mrs.) 227
  Georg 249, 286
  James 99
  Jno. 249
  John 249

Dauis (cont.)
  Nicko. 270
  Richard 212
  Samuel 107, 249
  Samuell 249
  Tobyas 312
  William 88, 177, 262
  William (Cpt.) 317,
    339
  Willm 123
  Wm. 355
  Wm. (Cpt.) 289, 339
Dauison, (?) 122
Davenport, (?) (Cpt.)
    285
  (?) (Mrs.) 72
  Jno. (Rev.) 388
  John 292
  John (Rev.) 361, 388
  Mary (Mrs.) 72
  Richard (Cpt.) 305
Daves, (?) 37
Davies, Ephraim 222
  James 12
  Rice 137
Davis, (?) 147, 168, 378
  (?) (Mrs.) 379
  Barbara (Mrs.) 56
  Barbary 141
  Barbary (Mrs.) 141
  Benjamin 285, 368, 370
  Benjamine 285
  G. 111
  Geo. 286
  George 56, 137, 141,
    160, 163, 285
  James 210
  Johanna (Mrs.) 210
  Johannah (Mrs.) 210
  John 56, 378
  Joseph 285
  Rice 164, 360
  Rich'd 209, 210
  Richard 81, 134, 209,
    210
  Samuell 56
  Sarah 195, 196, 209
  Sarah (Mrs.) 210
  Tho. 215
  Tobias 151, 195, 196,
    210
  Tobyas 210
  William 43, 48, 153,
    343, 390
  Willm 190
  Wm. 43, 48, 114, 140,
    182, 204, 206, 210,
    214
  Wm. (Cpt.) 368, 370
Davison, (?) 127, 146
Davy, (?) 179
Dawes, Ambrose 388
  Jo. 121
  William 390
  Wm. 149
Dawson, (?) 4
Day, Betty 43
  Hugh 285
  Jane (Mrs.) 285
  John 237
  Ralph 329
  Steeuen 99
  Susan (Mrs.) 329
  Wentworth 203
  William 285
De La Noe, Phillip 156
De Vere, John 6
Deaken, (?) 324

Deaman, John 321
  Samuell 321
Deane, (?) 136
  Stephen 108
  Tho. 281, 380
  Thomas 380
Dearing, Saml. 125
Death, Abigail (Mrs.) 37
Dedham, (?) 5
Deere, George 106
Deffet, John 154
Dell, (?) (Mrs.) 127
  Abigall (Mrs.) 59
  George 58, 112, 146
  George (Cpt.) 59
  Ralph 58
Deman, John 321
  Samuell 321
Demericke, John 121
Denicon, Edw. 266
  Edward 247, 257, 311
Dening, Ann (Mrs.) 52
Denison, (?) 123
  (?) (Maj.) 75
  (?) (Mrs.) 46, 89
  Edw. 196, 231
  Edward 157, 187, 195,
    196, 257, 266, 270,
    282, 283, 296
  George 191, 200
  Willm 162
  Wm. 94, 117, 126
Denman, Jno. 164
  Mary 164
  Mary (Mrs.) 164
Denmans, Jno. 164
Dennae, Tho. 90
Denning, Obediah 52
  William 52, 126
  Wm. 52
Dennis, James 120, 278
  Mary (Mrs.) 278
Dennison, Daniel 315
  Edw. 324
  Edward 274, 289, 324
  Elizabeth (Mrs.) 324,
    325
  Mary 324
  William 324
Denton, (?) 14
  (?) (Rev.) 14
  Richard 167
  Ruth (Mrs.) 167
Denyson, Willm 89, 94
  Willm. 86
Devotion, Edward 128
Dewer, Thomas 138, 158,
    386
Dewse, Franc 122
Dexter, Rich. 122
  Tho. (Jr.) 354
  Thomas (Jr.) 194
Dey, Wm. 260
Diar, Ann (Mrs.) 309
Dickerman, Abraham 179
  Ellen (Mrs.) 164
  Tho. 91
  Thomas 91, 164
  Wm. 156
Dickeson, Philemon 121
Dickson, Lydia 272
Dier, George 212
  Peter 120
  Thomas 123, 186
Dill, (?) 198
  Benjamin 234
  Dico 198
  George 198, 241, 242

Dill (cont.)
  Joseph 234
  Samuel 234
Dills, Joseph 198
Dinsdale, William 169
Dinsdall, William 342
Diven, John 149
Dixer, Nathaniell 378
  Samuell 207
  William 207
Dixison, Philemon 2
Doble, Tobias 385
Dod, Geo. 120
  Georg 77
  George 224, 225
  Mary (Mrs.) 224, 225
Dodson, Anthony 156
  George 156
Dodyson, Sarah (Mrs.) 5
Doeletell, John 190
Dogget, (?) 99
Dole, Richard 169
Dolittle, John 165
Dones, Jno. (Jr.) 97
Donning, Emman. 18
Dons, Thomas 186
Dor, Thomas 383
Dorifield, Barnabas 228
Dorman, John 347
Dorneing, Dormon 176
Dosset, Father 274
Doubty, George 99
Douce, (?) 379
Douglas, Henery 300
  Henry 179, 299
  John 299
  Juden (Mrs.) 299
  Judeth (Mrs.) 299, 300
Douines, Daniel 336
Doulittle, John 162
Dous, Relief 167
Douse, Francis 138
Dove, Math 111
Dovenies, Daniel 219,
    220
  Daniell 219
Dovenses, Daniell 219
Dowden, Leonard 368, 370
  Mercy (Mrs.) 368
Dowglas, Hennery 299
Dowlettell, John 166
Downes, Thomas 130
Dowse, Catharine (Mrs.)
    351
  Francis 107, 290, 351
  Franses 351
Drake, (?) 135, 141,
    276, 277, 313, 330,
    341, 344, 351, 352
  Samuel G. 345
Drew, Elisabeth 239
  Jemina (Mrs.) 239
  Jeminah (Mrs.) 239,
    240
  John 239
  Robert 215
Drewry, Hugh 111
Drinker, (?) 22
  Edward 92, 218, 224,
    248
  Elizabeth (Mrs.) 92
  James 92
  John 92
  Johns 92
  Phillip 92
Drinsdall, (?) 378
Drudgham, (?) 127
Drury, Hugh 121, 226

Drus, John 211
Dudley, (?) 47, 61, 70,
  81, 98, 126
  Ann 60
  Bradstreete 46
  Deborah 45
  Denison 46
  John 45, 46, 61, 127,
  146
  Joseph 45, 370
  Margaret 60
  Paule 45
  Samuell 46
  Samull 46
  Sarah 46, 47
  Tho 61, 95
  Tho. 46, 47
  Thomas 45, 46, 47, 60,
  61, 126
  Thomas (Gov.) 25, 121
  Thomas (Jr.) 148
  Thomas (Sr.) 34
  Woodbridge 46
Dudly, (?) 69
  Sarah (Mrs.) 74
Dudlye, Thomas 7
Duer, Tho. 123, 293
Dugdale, (?) 6
Dugles, Henry 299
  Judea (Mrs.) 299
Duke, Mary 111
Dumer, (?) 99
  Richard 31, 32
Dunbarr, John 37
Duncan, Natha. 123, 142,
  355
  Nathan. 142
  Nathaniel 168
  Nathaniell 36
Dunckin, (?) 128
Dunckle, Elnathan 389
Dunckles, Silence
  (Widow) 389
Dunckly, Elnathan 111
Dundee, Gilbert 378
Dunster, (?) 88, 95, 97
  Henry 98, 99
Dunton, (?) 352
Durdell, Hugh 122
Dvglas, Henry 299
  Thomas 299
Dwight, Elizabeth (Mrs.)
  183
  Jno 125
  John 40, 183, 184, 366
  Sarah 184
  Timothy 183, 184, 385,
  388
  Timothy (Sr.) 184
Dyar, Ann (Mrs.) 309
  Tho 58
  Thomas 186, 205, 298,
  299, 325
Dyars, Thomas 147
Dyer, (?) 176
  John 325
  Thomas 57, 105, 131,
  227, 238, 298
  Thos 53
  Thos. 57
Dyke, (?) 178
Dyon, Thomas 211
Eares, Robert 335
Earle, Ralph 58
East, Elisabeth 262
  Mary 262
  Roger 99
  Wm. 147

Easton, Nicholas 330
Eaton, (?) 99
  Abigall 144
  Abigall (Mrs.) 144
  Eliaser 363
  Elisabeth 363
  Jabesh 220
  Jno. 144
  John 104, 144
  Josiah 379
  Mary 144
Eddenden, Edmond 79, 96,
  175, 262, 286
  Edmund 79, 199
Eddendon, Edman 246
Eddie, John 25
Eddington, (?) 121
Eddye, John 25, 121
Edendon, Edmond 290
Edinsell, Thomas 128
Edlin, John 85
Edling, David Ludecius
  114
  David Ludecus 114
Edmonds, Will 156
Edmons, (?) 177
Edmunds, (?) 227
  (?) (Sr.) 363
  Robt 120
Eds-all, (?) 215
  Samuell 215
Edsell, Thomas 232
Edwards, Philip 255
  Robert 118
Edzer, (?) 378
Egginton, Jeremiah 198
Eggleton, Richard 264
Egings, Jeramiah 301
Eieres, (?) (Mrs.) 281
Eire, Dorothy 146
  John 145, 146
  Lydia 126
  Lydia (Mrs.) 126
  Maria 145, 146
  Martha (Mrs.) 145, 146
  Mary 145
  Simon 126, 145, 146
  Simon (Jr.) 126
  Symon 20, 155
  Thomas 146
Eirounes, Mathew 136
Elby, Giles 378
Eles, John 1
  Richard 1, 11
Eliab, Reb. (?) 5
Eliot, (?) 85, 88, 111,
  297
  Francis 221, 354
  Hanna 35
  Jacob 107, 206, 263,
  315, 354
  Jacob (Sr.) 194, 354
  John 86, 89, 184, 296
  John (Rev.) 353
  Margery (Mrs.) 353,
  354
  Mehittable 354
  Philip 29, 117
  Phill. 29
  Phillip 3, 11, 29, 30,
  90, 123
Eliote, (?) 3, 4
  Allin 4
  Jacob 4
  Philip 86
  Phillip 4
  ffrances 4
Eliott, Jacob 159, 194

Eliott (cont.)
  Jacob (Jr.) 354
  John 283
  Margerie (Mrs.) 353
  Mary 159
Eliut, (?) 105
  Elizabeth 143
Ellcocke, Anthony 215
Ellcott, Jacob 35
  Margery (Mrs.) 35
Ellen, Oliue 102
Elleott, Jacob 35
  Margery (Mrs.) 35
Ellice, Richard 104
Ellin, Daniel 332, 333
  Daniell 333
  Mary (Mrs.) 332, 333
  Nicholas 332, 333
Elliot, (?) 69
  Asaph 194
  Elizabeth (Mrs.) 133,
  183
  Francis 123, 221, 340
  Hannah 194
  Jacob 194, 258, 260,
  353, 354
  John 133, 157, 185
  Lydia 133
  Margery (Mrs.) 194,
  353, 354
  Mehetabel 354
  Mehitable 194
  Philip 183
  Philipp 183
  Phillip 51, 133, 134
  Sarah 133, 194
  Susanna 194, 354
Elliots, (?) 123, 334
  Elizabeth (Mrs.) 183
  Philip 183
Elliott, (?) 69, 174
  (?) (Mrs.) 173
  Asaph 194
  Francis 173, 255, 340
  Frauncis 251
  Hannah 194
  Jacob 35, 194, 256,
  342
  John 46, 174
  Margery (Mrs.) 194
  Mehitable 194
  Phillep 152
  Phillip 39, 133, 134
  Sarah 194
  Susanna 194
Ellis, (?) 12, 20, 89,
  257, 258
  Edward 257, 258, 305
  Elizabeth 368
  Elizebeth 370
  Joseph 389
  Margarett 304
  William 173
Ellise, Wm. 221
Elliway, (?) 160
  Wm. 140
Elly, Daniel 32
Else, Ellis 167, 168
Elton, (?) 150
Emans, (?) 378
Emeryes, Jno. 138
Emmons, Martha (Mrs.)
  233
Emons, (?) 137
  Alice 275, 276
  Benjamin 232, 275
  Elizabeth 232, 275
  Hanna 232

Emons (cont.)
  Joseph 275, 276
  Martha 275
  Martha (Mrs.) 233,
    275, 276
  Mary 275
  Obadia 232
  Obadiah 233, 275, 276
  Obadyah 276
  Samuel 232, 275, 276
  Thomas 232, 233, 275
Endecot, Elisabeth
  (Mrs.) 268
  Jno. 268, 305
  John 268, 290
  Zerubbabel 268
Endecott, Elizabeth
  (Mrs.) 310
  Jo. (Gov.) 48, 50, 133
  Jo. (Jr.) 226
  John 193, 267, 268,
    310, 316
  Zerubabel 267
Endicots, (?) 111
Endicott, Elizabeth
  (Mrs.) 266, 268, 310
  John 266, 267, 268,
    310, 377
  John (Sr.) 140, 266
  Zerobabel 267
  Zerubabel 267
Enges, Madott 169
English, Lorance 148
  Maudil 52
  Will 157, 168
  William 233, 276, 363
  Wm. 158, 276
Englishe, William 294
Eoster, Hopestill 109
Epps, (?) 213
Errington, Abra 99
Eson, Nicholas 330
Estic, Ester (Mrs.) 129
Estick, Ester (Mrs.) 129
Estwicke, Edw 127
Etherington, Thomas 294
Ethrington, Thomas 293,
  294
Euans, Mary 215
Euens, (?) 99
Euered, John 199, 363,
  379
Euerell, James 59, 242,
  272, 273, 299
Euerill, (?) 156, 379
  James 106, 123, 138,
    157, 169, 294
Euins, (?) 122
  Richard 212
Eurill, James 147
Evans, Dauid 215
  David 214, 215
  Elizabeth 214
  Henry 107
  Jonathan 214
  Mary 214
  Mary (Mrs.) 214
  Richard 211
  Willm. 120
Evard, (?) 215
Evens, Richard 211
Everel, James 242
Everell, Abiell 366
  James 123, 388, 389
Everill, Hannah 123
  Iames 42
  James 106, 116, 119,
    385

Everrell, James 42
Everrills, (?) 42
Ewer, Thomas 85
Eyers, An 171
  Beniamine 171
  Christian 171
  Dorothy 171
  Mary 171
  Rebekah 171
  Simond (Sr.) 172
  Symond (Sr.) 171
Eyes, Symond (Jr.) 171
F-, (?) 167
Fairbanks, (?) 108
  Jonas 153
Fairebanck, Richard 37
Fales, James 389
Far, Ellihar 379
Fare, Barnabas 119
Farebanck, George 328
  Grace (Mrs.) 328, 329
  John 329
  John (Jr.) 334
  John (Sr.) 334
  Jonas 329
  Jonathan 328, 329
  Jonathan (Sr.) 328,
    329
  Mary 328, 329
  Sarah 329
  Susan 329
Farmer, (?) 202, 234,
  251
Farnam, John 146, 177,
  336
  John (Sr.) 219
Farne, Miles 330
Farnham, (?) (Mrs.) 281
  Henry 151, 323
  Jno. 225, 310
  John 274
  John (Sr.) 274, 336
Farnhams, Joane (Mrs.)
  323
  John 272
Farnsworth, Joseph 128
Farnum, Jno. 364
  John 114, 127, 154,
    168, 212, 220
  John (Sr.) 220, 299
Farnworth, Elizabeth 152
  Ester 152
  Hannah 152
  Joseph 151, 152, 153
  Mary 152
  Mary (Mrs.) 152, 153
  Rebecca 152, 153
  Samuel 152
  Samuell 152
Faroh, John 227
Farrey, (?) 120
Farrington, John 139
Faulkner, David 156
  Thomas 157
Fawer, (?) 121
  Barnabas 147, 362
  Grace (Mrs.) 147, 362
Fawkner, David 157
Faxon, (?) 315
  Thomas 221, 315
  Thomas (Jr.) 212
  Thomas (Sr.) 212, 383
Fearing, Israel 250
  Israell 250
  John 122, 145, 249,
    250
  Margret (Mrs.) 249
  Margrett (Mrs.) 249

Fearing (cont.)
  Mary 250
  Sarah 250
Feild, Darby 37
  George 44
  Pate 156
  William 250
  Wm. 250
Felch, (?) 303
Fellowes, Richard 105,
  147, 378
Felt, (?) 6, 156
Fen, (?) 198
Fenne, Mary 163
  Mary (Mrs.) 163
Fenns, (?) (Mrs.) 163
Fering, John 145
Ferings, John 220
Fermace, Alice (Mrs.)
  129
Fernald, Renald 44
Fernig, John 170
Ferniside, Elizabeth
  (Mrs.) 155
  Jno. 263
  John 143, 168, 198,
    218, 220, 222, 263,
    356, 362
Ferring, John 145, 189,
  250
Ferringe, John 250
Fessenden, John 11
Fface, Robt 98
Ffairefield, Richard 32
Ffarnworth, Joseph 54
Ffawer, Barnabas 55, 83
  Eleazer 55
  Eliasar 55
  Grace (Mrs.) 55
Ffayerweather, Thomas 85
Ffeavor, Alice (Mrs.) 72
  William 72
Ffeild, (?) 97
  Robert 127
  Robt. 53
  Roftt 53
Ffellowes, Leonard 105
  Samuell 105
  William 105
Ffesington, John 99
Ffessington, John 11
Ffinson, Samuel 21
  Thomas 21
Ffisher, Anthony 40
  Daniell 104
Fflack, (?) 79
Ffletcher, Edw. 75, 100
  Edwd 55
  Edwd. 52
Fflint, (?) 51
  Tho 26
  Thomas 9, 10, 26
Ffoordam, (?) 14
  Robert (Rev.) 14
Ffoote, Joshua 60
Ffoster, (?) 58, 98
  Hopestill 50, 56, 91,
    103
  James 47, 48
  Tho. 54, 55
Ffote, Joshua 60
Ffoulsham, Jno. 81
Ffounel, John 99
Ffowle, George 9, 10
Ffowler, Henry 60
Ffrancklen, (?) 99
Ffreeman, Apphia 20
  Apphya 20

Ffrench, Nath 98
  Stephen 57
  Wm. 98
Ffrost, (?) 2
Ffry, Elizabeth 17
  Mary 17
  Wm. 17
Ffuller, John 99
Ffurnell, Stro. 97
Fickes, (?) 311
Field, Mary (Mrs.) 64
  Robt 120
  Zachery 99
Filbrooke, James 379
  Thomas 378
Finch, (?) 335
  John 378
  Samuel 152
Finder, Tho. 120
Finson, Samuel 21
  Thomas 21
Fish, (?) 378
  Jno. 112
Fishe, (?) 123
Fisher, (?) (Lt.) 387
  Ann (Mrs.) 331
  Anne 96
  Anthony 119, 212, 389
  Anthony (Jr.) 212
  Cornelius 256
  Daniel 183, 389
  Daniell 104, 130, 188,
    255, 256, 329, 331,
    332
  Edward 309
  Elizabeth 119, 331
  Elizabeth (Mrs.) 330
  Joane (Mrs.) 389
  John 96, 330, 331, 332
  Jonathan 331
  Joshua 331, 385
  Joshua (Lt.) 184
  Joshuah 334
  Josiah 389
  Josuah 331, 332
  Leah (Mrs.) 256
  Mary (Mrs.) 330, 331,
    332
Fisk, (?) (Rev.) 172
Fitch, Elizabeth 344
  James 344
  Richard 344
  Thomas 378
Fitche, Thomas 293, 294
Fitchew, Peter 116
  Petter 116
Flacke, Cotton 137
  Jane (Mrs.) 137
  Samuell 137
Fletcher, (?) 138
  (?) (Mrs.) 262
  Edw. 262, 294, 304,
    305
  Edward 126, 128, 237,
    285, 303, 304
  Elizabeth 304
  Mary (Mrs.) 304, 305
Flint, (?) 51, 342
  Henery 326
  Henry 228, 325, 326
  Henry (Rev.) 325
  Josiah 326
  Josiah (Rev.) 326
  Josias 326
  Margery 136, 254
  Margery (Mrs.) 326
  Seth 326
  Thomas 9

Flints, (?) 326
Flood, Lydia (Mrs.) 219
  Rich'd 219
  Richard 218
Floyd, Jno. 125
Flynt, (?) 125
Fogg, Ralph 6
Fogge, John (Sir) 6
Follett, William 113,
  138, 357
  Wm. 113
Foot, Caleb 146
  Elizabeth (Mrs.) 127
  Joshua 127
Foote, Caleb 122
  Joshua 146, 149
Forbes, (?) 355
  James 304
Ford, Stephen 242
  Tho. 120
  William 378
Forde, (?) 97
Fordham, Elizabeth
  (Mrs.) 14
  Hannah 14
  John 14
  Jonah (Rev.) 14
  Joseph 14
  Josiah 14
  Ro. 348
  Robert 14
  Robert (Rev.) 14
Forwell, (?) 317, 318
Foster, (?) 119, 122,
  193, 212, 235, 359
  (?) (Lt.) 194
  (?) (ensigne) 295
  Hopestill 153, 164,
    186, 194, 210, 212,
    245, 255, 265, 280,
    295, 305
  Hopestill (Cpt.) 295,
    374
  Hopestill (Lt.) 292
  Hopstill 51
  Thomas 347
  Timothy 167, 385
  hopestill 91
Foulsome, John 122
Fowler, John 347
Fowles, Joseph 325
Fox, Tho 156
Foy, Wll. 125
Frairy, Elizabeth (Mrs.)
  389
  John (Jr.) 389
  Theophilus 389
Francis, (?) 378
Francklin, John 164
  William 128, 165
Franckline, Phebe (Mrs.)
  165
  William 165
Franckling, John 164
Francklyn, Jno. 362
  John 362
Franersco, Franers 260
Franklin, (?) (Dr.) 92
  William 164
Frary, Elizabeth (Mrs.)
  291
  Hannah (Mrs.) 194, 354
  John 291
  Prudence 141
  Theoph. 354
  Theophilus 256, 263,
    342, 354
Frarye, (?) 291

Frarye (cont.)
  Elizabeth 291
  Elizabeth (Mrs.) 291
  Jno. 291
  Jo. 291
  John 291
  John (Jr.) 291
  Theophilus 258, 312
Fratchford, Thomas 98
Fray, George 122
Frayre, Theoph. 260
  Theophilus 260
Freake, Jno 215
  John 164, 214, 313
Fredericke, John 127
French, G. 111
  Jacob 383
  John 166, 255, 340
  Mary (Mrs.) 241
  Stephen 237
  Stephen (Sr.) 383
  Thomas 190
Frie, Elizabeth 197
Fris, John 156
Frissel, John 63
Frissell, James 243
Frissyll, John 90
Frothingham, Peter 385
  William 354
Fruysell, (?) 243
Fry, (?) 222
  Elizabeth 17
  Mary 17
  William 17
Fryar, George 302, 303
Fryer, Geo. 303
  George 302, 303
  Nath 179
  Nathaniell 308
Fugrame, William 128
Fuller, Edward 22
  Hannah (Mrs.) 200
  John 297
  Tho 133
  Thomas 132, 133, 178,
    200
Furnall, Strong 149
Furnell, Stronge 122
  William 378
Furnill, Strong 120
Gaige, Tho 120
Gallop, Ann 301
  Christobell 60
  Christovell 60
  Hannah (Mrs.) 60
  Jno. 97
  Joane 60, 100
  John 34, 60, 100, 101,
    108
  Joseph 100, 156
  Nathaniell 60, 100,
    153
  Sam'l 209
  Saml1. 60
  Samuell 100
Gallops, Samuell 101
Gamlen, Benjamin 228,
  229
  Elizabeth (Mrs.) 228,
    229
  Robert 228
Gamlin, (?) 88
  Robert 229
  Robt. 230
Ganet, Math. 110
  Nathl 111
Gard, John 215
Gardener, George 330

Gardner, Edward 149
  Elizabeth (Mrs.) 358
  George 358
  Peter 312
  Richard 127, 377
  Tho 110, 111
  Tho. 121, 377
Garet, Martine 159
  Prissilla (Mrs.) 159
Garett, Martine 159
  Prissilla (Mrs.) 159
Garfield, Edward 80
  Johannah (Mrs.) 333
Garis, Arthur 29
Garlick, (?) (Mrs.) 41
Garner, Richard ·146
Garnesey, Henry 210
Garnett, John 122
Garnsey, (?) 255
  Henry 212, 255
Garret, James (Cpt.) 161
  John 325
  Lydia (Mrs.) 212
  Mary 325
  Mary (Mrs.) 325
  Richard 212
  Robert 312, 325
  Robt. 325
  Sarah 325
Garrets, (?) 147
Garrett, (?) 122
  John 325
  Mary 325
  Mary (Mrs.) 325
  Richard 161
  Robert 325
  Robt. 325
  Sarah 325
  William 274
  Wm. 274
Garry, (?) 243
Garscay, Wm. 140
Gary, (?) 183
  Arthur 187, 270
  Ez. 389
  Frances (Mrs.) 270
  Nathaniell 270
  Sam(uel) 270
  Samuell 270, 334
  William 270, 271, 388
Garye, Arthur 243
Gates, Stephen 122, 139
Gatleife, Jonathan 235
  Prudent (Mrs.) 235
  Thomas 235
Gatliefe, Jonathan 235
Gatliff, Jonathan 235
  Prudent (Mrs.) 235
Gatliffe, Mary 235
  Thomas 235
Gatline, Thomas 234
Gattlife, Thomas 234
Gawod, Anne 16
Gay, Abigail 384
  Hezekiah 384
  John 178, 384, 385,
    389
  Jonathan 384
  Judith 384
  Nathaniel 384
  Samuel 384
Gaylord, William 84
Gee, Peter 179
Gennings, Jno. 111
Gent, John 378
Geor(ge), Anne (Mrs.)
  118
George, (?) (Mrs.) 177

George (cont.)
  Anne (Mrs.) 95
  John 95, 154
  Robert 95
  Susan 95
Georges, Peter 148
Gerarde, John 355
Gernsey, Henry 179
Gerrish, Johan 91
  Willi. 91
  William 90
  Willl. 91
Gibbins, Susanna (Mrs.)
  169
Gibbons, (?) (Gen.) 37,
  72
  (?) (Maj.) 128
  Edward (Gen.) 128, 166
  Edward (Maj.) 120
  Jothan 166
  Margarett (Mrs.) 166
  Susanna 166
Gibbs, (?) 138
  Benjamin 336
  Dennis 308
  John 308
  Mary (Mrs.) 157
  Robert 174, 177, 215,
    317, 368
  Robt. 363
Gibons, Willm 120
Gibs, Robt 247
Gibson, (?) 121, 346
  (?) (Mrs.) 48
  Christopher 113, 120,
    156, 164, 241, 251,
    265
  Margret (Mrs.) 48
  Robert 167
  Robt. 167
  Wm. 221
Giffard, John 138
Gifford, John 281
Gilbert, John 317, 318
Gilburt, (?) 312
Gile, Hannah (Mrs.) 131
  Mary 131
  Thomas (Jr.) 131
Gill, Arthur 113, 140,
  160, 357, 358
  Elizabeth 137
  Frances 160
  Jno. 83
  John 113, 135, 136,
    140, 160, 187, 232,
    358
  Obediah 137
  Tho. 160
  Thomas 122, 378
Gillam, Ben. 129, 303
  Benj 120, 127
  Benj. 120, 167
  Benj. (Sr.) 281
  Benjamine 220
  Hannah 308
  Zachariah 294
  Zechariah 293, 294
Gillams, Benjamine 220
Gillet, Deborah 388
  Hannah 229, 388
  John 248
Gillett, Hannah 229
Gilletts, Jno. 248
Gilliam, Benjamin (Sr.)
  215
Gillit, Elizabeth (Mrs.)
  229
  Hannah 229

Gillit (cont.)
  John 229
  Math 120
Gillman, Moses 179
Gillmon, Edw 110
Gills, Edw 111
Gillum, Ben 110
  Benjn. 146
  George 110
Gilman, Edw. 120, 121
  Edward 122
  Moses 139
Gimson, James 211
Giuing, Abraham 291
  Jno. 291
  John 291
  Mary 291
Gladman, Elkanah 281
  Elkanah (Jr.) 281
  Elkanah (Sr.) 281
Glascock, Rich. 307
Glendall, (?) 131
Glouer, (?) 41, 112,
    121, 123, 168
  Abigail (Mrs.) 147
  Anne (Mrs.) 136
  Habacucke 52
  Habakuck 235
  Habbacuk 234, 294
  Henery 147
  John 41, 52, 136
Glover, (?) 150, 379
  Anne (Mrs.) 176
  Habacucke 51, 52
  Habacuke 52
  Habakueke 51
  Habucucke 176
  Henery 147
  John 39, 51, 52, 54,
    127, 135, 176
  Mary (Mrs.) 162, 176
  Nath. 176
  Nathaniel 176
  Nathaniell 162
  Nathl 176
  Nathl. 51, 52, 176
  Pelatiah 51, 52
  Thos 52
  Thos. 51
Goble, John 302, 303
Gobner, Joseph 269
Godfrey, (?) 90
  Joseph 127
Goffe, Edw. 98
  Edward 98
Gold, Edward 123
  Elizabeth 269
  Francis 176
Golder, Francis 140
Goline, (?) 235
Goodale, John 248
Goodall, (?) 379
  Jno. 247, 248
  John 247, 248, 257
  Sarah (Mrs.) 247
Goodalle, Elizabeth 93
Goodgrome, Richard 203
Goodhouse, Peter 265
Goodier, (?) 53
Goodieur, Stephen 281
Goodrich, Margaret
    (Mrs.) 118
  William 118
Goodwin, (?) 127
  Edward 146, 157
Goodwine, Edwd. 160
  Thomas 179
Goodyear, Lydia (Mrs.)

Goodyear (cont.)
  281
Goodyeare, Samuell 127
Gookin, (?) (Cpt.) 51,
  54, 99, 200, 326,
  356
Gookins, (?) (Cpt.) 136
Gool, (?) 99
Goold, (?) (Mrs.) 276
  Jer 111
  Zaccheus 13
Goose, (?) (Mrs.) 120
  Peter 215
  Susan 129
  Susan (Mrs.) 129
Goram, John 378
Gore, (?) 12, 122
  Abigail 134
  Abigall 134
  Hannah 134
  John 122, 134, 359,
    365
  Mary 134
  Rhoda (Mrs.) 359, 365
  Rose (Mrs.) 134
  Samuel 134, 187
  Samuell 248
Gorgray, Wm. 160
Gornel, John 292
Gornell, John 56, 136,
  186, 209
Gornill, John 211
Gosse, John 117
Gould, Edward 379
  Frances 204, 348
  Jarvis 157
  Jeremy 14
  John 286
  Zacheus 267
Gouldsmith, John 92
Gouldston, Anne (Mrs.)
  118
  Henry 118
Gouldstone, Ann (Widow)
  118
Gounrs, (?) 45
Gour, Jo. Winthrop 346
Goure, John 122
Gove, Edward 93
  John 93, 127
  Mary 93
Grace, (?) 109
Grafton, John 215
  Joseph (Jr.) 308
Graner, Mordicha 137
Grant, Christo. 99
  Thomas 202
Graue, Hannah 51
Graues, Grace (Mrs.) 143
  James 127
  John 88
  Richard 263
  Richd. 22
Grave, (?) (Widow) 30
  Hanna 29, 30
  Iohn 29
  John 29, 117
  Jonathan 29, 30
  Marah 30
  Mary 29
  Samuell 29, 30
  Sarah 29, 30
Graves, (?) 379
  Richard 162
Gray, (?) 74
  Francis 177
  Peter 221
  Robert 120

Gredle, Richard 216
Gredlee, Richard 217
Greegss, Allice (Mrs.)
  216
  Ann 216
  James 216
  Sarah 216
Green, James 279
  John 113, 257
  Sam. 99
  Thomas 279
  Thomas (Jr.) 257
Greene, (?) 281
  (?) (Mrs.) 60
  Hen 149
  Jacob 110
  James 169
  John 28, 85, 92, 93,
    338, 348
  Joseph 378
  Nath. 121
  Nathaniell 311
  Percefell 99
  Ralph 106, 122
  Richard 215
Greeneleffe, (?) 242
Greenland, (?) 1
Greenleafe, (?) 215,
  317, 318
  John 317, 321
  Mary (Mrs.) 321
Greenleffe, Edmund 178
Greenleife, (?) 176, 255
  Edm. 91
Greenough, Dorothy 273
  Elizabeth 273
  Elizabeth (Mrs.) 272
  Thomas 251
  William 272, 273
Greenoway, Vrsly 10
Greens, (?) 93
Greenwood, Nathaniel 340
  Nathl. 56
Gregorie, Richard 302,
  303
Grenaway, John 377
  Mary (Mrs.) 377
  Susan 377
  Susannah 377
Grenaways, John 168
Grenleife, Edmond 91
Grey, Thomas 302
Grice, Charles 227, 228
  David 228
  John 228
  Margery (Mrs.) 228
Griches, (?) 235
Gridlee, Richard 217
Gridley, (?) 122, 124,
  129, 378
  Rich. 116
  Richard 126, 136, 143,
    150, 167, 196, 216,
    217, 286, 312, 319,
    320
Gridlie, Richard 385
Gridly, Joseph 219
  Lydia (Mrs.) 219
  Rich. 168
  Richard 218
  Richd. 161
Griffin, (?) 111
  Chare 99
  George 127
  John 127
  Thomas 191, 364
Griffinne, (?) 243
Griges, George 204

Griges (cont.)
  Thomas 90
Grigges, Alice (Mrs.)
  216
  James 216, 217
Griggs, Alice (Mrs.)
  163, 216
  Anne 163
  George 163, 216
  Grissell (Mrs.) 163
  Humphery 163
  Humphry 55
  James 163
  Joseph 152, 187
  Mary 163
  Sarah 163
  Wm. 111
Grigley, Richard 347
Grimes, (?) 99
Grimstone, Margaret 96
Grinaway, (John) 122
Grinnoway, (?) 108
Grocer, Jno. 247
  Thomas 247
Grocers, Thomas 247, 248
Groomes, (?) 122
Grose, (?) 129
  Clement 389
  Edmund 389
  Elizabeth 271
Gross, Clement 386
  Clement (Jr.) 386
  Elizabeth 271
Grosse, (?) (Widow) 122,
  126
  Clement 101, 147
  Clements 101
  Edmund 101, 147, 227
  Hanna 101
  I. 101
  Isaack 110, 227
  Isaake 227
  Isack 101
  Mary 227
  Mathew 147, 156
  Matthew 101
  Susan 227
  Susanna 101
  Tho 101
Grosses, Clement 380
Grout, John 130
  Sarah 130
  Sarah (Mrs.) 131
Grover, John 162
Grub, Thomas 121
Grubb, (?) 107
  Tho. 116, 128, 153
  Thomas 150, 237, 263,
    300, 389
Grunn, Elizabeth 181
  Francis (Mrs.) 181
  Jone 181
Gulifore, Lidia 111
Gullife, Jonathan 224
  Prudence (Mrs.) 224
  Thomas 224, 234
Gullison, Hugh 120
Gulliver, Jonathan 224
  Prudence (Mrs.) 224
  Thomas 224, 234
Gunnison, (?) 97, 122
  (?) (Mrs.) 363
  Hugh 37, 138
Gurly, William 127
Gurnell, Jno. 134
  John 176, 292, 374,
    385
Gurnet, Janet 238

Gurney, Jno. 149
John 148, 221, 355
John (Sr.) 221
Rebecca (Mrs.) 325
Gurnill, (?) 255
Gurwell, Phill. 120
Guy, (?) 120
Nicholas 13
Guye, Nicholas 13, 117
Gwin, Thomas 338
Habborne, John 13
Samuel 13
Hach, John 161
Hackburne, Abraham 12
Elizabeth 12
Hannah 12
Isaac 12
John 12
Joseph 12
Samuel 12
Haddings, George 98
Haddock, (?) 108
Haddon, Katherine 14
Hagborne, (?) 97
Abraham 12
Elizabeth 12
Elizth. 12
Lugg 12
Samuel 12
Hagburne, (?) 378
Sam 13
Hagburnes, (?) 129
Elizabeth 129
Hahones, (?) 359
Hake, Robert 128
Hale, (?) 218
Robert 28, 222
Hales, Thomas 7
Halgraue, (?) 123
Hall, (?) 93, 111
Edw 111
Edward 3, 72, 156
John 44, 158
Richard 359
Robert 85, 258
Tho. 99
Hallett, Angell 122
Hallsall, Georg. 379
George 149
Halsall, Geo. 122
George 128
Halsted, Edna 25
Henry 25
Nathan 117
Susan 44
William 25, 88
Halstone, (?) 99
Haly, Tho. 151
Thomas 312
Hambleton, William 379
Hament, (?) (Mrs.) 171
Elizabeth 171
John 171
hanna 171
Hamilton, W. 58
Hamlet, Wm. 99
Hammes, Mark 234
Hammon, John 138
Hamnore, Jno. 149
Hams, Anthony 122
Marke 120, 122
Hamund, (?) 99
Hanberry, (?) (Mrs.) 137
Wm. 104
Hanbury, (?) (Mrs.) 105,
127
John 105
Wm. 104

Hancock, Daniell 379
Hancocke, Matt. 99
Samll. 378
Handes, Marcke 112
Hands, (?) 242
Jo. 234
Mark 234
Marke 234, 242
Mary (Mrs.) 234
Mehitabell 234
Hanford, Nathaniel 110
Hanley, Thomas 243
Hanmore, John 156
Hanner, Marie 2
Hanniford, (?) 242
(?) (Mrs.) 234, 242
(?) (Widow) 242
Abigael 242
Abigail (Mrs.) 234
Abigaill (Mrs.) 234
Hannah 241
John 241, 242
Mary 241
Rose 241
Samuel 242
Samuell 241
Sarah 241
Hannifords, (?) 218
Hanniwell, Roger 120
Hannyford, (?) (Mrs.)
234
Hans, Marke 127
Hansett, John 30
Harbart, (?) 378
Harber, John 356
Harbert, To 379
Harbor, Hannah 54
Hannah (Mrs.) 356
Jno. 356, 357
Jno. (Sr.) 356
John 356
John (Jr.) 356
John (Sr.) 356
Harden, Abraham 125
Rich 111
Harder, Elisabeth 237
Elizabeth (Mrs.) 237
Hardier, Elizabeth 136
Elizabeth (Mrs.) 136,
237, 360, 361
Jno. 136
Lydia 361
Mary 136
Richard 136, 360, 361
Hardin, John 120, 121
Joseph 120
Harding, Abraham 141,
291, 387, 389
Elizabeth (Mrs.) 141,
389
Hannah (Mrs.) 387
John 156, 291, 389
Joseph 156
Mary 389
Robert (Cpt.) 138
William 317
Hardinge, (?) 291
Abraham 291
Elisabeth (Mrs.) 291
Elizabeth 291
Jno. 291
Jo. 291
John 291
Hardinges, John 291
Harine, Rich 121
Harker, John 120
Harkman, Timothy 343
Harlackenden, Roger 6

Harlakenden, Elizabeth 7
Elizabeth (Mrs.) 7
Nevile 7
Richard 7, 8
Roger 8
Sarah 7
Harlakynden, Thomas 6
Harmon, Thomas 122, 123
Harris, (?) 34, 355
Anthony 1
Daniell 1
Jno 111
Jo 1
John 302, 303
Mary 111
Robert 335
Robt. 335
Tho. 1, 11
Thomas 17, 60
Walter 17, 83, 103
William 1
Harrison, John 121, 179,
388
Harrod, James 232
Wm. 232
Hart, John 122, 127
Samuell 149
Harte, Jno 111
Hartwell, Will 156
Harvard, Jno. 144
Harvey, John 389
Mary 389
Thomas 389
William 389
Harvie, Joseph 6
William 378
Harvy, Martha (Mrs.) 166
William 166
Harvye, Joseph 6
Harwood, (?) 59, 121
Andrew 21
John 27
Rachell (Mrs.) 235,
236
Thomas 55, 129, 235,
236
Willomet 160
Haryman, Leonard 99
Hassell, Mansfield 73
Hassey, Cornet 271
Hastings, Thomas 89,
117, 118, 296
Hasty, Edward 120
Hatch, John 105
Hathorne, John 149
Nath. 259
Nathaniel 259
William 87
Hatley, William 105
Hatson, Thomas 212
Hatton, Elifall 308
Hauchin, Jeremiah 119
Haughe, Atherton 346
Haughs, Susan 111
Hauke, Mathew 125
Haukins, Jobe 111
Haule, Samuell 85
Havens, (?) (Mrs.) 135
Richard 107
Haward, John 166
Hawes, Edward 57, 183,
188
Eliazer 384
John 273, 274
Mary 273, 274
Obadiah 212
Obidiah 212
Richard 150, 212

Hawes (cont.)
Robert 273, 274
Thomas 273, 274
Hawke, Math 120
Mathew 82, 122, 132,
144, 145, 176
Matt. 125
Hawkes, (?) 378
Mathew 189, 250
Mathewe 49
Hawkinges, Job 388
Hawkins, (?) 22, 316
Abraham 272
Abrasa 93
Damarus 390
Elizabeth 390
Elizabeth (Mrs.) 93
James 120, 157, 212,
390
James (Sr.) 390
Job 103, 123, 156
Mary 390
Mary (Mrs.) 163, 390
Robert 85
Ruth 390
Sarah 390
Tho. 158
Tho. (Cpt.) 163
Thomas 127, 138, 163
Thomas (Cpt.) 163
Hawkner, Thomas 122
Hawks, Mathew 132, 215
Hawley, Elizabeth (Mrs.)
302
George 302
H. 303
Thomas 187
Wm. 146
Hawly, George 302
Henry (Col.) 301
Hawthorne, (?) (Cpt.)
267
Jno. 179
John 138
Hayman, John 270
Haynes, John 8
Hayns, Walter 87
Haythorne, (?) (Maj.)
268
Hayward, Huldah 253
Margery (Mrs.) 167
Samuel 390
William 166
Hazard, (?) 222, 359
John 218
Mary (Mrs.) 218
Healey, Willm. 122
Healy, (?) 120
William 105,
106
Heard, Jno. 110
John 121
Hearin, Mary (Mrs.) 246
Thomas 246
Hearsey, Willm. 122
Hearsie, William (Sr.)
139
Heath, (?) 4, 85, 89,
133, 156
(?) (Widow) 242, 243
Elizabeth (Mrs.) 242,
243
Hanna 38
Hannah 243
Isaac 39, 117, 126,
128, 143, 185, 325
Isaack 11, 127, 134,
184, 185

Heath (cont.)
Isaacke 184
Isack 84, 89, 102, 231
Isacke 3, 39
Mary 38, 39, 243
Peleg 151
Pelig 39
Robt. 22
Susanna (Mrs.) 41
William 29, 38
Willm 38, 39
Willnj. 29
Heathe, Edward 12
Heaths, Isaack 296
Heaton, (?) 256
Elieazer 169
Elisabeth 255
Jabez 390
Nathaniel 255
Nathaniell 255
Hebberd, (?) 189
Hebbert, Edward 176
Heborne, (?) 88
Hedge, (?) 122
Heivers, Abraham 385
Heiward, Geo. 118
Helds, William 149
Heley, William 96
Helly, William 127
Helmon, Josiah 306
Hely, Willm 107
Henbury, (?) 122
Henchman, Daniel 286
Henewood, James 110
Henfield, (?) 147
(?) (Cpt.) 42
Robt 121
Henniford, (?) 168
Henning, Thomas 304
Henry, (?) 109
Hensdall, Robert 129
Hensdell, Rob 128
Robert 141, 147
Herbery, Phillippe 311
Hersee, William 91, 96
Hersie, Elizabeth 139
Elizabeth (Mrs.) 139
Frances 139
Francis 139
James 139
John 139
Judith 139
William 138, 139, 174
William (Jr.) 138
William (Sr.) 138
Hersy, Wm. 293
Hervey, (?) 269
Hett, (?) 299
Samuell 299
Tho. 122
Hetth, William 11
Heward, Georg 26
Hewens, Jacob 164
Hewes, (?) (Lt.) 89
John (Lt.) 127
Joshua 13, 60, 89, 149
Josuah 88
Hewet, Thomas 174, 189
Heyers, Symon 117
Heylet, John 337
Lydia (Mrs.) 337
Heylett, Edmd. 191
Edmund 191
Lyddia (Mrs.) 191
Heyletts, Sumuell 191
Heyward, Georg 26
George 25
Heywood, Margery (Mrs.)

Heywood (cont.)
167
Hibbins, (?) 41, 45, 47,
51, 52, 54, 98, 112,
121, 123, 356
Ann (Mrs.) 76, 77
Jno 76
John 76
Jonathan 76, 77
Joseph 76
William 20, 75, 76,
107, 350
Wm. 52, 95
Hibbinses, (?) 122
Hickes, (?) 242, 378
Richard 241
Hide, Mary 282
Timothy 282
Hides, Sam. 99
Hieroms, (?) 131
Higginson, (?) 358
Sarah (Mrs.) 315
Hildreth, Richard 99
Hill, (?) 97, 110
(?) (Mrs.) 50
Frances (Mrs.) 37
Francis (Mrs.) 233
Hannah 37
Ignatius 142
James 162, 190, 291,
339
John 90, 111, 122,
156, 233, 311, 384
Mary 233
Peeter 160
Ralph 122
Samuel 338
Samuell 233
Tho. 293
Thomas 293
Val. 140
Valentine 136, 149
Vallentine 37
Hillard, Ann 105
Hille, Vallentyne 37
Hilleard, Elisebeth
(Mrs.) 96
Hiller, (?) (Mrs.) 96
Elisebeth (Mrs.) 96
Hills, (?) 49, 159
Joseph 87, 218
Tho. 293
Hilman, Jos. 307
Hilton, Edward 16
Willm 101
Hinckley, Tho. 176
Thomas 105, 176
Hincksman, (?) 276
Elizabeth (Mrs.) 232
John 276
Hincksmans, (?) 276
Hinckson, Walter 264
Wm. 98
Hindsall, Robert 215
Hinsdell, Robert 383
Hippen, William 77
Hitchborne, David 378
Hoare, R. 203
Hobart, Edward (Sr.) 220
Joshua (Cpt.) 220
Hobb, Joseph 390
Hobbert, Elisabeth
(Mrs.) 20
Hobbertt, Josua (Cpt.)
114
Hobert, Benjamin 19
Elisabeth (Mrs.) 19
Hannah 19

Hobert (cont.)
  Hanner 19
  Rachel 19
  Rachell 19
  Rachhell 19
  Robert 19
  Sarah 19
Hodsden, Nicho 111
Hodsman, Edward 144
Hoe, Abraham 128
Hoffes, (?) 244
Hogsfleshe, (?) 125
Hohnan, (?) 120
Holban, (?) 99
Holbrock, William 383
Holbrook, (?) 298
  John 222, 325
  John (Lt.) 299
  Tho 111
  Thomas 340
Holbrooke, Elizabeth
  (Mrs.) 147
  John 186, 343
  Wm. 147
Holdsworth, Joseph 388
  Joshua 388
Hole, John 215
Holebrooke, John 186
Holeman, (?) (Mrs.) 136
  Richd. 378
Holgraue, (?) 28, 120
Holgraues, (?) 28
Holgrave, (?) 28
Holland, (?) 102
  Angell 120
  John 39, 40, 83
Hollet, Angell 110
Holliday, John 281
Hollman, Thomas 283
Holloway, (?) 212, 343
  Benjamin 319
  Elisha 248
  Elizabeth (Mrs.) 248
  Esther 248
  Jno 156
  Mallachey 248
  Mary (Mrs.) 319
  Nehemiah 248
  Timothy 248
  William 129, 248, 319,
    320
  Wm. 55
Holly, (?) 204
  Samuel 17, 348
  Samuell 17, 204
Hollye, Samuell 348
Hollyes, Sara (Mrs.) 110
Hollyoke, Edward 166
  Eleazer 166
Holma, Jno. 160
Holman, Abigal 44
  Hannah 44
  Iohn 44
  Jno. 154, 160
  John 44, 121, 154, 160
  Mary 44
  Samuel 44
  Tho. 257
  Thomas 44
Holmes, Dauid 283
  Ebenezer 381
  George 85, 86
  Jane (Mrs.) 283
  Joseph 85
  Nathanael 365
  Obediath 98
Holsey, (?) 124
  Geo. 108

Holyoke, (?) 165
  Andrewes 165
  Edward 165, 166
  Edword 165
  Elizur 166
  Marten 165
  Martin 165
  Prenam 165
  Tuttle 165
Homes, Bathsheba 103
  Dauid 283
  David 283
  Jane (Mrs.) 283
  Margaret 283
  Margarett 103
  Mary 103
  Rachell 103
  Robt 99
  Thomas 103
  William 103
  William (Maj.) 103
Hoocker, (?) 88
Hooke, Francis 211
Hooker, (?) 3
Hooper, Chrispin 177,
    364
  Elizabeth (Mrs.) 304
Hope, (?) 313
Hophton, James 257
Hopkinns, William 296
Hopkins, (?) 108, 122,
    325
Hoppen, Stephen 102
Hoppin, Benjamen 278
  Delieurance 278
  Hannah 278
  Hannah (Mrs.) 277
  Jno. 278
  Joseph 278
  Oppertunity 278
  Sarah 278
  Stephen 187, 277, 278
  Thomas 278
Hoppkins, Steephen 111
Hord, John 204
Hords, John 204
Hornby, James 347
Horne, Humphrey 120
Horper, Tho. 168
Horton, Timothy 343
Hosking, Elias 53
Houchin, (?) 123, 202,
    268
  Jer. 147, 363
  Jeremiah 49, 126, 160
  Jeremy 126, 147, 227
Houchine, Thomas 220
Houchyes, (?) 236
Hougge, Richrd. 110
Hough, Daniel (Cpt.) 123
Houghes, (?) 263
Houghton, Ralph 208
Hourle, (?) (Widow) 122
House, Elizabeth 171
  Elizabeth (Mrs.) 171
  Samuell 171
Houtchin, Jeremie 31
How, (?) 21
  Abraham 83, 167
  Edward 19, 346
  Elizabeth (Mrs.) 143
  Joseph 199, 279, 280,
    287, 299, 386
  Margaret 21
  Margret 346
Howard, (?) 123, 343,
    379
  Geo 88

Howard (cont.)
  George 156
  Jo. 5
  John 156, 178
  Mary 253
  Robert 79, 130, 160,
    165, 215, 253
  Robrt. 79
  Robt 48
  Robt. 47, 48, 160
  Will. 172
  William 162, 171, 172
Howchin, Jer. 226, 368
  Jeremiah 111, 310,
    311, 317
Howe, Edward 22, 121,
    346
  Joseph 294
  Margaret 21
Howell, Edward (Lt.) 14
Howes, (?) 20
Howing, Elizabeth 113
Hows, Abraham 229
Howsen, (?) (Cpt.) 120
Hubbard, (?) 49, 122,
    123, 170, 171
  Edmund 122
  Elisabeth (Mrs.) 116
  John 352, 360
  Joseph 125
  Joshua 82, 125, 144
  Joshua (Cpt.) 125
  Joshua (Lt.) 122
  Joshuah (Cpt.) 258
  Josiah 145
  Peeter 170
  Peter 144, 145, 170,
    258, 259, 260
  Wm. (Jr.) 146
Hubbards, Edmond 250
Hubbart, (?) 96
Hubberd, Caleb 251
  Edmund 170
  Joshua 114
  Joshua (Cpt.) 258, 260
  Josiah 49
  Peter 144, 145, 258,
    259, 260
  Susanna (Mrs.) 258,
    259, 260
  Tho. 145
Hubbert, (?) 105
  Anthony 104
  Peter 84, 260
  Susanna (Mrs.) 260
Hubberts, Edmond 250
Hubborn, William 227
Huckins, Thomas 168
Hucstable, Macklin 120
Hudchinson, Elizabeth
    309
  Elizabeth (Mrs.) 309
Hudson, (?) (Lt.) 138
  Francis 127, 227
  Hannah 35
  John 35, 153
  Mary (Mrs.) 35, 36
  Ralph 35
  Thomas 36
  Will 138
  Will. 138
  William 36, 98, 161,
    168, 194, 386
  William (Lt.) 76, 177,
    196
  Willm 107
  Willm. (Lt.) 122
  Wm (Lt.) 199

409

Hudson (cont.)
Wm. 98, 138, 146, 147
Hudsons, (?) 52
Hues, (?) (Lt.) 89
John 207
Joshua 117
Huetts, Thomas 220
Hughson, Jno 104
Huginsworth, (?) (Widow) 99
Hull, (?) 151
Edward 277
George Vickry 215
Jno 52, 78, 105
Jno. 258
John 52, 79, 106, 126, 140, 146, 165, 190, 193, 194, 206, 217, 235, 237, 250, 258, 260, 276, 277, 286, 289, 300, 315, 338, 344
Robert 20, 86, 98, 105, 112, 116, 276, 277, 349
Robrt. 349
Robt 112
Robt. 75, 126, 277
Thomas 378
Tristram 378
Tristrom 110
Hulls, Tristram 269
Huly, Robert 111
Humfrey, James 197, 198, 223, 292
Joan 212
Jonas 197, 198
Susanna 197
Humfries, John 388
Humphery, Amiell 327
Amiells 327
Aniell 328
James 280, 328
Jane 327
Jane (Mrs.) 326, 328
William 327
Williams 326
Humpheryes, William 126
Humphrey, (?) 328
Isaac 374
Jane (Mrs.) 328
Jonas (Mrs.) 328
Patience 374
Humphreys, (?) 176
James 198
Jonas 198
Humphry, James 232, 283
Hun, An (Mrs.) 86
George 86
nathanell 86
Hunckin, Hercules 109
Hune, Nathaniell 378
Hunkins, John 207
Hunn, George 86
Hunne, George 86
Nathl. 119
nathanell 86
Hunt, Alice (Mrs.) 347
Edward 259
Elizabeth 161
Enoch 41
Ephraim 41, 53, 105
Ephrim 41
Helen 347
John 347
Robert 347, 348
Susan (Mrs.) 87, 347
Susanna (Mrs.) 347

Hunt (cont.)
Thomas 161, 347
Wm. 17
Hunters, William 263, 264
Hunting, Hannah 384
John 183
Huntley, John 187
Hurd, John 277
Hurst, (?) 138
Huse, (?) 110
Hust, (?) 120
Hutchin, Jerimy 178
Hutchine, George 99
Hutchinson, (?) 359
(?) (Cpt.) 193
Abigall 129
Abigell (Mrs.) 121
Ed. 363
Ed. (Jr.) 362
Edw. 224
Edw. (Cpt.) 198
Edward 63, 111, 113, 121, 126, 128, 129, 169, 189, 194, 209, 300, 309, 350
Edward (Cpt.) 182
Edward (Lt.) 76
Edward (Sr.) 112, 309
Eliakim 310
Elisha 309
Elizabeth 309
Elizabeth (Mrs.) 309
Hannah 309
Katherine 309
Richard 153, 225, 350
Samuel 225, 226, 308, 310, 350
Samuell 123
Susan (Mrs.) 309
Thomas 63
William 350
Hutchinsons, Edward 309
Edward (Cpt.) 181
Hutchison, Edward 149
Hutson, Francis 140
Hutton, Rich. 120
Ibitt, Robert 2
Igleden, (?) (Widow) 8
Stephen 8
Iles, Richard 11, 85
Indecott, (?) (Gov.) 253
Indecotte, (?) 108
Ingion, Mary 171
Inglish, William 276, 365
Ingollds, Francis 107
Ingolls, Barnett 162
Ingraham, William 388
Ireland, William 24, 272
Wm. 265
Irnes, Mathew 379
Irons, Browne 196
Elizabeth 196
John 196
Mathew 196, 197
Rebecka 196
Samuell 196
Thomas 196
Isaack, Joseph 6
Isack, Joseph 3
Isacke, Mary 99
Islip, Adam 355
Iverts, (?) 110
Ivey, James 125
Jno. 125
Iwitt, Thomas 158
Jacie, Henry 32

Jacklin, Edmond 276
Edmund 130, 148, 351
Susan (Mrs.) 281
Susana (Mrs.) 351
Jackson, (?) 3, 93, 111, 127
Abigail 386
Edmund 123, 167, 197, 227, 271
Edward 17, 120, 122, 204, 252, 253, 348
Elisha 271
Elizabeth 271
Elizabeth (Mrs.) 253
Hannah 154
John 17, 117, 167, 193, 348, 386
Jonathan 252
Mary (Mrs.) 271
Samll. 111, 149
Sara 112
Jacksone, John 204
Jacob, (?) (Mrs.) 189
Deborah 132
Elizabeth 132
Hannah 132
John 132
Joseph 132
Mary 132
Mary (Mrs.) 132
Nicho. 122
Nicholas 132
Sarah 132
Jacson, Edmund 233
Edw. 98
Richard 99
James, Ann (Mrs.) 315
Edward 161
Erasamus 120
Franc 122
Gaudy 315
ffrancis 81
Jameson, (?) 300
Jancks, Joseph (Sr.) 149
Janemet, (?) 338
Janson, Hannah 102
Jaquith, Abraham 57
Jarrett, Richard 118
Jarves, John 37
Jarvis, (?) 97
Jno 218
John 138, 218
Jason, Chr. 301
Jay, Mary 363
Jefferay, Will. 2
Jeffes, John 166
Jeffryes, Ann (Mrs.) 342
Jempson, James 211
Sarah (Mrs.) 211
Jeners, (?) 298
Jenison, Wm. 121
Jenkes, Jos. 122
Joseph (Jr.) 149
Jenner, Tho. 120
Jennings, William 21
Wm. 21
Jennison, William 21
Jesse, Henry 32
Jewell, Grisell (Mrs.) 54
Mary 163
Sam. 120
Samuell 163
Tho. 54, 55
Thomas 54, 163
Jewet, (?) 99
Joseph 22, 110
Maxamill 111

Jewett, (?) 164
  Ann (Mrs.) 346
  Joseph 107, 122, 136, 346
  Mary (Mrs.) 346
  Nic 22
Jo--life, John 215
Joanes, (?) 346
  Abraham 190
  Anne (Mrs.) 163
  Robert 81
  Thomas 198, 379
Joaness, Ann (Mrs.) 216
Joans, Thomas 198
Joel, Bridget 160
  Elizabeth 160
  Ellenor 160
  John 160
  Margaret 160
John(son), (?) (Cpt.) 168
Johns, (?) 301
  William 222
  Wm. 176
Johnson, (?) 59, 99, 111, 123, 177, 272, 286, 346, 363
  (?) (Cpt.) 76, 112, 128, 243, 363, 378
  (?) (Lt.) 74, 75
  (?) (Widow) 227, 378
  Abigail (Mrs.) 135
  Edward 34, 153
  Elizabeth 156
  Francis 120, 140
  Hannah 82, 83
  Isaac 156, 388
  Isaac (Cpt.) 157
  Isaack 127
  Isaack (Cpt.) 312
  Isack 152
  James 30, 54, 76, 77, 86, 98, 106, 107, 112, 118, 119, 125, 126, 130, 135, 150, 164, 167, 214, 219, 220, 221, 223, 224, 227, 233, 316, 317, 349
  James (Cpt.) 77, 130, 135, 167, 168, 177, 215, 224, 315
  James (Lt.) 147
  Jeames 105
  Jno. 126
  John 13, 46, 47, 81, 89, 102, 108, 122, 123, 128, 143, 151, 156, 157
  Katharine (Mrs.) 265
  Margaret (Mrs.) 170
  Margarett (Mrs.) 171
  Mary (Mrs.) 159, 281
  Mehetable 156
  Samuel 159
  Thomas 122, 170, 355
Johnsone, John 84
Johnsons, Samuell 159
Joice, William 98
Jollife, (?) 363
Jolliffe, John 177, 308
Jolyffe, Jno. 229
Jones, (?) 88, 107, 129, 194, 212, 243
  Alice 76
  Alice (Mrs.) 116, 347
  Anne (Mrs.) 207
  Caleb 385

Jones (cont.)
  Eldad 192
  Ellin (Mrs.) 280
  Hannah 279
  Isaack 243, 279
  Joseph 122
  Kingsley 192
  Margaret 76
  Rice 102, 207, 378
  Richard 116, 347
  Rise 215
  Robert 122
  Saml1 176
  Saml1. 212
  Samuel 192
  Samuell 192
  Samvell 192
  Tho. 122
  Thomas 34, 108, 138, 161, 194, 255, 264, 279
  Timothie 116
  Timothy 48
  Wm. 311
Jonnson, Isaac 156
Jonson, Hannah 386
  James F. 386
  Mary (Mrs.) 386
  Rebeckah 386
  Samuel 386
  Thomas 215
Jonsons, John 187
Jordan, (?) 99
  Abraham 57
  Anne 57
  James 57
  Mary 57
  Tho. 57
  Thomas 57
Joslenes, Thomas 96
Joy, John 100
  Tho. 127
  Thomas 122, 197
Joye, Joane (Mrs.) 60
Joyes, Thomas 227
Joylife, John 339
Joyliffe, Jno. 167, 308
  John 159, 214, 226, 360
Joyloffe, John 311
Judkin, Job 120, 277
Judkins, Job 179
Judson, Esther 132
  Mary 132
  Mary (Mrs.) 132, 133
  Samuell 132
  Sarah 132
Juell, John 161
Juets, (?) 346
Jupe, (?) 74
  Anthony 71, 74
  Benjamin 74
  Benjamine 71, 72, 74
  Grace (Mrs.) 71, 72
  Mary 71, 72, 74
  Nicholas 72
  Robt 99
Jutkins, Saml1. 379
Juttkins, Job 379
Kaine, Moses 111
Kaker, (?) 154
  Elizabeth 154
  Elizabeth (Mrs.) 154
  Ormanell 154
Kalsoe, Joane (Mrs.) 45
Kane, Aurther 110
  Ezra 126
Keagle, John 120

Keajnes, Robert (Cpt.) 36
Keane, (?) 73
Keaser, (?) 165
Keasur, Hannah 165
Keayne, (?) 350
  (?) (Mrs.) 378
  Anna 75
  Anne (Jr.) (Mrs.) 168
  Anne (Mrs.) 65, 70, 73
  Arthur 156
  Benj. (Maj.) 360
  Benjamin 74
  Benjamine 65, 67, 70, 71
  Benjamine (Maj.) 70, 71
  Dudley 70
  Dudly 69
  Hannah 71, 74
  John 74
  Josiah 122
  Robert 65, 73, 75, 360
  Robert (Cpt.) 73, 75, 360
  Robt (Cpt.) 52
  Wilson 67
Keden, Beniamin 207
Keeby, Henry 102
Keen, John 378, 379
Keene, Jo. 1
Keieke, Judith 35
Keift, (?) 14
Keine, (?) (Cpt.) 109
Kellie, David 219
  Elizabeth (Mrs.) 219
Kellon, Thomas 177
Kellond, Tho. 311
  Thomas 363, 364
Kelly, David 219
  Elizabeth (Mrs.) 219
Kelond, Tho 364
Kemball, Henry 97, 99
  John 117
  Tho 127, 149
Kemon, James 158
Kempsters, Daniel 99
Kempthorne, Danl 127
  Simon 37
Kemthorne, Simeon 227
Kendrick, George 110
Kennidge, Mathew 153
Kennwicke, William 161
Kent, John 188, 237
  Joseph 237
  Joshua 237, 238
  Mary (Mrs.) 238, 239
  Richd. 378
Keyes, Samuell 317
Keysar, George 165
Keysly, Jno 111
Kibby, Edward 138
  Gresill (Mrs.) 192
  Grissell (Mrs.) 192
  Henry 102, 183, 192
Kiers, (?) 117
Kilcop, (?) 138
  Wm. 55
Kilcup, Grace (Mrs.) 286
  William 286, 304
Kilcupp, Grace (Mrs.) 286
  William 286, 310
Kileup, Willm. 123
Killcup, Sarah (Mrs.) 129
  Wm. 129, 192
Killcupp, G. 111

411

Killcupp (cont.)
  Grace 286
  William 192, 286
Kimball, (?) 171
  Henry 149
  Thomas 146
King, (?) 221
  Dorothie (Mrs.) 41,
    121
  John 41, 121, 335
  Mary 179
  Ralph 178
  Ruth 41
  Samuell 330
  Sarah 41
  Sarah (Mrs.) 163, 217
  Susanna 41
  Thomas 117
  William 216, 217
  Wm. 161
Kingam, (?) 222
Kinge, (?) 99, 122
  Daniell 110
  Dorothy 41
Kingley, ffredome 54
Kingman, (?) 222
  (?) (Sr.) 122
  Edward 298, 299
  Edward (Jr.) 123
  Henrey 299
  Henry 166, 298, 299
  John 298, 299
  Thomas 298, 299
  Thomas T. 299
Kingsberry, John 104
Kingsbery, Henry 178
  John 178
  Josiph 178
  Margaret 200
Kingsberye, Jo. 5
Kingsbura, John 178
Kingsbury, John 178
  Josiph 178
  Margaret 200
  Margrett (Mrs.) 178
Kingsley, Alice (Mrs.)
    347
  John 48, 347, 359
  ffreedome 54
Kingsly, (?) 176
Kingston, Thomas 293
Kinsley, Alice (Mrs.)
    347
  John 41, 283, 347
  Stephen 283
  Steuen 356
  steuen 86
Kinslie, (?) 347
Kinsly, (?) 164
Kinston, Thomas 293
Kirbey, Willm (Jr.) 120
Kitchell, Robert 14
Kitchen, Robt. 363
Knap, James 179
Knight, (?) 98, 122,
    129, 164, 346
  Ann (Mrs.) 158
  Anna (Mrs.) 58
  Athagered 23
  Edward 58
  Francis 121
  John 346
  Joseph 287, 321
  Martha 58
  Mary (Mrs.) 346
  Mathew 111
  Richard 55, 90, 93,
    175, 196

Knight (cont.)
  Robert 58, 111, 120
  Robt. 37, 58, 111
  Wil 108
  Wm. 34
  ffrancis 101
Knights, (?) 99
  Athagered 23
Knite, John 346
  Mary (Mrs.) 346
Knocker, Geog 22
  Tho. 22
  Thomas 22
Knolls, (?) (Rev.) 26
Knowles, John 121
  Richard 149
Knowls, John 222
Knowlse, Elisabeth 19
  Mary 19
Knoxe, Willyam (Jr.) 95
Koker, Samll. 154
  Samuell 154
Kowdale, Edw. 107
Kymball, Charles 227
Ladd, Edward 153
Laddehorne, John 242
Laddyn, James 2
Lake, (?) 138
  Jno. 111, 179, 263
  John 77, 99, 120, 123,
    137, 219, 224, 300,
    303, 386, 388
  Tho 99, 153
  Tho. 55, 157, 229, 364
  Thomas 37, 109, 119,
    120, 128, 136, 140,
    177, 198, 206, 262,
    279, 281, 311, 364,
    390
  Thomas (Cpt.) 214,
    239, 280, 281, 287
  Thos 55, 390
Laland, Henry 387, 388
  Hopestill 387
Lamb, (?) 111
  Joshua 243
  Thomas 117
Lambert, James 61
  Thomas 378
Lambett, Jno. 149
Lambson, Barnabe 3
  Barnabey 3
  Bridge 3
  Isaac 3
  Joseph 3
  Mary 3
  Parish 3
  Sarah 3
  Sparahak 3
  Stone 3
Lamper, Henery 125
Lampere, (?) 122
Lamperry, Henry 177
Lampery, Henery 242
Lampory, Henry 363
Lamprey, Hen 157
  Henery 137
  Henry 127, 138
Lampsons, Barnebe 99
Lane, (?) 101
  Andrew 54
  Ann (Mrs.) 73
  Delsebelath (Mrs.) 207
  Dousabella (Mrs.) 207
  Edward 178
  Francis 206
  George 54, 139, 174
  Hannah 73

Lane (cont.)
  James 206, 207
  James (Jr.) 207
  James (Sr.) 207
  Jno. 263
  Job 138
  John 264
  Mary 54, 343
  Sampson 263, 264
  Samson 263
  William 54, 110, 128
  Willm. 122
  Wm. 54
Langdon, John 120, 309
  Sarah (Mrs.) 129, 309
  Sary (Mrs.) 129
Langer, Dinah 189
  Elizabeth 189
  Margarets 189
  Richard 189, 366
Langham, Jno. 77
Langhorne, (?) (Mrs.) 60
Langley, John 121, 122
Langly, Abell 278
Lapdell, Symon 378
Larch, John 389
Largine, (?) 378
Larkin, (?) 93
Lasell, (?) 198
  Elizabeth (Mrs.) 144
  Jno. 81
  John 122, 144
Lasells, James 77
Lason, John 57
Latham, Elizabeth (Mrs.)
    6
Latimer, Anne 217
Lattimore, Ann (Mrs.)
    216
  Anne (Mrs.) 216, 217
  Robert 216, 217
Lauer, Margery 238
Lauerett, Hannah 36
  Hudson 36
  John (Cpt.) 36
Laughton, Thomas 162
Laurence, (?) (Widow)
    164
  Elizabeth 164
  Nicholas 120
Lausun, (?) 99
Lawrance, Nicholas 177
Lawrence, Jno. 80
  Jo 22
  Lawson, Chr. 98
  Christo. 64
  Christopher 177
Lawsons, Christo. 64
Layton, Joseph 183
Leach, John 384
Leader, (?) 123, 198
  Abigal 226
  Ales (Mrs.) 226
  Rebecka 226
  Richd. 127
  Samuel 226
  Samuell 226
  Samuells 226
  Thomas 226
Leads, (?) 122
Leager, Anna (Mrs.) 210
  Anne (Mrs.) 211
  Bethia 210, 211
  Hannah 210, 211
  Jacob 210, 211
  Maries 211
Leapet, (?) 99
Leatchford, Tho. 349

Leauerett, Hudson 311
Leauett, John (Deacon)
    220
Leavitt, Jno. 125
Lechford, (?) 350
    Tho. 350
    Thomas 349
Lee, Edward 6
    Joseph 103
Leech, Ambrose 379
Leedes, Richard 56
Leeds, Richard 381
Legare, Jacob 211
Legat, Ann (Mrs.) 16
    John 16
Leigh, Thomas 37
Leisly, William 301
Leland, Tho. 177
Lemon, Mary 99
Lempry, Henry 364
Lenard, James 79
Leonard, Hen 111
    Phillip 149
Lepingwell, (?) 99
Lettin, Richard 118
Leueret, Elizabeth 36
    Jno. (Gen.) 289
    John 264, 302
    John (Cpt.) 36
    John (Gen.) 319
Leuerett, (?) (Gen.) 313
    Ann (Mrs.) 36
    Hudson 177, 364
    John 315
    John (Gen.) 315, 320,
        339
Leueretts, (?) (Cpt.)
    180
Leuerit, John (Cpt.) 136
Leueritt, Tho. 346
Lever, Margery 150
Leveret, (?) 378
    Jo. 124
    John (Cpt.) 213
Leverett, (?) (Gen.) 297
    (?) (Maj.) 216
    Ann (Mrs.) 107
    Hannah 36
    Hudson 36, 363
    Jno. 43, 208
    John 214
    John (Cpt.) 208
    Thomas 35, 107
Levins, John 98, 377
Lewes, (?) 101, 227
    John 169, 279
    Phillip 37
Lewis, (?) 29, 88, 121,
    305, 312, 344, 347
    John 120, 146, 154,
        379
Lewit, Tho. 122
Lials, Peeter 111
Lidget, (?) 303
Lidgett, Peter 311
Lilly, Edward 303
Lillye, Edward 281
Lilse, Ann (Mrs.) 312
Limbrey, John 201
Linchorne, Anne (Mrs.)
    224
    Robert 224
Linckhorne, Samuell 215
    Thomas 54
    William 187
Lincoln, Joane (Mrs.)
    144
    Stephen 144, 166

Lincoln (cont.)
    Stephen (Sr.) 144
    Thomas 170, 171
Lincolne, (?) 378
    Anne (Mrs.) 224
    Daniell 378
    Joane (Mrs.) 144
    Robert 224
    Sam. 121
    Samll. 379
    Stephen 144, 166
    Steuen 144
    Susanna 144
    Tho. 122
    Thomas 144, 171
Lincon, Joshua 189
    Margaret (Mrs.) 189
    Thomas 189
Lincorne, Thomas 81, 250
Lind, Simon 252, 253
Linde, Simon 251, 253
Lindon, (?) 378
Linkeolns, Thomas 220
Linkhorne, Thomas 260
Lion, (?) 215
Lippencut, Rich 120
Liscomb, Hannah (Mrs.)
    386
    John 386
Lisle, Alice (Mrs.) 312
    Allice (Mrs.) 313
    Francis 312
    Joseph 312
    Mary 312
Litlefeild, francis 366
Littlefield, Franc 120
    Francis 388
    Meribah (Mrs.) 388
Loaeren, Ann (Mrs.) 346
    John 346
Lobdell, John 190
Lobdin, John 145
Lobdon, John 122
Locke, Jno. 159
    Phillip 158
Locks, Bridget (Mrs.)
    321
Lockwood, John 5, 6
    Robert 121
    Robt. 117
Lodge, (?) 22
Loe, John 102
Loker, John 120
Londe, E- 161
Long, Anne (Mrs.) 107
    Anne (Mrs.) 157
    Jo. 116
    Joseph 152
    Mary (Mrs.) 54
    Philip 107, 114
    Phillip 138, 153, 157,
        378
    Robert 23, 91
    Robert (Sr.) 158
    Thomas 152
Longe, Philip 114, 121
Longhorne, Tho 99
Longs, Phillip 157
Looman, Anne (Mrs.) 154
Lopdell, Nicholas 27
Lorain, Tho. 84
Lorans, John 120
Lord, Rebecca (Mrs.) 64
    Rich 98
    Richard 53
    Robert 212
    Robt. 119
Loreing, Tho. 122

Loreing (cont.)
    Thomas 190
Loring, Jane (Mrs.) 190
    Tho. 105
    Thomas 190
Loringe, Tho 105
    Thomas 105
Lothrops, (?) 354
Louet, (?) 257
Louett, Daniel 257
Louetts, Daniel 258
Louewell, John 158
Louit, John 122
Love, John 378
Lovell, John 390
Lovells, (?) 220
Loveran, John 346
Loveren, John 346
Loverin, Thomas 346
Lovering, Ann (Mrs.) 346
    Anna (Mrs.) 346
    John 346
Lovermore, John 159
Lovetts, (?) 257
Lovewell, John 158
Lovran, John 21, 346
Low, Elizabeth 195
    John 124, 195
Lowden, Richard 385
Lowe, (?) 121
    Anthony 125
    Johannis 144
    John 119, 144
    Thomas 2
Lowel, John 379
Lowell, John 215, 248,
    379
Lowering, John 21
Lowle, Beniamine 90, 91
    Elizabeth 90, 91
    Elizabeth (Mrs.) 90
    James 90
    Jno. 91
    John 90, 91
    Joseph 90
    Mary 90, 91
    Peter 90
    Richard 90
Loyall, Francis 277
Loyd, Mary (Mrs.) 308,
    309
Loylyffe, John 229
Ludington, Wm 111
Ludken, William 351
Ludkin, Aaron 98, 122
    Elizabeth (Mrs.) 119
    George 98
    William 118, 119, 351
    Wm. 351
Luke, (?) 227
Lumpkin, (?) (Widow) 98
Lunn, Tho. 110
Lusher, (?) (Gen.) 300
    (?) (Maj.) 194, 200
    Elaizer 133
    Elea. 238
    Eleazar 370
    Eleazer 40, 57, 104,
        114, 125, 133, 144,
        166, 178, 239, 383,
        384
    Eleazer (Cpt.) 166
    Eliazar 184
    Eliazer 57, 144, 178,
        200, 218, 317, 329
    Eliazer (Cpt.) 57,
        132, 178
    Eliezar 183, 188

413

Luson, John 119, 183,
   187, 188, 366
   Martha (Mrs.) 188
   Robert 188
   Susan 188
   Thomas 188
Lux, (?) 90
   Humfry 97
Luxford, James 99, 117,
   156
Lyale, Robert 113
Lyme, Thos. 50
Lyncolne, Daniell 122
   Stephen 123
   Tho. 122
Lynd, (?) 379
   Simon 252, 253
Lynde, Simon 253
   Symon 235
   Thomas 113
Lyndes, Symond 311
Lyndon, Augustin 194
Lyne, (?) 348
   Thomas 28
Lynes, (?) 236, 303, 316
   Thomas 198
Lyon, Thomas 382
   William 334
   Willm 185
Mackartye, Thaddeus 281
Macon, Arther 177
Madder, (?) 225
Maddocks, (?) 123
Maddox, John 337
   Mary (Mrs.) 337
Mader, (?) (Mrs.) 242
Madocke, James 146
Madson, Thomas 152
Maduck, Edward 146
Magdalens, Mary 247
Magit, Joseph 99
Mahew, Jane 26
   Thomas 121
Maho, (?) 225
Mahoone, Dorman 212
   Mary (Mrs.) 212
Maineyerd, Elias 125
Maio, John 251
Maisters, John 5
Makepeace, (?) 123, 345
   Elisabeth (Mrs.) 278
   Elizabeth (Mrs.) 278,
   345
   Hannah 277, 278
   Hester 277, 278
   Mary 277, 278
   Thomas 119, 277, 278,
   345
   Waytawhile 278
   William 277
   Wm. 277
Makepeas, (?) 111
Makins, Thomas 179
Mallowes, John 215
Manfeild, John 152
Manfield, Mary 255
Maning, George 359
Mannig, Wm. (Sr.) 98
Manning, John 37
   William 263
   William (Sr.) 263
   Wm. 263
   Wm. (Jr.) 98
Mans, Wm. 98
Mansfeild, (?) 97
   John 73
   Mary 255
Mansfield, John 12, 27,

Mansfield (cont.)
   73, 315
   John (Sir) 73
   Mary 165
Marable, John 120
Marchant, (?) (Mrs.) 2
   John 120
   Marie 2
   Wm 111
Marion, Jno. 79
   John 185
Marrell, Isaac 185
Marret, Thomas 25, 121
Marrett, Tho. 99
Marrit, Thomas 25
Marsh, Elisebeth 91
   Elizabeth (Mrs.) 91
   Ephraim 145
   George 91
   John Whit 160
   Mary 91, 145
   Oneseferes 91
   Sarah 145
   Sarah (Mrs.) 145
   Tho. 139, 145
   Thomas 91, 132, 139,
   145
   Thos. 153
Marshall, (?) 123
   (?) (Deacon) 241, 342
   Dea 52
   Jno. 179
   John 220
   Micheson 108
   Tho 101, 102
   Tho. 35, 55, 107, 119
   Thomas 35, 90, 159,
   294
   Thos 55
   Thos. 126
Marshalls, Thomas 294
Marston, Benja. 363
Martin, (?) 122
   George 191
   John 192
   Lewis 368, 369
   Rebecka 191
   Sarah 232
Martine, Lewes 173, 174
   Lewis 173, 174, 369
   Michaell 154
   Robert 199
Martyn, Lewis 368
Mashe, Thomas 122
Mason, (?) (Lt.) 23, 95
   Arther 177
   Arthur 179, 214, 303,
   363
   Hugh 23, 117
   Ralph 149
   Raphe 125
   Richd. 179
   Robert 149
   Robin 179
   Robine 179
   Sampson 83, 136, 212
   Samson 192
   Samuell 343
   Sarah 149
   Sarah (Mrs.) 149
   Tho. 119
Massey, Jefferey 129
Masters, Abraham 6
   Elizabeth 6, 50
   John 5
   Katherin (Mrs.) 50
   Lidya 5
   Nathaniel 5

Masters (cont.)
   Nathaniell 6
   Peter 50
   Sarah 5
Masterson, Nathaniel 189
   Nathaniell 189
Mather, (?) 39, 48, 73,
   284, 330
   Abigail 62
   Cotton 62, 63
   Eleazer 61
   Eliazer 179
   Elizabeth 373
   I. 10
   Increase 61, 63, 208,
   343
   Increase (Dr.) 76
   Increase (Rev.) 63
   John 78, 151
   Katherine 374
   Marja 78
   Nathaniel 62
   Richard 50, 78, 193,
   238, 315, 343, 347,
   381
   Richard (Rev.) 78,
   193, 343, 377
   Richd. 52, 78
   Samuel 62
   Sarah 62
   Timothy 193, 194, 370,
   374
   elizabet 62
   mariah 62
Mathers, (?) 347
Mathewes, Doman 156
Mathue, Dorman 212
   Mary (Mrs.) 212
Mathues, frances 97
Matson, John 156, 242
   Thomas 305, 351
Matsons, Thomas 351
Matthews, Elizabeth
   (Mrs.) 389
   Hannah 389
   John 389
Mattock, Alice 279
   James 226, 279, 342
   Mary 279
   Mary (Mrs.) 279
   Samuel 279
Mattocke, Alice 279
   James 279
   Mary 279
   Mary (Mrs.) 279
   Samuel 279
Mattocks, (?) 355
Mattoek, James 225
Mattox, David 128
   Mary (Mrs.) 279
   Samuel 281
   Sarah (Mrs.) 128
Mattson, Tho. 226
Mattux, Ed 127
Matux, James 127
Maud, Daniel 43
Maude, Daniel 286
Maudsley, John 202
Mauerick, Rebecca (Mrs.)
   308, 309
   Samuel 310
   Samuell 37, 310
Mauericke, (?) 122
   Antipas 37
   Elias 272
   Moses 225
   Rebeckah (Mrs.) 225
   Sam. 111

414

Mauericke (cont.)
  Samuell 37
  Samuell (Jr.) 225
Mauerickes, (?) (Mrs.)
  225, 310
Mauricke, Samuell 149
Maverick, Abigale 1
  Anne 1
  Elias 92, 219
  Jane (Mrs.) 112
  John 1, 127
  Saml. 120
  Samuel (Jr.) 225, 310
  Samuell 58
Mavericke, Anipas 109
  Elias 224
  Saml. 58
  Samuell 111
Mawdsley, Ebenr. 370
Maxfeild, Clem. 255
Maxfield, Clement 164
Maxfields, Clemt. 164
  Mary (Mrs.) 164
Maxflld, Clement 255
May, George 388
  Jno. 390
  John 390
  Samuel 390
  Samuell 200
Mayew, Samuell 110
Mayhew, Math. 120
  Tho 149
  Thom. 19
  Thomas 37, 117
  Thos. 46
Mayhoo, (?) (Rev.) 172
Mayhu, (?) 89
Maynard, Elizabeth 167
  John 127, 161, 167,
  363
Mayo, (?) 177, 182
  John 172, 250
  Sam 250
  Sammuell 251
  Samuel 250
  Samuell 251
Mayoh, Samuell 250
Mayre, (?) 242
Mead, (?) 190
  Dauid 295
  Experience 295
  Gabrell 47
  Gabriel 294
  Gabriell 48, 294
  Israell 295
  Joanna (Mrs.) 294
  Lidia 295
  Patience 295
  Sarah 295
Meade, (?) 50
  Gabrell 295
Meader, (?) 243
Meades, Richard 187
Meadford, Robt 99
Meane, Ann (Mrs.) 11
  John 11
Means, Ann (Mrs.) 11
  John 11
Meare, Robert 153
Meares, (?) 223
  (?) (Mrs.) 224
  Jno 224
  Jno. 224
  John 223
  Mary 224
  Mary (Mrs.) 223
  Samuell 224
  Steven 113

Mears, Elizabeth 224
Medcalfe, (?) 74
  Thomas 329
Meddowes, (?) 110
Medefeild, (?) 354
Meede, Gabrell 50
Meene, (?) 99
Meere, Elizabeth (Mrs.)
  316
  Robert 316
Meeres, Elizabeth (Mrs.)
  316
  James 316
  Jno. 223
  John 316
  Mercy 224
  Rober(t) 175
  Robert 316
  Samuell 316
Meers, Elizabeth 224
  Elizabeth (Mrs.) 317
  James 224, 316
  Jno 169
  John 224
  Mercy 224
  Robert 316, 317
  Robt. 317
  Samuell 316
Meggs, John 17
Mein, Ann (Mrs.) 11
  John 11
Mekins, Thomas 98, 170
Mellowes, Abraham 119
  Edward 109
  Elizabeth (Mrs.) 345,
  346
  John 106, 214, 215
  Martha 43
  Oliver 345
  Olyvar 345
Mena, Ann (Mrs.) 11
  John 11
Mercer, Tho. 121
Merchant, (?) (Mrs.) 23
  John 117
  Wm. 23
Meriam, (?) 9, 371
Merriam, Robert 88
Merrick, John 96
Merricke, Elizabeth
  (Mrs.) 96
  Elizebeth 96
  John 96
Merrit, Deborah 78
  Elizabeth (Mrs.) 78
  James 61
Merry, (?) 12
  Mary (Mrs.) 162
  Walter 24, 162
Mesinger, (?) 177
Messenger, (?) 123
Messinger, Edward 379
  Henry 61, 120
Metcalfe, (?) 126
  Mary (Mrs.) 126
  Michael (Sr.) 74
  Michaell 125, 238, 239
Metson, Thomas 285
Mettem, (?) 177
Michalson, (?) 119
Michell, Jonathan 99
Michelson, (?) 122
Micherson, Edw. 99
Micho, Edward 306
Micklethwaite, Nathaniel
  350
Midge, (?) 378
Midlebrooke, Joseph 99

Midlton, (?) (Cpt.) 109
Mihills, (?) 288, 289
Milam, Abigail 287
  Constance 287
  Hannah 287
  Humphery 280, 287
  Humphrey 120, 288
  John 120
  Mary 287
  Mary (Mrs.) 287
  Sarah 287
Miles, (?) 385
  Experience (Widow) 385
  Richard 385
Mill, Jo 37
Millam, Jno. 149
Millard, Thomas 386
Miller, (?) 182
  Jeremiah 167
  Jeremy 168
  John 50, 386
  Joseph 99
  Lydia 269
  Robert 90, 269
  Robt. 269
  Tho. 263
  Thomas 386
  Timothy 90
Milles, John 37
  Richard 215
Mills, Jno 125
  Johanna 156
  John 15, 37, 111, 127,
  221
Milom, (?) (Mrs.) 27
  Humphrey 242
Miner, John 363
Minot, (?) 385
  James 385
  Jno. 134
  John 134, 153, 385
  Martha 385
  Samuel 385
  Stephen 385
Minott, (?) 39
  George 108
  James 279
  Jno. 208, 223
  John 133, 134, 164,
  167, 210, 233, 255,
  280, 305
  Stephen 305
  jo. 293
Miriam, Joseph 9
  Robert 9
  Robt. 25, 26
  Sarah (Mrs.) 9
Miriams, Joseph 10
Mirriam, John 187
Mitchel, Jonathan 315
Mitchell, (?) (Jdg.) 5
Mittison, Ed. 120
Mixture, Isacke 99
Mockcliet, Jno. 79
Modesly, Cicily (Mrs.)
  202
  John 202
Modsly, Elizabeth 202
  John 202
  Mary 202
  Sisilly (Mrs.) 202
  Sisily (Mrs.) 202
  Thomas 202
Monk, John 109
Monticue, John 154
Moody, (?) 207
Moone, (?) 97
  Robt 120

415

Moor, Hannah (Mrs.) 388
  Joseph 388
Moore, Goulden 99
  J. B. 76
  Jno 76, 77
  John 8
  Jonathan 77
  Joseph 120, 179, 215
  Richard 218
  ffrances (Sr.) 99
Moores, Jno. 79
More, Elizabeth 301
  Jeremiah 107
  Joseph 363, 364
  Josiph 177
  Joss 177
  Thomas 301
Morell, Isaac 187
  Jeremy 149
Morgin, James 117
Morice, Edward 184
Moricke, Elizabeth
    (Mrs.) 105, 106
  Jno 105
Mories, Benjamin 185
Morill, Isaac 187
Morley, John 156
Morrell, Abraham 196
  Ezekiell 157
  Isaac 94, 157, 166,
    195, 196
  Isaack 81, 134
  Isack 143
  Isacke 81
  Jeremiah 336
  Katherine 195
  Sarah 196
Morricke, Elizabeth
    (Mrs.) 105
  Jno 105
Morrill, (?) 212
  Isaac 151
Morris, Edward 152, 229,
    243, 266, 385, 390
  Thomas 165
Morrish, Rose (Mrs.) 241
Morrisse, Edward 243
Morry, Thomas 243
Morse, Abigall 130
  Ann (Mrs.) 49
  Annas (Mrs.) 130
  Bathia 130
  Daniell 49
  Elizabeth (Mrs.) 49,
    153
  Ephraim 130
  Ezrah 130
  Hannah (Mrs.) 198, 356
  Jno 111
  Jno. 130
  John 49, 104, 130,
    220, 390
  Joseph 49, 129, 130,
    198, 356
  Mary 49
  Nathaniell 130
  Ruth 130
  Saml. 49
  Samuell 49, 153, 349
Morton, Nicholas 378
Mory, Benjamin 185
  Mary 184
Moseley, Ebenezer 374
  Thomas 374
Moses, (?) 355
Moslyes, Hen 111
Moss, John 127
Mosse, John 72

Mosse (cont.)
  Joseph 150
  Mary 74
  Mary (Mrs.) 71, 72
Moulton, Robert 358
  Robert (Jr.) 359
  Robert (Sr.) 358
  Robt. 84
  Tho 22
Mountjoy, George 242
Mousall, John 95
  Ralph 93
Mousell, Raphe 85
Mowsall, John 95, 96
Mroly, (?) (Mrs.) 111
Mudd, Jno. 77
Mullings, George 120
Mumford, Edmund 247
  Edward 336
  Wm. 262
Muniage, Georg 25
Muning, Georg 25
Munjoye, George 161
Munjoys, Benjn. 141
  George 141
Munninge, George 109
Munninges, George 109
Munnings, G. 108
  George 127, 138, 146
  Hannah (Mrs.) 179
  Joanna (Mrs.) 138
  Johanna (Mrs.) 138
  Johannah (Mrs.) 138
  Mahalaleel 178, 179
  Mahalalell 179
  Mahaliell 179
  Susanna (Mrs.) 179
  Theophylus 138
  Vpshall 179
Munt, Elinor (Mrs.) 233
  Faith 293
  Mary 293
  Patience 293
  Thomas 233, 293
Mussell, Thomas 27
Mylam, Abigail 280, 287
  Constance 280, 287
  Hannah 280, 287
  Humphery 280, 288
  Humphry 280, 287
  Mary 280, 287
  Mary (Mrs.) 280, 287,
    288
  Sarah 280, 287
Mylame, Mary (Mrs.) 134
Myllum, Jno. 110
Mynot, George 40
Mynott, Jno. 210, 233,
    292
Myrrick, (?) 379
Myrricke, Thomas 138
Nailor, Edward 281
Nanneye, Robert 225
Nanny, Katherine (Mrs.)
    225, 226
  Mary 225
  Robert 215, 225, 226
  Samuel 225
Nash, (?) 127
  (?) (Mrs.) 127
  Isaack 149
  James 147, 265
  Jno. 110
  Robert 111, 379
Nashe, James 122
  Robt 102
  Robt. 122
Nason, Richard 294

Naulton, Jno. 148
  Samll. 148
  Samuell 148
Nauney, Robert 37
Naylor, Katherine (Mrs.)
    308
Neale, Henry 254
Needam, (?) 16
Needham, William 237,
    383
Needom, William 54, 356
  Wm. 55
Needome, William 154
Negar, Angola 73
Negars, Dipora 73
  Richard 73
Negoos, Jonathan 35
Negus, Benj 52
  Benjamin 165, 379
  Benjamine 38, 149, 175
  Benjn. 52
  Grace 362
  Jane (Mrs.) 362
  Jonath 54
  Jonathan 54, 129, 207,
    362
Nelson, Joan (Mrs.) 31
  Joane (Mrs.) 31
  Mercy 31
  Phillip 31
  Samuel 32
  T. 32
  Tho. 32
  Thomas 31, 32
Netheland, Willm. 116
Newberry, (?) 108
  Jane (Mrs.) 84
  Thomas 84
Newbery, (?) 52
  Francis 58
  Thomas 84
Newdigate, (?) 251
Newell, Abraham 215
  Jacob 243
  John 146, 296
Newells, Jacob 242
Newgate, (?) 44
  Ann 252
  Ann (Mrs.) 251
  Elizabeth 252, 253
  Hanna 252, 253
  Iohn 30
  Isobel 251
  Jno. 251
  John 251, 253
  Lewis 251
  Linde 253
  Nathaniel 251
  Nathaniell 251, 252,
    253
  Sarah 252, 253
  Willinam 252
Newgates, (?) 108
Newgats, (?) 111
Newland, Antho. 120
  Henry 79
Newlands, Anthony 220
Newman, (?) 50, 347
  Elizabeth (Mrs.) 17
  George 37
  John 161
  Samuel (Rev.) 347
Newmarsh, John 111
Newton, Rich. 99
Nicholls, David 110
  Rbt. 117
Nichols, Alice (Mrs.)
    231

Nichols (cont.)
  Mordecai 231
  Mordecay 231
  Randall 127, 138, 146
  Randell 179
Nickerson, Anne (Mrs.)
  131
  Will 157
  William 130, 131
Nicklas, Richard 161
Nickolls, Randoll 93
Nicoles, Thomas 99
Nicolls, Alice (Mrs.)
  231
  John 231
Nilles, (?) (Mrs.) 235
Nills, (?) (Mrs.) 235
Noble, Thomas 122
Nocholls, (?) (Widow)
  274
Nock, Thomas 22
Nocke, Thomas 154
Noice, Nicholas 90
Norcutt, Will 109
  Will. 379
Norden, Samll. 156
  Samuel 389
  Samuell 123, 242
  Sarah 389
Norman, John 28
  Thomas 203
  Willm. 122
Norrice, (?) 268
Northend, Ezechiel 31
Norton, (?) 60, 67, 75,
  76, 97, 99, 127,
  169, 172, 268, 362
  (?) (Mrs.) 60, 315
  (?) (Rev.) 72, 142
  Elizabeth (Mrs.) 213
  John 31, 140, 143,
  182, 212, 214, 355,
  362
  John (Rev.) 203, 214
  Joice 355
  Mary (Mrs.) 213, 214
  Nicho. 122
  Nicholas 111
  Ric. 125
  Richard 146, 161
  Richd. 161
  Richrd. 111
  Tho. 213
  Thomas 213
  William 213, 214
Nortons, (?) 44
  Thomas 213
Notley, Thomas 198
Noushole, Ralph 85
Nowel, Increase 13, 32
Nowell, (?) 21, 40, 45,
  47, 51, 54, 56, 57,
  58, 59, 64, 88, 112,
  116, 117, 119, 121,
  123, 356, 357
  (?) (Gov.) 128, 129
  George 169
  Incr 101
  Incr. 87, 88, 94, 106,
  346, 350
  Increace 8
  Increas 92
  Increase 9, 10, 11,
  12, 14, 16, 20, 23,
  26, 27, 28, 29, 30,
  31, 34, 87, 88, 90,
  91, 93, 95, 96, 98,
  99, 100, 101, 102,

Nowell (cont.)
  104, 105, 107, 108,
  110, 116, 117, 346,
  348
  Iner. 35
  Jno. 168
  John 127
Nowells, (?) 27
  George 271
Nowsall, Ralph 92
Noyce, Peter 31
  Robt 111
Noyes, Moses 359
  Peter 87
Nuberie, Thomas 84
Nucomb, Francis 221
Nuemarke, John 121
Nugaite, (?) 363
Nuten, John 368, 370
Nutt, (?) 307
  Rob 306
Oakes, (?) 129
Oaks, Tho. 99
Oates, Eliz. (Mrs.) 205
  Elizabeth (Mrs.) 205
  John 122, 190
Ockinton, Will. 378
Odlin, Jno. 385
  John 119, 384
Offley, (?) 3
Okes, Edw 98
Oldam, Rich. 98
Oldreges, (?) 164, 347
Oleiver, Petter 137
Olford, (?) 379
Oliner, Peter 215
Oliuer, (?) 110
  James 102, 122, 125,
  199, 247, 379
  James (Cpt.) 227, 248,
  261
  Peeter 177
  Peter 80, 187, 221,
  222, 262, 263, 311,
  339, 359
  Samuell 122, 125, 181
  Thomas 221
Oliuers, (?) (Cpt.) 236
Oliver, (?) 28, 109, 147
  Iohn 30
  James 30, 224, 317,
  386
  James (Cpt.) 224
  John 30, 90, 159, 221
  Peter 215, 220, 221,
  385, 386
  Sam. 120
  Tho. 30
  Thomas 30, 35, 135,
  221
Olivr, Pettr 354
Olliue, Henry 312
Olliuer, (?) 235
  James 199, 215
  Jeames (Cpt.) 214
  Peter 61, 215, 318,
  319, 320, 322, 343,
  359
  Thomas 36
Olliuers, Peter 309
Olliver, (?) 72
  (?) (Cpt.) 379
  Abigail 135
  Havens 135
  James 109, 135, 138
  James (Cpt.) 135, 138
  John 72, 135, 252
  Peeter 76, 135, 137,

Olliver (cont.)
  140, 214, 252, 253
  Peeter (Lt.) 140
  Peter 53, 11, 128, 140
  Peter (Lt.) 135
  Samuell 135
  Sarah (Mrs.) 253
  Thomas 135, 252
  Woollfall 135
Opie, Nicholas 153
Orgraue, Anne (Mrs.) 175
Oris, George 117
Orriss, Gorge 114
Osborne, Freesweed
  (Mrs.) 215
  Recompence 285
  William 161, 215
Osburne, William 215
Ostler, Nan 75
Otis, Jno 81
  John 97
Otties, John 97
Ottis, (?) (Mrs.) 205
  Allice 131
  Anne 131
  Elizabeth (Mrs.) 205
  Hannah 131
  Jno 174
  John 131
  Margaret 131
  Mary (Mrs.) 132
Ottise, Jno. 132
Owen, William 228
Owin, William 228
Pacey, Thomas 37
Packer, (?) 124
  Samuell 147
Pacy, (?) 60
  Sarah (Mrs.) 46, 47,
  168
  Thomas 120
Pacye, Sarah (Mrs.) 74
Paddens, Thomas 158
Paddock, (?) 22
Paddy, (?) 122, 368
  Benjamine 139
  Elizabeth 139, 140
  Hannah 139
  John 139, 140
  Mary (Mrs.) 139
  Mercy 139, 140, 368
  Nathaniell 139
  Samuell 139
  Thomas 139, 368, 370
  William 114, 139, 153,
  368, 370
  Willm 113
  Wm. 55
Paddyes, Wm. 147
Padge, Mary (Mrs.) 91
  Nicholas 215
Padishall, (?) 124
Padlefoote, Jonathan 99
Page, (?) 165
  (?) (Mrs.) 171, 172
  Edw 111
  Edward 156, 242, 281
  Edwd 157
  Elizabeth 171
  Elizabeth (Mrs.) 143
  John 171
  Mary 171
  Nicho. 202
  Nicholas 202
  Pheebee 171
  Samuell 171
Pagraue, (?) (Mrs.) 288
Paige, Anna (Mrs.) 75,

417

Paige (cont.)
  315, 360
  Nicho. 360
  Nicholas 75, 360
  Nickolas (Cpt.) 360
Paine, Agnes (Mrs.) 311
  Elizabeth 15
  Hanna 172
  Hanna (Mrs.) 171
  Hannah (Mrs.) 318
  John 171, 172, 173,
    213, 248, 265, 311
  John (Jr.) 311
  Judith (Mrs.) 15
  Mathew 127
  Moses 14, 15, 148,
    149, 173, 244, 326
  Peter 120
  Rob 108
  Sarah 341
  Sarah (Mrs.) 341
  Stephen 122, 127, 166
  Steuen 15
  Steven 14, 15
  Tho 149
  Thomas 318
  Tobias 340, 341
  Will 172
  William 149, 153, 163,
    171, 172, 341
  Willm. 120
  moses 14
Painter, Thomas 159
Pajne, Moses 15
Palmer, (?) (Widow) 200
  Abr. 85
  Abraham 113, 127
  Abram 22, 146
  Benjamin 199
  Benjamine 199
  Elihu 199, 200
  Elizabeth 199
  Elyhu 199
  George 161
  Gersham 199
  Grace 199
  Grace (Mrs.) 113
  Hannah 199
  John 122, 199
  Jonas 199
  Moses 199
  Nehemia 199
  Nehemiah 199
  Rebecca 199
  Walter 199, 200
  William 199
Palmeter, John 243
  John (Jr.) 257
Palsgraue, (?) 99, 347
  Anna (Mrs.) 337, 338
  Lydia 337
  Mary 177, 337
  Richard 337
Parill, Edward 117
Paris, Jno 120
Parish, John 99
Park, (?) 93
  (?) (Deacon) 312
  William 3, 98, 107,
    184
Parke, (?) 156
  (?) (Deacon) 296
  Jno. 157
  Rich. 99
  Thomas 111, 191, 364,
    365
  William 81, 89, 102,
    108, 127, 187, 191,

Parke (cont.)
  229, 231, 243, 289,
    364, 390
  William (Deacon) 296
  Wm. 270, 311, 377
  Wy. 117
  williame 364
Parkehurst, Geo. 117
  Susanna 117
Parkemane, Elias 125
Parker, (?) 121, 137,
    248, 316, 387
  Elisabeth 247
  John 290
  Margaret (Mrs.) 341,
    342
  Ralfe 215
  Ralph 120
  Richard 36, 75, 119,
    126, 142, 146, 150,
    159, 316
  Richd. 75
  Robert 99
  Sam. 122
  William 84
Parkers, (?) 66
Parkes, (?) 123
  Elisabeth 247
  William 112, 158
  William (Deacon) 289
  Willim 46
  Wm. 146, 255, 256
Parkhurst, George 117
  Susanna 117
Parkman, Bridget (Mrs.)
    218
  Elias 218
  Ellias 218, 379
Parks, (?) 85, 133
  William 89, 127, 211
  Wm. 374
Parmanter, Robert 244
Parmenter, Gm. 257
  Robert 173
  Robt 173
Parmenters, (?) 244
Parmeters, (?) (Mrs.)
    247
Parmiter, Gm. 248
Parris, John 105
Parrish, Thomas 2
Parrks, Will 86
Parson, Francis 369
  William 258, 388
Parthurst, Geo 111
Pason, Ed 127
  Edward 146, 335
Patching, (?) (Mrs.) 50
Pateshall, Robert 226
  Robeurt 177
  Robt 157
  Robt. 153
Patine, (?) 83
Patten, (?) 31, 83, 176,
    212
  Nathaniell 31, 133,
    192, 381
Pattens, Wm. 99
Patteshal, Rob't 218
Patteshalls, Rob't 218
Pattison, John 337
Patton, Nathaniell 163
Paul, Samll. 375
  Samuel 284
Paule, Samuel 284
  Samuell 328
Paull, Samuell 284, 328
Paver, (?) 347

Payne, (?) 346
  John 172, 215
  Matt 146
  Moses 15, 148
  Robt 99
  Stephen 81
  Tobias 341
  Willm 102
  Wm. 99, 143
Paynin, (?) 60
Payson, Giles 21
Payton, Bazeliell 119
  Mary 140
  Sarah 140
Peace, Peter 385
Peach, Alice 160
  John 118
Peache, Allice 160
Peacock, (?) 122, 312
Peacocke, Caleb 361
  Richard 148, 358, 361
  Richd. 50, 51
  Will. 378
  William 127, 151, 187
Peacockes, William 187
Peacocks, (?) 36
Peak, Dorcas (Mrs.) 266
  Jonathan 243
Peake, (?) 88, 242
  Christopher 80, 229,
    266
  Dorcas 266
  Dorcas (Mrs.) 266
  Ephraim 266
  Jonathan 266
  Joseph 266
  Sarah 266
  Thomas 167, 168
  William 127, 203
  Wm. 146
Pearce, Ester (Mrs.) 150
  Jno. 278
  Mary (Mrs.) 278
Pearose, James 378
Pears, Exercise 192
  John 191, 192
  Mary 192
  Mercy 192
  Nehemiah 192
  Rebecca (Mrs.) 191
  Samuell 192
Pearse, An 218
  Ann (Mrs.) 246
  Anne (Mrs.) 246
  George 212
  Hester (Mrs.) 379
  John (Sr.) 133
  Joseph 342
  Mary 246
  Mary (Mrs.) 212
  Michael 82
  Robert 246
  Thomas 48, 246
  Thos 48
  William 160, 201, 202,
    218, 233, 234, 240,
    242, 246, 273, 276,
    279, 280, 288, 324,
    335, 379
  William (Sr.) 249,
    273, 335
  Wm. 131, 160, 218,
    234, 242, 276, 279
Peas, Hen. 378
  John 154, 212
Pease, Henery 350
  Henery (Sr.) 350
  Henrey 351

418

Pease (cont.)
Henry 215, 350, 351,
352
Henry (Sr.) 351
John 215, 351
Joseph 342
Susana 351
William 160
henery 351
Peck, Joseph 152, 215
Simon 152
William 215
Pecke, (?) 122, 156
Pecks, Joanna (Mrs.) 49
Peddington, Olave 18
Peede, (?) 363
Peeke, (?) 122
Elizabeth 215
Peeteete, Jno. 168
Peirce, (?) (Widow) 379
Esther 380
Esther (Mrs.) 379
George 212
John 87, 102
John (Cpt.) 174
Mary 99
Mary (Mrs.) 212
Moses 380
Robert 378
Samuell 222
William 379
Wm. 379
Peiropoynt, John 187
Peirpoint, (?) 378
Peirse, (?) (Widow) 379
Ebenezar 380
Ebenezer 379, 381
Ester (Mrs.) 192
Esther 380, 381
Esther (Mrs.) 379
Hester 379
John 37, 111, 381
Moses 381
Nathaniel 379
Nathaniell 380, 381
William 192, 379, 380,
381
Wm. 379
Pelham, Herbert 24
Pell, (?) 147
Elizabeth 107
Joseph 107
William 330
Pellam, Willm. 117
Pelmeter, (?) 312
Father 312
Pemberton, Ja. 170
James 294
Pembleton, (?) 44
Bryant 207
Pembletons, (?) 207
Pemerton, James 72
Pen, (?) 72, 214
James 43, 110, 207,
253
Will 212
Pendelton, Joseph 37
Pendleton, (?) 111
Bryan 22
Bryan (Cpt.) 161
Joseph 38
Penn, (?) 59, 92, 109,
267, 274
Ja. 124
James 35, 36, 55, 60,
78, 90, 103, 109,
110, 146, 163, 165,
169, 177, 182, 190,

Penn (cont.)
194, 206, 208, 237,
272, 300, 315, 342,
353, 354, 388
Jeames 226
Willm. 123
Penne, (?) 363
James 35, 36, 42, 119,
362
Penns, (?) 141
Penny, Henry 168
Pennyman, James 243, 244
Joseph 243
Lydia (Mrs.) 244
Samuell 244
Pentecost, John 378
Penticost, (?) 99
John 22
Penye, William 116
Pepper, Jno. 388
Joseph 388
Robert 30, 80, 151,
152, 156, 157, 243,
312, 388
Robt. 51, 270
Perce, John 87
Michaell 122
Perin, Henery 58
Perkins, (?) 3, 131
Christopher 122
William 13
Permitor, John 6
Perpointe, (?) 83
Perpont, John 274
Perrey, (?) (Mrs.) 123
Perrie, Franc 121
Perriman, Thomas 41
Perry, (?) 97, 102
Francis 149
Isack 277
Jno. 311
John 11, 133, 229
Joseph 110
Mehetabell 354
Samuell 311
Seth 229, 354
Wm. 201
Person, Elizabeth (Mrs.)
308, 309
Pery, Samuell 230
Petecharie, Dauis 99
Peters, Hugh 350
Phelph, Henry 187
Phelps, Elizabeth 358
Henry 358
James 162
John 358
Philbricke, (?) 99
Philips, (?) 186
Eliazar 183
Georg 85
Henery Ensigne 290
Henrie 183
Henry 183
Mary (Mrs.) 183
Phillipes, John 278
Phillippes, John 274
Phillipps, Georg (Rev.)
20
Samuel 20
Phillips, (?) 172, 215
Ambrose 379
Anna (Mrs.) 9
Anne 9
Elizabeth 64
George 116
Henerye 9
Henr. 110

Phillips (cont.)
Henry 40, 181, 343
Jno. 149
John 147, 153, 162,
173, 179, 211, 249,
265
Joseph 384
Martha 64
Mary 64
Nathl 64
Nicholas 90, 121, 123,
390
Phebe 64
Rebecca 64
Sarah 64
Susanna (Mrs.) 63, 64
Tho 127
Thomas 122, 146
William 63, 166, 215
William (Lt.) 127, 242
Willm. 122
Wm 64, 110
Wm. 52, 136, 146, 147,
226
Wm. (Jr.) 127
Wm. (Lt.) 168
Zacharie 119
Zachary 146, 156, 157,
169
Zachery 123
Zackery 107
Zacre 363
Phillpot, (?) 111
Philpott, Wilim. 120
Philps, Thomas 101
Phippen, Benj 123
Phippeney, Joseph 120
Phippenie, Joseph 106
Phippeny, Benjamin 106
David 106
Gamaliel 106
George 106
Sara 110
Sarah (Mrs.) 106
Pickerin, Jeams 207
Pickerine, John 207
Pickrins, Jonathan 363
Pidge, (?) 182
Pierce, Elisabeth 21
John 102
Sarah (Mrs.) 206
Pierpoint, John 134
Robert 134, 312
Pierpont, John 378
Pig, Hany 20
John 20
Mary 21
Mathew 20
Saray 20
Thomas 20, 182
Pigg, (?) 182
Hany 20
John 182
Thomas 80
Pigge, (?) 182
Hannah 20
Henry 20
John 182
Nathew 20
Thomas 20, 182
Pilbeame, (?) 128
Pimer, Mathew 24
Philemon 24
Pimpton, Henry 41
Pincheon, (?) 84
Pinnion, Nicholas 149
Pirkines, Wm. 89
Pitcher, Andrew 186,

Pitcher (cont.)
  187, 365
  Experience 187
  John 187
  Jonathan 187
  Margaret (Mrs.) 186
  Nathaniel 187
  Ruth 187
  Samuel 187
  Samuell 187
Pitford, Peter 120
Pittman, William 149
Pitts, (?) 121, 378
  Edm. 132, 195
  Edmond 176, 250
  Edward 122
  Elizabeth (Mrs.) 147
  Robert 110
  Wy 125
Place, (?) 206, 207
  (?) (Mrs.) 50
  Alice 207
  Peter 207
Plimpton, Henry 41, 121
  John 144
Plimton, Elisabeth 31
  Thomas 31
Plinnys, (?) 131
Plinton, John 3
Plumb, Allexander 339,
  340
Plumbley, Joseph 235
Plumer, Ephraim 169
  John 169
  Mary 169
  Samuel 380
  Samuell 169, 342, 380
Plummer, Mary (Mrs.) 342
Poades, John 177
Pode, Edward 122
Poland, William 363
Pole, John 168, 378
Pollard, (?) 179
Polly, Jno. 243
Pomfret, William 44
Pond, Jonathan 113
  Martha 332
  Mary 332
  Mary (Mrs.) 232
  Robert 85, 232
  Robt. 212
  Sara 113
  Will 111
  William 153, 202, 211,
  232
  Wm. 153
Poole, Benjamin 237, 343
  Edward 237, 238
  Isaack 237
  Jacob 237
  John 237
  Joseph 237
  Mary 343
  Mary (Mrs.) 343
  Samuell 237, 238, 343
  Sarah 237
  Wm 111
Pope, (?) 111, 347
  (?) (Widow) 83
  Jane 83
  Jane (Mrs.) 209
  John 102, 164, 346,
  347
  John (Sr.) 103
  Joshua 102
  Mary 355
  Thomas 102
Pormort, (?) 101

Pormort (cont.)
  Philemon 24, 101
Pormorts, (?) 101
Pormortt, Philemon 286
Porter, (?) 151
  Abell 211, 312
  Edward 3, 85, 94, 135,
  263
  G. 111
  John 122, 137, 268
  edward 88
Portous, Robert 27
Post, Dorothy (Mrs.) 175
  Richd. 149
Potter, Geo. 51
  Jane 51
  Jno 51
  John 51
  Luke 25, 26
  William 51, 123, 152
Potterton, Sarah 281
Powell, (?) 123, 127,
  182, 183, 225, 262,
  309
  Edward 379
  Henry 105
  Mary 52
  Michael 105
  Michaell 40, 146
Powning, Eliza. (Mrs.)
  300
  Elizabeth (Mrs.) 300
  Hen. 167
  Henry 142, 173, 174,
  187, 190, 203, 204,
  300
Poyston, Tho. 22
Prate, Hil. G. 108
  Timothy 168
Pratt, (?) 140
  Hannah (Mrs.) 186
  John 91
  Samuell 186
  Tho 111
  Timothy 242
Pray, Quinton 149
Prays, (?) 255
Preist, Margarett 167
Preistley, (?) (Mrs.)
  137
Prentice, (?) 99
  Robert 311
  Thomas (Cpt.) 312
Prentise, Gowldinge 7
  Robert 151, 311
  Thomas 7
Prentiss, Robert 187
Prescote, John 117
Prescott, John 122, 208
  William 374
Prest, James 122
Preston, (?) (Dr.) 178
  (?) (Mrs.) 238
  Daniell 210, 238
  Edw 110
Prestons, (?) (Dr.) 89,
  178, 354
  Daniell 238
Presus, Charles 149
Price, Rich. 308
  Richard 214, 215, 216,
  251, 308
Prichard, (?) 26, 117
  Will 161
Prideaux, (?) (Mrs.) 315
  Bridget (Mrs.) 314
  Nicholas 314
Priest, Deliverance 254

Prince, Ann 177
  Anne 363
  Jno. 81
  John 120, 122, 190,
  237, 320
  Samuell 140
Princes, John 139
Prior, (?) (Mrs.) 119
Pris, Nicholas 49
Prise, Richard 250
Procter, Abigail 205
  Edeth (Mrs.) 205
  George 205, 206
  Hannah 205
  Mary 205
  Samuell 205, 206
  Sarah 205
Proctor, George 108
  Samuell 206
Prosser, Thomas 105
Prout, Margaret (Mrs.)
  335
  Timothy 335
  Timothy (Jr.) 335
  Timothy (Sr.) 335
Pryor, Joseph 156
Puddiford, Henry 220
Puddington, (?) (Widow)
  101
Puerchis, Oliuer 171
Puffer, (?) 354
Pulteney, (?) 355
Punchard, Fra. 302, 303
  Frances 302
Purchase, John 207
  Oliuer 221
  Oliver 164, 347
Purches, Olliuer 172
  Olliur 172
Purton, Elizabeth (Mrs.)
  106
  John 106
Putman, Thomas 87, 268
Py, Edw. 301
Pynchors, (?) 165
Pynson, William 100
Quencser, Edmond 125
Quick, William 27
Quincy, Edmond 276
  Edmund 212, 221
Quiney, John 276
Quinney, Edmond 276
Quinsey, Edmond 315
  Edmund 149, 173, 228
  Edward 383
  Joanna (Mrs.) 326
Quint, A. H. 44
Quintin, Henry 307
  Mary (Mrs.) 307
Quishin, Jeremiah 308
Quishion, Jeremiah 308
Rachell, Judah (Mrs.)
  167
  Robert 167
Rainer, (?) 99
Raines, Mary 343
Rainsford, (?) 3, 97,
  116, 206
  Edward 35, 60, 125,
  293, 342
  Edwd. 60
  Jonathan 225, 310
  Nathan 259
Rallings, Tho. 167
  Thomas 149, 218, 225
Ramsay, Henrie 200
Ramsden, Joseph 156
Ramsey, Henrie 201

Ramsey (cont.)
  Henry 200, 201
Rand, Robert 72
Randall, David 222
Randol, (?) 99
Rands, (?) (Mrs.) 27
Rane, John 186
  Mary (Mrs.) 186
Ranken, John 46
Rankins, John 126
Ransford, Edward 256
  Jonathan 177
  Nathan 259
Ratchell, Robert 167
Ratcliffe, (?) 248
Raulinge, John 95
Rawlens, Thomas 17
Rawlings, Jasper 149
  Thomas 218
Rawlins, (?) 122, 378
  Jasper 287
  Mary (Mrs.) 287
  Nathaniel 158
  Nathaniell 158
  Sarah (Mrs.) 158
  Thomas 158
Rawson, (?) 73, 77, 108,
  136, 214, 294, 312,
  337
  Ed. 246
  Edw 77, 86, 111, 113,
    120, 132, 133, 182,
    239, 242
  Edw'd 41
  Edw. 78, 80, 107, 114,
    115, 133, 137, 148,
    152, 158, 161, 170,
    174, 175, 201, 205,
    215, 216, 218, 219,
    222, 229, 243, 247,
    249, 255, 264, 268,
    283, 293, 295, 298,
    305, 308, 312, 313,
    318, 319, 320, 321,
    322, 326, 330, 339,
    340, 341, 342, 354,
    356, 362, 364
  Edward 35, 36, 37, 38,
    39, 40, 44, 45, 49,
    61, 74, 75, 76, 77,
    78, 81, 91, 93, 97,
    112, 113, 118, 119,
    120, 121, 123, 126,
    129, 132, 141, 143,
    150, 159, 172, 181,
    182, 188, 198, 199,
    203, 205, 207, 214,
    217, 233, 242, 243,
    244, 245, 247, 250,
    256, 259, 260, 281,
    285, 291, 293, 294,
    297, 300, 302, 303,
    311, 315, 338, 339,
    341, 356, 357, 358,
    359, 361, 362, 364
  Edwd 112
  Edwd. 37, 45, 47, 50,
    51, 101, 121, 123,
    220
  Edwdd. 56
  Elwd 41
  Ewd. 137, 200, 336,
    343
  Margaret 113
  Margarett 137, 359
  Peren 198
  Perin 225
  Rachel 188

Rawson (cont.)
  margaret 357
  peren 356
Ray, Simon 235
Rayes, John 97
  Simon 87
Raymond, John 215
Rayner, Robert 113
Raynold, Robert 126
Raynsford, (?) 3
  Ed. 101
  Edw. 159, 277
  Edward 212, 233
  Jonathan 215
Read, (?) 265
  Esdras 169
  Joseph 58
  Mary 128
  Thomas 168
  William 127, 128, 156,
    260, 342
  Wm. 156
Reade, John 14
  Mary 168
  William 112, 194
Redwood, Nicholas 311
Rees, John 106
Reeves, Thomas 117
Reinolds, Nathaniell 183
Remington, Jonathan 207
Renolds, (?) (Sr.) 72
  Edward 355
  Nath. 168
  Nathaniell 215, 272
Renolt, (?) 348
Replye, Abraham 81, 82
  Jno. 81, 82
  John 81, 82
  William 81
Reynolds, Mary 149
  Mary (Mrs.) 150
  Nathaniell 149, 150
  Robert 149, 150
  Ruth 149
  Sarah 149
  Sarah (Mrs.) 184
  Tabitha 149
Rice, Edmund 23
  Edward 23
  Philip 256
  Phillipe 256
Richard, William 186
Richards, (?) 99
  (?) (Mrs.) 137, 182
  Alce 105
  An 105
  Beniamine 105
  David 388
  Hannah 105
  James 105, 123
  Jno. 143, 177, 178,
    364
  John 105, 166, 173,
    364, 379
  Josephe 105
  Mary 105
  Samuell 105
  Thomas 105
  Welthian (Mrs.) 105
  William 298
Richardson, Amese 198
  Amos 107, 112, 229,
    240
  Ezekiel 95
  Ezekiell 95
  James 95
  John 16
  Josias 95

Richardson (cont.)
  Phebe 95
  Samuel 95
  Susanna (Mrs.) 95
  Theophilus 95
  Thomas 95
Richarson, Susanna 96
  Thomas 96
Richbell, John 103, 167
Richbill, John 215
Richeson, Amos 77, 134
  Amose 97
Richison, Amos 58, 149
Rider, Elizabeth (Mrs.)
    54
  Tho 54, 149
  Thomas 54
Rigbes, Samue 208
Rigbey, John 93
Rigby, Elizabeth 374
  Henry 183
  Samll. 179
  Samuel 374
Riggs, (?) 85
Rimington, (?) (Lt.) 152
Ripley, Abraham 152
  John 378
  Willm. 122
  Wm. 82
Ripleye, Jno. 82
Risby, William 378
Rise, (?) 23
  Edmund 23
Rivedon, Mounten 211
Roades, (?) (Mrs.) 281
  Jno 169
Robbins, Richard 99
Robbinson, John 219
  Sam'll 219
  Samuell 219
  Thomas 219
  William 218
  Willm 39, 187
Robenson, Willm. 121
Roberts, (?) (Widow) 137
  Jno. 112
  John 112, 154
  Samuell 112
  Symon 378
  Tho 111, 153
  Tho. 123, 127, 146
  Thomas 129
Robeson, William 44
Robinson, (?) 99, 141,
    142, 363
  (?) (Mrs.) 141, 142,
    177
  Elizabeth (Mrs.) 320,
    321, 322
  Franc 121
  James 263
  Jno. 52, 263
  John 219
  Jonathan 317
  Joseph 263
  Mary 263, 284, 317
  Nathaniel 317, 318
  Nathaniell 179, 317,
    318
  Samuel 142, 219
  Samuell 182, 333
  Samvell 219
  Tho. 168
  Thomas 167, 168, 263,
    321
  William 93, 179, 187,
    192, 212, 218, 246,
    333

Robinson (cont.)
  Willm 44
  Wm. 48, 136, 192, 218
Robison, James 379
  Jno. 53
  Mary (Mrs.) 143
Rock, Joseph 215, 222,
  362
  Josiph 177
Rocke, (?) 142, 363
  (?) (Mrs.) 141, 142
  Joseph 121, 141, 142,
    154, 161, 177, 263,
    362
Rockett, Ann 176
Rockwood, (?) (Widow)
  251
  Anne (Mrs.) 251
  Jo. 176
  Phoebe 251
  Richard 176
Roger, Edwd. 48
Rogers, (?) 31, 89, 107,
  122, 177, 363
  (?) (Rev.) 32
  Ezechiell 31
  Hannah 186
  Jeremiah 192
  Jno. 149
  John 57, 58, 99, 107,
    131, 132, 154, 156,
    160, 166, 185, 186
  John (Deacon) 365
  Judeth (Mrs.) 186
  Judith (Mrs.) 185, 186
  Liddia 186
  Mary 186
  Sarah 186
  Simmon 347
  Simon 256
  Susana 304
  Symon 390
  Thomas 21
  wm. 363
Rolleston, Simon 203
Rones, Thankful 192
Roote, (?) 151
  Ralph 260
Roper, John 92
Rose, John 179
Roseamond, (?) 109
Rosewell, (?) 285
Rouck, (?) 300
Rouse, (?) (Mrs.) 363
  Faithful 348
  Faithfull 156
  Suretrust (Mrs.) 348
Row, (?) 127
  Moses 220
  Robt. 339
Rowe, Jesop 339
  John 339
  Robt. 339
Rowell, Thomas 114
Rows, John 339
Roxbury, Jonson (Cpt.)
  215
Royall, Mary 371
  Mary (Mrs.) 371
  Samuell 271
  William 371
Royson, (?) 73
Rub, (?) 179
Ruck, Elizabeth (Mrs.)
  323, 324
  Joane 323
  John 63, 323
  Sam. 324

Ruck (cont.)
  Samuel 323
  Thomas 323, 324
  Thomas (Sr.) 324
Rucke, (?) 37, 123
  Joane 45
  John 45
  Samuel 45
  Tho. (Jr.) 45
  Tho. (Sr.) 45
  Thomas 37, 45, 112
  Thomas (Jr.) 45
  Thomas (Sr.) 45
Ruddock, (?) 303
  John 99
Rudgles, John 230
Rudick, Jollif 99
Rugels, Gorg 368, 370
  Samuell 368
Ruggles, (?) 85, 123,
  151
  Abigail 151
  Craft 151
  Georg 150
  George 368, 370
  Iohn 29
  John 29, 90, 134, 150,
    151, 230, 231
  John (Jr.) 152, 231
  John (Sgt.) 151
  John (Sr.) 150
  Margery (Mrs.) 230,
    231
  Mary (Mrs.) 151
  Saml1. 152
  Samuel 151
  Samuell 29, 151, 274,
    368
  Sarah 29
  Thomas 29, 151
Rugles, (?) 111
  Jno. 230
  John 39, 133, 231
  John (Sr.) 133, 230,
    231
  Margery (Mrs.) 230
Rush, Jasper 292
Rushworth, (?) (Mrs.)
  309
  Edward 308, 309
Russel, James 308
Russell, (?) 97, 99,
  122, 165, 182
  Boson 156
  Elizabeth 13
  Geo. 122
  Henry 13, 14
  Jane (Mrs.) 14
  John 85, 99
  Ralph 79
  Richard 23, 109, 110,
    120, 157, 168
Rust, Henry 122, 205,
  212, 217, 250, 318
  Mary (Mrs.) 388
  Nathaniel 388
Rutter, John 117
Sadler, Tho 102
Saffan, John 247
Saffin, (?) 310
Sailes, John 122
Sale, Edw. 298
  Edward 298
Salmon, Jabesh 384
Salter, (?) 260, 383
  Walter 107, 114, 157
  William 76, 77, 153,
    274, 320

Salter (cont.)
  Wm. 77, 268
Saltestone, (?) 97
Saltonstall, R. 109
  Richard 34, 109
  Robert 109
  Robt. 37
  Samuell 109
Sames, Ralph 154
Sampford, John 215
Sampson, (?) 123
  Hen 156
  Wm. 140
Samson, Jno. 140
  Thomas 96
Samuel, John 220
Sanbrock, Alce 100
  Samvell 100
  Thomas 100
  William 100
Sanbrooke, Thomas 100
Sandbrooke, Thomas 99
Sander, Edward 161
Sanders, Jno 48, 49
  John 48, 49, 90
  Martin 87, 361
Sanderson, Benjamin 385
  Robert 233, 293
  Robrt 293
  Robt. 277
  Robt. (Deacon) 337,
    338
Sandford, Elizabeth
  (Mrs.) 181
  John 181, 248
  Robert 379
  Samuell 181
  Sarah 248
Sandis, Henry 119
Sands, (?) 120
  (?) (Mrs.) 151, 224
Sandyes, Henry 110
Sandys, (?) (Mrs.) 262
  Henry 99
Sanford, (?) (Mrs.) 194
  Elisha 309
  Ezbon 309
  John 109, 188, 196
  Peleg 308
  Restram 309
  Richard 175
  Richd. 160, 212
  Robert 269, 378
  Robt. 269
  William 309
Sanfords, (?) 226
  Elizabeth (Mrs.) 181
  John 181
  Samuell 181
Sanger, Mary (Mrs.) 149
  Nathaniell 149
Sannders, George 306
  Margaret (Mrs.) 306
Satell, Kenricke 38
  Mary 38, 353
  Richard 38
  Thomas 38, 352, 353
Sattell, Richard 38
Sauage, (?) 120
  (?) (Cpt.) 310
  Dine 308
  Ephraim 308
  Faith 308
  Mary 308
  Tho. 120
  Thomas 125, 308, 317
  Thomas (Cpt.) 235,
    317, 339

Sauages, (?) (Cpt.) 310
Saualls, William 234
Sauige, (?) (Cpt.) 165
Sauill, Sarah 254
Saunderrs, Martin 360
Saunders, Elisabeth 237
George 281
John 12, 320, 339, 384
Martin 361
Martine 173
Martine (Sr.) 173
Martyn 237
Robert 131
William 384
Saunderson, Robert 246,
258
Saundrs, John 173
Joseph 149
Martine 173
Rachell (Mrs.) 173
Sautell, Richard 38
Tho. 38
Savage, (?) 330, 341,
344, 346, 350, 351,
352, 355, 356, 358,
359, 360, 361, 374,
377, 383, 384, 385,
388
(?) (Cpt.) 202
Th. 35
Tho. 35, 116, 121
Thomas 98, 109, 111,
112, 114, 140, 154,
158, 384
Thomas (Cpt.) 153,.
169, 335
Thomas (Sr.) 202
Savel, Bass 383
Benjamin 383
Hannah 383
John 383
Samuel 383
Sarah 383
Sarah (Mrs.) 383
William 383
William (Sr.) 383
Savory, Katherine (Mrs.)
131
Sawdy, Joha 168
John 167, 168
Sawer, (?) 129
Sawin, John 2
Sawinge, John 12
Sawjer, Tho. 99
Sayer, Thomas 144
Sayres, Job 281
Scant, William 54
Wm. 54
Scarbarrow, John 117
Scarborough, Samuel 359
Scarborow, Samuell 296
Scarbrough, Samuell 359
Scarebrow, John 86
Scarlet, (?) (Mrs.) 97
Samuell (Cpt.) 164,
166
Scarlett, (?) 177
(?) (Mrs.) 363
Samuell 214
Samuell (Cpt.) 164
Scath, Ann 105
John 105
Scathe, Anne 96
Elisebeth (Mrs.) 96
John 96
Scenter, John 271
Sarah (Mrs.) 271
Scotaway, (?) 124

Scott, (?) (Mrs.) 212
(?) (Widow) 356
Benjamen 356
Benjamin 356, 357
Elisabeth (Mrs.) 262
Elizabeth (Mrs.) 128
Robert 103, 128
Robrt 38
Robt. 126
Robte 107
Scotte, Robt 125
Scottew, Josh. 124
Scotto, Joshua 37, 158
Thomas 194
Tomas 182
Scottoo, Liddia 136
Scottow, (?) 142
John 194, 364
Joseua 106
Josh 157
Josh. 114, 138, 140,
194, 210, 303, 364
Joshua 120, 128, 129,
173, 177, 379
Josuah 303
Jushua 142
Sarah (Mrs.) 194
Tho. 153, 194
Thomas 182, 194, 277
Scottowe, Joshua 76
Tho. 120
Scudder, Jno. 164
John 108, 347
Search, (?) 272
(?) (Mrs.) 3
John 60, 100, 101,
240, 273, 305, 342
Seares, Daniell (Mrs.)
118
Mary 118
Searge, William 179
Searle, (?) 225
(?) (Col.) 248
Searles, (?) (Col.) 303
Seatchwell, (?) 32
Seauer, Robert 187, 270,
312
Robt. 271
Shubaell 312
Seaver, Robert 29, 152,
187, 210, 229, 390
Shuball 151
Seaward, Roger 157
Seawell, Rich. 301
Sedg(wick), (?) (Cpt.)
121
Sedgwick, (?) 348
(?) (Maj.) 93, 98
Robt. (Maj.) 37
Sedgwicke, Zacheus 281
Seelly, John 97
Seely, John 98
Seelyes, (?) 146
Seers, Jno. 97
Seirch, John 169
Sejuke, Robt. (Maj.) 37
Sellecke, Dauid 215
David 153
Jonathan 215
Sellick, David 113, 153
Sellicke, Dauid 127
Nath. 214
Sellocke, David 31
Semon, Hannah 16
Sems, Thomas 84
Sendal, Saml. 363
Sendall, Saml. 222
Samll 169

Sendall (cont.)
Samuel 167, 362
Samuell 217
Senderlin, John (Sr.)
299
Sensions, (?) 284
Senter, John 272
Sentyon, (?) 102
Sergent, Stephen 109
Serrnay, William 97
Seuer, Robert 127, 146
Severn, (?) 110
Sewall, (?) 344
Samuel 371, 372, 373,
374, 375, 381
Samuel (Jdg.) 63, 372,
374, 375
Sewell, Barbara (Mrs.)
181
David 181
Elizabeth 181
Reinold 181
Shapleigh, Nic. 97
Shaplej, (?) (Cpt.) 120
Shapley, (?) (Maj.) 363
Nicolas (Maj.) 177
Shapman, Richard (Sr.)
339
Sharman, Martha 159
Mary 159
Samuel 159
Sharp, Abigail 170
Abigaile 358
Abigaill (Mrs.) 170
Abigall (Mrs.) 170
John 170, 358
Mary 170, 358
Robert 128, 170, 358
Sharpe, Abigaile 358
Mary 358
Richard 388
Robert 111, 170
Sharpley, Nicolas (Cpt.)
177
Shattock, Samuel 112
Samuell 100
Shattocke, Wm. 136
Shattuck, (?) 10, 17
Lemuel 9
Shaw, (?) 317
John 53, 127, 138,
146, 177
Joseph 53, 137
Mary (Mrs.) 53
Shawe, Abraham 5
Jno. 125
John 5, 121
Joseph 5, 137
Martha 5
Mary (Mrs.) 137
Marye 5
Tho. 122
Shawes, (?) 191
Shaws, (?) 5
Sheafe, (?) 141, 379
Jacob 112, 127, 128,
140, 142, 147, 159,
168, 169, 170, 379
Margaret (Mrs.) 170
Margt. (Mrs.) 168
Sheafes, (?) 378
Sheaffe, Elizabeth 180,
182
Jacob 179
Margarett (Mrs.) 182
Mehittabell 182
Shearman, (?) (Mrs.) 215
Abigail 159

423

Shearman (cont.)
Abigaile 159
Ann 159
Elizabeth (Mrs.) 159
John 95, 99
Martha 159
Richard 159, 321
Sheath, Jaacob 112
Shedwell, (?) 378
Shefeld, Robert 127
Sheffield, Edmond 113
Edmund 123
Mary (Mrs.) 115
Shefieles, Robert 146
Shelly, Sarah 343
Sheopardson, Daniell 87, 88
Johanna 87
Lidia 87
Shepard, Edw. 99
Tho (Rev.) 99
Shepardson, Daniell 94
Sheperdson, Daniel 348
Shephard, (?) 7
Shepheard, Samuell 121
Thomas 8, 315
Shepherd, Samuell 117
Thomas 14
Shepherdson, Daniell 348
Sheppard, John 119
Margaret (Mrs.) 119
William 304
Sheppards, (?) 113
Shepperd, Margaret (Mrs.) 119
Sherborne, Henry 98
Sherman, (?) (Mrs.) 32
Abigail 27
Henry 37
Joh. 117
John 19, 97, 121, 315
Martha 159
Prissilla 159
Richard 159
Samll. 379
Samuel 158
Sherwood, (?) 102
Shippen, Edward 388, 390
Shipton, Thomas 304
Shirman, (?) (Rev.) 172
Shoare, Sampson 120, 123, 154
Samson 336
Shoomaker, Evarll. 215
Shore, Sampson 146
Shoreman, Samuell 88
Short, Clement 293
Shorte, Henry 93
Shove, George 137
Showell, David 169
Shrimpton, (?) 99, 119, 260
Abigail 261
Bethiah 261
Ebenezer 203, 261, 262
Edw. 203
Edward 202, 203, 261, 262
Elinor (Mrs.) 100
Elisabeth 261, 262
Elizabeth 203
Elizabeth (Mrs.) 203, 262
Ellenor (Mrs.) 262
Epafras 261, 262
Epaphras 203
Henery 100, 126, 128
Henry 140, 153, 161,

Shrimpton (cont.)
169, 173, 182, 187, 203, 260, 262
Jonathan 100, 202, 203, 262
Lidya 261
Lydia 203
Lydya 262
Mary 202, 203, 261, 262
Mary (Mrs.) 261
Saml. (Col.) 251
Samuel 262
Samuell 261, 343
Sarah 261
Silas 203, 261, 262
Shrimptons, Edw. 261
Shrimton, (?) 93
Shurt, Abraham 138
Shute, Marie 110
Richard 110
Robert 110
Saml. 381
Sara 110
Thomas 110
Sibb, (?) (Dr.) 89
Sibly, Sarah 184
Sibs, (?) (Dr.) 355
Sill, John 14, 99
Silliocke, (?) 123
Silsbee, Ann 359
Simkins, (?) 111
Ishabell (Mrs.) 158
Nicholas 158
Simknes, Nicholas 103
Simpkins, (?) (Cpt.) 122
Simpson, Robert 347
Sims, Zakeria (Rev.) 110
Simson, John 117, 203
Singleman, Henry 121
Singleton, Will. 385
Sirle, Daniell (Col.) 301, 302
Skarlet, Samuell 110
Skarlett, John 167
Skerry, Henry (Sr.) 129
Skidmore, Thomas 26
Skillinge, Deborah 215
Skiner, Edward 2
Skinner, Christopher 297
Edward 23
Jno. 287
John 287
Thomas 23
Skinners, Edward 23
Slanney, Mary 23
Smart, John 16
Smead, (?) (Widow) 164
Judith (Mrs.) 346
Visillah 164
William 102, 164, 347
Smedly, John 10, 90
Smeed, Judith (Mrs.) 164
William 164
Smeeds, Judith (Mrs.) 164
Wm. 164
Smith, (?) 99, 111, 176
(?) (Cpt.) 26
Abraham 195, 232
Alice (Mrs.) 232
Alice (Widow) 232
Alis (Mrs.) 232
B. 117
Christ 160
Christopher 160, 329
Edward 61
Elizabeth 160

Smith (cont.)
Franc 121
Francis 110, 195
George 329
Henry 43, 49, 190
Isaac 195
James 112, 137, 335
Jeremy 28
Jn 183
John 39, 136, 138, 140, 183, 195, 196, 220, 221, 255
Jone 335
Lawrence 153, 255
Mary 195, 255
Ralph 121, 189, 365
Richard 79, 194
Samuel 232
Sarah (Mrs.) 220
Temperance 130
Thomas 174, 187, 339, 379
Will 22
William 202, 311, 315
ffrances 99
Smithe, Lawrence 255, 281
Smyth, Daniell 122
John 122
Jone 41
Judeth 122
Ralph 122
Snawsell, Thomas 281
Snell, Hannah 335
Hannah (Mrs.) 335, 336
Jane 335
John 335
Susanna 335
Symon 335, 336
Snellin, (?) 129
Snelling, William 197, 377
Snook, James 57, 58
Margaret (Mrs.) 57
Snooke, Elizabeth (Mrs.) 57
James 57, 160
Joane 57
Marg'ret 160
Margaret (Mrs.) 160
Snow, Milca (Mrs.) 343
Milcha (Mrs.) 342
Thomas 342, 343
Sonart, (?) 378
Soulsby, (?) 359
Ann 359
Souther, (?) 147
Mary 104
Nathl. 53
Sarah (Mrs.) 147
Southick, (?) 111
Southwicke, John 162
Sowther, (?) 121
(?) (Mrs.) 147
Mathll. 123
Nath 128, 147
Natha. 42
Nathaniel 104
Nathaniell 42, 112, 137
Sarah (Mrs.) 147
Spall, Elizabeth 321
Mary 321
Thomas 321
Sparauhauke, John 99
Sparhawk, Nathaniel 11
Sparowe, Jo. 116
Sparowhauke, Ester 99

Sparowhauke (cont.)
Nathaniell 98
Sparowhauks, (?) 98
Wm. 98
Sparrowhawk, Nathaniel
98
Spaul, Thomas 26
Spaule, (?) (Mrs.) 32
Elizabeth 321
Thomas 27, 321
Spawle, Elizabeth 159
Mary 159
Speere, (?) 111
George 179
Spencer, (?) 120
Geo. 123
Gerarard 8
Roger 378
Stephen 179, 234
Tho. 294
Thomas 294
William 294
Wm. 294
Spere, Mary (Mrs.) 38
Speres, George 355
Sperlin, (?) (Cpt.) 146
Spicer, Dionisa (Mrs.)
306, 307, 308
Elizabeth 306
Jane (Mrs.) 306
John 306
Stephen 306, 307, 308
Spiers, John 58
Spoore, John 28
Spowell, William 156
Spowells, (?) (Mrs.) 80
Sprage, (?) 378
Ralph 85
Raphe 85
Sprague, Ralph 222
Richard 109, 385
Sprinckfeild, Emanuell
278
Mary (Mrs.) 278
Springe, John 95
Spur, Robert (Jr.) 375,
376, 382
Spurr, Robt. 48
Spurrs, John 37
Spurs, Jno. 110
Spyers, John 58
Squire, Barnard 147
Thomas 87, 107, 157
Stables, Saml. 125
Staines, Richard 233
Stalham, (?) 236
Stanborough, Josiah 121
Standish, Josiah 340
Stanes, (?) (Mrs.) 276
Richard 276
Stanley, Christopher 34,
35
Ruth (Mrs.) 137
Susan (Mrs.) 35
Stanton, Thomas 200
Thos. 102
Stapell, Jeffery 349
Staple, Jeffrey 349
Martha 349
Staples, Jeffrey 349
Martha 349
Star, (?) 99
Stare, (?) (Sr.) 363
Starke, Robert 118
Starkye, Nathaniell 215
Starr, (?) 123
(?) (Jr.) 147
(?) (Sr.) 147

Starr (cont.)
Comfort 53, 104, 126,
155, 156
Comfort (Sr.) 104
Elizabeth 155, 156
Hannah 155
John 155, 156, 175
Maynard 155
Robert 297
Tho 169
Thomas 155, 156, 169
William 297
Wm. 297
Starre, (?) 126
Comfort 126
Robert 297
Samuell 155
Thomas 155, 363
Staughton, Wm. 255, 305
Stearnes, Isack 117
Stearns, Nathaniel 388
Stebbin, John 81, 151,
312
Martin 377
Stebbinnes, John 257
Stebbins, (?) 112
John 185, 187, 282,
378, 379
Martin 110, 128, 377
Martine 126, 377, 378
Stebens, Martyn 378
Stebins, John 283, 324
Martin 113
Stedman, (?) 272
John 99, 272
Robt 99
Tho. (Sr.) 246
Steevens, Jona. 37
Stephens, David 37, 111
Jeremiah 229
Sterne, Isaac 121
Sternes, John 117
Sterns, (?) 378
Stet, (?) 99
Steuens, (?) (Dr.) 120
John 169, 342
Samuell 169, 342
Wm. 265
Steuenson, Wm. 49
Stevens, (?) 122
Geore 61
George 61
Jeremiah 229
Joseph 80
Mary (Mrs.) 80
William 161, 359
Wm. 359
Steward, Alexander 281
Stibbins, (?) 123
Stilson, (?) 99
Stimes, (?) 93
Stitson, Will 22
William 93
Stockbridge, Charles 136
Elizabeth 136
Ester 136
Hannah 136
John 136
Mary 136
Mary (Mrs.) 136
Sarah 136
Stockden, Edmund 312
Stocker, Thomas 110
Stockwell, Nehemiah 264
Stoddard, (?) 181, 202,
311, 343
Anth. 178
Antho. 36, 123

Stoddard (cont.)
Anthony 75, 98, 126,
127, 146, 153, 169,
179, 182, 262, 272,
311, 355, 363, 388
John 122
Stodder, (?) 107
Anthony 171, 172
Daniell 195
Hannah (Mrs.) 195
John (Sr.) 195
Samuell 195
Stodderd, Anthony 172
Stodders, (?) 28
Stoddrs, (?) 378
Stoder, (?) 124
Ston, John 211
Stone, (?) 218
(?) (Dr.) 379
Daniel 99, 305
Daniell 207
Gregory 11, 23, 98
Heugh 146
Hugh 127
Joane (Mrs.) 227
John 121, 227, 379
Jone (Mrs.) 227
Symon 85, 117, 121
Stonehard, John 117
Stones, John 225
Nicholas 386
Simon 227
Stonnard, John 102
Stonne, Anne (Mrs.) 19
John 19
Storer, Richard 276, 277
Story, (?) 350
George 350
Stoughton, (?) 108
(?) (Mrs.) 108, 212
Israel 33, 34, 84,
108, 346
Israell 164
Israell (Col.) 108
John 33
Judith 346
Thomas 34
William 33, 73, 255,
279, 359, 365
William (Gov.) 34
Stoughtons, (?) 245
(?) (Mrs.) 164
Stoune, (?) 2
Stovard, Siluester 120
Stow, Elizabeth 50
John 50, 84, 98, 102,
377
Nath. 98
Nathl. 50
Saml. 50
Thankfull 50
thankfull 50
Stowe, John 50, 120, 378
Marie 50
Sam. 50
Symon 25, 121
Thankfull 50
Thomas 50
thankfull 50
Stower, Abigail 28
Amy (Mrs.) 27, 117
Jone 28
Joseph 28
Nicholas 27, 117
Richard 28
ffar 28
ffarre 28
Stowers, John 117

Stowman, (?) 102
Stowton, Robert 24
Stowtones, (?) 102
Strange, John 162
Stranges, William 359
Strangeways, William 359
Stranguage, William 359
Stratton, Elefall 309
Stream, Beniamin 205
Streame, Benjamine 205
  Elizabeth (Mrs.) 205
  Tho. 205
  Thomas 205
Streete, (?) 97
Stronge, John 84
Stubbs, Abigail (Mrs.)
  26
  Joshua 120
  Richard 122
Stubes, (?) 379
Sturges, Edward 120
Stutly, Peeter 161
Sumer, Abigail (Mrs.) 22
  Tho. 22
Summer, Abigail (Mrs.)
  22
Sumner, (?) 164, 260,
  346
  Abigail (Mrs.) 22
  Robert 140
  Thomas 22
  William 198, 223, 245,
    285, 292
Sunderland, Jno. 110,
  160
  John 58, 118, 121,
    138, 166, 177, 188,
    189, 207, 215, 232,
    249, 342
  John. 118
Sunderlands, John 118
Sunderling, Jno. 149
Sundrland, John 215
Sute, Richard 149
Sutton, John 122
Swadden, Phillip 120
Swan, Henry 28
  Jo. 2
  John 14
  Thomas 323, 389
Swasey, John 120
Swayne, Jer 22
Sweate, (?) 269
  John 269
Sweden, Philip 122
Sweet, Jno. 167
  John 101, 220, 270
  Robert 161
  Wm. 146
Sweete, (?) 179
  Jno 113, 220
  Jno. 250, 358
  John 12, 27, 100, 101,
    113, 140, 160, 163,
    220, 273, 305, 357,
    358
Sweets, John 273
Swelus, Robert 15
Swet, John 127
Swetman, (?) 122
  Tho 99
  Tho. 120
  Thomas 119
Swett, John 385
Swift, (?) 99, 176, 343,
  347, 361
  Father 265
  Obadiah 193, 374, 376

Swift (cont.)
  Rest 373
  Thomas 212, 242, 333
Swifte, Rest 374
Swifts, (?) 264
Swinerton, (?) 257
  John 247, 248, 257
Symes, Zechariah (Sr.)
  315
Symonds, Samuel 114
  Samuell 20
  Walter 342
Symons, Samuel 14
Syth, (?) 179
Taboies, John 120
Tabor, Lidya (Mrs.) 5
Tabutt, (?) 379
Tailer, Henry 121
Tailor, Christopher 161
  Elisabeth (Mrs.) 32
  John 251
  Nicholas 32
  Nichols. 32
  Richard 256
Tainter, Joseph 13, 145,
  171, 172
Talby, Hannah 207
Tall, John 171
Tanner, (?) 99
Tapley, Edward 58
Tappan, Abraham 91
Tappin, (?) 176
Tapping, John 263
Taprill, Richard 161
Tare, Fardinando 149
  Richard 350, 351
  Sidracke 149
  Tho 149
Tarne, (?) 316
  Hannah 135
Tasker, Isac 120
Tauerne, Anchor 127
Tayer, Fardinado 254
  Margery (Mrs.) 254
  Sidrache 254
Tayler, Robt. 379
Taylor, (?) 99
  Henry 342
  James 10
  John 99, 251, 325
  John (Sr.) 325
  Rebecca 156, 325
  Rebecca (Mrs.) 325
  Richd. 156
  William 306
Taylors, (?) 327
  Gregory 121
Tearne, Deliverance 185
  Miles 185
Tellar, (?) (Mrs.) 243
Temple, John 388
  Thomas (Sir) 229
Terry, Thomas 277
Tey, John 3
Thacher, Thomas (Jr.)
  269
Thackster, Elizabeth
  (Mrs.) 132
  Thomas 81
Thaier, Cornelius 222
Thatcher, (?) 319
  Samuel 118
  Thomas 41
  Thomas (Rev.) 182
Thaxter, Elizabeth 125
  Elizabeth (Mrs.) 125
  Jno. 82
  John 82, 125, 189,

Thaxter (cont.)
  195, 250, 260, 334
  Samll. 125
  Samuell 125
  Sarah 125
  Tho. 125
  Tho. (Jr.) 125
  Thomas 122, 125
Thayer, (?) 253
  (?) (Dr.) 253
  Anna (Mrs.) 253
  Benjamin 254
  Cornelius 222
  David 254
  Deborah 253
  Ebenezer 253, 254
  Elizabeth 253
  Ephraim 254
  Experience 253
  Fardinando 254
  Ferdinando 253, 254,
    255
  Ferdinandoes 255
  Freelove 254
  Hannah 254
  Hannah (Mrs.) 253
  Huldah 254
  Huldah (Mrs.) 254
  Isaac 253, 254
  John 253
  Jonathan 254
  Josiah 254
  Margery (Mrs.) 253,
    254
  Mary 254
  Naomi 254
  Rachel 254
  Richard 176, 222, 350
  Samuel 254
  Sarah 254
  Shadrach 254
  Sydrach 254, 255
  Thomas 253, 254, 255
  Thomas (Jr.) 253
  Thomas (Sr.) 255
  Timothy 254
  Tryall 254
  William 254
  Zackerias 222
Thohinge, Beniamin 363
Thomas, (?) 11
  Alice (Mrs.) 198, 199
  Allice (Mrs.) 281
  Euan 58, 110, 122, 360
  Euen 177
  Evan 58, 137, 154,
    156, 198, 360
  Hugh 243
  John 215
Thomases, (?) 111
Thompson, (?) 125
  B. F. 14
  Benjamin 244
  John 109, 154, 379
Thomson, (?) 342
  Benjamin 237
  Edward 235
Thornehill, Tho. (Cpt.)
  177, 364
  Thomas (Cpt.) 363, 364
Thorner, Edward 161
  Henry 161
Thornhill, Tho. 364
  Thomas (Cpt.) 177, 363
  Timothy 364
Thornton, Geo. 376
  Mary (Mrs.) 118
  Peeter 118

Thornton (cont.)
Robin 179
Robt 179
Thorowgood, Tho. 123
Thomas 146
Throgmorton, (?) 102
Thronton, Peeter 118
Throwbridge, Elizabeth
374
Thurry, Tho. 127
Thurston, Jno. (Sr.) 387
John 388
John (Sr.) 388
Martha (Mrs.) 64
Mary (Mrs.) 387
Richard 127
Theophilus 389
Thomas 389
Thurstun, Benjamin 205,
211
Elisha 211
Thwing, Ben 379
Benia. 190
Beniamin 363
Benj 49
Benjamin 35, 36
Tice, Gouer (Mrs.) 57
Tichborne, Dauid 120
Ticknor, Hannah (Mrs.)
136
William 136
Tiler, Roger 149
Tileston, Tho. 233
Thomas 233, 371, 385
Thos. 376, 382
Thos. (Maj.) 375
Tilestone, Ruth 167
Thom. 108
Thomas 167, 246, 293,
371, 373
Till, Peter 312
Tilleston, Tho 120
Tilley, (?) 137
Tilly, (?) 378
(?) (Mrs.) 318
John 113, 126
William 360
Wm. 58, 137
Tillye, William 251
Tilson, Elizabeth 140
Tilston, Timothy 233
Tincker, John 36
Ting, (?) 227, 277
Edw. 75, 153
Edward 36, 78, 119,
126, 127, 146, 178,
179, 222
Tinge, (?) (Cpt.) 121
Edw. 75
Edward 42, 120, 122,
123, 311
William (Cpt.) 123
Willing (Cpt.) 123
Tinker, (?) 123
Jno. 97, 110
John 198, 348
Tinkers, Jno. 111
Titchburnes, Dauid 236
Titcomb, Elizabeth
(Mrs.) 342
Titcomes, William 342
Tite, Henery 48
Tode, John 121
Toker, Marce 110
Tolbut, William 125
Toleman, Thomas 381
Tolemans, (?) 212
Tolman, Hannah 176

Tolman (cont.)
Thomas 212
Tomas, (?) 124
Tome, John 161
Tomkins, (?) 164, 346
Tompkins, Ralph 346
Tompson, (?) 51, 169,
284
(?) (Mrs.) 98
Benjamin 286
Wllm 41
Tompsons, Willm 191
Tomson, (?) 75
Elizabeth 269
John 154
Samuel 237
Samuell 255
William 238
Tomsons, John 269
Toowill, Richard 218
Toowills, Rich'd 218
Toppan, (?) 16
Topping, (?) (Mrs.) 294
Toppins, Joh. 236
Torrey, (?) (Lt.) 122
Josiah 360
Sam. 232
William 114, 268
Torry, Phillip 127
Wm. 53
Tory, Phillip 146
Tounesend, Lyddja 37
Toung, Elizabeth (Mrs.)
77
James (Cpt.) 77
Towars, John 250
Tower, Leah (Mrs.) 388
William 388
Towers, John 220, 378
Towgood, Richard 37
Towne, Joan 129
Wm. 99
Townsend, Liddia 111
Townsin, Thomas 252, 253
Tracy, Peter 127, 146
Trapp, Thomas 173, 174,
369
Trarice, (?) (Mrs.) 281
Trask, (?) (Cpt.) 267,
268
W. B. 208, 290, 298
William B. 175, 183,
191, 195, 201, 223,
227, 230, 234, 241,
249, 257, 263, 269,
275, 281, 306, 314,
317, 323, 328, 334,
337, 341, 345, 349,
355, 357, 363, 368,
370, 377
Wm. B. 100, 108, 116,
124, 127, 135, 141,
147, 155, 163, 169
Traveegoe, Thomas 200
Travegoe, Thomas 200
Treadaway, Nathaniell 19
Natt. 99
Treadway, Mary 330
Nathaniel 330
Nathaniell 19
Treaveagoe, Jone (Mrs.)
200
Mary 200
Trenow, Ann 160
Trereise, (?) 121
Trescott, Thomas 154
William 179, 255
Wm. 154, 255

Tresler, Elinor (Mrs.)
358
Thomas 358
Treusdale, Richard 37
Trew, James 200
Trewbridge, Thomas 179
Treworgie, John 37
Nicholas 37
Treworgy, Jno 120
Treworthy, (?) 90
Trewsdell, Richard 123
Treyrice, (?) 117
Trigge, Richard 116
Trissell, James 152
Trobridge, Margret 373
William 215
Trowbridge, James 193,
374
True, Henry 121
Truesdale, Ri. 110
Rich 116
Richard 315
Truesdall, Rich 167
Rich. 113
Richard (Deacon) 362
Richd. 164
Truesdell, Peter 120
Trumball, John 120
Trumble, John 99
Trumbull, (?) 350
J. Hammond 350
Tho. 126
Trusdaile, (?) 363
Trusdale, Richard 177
Trusdall, (?) 59, 66
(?) (Deacon) 303
Richard 177, 294
Richard (Deacon) 256
Richd. 55, 179
Trusdell, Richard 150
Trusler, (?) (Mrs.) 358
Edward 358
Elinor (Mrs.) 358
Elizabeth 358
Ellinor (Mrs.) 358
Henry 358
Nicholas 358
Samuell 358
Thomas 358
Trutle, Catherin 301
Ralph 301
William 301
Truworthy, John 102
Tuchel, (?) 164
Benjamine 164
Joseph 164
Mary 164
Tuchill, (?) 164
Francis 164
Joshua 164
Tuchine, (?) 164
Tucke, (?) (Mrs.) 44
Joanna (Mrs.) 44
Robert 44
Tucker, (?) (Sr.) 189
Anne (Mrs.) 189
Jane 214
Jno (Sr.) 171
Jno. 81
John 170, 189, 190
John (Jr.) 189
John (Sr.) 189, 366
Mary 170, 171, 189
Robert 101, 107
Tuckerman, John 156, 378
Tuckers, Mary 171
Tuckey, Richard 201
Tuker, John 227

Turand, Mary (Mrs.) 206
Turel, John 232
Turell, Daniel 232, 240,
    249, 278
  Daniell 141, 152, 153,
    154, 201, 211, 212,
    248, 249
  Danl. 56
  John 232
Turfrey, Edward 359
Turill, Daniell (Jr.)
    368, 370
Turins, Danil 257
Turner, (?) 112, 120
  (?) (Lt.) 363
  (?) (Mrs.) 50
  Elisebeth (Mrs.) 91
  Elizabeth 37
  Elizabeth (Mrs.) 37,
    38
  Ephraim 236
  Faireweather 236
  Fairweather 236
  Georg 156
  Habacuk 37
  Humphrey 156
  Increase 56
  Isabell (Mrs.) 56,
    138, 186, 366
  Jefery 55
  Jeffery 56, 138
  Jno. 110
  John 37, 120, 137, 236
  Joseph 236
  Peeter 37
  Penelope (Mrs.) 237
  Praiseeuer 56
  Praiseever 56
  Robe't 37
  Robert 37, 135, 146,
    236, 237, 277
  Robt 38
  Robt. 123
  Robte 107
  Will. 280, 288
  William 280, 288
  Wm. 280, 288
Turners, (?) (Lt.) 196
Turnor, Robert 38
Turnrs., (?) (Lt.) 196
Turpin, Thos 120
Turrell, Dan. 265
  Daniell 232
  Jno. 232
Turrine, Daniell 179
Tuttell, Symon 156
Tuttills, Henry 250
Tuttle, John 166
Twelues, (?) 272
Twitchell, Benjamin 164
  Joseph 164
Tyler, (?) 111
Tyley, Samuel (Jr.) 370
Tyng, (?) 176
  (?) (Cpt.) 355
  Edw. 322
  Edward 73, 75, 177,
    321, 322, 368, 370
  William (Cpt.) 355
Tynge, Will 110
Underwood, Thomas 346
Upham, John 349
Upsall, Nich 101
  Nicholas 272
  Susanna 272
Usher, (?) 314
  Hezekiah 37, 262, 281,
    311

Usher (cont.)
  Hezekiah (Sr.) 229
Vahan, George 97
  James 156
  John 19
Vaine, Henry (Sir) 124
Van, Ridge 304
Vane, (?) (Mrs.) 124
Vassall, John 112
  Margaret 156
Vassell, Jno. 111
  John 123
Vasty, William 234
Vauhan, William 330
Vennar, Tho. 90
Venner, (?) 123
  Tho. 120
Verey, Hilliard 359
Vernon, Daniell 222
Vesey, Wm. 146
Vezie, William 326
Viall, John 127, 161,
    168, 197
Vicars, John 384
Vickars, Georg 106
Vickre, George 190
Vicory, Geo. 123
Viell, John 146
Vineing, John 160
Vmphrys, (?) 212
Vnderwood, Thomas 81,
    310
Voce, Robert 179
Vocy, William 127
Vose, Robt. 232
Voysy, (?) 128
Vpham, (?) 150, 151
  (?) (Mrs.) 272
  Phineas 380, 381
Vppam, John 14
Vppame, John 349
Vpsall, (?) 361
  Dorothy 273
  Dorothy (Mrs.) 272
  Elizabeth 272
  Nich 100
  Nicholas 272, 273
  Susanna 272
Vpshall, (?) 119
  Dorothy 60
  Nicho 111
Vrsilah, (?) 346
Vsher, (?) (Dr.) 355
  Hez. 317
  Hezekiah 109, 120,
    121, 190, 203, 204,
    214, 248, 339
Vttinge, Anne 8
Vty, Nath. 127
Vulet, Samll. 83
Wade, Henry 122
Wadsworth, Samuel 187
  Samuell 333
Wadworth, James 333
Waford, (?) (Widow) 7
Waiere, Richrd. 111
Waight, Gameliell 125
  Richard 41
Waire, Ben 121
Wait, Gamaliel 204
  Gamaliell 204
Waite, G. 111
  Gamalell 52
  Gamaliel 277
  Gamaliell 52, 150,
    216, 256
  John 386
  Rich 120

Waite (cont.)
  Rich. 121
  Richard 174
  Robert 111
Waits, Alexander 156
Wajte, Richard 37
Wakefeild, Obediah 352
Wakefield, John 99, 160
  Obadiah 352
Waker, (?) (Lt.) 111
  Isaac 90, 104
  Isaack 101, 102, 138
  Robt 106
Wakers, Isaac 138
Wakly, (?) 176
Walch, Gerard 161
Walden, (?) (Cpt.) 380
Walderne, Richard (Cpt.)
    161
Walderns, Richard 98
Waldren, (?) (Cpt.) 380
Waldrene, (?) 227
Wales, (?) 83
  Isabel 374
  Isabel (Mrs.) 377
  Jerijah 375, 381, 382
  Jno. 201
  John 197, 201
  Mary 377
  Nathaniel 197, 201,
    212, 377, 381, 382
  Nathaniel (Jr.) 374,
    377
  Nathaniel (Sr.) 377,
    382
  Nathaniell 197, 201
  Nathaniell (Jr.) 197
  Nathaniell (Sr.) 197
  Samuel 372, 375
  Susan 201
  Susan (Mrs.) 197, 377
  Susannah (Mrs.) 377,
    381
  Thomas 381
  Timothy 164, 197
Walker, (?) 121, 154,
    179, 336, 363
  (?) (Lt.) 122
  Anne (Mrs.) 167
  Asten (Cpt.) 127
  Augustion 22
  Austin 22
  Isaac 378
  Isaack 137, 388
  Isac 120
  Jacob 211
  Joseph 211
  Richard 107
  Richd. (Cpt.) 146
  Robert 36, 150, 194,
    197, 211, 255, 258,
    263
  Robrt 363
  Robt 125
  Robt. 277
  Sam 122
  Tho 156
  Tho. 153
  Thomas 36, 167
Walkers, Thomas 167
Walley, John 387
Wallis, Nathll. 168
Wallker, Robte 107
Walls, Mary 374
  Timothy (Jr.) 197
Wallsbe, David 228
Walsbee, David 221
Walsbie, Samuel 263

428

Walter, Laurence 121
  Richard 112
  Thomas 62
Walters, Joseph 278
  Martha (Mrs.) 278
  Richard 140
Waltham, (?) 53
  Ann 2
  Henery 2, 53
  Jonatham 53
  Phillyne 2
  Thomas 2
  William 2
Walton, (?) (Mrs.) 97
  George 44, 177
  Henr 98, 109
  Henry 32, 109
Waluer, Abra 98
Wantworth, William 44
Ward, (?) 9, 122, 320,
  378
  (?) (Cpt.) 96
  Benjamin 159, 312,
    318, 319
  Elizabeth 271
  Mary (Mrs.) 318, 319,
    320
  Obediah 179
  Samuell 81
Wardayle, Willm 101
Wardell, Elihu 388
  Elizabeth (Mrs.) 229,
    248, 388
  Leah 388
  Mary 388
  Meribah 388
  Rachel 388
  Uzall 388
  William 229, 248, 379,
    388
  Wm. 229
Wardells, William 229
Ware, (?) 149
  James 378
Warham, John 84
Warner, Tho. 120
  Thomas 168, 242
Warren, (?) 99
  Peter 233
Warrens, Peter 293
Warrish, Thomas 23
Warvicke, Henry 120
Warwick, Thomas 23
Warwicke, Henry 120
Waterman, (?) 243
  Richard 60
  Robte 107
  Thomas 81, 379
Watermans, (?) 334
Waters, Will. (Sr.) 379
Watkins, Jno. 111
  Tho. 227
  Thomas 219, 378
  Walter K. 387
Watrman, Tho. 230
Watson, (?) 92
  John 88, 94, 127, 183,
    282, 388
Watts, Jno. 281
  Will. 264
  Wm. (Col.) 264
Way, (?) 117, 122
  Aaron 272
  Aron 265, 272
  Eliazar 179
  Elizabeth 279
  George 138
  Henry 138, 279

Way (cont.)
  Richard 225, 248, 279
Waye, Aaron 224
  Rich. 311
  Tho 102
Wayle, Ricd 113
Waymouth, Jonathan 12
Wayt, Marshall 379
Wayte, Gamaliel 312
  Gamaliell 126
  Marshall 168
  Ri 128
  Richard 126, 128, 168,
    175, 285, 293
  Richd. 167, 168
  Richo. 294
Weale, Henry 168
  William 27
Weare, Elizabeth 137
  Elizabeth (Mrs.) 137
  Sarah 137
  William 137, 360
Weauers, (?) 237
Weaver, Edward 370
Webb, (?) 36, 51, 121,
  153
  Armitage 53
  David 381
  Elizabeth 180
  Henry 58, 99, 107,
    179, 182, 362
  Jane 180
  John 147, 153, 180,
    215, 379
  Jonathan 121, 378
  Joseph 130, 150, 151,
    192, 260, 380
  Margaret 179, 180
  Margarett 180, 182
  Margarett (Mrs.) 103
  Mehitabel 180
  Mehittabell 180
  Nehemiah 150
  Pearces 150
  Rebecca 53, 359
  Rebecca (Mrs.) 54
  Rebeccah (Mrs.) 140
  Rebeckha 359
  Richard 137, 150, 151
  Richd. 130
Webbe, Jo 116
Webber, Thomas 201
Webbs, (?) 66
Weborne, Thomas 177
Weden, Edwd. 149
Weebow, Stephen 168
Weeden, (?) 147
  Edw. 227
  Edward 73, 271
  Elizabeth (Mrs.) 271,
    272
Weekes, Amiell 327
  Ebenezer 327
  Elizabeth 327
  Geo 103
  Geo. 85, 93, 108
  George 83, 85, 109
  Jane 327
  John 327
  Joseph 153, 327
  Renue 327
  Thanckfull 327
  William 212
  Wlli 83
  Wm. 283
Weeks, (?) 111
  Amiell 328
  Emiel 328

Weeks (cont.)
  George 82, 328
  Joseph 328, 374
  Mary 374
  Renew 327
  William 327, 328
Weight, (?) 97
  Thomas 141
Weld, Ann (Mrs.) 282,
    283
  Barbara (Mrs.) 89
  Bethiah 282
  Daniel 15, 81, 98,
    115, 126, 281, 282,
    283
  Daniell 248, 281, 282
  Edmond 88, 89
  John 80, 88, 89, 187,
    282, 283, 312, 324
  Joseph 13, 84, 88, 89,
    282
  Sara 89
  Tho. 266
  Thomas 81, 88, 89,
    115, 151, 166, 185,
    195, 196, 210, 231,
    248, 266, 282, 283,
    296, 324, 386
  barbara (Mrs.) 88, 89
  daniell 89
  hannah 88
  mara 89
  mary 88
Welde, (?) 3, 86
  Tho 3
  Thomas 187, 350
Welds, Jno. 80
  John 210
Welke, Jno. 149
Welld, Thomas 243
Wellens, Thomas 27
Wellmoton, Ane 102
Wells, Edward 120
  Thomas 178
Welsh, Tho. 121
Welster, Willm 102
Wenborne, (?) 129
  Wm. 126, 156
Wensley, John 234
Wentworth, Willm 101
Weselld, John 127
West, (?) 111
  Bartholomew 309
Westgait, Adam 120
Westman, (?) 212
Westmerland, (?) 156
Weston, Edmund 156
  Francis 156
Weyborne, Elizabeth 78
  Elizabeth (Mrs.) 78
  James 78
  Jno 78
  Thomas 78, 79
  mary 78
Whale, Philemon 23
Wharton, Philip 378
  Phillepp 111
  Phillip 151, 154
  Phillippe 248
  Rich. 222
  Richard 221
Wheat, (?) 156
Wheatleigh, (?) 164
  Learnard 360
Wheatley, Gabriell 21
Wheel-wrights, (?)
  (Mrs.) 308
Wheeler, David 378

429

Wheeler (cont.)
  Georg 118
  George 156
  Joseph 17, 55, 118,
    204, 388
  Mary (Mrs.) 211
  Rebecca (Mrs.) 55
  Rebeccah (Mrs.) 128
  Roger 211
  Tho. 55, 116
  Thomas 55, 128, 156,
    277, 388
Wheelock, Ralph O. 49
Wheelocke, Gershom 195
  Hannah (Mrs.) 195
  Ralph 128, 141, 147,
    153
Wheelwright, (?) 286,
    350, 351
  (?) (Mrs.) 308, 309
  Elizabeth 308
  Hannah 308
  John 358
  Katherine 308
  Mary 308
  Rebecca 308
  Samll. 226
  Samuell 308
  Sarah 308
Whelclocke, Gershom 195
  Hannah (Mrs.) 195
Whelewright, John (Rev.)
    225
  Sam. 225
Wheple, Jno. 83
Whetcomb, P. 369
Whetcombe, James 369
Whetwell, (?) 129
  Wm. 146
Whight, John 3
Whipple, Matthew 213
Whit Marsh, John 160
Whitaker, Richard 355
White, (?) 108, 347
  Ann 301
  Charity 366
  Charity (Mrs.) 185
  Dorothy 301
  James 300, 301, 302
  James (Cpt.) 302, 303
  Jeames 301, 302, 303
  John 170, 301
  Joseph 186
  Josiah 301
  Ka. (Mrs.) 303
  Katherine (Mrs.) 301
  Nicho 111
  Nicho. 120
  Nicholas 197, 198
  Paul. 37
  Paull 111
  Phillip 27
  Susanna (Mrs.) 197
  Thomas 154, 186, 222,
    385
  Willm. 123, 301, 302
  Wm. 140, 160
Whiteing, Hannah (Mrs.)
    183
  Nathaniell 183, 184
Whiteinge, (?) 109
Whites, (?) 204
  Samuell 298
Whiting, (?) 73
  (?) (Mrs.) 384
Whitington, Richard 151
Whitman, (?) 122
  John 205

Whitman (cont.)
  Obadiah 325
Whitmans, (?) 186
Whitmarsh, John 147
  Nicho 160
  Nicholas 378
Whitmarshe, Nich. 121
Whitmore, Tho 149
Whitney, John 335
  Ruth (Mrs.) 149
Whiton, James 144
  Mary (Mrs.) 144
Whitt, (?) 235
  Perregrine 37
Whitte, Liddia (Mrs.)
    186
Whitten, James 122
Whitweld, William 127
Whyting, (?) 107
Wiatt, (?) (Mrs.) 215
Wiborne, Tho. 379
  Thomas 8
Wiburne, Thomas 8
Wieborne, James 79
  Thomas 79
Wier, Robt. 379
Wigeer, Hannah (Mrs.)
    389
Wigglesworth, Michael
    315
Wiggons, (?) (Cpt.) 109
Wight, Adam 127
  Ann (Mrs.) 128
  John 128
  Tho 153
  Thomas 129, 147, 332
  Thomas (Sr.) 389
Wilbor, Elizabeth (Mrs.)
    350
  Samuel 350
Wilbore, Joseph 79
  Samu. 350
  Samuell 79
  Shedrick 79
Wilborne, Mercy (Mrs.)
    143
  Thomas 390
Wilder, Edward 63
  Thomas 92, 316
  Thos. 92
Wilford, (?) 342
Wilkey, John 119, 120
Wilkie, Elizabeth (Mrs.)
    189
  John 121, 189, 366
Wilkins, (?) 165
Wilkinson, (?) (Widow)
    22
Willard, (?) 359
  (?) (Cpt.) 118
  (?) (Lt.) 10
  (?) (Maj.) 57
  J. 377
  Josiah 376
  Lyman 9
  Simon 9, 10, 118
  Symon 112, 118, 317
  Symon (Maj.) 112, 140
Willbore, Elizabeth
    (Mrs.) 79
  Joseph 79
  Samuel 79
  Samuell 79
  Shidrak 79
Willet, (?) 131
  Mary (Mrs.) 140
  Tho. (Cpt.) 140
  Thomas 140

Willett, Tho. (Cpt.)
    368, 370
Williames, John 317
Williams, (?) 97, 378
  (?) (Mrs.) 272
  (?) (Sgt.) 66
  Belknap 190
  David 204, 348
  Ebenezer 371, 375
  Henry Howell 251
  Hugh 158, 161
  Isaack 243
  John 152, 306, 317
  Mary (Mrs.) 190
  Math 122
  Michaell 122
  Nath. 129
  Nathaniel 43, 366
  Nathaniel (Sgt.) 178
  Nathaniell 55, 90,
    119, 122, 169, 177,
    179, 190
  Nathanl. 59
  Nathl. 48, 55
  Nathll. 128
  Nicholas 243
  Rich. 206, 313
  Richd. 206
  Robert 21, 128, 152,
    162, 215
  Roger 111
  Tho 28
  Thomas 28, 149
  Zebadiah 374
Willington, Mary (Mrs.)
    337
  Roger 337
Willis, (?) 162, 309
  Bridget 309
  Experience 384
  Jno. 277
  Jonathan 371
  Lawrance 277
  Lawrence 277
  Mary (Mrs.) 277
  Michael 384
  Mildred (Mrs.) 384
  Morse 384
  Nicolas 107
  Temperance 384
Willjams, Nathaniel 118
Willms, Thomas 101
Willockes, Hazillpenah
    53
Willougby, Fran 108
Willoughby, (?) 108
  Fra. 216
  Francis 127
  Hen. 307
  Henry 308
  ffrancis 87
Willoughbye, Fr. 264
Willows, (?) 99
Wills, Michaell 219,
    241, 251, 285
Willson, (?) 74, 84, 92,
    169
  (?) (Rev.) 172
  John 72, 75
  John (Rev.) 72
  John (Sr.) 75
  thomas 85
Wilmut, Benjamin 99
Wilshier, Tho 378
Wilshire, Tho. 122
Wilson, (?) 37, 67, 72,
    73, 111, 123, 378
  (?) (Mrs.) 384

Wilson (cont.)
(?) (Rev.) 76, 142, 165, 268
(?) (Widow) 221
Deborah 16
Edmond 314, 315
Edmond (Dr.) 314
Edward 85
Elizabeth 314
Elizabeth (Mrs.) 73, 314
Humfrey 16
Humphrey 16, 139
Jno. (Rev.) 110, 262
John 34, 36, 38, 73, 75, 112, 248, 314, 315, 317, 332, 352, 353
John (Jr.) 53, 214, 314
John (Rev.) 73, 74, 182, 253, 315, 319, 331
John (Sr.) 78, 140, 194, 315
John (Sr.) (Rev.) 314
Jonathan 201, 202
Joshua 16
Liddey 16
Mary 34, 314, 384
Mary (Mrs.) 38
Richard 55, 129
Samuel 16
Sarah 225, 314
Sarah (Mrs.) 55
Susanna 314
Thomas 16, 85, 378, 385
Will 85
Winborn, William 111
Winchester, Jno 80
Jno. 80
John 80, 96
Winchesteres, John 96
Winchship, Edward 11
Wincol, (?) 99
Winder, John 369
Windows, (?) 97
Wines, (?) 26
Wing, (?) 265
Jno. 210
Johanna (Mrs.) 36
John 265, 272
Robert 36
Winge, (?) 116
Jno. 264
Winkle, Thom. 117
Winship, Edward 11
Winsley, John 311
Samuell 102
Winslow, (?) 198
Edward 74, 75
Jno 169
John 177, 234, 311, 341, 364
John (Sr.) 225, 310
Saml. 127
Winslowe, (?) (Maj.) 215
Samll 110
Winsor, (?) (Mrs.) 276
Hannah 275
Martha 233, 275
Winter, John 117
Winters, John 121
Winthrop, (?) 34, 100, 162
(?) (Gov.) 21, 350, 361

Winthrop (cont.)
Adam 63, 109, 120
Deane 97, 162
Elizabeth (Mrs.) 120
Jo 97
Jo. 116, 346
Jo. (Gov.) 25
Joh. (Gov.) 26
John 18, 95, 98, 117
John (Gov.) 10, 13, 20, 21, 24, 27, 118, 121
John (Jr.) 350
John (Sr.) 34
Martha (Mrs.) 361
Sam. (Cpt.) 215
Steph. 19, 86
Stephen 17
Winthrope, Deane 215
Winthropp, Stee. (Mrs.) 97
Wipple, Jno. 111
Wise, Josep 379
Joseph 3, 127, 146, 151, 185, 187, 210, 243
Wiseman, James 111, 150
Wisewall, John 153, 179, 192, 199, 225, 272, 321
Wiswall, (?) 83, 91, 113, 321, 322
Enoch 153, 238, 284
Jno. 225, 310
John 54, 128, 136, 138, 157, 173, 174, 179, 190, 197, 210, 212, 219, 224, 238, 240, 248, 268, 276, 296, 300, 377, 386
John (Deacon) 321
John (Sr.) 272, 276, 386
Thomas 54, 238
Wiswalls, Enoch 238
John 238
Wiswell, Elizabeth 221
Enoch 284
John 276
Witham, Katherine 31
Witherell, (?) 99
Witherington, Philip 373
Withhead, Thomas 378
Withington, (?) 39, 179
Anna 284
Ebenezer 284, 370
Faith 284
Father 284
Henery 52
Henry 40, 133, 202, 283, 284
John 284
Margerie (Mrs.) 283, 284
Mary 284
Philip 371
Phillip 284, 371
Rich. 183
Richard 153, 183, 202, 211, 283, 284, 285, 376
Richd. 183
Richrd. 111
Wix, (?) 111
Woarye, Robert 22
Wods, (?) 187
Wolcott, (?) 85
Wollaston, (?) 281

Wood, (?) 123
Abigail 387
Anna (Mrs.) 387
Beththya 387
Edward 23
Eleazer 387
James 99
Jonathan 387
Martha (Mrs.) 213
Mary 387
Mehitabel 387
Nicholas 136, 387, 388
Richard 170, 171
william 25
Woodard, Peteer 184
Peter 184
Ralfe 91
Woodberey, Isaac 207
Woodbery, John 84
Woodbridge, (?) 286
(?) (Mrs.) 46
Woodcock, Jane (Mrs.) 260, 285
Richard 285
Wm. 222
Woodcocke, (?) 285, 379
Richard 285
Will. 378
Willm. 123
Wm. 222
Woodde, Isaac 113
Isaack 299
Rich. 113
Richard 149, 151, 158, 299, 320, 388
Wooddy, Isack 299
John 107, 114
Mary 113
Rich. 299
Richard 167
Woode, Isaac 387
Nicho. 83
Richard 387
Woodells, Elisebeth (Mrs.) 229
William 229
Woodford, (?) 257
Woodie, Isaac 387
John 387
Woodies, Richard 378
Woodmancey, John 146, 177
Woodmancy, John 127
Woodmansey, Bathia 286
John 123
Margarett (Mrs.) 286
Martha 286
Robert 286
Robt 286
Robt. 286
Woodmanseye, Jon. 311
Woodowes, Rich 121
Woods, Edward 153
John 89
Woodward, (?) 106, 122
Anne (Mrs.) 143
Nathanell 116
Nathaniel 131
Nathaniell 131
Peeter 184
Pet. 130
Peter 166, 182, 215, 238, 329, 332, 389
Peter (Jr.) 383
Peter (Sr.) 329
Petter 125
Rachell (Mrs.) 125, 235

Woodward (cont.)
  Ralp 220
  Ralph 220, 221, 250
  Robert 235
  Robt 125
  Robt. 119
  Sarah 221
  Thomas 342
  William 383
Woodwards, Ralph 250
Woodwell, Joseph 63
Woody, (?) 142, 299
  (?) (Sgt.) 379
  Isaac 387
  Isaack 115, 121
  Isac 120
  John 113, 387
  Mary 107, 115
  Ri. 299
  Richard 114, 115, 122,
    150, 166
  Richd. 179
Wooley, (?) 156
Woollfall, (?) (Mrs.)
    135
  Richard 135
Woord, John 221
Worker., (?) 124
Wormahill, Joseph 31
Wormhull, Joseph 111
  Miriam 111
Wormod, (?) 120
Wormwoode, (?) (Mrs.) 3
Worse, Robeurt 177
Wory, (?) 110
Wosley, (?) 363
Wright, Adam 146
  Cornelius 156
  Isaack 122
  Richard 12, 326
  Robin 179
  Robt 120
  Thomas 201
  Thos. 201
Wrighte, G. 108
Wullocks, (?) 127
Wyborne, Nathaniel 78
  Thom 78
  Thomas 78
  Thomas (Jr.) 78
Wycliffe, Agnes 22
  Ralph 22
Wyes, Anne 26
Wylder, Thomas 92
Wylie, John 3
Wyman, (?) 73
  Thomas B. 347
Yale, Dauid 37, 120
  David 34
Yard, Edward 322
Yarmouth, (?) 122
Yates, Jno 111
  Jno. 110
Yeamans, Shute Shrimpton
    251
Yeew, Tho 120
Yeo, Tho 102
  Thomas 106
Yeomanes, Edward 227
Yeomans, Edward 119
Yew, Thomas 106
Yonge, Joseph 122
  Rowland 120
Young, Meary (Mrs.) 213
Zechariah, (?) 179